ADVANCES IN
EXPERIMENTAL SOCIAL PSYCHOLOGY

VOLUME 22

ADVANCES IN
Experimental Social Psychology

EDITED BY
Leonard Berkowitz
DEPARTMENT OF PSYCHOLOGY
UNIVERSITY OF WISCONSIN—MADISON
MADISON, WISCONSIN

VOLUME 22

ACADEMIC PRESS, INC.
Harcourt Brace Jovanovich, Publishers
San Diego   New York   Berkeley   Boston
London   Sydney   Tokyo   Toronto

COPYRIGHT © 1989 BY ACADEMIC PRESS, INC.
ALL RIGHTS RESERVED.
NO PART OF THIS PUBLICATION MAY BE REPRODUCED OR
TRANSMITTED IN ANY FORM OR BY ANY MEANS, ELECTRONIC
OR MECHANICAL, INCLUDING PHOTOCOPY, RECORDING, OR
ANY INFORMATION STORAGE AND RETRIEVAL SYSTEM, WITHOUT
PERMISSION IN WRITING FROM THE PUBLISHER.

ACADEMIC PRESS, INC.
San Diego, California 92101

United Kingdom Edition published by
ACADEMIC PRESS LIMITED
24-28 Oval Road, London NW1 7DX

LIBRARY OF CONGRESS CATALOG CARD NUMBER: 64-23452

ISBN 0-12-015222-3 (alk. paper)

PRINTED IN THE UNITED STATES OF AMERICA
89 90 91 92   9 8 7 6 5 4 3 2 1

CONTENTS

Contributors ix

**On the Construction of the Anger Experience:
Aversive Events and Negative Priming
in the Formation of Feelings**

Leonard Berkowitz and Karen Heimer

    I. Introduction 1
   II. Approaches to Emotion and Anger 2
  III. A Cognitive-Neoassociationistic Analysis of Anger 7
  IV. The Present Research 13
   V. General Discussion 31
       References 35

Social Psychophysiology: A New Look

John T. Cacioppo, Richard E. Petty,
and Louis G. Tassinary

     I. Introduction 39
    II. Background 40
   III. An Alternative Conceptualization 43
   IV. Illustrating the New Look: Part I 43
    V. Illustrating the New Look: Part II 65
   VI. Sociological and Philosophical Obstacles 73
  VII. The New Look: Part III 77
 VIII. Conclusion 81
      References 83

**Self-Discrepancy Theory: What Patterns
of Self-Beliefs Cause People to Suffer?**

E. Tory Higgins

   I. Introduction 93
  II. Self-Discrepancy Theory 94

III.	Evidence for Hypothesis 1 of Self-Discrepancy Theory	99
IV.	Evidence for Hypothesis 2 of Self-Discrepancy Theory	120
V.	Summary and Concluding Remarks	128
	References	131

Minding Matters: The Consequences of Mindlessness–Mindfulness

Ellen J. Langer

I.	Overview	137
II.	Mindlessness and Mindfulness	138
III.	Mindlessnes-Mindfulness and Health	142
IV.	Mindlessness-Mindfulness and Performance	147
V.	Mindlessness-Mindfulness versus Related Concepts	151
VI.	Misconceptions about the Advantages of Mindlessness and the Disadvantages of Mindfulness	155
VII.	An Alternative View	157
VIII.	Preventing Mindlessness	165
IX.	Conclusions	167
	References	168

The Tradeoffs of Social Control and Innovation in Groups and Organizations

Charlan Jeanne Nemeth and Barry M. Staw

I.	Introduction	175
II.	Some Theoretical Considerations of the Strain toward Uniformity	176
III.	Ways of Achieving Uniformity	177
IV.	The Costs and Benefits of Achieving Uniformity	189
V.	Dissent, Performance, and the Quality of Decision Making	195
VI.	Social Control and Social Changes: Some Final Thoughts	204
	References	205

Confession, Inhibition, and Disease

James W. Pennebaker

I.	Introduction	211
II.	The Parameters of Trauma and Confession	212
III.	Confession: Its Effect on Mind and Body	222
IV.	A Theory of Inhibition and Confrontation	230
V.	Implications and Future Directions	236
	References	240

A Sociocognitive Model of Attitude Structure and Function

Anthony R. Pratkanis and Anthony G. Greenwald

I.	Introduction	245
II.	Identification of the Attitude Object: Engaging Attitude Functions	250
III.	Attitude as Heuristic	253
IV.	The Schematic Function of Attitudes	261
V.	The Self-Functions of Attitudes	267
VI.	Concluding Remarks	273
VII.	Summary	274
	References	275

Introspection, Attitude Change, and Attitude–Behavior Consistency: The Disruptive Effects of Explaining Why We Feel the Way We Do

Timothy D. Wilson, Dana S. Dunn, Dolores Kraft, and Douglas J. Lisle

I.	Introduction	287
II.	Thinking about Reasons Reduces Attitude–Behavior Consistency	289
III.	Why Does Thinking about Reasons Reduce Attitude–Behavior Consistency?	292
IV.	Self-Persuasion via Self-Reflection	296
V.	How and When Does Thinking about Reasons Influence Behavior?	301
VI.	Boundary Conditions on the Effects of Thinking about Reasons	308
VII.	Alternative Explanations for the Disruptive Effects of Thinking about Reasons	319
VIII.	Conditions under Which People Think about Reasons	326
IX.	How and When Will Thinking about Reasons Get Us into Trouble?	330
X.	Summary and Conclusions	334
	References	338

Index	345
Contents of Other Volumes	359

CONTRIBUTORS

Numbers in parentheses indicate the pages on which the authors' contributions begin.

LEONARD BERKOWITZ (1), Department of Psychology, University of Wisconsin, Madison, Wisconsin 53706

JOHN T. CACIOPPO (39), Department of Psychology, University of Iowa, Iowa City, Iowa 52242

DANA S. DUNN (287), Department of Psychology, Moravian College, Bethlehem, Pennsylvania 18018

ANTHONY G. GREENWALD (245), Department of Psychology, University of Washington, Seattle, Washington 98195

KAREN HEIMER (1), Department of Sociology, University of Wisconsin, Madison, Wisconsin 53706

E. TORY HIGGINS (93), Department of Psychology, New York University, New York, New York 10003

DOLORES KRAFT (287), Department of Psychology, University of Virginia, Charlottesville, Virginia 22903

ELLEN J. LANGER (137), Department of Psychology, Harvard University, Cambridge, Massachusetts 02138

DOUGLAS J. LISLE (287), Department of Psychology, University of Virginia, Charlottesville, Virginia 22903

CHARLAN JEANNE NEMETH (175), Department of Psychology, University of California, Berkeley, California 94720

JAMES W. PENNEBAKER (211), Department of Psychology, Southern Methodist University, Dallas, Texas 75275

RICHARD E. PETTY (39), Department of Psychology, University of Missouri, Columbia, Missouri 65211

ANTHONY R. PRATKANIS (245), Board of Psychology, University of California, Santa Cruz, California 95064

BARRY M. STAW (175), School of Business Administration, University of California, Berkeley, California 94720

LOUIS G. TASSINARY (39), Department of Psychology, University of Iowa, Iowa City, Iowa 52242

TIMOTHY D. WILSON (287), Department of Psychology, University of Virginia, Charlottesville, Virginia 22903

ON THE CONSTRUCTION OF THE ANGER EXPERIENCE: AVERSIVE EVENTS AND NEGATIVE PRIMING IN THE FORMATION OF FEELINGS

Leonard Berkowitz

DEPARTMENT OF PSYCHOLOGY
UNIVERSITY OF WISCONSIN
MADISON, WISCONSIN 53706

Karen Heimer

DEPARTMENT OF SOCIOLOGY
UNIVERSITY OF WISCONSIN
MADISON, WISCONSIN 53706

I. Introduction

An increasing body of evidence indicates that aversive stimuli can prompt aggressive reactions in humans as well as lower animals (Baron, 1977; Berkowitz, 1983a; Zillmann, 1979). Although the aggression is by no means inevitable (Bandura, 1973), under the right conditions, a remarkably broad range of decidedly unpleasant events can promote hostility or even open attacks on available targets. At the human level, for example, irritable cigarette smoke (Jones & Bogat, 1978; Zillmann, Baron, & Tamborini, 1981), foul odors (Rotton, Frey, Barry, Milligan & Fitzpatrick, 1979), high room temperatures (Baron & Bell, 1975), and disgusting scenes (White, 1979; Zillmann, Bryant, Comisky, & Medoff, 1981) have all been shown to increase the punishment given or hostility displayed to another person. Comparable findings have been reported in naturalistic investigations of the effects of atmospheric conditions on criminal violence. The urban riots in American cities during the late 1960s evidently were exacerbated by unusual summer heat (Baron & Ransberger, 1978; Carlsmith & Anderson, 1979), and high temperatures tend to increase other crimes of violence as well (Anderson & Anderson, 1984). Crime statistics also suggest that high temperatures and atmospheric pollution can even contribute to family disorders (Rotton & Frey, 1985).

It is important to recognize in all this that many of the aggressive actions recorded in these studies could not lessen the aversive stimulation to which the aggressors were exposed; the behavior is thus not always an attempt to eliminate or avoid the aversive situation (Berkowitz, 1983a; Berkowitz, Cochran, & Embree,

1981). Putting this another way, aversively stimulated aggression is often expressive rather than instrumental in nature. Other findings are consistent with this conception. Zillmann, Baron, and Tamborini (1981) showed that subjects exposed to unpleasant tobacco smoke tended to become highly hostile even though they had not been provoked beforehand and could not reasonably blame the target person for their discomfort. And then, too, Baron (1984) reported that deliberately provoked subjects became less hostile toward their tormentor after they had an irrelevant pleasant experience. It is as if the pleasant incident had made these people feel better, thereby lessening their negative affect-generated aggressive inclinations.

These observations raise important questions about the determinants and operation of emotions. How, we might ask, do aversive occurrences affect the neurophysiological motoric, and cognitive reactions often subsumed together under the general rubric "emotion"? In the interests of brevity and manageability, we here focus on emotional *experience,* and especially the experience of anger, so the question becomes, how do unpleasant events influence this type of feeling? Common sense and everyday life tell us that people often feel irritated, annoyed, and at times even angry, when they are afflicted by negative events. How are these experiences to be understood theoretically? Do the aversive incidents produce the annoyance, irritability, and anger directly, or do they have only an indirect influence on these feelings, such as by affecting the appraisal of other events so that annoyance–irritation–anger feelings are appropriate? And furthermore, what is the connection between these feelings and open aggression?

II. Approaches to Emotion and Anger

In recent years, there has been a veritable explosion in the number of books and articles on the topic of emotion, and space limitations do not allow us to review all of the theories of emotion in general or anger in particular that have been advanced in the past few decades. We restrict the present discussion to only a few analyses—those that seem to be attracting the most attention in contemporary social psychology and appear to be most pertinent to the questions we've raised about the effects of aversive events. To simplify matters, we divide these conceptions into two fairly broad categories, depending upon the importance they ascribe to cognitive processes. All of the theories recognize that cognitions can have a major role in the formation and operation of emotions. Indeed, if we confine ourselves to emotional experience, cognitive processes must be involved in some way. However, some formulations regard cognitions as necessary or at least the most important factor in the arousal of the emotional experience, whereas other theories, as Zajonc (1984a, p. 240) has noted, place much greater emphasis on "somatic factors and especially motor output."

A. THEORIES ASSIGNING PARAMOUNT ROLE TO COGNITIVE PROCESSES

The most popular approaches to the study of emotions in present-day social psychology assume that the person's thoughts and interpretations are virtually all-important in shaping the emotional experience. They do not entirely agree, however, as to just how cognitive processes exert this influence. One school of thought, represented by Schachter's (1964; Schachter & Singer, 1962) two-factor theory and Mandler's (1975) very similar conception, holds that the specific emotional experience is determined by the label the aroused persons apply to their bodily sensations. Appraisal theories (e.g., Averill, 1982; Lazarus, Averill, & Opton, 1970; Roseman, 1984), on the other hand, trace the experience to an "appraisal of the significance of a social encounter for one's well-being" (Lazarus, Coyne, & Folkman, 1984, p. 226). Let us look briefly at each of these perspectives.

1. Labeling–Attributional Conceptions

Schachter explicitly rejected the James–Lange contention that each emotion is associated with a particular pattern of physiological reactions. For Schachter, and also for Mandler (1975) who has accepted Schachter's analysis, cognitions shape an affectively neutral arousal state to produce the specific emotions. The emotion-precipitating event presumably creates only a diffuse and general excitation, which the aroused persons supposedly are motivated to interpret. Making use of whatever cues are available in the surrounding situation, they decide what specific emotion they are experiencing and label their feelings accordingly. The theory holds that this self-labeling then produces the differentiated emotional experience such as "anger" or "fear." In other words, the aroused individuals use the situational cues and their past experience in similar situations to infer what their emotional state must be. They would not experience anger, according to this perspective, simply because they were unhappy and/or not feeling well. Something in the surrounding situation supposedly has to give them a reason to believe they were angry before they would actually experience anger and act aggressively.

Schachter's cognition–arousal theory has received some empirical support in recent years, but it has also encountered serious problems (see Cotton, 1981; Leventhal & Tomarken, 1986; Reisenzein, 1983). Reisenzein (1983), for example, has argued that there is "no convincing evidence . . . that emotional states may result from a labeling of unexplained arousal." Other critics have objected to the two-factor theory's contention that people are not able to identify distinctive bodily and physiological reactions for the different emotional states. Thus, Epstein (1984) has shown that anger and other emotions are typically associated with distinctive bodily sensations, while Izard (1977) and Tomkins (1984), among others, have emphasized how distinctive motoric reactions contribute to the various emotional states.

2. Attribution–Appraisal Theories

The development of attributional ideas has resulted in a modification of Schachter's original theory. Proponents of this line of reasoning now typically maintain that the aroused people attribute their sensations to a particular cause and that this attribution then determines how they interpret their feelings. More recently, however, some writers, notably Weiner (1982, 1985; Weiner, Graham, & Chandler, 1982), have separated their attributional approach from Schachter's theory (see Weiner, 1982), bringing their analysis closer to appraisal theorizing. Weiner, perhaps the leading advocate of attributional conceptions of emotion, holds that the first stage in the formation of the negative emotions occurs when there is an unpleasant event, something representing a negative outcome. Theoretically, which specific emotions then arise depends upon the attributions that are made for this occurrence. Anger is supposedly felt when the negative outcome is attributed to a controllable cause internal to the perceived causal agent. Putting this in ordinary language, the theory says that people are most likely to become angry when they believe their negative outcome is due to another's deliberate action. Other studies of the appraisals that are typically involved in angering incidents have yielded findings consistent with this analysis, although with some relatively minor variations. On the basis of his research, Averil (1982, 1983) contends that anger usually grows out of a perceived deliberate misdeed. Smith and Ellsworth (1985) have reported supporting observations in a study in which university students were asked to recall emotional incidents from their past.

For appraisal theories, then, whether they are couched in attributional terms or not, a cognitive assessment of the situation is always involved in emotions. Lazarus has taken this position (Lazarus, Averill, & Opton, 1970; Lazarus, Coyne, & Folkman, 1984), insisting that the full emotional experience—consisting of "thoughts, action impulses, and somatic disturbances"—is impossible unless some form of cognitive appraisal has taken place. There must be some evaluation of the arousing stimulus' relevance for one's well-being.

We can easily combine all of these ideas in a summary statement about the consequences of aversive events: the afflicted persons should not feel angry unless they believe (1) someone was responsible for their suffering, (2) the negative occurrence need not have arisen otherwise, and (3) their tormentor had acted in a socially unjustified manner.

B. POSITIONS HOLDING THAT COGNITIVE APPRAISALS ARE NOT ALL-IMPORTANT

1. Feedback from Neuromuscular Reactions

Although a number of psychologists besides Lazarus insist on the centrality of cognitive appraisals in adult emotionality, other authorities argue that these assessments are not all-important in the formation of emotional experiences. They maintain that expressive–motoric reactions provide an important feedback into the emotion system, either contributing to the emotional experience or even being necessary for its creation. The James–Lange theory is of course the classic variation on this theme and emphasizes the feedback provided by the autonomic system. But more up-to-date versions, particularly the analyses advanced by Tomkins (1962, 1984) and Izard (1977), have generally placed the greatest stress on feedback from the face and other types of neuromuscular reactions. (See Leventhal & Tomarken, 1986, for an assessment of recent research into the effect of expressive reactions on emotions.)

In 1984, Tomkins traced innate forms of affect to certain patterns of neural stimulation from the body. Anger, he said, results from high levels of such stimulation. A brief quotation illustrates his argument: "a slap on the face is likely to arouse anger because of the very high density of receptors on the surface of the face. In contrast, a stab of pain elsewhere in the body may lack both the requisite density and duration to activate more than a cry of distress" (p. 176). It is not clear from this discussion whether Tomkins would predict that unpleasant noises, odors, and heat would produce angry feelings, although he conceivably might expect such an outcome if the aversive condition was sufficiently intense and persistent. At any rate, note that the anger is attributed to a pattern of neural stimulation and not to an appraisal of the unpleasant event.

2. "Preferences Need No Inferences"

Zajonc (1980, 1984a,b) is one of the best known exponents of the view that affective reactions are not always the product of cognitive appraisals. Defining cognition in information-processing terms as involving the transformation of sensory input "according to some more or less fixed code," and noting that this cognitive operation need not be conscious, intentional, or rational, he argues that (1) affect and cognition are separate and partially independent systems, and (2) affective judgments (preferences) can be made without any cognitive encoding.

Appraisal theorists have objected to Zajonc's contention because of their belief in the necessity of cognitive evaluations (e.g., Epstein, 1984; Lazarus, 1984; Lazarus, Coyne, & Folkman, 1984). The controversy is in large part a matter of how one defines "cognition." For Lazarus, cognition is involved when the emotion-generating stimulus is given some meaning even though this meaning is imparted on the basis of very little information, requiring very little information processing. This meaning, presumably having to do with the stimulus' significance for the person's well-being, and which supposedly can exist at a very low level, is said to be necessary if the stimulus is to create an emotional reaction. Zajonc (1984a,b) is bothered by the imprecision in Lazarus's usages of the term *cognition*. Insisting that this concept must have to do with a minimum amount of "mental work," he replies that Lazarus's definition of cognition is so vague and general that it is impossible to determine whether a cognitive appraisal actually occurred.

C. SOME CONCLUDING THOUGHTS ON THIS CONTROVERSY

We do not have to become involved in the details of the argument between Zajonc and his opponents, and we certainly do not have the time to examine all of the intricacies in the debate between the cognitive appraisal position and the neurophysiological–feedback conception. Nonetheless, it is appropriate to summarize where we stand in this general controversy.

First of all, it seems to us, any truly adequate account of emotions must recognize that the person's bodily–motor reactions, especially in the face, can influence emotional feelings. For example, in an experiment by Laird (1974), subjects induced to frown while they were looking at pictures of (Ku Klux) Klansmen increased in reports of angry feelings. After surveying the research into facial feedback effects, Leventhal and Tomarken concluded, "on the basis of our review, we tend to agree with Laird's assessment that expressive changes can alter subjective states" (1986, p. 580). Such an influence is undreamed of in the appraisal theory philosophy. The often-reported displays of emotionality in newborn infants, described by Darwin as well as more recent investigators (see Trevarthen, 1984), are also troublesome for the appraisal position, especially those versions (e.g., Averill, 1982, 1983) holding that emotions are primarily social constructions. As Tomkins has put it, the theories postulating that appraisal is "a necessary condition for affect activation" are "embarrassed" by these indications of the unlearned activation of affect (Tomkins, 1984, p. 170). If we adopt Zajonc's definition of cognition, we must acknowledge that the very young child apparently can feel angry without cognitively appraising the significance of the situation for his or her well-being and can show this anger (in some ways similar to the actions exhibited by enraged adults) even when she or he has not learned how an angry individual is expected to behave.

We also find the Tomkins–Izard approach attractive because it explicitly recognizes the likelihood of innate determinants of affect. This is especially important in considering the effects of aversive stimulation. There probably is very little learning involved in the displeasure we feel when the weather is hot and humid and/or foul odors bombard our nostrils. The heat and smell are inherently bothersome and undoubtedly produce negative affect because they are physiologically offensive rather than because they are given a particular psychological meaning.

III. A Cognitive–Neoassociationistic Analysis of Anger

Though cognitive–appraisal analyses hold that the anger stems only indirectly from the unpleasant occurrence (because an intervening appraisal is presumably necessary), Berkowitz has suggested (1983a,b) that negative affect leads directly to both (1) a primitive experience of anger and (2) aggressive inclinations, as well as to a variety of other basic feelings and action tendencies. According to this cognitive–neoassociationistic model, when people encounter an event they would prefer to avoid or escape (i.e., an aversive stimulus), either because of its inherent properties (e.g., unpleasant heat or a foul odor) or because of their own appraisal of the event (e.g., they might regard the occurrence as a threat or frustration or a disgusting scene), a sequence of reactions is initiated that varies with both time and thought. First of all, the aversive stimulation produces negative affect. Because of the associative linkages that exist between unpleasant feelings and particular somatic, expressive–motor, and cognitive reactions, this negative affect presumably then activates a variety of expressive–motor reactions, feelings, thoughts, and memories that are associated with *both* flight *and* fight (i.e., with inclinations to escape–avoid and to attack). A variety of factors—genetic, learned, and situational—supposedly determine the relative strengths of these two tendencies and their concomitants. Berkowitz also suggests that the experience of fear grows out of one's awareness of the escape-associated reactions, and that the experience of anger is based on the awareness of the aggression-associated expressive–motor responses, feelings, thoughts, and memories. However these emotional feelings are formed, fear and anger can exist together, although not necessarily to the same degree.

A. SOME CONCEPTUAL DISTINCTIONS

Some aspects of this model should be made explicit at this point. For one thing, in agreement with Buss (1961) and Feshbach and Feshbach (1986), it differentiates between *anger, instigation to aggression,* and *hostility,* contending that these terms refer to somewhat different, although correlated, processes. Thus, contrary to Averill's (1982) conception of anger as a syndrome encompassing both experience and action, the present formulation defines anger *only as an experience*. Moreover, the model also implies that the anger experience only *parallels and does not create* the instigation to aggression; the negative affect in itself supposedly produces this instigation, an inclination to harm some available target, preferably (but not only) the perceived source of the displeasure. Hostility, on the other hand, is viewed as an unfavorable judgment or opinion of another. Such a judgment obviously can have a number of different roots, but it can also arise from the negative ideas and memories that are activated by the negative affect. All of this means that although we would expect indicators of unpleasant feelings, anger, hostility, and aggression to be correlated, the correlations probably will not be perfect, and at any rate, aggression, and hostility can be differentiated conceptually.

B. ADDITIONAL EVIDENCE

A host of observations from many different social settings are consistent with this line of reasoning. Going beyond the evidence cited earlier, when Shaver, Schwartz, Kirson, and O'Connor (1987) asked university students to write accounts of their emotional experiences, the researchers found that many of the respondents traced their anger to a variety of unpleasant occurrences. The most frequently mentioned source of anger was some perceived misdeed, but the students also report becoming angry when their goal-directed activity was interrupted (i.e., when they were frustrated), when their expectations were violated, and even when they were under stress and fatigued. Furthermore, also in line with the present formulation, evidence suggests that at least some negative events can give rise to both fear and anger. The students studied by Diener and Iran-Nejad (1986) rated their feelings during whatever emotional episodes they encountered in their daily lives over a period of weeks, and they indicated that fear and anger often went together in these emotional incidents.

Perhaps more to the point, research into depression testifies to the frequent association of depression and anger (see Berkowitz, 1983a). Not a few clinical studies of depressed adults and children have reported that many of these persons are subject to impulsive outbursts of aggression and frequently express angry feelings. Their depression can contribute to their aggressive displays. Contrary to the traditional psychodynamic interpretation of depression as anger turned inward, experiments indicate that the depressive mood tends to generate angry feelings. This is clearly seen when a depressive mood is established experimentally, either through learned helplessness procedures, the Velten technique, or some other similar "thought priming" manipulation. In all of these cases, the people induced to be depressed also tend to describe themselves as being angry (see Hynan & Grush, 1986; Miller & Norman, 1979; Troccoli, 1986). Then too, this depression-heightened anger is at times associated with impulsive displays of overt aggression (Hynan & Grush, 1986).

C. SUBSEQUENT COGNITIVE PROCESSING

All this is not to say that anger, fear, and the other basic negative emotions never become clearly separated. We know from our everyday lives, as well as from a growing body of research (e.g., Russell, 1980; Smith & Ellsworth, 1985), that people frequently distinguish among the various negative emotional states. And furthermore, there also are physiological differences between these states (see Leventhal & Tomarken, 1986). The present formulation suggests that these more differentiated emotional experiences result from further cognitive processing, much of which is at a preconscious level (Dixon, 1981; Epstein, 1984), after the initial negative affect and the rudimentary fear and anger experiences. Appraisals, attributions, and other cognitions now come into play to further differentiate, enrich, or even suppress the negative-affect-produced feelings and action tendencies (Isen, 1984; Leventhal, 1982, 1984; Showers & Cantor, 1985).

1. Activating the "Deeper" Processing

This higher-order, relatively controlled processing does not always go into operation, however; people have to be motivated to think more extensively and more deeply about the various kinds of information they have received (Harkness, DeBono, & Borgida, 1985; Showers & Cantor, 1985). But when this controlled processing does function, the aversively stimulated persons consider their feelings and inclinations, the perceived causes of their arousal, the possible consequences of any action they undertake, and the goals they would like to attain. In this connection, we should note, Epstein (1984) believes that there is a sequence of appraisals in the formation of emotions and suggests that considerations as to what responses are possible in the situation are of major importance in differentiating one emotion from another. Other thoughts might also have an effect. As Bower and Cohen (1982) and Leventhal (1984) theorize, people's feelings may also be affected by the rules they have acquired regarding what feelings are to be expected and/or are appropriate in particular situations.

2. Attention to One's Feelings

Assuming, with Shiffrin and Schneider (1977), that controlled processes require the person's active attention, the present model proposes that the cognitive executive systems regulating the influence of negative affect on subsequent behavior are activated when attention is focused on the self and especially on one's feelings. Some support for this proposal can be found in the Carver and Scheier (1981) discussion of attention and self-regulation and also in the research by Wilson and his associates on the role of introspection in attitude–behavior consistency (Wilson, Dunn, Bybee, Hyman, & Rotondo, 1984), but recent experiments in Berkowitz's laboratory are especially apropos. In three separate studies, Troccoli (1986) demonstrated that subjects experiencing a negative mood were relatively unlikely to be severely openly hostile to a target person when they focused their attention on their feelings. By contrast, the negative mood led to comparatively strong hostility toward the target when the subjects were distracted so that they gave less attention to their feelings. The subjects' attention to their feelings evidently had activated control mechanisms enabling them to regulate the influence of their negative mood on their treatment of the target individual. Because the subjects probably realized that overt hostility was usually socially undesirable, when controlling themselves, they restrained their punitiveness. In line with all this, Hynan and Grush (1986) reported that characteristically impulsive subjects were more likely than their nonimpulsive counterparts to become highly aggressive when they were made depressed, presumably because the former were typically less self-reflective and therefore were less likely to regulate the impact of their negative mood on their actions.

In sum, aversively stimulated anger and the parallel aggressive inclinations need not be revealed openly. The suffering persons might restrain themselves and not attack an available target, even when they are aggressively inclined, if they are conscious of their feelings and are also aware that this action could have unpleasant consequences for them. They might even suppress their angry feelings if they think this experience is inappropriate in the given situation.

3. Differentiating among Anger, Irritation, and Annoyance

In addition to activating behavioral controls, the higher-order cognitive processing can also serve to shape the specific nature of the emotional experience, as was noted here previously. One consequence is that as this emotional experience develops, there is a differentiation among anger, irritation, and annoyance. These feelings are not separate in the initial reaction to negative affect, and they are distinguished at first—if any distinctions are made at all—primarily in terms of the experienced arousal level; the feeling is presumably encoded as annoyance when the arousal is weakest, whereas it is viewed as anger when the arousal is most intense. In this respect, we agree with Gilligan and Bower (1984, p. 577), who suggested that anger is much the same node in the memory network whether it is labeled by the experiencing person as annoyance or anger. Be this as it may, with additional thought and consideration of a variety of factors (including social rules as to when particular emotions are apt to arise or are proper), after the first few moments, people increasingly differentiate among annoyance, irritation, or anger. Thus, if they are exposed to moderately aversive stimulation in a socially legitimate manner (as in the present experiments), they might be willing to say they are annoyed and irritated but be somewhat reluctant to admit feeling angry. Nonetheless, over a broad variety of unpleasant occurrences, feelings of annoyance, irritation, and anger tend to go together so that they are not totally separate.

The higher-order processing can also enrich and complicate the rudimentary feelings by bringing other ideas and memories into play, thereby activating other expressive–motor responses and sensations, along with the initial ones. The basic annoyance–irritation–anger might then turn into, say, contempt or moral outrage.

4. Prototype-Guided Constructions

Whatever the exact nature of the experienced feeling, it is essentially constructed from a variety of inputs. The present analysis holds (in essential agreement with Leventhal's [1982, 1984] views) that people construct their feeling experience on the basis of a number of different sources—their bodily changes, expressive–motor responses, and thoughts and memories. They probably are guided in this construction by the widely shared prototype that exists regarding the particular emotion they believe they are experiencing. Recent research (e.g., Shaver *et al.*, 1987) indicates that many persons in our society possess a common conception as to just what is involved in the specific emotions. According to Shaver and his associates (1987), anger is one of the basic emotions in people's natural taxonomy of emotions—along with love (affection), joy (happiness), surprise, sadness, and fear—and most of us share ideas as to what kinds of events typically create anger and how this emotion is usually experienced. This suggests that if the aroused persons think of themselves as "angry" (the process emphasized by Schachter's two-factor theory), they will combine all of the various thoughts and sensations they have in keeping with their conception of how anger should feel. Because of this construction, experienced emotion is not only an inference, as attribution–appraisal theories would have it.

D. EMOTIONS AS NETWORKS IN MEMORY

In this last regard especially, the present conception of anger is generally influenced by the developing network analyses of emotion (e.g., Bower, 1981; Bower & Cohen, 1982; Lang, 1979; and especially Leventhal, 1982,1984), but it differs from these other formulations in two important respects. Most important, more than Leventhal (1984) and Bower and Cohen (1982), the model offered here emphasizes the possibility that the negative affect in itself can involuntarily evoke aggressive reactions. Berkowitz's research has even been guided by the working assumption that virtually any kind of unpleasant event can produce aggressive inclinations and their associated feelings, thoughts, and memories. Second, the present formulation tends to give somewhat greater attention to the changes in thoughts, memories, and feelings as cognitive processing becomes deeper and more extensive. But over and above these differences, all of these analyses basically regard the separate feelings as nodes (or units) in an associative network, with these nodes being linked to autonomic patterns, expressive–motor reactions, thoughts, and memories. All of these conceptions also suggest that the arousal of any one component in the network would also tend to activate the other components with which it is connected.

1. *Feeling-activated ideas*. This last point clearly means that if negative affect is linked to anger and aggressive inclinations, as the model contends, unpleasant feelings should give rise to aggression-related ideas, as well as to an angry mood and aggressive tendencies. Findings obtained in Brendan Rule's laboratory (Rule, Taylor, & Dobbs, 1987) support this possibility. In contrast to subjects who were situated in rooms having a comfortable temperature, men and women who were exposed to unpleasantly high ambient temperatures were more likely to express hostile ideas in response to appropriate cues.

2. *Thought-activated feelings*. The present cognitive–neoassociationistic network formulation can also account for the influence of thoughts on feelings. Observers of human behavior have long noted how people's thoughts can activate emotional reactions (e.g., Pavlov, 1927). Among the more recent examples, Bandura pointed out that people can frighten themselves with fear-provoking thoughts and can "become sexually aroused by generating erotic fantasies" (1973), p. 45), whereas Novaco's (1975) complex procedure for training anger control teaches persons, among other things, to employ emotion-calming ideas when they are provoked. The Velten (1968) mood-induction procedure is yet another illustration of how thoughts can induce particular feelings.

The network analyses basically explain such observations by holding that memory is a collection of networks in which substantive elements of thought and feelings are linked associatively (e.g., Bower, 1981; Bower & Cohen, 1982). Bringing any one thought element into focal awareness theoretically activates this node; but in addition, the activation also spreads along the associative pathways to other elements in the network. As a consequence, these other ideas and/or feelings are easily aroused and quick to come to mind. The research into priming effects is readily interpreted in this light (Berkowitz, 1984). Thus, after subjects constructed sentences using words having aggressive connotations, they tended to evaluate a target person relatively unfavorably (Wyer & Hartwick, 1980), presumably because the use of the aggression-related words had activated other aggression-related thoughts that colored the subjects' judgments of the target. And similarly, in another study (Carver, Ganellen, Froming, & Chambers, 1983), the participants constructing the aggressive sentences also tended to deliver the most intense electric shocks to a fellow student whenever that individual made a mistake. Their aggressive ideas evidently led to aggressive acts.

Unlike some discussions of the priming effect, which emphasize only the activation of ideas semantically related to the priming task, but very much in line with the network formulation just summarized, the present reasoning holds that the initial thought-generating assignment can activate feelings as well as thoughts. As a case in point, when thinking about good deeds, people can both develop more positive assessments of other persons and experience happy feelings (Veitch, DeWood, & Bosko, 1977). Certain kinds of ideas are especially likely to activate annoyance–irritation–anger (A–I–A) feelings. Because we are often angry when we attack someone, anger should be linked to aggression, and thoughts of aggression should tend to promote angry feelings. In other words, merely thinking of hurting someone deliberately—which is commonly regarded as an aggressive action—should tend to activate the anger experience (unless the aggression is viewed as wrong or dangerous.) Furthermore, if aversive events tend to generate annoyance, irritation, and anger, as we propose, ideas about decidedly unpleasant incidents could also arouse these particular feelings.

IV. The Present Research

The present article reports four experiments illustrating the utility of our cognitive–neoassociationistic analysis of anger. Consistent with our formulation, and in opposition to the cognitive–attributional perspective (e.g., Averill, 1982; Weiner, 1985), these studies indicate that feelings of annoyance, irritation, and anger can be produced both by exposure to decidedly unpleasant stimulation and by thoughts about aggression and/or unpleasant occurrences. This can happen, moreover, even when the encountered or imagined aversive events are not regarded as illegitimate and improper. Furthermore, these two effects typically tend to summate. Where the Schachter–Singer (1962) two-factor theory of emotion suggests that thoughts shape a relatively high arousal state (so that our two experimental variables—feelings and thoughts—should interact), the present results consistently show that aversive stimulation and ideas can operate somewhat independently of each other to affect the final experience.

In keeping with the reasoning spelled out earlier, the findings also indicate that the participants' A–I–A feelings were relatively uninfluenced by the conjectured high-order processing systems. Presumably because the subjects had to rate themselves on a good number of feelings items and also believed that the study was concerned with matters other than their emotions, they apparently were not especially aware of any particular feelings; when they had to make the requested ratings, they could recognize, more or less in passing, that they were annoyed and irritated, and they acknowledged the feelings. However, they did not dwell on these thoughts too long, and they did not attempt to control them.

The research described here also gives some (but lesser) attention to measures of overt aggression. This is done primarily to demonstrate that the experienced feelings can parallel open behavior, as Berkowitz has argued (1983b). However, it is important to realize that there is *no* claim that the A–I–A feelings *generate* the instigation to aggression; the feeling and behavioral systems can operate somewhat independently of each other. Demonstrating this relative independence, in some of the studies, the participants apparently restrained the public display of aggression even though they reported being fairly annoyed. While the research reported here does not directly address the factors that produce these restraints, other investigations from our laboratory (Troccoli, 1986) have demonstrated that people are especially apt to regulate their negative-affect-generated aggressive inclinations when they focus their attention on their unpleasant feelings. It is reasonable to propose, then, that the present subjects controlled themselves and held back in displaying open hostility as a result of much the same kind of self-attention. Presumably because some situational influences had made them aware of their feelings and aggressive inclinations, they evidently were reluctant to treat the available target harshly because they believed such an action would make them feel worse by arousing guilt and/or evaluation apprehension.

A. EXPERIMENT 1

The first experiment heightened the accessibility of anger-related ideas and feelings in two ways: through exposure to mildly or very aversive stimulation and/or by a priming task requiring subjects to write an essay advocating the use of punishment in training. In establishing this latter variation, we basically assumed that the thought of punishment would generally be associated with at least two ideas: (1) the deliberate injury of another, a notion having aggressive connotations, and (2) the notion that punishment frequently comes about in response to someone's erroneous or improper conduct—conduct that usually has an unpleasant meaning. Thus, because of these linkages with ideas of aggression and/or wrongdoing, in thinking about punishment, the participants presumably would also be primed to feel bad in general as well as, more specifically, irritated, annoyed, and perhaps even angry. Our expectation, contrary to what would be predicted from the Schachter–Singer two-factor theory of emotion, was that each experimental treatment would independently increase anger-related feelings rather than interact with the other treatment. This should happen, furthermore, even though the subjects had no reason to believe they had suffered illegitimately in being exposed to the cold water and/or the punishment-essay requirement. From the attribution–appraisal perspective, there was no basis for anger arousal.

1. Method

The subjects were 41 male undergraduates recruited from introductory psychology classes. Five of these men were excluded (2 from each of the cold-water conditions) because they each violated instructions and removed a hand from the water before they were told to do so, resulting in 9 subjects in each of the four experimental conditions.

As was standard in our early experiments in this research area, another male student (the experimenter's accomplice posing as a fellow subject) joined the naive participant in the laboratory waiting room. The two were met by the male experimenter, also an undergraduate, who escorted them to the laboratory and told them they would be serving in an investigation of the effects of physical discomfort on creativity and imagination. Explaining that the study was generally concerned with how imaginative supervisors were and how well they generally did their job when they were physically uncomfortable, the experimenter said the research was particularly focused on the effects of this discomfort on the supervisor's imagination and creativity. To establish this discomfort, one of the two, supposedly to be chosen randomly, would function as the supervisor and would have to carry out several tasks while keeping one hand in a tank of water. The subjects were assured the procedure, which would last approximately 7 minutes, would not produce any physical damage, and they were asked if they were willing to participate. All agreed to do so.

After the two men signed the preferred consent form, they were asked to draw lots for their roles, and the naive subject always found that he was to be the supervisor. The two were then assigned to separate cubicles, ostensibly to eliminate any verbal or nonverbal communication between them. When the "supervisor" was settled in his booth, the experimenter played an audiotape recorder giving the subject previously tape-recorded information about his two forthcoming tasks. The message drew the participant's attention to the tank of water on the desk next to him, and he was told (1) he would have to immerse his nondominant hand in the water up to his wrist when the signal was given, and (2) he was to keep the hand in the water throughout each task. In the first phase, the subject was informed, he was to demonstrate how creative he could be by writing an imaginative essay on a specified topic. During this time (the experimenter added) his partner, the "worker," would be trying to come up with solutions to several business-related problems that had been assigned to him. In the next phase, after the supervisor had written his essay, he would have to evaluate the worker's problem solutions, using the apparatus on the desk near the water tank.

In making these latter judgments in the second phase, the subject was to reinsert his hand in the water and give the worker feedback for each of his ideas by pressing either the "reward," the "punish," or the "ignore" button on the apparatus. The participant was told at this time that his response could range anywhere from five presses on the reward button (which supposedly would deliver five nickels to the worker) to five administrations of punishment (which would give the worker five unpleasant blasts of noise that he would hear over his earphones). If the subject preferred, he could ignore any of the "worker's" answers by pressing the ignore button on the apparatus when that answer was given.

Starting the experiment, the tape-recorded instructions then told the participant to put his nondominant hand in the water up to the wrist, and the subject found that the water was either a decidedly aversive 6°C or a much less aversive 23°C. He was then assigned the topic for his essay. In all cases, the prerecorded statement said the topic was "unusual" in order to assess the subject's creativity.

For the punishment priming condition, the instructions then noted that Americans generally do not like to punish people when they make mistakes but added that punishment could be effective if it is carried out properly. The subject was asked to write a brief essay "defending the use of punishment." He was to think of reasons why "punishment is sometimes desirable."

In the neutral priming group, on the other hand, the "unusual" topic was to describe the "joys of winter cold and snow" in the northern U.S. and say what was wrong with life in the Sunbelt states. Each subject was informed that he would have 5 minutes for this writing. Unbeknownst to the participant, the experimenter periodically looked through the one-way mirror in the cubicle door to make sure the subject was following the instructions.

At the end of the writing period, the subject removed his hand from the water and filled out a questionnaire requiring him to rate how he had experienced the water and how he had felt at that time. He also indicated how free he felt to remove his hand from the water, his attitudes toward the experiment and experimenter, and also responded to a manipulation check. Each item presented a 9-step bipolar scale anchored at the low end with the phrase "not at all" and at the high end with the words "very much."

There are two types of measures in the present study: Self-reported feelings and overt behaviors. In the former category, the first index established was designed to determine whether we had created the intended differences in the unpleasantness of the situation to which the participants were exposed. This was the *aversiveness index,* based on how the water was rated ("comfortable," "unpleasant," "tolerable," or "painful"). The next measure was a felt-anger index, the *A–I–A index,* consisting of the ratings of how "annoyed," "irritable," and "angry" the subjects had felt when their hand was in the water.

Although both indices had a satisfactory internal consistency (Cronbach's alpha typically being at least .9 throughout the series of studies), we also examined the results with annoyed, irritable, and angry taken separately to see if the effects would be less for the anger ratings than for the annoyed and irritable measures. On the basis of our preliminary experience with these items, we expected the subjects given the highly aversive stimulation to rate themselves as relatively highly annoyed, somewhat less irritable, and only moderately or slightly angry— although they should be higher on all three measures than the other participants exposed to the less aversive stimulation. Finally, the subjects' ratings of how "sad" and "distressed" they had felt were also analyzed. Although the present theoretical formulation leads us to expect *some* degree of positive intercorrelations among the various negative-affect items, we also inquired whether the men had differentiated among their negative feeling states to any extent.

As was indicated earlier, the behavioral measures were obtained in the second phase of the study immediately after the men rated their feelings. The tape-recorded instructions again asked the subjects to immerse their nondominant hand in the water, and the participants then heard another voice, supposedly the "worker's," slowly call off five solutions to each of the two business-related problems previously given him. The subjects were to evaluate each answer by delivering anywhere from five rewards (nickels) to five punishments (noise blasts) to the worker as a judgment of the quality of the solution. The measures refer to (1) the number of trials (i.e., solutions) on which rewards were given or on which punishments were delivered, and (2) the total number of rewards and total number of punishments administered over all trials. Because the subjects could choose to ignore any of the "worker's" solutions by pressing the ignore button, the number of punishment trials is not simply 10 minus the number of reward trials.

2. Results

a. Manipulation Effectiveness. The subjects' responses to several of the items on the questionnaire testify to the effectiveness of the experimental manipulations. First, the men exposed to the 6°C water temperature rated the water as significantly colder than did the subjects in the 23°C water group ($F[1,32] = 50.39$, $p < .001$). More interestingly, the subjects' ratings of the effectiveness of punishment, summarized on the second line of Table I, indicate that the propunishment

TABLE I
EFFECTS OF WATER TEMPERATURE AND ESSAY TOPIC: EXPERIMENT 1

Item[a]	Highly aversive water temperature		Less aversive water temperature		Significant effects[b]
	Punishment essay	Neutral essay	Punishment essay	Neutral essay	
Aversiveness index	6.0	6.7	4.4	2.4	T, T × E
Punishment effectiveness	4.8	4.3	5.0	3.0	E ($p = .07$)
Felt free	5.1	2.4	3.6	5.3	T × E
A–I–A index*	5.4	4.7	4.0	1.9	T, E
Annoyed*	6.0	5.4	4.7	2.2	T, E ($p = .06$)
Irritable*	6.2	4.9	3.6	2.0	T, E
Angry*	3.9	3.7	3.7	1.3	T, E
Sad*	4.0	2.3	2.3	1.3	T, E
Distressed*	5.4	5.0	3.2	2.2	T
Number of reward trials	6.4	8.0	6.7	7.9	E
Total rewards	13.0	24.8	15.2	15.8	E, T × E
Number of punishment trials*	2.7	1.3	1.7	0.9	T, E
Total punishment*	4.0	2.7	2.2	1.2	T

[a]For each item, the higher the score the stronger is the indicated reaction.
[b]T, temperature effect; E, essay topic effect.
*The planned comparison was significant at $p < .01$.

assignment had tended to activate ideas favorable to this disciplinary procedure. When the men were asked, "In your opinion, how effective is it usually to punish someone in order to get him to improve his performance?" those in the punishment-priming condition tended to answer more affirmatively than their counterparts in the neutral-priming group. Although this difference did not quite achieve statistical significance ($F[1,32] = 3.37$, $p < .07$), a Duncan Multiple Range test of the differences among the four means showed that there was a reliable difference between the punishment and the neutral essay groups under the less aversive water temperature. The main effect for essay probably did not attain the conventional .05 level of confidence because of the relatively strong belief in the efficacy of punishment in the highly aversive (6°C) neutral-priming group. The men's exposure to the unpleasantly cold water alone had apparently inclined them to think relatively favorably about punishment.

Another finding is also consistent with our thesis that aversive stimulation increases the accessibility of ideas semantically associated with anger and aggression. If this phenomenon exists, we reasoned, the 6°C water should have facilitated the writing of the propunishment essay and made the neutral essay somewhat more difficult to compose. Evidence directly supporting this assumption could not be found in the content of the written statements, perhaps because the essays were typically brief and only a small number of subjects were in each condition. Nevertheless, the participants tended to write significantly longer statements favoring the use of punishment in the aversive water temperature condition (mean = 66.1 words) than under the more tolerable water temperature (mean = 53.1 words; $t[1,16] = 3.00$). Those assigned the neutral essay were not affected by the unpleasantness of the water temperature and tended to write about 73 words in both temperature groups.

Also in accord with our contention are the results obtained with the questionnaire item asking the subjects how free they felt to remove their hand from the water during the essay-writing task. In replying to this question, the participants might have been responding not only to the pressure they thought the experimenter was putting on them but also their willingness to carry out the desired action. They might have felt freer, in other words, if they wanted to do what was asked of them. The third line of Table I shows that the subjects felt the lowest level of pressure when the essay topic was presumably consistent with the temperature-generated inclinations (i.e., in the 6°C highly aversive, punishment-essay and the 23°C mildly aversive, neutral-essay groups), and that they felt the greatest pressure when the water temperature and essay topic were not consistent. This interaction was significant in the analysis of variance, $F(1,32) = 5.36$, $p = .02$, and the men exposed to the painfully cold water reliably reported feeling under less pressure when writing in favor of punishment than when composing the neutral essay. Taken together, all of these findings suggest that the subjects did not regard it as especially onerous to argue in favor of punishment when their hand was in the aversively cold water. The participants' evaluations of the experimenter and the experiment, obtained at the end of the session, are in keeping with this assessment. The conditions did not differ significantly in how favorably the men rated the experimenter or the investigation itself.

b. Feelings. The reasoning guiding the present research holds that both experimental variations—the priming task as well as the aversive stimulation—should have affected (1) the unpleasantness of the subjects' experience, (2) how annoyed, irritated, and perhaps even angry they said they felt, and (3) other negative feelings as well. The results obtained with the self-reported feelings items, summarized in Table I, are generally in line with this expectation.

Not surprisngly, the analysis of variance of the aversiveness ratings revealed a highly significant main effect for water temperature ($F[1,32] = 46.70, p < .001$) as well as a significant interaction ($F[1,32] = 10.59, p = .003$). According to a Duncan Multiple Range test with this index (not shown in the table), the punishment essay resulted in reliably more unpleasant ratings on this measure than did the neutral essay only under the less painful water temperature. A ceiling effect of some sort might have kept the people in the highly aversive water temperature condition from admitting more discomfort so that the additional impact of the punishment essay was not detected.

The results with the ratings of how "annoyed," "irritable," and "angry" the participants felt are very much as predicted. The A–I–A index yielded significant main effects for both temperature ($F = 12.3, p = .001$) and essay topic ($F = 5.5, p = .02$), as did the separate items "angry" (both $Fs = 4.2, p = .04$), and "irritable" ($Fs = 14.4, p < .001$, and $3.9 p = .05$, for temperature and essay, respectively). On the item, "annoyed," the temperature variation led to a significant effect ($F = 8.2, p = .007$), but the essay variation was only nearly significant ($F = 3.6, p = .06$). Because of the clear-cut expectations with these measures, planned comparisons were also carried out to test the prediction that the men in the highly aversive water-temperature–punishment essay condition would report the strongest feeling of annoyance–irritability–anger, while these feelings would be weakest in the highly aversive (23°C) neutral-essay group. The predictions were confirmed significantly for all measures: A–I–A ($t[32] = 4.16$), annoyed ($t[32] = 3.38$), irritable ($t = 4.10$), and angry ($t = 2.93$). This consistent pattern also testifies to the basic commonality among the three A–I–A feelings.

The findings with the remaining two feelings items were also pretty much as expected. Both experimental variables produced significant main effects on the men's ratings of how sad they felt (both F's $= 5.8, p = .02$), and the planned comparison was also significant ($t = 3.42$). On the other hand, for the measure of distress, only the water temperature variation yielded a significant main effect ($F = 9.2, p = .004$), although here too the planned comparison was significant ($t = 2.80$).

c. Rewards and Punishments. Analyses of variance were also carried out on the rewards and ounishments measures to determine whether the results obtained with the feelings items would parallel the way the subjects evaluated the "worker's" performance. These analyses indicated that the delivery of rewards and the administration of punishments operated somewhat differently.

As can be seen at the bottom of Table I, the essay topic was the primary influence on the rewards given. In comparison to the people assigned the neutral topic, the participants who argued in favor of punishments subsequently delivered rewards on fewer trials ($F[1,32] = 7.81, p < .01$) and gave fewer rewards overall ($F = 6.37, p = .02$). Temperature also interacted significantly with essay topic on this latter measure ($F = 5.27, p = .03$), because (for some reason) those in the aversive-water-temperature–neutral-priming condition were the most rewarding of all. For the punishment measures, on the other hand, both the unpleasantness of the water temperature to which the subjects were exposed and the essay priming exerted an influence. Pointing to the role of the aversive stimulation, the men in the 6°C water group were punitive on more trials than their counterparts in the warmer water condition ($F = 4.07, p = .05$) and also administered a greater total number of punishments ($F = 4.12, p = .05$). In the analysis of variance, the essay topic had a significant impact on only the number of trials in which punishments were given ($F = 8.69, p \leq .01$). However, the paired comparisons showed, as predicted, that the subjects in the aversive-water-temperature–punishment-priming group were punitive on more trials and administered a greater number of punishments overall than the people in any of the other conditions, while the participants in the less aversive-water-temperature–neutral-priming group were least punitive on both measures ($t = 3.56$ and 2.52, $p < .01$, respectively).

d. Correlations between Feelings and Actions. The correlations between the feelings measures and the total numbers of rewards and punishments administered, summarized in Table II, also testify to the differences between the rewarding and punishing behaviors in this study. In general, the men's negative feelings seemed to affect how harsh they were toward their partner but not how many rewards they gave him. They were inclined to be punitive rather than merely withhold rewards if they felt bad. Whatever the specific reason for this, the subjects' feelings evidently had some influence on their subsequent actions. The table also indicates that not all of the negative feelings had the same effects. The participants' experienced sadness was not significantly related to their later punitiveness. And further, even though the three A–I–A components were significantly intercorrelated (between .62 and .68), only the felt annoyance and irritability ratings significantly predicted the total number of punishments (r's $= .37$ and $.34$, respectively, $p < .05$). At least some of the men who had been aware of their angry feelings might have attempted to restrain their punitiveness. Thinking of themselves as "angry," they might have believed such an emotion was too strong a feeling under the given circumstances. This consciousness of the desirability of being appropriate could have led them to control their actions

TABLE II
CORRELATIONS BETWEEN FEELINGS MEASURES AND TOTAL NUMBERS OF REWARDS AND PUNISHMENTS: EXPERIMENT 1[a]

Feelings	SD[b]	Total rewards	Total punishments
A–I–A	2.2	−.15	.32*
Annoyed	2.7	−.06	.37*
Irritable	2.6	−.18	.34*
Angry	2.1	−.16	.10
Aversiveness index	3.1	.17	.32*
Sad	1.8	−.13	.14
Distressed	2.7	−.12	.40**

[a]The indicated Pearson product–moment correlations are based on all 36 cases in the experiment.
[b]SD = Standard deviation of each of the 9-step feelings ratings.
*$p = .05$.
**$p = .02$.

somewhat. On the other hand, those who thought themselves "distressed" were evidently not as strongly motivated to regulate their punishments, presumably because they did not regard this particular feeling as improper or unwarranted. Consequently, their negative affect could be translated into aggressive behavior ($r = .40, p < .02$).

B. EXPERIMENT 2

The preceding experiment assumed that the idea of punishment would have both unpleasant and aggressive associations. However, while many persons probably do think of punishment as the deliberate injury of another, and thus impart an aggressive meaning to the word, it undoubtedly has other meanings as well, such as "an educative procedure carried out in the best interests of those being disciplined." This type of meaning does not necessarily have aggressive implications. The second experiment addressed this ambiguity by attempting to focus the participants' thoughts more directly on the aggressive aspects of punishments. Some of the subjects were required to think of how punishment could hurt those being disciplined, whereas others had to concentrate on the ways in which punishment might be helpful. In both cases, the notion of punishment is associated with wrongdoing and mistakes, but in the former condition, the participants were more apt to be also reminded of the possibly aggressive nature of the act as well as the disciplined individual's suffering. Because of these latter connotations, in thinking of how punishment could be hurtful, the subjects presumably would be primed to feel irritable, annoyed, and perhaps even angry, and might also experience other negative feelings as well.

1. Method

Fifty undergraduate men served in the study but the data for six were discarded, three in each of the two temperature-level conditions, because they violated instructions and did not keep their hand fully immersed in the water. Consequently, there are 11 men in each group in the 2 × 2 design.

The cold stressor procedure followed in the first experiment was also employed in this study. However, because this investigation actually had been conducted more than a year before Experiment 1, there were some differences: The less aversive water temperature in this experiment was 18°C (instead of 23°C.), whereas the highly aversive water temperature was the same 6°C. Also, the final questionnaire used in this earlier experiment did not contain several of the items used in the previously reported investigation. Otherwise, the subjects were given much the same information and instructions.

The major procedural difference had to do with the kind of essays the subjects wrote. In the punishment-hurts essay condition, the "unusual" essay topic was to say why it was at times desirable to punish someone in a hurtful manner. On the other hand, in the punishment-helps essay group, they were to explain why punishment could be helpful to those being trained.

2. Results

a. Manipulation Checks. Even though the water temperature variation was not especially great in absolute terms (only 12°C), it produced highly significant main effects for water temperature on two relevant items. The participants exposed to the highly aversive treatment rated the water as significantly colder, and said they had enjoyed the experiment reliably less, than the subjects in the less aversive water temperature condition ($F[1,40] = 38.67$, $p < .001$, and 4.56, $p = .04$, respectively). No other significant effects were obtained with these items.

A major problem in this study, as in the previously reported one, has to do with the men's attitudes toward their essay assignment. More specifically, it is important to ascertain whether it was especially difficult or unpleasant for the subjects to write the essay arguing for the desirability of hurtful punishment. In the preceding experiment, it will be recalled, the subjects in the highly aversive water temperature condition apparently did not regard the punishment-essay task as especially onerous. The same amount of evidence, one way or another, is not available in this study, but some findings indicate that the participants were not under heavy stress when they wrote their punishment-hurts essay during the highly aversive water temperature condition. For one thing, as was just mentioned, the essay topic did not affect the participants' rated enjoyment of the experiment.

But more important, the results with the item assessing the subjects' liking for the experimenter suggest that the men exposed to the painfully cold water actually might have obtained some gratification in thinking about hurting someone. The analysis of variance of the item ratings revealed a significant interaction ($F[1,40] = 6.43, p = .01$), and the condition means are reported in the first data line of Table III. The subjects exposed to the less unpleasant water temperature expressed a reliably lower liking for the experimenter when they wrote about injurious rather than helpful punishment (by Duncan Multiple Range test, $p < .05$). It is as if the people in the former condition greatly resented the experimenter's requirement that they argue in favor of hurting someone. However, this pattern was reversed in the highly aversive water temperature group. Here, those asked to write about the merits of hurtful punishment tended to like the experimenter somewhat (but not significantly) more than their counterparts given the same aversive stimulation but who had to think about helpful punishment. Because of this reversal, the (6°C) highly aversive–punishment-hurts essay subjects rated the experimenter significantly more favorably (by Duncan Multiple Range test, $p < .05$) than the people writing the same essay under the more tolerable water temperature. Again, at the very least, these results indicate that the men given the painful cold stressor treatment did not find it unpleasantly difficult to advocate harmful punishment.

b. Feelings Measures. The results obtained by analyses of variance of the feelings ratings were basically in accord with our theoretical expectations. On the aversiveness index (the second data line in Table III), there was a significant main effect for water temperature ($F[1,40] = 32.27, p < .001$) and a near-significant effect for essay topic ($F[1,40] = 3.77, p = .06$), indicating that both

TABLE III
EFFECTS OF WATER TEMPERATURE AND ESSAY TOPIC: EXPERIMENT 2

Measure	Highly aversive water temperature punishment		Less aversive water temperature punishment		Significant effects
	Hurts	Helps	Hurts	Helps	
Like experimenter	7.3	6.6	6.1	7.4	T × E
Aversiveness index*	7.0	5.9	4.5	4.2	T, E (.06)
A–I–A index*	5.9	4.2	4.2	3.5	T, E
Annoyed*	6.6	5.3	5.4	3.8	T, E
Irritable*	6.4	4.7	4.5	3.7	T, E
Angry	4.5	2.6	2.7	2.9	—
Sad	3.3	3.0	2.6	2.8	—
Distressed*	6.3	3.2	3.5	3.1	T, E, T × E

*The planned comparisons involving these measures (testing the prediction that the groups in the first and fourth columns would have the strongest and weakest feelings) yielded significant ($p < .01$) t values.

manipulations had independently affected the unpleasantness of the subjects' experience. Apparently feeling bad because of the negative ideas and feelings activated by these two treatments, the people in the highly aversive-water-temperature–punishment-hurts group reported a stronger unpleasant experience than the participants in any other condition. Further, the planned comparison testing the expected condition differences among the four groups was also significant ($t[40] = 5.47, p < .001$).

The planned comparisons carried out with the A–I–A index scores and the component items "annoyed" and "irritable" were also significant, as predicted (t's[40] = 3.18, 3.24, and 3.14, respectively, $p < .01$). In the case of the "angry" ratings, however, though the people in the highly aversive-water-temperature–punishment-hurts group did have the highest scores, those exposed to the more tolerable water temperature while writing the punishment-helps essay did not have the expected lowest ratings. Nor did the "sad" ratings yield a significant planned-comparison result. By contrast, there was the expected significant outcome for the participants' ratings of how "distressed" they felt ($t = 3.66, p < .001$). These different findings suggest that the men had differentiated among the negative items to some extent.

c. Behavioral Measures. Unlike the preceding study, the analyses of variance of the rewards and punishments scores in this experiment did not yield any significant effects. Perhaps because their assigned essay topic had somehow made the participants in this investigation think about the possibly hostile nature of any punishments they administered to the worker (especially when they were explicitly asked to advocate injurious punishment), the men in this particular experiment apparently controlled their actions to a considerable degree. At any rate, while the present investigation did not replicate the earlier behavioral findings reported by Berkowitz *et al.* (1981), at the very least, it did demonstrate that the thought of injurious punishment can activate feelings associated with annoyance, irritability, and perhaps even anger.

C. EXPERIMENT 3

Where the subjects in the previously reported studies had all been men, the participants in the final two experiments in this series were women. The aforementioned investigations by Berkowitz *et al.* (1981) had indicated that the aversive-cold-stressor treatment tends to heighten the accessibility of A–I–A-related thoughts and feelings in women as well as men, but we also wanted to determine how a thought-priming experience would combine with the aversive stimulation to affect the women's feelings and actions. In this case, however, the priming was produced by asking the subjects to imagine a particular incident rather than by requiring them to write a brief essay.

1. Method

The participants were 40 undergraduate women who were recruited in the same manner as the male subjects in the earlier experiments. There were 10 persons in each of the four experimental conditions.

Unlike the previous studies, which employed a confederate posing as a fellow subject, the last two experiments only pretended to have this second individual. After the (female) experimenter had explained that the study sought to investigate the effects of unusual physical conditions on thought processes and supervisory effectiveness, a knock was heard at the laboratory door. The experimenter commented that "the other subject" had finally arrived, went to the door, opened it, and told the person supposedly there to wait in the adjoining room. Returning to the participant, she then informed the woman about both the cold-stressor situation and the way in which her imagination would be "stimulated" by having her think about a particular situation.

The subject entered the "supervisor's" cubicle and was instructed by the experimenter's previously tape-recorded voice to immerse her nondominant hand in the water tank next to the desk. In this third experiment, the water temperature was either a highly aversive 7°C or a less aversive 23°C. The participant then received her "thought-stimulating" assignment, supposedly while her partner, the "worker," was dealing with the problems given to her. With her hand in the water, the subject read a card on her desk describing a particular situation and was asked to imagine the incident and speak her thoughts aloud. In half of the cases (annoying-incident condition) she was to imagine a situation our prior testing had found to be highly annoying to many women: She had been "stood up" by a former boyfriend who had asked to meet her for a cup of coffee but failed to show up for the appointment. The remaining subjects (neutral-incident condition) were to think of themselves taking a bus ride through the countryside.

At the end of 5 minutes, the experimenter's tape-recorded voice instructed the participant to take her hand from the water and answer the questionnaire in the folder on the desk. The 9-step bipolar items, similar to those used in the earlier studies, asked the subject to rate her feelings at the time her hand was in the water. A new score, the *pleasantness index,* was established based on the items "happy," "relaxed," and "comfortable" to replace the no-longer-available aversiveness index.

When the questionnaire was completed, the subject reimmersed her hand in the water tank and heard another woman (ostensibly the "worker") read off her 10 ideas for solving the two business-related problems that had been assigned to her. As in the first two studies, the participant was to evaluate each solution by giving the "worker" a response ranging from five rewards to five punishments, although she could also ignore any idea by pressing the "ignore" button. The measures here were the total number of rewards and punishments delivered to the "worker" over the 10 trials. Finally, at the completion of this phase, after the subject took her hand from the water, she responded to another questionnaire indicating her attitude toward her partner, the experiment, and the experimenter.

2. Results

a. Difficulty of Priming Task. As in the earlier studies, there is no reason to believe that the present conditions differed in terms of how difficult it was to carry out the priming task. Analyses of variance of the scores on the item asking the subjects how easy it was to imagine the described incident did not reveal any significant effects. Nor did the conditions differ in reactions to the questions assessing the women's attitudes toward the experiment and the experimenter.

b. Feelings. Both experimental treatments influenced the subjects' reported feelings generally in the expected manner. With the exception of the women's reported sadness, all of the feelings items yielded a significant planned comparison. The people's exposed to the highly aversive water temperature while imagining the annoying incident tended to have the most unpleasant feelings, whereas those in the less-aversive-water-temperature–neutral-incident condition typically had the least negative feelings. (The t values in the planned comparisons are 4.24 for the pleasantness index, 5.94 for the A–I–A measure, 4.40, 5.71, and 5.21 for the three A–I–A component items, and 3.00 for the "distressed" rating; for 36 df, $p < .01$ in every case.)

However, there are also indications that the A–I–A items tended to be somewhat more sensitive to the annoying priming task than were the other feelings measures. As can be seen in Table IV, the difference between the annoying priming and neutral priming groups in the less aversive water temperature condition was relatively small on the unpleasantness and felt-distress measures, but it was much more substantial on the A–I–A items. Thus, where the priming variation produced reliable differences on every feeling measure under the painfully cold water temperature, by Duncan Multiple Range test, only the A–I–A index and felt-anger scores gave rise to significant priming differences under the mildly aversive water treatment. But still, the effects of the two experimental treatments combined so that the women required to think of the two experimental treatments combined so that the women required to think of the annoying incidence while exposed to the painfully cold water had the highest scores on the A–I–A index and items as well as on felt distress.

c. Reactions to Other Person. Presumably because of these activated feelings (and the associated ideas), the priming task also affected the number of rewards and punishments the participants gave the "worker". Over all groups, those who thought and talked about the annoying event administered reliably fewer rewards and more punishments than their counterparts in the neutral priming condition. (For total rewards, $F[1,36] = 3.93$, $p = .05$, whereas for total punishments, $F = 3.90$, $p = .05$. There were no other effects.) Table IV also reveals an

TABLE IV
EFFECTS OF WATER TEMPERATURE AND IMAGINED INCIDENT: EXPERIMENT 3

Measure[a]	Highly aversive water temperature incident		Less aversive water temperature incident		Significant effects
	Annoying	Neutral	Annoying	Neutral	
Pleasant index*	2.2	4.7	5.2	5.3	T, I, T × I
A–I–A index*	6.0	3.3	3.1	1.6	T, I
Annoyed*	6.3	4.0	3.7	1.9	T, I
Irritable*	6.8	3.9	3.0	1.6	T, I
Angry*	4.9	1.9	2.7	1.2	T, I
Sad	3.4	2.9	2.7	2.1	—
Distressed*	5.4	3.1	3.1	2.4	T, I
Total rewards[b]	10.5[ab]	11.0[ab]	8.1[a]	13.0[b]	I
Total punishments	7.1	4.8	8.4	5.5	I
Like partner[b]	6.7[a]	5.8[ab]	5.6[b]	6.5[ab]	T × I

[a] For each measure the higher the score the more the indicated characteristic applies.

[b] Cells not having a common subscript are significantly different ($p < .05$) by Duncan Multiple Range test.

*The planned comparison, testing the prediction that the groups in the first and fourth columns would have the highest and lowest feelings, was significant at $p < .01$.

unexpected result with these measures. Even though the women asked to think of the annoying incident while exposed to the highly aversive water temperature were most distressed, annoyed, irritable, and angry of all the groups, they actually tended to be somewhat *more* rewarding and *less* punitive than their counterparts facing the less painful stimulation. One possibility is that subjects in the former group had become very aware of their feelings as they listened to their partner's problem solutions, realized that they had little basis for their relatively hostile inclinations, and leaned over backwards, so to say, not to be harsh to the other person. The significant interaction ($F[1,36] = 5.62$, $p = .02$) obtained with the measure assessing the subjects' attitude toward their partner (based on their postevaluation ratings of how good a job they thought their partner had done, and whether they were willing to serve in another study with this person) is consistent with this interpretation. As the last line of Table IV shows, the participants imagining the annoying incident in the highly unpleasant water temperature condition were generally most favorable to the "worker," and expressed a reliably more positive final opinion of her than did the women also imagining the annoying incident under the less painful water condition. People do not always act in accord with their negative feelings, especially if they are aware of their feelings and regard them as inappropriate under the given circumstance. At times, as apparently happened here, they may even try so hard to be fair or not improperly unkind that they manifest a positive attitude they do not actually possess.

D. EXPERIMENT 4

The last experiment in this series addresses a question running through all of the preceding studies: Just what effect did the aversive stimulation have on the subjects? Our contention has been that the negative affect generated by the painfully cold water had led not only to the feelings of distress and displeasure but also to the annoyance, irritability, and anger reported by many of the participants, as well as to aggressive inclinations. But there obviously is another possibility. Rather than producing these effects fairly directly, some might say, the cold stressor situation could have created only a general arousal, which intensified the feelings evoked by other influences. For example, subjects given the negative priming might have believed they were being treated unfairly (although there was no evidence of this at all in their attitudinal reactions), and the high general arousal produced by the water could have energized their resentment and hostile tendencies. The final experiment investigated this possibility. Instead of undergoing the cold-stressor procedure employed in the other studies, the subjects were required to engage in an affectively neutral activity designed to create differences in their general arousal level. We believed the high arousal would intensify the annoyed, irritability, angry feelings activated by the imagined annoying incident. However, because the arousal in this study was presumably affectively neutral, this heightening of the A–I–A feelings in the high-arousal–annoying-priming group should be somewhat less than the intensification of the A–I–A feelings in the aversively stimulated–annoying-priming condition of the previous experiment (where the two A–I–A-generating effects summated).

1. Method

The subjects in this experiment were 40 undergraduate women, as in Experiment 3, and the same female experimenter conducted the investigation. The cover story was also the same: The research supposedly was an examination of the effects of unusual physical conditions on thought processes and supervision. However, as a change in the procedure, the "unusual condition" here was physical exertion; the participants were required to squeeze a hand dynamometer to a specified force level and then relax their grip, doing this repeatedly throughout the time they were imagining and talking about the assigned incident. Evidence indicates that handgrip exercise such as this typically increases systolic and diastolic blood pressure as well as skin blood flow and heart rate (Koslowski, Brzesinska, et al., 1973).

A 2 × 2 experimental design was established. The women in the high-arousal condition were asked to squeeze the hand dynamometer until the needle on the device registered 10 kg of force and then allow the needle to return to 0, wheras the others (low arousal group) were told to squeeze the dynamometer to 2 kg of force and then relax their grip. This squeezing and releasing was repeated throughout the 5 minutes of the priming activity. In this latter assignment, exactly the same as that employed in Experiment 3, half of the subjects had to imagine and talk about the annoying incident in which a former boyfriend stood them up (imagined-annoying-incident condition), whereas the others were to imagine and describe a bus ride through the countryside (neutral-incident condition).

At the end of the 5 minutes, the experimenter entered the cubicle, recorded the subject's pulse rate, and administered the brief questionnaire on feelings used in the previously described study. When this was completed, the experimenter's tape-recorded voice instructed the naive participant to resume the hand dynamometer procedure and the subject then heard her "worker" read off the standard 10 solutions to the two business-related problems. Again, she was to evaluate each answer by giving the other woman anywhere from five rewards to five punishments. Finally, at the end of the session, after the participant had stopped squeezing the hand dynamometer and her pulse was recorded, she responded to another questionnaire in which she indicated her attitude toward the experiment, experimenter, and her partner. The third index used the same items employed in the liking-for-partner measure in the preceding study.

2. Results

a. Evidence of Arousal Differences. There are at least two clear indicators of the differences in arousal produced by the hand dynamometer task. First, the readings of the subjects' pulse rate at the completion of the imagination priming (and before they rated their feelings) revealed a significant main effect for the arousal variation ($F[1,36] = 4.20$, $p = .04$) and no other effects. The women asked to squeeze the dynamometer at the 10 kg force level had a reliably faster pulse rate than their counterparts given the less effortful requirement. Similarly, the participants in the high arousal condition indicated that it had been easier for them to imagine the specified incident than it had been for the subjects in the low arousal group (according to their ratings made right after they had reported their feelings; $F[1,36] = 4.17$, $p < .05$; there was no other significant effect in the analysis of these ratings.)

The arousal level differences were not as clear-cut at the end of the second phase, when they had finished evaluating the "worker's" problem solutions. Although the mean pulse rates in the four conditions were approximately the same at this later time, as can be seen in Table V, the arousal effect was no longer significant ($F[1,36] = 2.65$, $p = .11$) because of the greater variability in scores.

All in all, the least we can say is that the dynamometer task had not been much of a distraction for the subjects. More than this, however, the task actually might have facilitated the priming effect at the higher work level, especially early in the session.

b. Feelings. What conclusions are drawn from the feelings measures depends

TABLE V
Effects of Arousal Level and Imagined Incident: Experiment 4

	Low arousal		High arousal		
Measure[a]	Annoying incident	Neutral incident	Annoying incident	Neutral incident	Significant effects[b]
Pulse					
Time 1	76.2	69.6	81.0	82.8	A
Time 2	75.0	71.4	78.0	82.8	—
Imagine easy	5.2	6.6	6.7	7.9	A
Pleasant index	3.2	5.2	3.0	5.5	I
A–I–A index	4.5	2.6	4.9	1.9	I
Annoyed	4.7	3.1	5.3	2.4	I
Irritable	4.4	3.1	5.0	2.1	I
Angry	4.4	1.6	4.4	1.2	I
Sad	3.8	2.0	3.1	2.7	—
Distressed	4.5	2.7	3.7	2.3	I
Like partner	7.1	6.5	5.9	7.4	A × I

[a]For each measure the higher the score the more the indicated characteristic applies.
[b]A, arousal level; I, imagined incident.

on how conservative we want to be. If we consider only the results of the analyses of variance, it appears that only the imagined incident had exerted a significant impact on these measures. In comparison to those in the neutral-imagined-incident condition, the subjects who thought and talked about the annoying event rated themselves as feeling less pleasant ($F = 30.16, p = .001$), more distressed ($F = 6.19, p = .02$), and more annoyed ($F = 10.38, p = .003$), irritable ($F = 7.62, p = .008$), and angry ($F = 18.32, p \leq .001$). (As in the last-mentioned study, there were no significant effects with the "sad" item.) However, a closer examination of the condition means is warranted because we had expected the people in the high-arousal–imagined-annoying-incident group to be most annoyed, irritable, and angry of all the subjects. The planned comparisons testing this prediction were significant for the A–I–A index ($t(36) = 2.77, p < .01$), for "annoyed" ($t(36) = 2.42, p < .02$), and for "irritable" ($t(36) = 2.07, p < .05$), but not for the felt-anger item. As the table also indicates, this group did not report the most distressed feelings, suggesting something of a difference in this study between distress and the A–I–A feelings.

    c. Reactions to Other Person. Unlike the previous experiment, there were no significant effects on the rewards and punishments measures in this investigation. However, the somewhat more subtle liking-for-partner index did yield some condition differences. The two experimental variables interacted significantly ($F = 6.84, p < .025$) so that the women imagining the annoying incident while under high arousal expressed the lowest liking for their partner of all the groups (planned comparison $t = 2.41, p < .02$). In this case, then, the expressed opinions were in line with the subjects' feelings of annoyance and irritability. Further evidence of this feeling-expressed–liking consistency can be seen in the correlations between the feelings scores and the liking-for-partner index over all subjects. Although each of the A–I–A feelings were negatively related to this expressed liking, the highest correlations were with the felt annoyance measure ($r = -.24$, ns [not significant]) and felt irritability ($r = -.38, p = .05$). The other negative affect items yielded essentially zero-order correlations with this liking.

V. General Discussion

Taken together, the results of the four experiments provide good support for Berkowitz's cognitive–neoassociationistic conception of anger. This formulation developed from the network analyses of emotion now being advanced by Bower (1981; Bower & Cohen, 1982; Gilligan & Bower, 1984), Lang (1979) and Leventhal (1982, 1984), but it extends these ideas to deal with the effects of aversive stimulation in particular. Basically, the reasoning holds that aversive events produce a negative affect, and that this affect, regardless of its source, tends automatically to activate both flight and fight tendencies and their associated physiological reactions, expressive–motor responses, thoughts, and memories. These relatively primitive (and perhaps unlearned) reactions can then be enriched, differentiated, intensified, or suppressed by additional processing systems if the latter are brought into operation by further thought. Presumably because this additional processing did not occur to any great extent in this series of experiments, exposure to the decidedly unpleasant cold water generally led to stronger feelings of annoyance, irritation, and anger than did the more tolerable water-temperature condition. This was not merely the result of the subjects' high general arousal level; the affectively neutral arousal generated in the last experiment did not produce these feelings.

From the present perspective, attributions regarding the source of the negative feeling are not the all-important determinants of anger that some theorists maintain (e.g., Averill, 1982; Weiner, 1985). We can see this in the first two experiments. The subjects' A–I–A feelings were significantly increased by both the exposure to the highly unpleasant cold water and the essays they wrote in favor of punishment, even though there was little reason for them to believe that either of these treatments was illegitimate and improper. Moreover, the essay topic had little direct connection with any misdeeds the subjects might have suffered in the past; the punishment essay presumably activated the A–I–A feelings because of the semantic linkage between punishment on one side and anger and aggression on the other. Our findings also suggest that specific emotional feelings can arise in ways not postulated by the Schachter–Singer (1962) two-factor theory of emotions. Where this latter model holds that people's specific emotions are shaped by the inferences they make about their internal sensations on the basis of their beliefs about the causes of these sensations, the separate effects of both independent variables in the first two experiments indicate that certain kinds of thoughts might arouse particular feelings without the mediation of these attribution-derived inferences.

All this is not to say, of course, that people are not angrily stirred up by thoughts of wrongs done to them and/or by their attributing their negative outcomes to another's deliberate transgression. These effects undoubtedly do occur. Very much in line with everyday experiences, the third experiment demonstrated that thoughts of a specifically annoying occurrence can promote angry feelings. Nevertheless, other kinds of ideas not directly linked to the controllable wrongs one has suffered can also give rise to these feelings. As for the role of attributions, the present analysis maintains that these beliefs can influence the emotional response in two ways: by affecting (1) the intensity of the initial displeasure, and/or (2) the deeper, more elaborated processing of the various informational and sensory inputs—if the attributions have any impact at all. Once the initial negative affect is felt, emotional reactions occur, although these can be weakened or strengthened and/or further differentiated through the additional processing.

In sum, the present reasoning holds that different levels of processing can influence the anger experience resulting from an aversive event. When there is relatively little thought, the negative affect generated by this occurrence automatically produces feelings of annoyance, irritability, and anger, while much more elaborated thought can complicate the reactions considerably, as we have noted. We also believe the participants in our research did not do the same amount of thinking about all of the measures employed in these studies. As was suggested earlier, they might well have given much less thought to their ratings of how they felt during the session than to the rewards and punishments they delivered to their partner. The subjects had to rate many feelings items, and these seemed to be an unimportant part of the study. As a consequence, the subjects presumably made little attempt to regulate their reports of their feelings. By contrast, they evidently were much more aware of what they were doing when they administered rewards and punishments to their "worker," especially in the three experiments mentioned last. They apparently recognized that they were being evaluated (even if only as a "supervisor") and presumably tried to make a good impression. In thinking about the rewards and punishments, especially in the last mentioned studies, they controlled their behavior to suit their purposes. The consequence was that their actions did not always parallel their feelings. They could have been feeling annoyed–irritated–angry, but they did not show this in how they treated the other student.

Some readers might regard the interrelationships among the various feeling measures as a problem. The present formulation expects many different kinds of negative feelings to be correlated with each other, especially during the initial, relatively primitive reaction to the aversive event. Theoretically, an unpleasant occurrence generates a variety of unpleasant feelings. But where we believe these feelings tend to become differentiated and separately recognizable out of the initial negative affect, at least to some degree, as differentiated action tendencies, thoughts, and memories arise, the intercorrelations could conceivably reflect only a general feeling of displeasure. According to this view, the subjects might have known only that they felt bad and indicated this by rating themselves as high on almost every negative feeling item. For us, however, the findings obtained over the four experiments indicate some degree of differentiation. As a case in point, the item "sad" did not yield significant condition differences in the last three studies, unlike the other negative feelings measures; the aversively stimulated people felt bad but they also knew they were not "sad." Moreover, as the summary tables indicate, we also obtained somewhat different results with the item assessing feelings of distress than with the A–I–A items. Thus, the priming treatment employed in Experiment 3 tended to have a greater impact on the A–I–A measures than on the felt-distress and sadness items; similarly, in the first two experiments, the results with the felt-distress measure were somewhat different from those obtained with the annoyance and irritability ratings. And finally, we might note, in the last experiment, the subjects' feelings of annoyance and irritability were more strongly correlated with their expressed attitude toward their partner than were any of the other feelings measures.

This differentiation was by no means entirely complete, however, particularly in the case of the three A–I–A feelings. Where some analysts maintain that annoyance and anger are distinct emotions, our findings throughout the experiments reported here suggest that these feelings have a good deal in common: The correlations between these measures in every experiment were never lower than the high .60s, the internal consistency of the A–I–A scales (Cronbach's alpha) was always in the .90s, and the experimental treatments produced the predicted significant planned comparisons for all three items in Experiments 1 and 3. Nonetheless, the subjects evidently did differentiate among the three A–I–A feelings to some degree, presumably as they thought more about what they were experiencing. Over most of the conditions, they consistently reported themselves as more annoyed and irritable than angry, and the planned comparison was not significant for the "anger" item in the second study. It is as if the participants had become highly aware of their particular feelings in at least some of these cases, decided that strong anger was not appropriate under the circumstances, and restrained the open admission of their anger.

Yet another question has to do with the priming effects noted in our research. In all four studies, the participants asked to undergo the aggressive-priming task reported significantly stronger A–I–A feelings soon afterward than the people given the neutral-priming task. While this outcome is entirely in line with the present network conception, some readers might wonder that such an effect was observed at all. They could argue, for example, that the experimental situation might have helped create the priming effect. The subjects were prepared to administer rewards and punishments to their partner, and the thought of the punishments could have facilitated the A–I–A feelings. We believe that such a thought-produced facilitation could have occurred. However, we also note that this is actually yet another priming effect, although one that was common to all of the experimental conditions. The present analysis says nothing about how powerful the influence of the aggressive thoughts on experienced feelings will be, only that there will be *some* influence. It could be that the experimental situation somehow made it easier for us to detect such an effect, but all we wanted to do was see whether it could arise at all. Other research could then determine what conditions affect the magnitude of the feelings that are activated by aggressive ideas.

Other critics might be concerned about the possible operation of demand characteristics. They could ask whether the participants had only complied with our obvious expectations. In replying to such a question, we do not offer yet another general discussion of demand characteristics (see Berkowitz & Donnerstein, 1982); we confine ourselves to the present data. In our view, the total pattern of findings obtained over the four studies argues against such a mere compliance explanation.

First of all, there are the inconsistent results with the rewards and punishments measures. As it became clearer that the experimenter might be interested in the subjects' aggressive behavior—because of the nature of the essay they were asked to write (in Experiment 2 as compared with Experiment 1, for example)—the participants were actually *less* apt to give us the rewards and punishments we might have expected. Then too, some of the results with these measures seem to be too complicated to be produced by a mere demand compliance. Thus, in the third experiment, the results were better with the rewards than with the punishments measures, which demand advocates probably would not have predicted, and they were best of all in the less-aversive-water-temperature condition rather than under the condition of highly unpleasant water temperature. If the subjects did not "go along" with our probable expectations on the reward and punishment tasks, why would they have complied with our supposed expectations on the feelings measures? The results with several of the questionnaire items also appear too complex to be explained in demand terms, most notably the significant interactions obtained on a number of items (the liking-for-partner ratings in Experiments 3 and 4, and the felt-pressure rating in Experiment 1 and liking-for-experimenter rating in the second study). Given the questions that can be raised about the pervasiveness of demand compliance (see Berkowitz & Donnerstein, 1982), those who would insist that the present findings are due merely to demand compliance should provide some evidence that such an artifact had indeed operated in this research. We do not see this evidence.

References

Anderson, C., & Anderson, D. (1984). Ambient temperature and violent crime: Tests of the linear and curvilinear hypotheses. *Journal of Personality and Social Psychology,* **46,** 91–97.

Averill, J. (1982). *Anger and aggression: An essay on emotion.* New York: Springer-Verlag.

Averill, J. (1983). Studies on anger and aggression: Implications for theories of emotion. *American Psychologist,* **38,** 1145–1160.

Bandura, A. (1973). *Aggression: A social learning analysis.* Englewood Cliffs, NJ: Prentice-Hall.

Baron, R. (1977). *Human aggression.* New York: Plenum.

Baron, R. (1984). Reducing organizational conflict: An incompatible response approach. *Journal of Applied Psychology,* **69,** 272–279.

Baron, R., & Bell, P. (1975). Aggression and heat: Mediating effects of prior provocation and exposure to an aggressive model. *Journal of Personality and Social Psychology* **31,** 825–832.

Baron, R., & Ransberger, V. (1978). Ambient temperature and the occurrence of collective violence: The "long, hot summer" revisited. *Journal of Personality and Social Psychology* **36,** 351–360.

Berkowitz, L. (1983a). Aversively stimulated aggression. *American Psychologist,* **38,** 1135–1144.

Berkowitz, L. (1983b). The experience of anger as a parallel process in the display of impulsive, "angry" aggression. In R. Green & E. Donnerstein (Eds.), *Aggression: Theoretical and empirical reviews.* New York: Academic Press.

Berkowitz, L. (1984). Some effects of thoughts on anti- and prosocial influences of media events: A cognitive–neoassociation analysis. *Psychological Bulletin,* **95,** 410–427.

Berkowitz, L., Cochran, S., & Embree, M. (1981). Physical pain and the goal of aversively stimulated aggression. *Journal of Personality and Social Psychology,* **40,** 687–700.

Berkowitz, L., & Donnerstein, E. (1982). External validity is more than skin deep: Some answers to criticism of laboratory experiments. *American Psychologist,* **37** 245–257.

Bower, G. (1981). Mood and memory. *American Psychologist,* **36,** 129–148.

Bower, G., & Cohen, P. (1982). Emotional influences in memory and thinking: Data and theory. In S. Fiske & M. Clark (Eds.), *Affect and social cognition.* Hillsdale, NJ: Erlbaum.

Buss, A. (1961). *The psychology of aggression.* New York: Wiley.

Carlsmith, J., & Anderson, C. (1979). Ambient temperature and the occurrence of collective violence: A new analysis. *Journal of Personality and Social Psychology,* **37,** 337–344.

Carver, C., Ganellen, R., Froming, W., & Chambers, W. (1983). Modeling: An analysis in terms of category accessibility. *Journal of Experimental Social Psychology,* **19,** 403–421.

Carver, C., & Scheier, M. (1981). *Attention and self-regulation.* New York: Spring-Verlag.

Cotton, J. L. (1981). A review of research on Schachter's theory of emotion and the misattribution of arousal. *European Journal of Social Psychology,* **11,** 365–397.

Diener, E., & Iran-Nejad, A. (1986). The relationship in experience between various types of affect. *Journal of Personality and Social Psychology,* **50,** 1031–1038.

Dixon, N. F. (1981). *Preconscious processing.* New York: Wiley.

Epstein, S. (1984). Controversial issues in emotion theory. In P. Shaver (Ed.), *Review of Personality and Social Psychology* (Vol. 5, pp. 64–88). Beverly Hills, CA: Sage.

Feshbach, S., & Feshbach, N. (1986). The role of fantasy and other cognitive processes in the regulation of children's aggression. In R. Blanchard & D. Blanchard (Eds.), *Advances in the Study of Aggression, Vol. 2.* (pp. 121–164). Orlando, FL: Academic Press.

Gilligan, S., & Bower, G. (1984). Cognitive consequences of emotional arousal. In C. Izard, J. Kagan, & R. Zajonc (Eds.), *Emotions, cognition, and behavior.* Cambridge, UK: Cambridge University Press.

Harkness, A., DeBono, K., & Borgida, E. (1985). Personal involvement and strategies for making contingency judgments: A stake in the dating game makes a difference. *Journal of Personality and Social Psychology, 49,* 22–32.

Hynan, D., & Grush, J. (1986). Effects of impulsivity, depression, provocation, and time on aggressive behavior. *Journal of Research in Personality, 20,* 158–171.

Isen, A. (1984). Toward understanding the role of affect in cognition. In R. Wyer & T. Srull (Eds.), *Handbook of social cognition* (Vol. 3). Hillsdale, NJ: Erlbaum.

Izard, C. E. (1977). *Human emotions.* New York: Plenum.

Jones, J., & Bogat, G. (1978). Air pollution and human aggression. *Psychological Reports, 43,* 721–722.

Kozlowski, S., Brezezinska, Z., Nazar, K., Kowalski, W., & Franczyk, M. (1973). Plasma catecholamines during sustained isometric exercise. *Clinical Science and Molecular Medicine, 45,* 723–731.

Laird, J. D. (1974). Self-attribution of emotion: The effects of expressive behavior on the quality of emotional experience. *Journal of Personality and Social Psychology, 29,* 475–486.

Lang P. (1979). A bio-informational theory of emotional imagery. *Psychophysiology, 16,* 495–512.

Lazarus, R. S. (1984). On the primacy of cognition. *American Psychologist, 39,* 124–129.

Lazarus, R. S., Averill, J. R., & Opton, E. M., Jr. (1970). Toward a cognitive theory of emotions. In M. Arnold (Ed.), *Feelings and emotions.* New York: Academic Press.

Lazarus, R. S., Coyne, J. C., & Folkman, S. (1984). Cognition, emotion and motivation: The doctoring of Humpty-Dumpty. In K. R. Scherer & P. Ekman (Eds.), *Approaches to emotion* (pp. 221–237). Hillsdale, NJ: Erlbaum.

Leventhal, H. (1984). A perceptual-motor theory of emotion. In L. Berkowitz (Ed.), *Advances in experimental social psychology* (Vol. 17, pp. 117–182). New York: Academic Press.

Leventhal, H. (1984). A perceptual-motor theory of emotion. In L. Berkowitz (Ed.), *Advances in experimental social psychology* (Vol. 17, pp. 117–182). New York: Academic Press.

Leventhal, H., & Tomarken, A. (1986). Emotion: Today's problems. *Annual Review of Psychology, 37,* 565–610.

Mandler, G. (1975). *Mind and emotion.* New York: Wiley.

Miller, I., & Norman, W. (1979). Learned helplessness in humans: A review and attribution theory model. *Psychological Bulletin, 86,* 93–118.

Novaco, R. (1975). *Anger control.* Lexington, MA: Heath, Lexington Books.

Pavlov, I. (1927). *Conditioned reflexes.* (G. Anrep, Trans. and Ed.) London: Oxford University Press.

Reisenzein, R. (1983). The Schachter theory of emotion: Two decades later. *Psychological Bulletin, 94,* 239–264.

Roseman, I. J. (1984). Cognitive determinants of emotion: A structural theory. In P. Shaver (Ed.), *Review of personality and social psychology* (Vol. 5, pp. 11–36). Beverly Hills, CA: Sage.

Rotton, J., & Frey, J. (1985). Air pollution, weather, and violent crimes: Concomitant time-series analysis of archival data. *Journal of Personality and Social Psychology, 49,* 1207–1220.

Rotton, J., Frey, J., Barry, T., Milligan, M., & Fitzpatrick, M. (1979). The air pollution experience and physical aggression. *Journal of Applied Social Psychology, 9,* 397–412.

Rule, B. G., Taylor, B., & Dobbs, A. R. (1987). Priming effects of heat on aggressive thoughts. *Social Cognition, 5,* 131–144.

Russell, J. A. (1980). A circumplex model of affect. *Journal of Personality and Social Psychology, 39,* 1161–1178.

Schachter, S. (1964). The interaction of cognitive and physiological determinants of emotional state. In L. Berkowitz (Ed.), *Advances in experimental social psychology* (Vol. 1). New York: Academic Press.

Schachter, S., & Singer, J. (1962). Cognitive, social, and physiological determinants of emotional state. *Psychological Review,* **69,** 379–399.

Shaver, P., Schwartz, J., Kirson, D., & O'Connor, C. (1987). Emotion knowledge: Further exploration of a prototype approach. *Journal of Personality and Social Psychology,* **52,** 1061–1086.

Shiffrin, R., & Schneider, W. (1977). Controlled and automatic human information processing: II. Perceptual learning, automatic attending, and a general theory. *Psychological Review,* **84,** 127–190.

Showers, C., & Cantor, N. (1985). Social cognition: A look at motivated strategies. *Annual Review of Psychology,* **36,** 275–305.

Smith, C., & Ellsworth, P. (1985). Patterns of cognitive appraisal in emotion. *Journal of Personality and Social Psychology,* **48,** 813–838.

Taylor, B. (1985). *Scripts for aggression.* Unpublished bachelor's thesis, Department of Psychology, University of Alberta, Edmonton.

Tomkins, S. S. (1962). *Affect, imagery, consciousness.* New York: Springer.

Tomkins, S. S. (1984). Affect theory. In K. R. Scherer & P. Ekman (Eds.), *Approaches to emotion* (pp. 163–195) Hillsdale, NJ: Erlbaum.

Trevarthen, C. (1984). Emotions in infancy: Regulators of contact and relationships with persons. In K. R. Scherer & P. Ekman (Eds.), *Approaches to emotion* (pp. 129–157). Hillsdale, NJ: Erlbaum.

Troccoli, B. (1986). *Mood induction and feelings awareness in the expression of hostility.* Unpublished doctoral dissertation, University of Wisconsin—Madison.

Veitch, R., DeWood, R., & Bosko, K. (1977). Radio news broadcasts: Their effects on interpersonal helping. *Sociometry,* **40,** 383–386.

Velten, E. (1968). A laboratory task for induction of mood states. *Behavior Research and Therapy,* **6,** 473–482.

Weiner, B. (1982). The emotional consequences of causal attributions. In M. C. Clark & S. T. Fiske (Eds.), *Affect and cognition* (pp. 185–209). Hillsdale, NJ: Erlbaum.

Weiner, B. (1985). An attributional theory of achievement motivation and emotion. *Psychological Review,* **92,** 548–573.

Weiner, B., Graham, S., & Chandler, C. (1982). Pity, anger, and guilt: An attributional analysis. *Personality and Social Psychology Bulletin,* **8,** 226–232.

White, L. (1979). Erotica and aggression: The influence of sexual arousal, positive affect, and negative affect on aggressive behavior. *Journal of Personality and Social Psychology,* **37,** 591–601.

Wilson, T., Dunn, D., Bybee, J., Hyman, D., & Rotondo, J. (1984). Effects of analyzing reasons on attitude-behavior consistency. *Journal of Personality and Social Psychology,* **47,** 5–16.

Wyer, R., & Hartwick, J. (1980). The role of information retrieval and conditional inference processes in belief formation and change. In L. Berkowitz (Ed.), *Advances in experimental social psychology* (Vol. 13). New York: Academic Press.

Zajonc, R. B. (1980). Feeling and thinking: Preferences need no inferences. *American Psychologist,* **35,** 151–175.

Zajonc, R. B. (1984a). The interaction of affect and cognition. In K. R. Scherer & P. Ekman (Eds.), *Approaches to emotion* (pp. 239–246). Hillsdale, NJ: Erlbaum.

Zajonc, R. B. (1984b). On the primacy of affect. *American Psychologist,* **39,** 117–123.

Zillmann, D. (1979). *Hostility and aggression.* Hillsdale, NJ: Erlbaum.

Zillmann, D., Baron, R., & Tamborini, R. (1981). Social costs of smoking: Effects of tobacco smoke on hostile behavior. *Journal of Applied Social Psychology,* **11,** 548–561.

Zillmann, D., Bryant, J., Comisky, P., & Medoff, N. (1981). Excitation and hedonic valence in the effect of erotica on motivated intermale aggression. *European Journal of Social Psychology,* **11,** 233–252.

SOCIAL PSYCHOPHYSIOLOGY: A NEW LOOK

John T. Cacioppo
DEPARTMENT OF PSYCHOLOGY
THE OHIO STATE UNIVERSITY
COLUMBUS, OHIO 43210

Richard E. Petty
DEPARTMENT OF PSYCHOLOGY
THE OHIO STATE UNIVERSITY
COLUMBIA, OHIO 43210

Louis G. Tassinary
DEPARTMENT OF PSYCHOLOGY
UNIVERSITY OF IOWA
IOWA CITY, IOWA 52242

I. Introduction

Social psychophysiology represents a metatheoretical orientation in which there is a joint consideration of the inherent biopsychosocial nature of mentation, emotion, and behavior, and a goal of formulating integrative accounts of these phenomena (Cacioppo & Petty, 1983). Movement toward the development of this orientation appeared promising two decades ago, with the appearances of Shapiro and Crider's (1969) article entitled "Psychophysiological Approaches to Social Psychology" in the *Handbook of Social Psychology* and of Shapiro and Schwartz's (1970) article entitled "Psychophysiological contributions to social psychology" in the *Annual Review of Psychology*. These articles were largely ignored by social psychologists, however, and progress toward thinking about social psychophysiology as a metatheoretical perspective rather than as a technically cumbersome methodological tool was stalled for over a decade (see Cacioppo, 1982; Cacioppo & Petty, 1986).[1]

---

[1]Consider, for instance, that despite what appeared two decades ago to be an increase in sophistication and interest among social psychologists in psychophysiological approaches, little social psychophysiological research actually occurred, and these early chapters were never revised or updated. Elsewhere, we have discussed the absence of analytical frameworks within which to create treatment comparisons and interpret psychophysiological data as a factor contributing to this dearth of research, and we have outlined and illustrated several analytic frameworks for psychophysiological research on social processes (Cacioppo & Petty, 1986). Hence, these issues are not discussed further here.

Our goal here is to take another look at, and to describe and elaborate a new look for, social psychophysiology. We begin by reviewing briefly the history of research utilizing psychophysiological concepts and measures to address social psychological questions, and we illustrate how reconceptualizing the psychophysiological enterprise can provide a noninvasive means of tracking processes by which the social world impinges on individual action and experience. Next, we survey evidence that interest within social psychology in psychophysiological concepts and techniques has been restricted not only by technical obstacles, but also by sociological and philosophical factors. Finally, research is summarized suggesting not only that psychophysiology has contributions to offer social psychology, but also that theoretical principles that have emerged from analyses of social behavior can be used to extend our understanding of fundamental psychophysiological phenomena and applied problems such as those in the area of health.

II. Background

Traditionally, social psychologists have been interested in the reportable and overt behavioral effects of human association and interaction. Social psychology itself is partitioned into conceptual areas of research such as attitudes, attraction, altruism, aggression, attribution, and so on. The emphasis in research tends to be on the manipulation of independent variables, the control or measurement of potential independent variables, and the collection of verbal report as the dependent variable (e.g., Carlsmith, Ellsworth, & Aronson, 1976; Ellsworth, 1977). This tradition was bequeathed to us by the founders of our discipline. For example, Gordon Allport, in his presidential address on September 4, 1946 before the first annual meeting of the Division of Personality and Social Psychology, observed that (1) investigations in personality and social psychology had quickly established scientific dignity; (2) important advances would be hindered by the adoption of the models, postulates, methods, or language of the physical sciences; and (3) verbal reports by individuals, although imperfect, promise both insight into social behavior and a depiction of human behavior that should prove socially useful (Allport, 1947).

The field of psychophysiology, in contrast, has evolved largely through the efforts of neurophysiologists, electrical engineers, experimental psychologists, clinical psychologists, and psychiatrists (e.g., Kaplan & Bloom, 1960; Porges & Coles, 1976). The diverse goals and interests of these individuals, coupled with the formidable technical obstacles confronting these early investigators, led quite predictably to a partitioning of the discipline not into psychologically interesting conceptual areas of research, but rather into anatomical–measurement areas (e.g., electrodermal, cardiovascular, electrocortical). As might be expected, the early definitions of psychophysiology were in operational terms such as research in which the polygraph was used (see Sternbach, 1966). Although the stated goal of psychophysiology subsequently became the use of noninvasive procedures to study the interrelationships between physiological events and human cognition, emotion, and behavior, the one common thread linking early psychophysiologists was their equipment and recording technique, and this remains a point of common discussion and research in the field today.[2]

Our interest in psychophysiology originated in our attempt to extend our understanding of attitudes and social cognition (Cacioppo, 1979, 1982; Cacioppo & Petty, 1979a, 1981a, 1982, 1983, 1986; Cacioppo, Petty, & Geen, in press; Cacioppo & Sandman, 1981; Petty & Cacioppo, 1986). We initially anticipated the promise of this approach to include the following: (1) the conceptual richness and intricate paradigms that characterize social psychology could be used to provide an interpretable ecological context for psychophysiological data; (2) the physiological knowledge base, technical sophistication, and real-time quantitative measurements that characterize psychophysiology could be used to test and extend existing theories in social psychology; and (3) the basic principles and phenomena of each discipline could ultimately be integrated to better understand human behavior—or what the Laceys (e.g., Lacey, Kagan, Lacey, & Moss, 1963) termed organismic–environmental transactions (see Cacioppo, Tassinary, & Fridlund, 1989). For instance, physiological responses, in contrast to measures such as response latencies or verbal reports, can be collected continuously without the individual having to do anything special. The detection and quantification of physiological signals can be performed with the assistance of computers more sensitively, reliably, and quickly than can fine-grained analyses of overt behavior. And analyses of subtle physiological response patterns and their time course may provide a means of differentiating underlying mechanisms of control even where overt behavior may be completely undifferentiated (see Cacioppo & Petty, 1986; Cacioppo & Tassinary, in press).

The notion that there are lawful relationships among physiological, psychological, and social processes is far from new, of course, dating at least as far back as the third century B.C. when the Greek physician Erasistratos used his

---

[2]As noted elsewhere (Cacioppo, 1984; Cacioppo & Petty, 1986), another obstacle to early efforts at integrative social psychophysiological research was the physiological background, technical sophistication, and elaborate and often troublesome instrumentation that was needed for collecting, reducing, and analyzing interpretable psychophysiological data in already complex social-psychological contexts. Tremendous advances have been made in the technical aspects of psychophysiological research, however. Standards for psychophysiological research have now been published for electrodermal (Fowles, Christie, Edleberg, Grings, Lykken, & Venables, 1981), cardiovascular (Jennings, Berg, Hutcheson, Obrist, Porges, & Turpin, 1981), and electromyographic (Fridlund & Cacioppo, 1986) recordings in humans (see also, Cacioppo & Tassinary, 1989; Coles, Donchin, & Porges, 1986; Martin & Venables, 1980). Moreover, advances in integrated circuits and computer hardware and software have made relatively inexpensive, user-friendly psychophysiological laboratories a reality and have greatly reduced the technical obstacles in psychophysiological research.

observations of peripheral physiological responses, such as the disruption of a regular heartbeat in a young man when his stepmother visited, to isolate the social cause of the individual's malady—"lovesickness" (Mesulam & Perry, 1972). However, psychophysiological studies of social behavior did not begin to appear in the social sciences until approximately a half century ago when, for instance, (1) Riddle (1925) studied deception and small group behavior by monitoring the respiratory rhythms of people bluffing during a poker game; (2) Smith (1936) studied social influence by monitoring the skin resistance responses (SRRs) of individuals as they were confronted by the information that their peers held attitudes that were discrepant from their own; and (3) Rankin and Campbell (1955) studied racial prejudice by monitoring the SRRs of individuals as they were exposed to white and black experimenters.

Despite the interesting findings of these early investigations, the emphasis was on identifying the physiological correlates of social psychological constructs and on the use of psychophysiological procedures for the purpose of construct validation (see Shapiro & Schwartz, 1970). The promise of the psychophysiological enterprise in this endeavor appeared to be considerable:

> At the very simplest level, the attraction of social psychologists to physiological techniques is not hard to understand. The techniques provide nonverbal, objective, relatively bias-free indices of human reaction that have some of the same appeal as gestural, postural, and other indicators of covert response. (Shapiro & Schwartz, 1970, pp. 89–90)

The key phrase here, as noted by Shapiro and Schwartz, is "*relatively* bias-free indices." Although physiological measures may be less susceptible to direct cognitive control than verbal or overt behaviors, physiological responses are vulnerable to instructional sets, intentional distortion, and social biases (see Cacioppo et al., 1989; Sternbach, 1966; Tognacci & Cook, 1975).

The fact that physiological indices are not linked invariantly to psychological processes or states proved a disappointment to some and resulted in suggestions that psychophysiology had failed to fulfill its promise (see Lindzey & Aronson, 1985; Stewart, 1984). These grim conclusions appeared justified because the establishment of any dissociation between a physiological measure and a psychological process or state invalidates the psychophysiological enterprise when the original investigation is designed to demonstrate an invariant relationship.[3]

---

[3] An "invariant" relationship between two variables refers here to isomorphia mapping. That is, if A and B are construed abstractly, then to say that there is an invariant relationship between the two means that: (1) B is present if and only if A is present, and (2) A is present if and only if B is present, whether or not they are causally related in an independent issue (see Wheeler, 1974).

Another somewhat more contemporary model might be termed "psychological invariants." Briefly, it may be acknowledged that there are one or more metabolic antecedents to physiological responses (e.g., heat leads to thermoregulatory adjustments and increased electrodermal activity [EDA]), but only one psychological process or event that is associated with a change in the physiological response

III. An Alternative Conceptualization

Although some still cling to a view of the psychophysiological enterprise as a search for invariants, this view is, in our opinion, an outdated, overly simplistic, and unnecessarily reductionistic characterization (see Cacioppo & Petty, 1981a, 1985). As Donchin (1982) noted;

> It is more sensible to view the psychophysiological measures as manifestations of processes evoked, or invoked, in the organism. Such processes may, or may not, be part of some information processing activity. When they are, their attributes may, or may not, be monotonic functions of some, arbitrarily selected, performance measure. When such functions are found they are of use to the extent that it is possible to address issues of theoretical import by employing psychophysiological measures as a source of data about the organism. (pp. 457–458)

This alternative, albeit less spectacular, conceptualization of the psychophysiological enterprise makes no pretense of promising someday to describe social behavior as a list of physiological correlates of psychological events. Nevertheless, it is quite feasible to make strong inferences about a person's cognitions, emotions, and conations from physiological response profiles, but these inferences can only be made within the framework of a very structured situation. Knowledge of psychophysiological principles as well as an understanding of the physiological and bioelectrical basis of the phenomena can therefore contribute to the value of the application of psychophysiology to the study of social processes and behavior.[4]

IV. Illustrating the New Look: Part I

Research on the messages carried by *incipient* (i.e., visually unobservable) facial actions illustrates the application of this alternative conceptualization of the psychophysiological enterprise. Before proceeding to this research, however, we need to say a bit more about the theoretical basis for the specific psychophysiological relationships with which we deal herein.

(e.g, arousal leads to increased EDA, and any increase in EDA that results, from the manipulation of psychological factors marks the presence of arousal). Our discussion of invariants is designed to apply to either of these conceptualizations. Interested readers may wish also to see Cacioppo and Tassinary (1989, in press).

[4]Interested readers should see Cacioppo and Tassinary (1989, in press) for a full explication of these statements.

A. RESPONSE PATTERNING

The first century of research on the psychophysiology of behavioral processes dealt with perception, nocturnal dreams, imagination, learning, and problem solving, most of which, at one time or another, were used to elicit responses in the somatic, autonomic, and central nervous systems. A characteristic finding, in part due to the intense nature of the independent variables and the insensitive nature of the dependent measures employed, was that physiological responding increased relative to baseline levels when emotionally evocative stimuli were presented or when people performed motor and cognitive tasks. As a result, several elaborate theories regarding task performance and arousal (in one of its many forms) were developed (see Fowles, 1980).

There were notable exceptions, however, to the focus on and evidence for general physiological arousal. In an illustrative study, Chester Darrow (1929) measured multiple physiological responses simultaneously while subjects performed a variety of tasks (e.g., mental arithmetic, being exposed to the sound of a sudden gun shot, attending to weak stimulation). Darrow observed that the notion of general arousal, though evidenced during many tasks, failed to account for much of the systematic variance in physiological responding. As measurement procedures achieved greater sensitivity and standardization, a greater range of stimulus intensities was examined, and the general finding was, in retrospect, not particularly surprising: The human organism responds to extremely intense stimuli in a fairly stereotyped fashion, whereas it responds to mildly to moderately intense stimuli in a more physiologically differentiated fashion (e.g., Cacioppo & Sandman, 1978; Ekman, Levenson, & Friesen, 1983; Lacey *et al.*, 1963; see Jennings, 1986; Lynn, 1966). Two early principles accounting for the differentiated patterns of physiological responding were (1) *individual response stereotypy*, which refers to the tendency for the same individual to display a prototypical profile of physiological response to all forms of stimulation; and (2) *stimulus response stereotypy*, which refers to the tendency for a situation or stimulus to elicit a common pattern or profile of response from people in general. More recently, two components of individual response stereotypy have been identified: (1) *individual consistency*—individuals display a reliable hierarchy of physiological responses across stimuli; and (2) *individual uniqueness*—distinct groups of individuals (e.g., hypertensives vs. normotensives) display responses or patterns of responses that are consistent within groups and differentiated across groups (Fredrikson *et al.*, 1985).

Additional principles were necessary, however, to account for the fact that particular elementary psychological operators—such as attention, positive or negative affect, imagery, and interpreting and encoding incoming verbal information (which are induced by a wide variety of stimuli)—also tended to invoke distinctive patterns of physiological activity. The notions of orienting, defensive, and startle responses were embraced, and specifying the antecedents, parameters, and consequences of these response syndromes continues to be an active area of research (e.g., Jennings, 1986; Lynn, 1966; Turpin, 1986).

In addition, theoretical analyses of efferent activity during problem solving, imagery, and emotion dating back to Darwin and William James have shared assumptions regarding the specificity and adaptive utility of somatic responses (e.g., see McGuigan, 1978; Schwartz, 1975). To better specify these links, R. C. Davis (1939) postulated the principle of *focus of muscular responses*, which holds that each task that a subject performs is accompanied by a focus of muscular activity. Davis's principle of focus of muscular response does not, however, predict where a focal point might be located or why.

Several years ago, we proposed an elaboration of Davis's postulate, which possessed greater explanatory and predictive power to account for the fact that particular elementary psychological operators tended to manifest in distinctive patterns of somatic activity (Cacioppo & Petty, 1981a). This model consisted of a set of five principles that drew on Davis's principle of focus of muscular response and extended Darwin's principles of serviceable associated habit and of antithesis to the level of unobservable somatic actions and patterns. The set of principles was summarily referred to as the "model of somatic patterning:"

1. *There are foci of somatic activity in which changes mark particular psychological processes.* For instance, a student who closes her or his eyes and vividly imagines watching a professor pace forward and back in the room during a lecture might show localized electromyographic (EMG) activity over the orbicularis oculi muscle region (around the eye; see Fig. 1) as if the student were actually squinting and relaxing in order to focus on the pacing professor.

2. *Inhibitory as well as excitatory changes in somatic activity can mark a psychological process.* For instance, in the preceding example, the act of imagining that she or he was watching a professor pacing forward and back in the room led to an increase in periocular EMG activity; however, if the student were to imagine the professor standing motionless and speechless in the middle of the room, this stationary image could actually lead to a diminution of periocular activity.

3. *Changes in somatic activity are patterned temporally as well as spatially.* Thus, consider the case in which a professor was pacing forward and back during her or his lecture, but who, during the course of making a point slowed and then stopped; a student who is imagining this scenario would show predictable changes in EMG activity over the periocular muscle region across time (temporal specificity)—and these changes would be localized rather than expressed generally across somatic sites (spatial specificity).

4. *Changes in somatic activity become less evident as the distance of measurement from the focal point increases.* Thus, in the preceding example, any

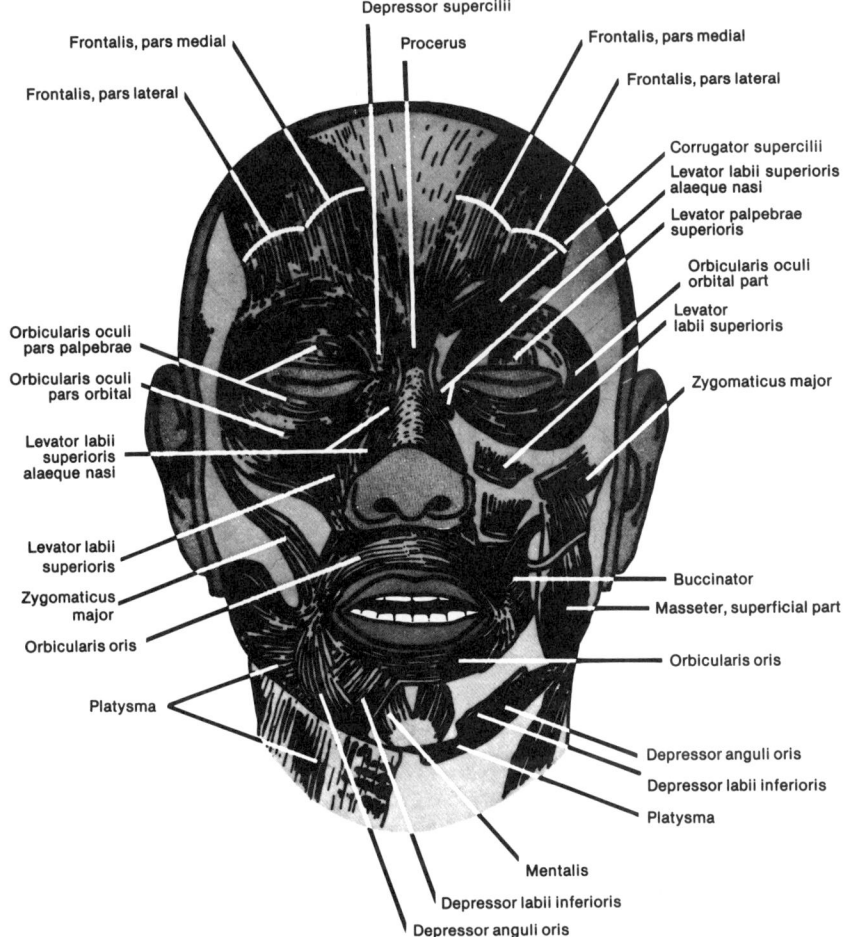

Fig. 1. Schematic representation of selected facial muscles. Overt facial expressions of emotion are based on contractions of the underlying musculature that are sufficiently intense to result in visibly perceptible dislocations of the skin and facial landmarks. The more common visible effects of strong contractions of the depicted facial muscles include the following (from Cacioppo, Martzke, Petty, & Tassinary, 1988).

1. *Muscles of the lower face.* Depressor anguli oris—pulls the lip corners downward; depressor labii inferioris—depresses the lower lip; orbicularis oris—tightens, compresses, protrudes, and/or inverts the lips; mentalis—raises the chin and protrudes the lower lip; platysma—wrinkles the skin of the neck and may draw down both the lower lip and the lip corners.

2. *Muscles of the mid-face.* Buccinator—compresses and tightens the cheek, forming a "dimple"; levator labii superioris alaeque nasi—raises the center of the upper lip and flares the nostrils; levator labii superioris—raises the upper lip and flares the nostrils, exposing the canine teeth; masseter—adducts the lower jaw; zygomaticus major—pulls the lip corners up and back.

localized changes in EMG activity over the periocular region would be more measureable at sites proximal rather than distal to the source of the bioelectrical signals (e.g., near to, rather than far from, the orbicularis oculi muscle).

5. *Foci can be identified a priori by (1) analyzing the overt reactions that initially characterized the particular psychological process of interest, but that appeared to drop out with practice, and (2) observing the somatic sites that are involved during the "acting out" of the particular psychological process of interest.* There are, of course, individual differences in the elementary psychologic operations initiated by a stimulus. For instance, most people who are asked to imagine a spiral respond by visualizing an exemplar, although some individuals (e.g., mathematicians) may respond by recalling the mathematical function for a spiral. This individual difference can be a source of error in a priori specifications of somatic foci. Hence, ideographic procedures can be useful to help ensure the particular psychological operation of interest was invoked in response to the experimental stimulus.

B. THE FACIAL RESPONSE SYSTEM

Given that somatic effectors (the striated muscles) provide the final pathway through which people interact with and modify their physical and social environments, it perhaps should not be surprising that analyses of the patterns of efferent neural discharges ("efference") may be informative to social psychologists. To be sure, the pattern of efference is not always as intended (e.g., as when one performs clumsily), not always a veridical reflection of goals (e.g., as when one deceives), and not always obvious (e.g., as when one hides the display of feelings through masking or inhibition), and these influences are important to recognize when specifying under what conditions a given pattern of efference will mark a particular psychological process. But without efference, individuals do not communicate, do not affiliate, do not proliferate, do not interact—in short, are not social.

From a social psychological perspective, the muscles of facial expression may be especially noteworthy, in that these somatic effectors serve such important communicative functions (Fridlund, in press). Even their structure is suggestive

---

3. *Muscles of the upper face.* Corrugator supercilii—draws the brows together and downward, producing vertical furrows between the brows; depressor supercilii/procerus—pulls the medial part of the brows downward and may wrinkle the skin over the bridge of the nose; frontalis, pars lateral—raises the outer brows, producing horizontal furrows in the lateral regions of the forehead; frontalis, pars medial—raises the inner brows, producing horizontal furrows in the medial region of the forehead; levator palpebrae superioris—raises the upper eyelid; orbicularis oculi, pars orbital—tightens the skin surrounding the eye, causing "crows-feet" wrinkles; orbicularis oculi, pars palpebrae—tightens the skin surrounding the eye, causing the lower eyelid to raise.

of this communicative function: the muscles of mimicry are linked to connective tissue and fascia rather than to skeletal structures; their influence on the social environment, therefore, is mediated by the construction of facial configurations rather than by direct action through the movement of the skeletal structure (Rinn, 1984).[5] Tomkins (1962), Izard (1971), and Ekman and Friesen (1975) have pioneered work on the face as a multisignal–multimessage response system.

Ekman and Friesen (1975), for instance, have conceptualized the face as a source of (1) static, (2) slow, (3) artificial, and (4) rapid signals. Carried by the rapid signals alone are a variety of messages; individuals have a good deal of control over most of these. The perioral musculature (e.g., orbicularis oris—see Fig. 1), for instance, is densely innervated by the facial (7th cranial) nerve and is capable of extraordinary specificity and flexibility (e.g., as in the case of verbal articulation). Nonverbal facial messages include *emblems* (symbolic communication—e.g., wink), *manipulators* (self-manipulative associated movements—e.g., lip bite), *illustrators* (actions accompanying–highlighting speech—e.g., raising the brows), *regulators* (nonverbal communication modulators—e.g., nods), and distinctive emotions (Ekman & Friesen, 1975).

Regarding the latter, the states of happiness, sadness, fear, anger, disgust, and surprise have been linked to distinctive facial displays across cultures and infants, whereas variability in facial efference and emotion has been linked to several sources, including differences in the emotion(s) evoked by a stimulus, differences in the timing of the emotional reaction, and differences due to display rules (e.g., Ekman, 1972, 1982; Ekman *et al.*, 1987; Izard, 1977; Scherer & Ekman, 1982; Steiner, 1979).

1. Facial Efference

Of course, not all intra- or interpersonal processes are accompanied by visually or socially perceptible expressive facial actions, and this fact has limited the utility of research linking facial actions to underlying psychological processes (e.g., Graham, 1980; Love, 1972; Rajecki, 1983). Graham (1980), for instance, employed Ekman and Friesen's (1978) comprehensive facial action coding system in an attempt to investigate emotional responses to advertisements. Unfortunately, few facial actions indicative of emotions were visually observed, and those that were observed failed to provide theoretically interesting information about how the viewers were processing the advertisements. Closer analyses of the construc-

---

[5]The presumed adaptive utility underlying the evolution of facial actions and expressions is twofold: (1) facial configurations provide a nonverbal means of communication among and across species, and (2) they serve to provide feedback regarding intrapersonal experience and behavior. Discussions of these functions are beyond the scope of the present article, but interested readers might wish to consult Buck (1980), Cacioppo, Petty, Losch, and Kim (1986b, pp. 266–267), Dimberg (1986), Ekman (1973), Izard (1977), Laird (1984), or Zajonc (1985) for more information.

tion of facial expressions reveals, however, that they are the result of (1) movements of facial skin and connective tissue due to the contraction of facial muscles, which create folds, lines, and wrinkles in the skin, and (2) the movement of facial landmarks, such as the brows and corners of the mouth (e.g., Ekman & Friesen, 1978; Izard, 1971; Rinn, 1984). Although muscle activation must occur if these facial feature distortions are to be achieved, it is possible for muscle activation to occur in the absence of any overt facial action if the activation is weak or transient, or if the overt response is aborted. Indeed, the efferent discharges that are too subtle or fleeting to be identifiable under normal conditions of social interaction may be of interest both because of their prevalence and because they are less likely to undergo the same distortions as overt expressions and actions. Several major facial muscles and actions are outlined briefly in Fig. 1.

Surface EMG is a psychophysiological technique that allows the measurement of both covert and overt facial efference.[6] The validity of this technique is based on the following anatomy and physiology. Briefly, a striated muscle consists of millions of fibers housed in connective tissue and is activated by a specific motor nerve. The motor nerve, in turn, consists of many tiny motoneurons, which terminate on muscle fibers at a region called the motor end plate. These motoneurons have differential critical firing thresholds, such that either progressively larger units are added to or progressively smaller units are subtracted from the total output of a motoneuron pool (size principle; Henneman, 1980). When a particular motoneuron is depolarized, a neural impulse travels to the end plate region, and the chemical transmitter acetylcholine initiates a self-propagating muscle action potential (MAP), which activates the physiochemical mechanism that causes the fiber to contract. Whenever a MAP passes along a muscle fiber, an electrical potential is created, which can be measured at the skin.

---

[6]It is worth emphasizing that EMG and visual (e.g., videotape) facial scoring procedures are complementary rather than exclusionary (see Cacioppo, Tassinary, & Fridlund, 1989; Ekman, 1982; Fridlund & Izard, 1983). For instance, EMG allows the measurement of minute changes in efferent neural discharges to particular facial muscle regions, whereas visual scoring procedures such as Ekman and Friesen's (1978) facial action coding system provide a sensitive and comprehensive means of examining observable facial actions. Although we commonly obtain unobtrusive video recordings as well as EMG recordings in our research, our focus thus far has been on changes in facial efference that are not socially perceptible. The judges who view and rate the video recordings for emotional signals have ranged from the subjects who participated in the study through an independent group of subjects and laboratory personnel to a practicing clinical psychologist with extensive experience in detecting and decoding subtle emotional messages from clients. Data provided by Ekman, Schwartz, and Friesen (1982, as cited in Ekman, 1982) suggest that responses of the magnitude we have been investigating are also not detectible using comprehensive, frame-by-frame analyses of facial action units. The supposition here, however, is not that more evocative stimuli would not elicit observable facial actions or expressions, but rather that it is possible for muscle activation to occur in the absence of an overt facial expression or action if either the activation is weak or the overt response is aborted.

The acetylcholine is quickly eradicated by the enzyme cholinesterase, and MAP activity and muscle fiber contraction cease without additional neural activity. Contraction of muscle fibers also activates skin receptors, which provide afferent feedback about facial muscle activity. Although the details of the individual MAPs are lost in surface EMG recordings, the discrete microvolt discharges from individual MAPs summate spatially and temporally during motor unit recruitment to yield an aggregate that, with proper placement and amplification, can indicate the action (or inaction) of motoneuron pools. (For further information about surface EMG, see Cacioppo *et al.,* 1989; Fridlund & Cacioppo, 1986).

Consistent with the foregoing model of somatic patterning, research using facial EMG recordings has revealed several interesting somatic links to fundamental psychological operations. (1) *Cognitive dimension:* somatic links to semantic working memory—somatic activity over the perioral region is greater during cognitive deliberations (e.g., silent language processing, mental arithmetic) than during automatic or visual processing; (2) *affective dimension:* somatic links to valence of the organismic–environmental transaction—somatic activity over the muscles of mimicry (e.g., corrugator supercilii, or brow region) varies as a function of emotions; and (3) *intensity dimension:* somatic links to gradations of response—the amount of somatic activity over the perioral region varies as a function of the load on the articulatory loop, and the amount of activity over the facial muscles of mimicry varies as a function of the intensity of an emotional reaction.

2. Skeletomuscular Patterning during Action and Imagery

In an illustrative study (Cacioppo, Petty, & Marshall-Goodell, 1984), subjects were led to believe that they were participating in research on involuntary neural responses during "action and imagery." Numerous dummy electrodes were also placed on the subjects to deflect attention from the facial placements and to lend credence to the cover story. Subjects on any given trial either: (1) actually lifted what was described as being a "light" (16 gram) or "heavy" (35 gram) weight (action); (2) imagined lifting the "light" or "heavy" weight (imagery); (3) silently read a neutral communication as if they agreed or disagreed with its thesis (action); or (4) imagined reading an editorial with which they agreed or disagreed (imagery).

Based on the model of somatic patterning, we expected the following: (1) perioral (orbicularis oris) EMG activity would be greater during the communicative attitudinal tasks than during the physical tasks, and (2) the emotional processes invoked by the positive and negative attitudinal tasks would lead to distinguishable patterns of EMG activity over the brow (corrugator supercilii), cheek (zygomaticus major), and possibly the nose (levator labii superioris—which is involved in expressions of disgust) regions (see Fig. 1), whereas the simple phys-

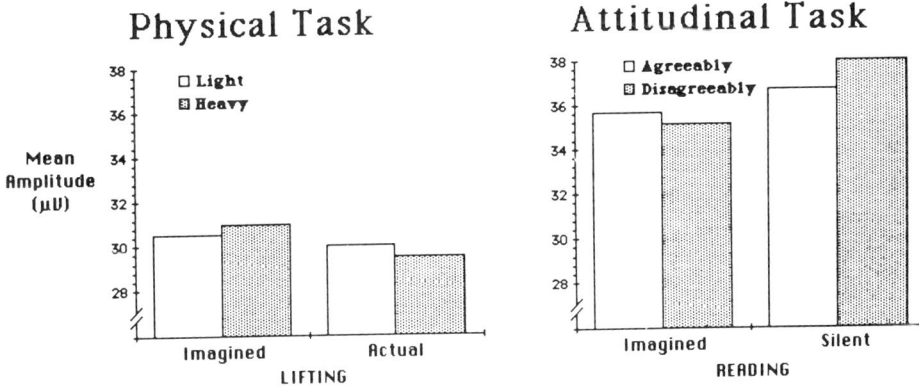

Fig. 2. Mean EMG amplitude over the perioral muscle region during physical and attitudinal tasks. (Adapted from Cacioppo, Petty, & Marshall-Goodell, 1984.)

ical tasks would lead to distinguishable EMG activity over the superficial forearm flexors (whose actions control flexion about the wrist).[7]

Imagining the performance of tasks, rather than actually performing the tasks, was, of course, associated with lower mean levels of EMG activity. More importantly, and consistent with the model of somatic patterning, multivariate analyses revealed that the site and overall form of the task-evoked EMG responses were generally similar across the levels of this factor. Analyses further revealed support for both predictions. As illustrated in Fig. 2, perioral EMG activity was higher during the attitudinal (language) than physical (nonlanguage) tasks even though the tasks required no overt verbalization. Moreover, EMG activity over the brow, cheek, and nose-wrinkler muscle regions in the face varied as a function

---

[7]We refer to general anatomical regions (e.g., cheek, brow, forearm, back) when specifying recording sites and avoid technical considerations for didactic purposes only. This is not to suggest that factors such as the specific site and orientation of the electrodes are unimportant. The bioelectrical activity from deep or proximal muscles can give the same appearance in a surface EMG recording as the activation of an underlying superficial muscle, and for this reason one should refer only to the EMG activity detected over muscle (e.g., Corrugator supercilii) regions. However, factors such as the exact site and orientation of the electrodes, the size of the electrodes, the interelectrode distance, the interelectrode impedance, and so on are important in that they determine the validity and sensitivity of surface EMG recordings as measures of the localized activation of muscle regions (Tassinary, Cacioppo, & Green, 1989). The placements specified in Table I and illustrated in Fig. 1, for instance, are not arbitrary, but rather are based on the available anatomical and empirical research on the relationship between specific facial actions and surface EMG activity. It perhaps should also be noted that data reduction involves the identification and assessment and/or removal of recording artifacts. For instance, eye blinks can appear as transient bursts of EMG activity when recording in proximal regions, and these segments should be quantified (e.g., counted, integrated) and analyzed (to assure equivalence across experimental conditions) if not also removed from the EMG recordings over proximal muscle regions not directly involved in the eye blink (see Cacioppo et al., 1988, 1989, in press; Fridlund & Cacioppo, 1986).

of whether subjects thought about the topic in an agreeable or disagreeable manner (see Fig. 3), EMG activity over the superficial forearm flexors was higher during the physical than the attitudinal tasks, and EMG activity over the forearm (but not over the facial muscles) varied across the simple physical tasks (see Fig. 4).

To probe whether our cover story and tasks were effective or whether subjects had suspicions regarding facial efference being the focus of the study, subjects were interviewed at the end of each session and were asked specifically what they believed to be the experimental hypothesis. Because subjects might reason that they should not disclose how much they "knew", we emphasized that it was important that they respond honestly and accurately. The postexperimental interviews failed to reveal any evidence for the operation of experimental demands. All subjects appeared convinced of the cover story (e.g., that the sensors were used to detect involuntary physiological reactions), and no subject articulated anything resembling the experimental hypothesis. Instead, the postexperimental

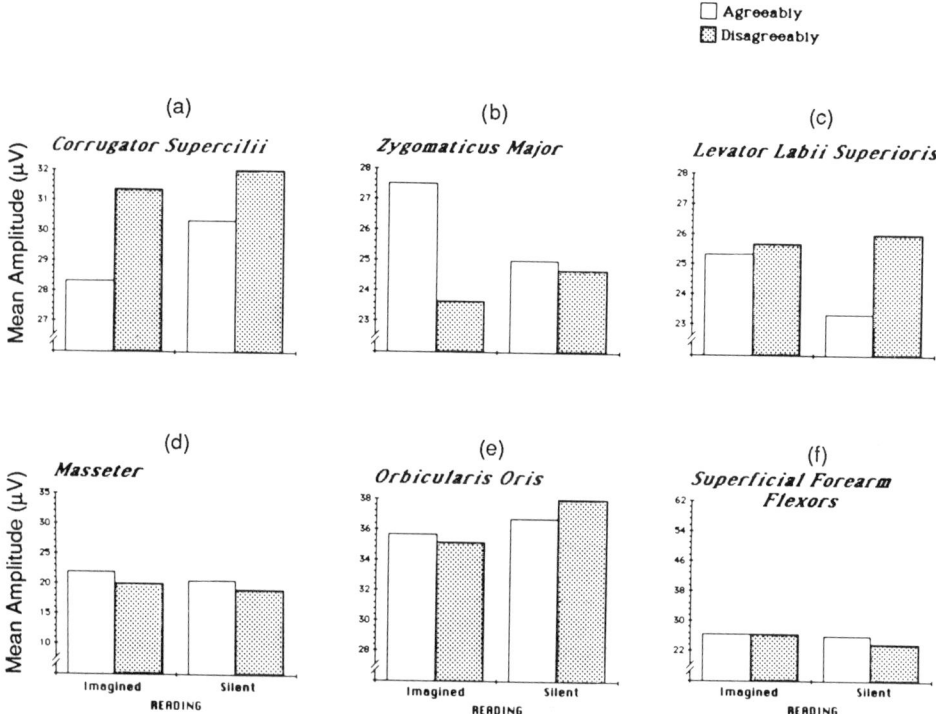

Fig. 3. Mean EMG amplitude over the brow (a), cheek (b), nose (c), jaw (d), perioral (e), and forearm (f) muscle regions as a function of attitudinal task. (Adapted from Cacioppo, Petty, & Marshall-Goodell, 1984.)

interviews of subjects indicated that they tended to organize the experimental trials in terms of whether they imagined or performed some task (e.g., lifting a weight or silently reading a text) rather than in terms of whether the task was physical or attitudinal.

Finally, following the study, two judges viewed videotapes of subjects during trials on which the subjects performed positive and negative attitudinal tasks. The judges' task was to guess the valence of the task performed on each trial, based on their observations of the subjects' facial display during the trial (i.e., when EMG recordings were obtained; see Footnote 6). Judges performed at chance level. It is unlikely that subjects deduced and chose to support the experimental hypothesis by making socially imperceptible facial responses to the attitudinal (but not to the physical) tasks. Indeed, Hefferline, Keenan, and Harford (1959) found that they could operantly condition an invisibly small thumb-twitch even though subjects remained ignorant of their behavior and its effect; and they

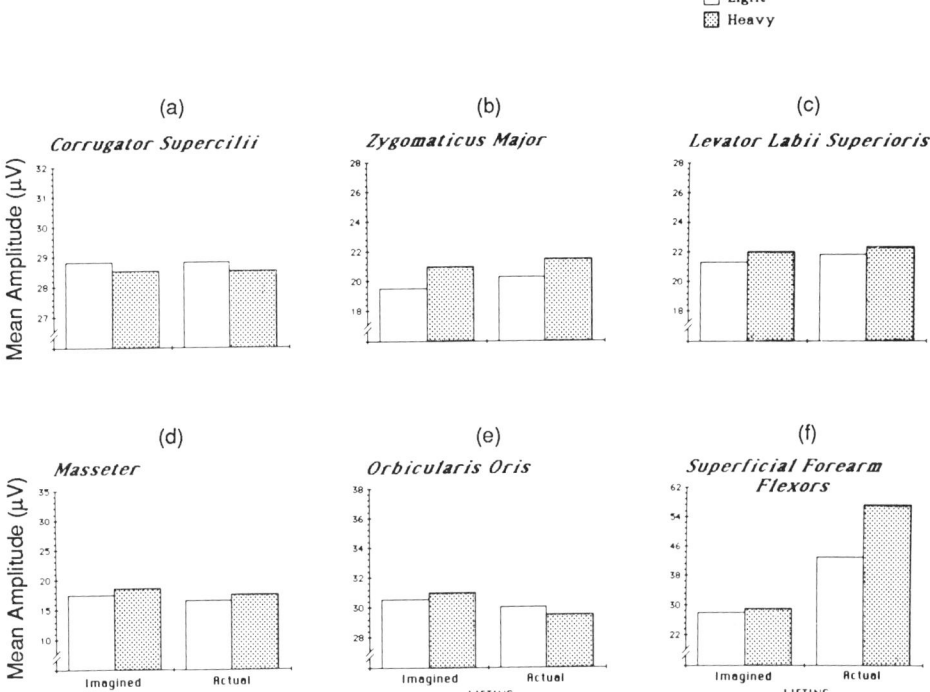

Fig. 4. Mean EMG amplitude over the brow (a), cheek (b), nose (c), jaw (d), perioral (e), and forearm (f) muscle regions as a function of physical task. (Adapted from Cacioppo, Petty, & Marshall-Goodell, 1984.)

reported that subjects could not produce this covert behavior *in the absence of EMG feedback* when deliberately trying to do so (see McCanne & Anderson, 1987). Together, these data suggest both that experimental demands are not necessary for the selective facial EMG activation observed during emotional processing and imagery and, more interestingly, that social cognition and affect can have discriminable effects on facial EMG patterning.

3. Perioral EMG Activity as a Function of Semantic Working Memory

The data displayed in Fig. 2 are consistent with the notion that problem solving and silent language processing influence perioral EMG activity (see reviews by Garrity, 1977; McGuigan, 1970). However, these data, like previous research, do not provide strong evidence regarding the specificity of the relationship between perioral EMG activity and information processing because the type of stimulus presented and/or the type of subject employed has been varied along with the extent of linguistic processing presumably manipulated. For instance, although poor readers have shown greater perioral EMG activity while reading than good readers (e.g., Edfeldt, 1960; Faaborg-Anderson & Edfeldt, 1958), it is unclear whether this effect resulted from differences in (1) the cognitive work involved either in comprehending or in encoding the material, (2) the manner in which the material is being processed, (3) attentional differences in the readers, (4) differences in apprehension, and/or (5) other factors.

In most of our initial investigations of perioral EMG activity, we employed the instructional manipulations used commonly to vary the load on semantic working memory as part of the encoding process. The paradigm involves presenting target words (e.g., trait adjectives) to subjects while randomly varying the question pertaining to each trait word (Craik & Tulving, 1975). In this paradigm, somatic responses attributable to features of subjects and stimuli are assigned to the error term, and what generally remains is variance due to the instructional factor (the "cue question"), which serves as the operationalization of the predominant type of informational analysis operating during the presentation of the target word (see Baddeley, 1978; Cermak & Craik, 1979). Results of research in this paradigm have generally shown that the more *semantic* (i.e., meaning-oriented) the cued analysis, the more likely subjects are to remember the stimulus word (see review by Craik, 1979), although these effects are especially evident when semantic processes are cued both at the time of encoding and at the time of retrieval (Morris, Bransford, & Franks, 1977; Tulving, 1978). These data have been interpreted as indicating the existence of qualitatively different processes by which incoming information is related to one or more existing domains of knowledge (Cermak & Craik, 1979; Craik, 1979).

The purpose of our initial study on semantic processing was to determine whether perioral (orbicularis oris) EMG activity was higher when subjects performed tasks requiring that they think about the meaning and self-descriptiveness of a word rather than about the orthographic appearance of the word (Cacioppo & Petty, 1979b). EMG activity over a nonoral muscle region (superficial forearm flexors of the nonpreferred arm) and heart rate were also recorded to determine whether task-evoked changes in EMG activity were specific or general (e.g., part of a diffuse arousal response). Subjects were shown cue questions asking them whether or not the succeeding trait adjective was printed in uppercase letters, or whether or not the word was self-descriptive. Half of the trait adjectives were printed in uppercase letters, and half were printed in lowercase; and half of the trait adjectives were highly self-descriptive, whereas half were not at all self-descriptive. Subjects responded yes or no by pressing one of two microswitches.

Results revealed several interesting results (see Fig. 5). First, the self-referent task led to better recall than the orthographic task, replicating previous studies in social psychology (e.g., Rogers, Kuiper, & Kirker, 1977). Second, the self-referent task led greater increases in perioral EMG activity than the orthographic task. Third, neither EMG activity over the forearm muscle group nor heart rate varied as a function of the orienting task, making it unlikely that the association between self-referent processing and perioral EMG activity was due to subjects being generally more tense or activated when performing the self-referent than the orthographic task.

This orienting-task paradigm has also been used to investigate the possible existence of different processes by which incoming information is related to one

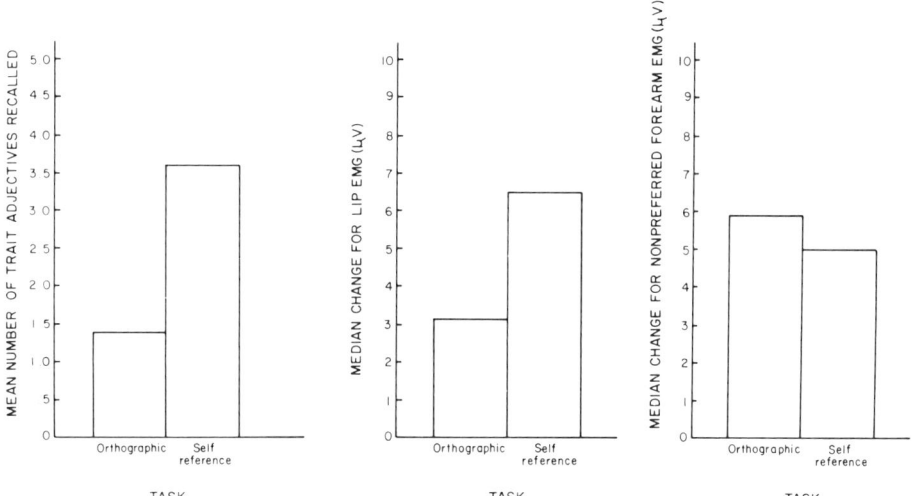

Fig. 5. Mean recall performance (left panel) and median change from an initial baseline for EMG activity during the processing interval for perioral (middle panel) and nonpreferred forearm (right panel) muscle regions, as a function of an orienting task. (From Cacioppo & Petty, 1981a.)

or more existing domains of social knowledge. Studies have shown that trait words are better recalled when rated for their descriptiveness of oneself or one's best friend than of people about whom one has little or no direct knowledge (e.g., Bower & Gilligan, 1979; Keenan & Baillet, 1980). These data have been interpreted as indicating structural differences in domains of social knowledge in memory. As Ferguson, Rule, and Carlson (1983) note, the domains of knowledge (e.g., one's self) accessed by tasks (e.g., self-referent task) that produce relatively better recall of the incoming stimuli are thought to be characterized by greater *elaboration* (i.e., more associations), *integration* (i.e., stronger interassociative bonding), and/or *differentiation* (i.e., more chunking of associations into distinct, but related, subsets).

Ferguson *et al.* further reported data from this paradigm using a between-subjects design showing that self-referent and evaluative orienting tasks yielded similar response latencies and levels of recall. They argued that (1) evaluation constitutes a central dimension along which incoming information (such as trait words) is categorized and stored, and (2) both evaluative and self-referent tasks facilitated the use of the evaluative dimension and minimized the use of other irrelevant dimensions in rating traits. This led them to conclude that, given the centrality of the evaluative dimension in the organization of memory, "no unique memorial status need be attributed to the self or familiar others" (Ferguson *et al.*, 1983, p. 260).

In an experiment bearing upon both the effects of effortful semantic processing on perioral EMG activity and on Ferguson *et al.*'s analysis, subjects were exposed to 60 trait adjectives spanning a range of likeability (Cacioppo & Petty, 1981b). Each trait adjective was preceded by one of five cue questions, which defined the processing task. The cue questions were (1) "Does the following word rhyme with _____" (rhyme), (2) "Is the following word spoken louder than this question?" (volume discrimination), (3) "Is the following word similar in meaning to _____?" (association), (4) "Is the following word good (bad)?" (evaluation), and (5) "Is the following word self-descriptive?" (self-reference). Finally, as in all of our facial EMG research, subjects in this study knew bioelectrical activity was being recorded, but they did not realize that activity over which they had voluntary control was being monitored.

Results revealed that mean recognition confidence ratings were ordered as follows: self-reference, evaluation, association, rhyme, and volume discrimination (see Fig. 6). Importantly, all means except the last two differed significantly from one another. These data, which were obtained using a within-subjects rather than a between-subjects design, have been conceptually replicated by McCaul and Maki (1984) and by Cacioppo, Petty, and Morris (1985), and they argue against Ferguson *et al.*'s contention that evaluative and self-referent processing are fundamentally the same.

In addition, we found the following:

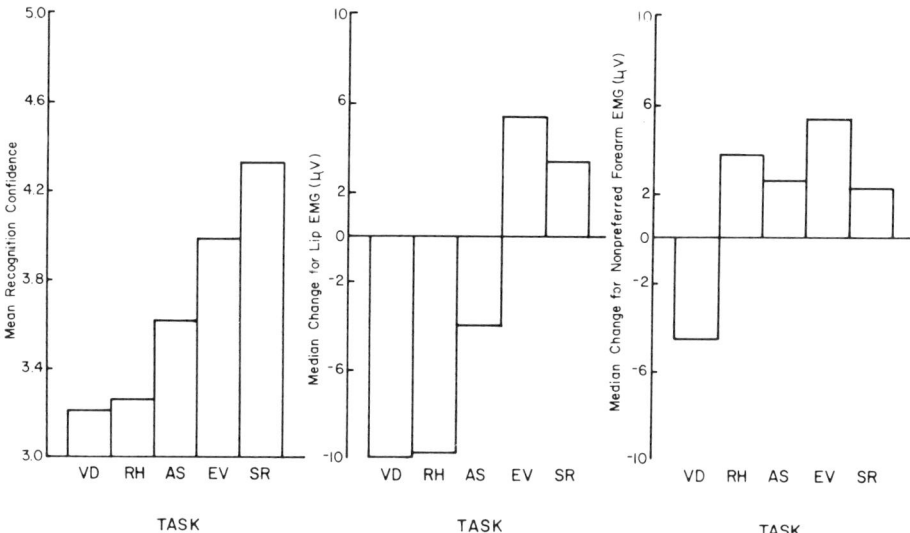

Fig. 6. Mean recognition confidence (left panel) and median change from prestimulus levels for EMG activity during the processing interval for perioral (middle panel) and nonpreferred forearm (right panel) muscle regions as a function of orienting task. (VD = volume discrimination; RH = rhyme; AS = association; EV = evaluation; and SR = self-reliance). (Adapted from Cacioppo & Petty, 1981b.)

1. The mean amplitude of perioral (orbicularis oris) EMG activity was lowest for the nonsemantic tasks of rhyme and volume discrimination, intermediate for the task of association, and equally high for the tasks of evaluation and self-reference (we subsequently found that these, too, could be differentiated using psychophysiological measures by analyzing the form rather than simply the mean amplitude of the EMG responses—Cacioppo et al., 1985; see Cacioppo & Dorfman, 1987)
2. Cardiac activity and the mean amplitude of EMG activity over a peripheral muscle region (i.e., nonpreferred superficial forearm flexors region) did not vary as a function of the type of task performed
3. The association between task and perioral EMG activity was temporally specific, with task-discriminating EMG activity observed only while subjects analyzed the aurally presented trait adjectives and formulated their response.

Together, these results suggest that (1) perioral EMG activity varies as a function of the load on semantic working memory; and (2) not only are there structural differences in domains of social knowledge in long-term memory, but the short-term language processes activated in concert with these knowledge structures differ.

4. Facial EMG Activity as a Function of Persuasive Appeals

Given evidence that perioral EMG activity varies as a function of short-term semantic processing and that EMG activity over selected facial muscle regions (e.g., corrugator supercilii, zygomaticus major) can discriminate between positive and negative emotional states, we reasoned that facial EMG measures might prove informative regarding elementary processes evoked by the anticipation and presentation of personally involving persuasive communications. Elsewhere, for instance, we have outlined specific conditions under which recipients of persuasive communications "cognitively respond" to message arguments, generating new associations, links, and implications central to the merits of an advocacy rather than basing attitudes on relatively simple peripheral cues (e.g., see Petty & Cacioppo, 1981, 1986). Miller and Baron (1973), on the other hand, argued that these conditions did not elicit extensive cognitive activity (see, also, Langer, Blank, & Chanowitz, 1978; Miller, Maruyama, Beaber, & Valone, 1976). Experimental results based on subjects' reported attitudes and the thoughts and ideas they listed in retrospective verbal protocols ("thought listings") provided support for the former position (Petty & Cacioppo, 1977; see Cacioppo & Petty, 1981c; Cialdini & Petty, 1981), but others have expressed reasonable concerns that these data could reflect post hoc rationalizations produced in response to postexperimental questioning rather than processes evoked by the persuasive communication (e.g., Miller & Coleman, 1981).

An initial study supported the applicability of psychophysiological principles and procedures to the particular paradigm of interest: localized increases in perioral EMG activity were observed when individuals followed the experimental instruction to "collect their thoughts" about an impending counterattitudinal editorial (Cacioppo & Petty, 1979a, Experiment 1; see Fig. 7).

A follow-up study was conducted in which subjects simply anticipated and heard a proattitudinal, counterattitudinal, or neutral communication (Cacioppo & Petty, 1979a, Experiment 2). Students were recruited for what they believed was an experiment on "biosensory processes," and, as in the previous research, they were unaware that somatic responses were being monitored. After subjects adapted to the laboratory, we (1) obtained recordings of basal EMG activity, forewarned subjects that in 60 sec they would be hearing an editorial with which they agreed, an editorial with which they disagreed, or an unspecified message; (2) obtained another 60 sec of physiological recording while subjects sat quietly; and (3) obtained yet another 120 sec of data while subjects listened to a proattitudinal appeal, counterattitudinal appeal, and a news story about an archeological expedition. Subjects were not told to collect their thoughts in this study, but rather somatovisceral activity was simply monitored while subjects awaited and listened to the message presentation. This allowed us to assess the extent to which spontaneous perioral activity accompanied the anticipation of a persuasive communication.

As expected, subjects evaluated more positively and reported having more favorable thoughts and fewer counterarguments to the proattitudinal than to the counterattitudinal advocacy. Although unexpected, we also found that subjects reported enjoying the "neutral" news story about an obscure archeological expedition as much as they did the proattitudinal editorial. Analyses of perioral EMG indicated that perioral activity increased following the forewarning of an impending and personally involving counterattitudinal advocacy, and it increased for all conditions during the presentation of the message. This selective increase of perioral EMG activity during the postwarning–premessage period provided convergent evidence for the view that people engage in anticipatory cognitive activity to buttress their beliefs when they anticipate hearing a personally involving, counterattitudinal appeal. Moreover, as illustrated in Fig. 8, the pattern of subtle facial EMG activity was found to reflect the positive–negative nature of the persuasive appeal before and during the message. Presentation of the proattitudinal and "neutral" messages was accompanied by a pattern of facial EMG activity similar to that found to accompany pleasant emotional imagery, whereas both the anticipation and presentation of the counterattitudinal message was associated with a pattern of EMG activity similar to that found to accompany

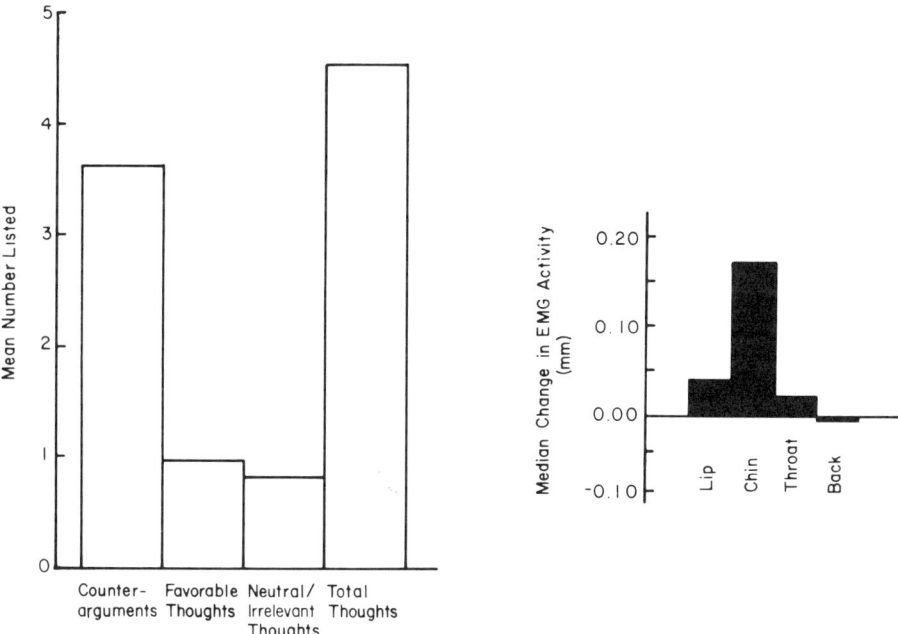

Fig. 7. Mean cognitive responses following the "collect thoughts" interval (left panel) and median changes in EMG activity from prewarning to the "collect thoughts" interval (right panel). (From Cacioppo & Petty, 1981a.)

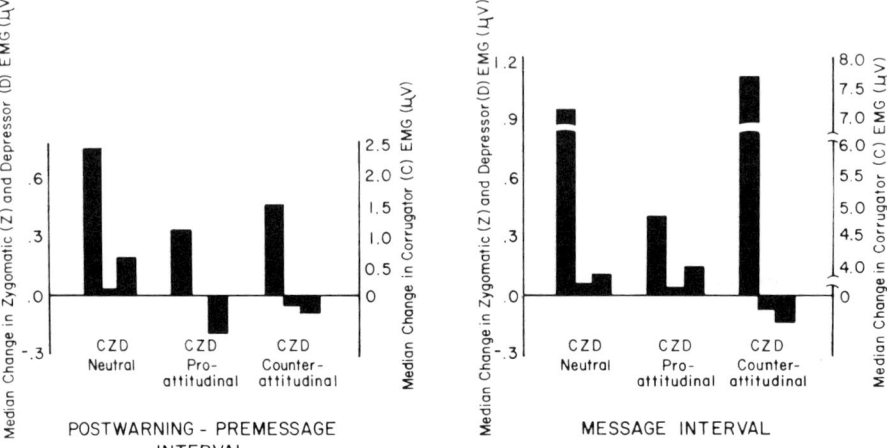

Fig. 8. Median change from prewarning baseline for brow (C), cheek (Z), and depressor (D) EMG activity during the postwarning–premessage (left panel) and message (right panel) intervals. The data are displayed separately for subjects in the neutral, proattitudinal, and counterattitudinal groups. (From Cacioppo & Petty, 1981a).

unpleasant emotional imagery. In sum, a psychophysiological approach proved useful in addressing theoretical question that had been resistant to customary approaches.

5. Toward a Coalition Model of Emotion

The psychophysiological approach adopted in the foregoing research differed from traditional psychophysiological applications in social psychology in that psychometric as well as physiological features of the measures were emphasized. Moreover, physiological measures have traditionally been viewed in social psychology as useful only in assessing general arousal and therefore incapable of distinguishing between positive and negative emotional states (e.g., see Fishbein & Ajzen, 1975; Rosenberg & Hovland, 1960). The studies reviewed thus far, however, suggest facial efference (as measured by EMG activity) is influenced differentially by positive and negative emotional states, even in situations where there are no changes in overt facial action and autonomic activity.

From these studies, coupled with previous research, we have begun to think of emotion as a coalition of normally loosely coupled control mechanisms that (1) are brought about temporarily to achieve a common purpose (flexible adaptation to an environmental challenge—imagined or real), and (2) produce a generally predictable sequence of recruitment of peripheral response components (e.g., see Cacioppo et al., 1984). For instance, the peripheral physiological elements of emotion and the order of recruitment of these elements appear at present to be as follows: (1) subthreshold activation of specific facial muscle regions (e.g., the corrugator supercilii region), which reflect the threat–assurance, or valence, of the emotion; (2) visceral activation begins to exceed threshold levels; (3) accumulating activation of these initially incipient facial actions (due to the increased frequency of MAPs and/or to larger MAPs being recruited) and subthreshold activation of additional, specific facial muscles, which also vary as a function of the emotion (or emotional blend); (4) readily recognizable (e.g., socially perceptible) overt expressions of emotion; and, according to the findings of Ekman *et al.* (1983), (5) autonomic differentiation of some emotional states.

The separate mechanisms of control for autonomic and somatic–expressive responses can introduce variability in this recruitment sequence, as for instance somatic responses are particularly vulnerable to voluntary control or masking. Nevertheless, changes in the central mechanisms of emotion (e.g., activity in the basolateral limbic circuit, dorsomedial thalamus, frontal pathways to limbic and core brain centers) are posited both to precede the peripheral manifestations and to be influenced by the efferent commands and consequent feedback (e.g., through its influence on the septohypothalamomesencephalic continuum).

In addition, an individual's awareness of an emotion is conceived as capable of emerging—or failing to emerge—at any point in the sequence of peripheral physiological manifestation, depending on factors such as focus of attention, available processing resources, and repressive style. That is, the peripheral manifestations of emotion are conceptualized as being contributory rather than necessary or sufficient to activate the subjective component of emotion (see Cacioppo & Petty, 1982; Cacioppo, Petty, Losch, & Kim, 1986, pp. 266–267). This proposition is based on two general heuristics that have emerged from neuroscience research (e.g., Kalat, 1984; Mueller, 1984). First, the reptilian (brain stem and basal ganglia), paleomammalian (limbic system), and neomammalian (neocortex) brain can each independently contribute to peripheral physiological elements of emotion. Second, the subjective component of emotion can be influenced by actions of the former two, but it relies much more fundamentally on an intact neomammalian brain.

This latter observation underlies many contemporary social psychological investigations of emotion. Smith and Ellsworth (1985, 1987), for instance, expected people's reports of emotion to be predicted by the manner in which individuals cognitively appraised the evocative stimulus and circumstance; results from both studies supported these expectations. The conditions under which cognitive appraisal represents a readout of the influences of lower central processes rather than serving as a causal variable in emotion remains uncertain at present.

At present, the coalition model (1) makes such questions salient, (2) provides a theoretical structure for organizing response patterns evoked by emotional stimuli, and (3) outlines in a general way how organizational and specific implementation rules result in emotion. Briefly, various response components of emotion, such as the subjective, autonomic, somatic–expressive, are conceptualized as being governed by only partially overlapping mechanisms of action, with consequent effects on response components ranging from strongly inhibitory to strongly excitatory (see Fig. 9). To ask what are the response characteristics of emotion and by what process did they manifest is to ask what are the rules governing the coalition. Within this framework, theories of emotion can be conceived as specifications of the organizational rules governing (at least parts of) the coalition. For instance, James's (1890), Cannon's (1927), and Schachter and

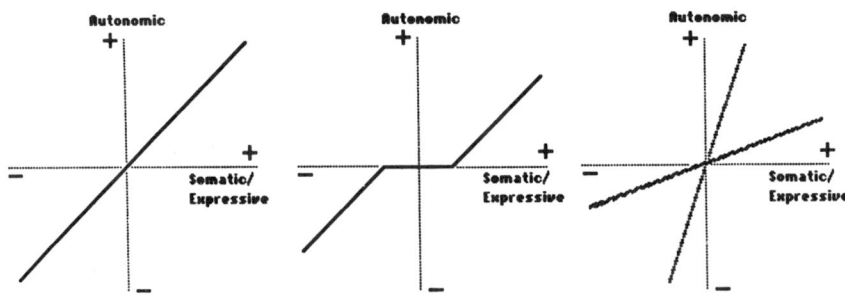

Fig. 9. Illustrative response component by influence matrix (upper panel), and depictions of a response space produced by the unitary organizational rule (lower left panel), unitary rule with a criterion threshold parameter (lower middle panel), and unitary rule with a slope parameter (lower right panel). For simplicity, only the bivariate response space for the autonomic and somatic–expressive response components has been depicted.

Singer's (1962) theories of emotion posit a positive relationship between changes in the autonomic and subjective components of emotion, with James also emphasizing corresponding changes in the somatic–expressive component. The general rule of organization governing the coalition in all three theories could therefore be described as unitary: "all for one and one for all" (see bottom, left panel of Fig. 9). It is the specific rules of implementation (i.e., rules governing the temporal sequence and causal role of each of the components) that differentiate these theories.

The simple organizational rule depicted in the bottom, left panel of Fig. 9 cannot account for the aforementioned hierarchy of peripheral physiological manifestations. Like the behavior of coalitions generally, however, the behavior of the coalition of the control mechanisms underlying emotions can be governed by multiple rules (and by single rules with multiple parameters) at any given time, the weight of each of which can vary dynamically. For instance, the hierarchical manifestation of autonomic and somatic–expressive responses can be explained by the addition of a parameter governing criterion thresholds in which "all are not created equal."[8] The bottom, middle panel of Fig. 9 depicts the bivariate (autonomic and somatic–expressive) response space for the unitary organizations rule, where the criterion threshold for facial efferent discharges is lower than that for autonomic activation.

As a final example, the externalizing–internalizing distinction in the "emotional discharge model" posits an inverse relationship between somatic–expressive and autonomic activity between subjects and a positive relationship between these components within subjects (e.g., see Buck, 1980; Notarius, Wemple, Ingraham, Burns, & Kollar, 1982). Although the moderating variable for this outcome has not yet been well specified, the effect suggests the existence of an organizational parameter that differs reliably across individuals. Specifically, the organizational parameter underlying the internalizer–externalizer distinction can be viewed as controlling the *rate* of activation of the autonomic versus somatic–expressive response components, manifesting as differences in the *slope* of the vector defining the bivariate response space for autonomic and somatic–expressive comonents. It is easy to show that the family of vectors in this response space, with slopes between one and infinity, result in descriptions of the the responses of "internalizers," whereas the family of vectors with slopes between zero and one result in descriptions of the responses of "externalizers" (see Fig. 9, bottom, right panel).

To summarize thus far, although the notion of a unitary organizational rule (activation) is embraced as a hypothetical construct in the present model, response patterns, rather than general and diffuse activation across response components,

---

[8]See Cacioppo, Martzke, Petty, and Tassinary (1988) for an extended discussion of the conception of continuous flow to viable response components, with variable criterion thresholds applied to physiological activity during affect-laden information processing.

are expected and explained in terms of the operation of general organizational rules and their parameters. According to the coalition model, therefore, individuals can exhibit a range of responses to an emotionally evocative stimulus, including such disparate combinations as a clear and reportable awareness of a discrete emotion co-occurring with little or no evidence of peripheral physiological response or expression, or the absense of subjective awareness of an emotional response to a stimulus co-occurring with peripheral physiological evidence of emotional evocation. Moreover, the parameters applied to a general organizational (e.g., the unitary) rule are not merely descriptive, but also represent theoretical constructs. For instance, the hierarchical manifestation of peripheral responses as emotional evocation increases is explained in terms of a threshold parameter suggesting a *gating mechanism* governing the manifestation of peripheral physiological responses, and the internalizer–externalizer distinction is explained by the actions of an independent slope parameter—suggesting a rate-governing *gain mechanism*. Finally, it is possible to describe individual response stereotypy in terms of these gating and gain mechanisms. One interesting implication of such an application is that the internalizer–externalizer distinction is not unique to emotional discharge, but rather is simply a special case of individual response stereotypy (or, more specifically, individual uniqueness).

The foregoing model of somatic patterning fits well within this framework, as it specifies the organizational rules linking the somatic–expressive and subjective response components.[9] For instance, the subtle, transient patterns of facial EMG activity we have found to be evoked by mild emotional stimulation have also been found to vary in magnitude with the intensity of the feelings expressed about the emotional stimuli (Cacioppo, Petty, Losch, & Kim, 1986b). In an illustrative experiment, subjects were exposed to slides of moderately unpleasant, mildly unpleasant, mildly pleasant, and moderately pleasant scenes. Subjects viewed each slide for 5 sec and rated how much they liked the scene that was depicted, how familiar the scene appeared, and how aroused it made them feel. Judgments of the video recordings of subjects' facial actions during the 5-sec stimulus presentations indicated that the scenes were sufficiently mild to not evoke socially perceptible facial expressions. Nevertheless, analyses revealed that EMG activity over the brow (corrugator supercilii) and periocular (orbicularis oculi) muscle regions differentiated the direction and intensity of people's emotional reaction to the scenes: the more subjects like the scene, the lower the level of EMG activity over the brow region; moreover, EMG activity was higher over

---

[9]Although the model of somatic patterning is usually viewed in terms of its predictions regarding what somatic sites are likely to be activated by specific thoughts, images, and emotions, elsewhere we have discussed how the somatic actions may also influence the eliciting state (see Cacioppo, Petty, Losch, & Kim, 1986b, pp. 266–267). For the sake of brevity, we neither delve into the implementation rules concerning these response components nor detail the parameters (e.g., response thresholds with a criterion level that varies with available attentional capacity) that modify these organizational rules to enable admixtures such as incipient somatic–expressive evidence of emotion in the absence of the subjective component.

the periocular region when moderately pleasant than mildly pleasant or unpleasant stimuli were presented.[10] EMG activity over the cheek (zygomaticus major) region also tended to be greater for liked than disliked scenes, with EMG activity being significantly higher when liked than disliked scenes were presented (see Fig. 10). Importantly, neither EMG activity over the brow region nor EMG activity over the cheek region covaried with reported arousal, nor did EMG activity over the perioral (orbicularis oris) region or a peripheral muscle region (superficial forearm flexors) vary as a function of stimulus likeability. These data, therefore, are more consistent with the view of response patterning and gradations than with the view that somatic activity simply increases in a unitary fashion when affect is aroused.

V. Illustrating the New Look: Part II

A. ERRORS OF INFERENCE

In the psychophysiological enterprise as outlined thus far, the manipulation of a specific psychological operation (such as the extent or the affectivity of information processing) is viewed as being *an* antecedent rather than *the* antecedent of the somatovisceral reactions. What is known about the systems underlying the physiological end point and the context in which the measures are obtained are also considered in order to derive specific hypotheses with limited ranges of construct validity and application. For instance, Ekman (1972) and Friesen (1972) have demonstrated that facial actions are clearly controllable and serve deceptive as well as communicative and emotionally expressive functions. In addition, the EMG patterning observed in this research is subtle and is easily

---

[10]EMG recordings from the periocular (orbicularis oculi) muscle region have been shown to be heightened by expressions of pain, squinting, and so forth (e.g., see Fridlund & Izard, 1983). Activity over this region might be thought, therefore, to reflect variations in fixation rather than incipient facial actions associated with affect. EMG activity over this muscle region was greater when positive than when negative stimuli were presented, however, even when a focal point was used (see Cacioppo *et al.*, 1986b, Pilot Study). Yet another interesting account for these data is based on Darwin's (1872/1965) observations and Ekman and Friesen's (1982) research on "felt" smiles. Darwin suggested that people display a smile—whether happy or not—when they wish to present a happy image but that people display both a smile and crow's feet at the outer edges of their eyes when they feel happy. The common elements in the facial expressions of the person who actually experiences a positive emotion are the actions of two muscles: "the zygomatic major pulling the lip corners upwards towards the cheekbone; and the orbicularis oculi which raises the cheek and gathers skin inwards from around the eye socket" (Ekman & Friesen, 1982, p. 242). Because there was no reason in the experimental setting for subjects to feign positive affective reactions to the experimental stimuli, it was suggested that the heightened EMG activity over the orbicularis oculi region, which we found to differentiate the affective nature of the experimental stimuli, may have been related to the variations in the subjects' positive feelings regarding the stimuli.

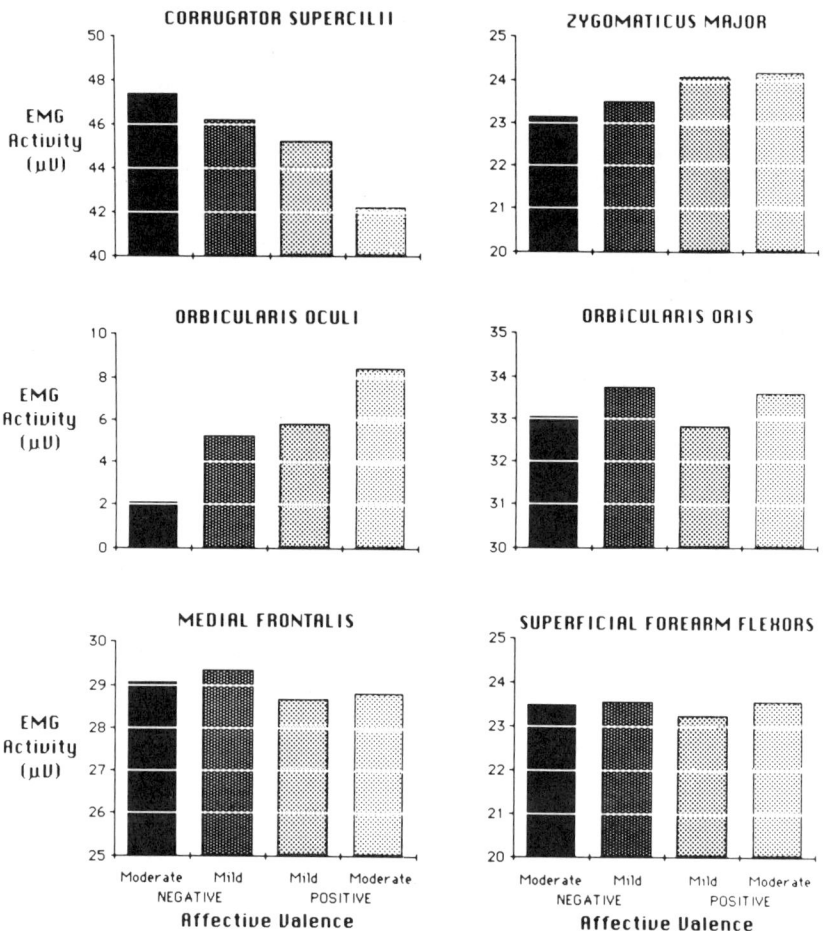

Fig. 10. Mean EMG amplitude over the brow (upper left), cheek (upper right), ocular (middle left), perioral (middle right), forehead (lower left), and forearm (lower right) muscle regions as a function of affective valence and intensity. (Adapted from Cacioppo, Petty, Losch, & Kim, 1986b.)

distorted, requiring optimal experimental conditions to obtain (see Cacioppo & Petty, 1987; Cacioppo *et al.*, 1989; Fridlund & Cacioppo, 1986).

Psychophysiological assessments are often viewed as being useful within social psychology, however, only to the extent that investigators can infer the presence or absence of a particular antecedent or process (e.g., affect) when a target physiological response (e.g., increased skin conductance) is observed.

Yet evidence that an event or process is associated with a particular physiological response is *a necessary but not a sufficient condition* for such an inference.

This is due to the fact that a statement and its converse are not logically equivalent. Thus, knowledge that a statement is true (i.e., A implies B) does not imply that the converse is true (i.e., B implies A). Hence, except in the rare circumstance in which one is dealing with an invariant (single-cause, single-effect) relationship (see Footnote 3), establishing that the manipulation of an event or process ("A") leads to a particular physiological response or profile of responses ("B") does not logically imply that "B predicts A."[11] For example, increased electrodermal activity (EDA) is evoked by a variety of factors, ranging from stress to novelty to arousal to significant events. To infer that a person was emotionally aroused based simply on increased EDA, therefore, is to commit the logical error of affirmation of the consequent (Runes, 1961).

How can one minimize dubious inferences while using physiological responses as markers of psychological operations? Although beginning with psychophysiological hypotheses that are compatible with the physiological system from which the responses are being measured is important, so too is viewing the problem as one of identifying the *diagnostic* (sensitivity and specificity) value of the physiological measures (i.e., a conditional probability problem). For instance, the interpretation of physiological data is aided by knowing not just that the manipulation of some psychological operation of interest leads to a particular physiological response. For accurate interpretation, the experimenter should also know both the likelihood within the assessment context that the target physiological response would be observed in the absence of the psychological operation of interest, and the likelihood that the manipulation of the psychological operation leads to something other than the target physiological response (Cacioppo & Tassinary, in press). Importantly, a physiological reaction (or pattern) that has few antecedents has a wider range of validity (i.e., interpretability) than one with a myriad of antecedents, and for this reason, analyses of response patterns and/or response waveforms can often prove valuable (Cacioppo et al., 1983; Cacioppo & Dorfman, 1987). Startle, orienting, and defense reactions all lead to increased EDA, for example, but they differ with respect to the pattern of somatovisceral activity (e.g., heart rate response, SCR, postural changes) as they unfold over time.

These concerns led us to develop a paradigm in which we could collect information (1) regarding the presence or absence of the psychological operation of interest, given the manifestation of the target physiological response, and (2) regarding the presence or absence of the psychological operation of interest in the absence of the target physiological response. There are now several studies that can be conceptualized within this approach to examine the psychophysiological outcomes discussed thus far.

[11]It should be obvious that investigators who wish to infer the presence or absence of a psychological event or process based on psychophysiological data are confronted by this problem even in the unusual case in which the psychological event of interest ("A") is *always* followed by a given physiological response or profile of responses ("B").

B. FACIAL EMG AS A MARKER OF AFFECT

The research reviewed herein has linked EMG activity over facial muscle regions such as the brow (corrugator supercilii) and cheek (zygomaticus major) to emotional imagery and to emotional reactions to auditory, visual, and social stimuli. The question addressed in a recent study was whether distinctive bursts of activity over the brow region during a clinical interview were associated with more negative thoughts and images than periods in which EMG activity over this region was quiescent (Cacioppo, Martzke, Petty, & Tassinary, 1988).

In addition, previous research has examined the spatial pattern of facial EMG activity evoked by variations in emotion, but this approach can be insensitive when individuals are speaking (e.g., due to the EMG cross talk recorded over the zygomaticus major muscle region, which is attributable to overt articulatory movements and to false smiles) or very mild emotions are involved (e.g., see Cacioppo *et al.*, 1986b; Tassinary, Cacioppo, & Geen, 1989). A potentially important and complementary approach involves specifying with greater precision the form of the EMG responses over the corrugator supercilii muscle region that is predictive of variations in emotion. Such an approach widens (or, in the worst case, leaves unchanged) the range of validity of somatic markers of emotion. Because the goal in this study was to predict mild variations in people's emotional experience as they were speaking during an interview, attention was given to the manner in which the EMG response over the corrugator supercilii muscle region unfolded over time (i.e., its form) while matching for the gross level of EMG activity observed over the zygomaticus major and medial frontalis muscle regions.

Four forms of phasic EMG activity over the corrugator supercilii muscle region were identified during pilot testing. The first represented basal levels of EMG activity over the corrugator supercilii muscle region and was included to establish baselines for reports of emotional experience (EMG Controls or "pseudotrials;" see Johnson & Lubin, 1972). The second represents an acicular burst of EMG activity over the corrugator supercilii muscle region (an *EMG spike*). Acicular EMG responses could be expected to occur for a variety of reasons. Increases in muscle tonus (which might result from sustained attention to a task) result in changes in spontaneous EMG responding, which can manifest as very brief semistochastic unimodal EMG pulses or spikes (i.e., less than a couple seconds in duration). Such activity is said to be spontaneous, or "nonspecific," because the spikes occur in the absence of any known precipitating or associated thought, emotion, or intention (e.g., see Sternbach, 1966, p. 68). Eye-blinks can also manifest in this form. In addition, a fleeting emotion could lead to this form of EMG response, but the transient nature of the emotion, coupled with the various nonemotional determinants of EMG spikes, should weaken the prediction of an individual's emotional experience based on the appearance of an EMG spike during an interview.

The final two forms of EMG response were defined as (1) a relatively smooth response less than 5 sec in duration, marked by a gradual onset and offset (an *EMG mound*), and (2) a ballistic EMG response also less than 5 sec in duration, which manifests more like a cluster of two or more partially overlapping EMG spikes than an EMG mound (an *EMG cluster*). Facial actions include those that serve primarily an interpersonal communicative function (e.g., raising of the brows while speaking, to emphasize nonverbally a point made verbally), as well as those, to paraphrase Darwin, that are in direct or indirect service of personal sensations and desires (e.g., see Darwin, 1872/1965, p. 28). Interpersonal communication—verbal and nonverbal—is facilitated by the transmission of high-fidelity signals. In the service of producing clear, unambiguous signals, the train of MAPs that are recruited with interpersonal communicative intent (or of a similar but more feeble state of intention) may be characterized by a relatively smooth sequence of activation (e.g., EMG mounds in contrast to EMG clusters). Of course, there need not be a contradiction between the facial actions that serve interpersonal communication and those that originate from personal sensations or desires; moreover, emotions can rise and fall gradually and, accordingly, may also be associated with relatively smooth increments and decrements of EMG activation. The important point here, however, is that phasic EMG clusters over the corrugator supercilii muscle region are less likely than EMG spikes or mounds to be the consequence of nonemotional events (e.g., spontaneous activation, paralinguistic signalling) and, hence, may be especially likely to mark variations in emotions during an interview.

To summarize, four specific forms of phasic EMG activity over the corrugator supercilii muscle region were investigated as blocking variables in the present research: (1) basal levels of activity, (2) spikes, (3) mounds, and (4) clusters. Because relatively few nonemotional antecedents were thought to exist for EMG clusters over the corrugator supercilii muscle region during an interview, the emotional experiences marked by EMG clusters were predicted to differ from those marked by basal levels, and the emotional experiences marked by EMG spikes and mounds were predicted to fall between these extremes.[12]

---

[12]Indeed, reports of negative thoughts and ideas that followed isolated spikes of EMG activity over the brow region tended to obtain only when individuals were asked immediately afterward to describe what they had just been thinking about, and the negative thoughts that were reported were sometimes described as having been passing through the background rather than the foreground of their stream of consciousness. The videotape reconstruction procedure we employed provided an insensitive test of the link between isolated EMG spikes and negative affect, however, because our pilot data had indicated these thoughts and ideas were fleeting and easily forgotten when a time delay was introduced between the appearance of the EMG spike and the cognitive assessment. We nevertheless decided to introduce such a delay, to minimize the reactive nature of the assessment procedures. In an attempt to gather preliminary data regarding isolated EMG spikes over the brow region and fleeting feelings of negative affect, however, we also administered the Byrne, Barry, and Nelson (1963) repression–sensitization scale to subjects several days prior to their participation in the study. We reasoned that repressors might be less likely than nonrepressors to have access to

Fifteen undergraduate women were recruited to participate in a study on self-disclosure. Following a recruitment meeting, during which time the procedures were described and a cover story was presented, subjects were brought into the laboratory and interviewed individually while unobtrusive video recordings and recordings of facial EMG activity were obtained. Subjects were seated in a dimly illuminated room and were asked to close their eyes and relax throughout the interview. Following adaptation to the lab, subjects were asked to talk about themselves with the goal of disclosing their "true self." The interviewer, an advanced clinical psychology student who was located in a separate room and was blind to the experimental condition, sought descriptions ranging from the superficial (e.g., physical attributes, demographics) to the intimate (e.g., perceived strengths and inadequacies, traumatic experiences). Throughout the interview, two other experimenters blind to the experimental hypothesis and to the subjects' self-disclosures, identified exemplars of each of four types of EMG responses over the brow region: (1) *control*—quiescent period at least 10 sec in duration; (2) *spike*—unimodal response with sharp onset and offset; (3) *mound*—smooth response no longer than 5 sec, characterized by a gradual onset and offset; and (4) *cluster*—multimodal response from 1 to 3 sec, characterized by an abrupt onset and offset. To assure these periods were otherwise comparable, exemplars were selected only if the individual was speaking, and EMG activity over the corrugator region did not reflect a blink or generalized activation of the facial muscles.

Immediately following the interview, the interviewer conducted a videotape reconstruction with the subject. Subjects watched and listened to the entire videorecording, which was paused at 20 separate segments (5 randomly selected exemplars from each of the four preceding response types). At each pause, subjects were asked to report what thoughts and images "flashed through their minds" at that moment during the interview, and the entire videotape reconstruction was audiotaped. Subjects returned within a few days for a final session, at which time they rated each of the 20 verbal descriptions that were recorded during the

---

any fleeting negative thoughts or feelings that accompanied an isolated EMG spike over the brow region (see Bonanno & Singer, 1986). To test this reasoning, subjects were subsequently classified as repressor or nonrepressor based on a median split of their scores on the Byrne *et al.* (1963) repression–sensitization scale, and subjects' ratings of the thoughts and images that covaried with EMG spikes and control intervals were contrasted. Analyses of variance revealed an interaction: repressors and nonrepressors rated similarly the insightful nature of the thoughts and ideas that occurred in the absence of EMG activity over the brow region (i.e., during control periods). However, the repressors tended to rate the thoughts and images covarying with EMG spikes over the brow region as less insightful than those that occurred during control intervals, whereas the nonrepressors exhibited the opposite pattern. Hence, it is possible that a *subset* of the EMG spikes over the brow region marked more transient negative affect, which subjects failed to recall or repressed during videotape reconstruction. Such a possibility awaits further research.

videotape reconstruction along an abbreviated version of the differential emotions scale. All ratings were made on 7-point scales, and the results of these ratings are summarized in Fig 11. Multivariate and univariate analyses revealed that the rating of the reported associations varied as a function of the type of EMG burst: Recollections during the transient spike and control periods were equivalently positive; those during EMG clusters were rated as being more negative; and those during EMG mounds were rated between these extremes. These results support the notion that specific forms of EMG activity over the brow region, when identified within a particular pattern of facial EMG activity, can serve as an episodic marker of negative affect when individuals were unaware of the target physiological response and of the experimental hypothesis (and, hence, were unlikely to engage somatic actions that would inhibit or mask the responses of interest).

In sum, we have suggested that inferences about a person's cognitive and emotional processes can be formed based on physiological profiles within structured situations, and we have discussed procedures for testing such inferences and any factors that limit these inferences.

C. PERIORAL EMG AS A MARKER OF SILENT LANGUAGE PROCESSING

Interestingly, Shimizu and Inoue (1986) have completed a study of sleep and dreams that bears on the utility of perioral EMG activity as a marker of silent language processing. Electroencephalographic (EEG), electrooculargraphic (EOG), perioral EMG, and nonoral EMG activity were recorded as subjects slept. Subjects were awakened during either rapid eye movement (REM) or Stage 2 sleep—as determined by inspection of the EEG and EOG recordings. When subjects reported dreaming, subjects were asked whether or not they had been speaking in their dreams. Dream recall during REM sleep occurred in approximately 80% of the awakenings, and it occurred during Stage 2 sleep in approximately 28% of the awakenings. Awakenings without dream recall were excluded from further analyses, as were awakenings preceded by phasic discharges in the perioral musculature that were accompanied by any whispering or vocalization. Results revealed that when phasic discharges over the perioral musculature were observed within the 30 sec preceding the awakening, subjects reported having been speaking in their dreams in 88% of the awakenings from REM sleep and 71% of the awakenings during State 2 sleep. Moreover, when phasic discharges over the perioral musculature were not observed within the 30 sec preceding the awakening, subjects reported having been speaking in their dreams in only 19% of the awakenings from REM sleep and in 0% of the awakenings during Stage 2 sleep.

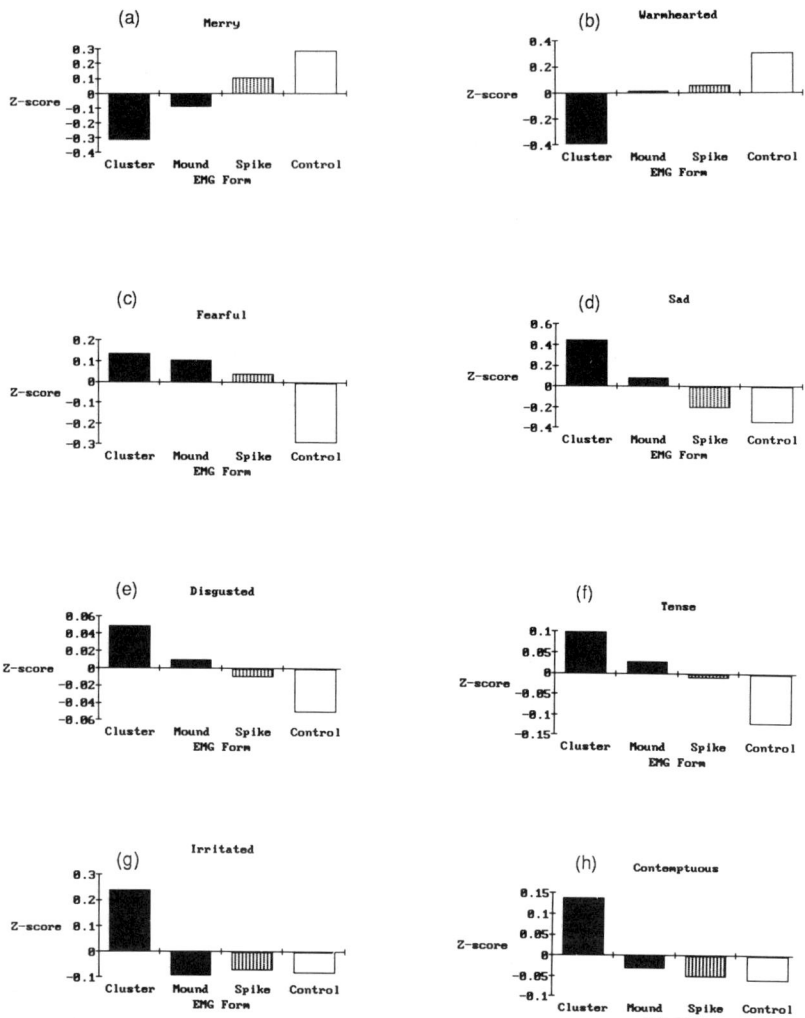

Fig. 11. Mean ratings of the feelings aroused during segments of the interview marked by particular forms of EMG response over the *corrugator supercilii* muscle region. Moments of the interview about which subjects were questioned were selected, based on the individuals speaking about themselves, showing no signs of blinking or general facial tensing, and evincing one of four specific forms of EMG response over the corrugator supercilii muscle region. Ratings were expressed on scales labeled merry/gleeful/amused (a), warmhearted/joyful/elated (b), fearful/scared/afraid (c), sad/downhearted/blue (d), disgusted/turned-off/repulsed (e), tense/anxious/nervous (f), irritated/angry/mad (g), contemptuous/scornful/disdainful (h). Each subject's ratings on each scale were standardized across the 20 segments of the interview during which she was asked to express how she felt. (From Cacioppo, Martzke, Petty, & Tassinary, 1988.)

In sum, previous research had indicated that negative emotional reactions influenced the EMG activity over regions of the muscles of mimicry (e.g., the brow) and that silent language and numeric loads on working memory influenced the EMG activity over the perioral muscle region. The research reviewed in this section further suggests that EMG discharges over the brow and over the perioral muscle region can be used to mark episodes of negative affect and silent language processing, respectively. Together, these studies have implications for the specificity and sensitivity of somatic markers when individuals cannot report, will not report, or do not know what to report about ongoing cognitive and emotional operations.

VI. Sociological and Philosophical Obstacles

A. THE BABY AND THE BATHWATER

The conceptualization of the psychophysiological enterprise as concerning in part the identification of episodic markers of behaviorally relevant cognitive and affective processes is a fairly recent development in psychophysiology and is still sometimes misunderstood (see Cacioppo & Petty, 1986; Cacioppo & Tassinary, in press; Donchin, 1982). At least part of this misunderstanding has a factual basis and a long history. For instance, Allport cited the following as being said by Carlston during a then-recent presidential address to the American Psychological Association:

> I believe that robotic thinking helps precision of psychological thought, and will continue to help it until psychophysiology is so far advanced that an image is nothing other than a neural even, and object constancy is obviously just something that happens in the brain. (Allport, 1947, p. 185)

Allport (1947), on the other hand, was concerned about general social problems and moral issues. It is therefore understandable, given the climate of the times, why Allport, in his inaugural presidential address to APA's Division of Personality and Social Psychology, might have equated psychophysiology with simplistic mechanistic thinking and criticized it (along with animal and infant research) as being reductionistic, inadequate, and a waste of time and energy for those interested in relevant social behavior.

Allport's (1947) criticisms of reductionism and of the search for psychophysiological invariants to explain social behavior, as well as his early defense of social cognition in the face of the juggernaut of American behaviorism, were important and influential. But rather than questioning the charge that the promise of psychophysiology was to generate a list of physiological invariants, Allport rejected the entire approach to the study of social behavior:

> In taking stock of the situation I observe how many of us seem so stupefied by admiration of physical science that we believe psychology in order to succeed need only imitate the models, postulates, methods and language of physical science. If someone points out the present inutility of mechanical models in predicting anything but the most peripheral forms of human behavior, we are inclined to reply: "Wait a thousand years." (Allport, 1947, p. 182)

B. THE LONG SHADOWS OF INTELLECTUAL FOCUS

There were long shadows cast by the early dismissal of organismic factors as being relevant to the study of social processes and behavior. Even when important formulations were developed that sought to integrate knowledge from multiple domains (e.g., Schachter & Singer, 1962), these formulations were soon stripped of any serious treatment of the organismic domain. Valins (1966), for instance, proposed that actual sensations or changes in physiological arousal were superfluous in emotion, and that instead, the simple belief that a change in physiological arousal occurred was necessary and sufficient to influence emotion by invoking the search for an emotional label. Several years later, Bem (1972) argued persuasively that people are typically insensitive to internal information and cues and, therefore, they were essentially in the same position when trying to understand their own actions as were observers. Psychophysiological concepts and procedures obviously have little place in such formulations.[13]

Schachter and Singer's (1962) integrative cognitive, social, and physiological theory of emotions also did much to advance the concept of physiological arousal as a factor to be reckoned with in analyses or social processes and behavior. Inspection of existing social psychological textbooks and the recent *Handbook of Social Psychology* reveals, for instance, that the only physiological construct to have had a major impact on theory and research in social psychology is the notion of arousal, a hypothetical construct that represents the intensive component of behavior. Furthermore, changes in physiological arousal have been conceptualized as being general, diffuse, and misattributable if not reportable, which makes their measurements technically simple and their interpretations straightforward: Any single physiological response, performance on drive-sensitive tasks,

---

[13]Note, too, that at no point was it demonstrated that physiological factors were not contributory, only that they were not *necessary* to obtain the outcome reported by Schachter and Singer (1962). The conclusion drawn by many from these studies, however, was that physiological factors were unimportant.

misattributions of bodily sensations, on simple self- reports of bodily sensations was thought to index a person's arousal–drive at that momemt in time. This conceptualization has led to most studies of physiological processes and social behavior being conducted with little need for physiological recording or concern about the underlying physiological or bioelectrical mechanisms.

Moreover, there is little hint that matters are rapidly improving. In reviewing the literature on cognitive dissonance a decade ago, Kiesler and Pallak (1976) noted in a strikingly contemporary tone (e.g., see Elkin & Leippe, 1986) that:

> We use the terms motivation (drive) and arousal loosely and interchangeably. . . . We recognize the continuing controversy regarding these concepts in the literature in experimental psychology. . . . Our simplistic use of the terms does not imply a theoretical stance on our part, but rather reflects the state of the art in social psychology. (p. 1015)

Although this use by social psychologists may have appeared reasonable at one time, it is important to note that, whether intended or not, this viewpoint *does* represent a theoretical stance—and one that strikes contemporary investigators in other fields as inexplicable if not somewhat naive. As Fowles (1980) summarized in a review of the literature on physiological arousal not long after the appearance of Kiesler and Pallak's review:

> The effect of attempting to assimilate all of these traditions to a single arousal theory was to create a model in which the reticular activating system was assumed to serve as a generalized arousal mechanism which responded to sensory inputs of all kinds, energized behavior, and producted both EEG and sympatheitc nervous system activation. . . . As is well-known, this model failed the empirical test rather badly. (p. 88)

All the more striking is that advances in the area of experimental psychology pertaining to cognition have had a large impact on conceptualizations in social psychology during the past decade, while cognitive psychologists and artificial intelligence researchers have begun to show increasing interest in the ''wetware'' (neural circuitry) of the human organism.

Even the early attraction of psychophysiological conceptualizations and procedures to social psychologists for purposes of construct validation proved a virtual dead end. When physiological procedures were used *successfully* to validate a social psychological construct, there was little reason to continue using these relatively complex, expensive, and time-consuming procedures to investigate the construct because the validity of the construct had been established, at least to the extent possible using psychophysiological procedures. Therefore, the simpler, less expensive, and less time-consuming verbal or behavioral measures traditionally used by social psychologists had been exonerated as being just as informative. The important concept of residual arousal, for instance, has received wide acceptance and application within social psychology, but the construct validity of this important concept is based almost entirely on a single pilot study reported by Cantor, Zillmann, and Bryant (1975), in which both self-report and physiological data were recorded (cf. Cacioppo, Tassinary, Stonebraker, & Petty, 1987).

The situation proved no better when the application of psychophysiological procedures *failed* to confirm the validity of a verbal measure of a social construct. Breckler (1984), for instance, argued that studies of the attitude tripartite should measure responses from a variety of domains, and in Experiment 1, he recorded heart rate as a measure of the "affective" component of attitudes. Analyses revealed that heart rate was unrelated to his other measures of the affective component. Having failed to confirm the expected link between heart rate and the "affective component" of attitudes, Breckler (1984) conducted a "verbal report analogue" (p. 1200) of his first experiment while deleting all physiological measures in the replication. The deletion of physiological measures produced a pattern of data more friendly to the tripartite conceptualization.

C. OPERATIONAL AND CONCEPTUAL DISCONFIRMABILITY

The empirical disconfirmation of a theoretical prediction can be attributable to a variety of factors, not the least of which is a suspect relation between psychophysiological data and the theoretical construct of interest. Indeed, the relation between social psychological theory and psychophysiological data have been and often continue to be criticized for: (1) naive or questionable operationalizations (e.g., heart rate as an index of affect); (2) inappropriate, artifactual, or insensitive measurement procedures (e.g., heart rate is under tight homeostatic control; the size of SRRs can be affected dramatically by the background level of skin resistance); and (3) naive or inappropriate interpretations (e.g., inferring evidence for general arousal when only one physiological response was monitored or when more than one response was monitored but only one showed significant or expected changes as a function of the treatment). Consequently, unexpected data in construct validation studies have led to the discrediting of the psychophysiological conceptualizations and/or procedures rather than of the theory itself.

The point is not to reify physiological responses, but rather to give them the same thought and attention that we give our verbal and behavioral measures. As when using verbal or behavioral measures, conceptual disconfirmability, and hence theoretical advances in understanding social behavior based on psychophysiological investigations, requires that the relation between concepts and operations first be established confidently (see Greenwald, Pratkanis, Leippe, & Baumgardner, 1986).

Having noted this, yet further hindrances become immediately obvious: (1) there is no apparent purpose in social psychologists learning about or using psychophysiological theory and techniques unless or until the links between psychophysiological data and social psychological constructs have been clearly established; and (2) there is little incentive for psychophysiologists to begin the arduous task of establishing these relationships when there is little interest in or audience for the effort.[14] In the next section, we review evidence suggesting that these obstacles are neither peculiar nor inexorable.

VII. The New Look: Part III

Research on theoretical processes in social psychology ranging from the arousal of cognitive dissonance to the cue processing underlying the sleeper effect has traditionally relied on people's self-reports to assess the efficacy of the experimental manipulations, the effects of these manipulations on verbal and overt behavior, and the operation of the assumed intervening sequence of events. One feature of this research is that ingenious experimental designs have been employed to allow inferences to be drawn regarding the processes underlying these verbal and/or behavioral data. However, these inferences are themselves often followed by ingenious counterarguments and occasionally by theoretical impasses. The number of seemingly irreconcilable debates in social psychology has fueled concerns about the nature of the social sciences generally and social psychology in particular, including aspects of its stability, methodology, and epistemology (e.g., Gergen, 1973; Greenwald, 1975; McGuire, 1973, 1985).

These conditions might be thought sufficient to lead to the consideration, if not embracing, of alternative approaches. Not so, according to Kuhn (1970), who suggests that there is a strong resistance to new paradigms inherent in established disciplines. For instance, social psychological constructs are generally defined in a manner that capitalizes on the methodologies and measures most readily available, thereby maximizing their testability and influence—and minimizing the relevance of alternative domains of knowledge, such as psychophysiological concepts and procedures. Hence, theoretical constructs such as

---

[14]It is of interest to note that major figures in psychophysiology as well as in social psychology contributed unwittingly to this dilemma. We have already noted that Gordon Allport (1947) equated psychophysiology with simplistic, mechanistic thinking. A dozen years later, Lacey (1959) cogently criticized poorly controlled psychophysiological studies of psychotherapeutic interactions—social interactions of interest to psychophysiologists of that day—and he called for more highly controlled investigations of psychophysiological measurement and relationships. Allport's influential presidential address and subsequent writings cast verbal reports in the starring role and cast psychophysiological concepts and measures as irrelevant to the study of social processes and behavior. Lacey's appeal, on the other hand, diminished the incentive for psychophysiologists investigating relatively abstract and intractable social constructs and processes. It is perhaps understandable, therefore, why more was said about physiological factors and mechanisms in the original textbooks on social psychology than in contemporary textbooks and why more was said about social and cultural factors in the original texts in psychophysiology than in the texts that have appeared in the intervening two decades.

physiological arousal become conceptualized in attributional terms, and their influence on individual and group behavior is investigated primarily by using verbal reports and misattribution paradigms (cf. Lindzey & Aronson, 1985; Reisenzein, 1983).

In sum, analyses of the nature of scientific progress anticipates the resistance of established disciplines to new paradigms because, for instance, existing theories oftentimes make no clear predictions regarding these new measures. This is best viewed as an unintentional consequence of the best of scientific intentions (e.g., in the name of disconfirmability, parsimony).

A. EMPIRICAL ANOMALIES

The conflicting demands of avoiding a policy of immunizing perspectives against refutation while maintaining testable theories and not succumbing too easily before they have been able to make their contributions to the growth of science have long been recognized by philosophers of science. It is noteworthy in this context, however, that a key condition supporting the development of new or more complex perspectives is the observation of phenomena that cannot be assimilated easily into existing paradigms. The growth of systematic research on the relationships between social processes and psychophysiological measures or mechanisms, therefore, may be necessary but not sufficient to foster the consideration of the organism, as well as the individual, when studying social processes and behavior. Ultimately, the prospects for the growth within social psychology of a metatheoretical orientation, wherein there is an integrated consideration of the biopsychosocial aspects of mentation, emotion, and behavior, depends on the ability of this perspective to reveal and explain new and interesting phenomena. In our view, there are promising signs that such is the case.

Consider, for instance, that attitudes and emotions have traditionally been defined, at least within social psychology, in terms of what people report believing or feeling. Constructs such as "unconscious emotion," therefore, are a contradiction in terms, and clinical phenomena such as *prosopagnosia*—a neurological condition of individuals who are unable to recognize visually the faces of familiar persons, exhibiting large skin conductance responses (SCRs) to faces of persons they had previously known but were not able to recognize (Tranel & Damasio, 1985)—stand as empirical anomalies. So, too, do (1) studies on the effects of environmental noise during various sleep stages, which reveals that sleeping subjects exhibit subtle patterns of facial efference remarkably similar to those observed in waking subjects confronted by unpleasant stimuli (Sumitsuji, Nan'no, Kuwata, & Ohta, 1980); (2) studies showing that subtle adjustments of bodily response, such as head nodding (Wells & Petty, 1980) or transient and specific variations in heart rate (Cacioppo, 1979), can influence attitudes and persuasion; (3) studies showing that emotion can be characterized by specific rather than general and diffuse physiological responses (e.g., Cacioppo, Petty, Losch, & Kim, 1986b; Ekam *et al.*, 1983); and (4) studies demonstrating physiological (Tassinary, Orr, Wolford, Napps, & Lanzetta, 1984) and behavioral (Greenwald, Klinger, & Liu, 1987) effects of the processing of emotionally laden words whose presentation cannot be reported.

Empirical anomalies within psychophysiology also exist which call for a consideration of social factors. For instance, there is now evidence for a moderating role of social factors (e.g., mere presence) on stimulus changes and physiological reactivity in studies of both autonomic (e.g., Fowles, Roberts, & Nagel, 1977; see, also, Moore & Baron, 1983) and somatic response systems (e.g., Ekman, 1972; Yarczower & Daruns, 1982); and for the role of social factors (e.g., position in a social hierarchy) on the relationship between physiological changes and behavior (e.g., Haber & Barchas, 1984; see, also, Zillmann, 1983).

B. A CHANGING ZEITGEIST

The social and political zeitgeist has also been more influential in social psychology than in many sciences, presumably because of the close relationship between social psychological interests and social events (Jones, 1985). It is significant, therefore, that a major development in Western societies over the past several years is the realization that the leading causes of disability and death (e.g., heart disease, cancer, accidents) have substantial social and behavioral components. The resulting emphasis on preventive medicine and on the social and behavioral factors related to public health has stimulated interest among social scientists in physiological concepts and techniques (e.g., Fleming, Baum, & Singer, 1984; Van Egeren, 1984). A second important consequence is that attention is being given to questions regarding (1) which, when, and how physiological mechanisms moderate the effect of social stimuli on individual action and experience; and (2) which, when, and how social factors and systems moderate the effect of environmental stimuli on physiological reactivity and disease.

Again, not only does psychophysiology have contributions to offer social psychology, but also theoretical principles that have emerged from analyses of social behavior can be used to extend our understanding of psychophysiological phenomena—such as how it is that people detect and interpret the signs (bodily changes detected through exteroceptive sensory channels) and symptoms (bodily changes detected through interoceptive or proprioceptive sensory channels) of disease (e.g., Cacioppo, Andersen, Turnquist, & Petty, 1986a; Leventhal, Meyer, & Nerenz, 1980).

As a case in point, consider one of the most eloquent of social psychological theories—social comparison theory. Although Festinger (1954) proposed his theory of social comparison to stipulate why individuals compared their own opinions and abilities with those of others, with whom these comparisons were made, and with what effects these comparisons were made, this work served as the springboard for the next three decades of social psychological research on the problem of explicating the cognitive and emotional processes that are initiated by the detection of unexpected bodily events (e.g., see Riesenzein, 1983; Schachter, 1959; Schachter & Singer, 1962).

We have also drawn on this work to suggest that not only do people attempt to evaluate their abilities and opinions to achieve or maintain an explicable social condition, but they also actively evaluate their bodily signs and symptoms to achieve or maintain an explicable physiological condition. Specifically, it was noted that the process of social comparison typically involves comparing one's abilities and opinions with those of others, and it was proposed that the process of psychophysiological comparison typically involves comparison of signs and symptoms (1) that those individuals attribute to a situation or stimulus—or what could be termed "implicit stimulus response stereotypy"—and (2) that those individuals attribute to themselves—or what could be termed "implicit individual response stereotypy" (Cacioppo, 1983). We subsequently identified general principles governing the appraisals of individuals confronted with the signs and symptoms of disease (Cacioppo, Andersen, Turnquist, & Petty, 1986a; Cacioppo, Andersen, Turnquist, & Tassinary, in press). These principles, which are summarized in Table I, portray psychophysiological comparison processes as being pervasive, influential, and in many cases biased to support a positive view of oneself and one's physiological condition (see Table I).

A study of 54 women who had just been diagnosed as having gynecologic cancer provided an examination of several of these principles (Cacioppo, Andersen, Turnquist, & Petty, 1986a). Patients were interviewed individually within 36 hours of their admission to the hospital by an interviewer who was blind to the experimental hypotheses. The interviews, which were conducted prior to the onset of any medical treatment, inquired about the signs and symptoms patients noticed, their perceived causes for and interpretation of these bodily changes, their desire–motivation to seek further information about or treatment for the signs and symptoms, and so forth.

The results indicated that principles derived from social psychological analyses of behavior—such as the postulates of logical and hedonic consistency—provided pointers to, if not explanations for, patient decision making and delay. For instance, we found that patients tended to generate explanations for unexpected bodily changes according to prototyped conceptions they have of daily activities and physical diseases (see, also, Bishop & Converse, 1986; Leventhal et al., 1980; Safer, Tharps, Jackson, & Leventhal, 1979). In addition, however, we found that the more innocuous the account generated initially for their signs and symptoms (e.g., normal life events, not cancer), the less their motivation to continue searching for an explanation, and the longer the delay in seeking appraisal.

Perhaps more important than the ultimate validity of the specific principles

TABLE I
PSYCHOPHYSIOLOGICAL COMPARISON PROCESSES

1. People are motivated to maintain an explicable physiological condition.
2. Symptoms are not necessarily either perceived as neutrally arousing or perceived accurately in terms of their physiological etiology.
3. The strength of the motivation to understand and evaluate the symptoms is a function of their unexpectedness, salience, personal relevance, and perceived consequences.
4. Symptom interpretation involves a comparison of the symptoms with the known consequences of salient contextual stimuli (e.g., pathogens, medication), and physiological conditions (e.g., fatigue, allergies, diseases—i.e., illness prototypes).
5. Symptom interpretation is governed in part by logical consistency. For instance, the probability of a specific illness inference is a direct function of its accessibility and an inverse function of the discrepancy between the symptoms and the illness prototype.
6. Symptom interpretation is governed in part by hedonic consistency. For instance, innocuous explanations (e.g., accounts depicting the symptoms as transient or self-correcting) more greatly diminish the individual's motivation to obtain an explicable physiological condition to a greater degree, ceteris paribus, than do highly threatening accounts.
7. The more diffuse the symptoms, the greater the number of potential comparisons and, consequently, the greater the likelihood of erroneous interpretations of the symptoms and the more susceptible to change are these inferences.
8. If an illness prototype cannot be identified initially that is believed to have effects similar to the detected bodily changes, then the prototype that maximizes the aforementioned logical and hedonic parameters will influence subsequent attention to and production and detection of the expected symptoms.
9. If a comparison cannot be identified initially that is believed to have effects similar to the detected bodily changes, then the detected symptoms will influence the idiosyncratic physiological consequences attributed to the prototype that maximizes the aforementioned logical and hedonic parameters.

outlined in Table I, however, is the suggestion from these and related approaches (e.g., Leventhal *et al.;* 1980; Matthews, Siegel, Kuller, Thompson, & Varat, 1983; Mechanic, 1972; Pennebaker, 1982) that a consideration of social, psychological, and physiological factors and knowledge domains need not result in reductionism but rather can lead to new, interesting, and integrative insights into human nature.

VIII. Conclusion

We have traced the transition of "social psychophysiology" from a reductionistic search for physiological invariants to an esoteric methodological tool for purposes of validating social psychological constructs to a metatheoretical orientation wherein there is a joint and integrative consideration of the inherent biopsychosocial nature of mentation, emotion, and behavior. We argued that physiological measures can fruitfully be conceptualized as manifestations of processes invoked as part of an organismic–environmental transaction (see, also, Donchin, 1982). Such processes may or may not be part of psychological activity, and may or may not be responsive to or influential in human association and interaction. When measures within limited contexts are identified that are related to social psychological processes or events, the nature of the relationship may or may not be monotonic. When the functional relationship within the measurement context across these various levels of representation is found, it is of use to the extent that it is possible to address issues of theoretical import by employing psychophysiological measures as a source of data about the social organism. That is, the goal is not simply to catalog the physiological manifestations of social behavior.

We also noted that inferences regarding the presence or absence of a particular antecedent or process (e.g., arousal) based on a particular target physiological response (e.g., SCRs) can be misleading unless one also considers (1) the nature of the relationship between the psychological process or event of interest and the physiological response being measured (e.g., negatively evocative stimuli have often been found also to heighten SCR), (2) the likelihood of other factors within the measurement context eliciting the observed physiological response (e.g., SCR activity is heightened when individuals become startled, alerted, conflicted, ecstatic, warm, etc.), and (3) the likelihood that the antecedent of interest leads to something other than the target physiological response (e.g., mildly evocative negative stimuli may heighten activity over the brow region while failing to alter EDA).

Furthermore, although the assignment of psychological meaning to a physiological response does not depend logically on knowledge of the physiological mechanism underlying the response, the physiological basis of the responses of interest are often well articulated and can contribute to psychometric and social psychological inquiries by its: (1) intimation or stimulation of theory and operationalizations; (2) discrimination of signal from artifact; (3) provision for safety of the individuals involved; (4) stipulations for the acquisition and analysis of digital arrays and descriptive parameters that are reliable and valid representations of the physiological events of interest; and (5) guidance of feasible inferences based on physiological data.

Illustrative research was reviewed demonstrating the use of facial EMG to help track the means by which the social world impinges on individual action and experience in studies ranging from self-referent processing to self-disclosure to communication and persuasion. However, given the inherent resistance of established disciplines to new paradigms (e.g., because in the service of parsimony and disconfirmability, theories within a discipline often make no clear predictions regarding new domains) the growth of systematic research on the relationships between social processes and psychophysiological data is necessary but not sufficient to foster our considering the organism as well as the individual when studying social processes and behavior. Ultimately, therefore, the prospects for a social psychophysiological approach to human nature depend on its ability to uncover and explain new and interesting phenomena. Promising signs were reviewed that just such a circumstance might be developing.

Finally, it was noted that the social and political zeitgeists have been more influential in social psychology than in many other sciences, understandably, as Jones (1985) argues, because many of the phenomena of interest and in dire need of explanation are played out in the social and political arena (e.g., Latane & Darley, 1970; Milgram, 1963). The recent realization that the leading causes of disability and death in Western civilization have substantial social and behavioral components, and the emergence of interest and research on the social and behavioral factors related to public health, are therefore significant. These developments have stimulated interest among social psychologists not only in physiological concepts and techniques, but also in questions regarding which, when, and how physiological mechanisms moderate the effect of social stimuli on individual action, experience, and health. The long tradition of basic research and theory within social psychology is serving this emerging zeitgeist well, as social psychological principles are providing an important legacy for health as well as for psychophysiological research.

Acknowledgments

This article is based on an invited address delivered by J. T. Cacioppo at the annual meeting of the American Psychological Association, Washington, DC, 1986. The research cited in, and preparation of, the address and article were supported by National Science Foundation Grant Nos. BNS-8444909 and BNS-8517658.

References

Allport, G. W. (1947). Scientific models and human morals. *Psychological Review*, **54**, 182–192.
Aronson, E., Brewer, M., & Carlsmith, J. M. (1985). Experimentation in social psychology. In E. Aronson & G. Lindzey (Eds.), *Handbook of social psychology* (3rd ed., Vol. 1). Hillsdale, NJ: Erlbaum.
Aronson, E., & Lindzey, G. (Eds.). (1985). *Handbook of social psychology* (3rd ed., Vol. 1). Hillsdale, NJ: Erlbaum.
Baddeley, A. D. (1978). The trouble with levels: A reexamination of Craik and Lockhart's framework for memory research. *Psychological Review*, **85**, 139–152.
Bem, D. J. (1972). Self-perception theory. *Advances in Experimental Social Psychology*, **6**, 1–62.
Bishop, G. D., & Converse, S. A. (1986). Illness representations: A prototype approach. *Health Psychology*, **5**, 95–114.

Bonanno, G. A., & Singer, J. L. (1986). *Repressive personality style: Theoretical and methodological implications for health psychology*. Unpublished manuscript, Yale University.

Bower, G. H., & Gilligan, S. G. (1979). Remembering information related to one's self. *Journal of Research in Personality*, **13**, 420–432.

Breckler, S. J. (1984). Empirical validation of affect, behavior, and cognition as distinct attitude components. *Journal of Personality and Social Psychology*, **47**, 1191–1205.

Brock, T. C. (1967). Communication discrepancy and intent to persuade as determinants of counterargument production. *Journal of Experimental Social Psychology*, **3**, 269–309.

Buck, R. (1980). Nonverbal behavior and the theory of emotion: The facial feedback hypothesis. *Journal of Personality and Social Psychology*, **38**, 811–824.

Byrne, D., Barry, J., & Nelson, D. (1963). Relation of the revised repression–sensitization scale to measures of self-deception. *Psychological Reports*, **13**, 323–334.

Cacioppo, J. T. (1979). Effects of exogenous changes in heart rate on facilitation of thought and resistance to persuasion. *Journal of Personality and Social Psychology*, **37**, 489–498.

Cacioppo, J. T. (1982). Social psychophysiology: A classic perspective and contemporary approach. *Psychophysiology*, **19**, 241–251.

Cacioppo, J. T. (1983, May). Psychophysiological comparison theory: The physical, psychological, and social meanings of symptoms. In H. Leventhal (Chair), *The physical, psychological, and social meanings of symptoms*. Presented at the meeting of the Midwestern Psychological Association, Chicago, IL.

Cacioppo, J. T. (1984). Sociopsychophysiology. In R. J. Corsini (Ed.), *Wiley encyclopedia of psychology* (Vol. 3, pp. 349–351). New York: John Wiley & Sons.

Cacioppo, J. T., Andersen, B. L., Turnquist, D. C., & Petty, R. E. (1986a). Psychophysiological comparison processes: Interpreting cancer symptoms. In B. L. Andersen (Ed.), *Women with cancer: Psychological perspectives* (pp. 141–171). New York: Springer-Verlag.

Cacioppo, J. T., Andersen, B. L., Turnquist, D. C., & Tassinary, L. G. (in press). Psychophysiological comparison theory: On the experience, description, and assessment of signs and symptoms. *Patient Education and Counseling*.

Cacioppo, J. T., & Dorfman, D. D. (1987). Waveform moments analysis in psychophysiological research. *Psychological Bulletin*, **102**, 421–438.

Cacioppo, J. T., Marshall-Goodell, B., & Dorfman, D. D. (1983). Skeletal muscular patterning: Topographical analysis of the integrated electromyogram. *Psychophysiology*, **20**, 269–283.

Cacioppo, J. T., Martzke, J. S., Petty, R. E., & Tassinary, L. G. (1988a). Specific forms of facial EMG response index emotions during an interview: From Darwin to the continuous flow hypothesis of affect-laden information processing. *Journal of Personality and Social Psychology*, in press.

Cacioppo, J. T., & Petty, R. E. (1979a). Attitudes and cognitive response: An electrophysiological approach. *Journal of Personality and Social Psychology*, **37**, 2181–2199.

Cacioppo, J. T., & Petty, R. E. (1979b). Neuromuscular circuits in affect-laden information processing. *Pavlovian Journal of Biological Science*, **14**, 177–185.

Cacioppo, J. T., & Petty, R. E. (1981a). Electromyograms as measures of extent and affectivity of informational processing. *American Psychologist*, **36**, 441–456.

Cacioppo, J. T., & Petty, R. E. (1981b). Effects of extent of thought on the pleasantness ratings of p–o–x triads: Evidence for three judgmental tendencies in evaluating social situations. *Journal of Personality and Social Psychology*, **40**, 1000–1009.

Cacioppo, J. T., & Petty, R. E. (1981c). Social psychological procedures for cognitive response assessment: The thought listing technique. In T. V. Merluzzi, C. R. Glass, & M. Genest (Eds), *Cognitive assessment* (pp. 309–342). New York: Guilford Press.

Cacioppo, J. T., & Petty, R. E. (1982). A biosocial model of attitude change: Signs, symptoms, and undetected physiological responses. In J. T. Cacioppo & R. E. Petty (Eds.), *Perspectives in cardiovascular psychophysiology* (pp. 151–188). New York: Guilford Press.

Cacioppo, J. T., & Petty, R. E. (Eds.). (1983). *Social psychophysiology: A sourcebook*. New York: Guilford Press.
Cacioppo, J. T., & Petty, R. E. (1985). Physiological responses and advertising effects: Is the cup half full or half empty? *Psychology and Marketing*, **2**, 115–126.
Cacioppo, J. T., & Petty, R. E. (1986). Social processes. In M. G. H. Coles, E. Donchin, & S. Porges (Eds.), *Psychophysiology: Systems, processes, and applications* (pp. 646–679). New York: Guilford Press.
Cacioppo, J. T., & Petty, R. E. (1987). Stalking rudimentary processes of social influence: A psychophysiological approach. In M. P. Zanna, J. M. Olson, & C. P. Herman (Eds.), *Social influence: The Ontario symposium* (Vol. 5, pp. 41–74). Hillsdale, NJ: Erlbaum.
Cacioppo, J. T., Petty, R. E., & Geen T. R. (in press). Attitude structure and function: From the tripartite to the homeostatis model of attitudes. In A. R. Pratkanis, S. J. Breckler, & A. G. Greenwald (Eds.), *Attitude structure and function*. Hillsdale, NJ: Erlbaum.
Cacioppo, J. T., Petty, R. E., Losch, M. E., & Kim, H. S. (1986b). Electromyographic activity over facial muscle regions can differentiate the valence intensity of affective reaction. *Journal of Personality and Social Psychology*, **50**, 260–268.
Cacioppo, J. T., Petty, R. E., & Marshall-Goodell, B. (1984). Electromyographic specificity during simple physical and attitudinal tasks: Location and topographical features of integrated EMG responses. *Biological Psychology*, **18**, 85–121.
Cacioppo, J. T., Petty, R. E., & Morris, K. J. (1985). Semantic, evaluative, and self-referent processing: Memory, cognitive effort, and somatovisceral activity. *Psychophysiology*, **22**, 371–384.
Cacioppo, J. T., & Sandman, C. A. (1978). Physiological differentiation of sensory and cognitive tasks as a function of warning, processing demands, and reported unpleasantness. *Biological Psychology*, **6**, 181–192.
Cacioppo, J. T., & Sandman, C. A. (1981). Psychophysiological functioning, cognitive responding, and attitudes. In R. E. Petty, T. M. Ostrom, & T. C. Brock (Eds.), *Cognitive responses in persuasion* (pp. 81–104). Hillsdale, NJ: Erlbaum.
Cacioppo, J. T., & Tassinary, L. G. (in press). The concept of attitude: A psychophysiological analysis. In H. L. Wagner & A. S. R. Manstead (Eds.), *Handbook of psychophysiology: Emotion and social behaviour*. Chichester: Wiley.
Cacioppo, J. T., & Tassinary, L. G. (1989). *Principles of psychophysiology: Physical, social, and inferential elements*. Cambridge: Cambridge University Press, in press.
Cacioppo, J. T., Tassinary, L. G., & Fridlund, A. J. (1989). The skeletomotor response system: Surface electromyography. In J. T. Cacioppo & L. G. Tassinary (Eds.), *Principles of psychophysiology: Physical, social, and inferential elements*. Cambridge: Cambridge University Press, in press.
Cacioppo, J. T., Tassinary, L. G., Stonebraker, T. B., & Petty, R. E. (1987). Self-report and cardiovascular measures of arousal: Fractionation during residual arousal. *Biological Psychology*, **25**, 135–151.
Cannon, W. B. (1927). The James–Lange theory of emotions: A critical examination and an alternative theory. *American Journal of Psychology*, **39**, 106–124.
Cantor, J. R., Bryant, J., & Zillmann, D. (1974). Enhancement of humor appreciation by transferred excitation. *Journal of Personality and Social Psychology*, **30**, 812–821.
Cantor, J. R., Zillmann, D., & Bryant, J. (1975). Enhancement of experienced sexual arousal in response to erotic stimuli through misattribution of unrelated residual excitation. *Journal of Personality and Social Psychology*, **32**, 69–75.
Carlsmith, J. M., Ellsworth, P. C., & Aronson, E. (1976). *Methods of research in social psychology*. Reading, MA: Addison-Wesley.
Cermak, L. S., & Craik, F. I. M. (Eds.). (1979). *Levels of processing in human memory*. Hillsdale, NJ: Erlbaum.

Cialdini, R. B., & Petty, R. E. (1981). Anticipatory opinion effects. In R. E. Petty, T. M. Ostrom, & T. C. Brock (Eds.), *Cognitive responses in persuasion* (pp. 217–236). Hillsdale, NJ: Erlbaum.

Coles, M. G. H., Donchin, E., & Porges, S. (Eds.). (1986). *Psychophysiology: Systems, processes, and applications*. New York: Guilford Press.

Craik, F. I. M. (1979). Human memory. *Annual Review of Psychology*, **30**, 63–102.

Craik, F. I. M., & Tulving, E. (1975). Depth of processing and the retention of words in episodic memory. *Journal of Experimental Psychology: General*, **104**, 268–294.

Darrow, C. W. (1929). Electrical and circulatory responses to brief sensory and ideational stimuli. *Journal of Experimental Psychology*, **12**, 267–300.

Darwin, C. *The expression of the emotions in man and animals*. (originally published, 1872). Chicago: University of Chicago Press, 1965.

Davis, R. C. (1939). Patterns of muscular activity during "mental work" and their constancy. *Journal of Experimental Psychology*, **24**, 451–465.

Dimberg, U. (1986). Facial reactions to fear-relevant and fear-irrelevant stimuli. *Biological Psychology*, **23**, 153–161.

Donchin, E. (1982). The relevance of dissociations and the irrelevance of dissociationism: A reply to Schwartz and Pritchard. *Psychophysiology*, **19**, 457–463.

Edfeldt, A. W. (1960). *Silent speech and silent reading*. Chicago: University of Chicago Press.

Elkin, R. A., & Leippe, M. R. (1986). Physiological arousal, dissonance, and attitude change: Evidence for a dissonance–arousal link and a "don't remind me" effect. *Journal of Personality and Social Psychology*, **51**, 55–65.

Ekman, P. (1972). Universal and cultural differences in facial expressions of emotion. In J. Cole (Ed.), *Nebraska symposium on motivation, 1971* (Vol. 19). Lincoln: University of Nebraska Press.

Ekman, P. (1973). *Darwin and facial expression: A century of research in review*. New York: Academic Press.

Ekman, P. (1982). *Emotion in the human face* (2nd ed.). Cambridge: Cambridge University Press.

Ekman, P., & Friesen, W. V. (1975). *Unmasking the face*. Englewood Cliffs, NJ: Prentice-Hall.

Ekman, P., & Friesen, W. V. (1978). *Facial coding action system (FACS): A technique for the measurement of facial actions*. Palo Alto, CA: Consulting Psychologists Press.

Ekman, P., & Friesen, W. V. (1982). Felt, false, and miserable smiles. *Journal of Nonverbal Behavior*, **6**, 238–252.

Ekman, P., Friesen, W. V., O'Sullivan, M., Chan, A., Diacoyanni-Tarlatzis, I., Heider, K., Krause, R., LeCompte, W. A., Pitcairn, T., Ricci-Bitt, P. E., Scherer, K., Tomita, M., & Tzavaras, A. (1987). Universals and cultural differences in the judgments of facial expressions of emotion. *Journal of Personality and Social Psychology*, **53**, 712–717.

Ekman, P., Levenson, R. W., & Friesen, W. V. (1983). Autonomic nervous system activity distinguishes among emotions. *Science*, **221**, 1208–1210.

Elkin, R. A., & Leippe, M. R. (1986). Physiological arousal, dissonance, and attitude change: Evidence for a dissonance-arousal link and a "don't remind me" effect. *Journal of Personality and Social Psychology*, **51**, 55–65.

Ellsworth, P. C. (1977). From abstract ideas to concrete instances: Some guidelines for choosing natural research settings. *American Psychologist*, **32**, 604–615.

Englis, B. G., Vaughan, K. B., & Lanzetta, J. T. (1982). Conditioning of counter-empathic emotional responses. *Journal of Experimental Social Psychology*, **18**, 375–391.

Faaborg-Anderson, K., & Edfeldt, A. W. (1958). Electromyography of intrinsic and extrinsic laryngeal muscles during silent speech: Correlation with reading activity. *Acta Otolaryngologica*, **49**, 478–482.

Ferguson, T. J., Rule, B. G., & Carlson, D. (1983). Memory for personally relevant information. *Journal of Personality and Social Psychology,* **44,** 251–261.
Festinger, L. (1954). A theory of social comparison processes. *Human Relations,* **7,** 114–140.
Fishbein, M., & Ajzen, I. (1975). *Belief, attitude, intention, and behavior: An introduction to theory and research.* Reading, MA: Addison-Wesley.
Fleming, R., Baum, A., & Singer, J. E. (1984). Toward an integrative approach to the study of stress. *Journal of Personality and Social Psychology,* **46,** 939–949.
Fowles, D. C. (1980). The three arousal model: Implications of Gray's two-factor learning theory for heart rate, electrodermal activity, and psychopathy. *Psychophysiology,* **17,** 87–104.
Fowles, D. C., Christie, M. J., Edelberg, R., Grings, W. W., Lykken, D. T., & Venables, P. H. (1981). Publication recommendations for electrodermal measurements. *Psychophysiology,* **18,** 232–239.
Fowles, D. C., Roberts, R., & Nagel, K. E. (1977). The influence of introversion/extroversion on the skin conductance response to stress and stimulus intensity. *Journal of Research in Personality,* **11,** 129–146.
Fredrikson, M., Danielssons, T., Engel, B. T., Frisk-Holmberg, M., Strom, G., & Sundin, O. (1985). Autonomic nervous system function and essential hypertension: Individual response specificity with and without beta-adrenergic blockade. *Psychophysiology,* **22,** 167–174.
Fridlund, A. J. (in press). Evolution and facial action in reflex, emotion, and paralanguage. In P. K Ackles, J. R. Jennings, & M. G. H. Coles (Eds.), *Advances in psychophysiology* (Vol. 4). Greenwich, CT: JAI Press.
Fridlund, A. J., & Cacioppo, J. T. (1986). Guidelines for human electromyographic research. *Psychophysiology,* **23,** 567–589.
Fridlund, A. J., & Izard, C. E. (1983). Electromyographic studies of facial expressions of emotions and patterns of emotion. In J. T. Cacioppo & R. E. Petty (Eds.), *Social psychophysiology: A sourcebook* (pp. 243–286). New York: Guilford Press.
Friesen, W. V. (1972). *Cultural differences in facial expression in a social situation: An experimental text of the concept of display rules.* Unpublished doctoral dissertation, University of California, San Francisco.
Garrity, L. I. (1977). Electromyography: A review of the current status of subvocal speech research. *Memory & Cognition,* **5,** 615–622.
Gergen, K. J. (1973). Social psychology as history. *Journal of Personality and Social Psychology,* **26,** 309–320.
Graham, J. L. (1980). A new system for measuring nonverbal responses to marketing appeals. *1980 AMA Educator's Conference Proceedings,* **46,** 340–343.
Greenwald, A. G. (1968). Cognitive learning, cognitive response to persuasion, and attitude change. In A. Greenwald, T. Brock, & T. Ostrom (Eds.), *Psychological foundations of attitudes.* New York: Academic Press.
Greenwald, A. G. (1975). Consequences of prejudice against the null hypothesis. *Psychological Bulletin,* **82,** 1–20.
Greenwald, A. G., Klinger, M. R., & Liu, T. J. (1987). *Unconscious processing of word meaning.* Unpublished manuscript, University of Washington.
Greenwald, A. G., Pratkanis, A. R., Leippe, M. R., & Baumgardner, M. H. (1986). Under what conditions does theory obstruct research progress? *Psychological Review,* **93,** 216–229.
Haber, S. N., & Barchas, P. R. (1984). The regulatory effect of social rank on behavior after amphetamine administration. In P. R. Bachas (Ed.), *Social hierarchies.* Westport, CT: Greenwood Press.
Hefferline, R. F., Keenan, B., & Harford, R. A. (1959). Escape and avoidance conditioning in human subjects without their observation of the response. *Science,* **130,** 1338–1339.

Henneman, E. (1980). Skeletal muscle: The servant of the nervous system. In V. B. Mountcastle (Ed.), *Medical physiology,* 14th ed., vol. 1 (pp. 674–702). St. Louis: Mosby.
Izard, C. E. (1971). *The face of emotion.* New York: Appleton-Century-Crofts.
Izard, C. E. (1977). *Human emotions.* New York: Plenum.
James, W. (1890). *The principles of psychology* (Vol. 2). New York: Holt.
Jennings, J. R. (1986). Memory, thought, and bodily response. In M. G. H. Coles, E. Donchin, & S. W. Porges (Eds.), *Psychophysiology: Systems, processes, and applications* (pp. 290–308). New York: Guilford Press.
Jennings, J. R., Berg, K. W., Hutcheson, J. S., Obrist, P., Porges, S., & Turpin, G. (1981). Publications guidelines for heart rate studies in man. *Psychophysiology,* **18,** 226–231.
Johnson, L. C., & Lubin, A. (1972). On planning psychophysiological experiments: Design, measurement and analysis. In N. S. Greenwald & R. A. Sternbach (Eds.), *Handbook of psychophysiology* (pp. 125–158). New York: Holt, Rinehart & Winston.
Jones, E. E. (1985). Major developments in social psychology during the past five decades. In G. Lindzey & E. Aronson (Eds.), *The handbook of social psychology* (3rd ed., pp. 47–107). New York: Random House.
Kalat, J. W. (1984). *Biological psychology* (2nd ed.). Belmont, CA: Wadsworth.
Kaplan, H. B., & Bloom, S. W. (1960). The use of sociological and social-psychological concepts in physiological research: A review of selected experimental studies. *Journal of Nervous and Mental Disorders,* **131,** 128–134.
Keenan, J. M., & Baillet, S. D. (1980). Memory for personally and socially significant events. In R. S. Nickerson (Ed.), *Attention and performance* (Vol. 8). Hillsdale, NJ: Erlbaum.
Kiesler, C. A., & Pallak, M. S. (1976). Arousal properties of dissonance manipulations. *Psychological Bulletin,* **83,** 1014–1025.
Kuhn, T. S. (1970). *The structure of scientific revolutions* (2nd ed.): Vols. 1 and 2. Foundations of the unity of science (Vol. 2, No. 2). Chicago: University of Chicago Press.
Lacey, J. I. (1959). Psychophysiological approaches to the evaluation of psychotherapeutic process and outcome. In E. A. Rubinstein & M. B. Parloff (Eds.), *Research in psychotherapy* (Vol. 1). Washington, DC: American Psychological Association.
Lacey, J. I., Kagan, J., Lacey, B. G., & Moss, M. A. H. (1963). The visceral level: Situational determinants and behavioral correlates of autonomic response patterns. In P. N. Knapp (Ed.), *Expression of the emotions in man* (pp. 161–196). New York: International University Press.
Laird, J. D. (1984). A real role of facial response in the experience of emotion: A reply to Torrangeau and Ellsworth, and others. *Journal of Personality and Social Psychology,* **47,** 909–917.
Langer, E., Blank, A., & Chanowitz, B. (1978). The mindlessness of ostensibly thoughtful action: The role of "placebic" information in interpersonal interaction. *Journal of Personality and Social Psychology,* **36,** 635–642.
Latane, B., & Darley, J. M. (1970). *The unresponsive bystander: Why doesn't he help?* New York: Appleton-Century-Crofts.
Leventhal, H., Meyer, D., & Nerenz, D. (1980). The common sense representation of illness danger. In S. Rachman (Ed.), *Contributions to medical psychology* (Vol. 2). New York: Pergamon.
Lindzey, G., & Aronson, E. (1985). *Handbook of social psychology* (3rd ed.). New York: Random House.
Love, R. E. (1972). *Unobtrusive measurement of cognitive reactions to persuasive communications.* Unpublished doctoral dissertation, Ohio State University, Columbus.
Lynn, R. (1966). *Attention, arousal and the orientation reaction.* Oxford: Pergamon.
Martin, I. & Venables, P. H. (Eds.). (1980). *Techniques in psychophysiology.* Chichester: Wiley.
Matthews, K. A., Siegel, J. M., Kuller, L. H., Thompson, M., & Varat, M. (1983). Determinants of decisions to seek medical treatment by patients with acute myocardial infarction symptoms. *Journal of Personality and Social Psychology,* **44,** 1144–11561

McCanne, T. R., & Anderson, J. A. (1987). Emotional responding following experimental manipulation of facial electromyographic activity. *Journal of Personality and Social Psychology, 52,* 759–768.
McCaul, K. D., & Maki, R. H. (1984). Self-reference versus desirability ratings and memory for traits. *Journal of Personality and Social Psychology, 47,* 953–955.
McGuigan, F. J. (1970). Covert oral behavior during the silent performance of language tasks. *Psychological Bulletin, 74,* 309–326.
McGuigan, F. J. (1978). *Cognitive psychophysiology: Principles of covert behavior.* Englewood Cliffs, NJ: Prentice-Hall.
McGuire, W. J. (1973). The yin and yang of progress in social psychology: Seven koan. *Journal of Personality and Social Psychology, 26,* 446–456.
McGuire, W. J. (1985) Attitudes and attitude change. In G. Lindzey & E. Aronson (Eds.), *The handbook of social psychology* (3rd ed.). Reading, MA: Addison-Wesley.
Mechanic, D. (1972). Social psychologic factors affecting the presentation of bodily complaints. *The New England Journal of Medicine, 286,* 1132–1139.
Mesulam, M., & Perry, J. (1972). The diagnosis of lovesickness: Experimental psychophysiology without the polygraph. *Psychophysiology, 9,* 546–551.
Milgram, S. (1963). Behavioral study of obedience. *Journal of Abnormal and Social Psychology, 67,* 371–378.
Miller, N., & Baron, R. S. (1973). On measuring counterarguing. *Journal for the Theory of Social Behavior, 3,* 101–118.
Miller, N., & Coleman, D. (1981). Methodological issues in analyzing the cognitive mediation of persuasion. In R. E. Petty, T. M. Ostrom, & T. C. Brock (Eds.), *Cognitive responses in persuasion.* Hillsdale, NJ: Erlbaum.
Miller, N., Maruyama, G., Beaber, R., & Valone, K. (1976). Speed of speech and persuasion. *Journal of Personality and Social Psychology, 34,* 615–625.
Moore, D., & Baron, R. S. (1983). Social facilitation: A psychophysiological analysis. In J. T. Cacioppo & R. E. Petty (Eds.), *Social psychophysiology: A sourcebook.* New York: Guilford Press.
Morris, C. D., Bransford, J. D., & Franks, J. J. (1977). Levels of processing versus transfer appropriate processing. *Journal of Verbal Learning and Verbal Behavior, 16,* 519–533.
Mueller, J. (1984). Neuroanatomic correlates of emotion. L. Temoshok, C. Van Dyke, & L. S. Zegans (Eds.), *Emotions in health and illness* (pp. 95–121). New York: Grune & Stratton.
Notarius, C. I., Wemple, C., Ingraham, L. J., Burns, T. J., & Kollar, E. (1982). Multichannel responses to an interpersonal stressor: Interrelationships among facial display, heart rate, self-report of emotion, and threat appraisal. *Journal of Personality and Social Psychology, 43,* 400–408.
Pennebaker, J. W. (1982). *The psychology of physical symptoms.* New York: Springer-Verlag.
Petty, R. E., & Cacioppo, J. T. (1977). Forewarning, cognitive responding and resistance to persuasion. *Journal of Personality and Social Psychology, 35,* 645–655.
Petty, R. E., & Cacioppo, J. T. (1981). *Attitudes and persuasion: Classic and contemporary approaches.* Dubuque: Wm. C. Brown.
Petty, R. E., & Cacioppo, J. T. (1986). *Communication and persuasion: Central and peripheral routes to persuasion.* New York: Springer-Verlag.
Porges, S. W., & Coles, M. G. H. (1976). *Psychophysiology: Benchmark papers in animal behavior* (Vol. 6). Stroudsburg, PA: Dowden, Hutchinson, and Ross.
Rajecki, D. W. (1983). Animal aggression: Implications for human aggression. In R. G. Geen & E. J. Donnerstein (Eds.), *Aggression: Theoretical and empirical reviews* (Vol. 1, pp. 189–211). New York: Academic Press.
Rankin, R. E., & Campbell, D. T. (1955). Galvanic skin responses to Negro and white experimenters. *Journal of Abnormal and Social Psychology, 51,* 30–33.

Reisenzein, R. (1983). The Schachter theory of emotion: Two decades later. *Psychological Bulletin*, **94**, 239–264.
Riddle, E. M. (1925). Aggressive behavior in a small social group. *Archives of Psychology*, **78**.
Rinn, W. E. (1984). The neuropsychology of facial expression: A review of the neurological and psychological mechanisms for producing facial expression. *Psychological Bulletin*, **95**, 52–77.
Rogers, T. B., Kuiper, N. A., & Kirker, W. S. (1977). Self-reference and the encoding of personal information. *Journal of Personality and Social Psychology*, **35**, 677–688.
Rosenberg, M. J., & Hovland, C. I. (1960). Cognitive, affective, and behavioral components of attitude. In M. H. Rosenberg, C. J. Hovland, W. J. McGuire, R. P. Abelson, & J. W. Brehn (Eds.), *Attitude organization and change: An analysis of consistency among attitude components* (pp. 1–14). New Haven: Yale University Press.
Rosenberg, M. J., Hovland, C. I., McGuire, W. J., Abelson, R. P., Brehm, J. W. (1960). *Attitude organization and change*. New Haven: Yale University Press.
Runes, D. D. (Ed.). (1961). *Dictionary of philosophy*. Paterson: Littlefield, Adams.
Safer, M. A., Tharps, Q. J., Jackson, T. C., & Leventhal, H. (1979). Determinants of three stages of delay in seeking care at a medical clinic. *Medical Care*, **17**, 11–29.
Schachter, S. (1959). *The psychology of affiliation*. Stanford: Stanford University Press.
Schachter, S., & Singer, J. E. (1962). Cognitive, social, and physiological determinants of emotional state. *Psychological Review*, **69**, 379–399.
Scherer, K. R., & Ekman, P. (1982). *Handbook of methods in nonverbal behavior research*. Cambridge: Cambridge University Press.
Schwartz, G. E. (1975). Biofeedback, self-regulation, and the patterning of physiological processes. *American Scientist*, **63**, 314–324.
Selye, H. (1976). *The stress of life*. New York: McGraw-Hill.
Shapiro, D., & Crider, A. (1969). Psychophysiological approaches to social psychology. In G. Lindzey & E. Aronson (Eds.), *The handbook of social psychology* (Vol. 3, 2nd ed.). Reading, MA: Addison-Wesley.
Shapiro, D., & Schwartz, G. E. (1970). Psychophysiological contributions to social psychology. *Annual Review of Psychology*, **21**, 87–112.
Shimizu, A., & Inoue, T. (1986). Dreamed speech and speech muscle activity. *Psychophysiology*, **23**, 210–214.
Smith, C. A., & Ellsworth, P. C. (1985). Patterns of cognitive appraisal in emotion. *Journal of Personality and Social Psychology*, **48**, 813–838.
Smith, C. A., & Ellsworth, P. C. (1987). Patterns of appraisal and emotion related to taking an exam. *Journal of Personality and Social Psychology*, **52**, 475–488.
Smith, C. E. (1936). A study of the autonomic excitation resulting from the interaction of individual opinion and group opinion. *Journal of Abnormal and Social Psychology*, **30**, 138–164.
Steiner, J. E. (1979). Human facial expression in response to taste and smell stimulation. *Advances in Child Development and Behavior*, **13**, 257–295.
Sternbach, R. A. (1966). *Principles of psychophysiology*. New York: Academic Press.
Stewart, D. W. (1984). Physiological measurement of advertising effects. *Psychology and Marketing*, **1**, 43–48.
Sumitsuji, N., Nan'no, H., Kuwata, Y., & Ohta, Y. (1980). The effects of the noise due to the jet airplane to the human facial expression (EMG study), EEG change and their manual responses at the various sleeping stages of the subjects. *Electromyography and Clinical Neurophysiology*, **20**, 49–72.
Tassinary, L. G., Cacioppo, J. T., & Geen, T. R. (1989). A psychometric study of surface electrode placements for facial electromyographic recording: I. The brow and cheek regions. *Psychophysiology*, in press.
Tassinary, L. G., Orr, S., Wolford, G., Napps, S., & Lanzetta, J. T. (1984). The role of awareness in affective information processing: An exploration of the Zajonc hypothesis. *Bulletin of the Psychonomic Society*, **22**, 489–492.

Tognacci, L. N., & Cook, S. (1975). Conditioned autonomic responses as bidirectional indicators of racial attitude. *Journal of Personality and Social Psychology,* **31,** 137–144.

Tomkins, S. S. (1962). *Affect, imagery, consciousness: Vol. 1. The positive affects.* New York: Springer.

Tranel, D., & Damasio, A. J. (1985). Knowledge without awareness: An automatic index of facial recognition by prosopagnosics. *Science,* **228,** 1453–1454.

Tulving, E. (1978). Relation between encoding specificity and levels of processing. In L. S. Cermak & F. I. M. Craik (Eds.), *Levels of processing in human memory* (pp. 19–91). Hillsdale, NJ: Erlbaum.

Turpin, G. (1986). Effects of stimulus intensity on autonomic responding: The problem of differentiating orienting and defense reflexes. *Psychophysiology,* **23,** 1–14.

Valins, S. (1966). Cognitive effects of false heart rate feedback. *Journal of Personality and Social Psychology,* **4,** 400–408.

Van Egeren, L. F. (1984). Social processes, biology, and disease. In W. M. Waid (Ed.), *Sociophysiology* (pp. 249–282). New York: Springer-Verlag.

Wells, G. L., & Petty, R. E. (1980). The effects of overt head movements on persuasion: Compatibility and incompatibility of responses. *Basic and Applied Social Psychology,* **1,** 219–230.

Wheeler, J. A. (1974). The universe as a home for man. *American Scientist,* **62,** 683–691.

Yarczower, M., & Daruns, L. (1982). Social inhibition of spontaneous facial expressions in children. *Journal of Personality and Social Psychology,* **43,** 831–837.

Zajonc, R. B. (1985). Emotion and facial efference: A theory reclaimed. *Science,* **228,** 15–21.

Zillmann, D. (1983). Transfer of excitation in emotional behavior. In J. T. Cacioppo & R. E. Petty (Eds.), *Social psychophysiology: A Sourcebook* (pp. 215–242). New York: Guilford Press.

SELF-DISCREPANCY THEORY: WHAT PATTERNS OF SELF-BELIEFS CAUSE PEOPLE TO SUFFER?

E. Tory Higgins

DEPARTMENT OF PSYCHOLOGY
NEW YORK UNIVERSITY
NEW YORK, NEW YORK 10003

I. Introduction

It is a common experience that unpleasant thoughts can produce unpleasant feelings. When the unpleasant thoughts are about oneself, the feelings can be especially distressing and even debilitating. The notion that negative thoughts about oneself can be a source of emotional distress has a long history in psychology (e.g., Adler, 1964; Horney, 1946; James, 1948/1890; Sullivan, 1953) and continues to be considered so fundamental that many recent perspectives on the psychological nature of severe distress are based upon it (e.g., Abramson, Seligman, & Teasdale, 1978; Bandura, 1977; Beck, Rush, Shaw, & Emery, 1979; Ellis, 1962).

These recent perspectives on the relation between self and affect generally emphasize people's beliefs about who they are now or will become and their attributions for these current and future actual selves (see also Kuiper, Derry, & MacDonald, 1982; Markus & Nurius, 1986; Weiner, 1986). Other perspectives on the motivational consequences of self-related beliefs have focused on the interrelation among different sorts of information about the actual self. Some theories, for example, have considered the effect of inconsistencies between one's perceived actual self and feedback related to these self-perceptions (e.g., Aronson, 1969; Bramel, 1968; Rogers, 1959; Swann, 1983; Wicklund & Gollwitzer, 1982). Other theories propose that people need consistency among their perceived actual-self attributes in order to form a coherent and unified self-concept (e.g., Allport, 1955; Brim, 1976; Epstein, 1973; Harter, 1986; Lecky, 1961; Morse & Gergen, 1970; Snygg & Combs, 1949).

Unquestionably, people's conceptions of their *actual-self attributes* (current or future) or people's *self-concepts* are a major source of emotional–motivational problems. But people differ in the kinds of emotional problems that they tend to have. By considering the negativity or inconsistency of actual-self attributes alone, how is it possible to understand why some persons are more likely to suffer from dejection-related problems, such as sadness and disappointment, whereas others are more likely to suffer from agitation-related problems such as fear and restlessness? And is it the case that people's emotional problems are related only to aspects of the actual self, or are they related to other types of self-beliefs as well? Indeed, even when such problems are associated with the actual self, is it actual-self attributes alone that produce such problems or is it the *relation* between actual-self beliefs and other types of self-beliefs?

To address these questions, it is necessary to have a model of the relation between self and affect that goes beyond the actual self. My colleagues and I have proposed and tested one such model, which we call "self-discrepancy theory" (e.g., Higgins, 1987; Higgins, Bond, Klein, & Strauman, 1986a; Higgins, Klein, & Strauman, 1985b). The purpose of this article is to describe the original model and review the empirical support for it. Another purpose is to expand and modify the model in order to address more adequately the conceptual issues underlying the preceding questions and to introduce a new perspective on the relation between self and affect.

II. Self-Discrepancy Theory

The basic premise of self-discrepancy theory is that it is the relations between and among different types of self-beliefs or self-state representations that produce emotional vulnerabilities rather than the particular content or nature of the actual self or of any other individual self-belief. To distinguish among different types of self-state representations, self-discrepancy theory proposes two psychological parameters: *domains of the self* and *standpoints on the self*. In the original version of the model (see Higgins, 1987), three types of self-domains were identified: (1) the *actual* self, which is your representation of the attributes that someone (yourself or another) believes you actually possess; (2) the *ideal* self, which is your representation of the attributes that someone (yourself or another) would like you, ideally, to possess (i.e., a representation of someone's hopes, wishes, or aspirations for you); and (3) the *ought* self, which is your representation of the attributes that someone (yourself or another) believes you should or ought to possess (i.e., a representation of someone's sense of your duty, obligations, or responsibilities). Two types of standpoints on the self were also identified: (1) your *own* personal standpoint; and (2) the standpoint of some significant *other* (e.g., mother, father, spouse, close friend).

Different types of self-state representations were identified by combining each of the different types of self-domains with each of the different types of standpoints on the self. The following six basic types of self-state representations were thus identified: actual/own, actual/other, ideal/own, ideal/other, ought/own, and ought/other. The first two self-state representations, and particularly the actual/own self-state, constitute what is typically known as a person's *self-concept* (see Wylie, 1979). The four remaining self-state representations are self-directive standards or *self-guides* (see Higgins, Strauman, & Klein, 1986b, for a review of different kinds of standards). The psychological literature has historically distinguished among various facets of the self (see, for example, Erikson, 1950/1963; Greenwald & Pratkanis, 1984; Markus & Wurf, 1987; Piers & Singer, 1971; Rogers, 1961; Schafer, 1967; Sullivan, 1953). Yet, with a few notable exceptions (e.g., James, 1890/1948), there has been little attempt to relate different types of self-state representations to different kinds of emotional problems. Moreover, no explicit model has been proposed that predicts which kinds of emotional problems should be associated with which types of self-state interrelations. Self-discrepancy theory was developed in an attempt to provide such a model.

A. MOTIVATIONAL ASSUMPTIONS OF SELF-DISCREPANCY THEORY

Self-discrepancy theory contains both motivational and information-processing assumptions. There are two major motivational assumptions. First, self-discrepancy theory assumes that *people are motivated to reach a condition in which their self-concept matches their personally relevant self-guides*. Like other homeostatic theories concerning discrepancies from standards (e.g., Rogers, 1961) or cognitive inconsistencies (e.g., Festinger, 1957), it generally assumes that the discomfort associated with a self-discrepancy increases as the magnitude of the discrepancy increases. Specifically, it assumes that the greater the divergence between the attributes of one self-state representation and those of another, the greater the discomfort. The theory also assumes that there are individual differences in the self-guides that persons are especially motivated to meet. It is postulated that both the source of this motivation to match self-guides and the individual differences in relevant self-guides derives from the early socialization history of each person (to be described later).

The general notion that standards involving hopes and wishes or duties and obligations are motivating has a long history. It was perhaps James (1890/1948) who first pointed out that standards both directly prompt action and, through their use in self-evaluation, arouse emotions that are themselves motivating. It is assumed by control theory and theories of objective self-awareness that people self-regulate through a discrepancy-reducing negative feedback process, the function of which is to minimize differences between a current state of affairs and some other reference value (e.g., Carver & Scheier, 1981; Duval & Wicklund, 1972; Miller, Galanter, & Pribram, 1960; Wiener, 1948). Theories of level of aspiration, although focusing on the relation between performance and standard setting (see Festinger, 1942; Lewin, 1935; Rotter, 1942), have also assumed that people need high-level goals to motivate performance.

The first motivational assumption of self-discrepancy theory, then, is that persons are motivated to bring their current state into line with some valued end-state, to reach a condition in which their current actual self matches their self-guides. But self-discrepancy theory extends these previous models by postulating that there are individual differences in the types of self-guides that persons are especially motivated to meet, which in turn is a source of individual differences in emotional–motivational predispositions.

Self-discrepancy theory also differs from previous models in making the following, second motivational assumption: *relations between and among different types of self-state representations represent different kinds of psychological situations, which in turn are associated with distinct emotional–motivational states.* It has been noted in the literature that belief inconsistencies reflect personal costs and problems and not simply a failure to achieve internal consistency or a "good Gestalt fit" (e.g., Abelson, 1983; Holt, 1976; Kemper, 1978; Plutchik, 1962; Schlenker, 1985). Self-discrepancy theory shares this viewpoint and proposes that different types of self-discrepancies reflect different types of negative psychological situations. To begin with, consider the negative psychological situations associated with self-concept:self-guide discrepancies, such as a discrepancy between a person's actual/own and ideal/own self-state representations.

People's reactions to their own performance are determined not solely by the features of the performance, but also by the meaning or significance of the performance to them. More generally, it is well known that psychological situations are a function of both the nature of events and people's interpretations of those events (Asch, 1952; Lewin, 1951; Merton, 1957), and the same event can be interpreted differently by different people (Kelly, 1955; Klein, 1970; Murray, 1938). Similarly, self-discrepancy theory assumes that the personal impact of self-perceived attributes is determined by the personal significance of possessing those attributes. The significance of possessing the attributes, in turn, is assumed to depend not on the nature of the attributes per se but on their relation to the person's self-guides. Thus, it is assumed that different negative psychological situations associated with the self-concept derive from the relations between the self-concept and different types of self-guides.

Although negative psychological situations are also expected to vary as a function of self-guide standpoint (i.e., "own" vs. "other"), there are two basic negative psychological situations that are associated with differences in self-guide domain for both types of self-guide standpoint. The self-discrepancies associated with these two basic negative psychological situations are as follows:

1. Actual/own self versus ideal self (own and other standpoint): If a person possesses this discrepancy, the current state of his or her actual attributes, from the person's own standpoint, does not match the ideal self that is personally desired or hoped for or that the person believes that some significant other person wishes or hopes that she or he would attain. This discrepancy represents one of two basic kinds of negative psychological situations that are associated with negative emotional–motivational states (see, for example, Mowrer, 1960)—*the absence of positive outcomes* (actual or expected). This kind of negative psychological situation has been associated with sadness, disappointment, dissatisfaction, or more generally, dejection-related emotional–motivational problems (see Jacobs, 1971; Lazarus, 1968; Mowrer, 1960; Roseman, 1984; Stein & Jewett, 1982). Thus, it is hypothesized that *people possessing actual/own:ideal (own or other) self discrepancies are vulnerable to dejection-related problems.*

2. Actual/own self versus ought self (own and other standpoint): If a person possesses this discrepancy, the current state of his or her attributes, from the person's own standpoint, does not match the state that she or he personally believes it is his or her duty or obligation to attain or believes some significant other person considers to be his or her duty or obligation to attain. Because violation of self- or other-prescribed duties or obligations is associated with self- or other-administered sanctions (i.e., punishment, criticism), this discrepancy represents the other basic kind of negative psychological situation that is associated with negative emotional–motivational states—the *presence of negative outcomes* (actual or expected). This kind of negative psychological situation has been associated with fear, worry, tension, or more generally, agitation-related emotional–motivational problems (see Jacobs, 1971; Lazarus, 1968; Mowrer, 1960; Roseman, 1984; Stein & Jewett, 1982). Thus, it is hypothesized that *people possessing actual/own:ought (own or other) discrepancies are vulnerable to agitation-related problems.*

B. INFORMATION-PROCESSING ASSUMPTIONS OF SELF-DISCREPANCY THEORY

In addition to the motivational assumptions, self-discrepancy theory makes distinctive information-processing assumptions. First, the theory assumes that *a self-discrepancy is a cognitive structure interrelating distinct self-beliefs*. Second, it assumes that *the likelihood that a self-discrepancy will produce psychological distress depends on its level of accessibility.*

Even though a self-discrepancy is assumed to represent a motivationally significant psychological situation, it is also assumed to be a cognitive structure because it involves an interrelation among the attributes in one self-state representation and those in another. (See Sorrentino & Higgins, 1986, for a discussion of cognitive-motivational synergistic constructs.) As a cognitive structure, a self-discrepancy should function like any other cognitive structure. And one property of cognitive structures (or any construct) is that they vary in accessibility, or in the likelihood that they will be used in information processing, such as to interpret events (for reviews, see Higgins & King, 1981; Wyer & Srull, 1981, 1986).

Various factors can determine the accessibility of a cognitive structure, including how recently it has been activated. It has been well established that exposure to a prior stimulus, such as a verbal description, that activates a stored construct—a *priming* manipulation—increases the likelihood that people will subsequently use the construct to interpret construct-related events. That is, priming a construct temporarily increases its accessibility (e.g., Bargh, Bond, Lombardi, & Tota, 1986; Higgins, Bargh, & Lombardi, 1985a; Higgins, Rholes, & Jones, 1977; Srull & Wyer, 1979, 1980). In addition to its accessibility, the likelihood that a stored construct will be activated also depends on the relation between its "meaning" and the properties of the stimulus event. Thus, a self-discrepancy, like any stored construct, will not be used to interpret an event unless it is *applicable* to the event (see Higgins & Bargh, 1987; Higgins *et al.*, 1977).

Like other cognitive structures, an accessible self-discrepancy can influence subsequent responding automatically and without awareness (see Bargh, 1984; Bargh & Pietromonaco, 1982; Bargh & Pratto, 1986; Higgins & King, 1981; Higgins, King, & Mavin, 1982; for a similar perspective, see Kelly, 1955). Indeed, persons need not be aware of the accessibility of their self-discrepancies or even of their availability (i.e., existence). Thus, self-discrepancy theory assumes that the negative psychological situations embodied in self-discrepancies can be activated without people being aware either of the discrepancies or of their impact on their emotional–motivational responses. Other implications of the assumption that self-discrepancies are cognitive structures are discussed in a subsequent section of this article.

Combining this set of motivational and information-processing assumptions leads to the following general hypothesis of self-discrepancy theory (Higgins, 1987): *The greater the magnitude and accessibility of a particular type of self-discrepancy possessed by an individual, the more the individual will suffer the kind of discomfort associated with that type of discrepancy.* For the purpose of reviewing the empirical support for the theory, this general hypothesis will be considered in terms of the following two component hypotheses:

Hypothesis 1: The greater the magnitude of a particular type of self-discrepancy possessed by an individual, the more the individual will suffer the kind of discomfort associated with that type of discrepancy.

Hypothesis 2: The greater the accessibility of an available type of self-discrepancy possessed by an individual, the more the individual will suffer the kind of discomfort associated with that type of discrepancy. The evidence for each of these hypotheses is considered in turn.[1]

III. Evidence for Hypothesis 1 of Self-Discrepancy Theory

Scattered throughout the previous literature are reports of associations between particular types of discrepant self-beliefs and particular kinds of discomfort that are generally consistent with the predictions of self-discrepancy theory (e.g., James, 1890/1948; see Higgins, 1987, for a review). However, the effect of the *magnitude* of different types of self-discrepancies on the intensity of different kinds of discomfort has been tested only in our own studies.

A. HYPOTHESIS 1 AND EMOTIONAL–MOTIVATIONAL PROBLEMS

In our first study (Higgins *et al.*, 1985b), undergraduates filled out a questionnaire designed to measure their self-discrepancies, the "Selves Questionnaire," as well as a variety of questionnaires that measured various kinds of emotional–motivational problems. The Selves Questionnaire simply asks respondents to list up to 10 attributes for each of a number of different self-states. It is administered in two parts, the first involving the respondent's own standpoint and the second involving the standpoints of the respondent's significant others (e.g., mother, father). On the first page of the questionnaire, the actual, ideal, and ought self-states are defined (as described earlier). On each subsequent page, there is a question about a different self-state, such as "Please list the attributes of the type of person *you* think you *actually* are" or "Please list the attributes of the type of person your *Mother* thinks you *should or ought* to be."

The questionnaire had respondents spontaneously list the attributes associated with each of their self-states, rather than using a nonidiographic checklist procedure, in order to increase the likelihood that respondents' accessible and personally important attributes would be obtained. In different studies, controls for

---

[1] It should be noted that the presentation of distinct hypotheses concerning the "magnitude" and the "accessibility" of self-discrepancies does not imply that self-discrepancy theory assumes that these two variables are totally independent. Indeed, according to Higgins and King's (1981) model of the determinants of accessibility, it would be expected that greater magnitudes of self-discrepancy would generally be associated with higher levels of chronic accessibility. Nevertheless, the "magnitude" and the "accessibility" of self-discrepancies are distinct variables, as evidenced by the priming studies described later in the article, in which the momentary accessibility of self-discrepancies is increased by manipulations that are independent of the magnitude of subjects' self-discrepancies.

the personal relevance of different standpoints were also included (see Higgins, 1987). It is important to note that respondents were not asked to recall or make judgments concerning their self-discrepancies. Indeed, they were not even asked to interrelate their different self-states. They were simply asked to describe, separately, particular self-state attributes. It was the coders of the questionnaire who subsequently determined whether a respondent's questionnaire revealed any self- discrepancies. Thus, it was not necessary for respondents to be aware of whether or not they possessed self-discrepancies in order for self-discrepancies to be obtained.

The basic coding procedure for calculating the magnitude of a self-discrepancy involved a two-step procedure:

1. For each self-discrepancy, the attributes in one self-state (e.g., actual/own) were compared to the attributes in the other self-state (e.g., ideal/mother) to determine which attributes were synonyms and which were antonyms, according to Roget's thesaurus. Attributes across the two self-states that were neither synonyms nor antonyms were considered to be *nonmatches*. In the Higgins et al. (1985b) study, synonyms were considered to be *matches* and antonyms were considered to be *mismatches*. In subsequent studies, respondents were asked to rate for each listed attribute the extent to which the standpoint person (self or other) believed they actually possessed or ought to possess or wanted them to possess that attribute. This allowed a distinction to be made between *true matches*, in which the attributes in a pair not only were synonyms but also had the same basic extent rating, versus *synonymous mismatches*, in which the attributes in a pair were synonyms but varied considerably in extent (e.g., actual/own: "slightly attractive" versus ideal/own: "extremely attractive").

2. The magnitude of self-discrepancy for the two self-states was calculated by summing the total number of mismatches and subtracting the total number of matches.[2] (When the "extent" measure was added in subsequent studies, antonymous mismatches were weighted twice that of synonymous mismatches; see for example, Study 2 in Higgins et al., 1986a).

Our method of measuring people's self-discrepancies differs from previous methods for measuring self-concept negativity or low self-esteem. First, it is a completely idiographic method, in that the procedure for generating both the list

---

[2]Because of the substantial number of nonmatching attributes and the variation in this number across different individuals' self-discrepancies, there is no necessary relation (either negative or positive) between the number of a respondent's matching attributes and the number of his or her mismatching attributes for any particular type of self-discrepancy. Our studies, in fact, have consistently found only small and nonsignificant relations between the number of matching attributes and the number of mismatching attributes in subjects' self-discrepancies. Thus, the potential loss in reliability associated with difference-score measures (see Cohen & Cohen, 1975) is less of a disadvantage for the self-discrepancy measure than for discrepancy measures that include all attributes in calculating difference scores.

of actual self-attributes and the list of self-guides attributes (e.g., ideal/own attributes) is unconstrained and spontaneous. In addition, the two lists of attributes are independently generated and can contain different attributes. By contrast, an experimenter-provided checklist procedure has neither of these features. Second, because the method distinguishes among matches, mismatches, *and* nonmatches, and because nonmatches are generally as frequent as either matches or mismatches, typically only a subset of the listed actual self-attributes are used in the final measure of the magnitude of a self-discrepancy. This method assures that only personally significant or important actual self-attributes, as defined by their being related to a subject's personal guides, are included in the final measure. By contrast, checklist and other procedures typically include all of the actual self-attributes listed. Third, by classifying actual self-attributes as matches, mismatches, or nonmatches, depending on their relation to a particular self-guide, the method involves no a priori assumptions concerning the positivity or negativity of a particular actual self-attribute. Indeed, the same actual self-attribute could be a match ("positive") in relation to one self-guide and be a mismatch ("negative") in relation to another self-guide. This feature of the method again reflects the highly idiographic nature of the method as well as its sensitivity to the multiple roles that a single actual self-attribute can play in an individual's phenomenology. By not relating actual self-attributes to different self-guides, previous methods have also not possessed this feature.

In addition to filling out the Selves Questionnaire, the subjects in the Higgins *et al.* (1985b) study also responded to a number of questionnaires measuring chronic discomfort and emotional problems, including the Beck Depression Inventory (BDI; Beck, Ward, Mendelson, Mock, & Erbaugh, 1961), the Blatt Depressive Experiences Questionnaire (BDEQ; Blatt, D'Afflitti, & Quinlan, 1976), the Hopkins Symptom Checklist (HSCL, Derogatis, Lipman, Rickels, Uhlenhuth, & Covi, 1974), and an Emotions Questionnaire we developed to measure chronic experience of negative emotions that asked subjects how often they felt a particular kind of depressive or anxious emotional state.

Strong support for Hypothesis 1 was found in this study. A measure of overall actual:self-guide discrepancy was significantly correlated with each of the measures of discomfort (correlations ranging from .32, $p < .02$, to .49, $p < .001$), with the intensity of subjects' chronic discomfort being greater as the magnitude of their overall discrepancy increased. In addition, distinct patterns of correlations were found for actual:ideal versus actual:ought discrepancies. Partial correlational analyses were performed where the contribution of alternative self-discrepancies to the relation between a particular self-discrepancy and a symptom was statistically removed. These analyses revealed both (1) that as the magnitude of subjects' actual:ideal discrepancies increased, the intensity and frequency of their suffering from dejection-related symptoms increased (e.g., dissatisfied, lack of pride, feeling blue, feeling no interest in things), and (2) that as the magnitude of subjects' actual:ought discrepancies increased, the intensity and frequency of their suffering from agitation-related symptoms increased (e.g., suddenly scared for no reason, heart pounding or racing, irritability, spells of terror or panic).

These basic findings were replicated in subsequent studies that extended and improved upon the Higgins *et al.* (1985b) study in a number of respects. Most important, the subsequent studies measured subjects' chronic discomfort and emotional problems weeks after their self-discrepancies were obtained. In one study (Strauman & Higgins, 1989, Study 1), a series of factor analyses were performed on the items in the aforementioned questionnaires, measuring chronic discomfort in order to identify distinct item clusters. Two distinct clusters were found, one reflecting a *disappointment–dissatisfaction emotional syndrome* (e.g., disappointed in oneself; not making full use of one's potential abilities; very satisfied with oneself and one's accomplishments [reversed scoring]), and the other reflecting a *fear–restlessness emotional syndrome* (e.g., feeling afraid to go out of one's house alone; feeling one is or will be punished; feeling so restless one cannot sit down). Consistent with Hypothesis 1, partial correlational analyses revealed unique, distinct, and significant relations between these emotional syndromes and specific types of self-discrepancies (partial r's of .30 to .35, $p \leq$ .01). Specifically, as the magnitude of subjects' actual/own:ideal/own discrepancy increased, their suffering from the disappointment–dissatisfaction syndrome increased, and as the magnitude of subjects' actual/own:ought/other discrepancy increased, their suffering from the fear–restlessness syndrome increased.

In another study (Strauman & Higgins, 1989, Study 2) Hypothesis 1 was tested with respect to undergraduates' vulnerability to suffering from mild depression versus social anxiety. A latent variable analysis was used to evaluate simultaneously the validity of the predicted constructs (see Bentler, 1980). One month after filling out the Selves Questionnaire, undergraduates filled out a battery of measures that comprised both the latent variable for depression—the BDI and the HSCL depression subscale—and the latent variable for social anxiety—the Fear of Negative Evaluation scale (FNE), the Social Avoidance and Distress scale (SAD) (for both scales, see Watson & Friend, 1969), and the HSCL interpersonal sensitivity subscale.

The only model to provide an acceptable fit to the sample data ($p > .15$) was the hypothesized causal structure shown in Fig. 1. Consistent with Hypothesis 1, as the magnitude of subjects' actual/own:ideal/own discrepancy increased, their suffering from depression symptoms increased, and as the magnitude of subjects' actual/own:ought/other increased, their suffering from social anxiety symptoms increased. Each of these relations was independent of any relation between the alternative discrepancy and the symptoms. Moreover, actual/own:ideal/own discrepancy was not related to social anxiety and actual/own:ought/other was not related to depression.

In the most recent study testing Hypothesis 1 (Strauman, 1989), clinical samples

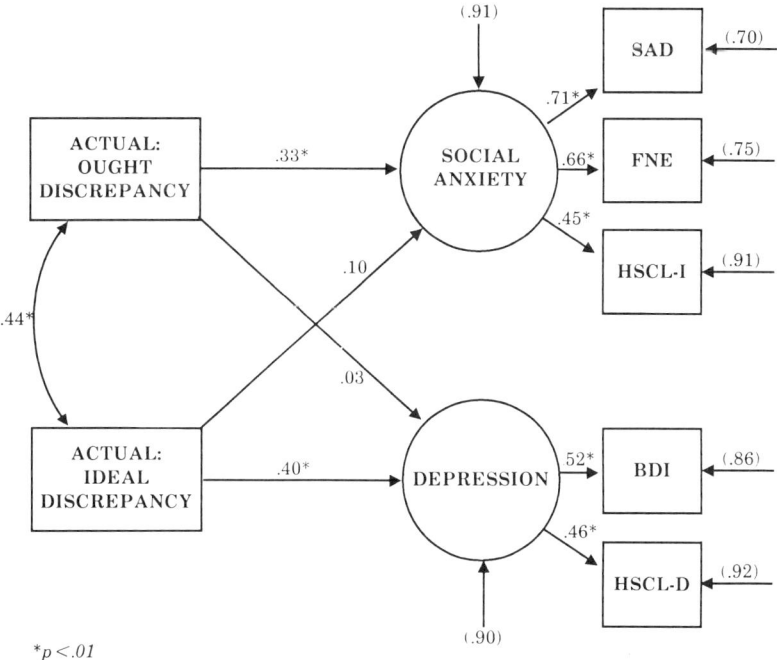

Fig. 1. Latent-variable model relating type of self-discrepancy (e.g., actual/own:ideal/own discrepancy; actual/own:ought/other discrepancy) to kind of emotional problem (e.g., depression; social anxiety). (SAD = Social Avoidance and Distress scale; FNE = Fear of Negative Evaluation scale; HSCL = Hopkins Symptom Checklist, I = interpersonal sensitivity subscale, D = depression subscale; BDI = Beck Depression Inventory.)

were used in order to determine whether the hypothesized distinct vulnerabilities would hold for people who suffered from extreme levels of chronic emotional–motivational problems. Samples of normal undergraduates, clinically diagnosed depressed patients, and clinically diagnosed social phobic patients were given standard measures of depression (Hamilton, 1960) and social anxiety (Liebowitz, Gorman, Fyer, & Klein, 1985) and the Selves Questionnaire. As shown in Table I-A, the samples varied on the measures of depression and social anxiety in the expected directions. The critical prediction of the study was that the depressed patients would have the highest level of actual/own:ideal/own discrepancy, the social phobic patients would have the highest level of actual/own:ought/other discrepancy, and the normal undergraduates would have the lowest levels of both types of discrepancies. As shown in Table I-B, these predictions were confirmed. Thus, Hypothesis 1 holds for clinical levels of emotional–motivational problems as well.

TABLE I
CLINICAL CHARACTERISTICS AND TYPE OF SELF-DISCREPANCY
ASSOCIATED WITH SUBJECT GROUPS

	Subject groups		
Measures	Normals	Social phobics	Depressives
A. Characteristics[a]			
Hamilton Depression Scale	2.9_a	6.3_b	15.3_c
Anxiety Subscale of Social Phobia Scale	13.9_a	36.0_c	22.8_b
B. Type of self-discrepancy[b]			
Actual/own:ideal/own	1.00_b	1.50_b	2.70_c
Actual/own:ought/other	0.67_a	1.67_b	0.20_a

[a]Different subscripts indicate significant differences among groups within each row.
[b]Different subscripts indicate significant differences among all six cell means.

B. SOCIALIZATION OF SELF-BELIEFS AND THEIR MOTIVATIONAL SIGNIFICANCE

Hypothesis 1 has also been tested in studies that considered an additional type of self-belief that contributes to emotional–motivational vulnerability (Higgins, Klein, & Strauman, 1987)—individuals' beliefs about the negative consequences of possessing a self-discrepancy. This additional type of self-belief derives from the socialization history of individuals' self-regulatory and self-evaluative processes, which are now briefly described (for a fuller account, see Higgins, 1989).

At 18 to 24 months of age, a dramatic shift in children's ability to mentally represent events occurs (see Bruner, 1964; Case, 1985; Fischer, 1980; Piaget, 1951; Werner & Kaplan, 1963). During this period, which is associated with the emergence of symbolic representation (see Huttenlocher & Higgins, 1978), children become capable of recognizing the higher-order relation that exists between two other relations. As a consequence of this increase in representational capacity, children can now consider the bidirectional relationship between themselves and another person (e.g., the child's mother) as a relation between two distinct mental objects, the self-as-object and the other-as-object (see Bertenthal & Fischer, 1978; Harter, 1983; Lewis & Brooks-Gunn, 1979). Thus, children can now represent the following relation between two relations:

1. The relation between a particular kind of self-feature (action, response, physical appearance, etc.) and a particular kind of response by another person, such as the relation between the child making a fuss or mess at mealtime and the mother frowning, yelling, or leaving.

2. The relation between a particular kind of response by another person and a particular kind of psychological situation they will experience, such as the relation between the mother frowning, yelling, or leaving and the child experiencing a negative psychological situation.

At this period, then, children can represent *self–other contingencies:* when I display feature X, response Y of person A is likely to occur; response Y of person A is associated with my experiencing psychological situation Z. This self–other contingency knowledge is the early precursor of self-guides. It is used by children for self-regulation in order to approach or avoid different psychological situations.

At 4 to 6 years of age, another dramatic shift occurs in children's mental representations (see Case, 1985; Feffer, 1970; Fischer, 1980; Flavell, Botkin, Fry, Wright, & Jarvis, 1968; Piaget, 1965; Selman & Byrne, 1974; Werner, 1957), a change that is associated with the shift from the absence to the presence of role-taking or perspective-taking ability (for reviews, see Higgins, 1981; Shantz, 1983). Children at this stage possess an executive control structure that permits the coordination of two systems of interrelations that are qualitatively distinct (see Case, 1985; Higgins, 1981). Children are increasingly able to infer the thoughts, expectations, motives, and intentions of others (see Shantz, 1983) and to use sources of information beyond the immediate contextual features when judging the actions of self and others (see Dweck & Elliott, 1983; Ruble & Rholes, 1981; Shantz, 1983). Children can now interpret and evaluate their actions in relation to some internal standard.

These changes produce major changes in children's self–other contingency knowledge, and thus in their self-evaluative and self-regulatory processes. Children can now monitor, plan, and evaluate one of their features in relation to the type of feature that they infer is valued or preferred by another person. That is, they can self-regulate and self-evaluate in terms of a standard or guide for their features that is associated with another person's viewpoint or standpoint on them. Children can understand now that the relation between self-feature X and other-response Y is mediated by the relation between self-feature X and a significant other's standpoint on self-feature X. Thus, children are now able to possess true self-guides.

It is not enough, however, for children to have the representational capacity for self-guides. They must also have the opportunity and motivation to acquire and use self-guides. The characteristics of child–caretaker interaction that influence the opportunity for children to acquire self–other contingency knowledge are described elsewhere (Higgins, 1989). The motivation for children to acquire self–other contingency knowledge and self-guides depends upon the psychological situation Z component that is associated with the other-response Y component of the self–other contingency knowledge.

Caretaker–child interactions vary in the psychological situations they produce in the child. The basic difference between caretaker–child interactions that involve a positive versus a negative psychological situation for the child is that positive interactions reflect a *match* between a child's features and those child features valued by the caretaker (as perceived by the child), whereas negative interactions reflect a *mismatch*. When a match occurs, the caretaker is likely to respond to the child in a manner that places the child in a positive psychological situation (e.g., hugging, holding, reassuring). When a mismatch occurs, the caretaker is likely to respond to the child in a manner that places the child in a negative psychological situation (e.g., punishing, criticizing, withholding).

A child is most likely to acquire self–other contingency knowledge and self-guides associated with positive psychological situations when his or her caretakers manage the circumstances of interaction so as to maximize the likelihood of the child instantiating an attribute valued by the caretakers, which would lead to a positive response by the parents toward the child. As a result of such interactions, the child would learn self–other contingencies associated with child-attribute:caretaker-guide matches and positive psychological situations. Consistent with this expectation, the socialization literature suggests that caretaker–child interactions with such properties (including parental sensitivity, parental acceptance, and induction accompanied by displays of positive affect, caretaker–child sharing of scripts and interaction goals, and parental engineering and planning of the child's situation) are associated with children's acquisition of strong self-guides as revealed in their positive influence on children's self-regulation (see Maccoby & Martin, 1983; Radke-Yarrow, Zahn-Waxler, & Chapman, 1983).

There are different types of positive psychological situations that children can experience in their interactions with caretakers. The two basic types are the *presence of positive outcomes* and the *absence of negative outcomes*. An example of the former would be a child smiling at the mother, the mother picking up and hugging the child, and the child feeling happy and satisfied. An example of the latter would be a child crying out in distress, the mother responding by removing the distress and reassuring the child, and the child now feeling safe and secure. The literature provides little information about the types of caretaker–child interactions that produce different positive reactions in children. It may be that some parents are more oriented to manage their child's environment so as to minimize the likelihood that their child will experience a negative outcome (e.g., "child-proofing" the house; teaching how "good manners" minimize social conflict), whereas other parents are more oriented to manage their child's circumstances so as to maximize the likelihood that their child will experience a positive outcome (e.g., buying "age-appropriate" toys; setting up opportunities for the child to engage in prosocial activities).

The two basic types of negative psychological situations that children experience in their interactions with their caretakers are the *absence of positive outcomes* and the *presence of negative outcomes*. A classic example of a caretaker style associated with the former would be "love withdrawal," and a classic example of the latter would be "punishment." A more extreme example of the former would be "child neglect," and a more extreme example of the latter would be "child abuse" (see Higgins, 1989). Mahler, Pine, and Bergman (1975) provide case studies exemplifying each of these types. In the case of "Teddy," his mother is described as being generally insensitive to Teddy's needs, giving him minimal care and attention, being ambitious for him and disappointed when his progress is slow, which is likely to be associated with Teddy experiencing the absence of positive outcomes. In the case of "Sam," his mother is described as being intensely overstimulating, playing roughly to get his attention, dominating him, and disapproving of what she perceives to be Sam's willfulness, all of which are likely to be associated with Sam experiencing the presence of negative outcomes.

Self-discrepancy theory would predict that children who chronically experience the absence of positive outcomes would be vulnerable to dejection-related problems, whereas children who chronically experience the presence of negative outcomes would be vulnerable to agitation-related problems. Consistent with these expectations, Mahler et al. (1975) report that Teddy was lethargic, relatively unresponsive, subdued in motor activity and exploration, sad-looking, and so on, whereas Sam was fretful, frantic, frenzied, noisy, frequently uncontrolled and agitated in play, hyperactive, panicky, and so on.

Self-discrepancy theory assumes that children are motivated to approach the positive psychological situations and avoid the negative psychological situations associated with their caretakers' responses to them. To do so, children must learn to anticipate these responses and discover how their own self-features influence the likelihood that these responses will occur. They can best do this by learning which self-features are valued or preferred by the caretakers. In order to obtain positive outcomes, children attempt to learn what self-features their caretakers would ideally like them to possess, the self-features their caretakers hope for or wish for—the ideal self-guide. In order to avoid negative outcomes, children attempt to learn what self-features their caretakers believe they should possess, believe it is their duty or obligation to possess—the ought self-guide.

Children are motivated to match or instantiate an ideal or ought self-guide attribute in order to experience positive psychological situations. They are also motivated to reduce or avoid instantiating a mismatch with an ideal or ought self-guide attribute in order to reduce the likelihood of experiencing negative psychological situations. As mentioned, children have different experiences of caretaker–child interaction that orient them either to approach positive psychological situations or to avoid negative psychological situations, and different experiences that orient them to the presence or absence of positive outcomes (the ideal self-guide) or to the absence or presence of negative outcomes (the ought self-guide).

In sum, in order to approach the positive and avoid the negative psychological situations Z associated with other-responses Y, children are motivated to learn what kinds of self-features are expected, valued, and preferred by the significant others in their lives. By 4 to 6 years of age, then, children are both able and motivated to possess self-guides and self–other contingency knowledge concerning the self-features that significant others value and the consequences of meeting or not meeting these self-features. There are individual differences, however, both in which type of self-guide children are especially motivated to meet (i.e., ideal vs. ought) *and* in children's beliefs concerning the consequences of meeting or not meeting their self-guides (i.e., how significant others are likely to respond and the type and intensity of psychological situation they are likely to experience as a consequence).

Self-discrepancy theory predicts that both kinds of individual differences in self-beliefs influence people's emotional–motivational vulnerability. I now review the evidence for the relation between people's self-beliefs concerning the negative consequences of failing to meet others' guides for them and their emotional–motivational vulnerabilities.

C. BELIEFS ABOUT THE NEGATIVE CONSEQUENCES OF POSSESSING SELF-DISCREPANCIES

To date, there has been only preliminary testing of Hypothesis 1 concerning the combined impact of the magnitude of people's self-discrepancies and people's beliefs about the negative consequences of possessing such self-discrepancies. In one study (see Higgins *et al.*, 1987), undergraduates filled out the Selves Questionnaire and the Socialization Questionnaire weeks before responding to the BDI and the HSCL. The 14-item Socialization Questionnaire attempted to measure subjects' beliefs about the consequences of discrepancies between their self-attributes and significant others' guides for them (i.e., their self–other contingency knowledge). The questionnaire first defined parents' *ideals* and *oughts* for their children. It then asked subjects the following kinds of questions: (1) "Have you ever felt unloved because you didn't live up to your parents *ideals* for you? To what extent?" (2) "Have you ever felt you would be emotionally abandoned if you didn't live up to your parents' *ideals* for you? To what extent?" (3) "Did you ever believe that your parents would reject you if you didn't live up to their *oughts* for you? To what extent?" Each question was answered on a 5-point scale that ranged from 0 (not at all) to 5 (a great deal).

Each subject's scores for the ideal questions were averaged to form an overall measure of the strength of the subject's belief about the negative consequences of an actual-self-discrepancy from their parents' ideals for them (strength of ideal-outcome contingency beliefs), and each subject's scores for the ought questions were averaged to form an overall measure of the strength of the subject's belief about the negative consequences of an actual-self-discrepancy from their parents' oughts for them (strength of ought–outcome contingency beliefs). For each measure, the ideal-outcome contingency beliefs and the ought-outcome contingency beliefs separately, the subjects were divided using median splits into those who strongly believed that self-discrepancies from parental guides was associated with negative consequences (e.g., being abandoned or rejected) and those who did not. On the basis of their responses to the Selves Questionnaire, the subjects were also divided, using tertiary splits into three levels of actual/own:ideal discrepancy (combining both ideal/own and ideal/other discrepancies) and three levels of actual/own:ought discrepancy (combining both ought/own and ought/other discrepancies). We then performed a Level-of-Actual:Ideal-Discrepancy × Strength-of-Ideal-Outcome-Contingency-Beliefs analysis of covariance (with level of actual:ought discrepancy as the covariate) and a Level-of-Actual:Ought-Discrepancy × Strength-of-Ought-Outcome-Contingency-Beliefs analysis of covariance (with level of actual:ideal discrepancy as the covariate) on the measure of emotional–motivational problems.

A squared multiple correlation (R^2) was used as a summary statistic of the amount of variance of the two dependent variables, which was accounted for by the main effects and interactions of the two independent variables. The results of this summary statistic supported Hypothesis 1. Higher levels of actual:ideal discrepancy plus stronger ideal-outcome contingency beliefs were significantly related to higher levels of depression on both the BDI and the HSCL depression subscale (the zero-order multiple correlations *[R]* ranged from .52 to .62), but they were not reliably related to greater levels of fear/anxiety-related problems. In contrast, higher levels of actual:ought discrepancy plus stronger ought-outcome contingency beliefs were significantly related to greater chronic levels of fear/anxiety on both the HSCL anxiety subscale and the HSCL paranoid subscale (the zero-order multiple correlations *[R]* ranged from .47 to .49), but they were not reliably related to greater levels of depression.

In addition to providing support for Hypothesis 1, the results of this study provide evidence of another self-belief that is associated with emotional–motivational vulnerabilities—a person's self–other contingency knowledge or beliefs concerning the likelihood of negative interpersonal consequences from a failure to meet significant others' guides for him or her. This study found that subjects' outcome-contingency beliefs were significantly and independently related to their symptoms. Indeed, on the BDI, there was a significant Actual:Ideal Discrepancy × Strength-of-Ideal-Outcome-Contingency-Beliefs interaction ($p < .001$), which reflected the fact that only the group of subjects who possessed both a high magnitude of actual/own:ideal discrepancy *and* strong beliefs concerning the negative consequences of possessing such a discrepancy had a mean BDI score in the moderately depressed range ($M = 25.0$ vs. M's less than 9 for the other groups of subjects).

The Socialization Questionnaire used in this study also contained a couple of items measuring subjects' commitment to their parents' self-guides for them: (1) How committed are you to being the type of person your parents would *Ideally* like you to be? To what extent? (2) How much do you currently care about being the type of person your parents *ideally* would have liked you to be? To what extent? The study found that across all subjects, the stronger the subjects' expressed commitment to their parents' ideal for them, the higher was their level of depression (BDI, $p = .01$; HSCL depression subscale, $p = .05$). In contrast, subjects' expressed commitment to their parents' ought for them was not correlated with their level of depression (p's $> .20$). It might also be noted that the one subject who was in the highest tertial on all three predictors—actual/own:ideal discrepancy, ideal-outcome contingency, and ideal commitment—also had the highest BDI in the sample, an extreme score of 35.

In a 1987 study, the association between people's self–other contingency knowledge and vulnerability to depression was examined further (Higgins & Tykocinsky, 1987). One limitation of the Higgins *et al.* (1987) study was that the questions concerning self–other contingencies were not designed specifically to distinguish between the two types of negative psychological situations associated with such contingencies—the absence of positive outcomes versus the presence of negative outcomes. As discussed earlier when describing different socialization patterns, different types of caretaker–child interactions are associated with children experiencing different types of psychological situations.

The History and Background Questionnaire was constructed that measured respondents' self–other contingency beliefs for parent–child interactions associated with either the absence of positive outcomes if they failed to meet their parents' ideal for them or the presence of negative outcomes if they failed to meet their parents' ought for them. The questions measuring beliefs about ideal-discrepancy–absence-of-positive-outcomes contingencies were as follows:

1. When you were growing up, did you believe that you would *lose your mother's affection* (or, in a separate question, *lose your father's affection*) if you failed to be the type of person she (he) wanted or hoped you would be? How much did you believe this?
2. When you were growing up, did you believe that you would *lose your mother's respect* (or, *lose your father's respect*) if you failed to be the type of person she (he) wanted or hoped you would be? How much did you believe this?

The questions measuring beliefs about ought-discrepancy–presence-of-negative-outcomes contingencies were as follows:

1. When you were growing up, did you believe that *your mother would punish you* (or *your father would punish you*) if you failed to be the type of person she (he) believed it was your duty or responsibility to be? How much did you believe this?
2. When you were growing up, did you believe that *your mother would criticize you* (or, *your father would criticize you*) if you failed to be the type of person she (he) believed it was your duty or obligation to be? How much did you believe this?

Each question was answered on a 5-point scale from 0 (not at all) to 4 (very much). Subjects' scores on the four ideal-outcome contingency questions were combined and their scores on the four ought-outcome contingency questions were combined. We predicted that subjects' level of chronic dejection-related problems, as measured by the BDI, would be associated with the strength of their ideal-outcome contingency beliefs but not with the strength of their ought-outcome contingency beliefs. As predicted, the stronger were subjects' beliefs when they were growing up that failure to meet their parents' ideal for them would lead to the absence of positive outcomes, the more they currently suffered from depression (r [61] = .37, $p < .01$). In contrast, the strength of subjects' beliefs when they were growing up that failure to meet their parents' ought for them would lead to the presence of negative outcomes was not associated with their current level of depression (r [61] = .08, $p > .10$). This difference in correlations was significant ($p < .05$).[3] The null effect for subjects' ought-outcome contingency beliefs indicates that the significant effect for subjects' ideal-outcome contingency beliefs was not simply a result of subjects' current negative mood producing a negative bias when responding to the History and Background Questionnaire. Moreover, on measures of how frequently subjects felt "anxious" and "uneasy," the opposite pattern was found, with the strength of subjects' ought-outcome contingency beliefs being more strongly related to these agitated emotions (both r's > .35, $p < .01$) than was the strength of subjects' ideal-outcome contingency beliefs (both p's > .05).

Thus, people's beliefs about their actual self are not the only kind of self-belief that predicts emotional problems. Self-beliefs concerning the likely responses of significant others to possessing discrepant attributes also contribute to people's vulnerability. This is one example of how people's self-beliefs beyond their beliefs about their actual self, or their self-concept, influence their vulnerabilities. Let us now consider some other evidence of vulnerabilities from self-beliefs beyond just the self-concept.

D. "DISCREPANCY" AS A CONTRIBUTING FACTOR IN VULNERABILITIES

The evidence reviewed previously of distinct vulnerabilities associated with actual:ideal versus actual:ought discrepancies clearly indicates the importance of considering self-beliefs other than just the self-concept. Given that subjects' actual/

---

[3]It should be noted that there are no items on the BDI that refer to loss of others' affection or loss of others' respect, but there are items that refer to punishment and criticism. Thus, if the strength of the associations between the items in the History and Background Questionnaire and those in the BDI were due to contamination or similarity of items, then the pattern of results should have been in the *opposite* direction.

own selves are used to measure both types of discrepancies, if the actual/own self (i.e., self-concept) were the only self-belief that mattered, then correlations with different kinds of emotional–motivational problems should not be found. This is especially true when the contribution to the correlation from the alternative type of self-discrepancy (measured in relation to the same actual/own self) is partialled out. But as the results clearly indicate, it is the *relation* between attributes in the actual self and attributes in different types of self-guides that is critical.

By definition, self-discrepancy theory is a *discrepancy* theory. Not only has the literature emphasized the emotional–motivational implications of the self-concept rather than other kinds of self-beliefs, but also some people have questioned whether measuring discrepancies contributes anything beyond measuring just the negativity of self-concepts (e.g., Hoge & McCarthy, 1983; Wells & Marwell, 1976; Wylie, 1961, 1979). One reason why some discrepancy measures may contribute little beyond the self-concept is that subjects are given a preselected set of attribute dimensions and are asked to place their actual selves and ideal selves along each dimension. This nonidiographic measure forces subjects to respond to all the attribute dimensions, regardless of their personal relevance. Under such circumstances, it would not be surprising for there to be high agreement among subjects that they would ideally like to be on the positive end of each dimension. This method increases the likelihood that the only individual differences observed would be a function of where on the dimensions subjects placed their actual selves; that is, the discrepancy scores would contribute little beyond the actual self scores.

In contrast to this type of discrepancy score, our measure of actual self-discrepancies, following the logic of the theory, measures the *relation* between each attribute in a subject's idiographic actual self and each attribute in one of the subject's idiographic self-guides (i.e., the matches and mismatches). Because the measure of subjects' ideal or ought selves is idiographic (and measures only accessible attributes), individual differences are more likely to be found. Thus, even subjects with identical self-concepts can have different scores on this measure because the relation between their self-concepts and their self-guides can still be different.

In a 1987 study, we used our measure of self-discrepancies to reexamine whether a discrepancy measure contributes anything beyond a measure of global self-concept negativity (Moretti & Higgins, 1987). Global self-concept negativity was calculated by coding each of the attributes listed by a subject (in response to the actual/own question) as being either positive or negative, according to Anderson's (1968) norms of attribute likability (i.e., the social desirability of attributes). Subjects' responses to the Selves Questionnaire were used to calculate their actual/own:ideal discrepancy scores (combining their ideal/own and ideal/other discrepancies). Two well-known measures of self-esteem, the Rosenberg Self-Esteem Scale (Rosenberg, 1965) and the Coopersmith Self-Esteem Scale

(Coopersmith, 1967), were used as the dependent measures and were collected a few weeks later.

The relation between actual:ideal discrepancy and each of the self-esteem measures was calculated, with the contribution of global self-concept negativity to each correlation from its association to both level of discrepancy and level of self-esteem being partialled out. If the discrepancy measure contributes nothing beyond self-concept negativity, then this analysis should reveal nothing. Instead, highly reliable associations were found (partial r's ranged from $-.45$ to $-.50$, all p's $< .01$), indicating that the higher the magnitude of subjects' actual:ideal discrepancies, the lower was their self-esteem, even when the contribution of self-concept negativity to this relation was statistically removed. In contrast, when the contribution of actual:ideal discrepancy was statistically removed from the correlation between global self-concept negativity and the measures of self-esteem, no significant effects remained.

Self-discrepancy theory differs from self-concept negativity perspectives by defining positivity and negativity only in relation to a self-guide, where a match to a self-guide is positive and a mismatch to a self-guide is negative. Indeed, the same self-concept attribute could be positive in relation to one self-guide and negative in relation to another self-guide. Self-concept attributes that have no relation to a self-guide are classified as nonmatches and are considered to be neither positive or negative from the perspective of self-discrepancy theory. According to the theory, then, a high number of socially undesirable nonmatches should not be related to low self-esteem, but a high number of socially undesirable mismatches should be related. From the perspective of self-concept negativity, however, all undesirable self-concept attributes should be related to low self-esteem. The results of the Moretti and Higgins (1987) study clearly supported the prediction made by self-discrepancy theory. As shown in Table II, negative or socially undesirable mismatches were significantly related to low self-esteem (both p's $\leq .001$) but negative nonmatches were not. Thus, not all socially undesirable self-concept attributes are associated with people feeling bad about themselves. But those that are mismatches to an ideal self-guide do show this relation. Table II also shows that whereas positive or socially desirable matches were significantly related to high self-esteem (both p's $\leq .01$), positive nonmatches were not. Thus, not all socially desirable actual self-attributes are associated with people feeling good about themselves. But those that are matches to an ideal self-guide do show this relation.

Perhaps the most compelling evidence for the contribution of self-discrepancies to people's vulnerabilities beyond their self-concepts would be evidence of a relation between self-discrepancies and emotional–motivational problems that did not even involve the self-concept. Self-discrepancy theory, after all, is a general model of the relations between self-beliefs and thus should apply to cases where the discrepancy is between self-beliefs other than the self-concept. One such case would be emotional—motivational problems associated with a conflict

TABLE II
RELATION OF (HIGH) SELF-ESTEEM TO SELF-CONCEPT ATTRIBUTES,
DEFINED IN TERMS OF SOCIAL DESIRABILITY
AND RELATION TO IDEAL/OWN

Social desirability Relation to ideal/own	Rosenberg Self-Esteem Scale	Coopersmith Self-Esteem Scale
Positive attributes		
Match	.43*	.50**
Mismatch	−.21	−.09
Nonmatch	−.17	−.02
Negative attributes		
Match	.12	.13
Mismatch	−.53**	−.55**
Nonmatch	−.13	−.13

*$p \leq .01$. **$p \leq .001$.

between an individual's self-guides that is independent of any conflict between these self-guides and the self-concept. Let us now consider this type of self-discrepancy.

E. SELF-GUIDE: SELF-GUIDE DISCREPANCIES AND VULNERABILITY TO CONFUSION-RELATED PROBLEMS

In its simplest form, a discrepancy between two self-guides represents an approach–approach conflict, in which a person is motivated to reach two valued end-states that cannot be approached simultaneously (see Lewin, 1935). When the valued end-states are opposite to each other, as when there is a mismatch between the attributes of two self-guides, a distinct negative psychological situation is created (see Miller, 1944)—*a double approach–avoidance conflict*. For example, a daughter might have a conflict between her personal wish to be assertive and her father's belief that she ought to be passive, which would involve an ideal/own:ought/other discrepancy (see Horney, 1946). In such cases, meeting one self-guide means failing to meet the other self-guide. Thus, both self-guides have a latent aspect, which is the negative psychological situation associated with failing to meet the alternative conflicting self-guide (e.g., punishment from failing to meet the ought/other self-guide or disappointment in oneself from failing to meet the ideal/own self-guide).

According to the underlying logic of self-discrepancy theory, to predict the emotional–motivational consequences of possessing a self-guide:self-guide discrepancy, one should consider the implications of someone chronically experiencing the negative psychological situation represented by the discrepancy—in this case, the consequences of chronically experiencing a double approach-avoidance conflict (see Van Hook & Higgins, 1988). This type of conflict has been associated in the response-competition literature with a number of emotional–motivational consequences, including vacillation, blocking, and entrapment in the conflict area (see Epstein, 1978; Heilizer, 1977; Miller, 1959). There would be some motivation to "flee the field" entirely (Lewin, 1935), which could produce distractibility, or to reject one end-state (or self-guide) at a time, in order to pursue at least temporarily the alternative end-state, which could be experienced as rebelliousness.

Thus, it was predicted that people who possessed a conflict between self-guides would, in comparison to people without such a conflict, report being more confused, muddled, unsure of themselves and their goals, distractible, and rebellious. This cluster of symptoms, in turn, resembles clinical descriptions of the hysterical personality style (e.g., Horowitz, 1976; Margaro & Smith, 1981; Shapiro, 1965). Thus, it was also predicted that people who possessed a chronic conflict between self-guides would have higher levels of this personality disorder than those who did not.

Although a self-guide:self-guide discrepancy can itself be independent of any relation between the self-concept and the conflicting self-guides, it is possible that the conflict could have long-term consequences for the self-concept. Because there would be vacillation in the predominance of the conflicting self-guides, there would be vacillation or inconsistency in which self-guide was used for self-evaluation. Given that the self-guides are opposite, the same attribute would be evaluated as a success when one self-guide was used, but as a failure when the other self-guide was used, which, over time, is likely to yield identity confusion and self-perceptions of possessing only moderate levels of mismatching attributes (i.e., neither a clear success nor a clear failure on the attribute). This latter effect would be revealed in a subject's extent ratings of his or her actual–own attributes, where the extent ratings of those actual–own attributes that also appear in a self-guide:self-guide mismatch would be lower or more moderate than the extent ratings of the remaining actual/own attributes.

Two studies were conducted to test these predictions (see Van Hook & Higgins, 1988). Undergraduates who possessed self-guide:self-guide discrepancies were compared to a control group of undergraduates who did not. Each of the preceding predicted relations between possessing self-guide:self-guide discrepancies and suffering from confusion-related and hysterical personality symptoms was confirmed. Moreover, through the use of both statistical and sampling methods, these relations were shown to be independent both of subjects' level of other kinds of emotional–motivational problems (i.e., dejection-related, agitation-related, anger-related problems) and of their level of actual/own:self-guide discrepancies (i.e., actual–own:ideal discrepancies and actual–own:ought discrepancies).

This study, then, both supports Hypothesis 1 of self-discrepancy theory and provides evidence that relations between self-beliefs that do not include the self-concept can be associated with unique personal problems. Further evidence of the impact of new self-belief relations on people's vulnerabilities was recently obtained as part of the Higgins and Tykocinsky (1987) study. The impact of relations involving two new self-beliefs were considered—people's beliefs about the type of person they can be, and people's beliefs about the likelihood that they would meet their self-guides.

F. VULNERABILITIES RELATED TO THE CAN SELF AND THE (EXPECTED) FUTURE SELF

Descriptions of self-beliefs in the literature have not been restricted to the current, actual self. They have also included people's beliefs about what they can and cannot do, of what type of person they might become or expect to become. These potential (James, 1890/1948) or possible (Markus & Nurius, 1987) selves have been described as having important motivational effects (Bandura, 1982; Lewin, 1935; Markus & Nurius, 1986; for a review, see Markus & Wurf, 1987). Previous models, however, have not descried how the *relations* between these types of self-beliefs and other types of self-beliefs produce emotional–motivational predispositions. In addition, previous models have rarely distinguished between the emotional–motivational vulnerabilities associated with these types of self-beliefs and those associated with other types of self-beliefs, such as different types of self-guides or imaginary, fantasized selves (see Freud, 1923/1961; Levinson, 1978). Indeed, as Markus and Nurius (1986) point out, until recently, it has been unusual for these types of self-beliefs even to be directly measured.

Because they contribute to how people define their psychological situations, self-discrepancy theory needs to be expanded to include these additional types of self-beliefs and their relations to other self-beliefs. Specifically, *two new domains of the self* need to be added:

1. The *Can* self, which is your representation of the attributes that someone (yourself or another) believes you *can* possess (i.e., a representation of someone's beliefs about your capabilities or potential)
2. The (expected) *Future* self, which is your representation of the attributes that someone (yourself or another) believes you are likely to possess in the future (i.e., the type of person someone expects that you *will* become).

For the purpose of this article the discussion of these domains of the self are restricted to self-state representations involving the individual's *own* standpoint.

Although previous descriptions of the self have included these types of self-beliefs (e.g., Bandura, 1982; Markus & Nurius, 1986), to my knowledge, no previous model of the self has either explicitly distinguished among the actual, can, and (expected) future self-state representations in assessing aspects of the self or made differentiated predictions concerning how their relations to other self-state representations produce vulnerabilities. Markus and Nurius (1986) assessed both subjects' "now self" and their "probable possible self," which are most similar to the actual self and (expected) future self, respectively. A separate can self was not assessed, and how the *relations* among these self-state representations was associated with emotional–motivational problems was not examined.

Bandura (e.g., 1982) identifies perceived self-efficacy as a motivational factor and distinguishes it from actual capabilities or actual performance. It is not clear whether perceived self-efficacy as a self-belief is more similar to the can self or to the (expected) future self. Bandura (1982) describes this self-belief as an appraisal of one's own capabilities and as a judgment about how well one can organize and execute a course of action. Although this description sounds closer to the can self, Bandura (1982) also suggests that it is one's effective personal force (see Heider, 1958) or even one's expectations of personal agency that is being judged, which seems closer to the (expected) future self. In any case, Bandura does not distinguish between the can self and the (expected) future self, nor are these self-beliefs related to other self-beliefs in predicting emotional–motivational predispositions. It should be noted, however, that in many of the types of performance situations to which perceived self-efficacy is applied, such as perceived capability to solve particular kinds of arithmetic problems (Bandura & Schunk, 1981), the can and (expected) future selves may be intertwined.

For the kinds of self-attributes and self-attribute relations of concern to self-discrepancy theory, however, it is important to distinguish between the can and future selves. In general, one might expect that a positive future self would be associated with positive affect and high self-esteem. Indeed, Markus and Nurius (1986) report that the magnitude of their subjects' positive probable selves was positively correlated with positive affect and self-esteem. According to self-discrepancy theory, however, the positivity of a person's future self is not determined by social norms (see Markus & Nurius, 1986), but rather by its relation to the person's self-guides. Moreover, it would be the interrelational pattern among the future self, a self-guide, *and* the self-concept (i.e., the chronic actual self) that would be critical. From the perspective of self-discrepancy theory, then, the question would be "What is the psychological situation represented by the following pattern: the future self matches the ideal self *but* the actual self is discrepant from both?" It could be argued that this pattern represents chronic disconfirmation of positive expectancies, which should be associated with severe disappointment and discouragement. Thus, although positive expectancies might generally be associated with positive affect, there may be particular chronic cases, such as the one just described, in which positive expectancies are associated with negative affect.

The predictions for the can self are also complex. One might expect that the more positive the can self, the better someone would feel. Indeed, perspectives on the self that do not consider the relation among self-beliefs would presumably predict that individuals with positive beliefs about their capabilities would be less vulnerable to emotional problems than individuals with less positive beliefs about their capabilities. But, according to the logic underlying self-discrepancy theory, it is the psychological situation represented by the relation among self-beliefs that is critical for predicting vulnerabilities.

Consider, for example, a woman who has a low can/own:ideal/own discrepancy but a high actual/own:can/own discrepancy. According to self-discrepancy theory, this person would have a positive can/own self because it meets her own ideal self. But what psychological situation is represented in this pattern of self-belief relations as a whole? This is a person who believes that she is capable of being the type of person she would ideally like to be but she is not actually meeting her potential. This is a depressing situation (e.g., "What's wrong with me? I know I can be what I would like to be but I am not doing it"). In fact, the psychological situation of believing that one is not meeting one's potential has been associated with depression (see Blatt *et al.*, 1976).

It should be noted that although self-discrepancy would predict dejection-related symptoms in this case, this does not necessarily mean that the person's motivation would be low. Negative affect need not be associated with low motivation. Indeed, high need achievers may be highly motivated by their dissatisfaction with their current level of performance (see Higgins *et al.* 1986b). Similarly, mild depressive symptoms, such as disappointment, dissatisfaction, self-blaming, may motivate someone to try harder (e.g., "What's wrong with me? Why am I so lazy? I know I can do better. I've got to try harder!"). Self-discrepancy theory proposes that particular self-discrepancies produce particular negative psychological situations that are associated with particular emotional–motivational states. These states involve suffering, but suffering does not necessarily imply low motivation. Often, in fact, it is associated with extremely high motivation, such as the motivation to escape when experiencing fear, the motivation to succeed after experiencing dissatisfaction from failure, or the motivation to resolve inconsistencies when experiencing unpleasant tension from dissonance. Indeed, even those suffering from the motivational problems associated with a self-guide:self-guide discrepancy (e.g., confusion, uncertainty over goals, distractibility) are highly motivated.

The impact of people's future self and can self in relation to other self-beliefs on people's chronic emotional–motivational states has only begun to be examined. In the Higgins and Tykocinsky (1987) study, subjects were directly asked to "list the attributes of the type of person *you* think you *can* be" as part of the Selves Questionnaire (after being asked to list their actual/own attributes). Thus, it was possible to measure subjects' can/own:ideal/own discrepancies. The results indicated that the *smaller* subjects' can/own:ideal/own discrepancies, the *higher* were their levels of depression as measured weeks later (r [60] = $-.39$, $p <$ .01). Thus, the subjects' beliefs that they possessed positive capabilities was associated with suffering!

As discussed earlier, self-discrepancy theory would predict this relation to the extent that people who possessed *both* a small can/own:ideal/own discrepancy *and* a large actual/own:can/own discrepancy (i.e., "I have the capacity to be the kind of person that I would ideally like to be, but I am *not* fulfilling my potential") were especially likely to suffer from depression and dejection-related symptoms. A simultaneous multiple regression analysis (including as factors, actual/own:ideal/own discrepancy, can/own:ideal/own discrepancy, actual/own:can/own discrepancy, and their interactions) revealed that the interaction between can/own:ideal/own discrepancy and actual/own:can/own discrepancy, independent of level of actual/own:ideal/own discrepancy and the other factors, was indeed uniquely related to depression and chronic dejection-related emotions, as measured weeks later. As shown in Table III, a low level of can/own:ideal/own discrepancy combined with a high level of actual/own:can/own discrepancy was predictive of the highest levels of depression and chronic dejection-related emotions. Thus, a pattern of self-beliefs involving the relations among attributes in *three* self-states represented a meaningful negative psychological situation ("unfulfilled potential to be the kind of person I would ideally like to be"), which was associated with suffering. Moreover, in this pattern, two of the three self-states (can/own and ideal/own) involve self-beliefs distinct from the self-concept.

The results of this study, then, are consistent with the predictions of self-discrepancy theory concerning the role of people's can self in relation to other

TABLE III
MEANS OF SYMPTOMS INVOLVING INTERACTIONS OF CAN:IDEAL AND ACTUAL:CAN DISCREPANCIES IN PREDICTING DEPRESSION (BDI) AND DEJECTION[a]

	High can:ideal		Low can:ideal	
	High actual:can	Low actual:can	High actual:can	Low actual:can
Depression	8.2	9.3	19.9	8.3
Overall dejection[b]	1.6	1.5	2.6	1.5
(Feeling) low	0.8	1.3	2.4	1.1
Disappointed	1.3	1.8	2.7	1.5
(Not) happy	1.8	1.8	2.6	1.4
(Not) satisfied	1.7	2.1	3.2	1.8
(Not) optimistic	1.7	1.8	2.7	1.9

[a] The table includes only those interactions of can:ideal and actual:can discrepancies that are significant ($p <$ .05) when level of actual:ideal discrepancy is statistically controlled.

[b] All emotions were rated on a scale from 0 (almost never) to 4 (almost always). (Can:ideal = can/own:ideal/own discrepancy; actual:can = actual/own:can/own discrepancy; actual:ideal = actual/own:ideal/own discrepancy.)

self-beliefs as a source of vulnerability. These results indicate that "positive" self-beliefs, including even beliefs about one's capabilities, are not always related to positive emotional states. The results also require a modification of Hypothesis 1 because as the magnitude of can/own:ideal/own discrepancy increased, suffering did *not* increase.

As discussed earlier, a fundamental assumption underlying self-discrepancy theory is that particular relations among self-beliefs represent, as a whole, a particular type of psychological situation, and it is the psychological situation that is the source of people's emotional–motivational predispositions. The results of this study are consistent with this assumption, as the prediction was based on the psychological situation represented by a can/own:ideal/own nondiscrepancy, combined with an actual/own:ideal/own discrepancy, and the prediction was confirmed. But it is also clear that discrepancies between self-beliefs do not always represent a negative psychological situation, especially when they are part of a larger system of self-beliefs. The general hypothesis of self-discrepancy theory, then, needs to be revised as follows: *The greater the extent and accessibility of a particular pattern of self-beliefs possessed by an individual, the more the individual will experience the emotional–motivational states associated with the type of psychological situation represented by that pattern.*

In addition to reflecting more accurately the basic assumptions of self-discrepancy theory, this new general hypothesis has the clear advantages of explicitly predicting *positive* as well as negative emotional–motivational predispositions and of considering interrelations among more than two self-beliefs at a time. With this new general hypothesis in mind, let us turn then to examine Hypothesis 2 of the theory.

IV. Evidence for Hypothesis 2 of Self-Discrepancy Theory

In order for the vulnerability associated with a particular self-belief pattern to eventuate in an episode (i.e., an occurrence of suffering), the self-belief pattern must be activated. Earlier in this article, various factors were described that can increase the likelihood that a stored construct will be activated. One source of activation is the *applicability* of the construct to a stimulus event. According to self-discrepancy theory, the interrelations among attributes constituting an actual/own:self-guide discrepancy represent, as a whole, a negative psychological situation that functions as a construct. Thus, the negative psychological situation represented by such a discrepancy, and the emotional–motivational state associated with it, are more likely to be activated when the negative psychological situation is applicable to a stimulus event than when it is nonapplicable. This prediction was tested in a study by Higgins *et al.* (1986a).

Undergraduates were asked to imagine either a positive event in which performance matched a common standard (e.g., receiving a grade of A in a course) or a negative event in which performance failed to match a common standard (e.g., receiving a grade of D in a course that was necessary for obtaining an important job). It was predicted (1) that the negative psychological situation represented by an actual/own:self-guide discrepancy would be applicable to the negative event but not to the positive event, and thus (2) that significant relations between the magnitude of subjects' discrepancies and changes in their moods would only be found when subjects focused on a negative event. Subjects' self-discrepancies were measured by the Selves Questionnaire a few weeks earlier as part of a general battery of measures. Subjects' actual/own:ideal/own and actual/own:ought/own discrepancies were measured, where domain varies but standpoint is controlled.

We predicted that in the negative event condition, in which negative psychological situations are applicable, the greater was the magnitude of a particular type of discrepancy possessed by an individual, the more she or he would experience the kind of state associated with the psychological situation represented by that discrepancy—dejection-related symptoms (e.g., feeling discouraged, blue, dissatisfied; a decrease in writing speed) in the case of actual/own:ideal/own discrepancy, and agitation-related symptoms (e.g., feeling afraid, desperate; an increase in writing speed) in the case of actual/own:ought/own discrepancy. In order to measure change in state, subjects' mood and writing speed were measured both before and after they engaged in imagining the positive or negative event. To measure change in mood, the contribution to subjects' postmanipulation mood from their premanipulation mood was statistically removed. To measure change in behavior, subjects' percentage increase in writing speed was calculated, and the contribution of subjects' premanipulation mood was again statistically removed.

The partial correlational analyses on the mood "change" measures are shown in Table IV, in which the contribution to the relation between one type of discrepancy and a mood measure from their common association to the other type of discrepancy was also statistically removed. As Table IV shows, the predictions were confirmed. The magnitude and type of subjects' actual–own:self-guide discrepancies predicted the amount and particular kind of change in mood that they would experience weeks later. Moreover, these relations were only clearly evident when subjects focused on an event to which the negative psychological situations represented by the discrepancies were applicable (i.e., the negative event condition).

The same basic pattern of results was also found for the writing-speed measure. As predicted, a significant negative relation between the magnitude of subjects' actual/own:ideal/own discrepancies and writing speed was found in the negative event condition. No significant correlation was found in the positive event condition, and this difference in correlations between the negative and positive event

TABLE IV
PARTIAL CORRELATIONS BETWEEN TYPES OF SELF-DISCREPANCIES AND TYPES OF
POSTMANIPULATION MOOD IN THE POSITIVE EVENT AND NEGATIVE EVENT CONDITIONS[a]

Type of post mood Type of self-discrepancy	Guided-imagery manipulation task			
	Positive event		Negative event	
	Dejection emotions	Agitation emotions	Dejection emotions	Agitation emotions
Actual:ideal	.17	.13	.39***	−.33**
Actual:ought	.05	.26*	−.04	.46***

[a] Partial correlations shown have premanipulation mood and the alternative type of self-discrepancy partialled out of each.
*$p < .10$. **$p < .05$. ***$p < .01$.

conditions was significant ($p < .05$). Moreover, the pattern of correlations for subjects' actual–own:ought–own discrepancies was in the opposite direction (see Higgins *et al.*, 1986a).

If self-discrepancies are unitized cognitive structures (see Fiske & Dyer, 1985; Hayes-Roth, 1977), then it should also be possible to activate an entire self-discrepancy by activating only one of its major components. Thus, activation of a self-guide that is part of an actual/own:self-guide discrepancy should, through spreading activation among interconnected parts (see Collins & Loftus, 1975), be sufficient to activate the whole discrepancy. And activation of the discrepancy should induce the specific kind of state associated with the type of psychological situation holistically represented by the discrepancy.

In addition, according to Hypothesis 2 of self-discrepancy theory, the greater the accessibility of a particular type of self-discrepancy, the more the individual possessing the self-discrepancy should experience the state associated with the type of psychological situation represented by the discrepancy. Thus, if an individual possesses more than one type of self-discrepancy, she or he should experience the emotional–motivational state associated with whichever self-discrepancy is temporarily more accessible. These predictions were tested in another study by Higgins *et al.* (1986a).

Four to 6 weeks before the experimental session, undergraduates completed the Selves Questionnaire, and on the basis of their responses, two groups of subjects were recruited for the experiment—subjects who were relatively high on both actual:ideal discrepancy (combining both ideal/own and ideal/other) and actual:ought discrepancy (combining both ought/own and ought/other), and subjects who were relatively low on both types of discrepancies. As part of an ostensible study on life span development, subjects were asked either to describe the kind of person that they and their parents would ideally like them to be and

TABLE V

MEAN CHANGE IN DEJECTION-RELATED EMOTIONS AND AGITATION-RELATED EMOTIONS
AS A FUNCTION OF LEVEL OF SELF-CONCEPT DISCREPANCIES AND TYPE OF PRIMING[a]

Self-concept discrepancies	Ideal priming		Ought priming	
	Dejection	Agitation	Dejection	Agitation
High actual:ideal and actual:ought discrepancies	3.2	−0.8	0.9	5.1
Low actual:ideal and actual:ought discrepancies	−1.2	0.9	0.3	−2.6

[a] Each emotion was measured on a 6-point scale from *not at all* to *a great deal*, and there were eight dejection emotions and eight agitation emotions. The more positive the number, the greater the increase in discomfort.

the attributes that they hoped they would have (the ideal-priming condition), or to describe the kind of person that they and their parents believed they ought to be and the attributes that they believed it was their duty or obligation to have (the ought-priming condition). Both before and after this priming manipulation, the subjects filled out a mood questionnaire that contained both dejection-related emotions and agitation-related emotions. The subjects rated the extent to which they now were feeling each emotion on a 6-point scale that ranged from not at all (0) to a great deal (5).

As shown in Table V, the results of the study revealed a significant three-way interaction that was consistent with our predictions. For subjects who had self-discrepancies available to be activated (i.e., subjects who were high in both types of self-discrepancies), activation of a self-guide through priming was sufficient to produce an increase in discomfort. Moreover, the kind of discomfort that these subjects experienced depended on which type of self-guide was activated, with subjects experiencing an increase in dejection-related emotions when the ideal self-guide was activated and an increase in agitation-related emotions when the ought self-guide was activated.

The results of this study are consistent with the notion that self-discrepancies are cognitive structures, but it is possible that this structure can only be activated and induce emotional–motivational states when people are made to think about themselves in motivational terms (i.e., think about their hopes or duties). The results of some recent studies, however, indicate that this is not the case.

One set of three studies (Higgins, Van Hook, & Dorfman, 1987) tested whether actual/own self-attributes themselves form a cognitive structure similar to that underlying semantic memory. In each study, purported to be investigating the Stroop interference effect, undergraduates were presented with a series of slides of target words printed in different colored inks and were asked to name the color of each word as quickly as possible. Prior to each slide, subjects were given a memory-load word that they repeated back after naming the color of the target word. The critical experimental manipulation was the relation between the memory load word, which functioned as the prime, and the target word. In each study there were self-related target traits primed either by other self-related traits or by self-unrelated traits, and object category targets primed either by semantically related categories or by semantically unrelated categories.

In this modified Stroop paradigm (see Warren, 1972), structural interconnectedness among category attributes themselves, where self-attributes would form one category, should produce slower response times for prime-target category pairs. This is because when the prime word and the target word are interconnected members of the same category, exposure to the prime word should automatically increase the accessibility of the target word's meaning, which would make it difficult for subjects to attend to only the color of the target word and ignore its meaning. With this paradigm, then, it is possible to demonstrate that preestablished interrelations among category members in long-term memory automatically influence performance on the task despite the performers' active goal or strategic orientation (in this case to respond as quickly as possible by ignoring the word's meaning).

In every study, the color-naming response times were slower for semantically related than semantically unrelated object category pairs, replicating the results of Warren (1972) and validating the paradigm. There was, however, no evidence of general interconnectedness among each subject's self attributes. Instead, there was evidence of structural organization around each subject's problematic self-attributes. Specifically, color-naming response times were significantly slower for self-attribute pairs involving a mismatching attribute (i.e., an actual/own attribute that was discrepant from one of the individual's self-guides) than for self-attribute pairs without a mismatching self-attribute.

The results of these Stroop studies suggest that self-discrepancies do form cognitive structures that can be automatically activated without having to make people think about themselves in motivational terms. In these studies, though, the emotional–motivational consequences of automatic activation of self-discrepancies were not examined. Such consequences were examined in our next set of studies.

If self-discrepancies are unitized cognitive structures that have bidirectional links among the attributes, then it should be possible to activate the entire self-discrepancy by simply activating a single attribute in the structure. Moreover, if a mismatch between an actual/own attribute and a self-guide attribute constitutes a cognitive structure, then activating the self-guide attribute should activate the negative psychological situation represented by the discrepancy and thus induce discomfort even though the self-guide attribute is itself a positive attribute. And, as discussed earlier, it should be possible to activate the discrepancy in a task that is purportedly non-self-relevant. Three studies have been conducted to test these predictions (see Strauman, 1989; Strauman & Higgins, 1987).

Each study used a covert, idiographic priming technique to activate self-attributes in a task supposedly investigating the "physiological effects of thinking about other people." Subjects were given phrases of the form, "An X person _____" (where X would be a trait adjective such as "friendly" or "intelligent"), and were asked to complete each sentence as quickly as possible. For each sentence, each subject's total verbalization time and skin conductance amplitude were recorded. Subjects also reported their mood on scales measuring dejection-related and agitation-related emotions at both the beginning and end of the session. In two of the studies, subjects were preselected on the basis of their responses to the Selves Questionnaire obtained weeks before the experimental session. Subjects were selected who were either high in actual:ideal discrepancy (combining ideal/own and ideal/other in one study and using ideal/own alone in the other study) and low in actual:ought discrepancy (combining ought/own and ought/other in one study and using ought/other alone in the other study), or high in actual:ought discrepancy and low in actual:ideal discrepancy.

Study 1 found that priming subjects' self-guide attributes produced a dejection syndrome in subjects with an actual:ideal discrepancy—an increase in dejection-related emotions (accompanied by a decrease in agitation-related emotions), a decrease in standardized skin conductance amplitudes, and a slight decrease in total verbalization time. In contrast, priming self-guide attributes produced an agitation syndrome in subjects with an actual:ought discrepancy—a slight increase in agitation-related emotions (accompanied by a decrease in dejection-related emotions), an increase in standardized skin conductance amplitudes, and an increase in total verbalization time.

Study 1 also found that priming subjects' ideal mismatches, regardless of a subject's predominant self-discrepancy, generally decreased subject's standardized skin conductance amplitudes and decreased their total verbalization time relative to non-self-relevant priming. In contrast, priming subjects' ought mismatches generally increased subjects' standardized skin conductance amplitudes and increased their total verbalization times relative to non-self-relevant priming. These differences between ideal and ought priming were both significant ($p < .05$). Thus, it is the activation of particular types of self-discrepancies that produces particular kinds of syndromes. It is simply that certain kinds of people are predisposed both to possessing particular types of self-belief patterns and to experiencing particular kinds of syndromes when any aspect of the self is activated.

Study 2 in this series further explored whether a mismatching attribute specifically must be activated in order to produce an emotional syndrome or whether priming any attribute from someone's ideal or ought self-guide would be sufficient. Study 2 also controlled more stringently for possible effects of the content of priming stimuli by yoking subjects such that the same priming stimuli were used for different subjects who varied in whether the primes were self-related or not. There were three priming conditions as a between-subject variable and two types of attributes as a within-subject variable used in this study.

Subjects were randomly assigned to one of the following priming conditions: (1) nonmatching priming, in which the trait adjectives were attributes in a subject's self-guide but the attributes did not appear in the subject's actual/own self-concept; (2) mismatching priming, in which the trait adjectives were attributes in a subject's self-guide and the value of these attributes in the subject's actual/own self-concept was discrepant from the value in the self-guide; and (3) yoked (mismatching) priming, in which the trait adjectives were attributes that did not appear in either a subject's self-guide or actual/own self-concept but were the *same* attributes that appeared as the trait adjectives for some other subject in the mismatching priming condition. These attributes defined the subject-related attributes. All subjects also received the same set of subject-unrelated trait adjectives, which were attributes that did not appear in any of the subjects' self-guides or actual/ own self-concepts.

In the mismatching priming condition, Study 2 replicated the basic pattern of results found in Study 1—a dejection-related syndrome (i.e., mood, skin conductance amplitude, and total verbalization time, all changing in the dejection-related direction) for the actual:ideal discrepant subjects and an agitation-related syndrome for the actual:ought discrepant subjects. For the standardized skin conductance amplitude measure and the total verbalization time measure, Study 2 permitted a trial-by-trial analysis of the effects of priming actual/own:self-guide mismatches. These results are shown in Fig. 2 and 3. As is evident from these figures, there was a striking shift into and out of the syndromes as subjects received (subject-related) mismatching priming versus subject-unrelated

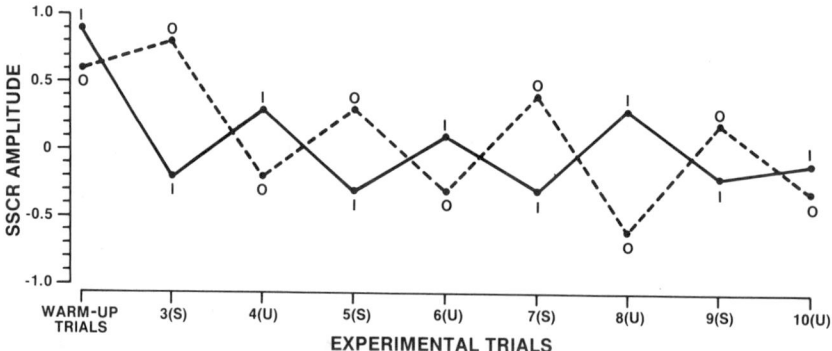

Fig. 2. Standardized spontaneous skin conductance response (SSCR) amplitude during warm-up and experimental trials for subjects in the mismatch priming condition. (I = actual/own:ideal/own-discrepant subjects' central tendency; O = actual own:ought/other-discrepant subjects' central tendency; S = subject-related trial; U = subject-unrelated trial.)

priming, respectively. Moreover, the direction of the shifts were opposite for the actual:ideal discrepant subjects than for the actual:ought discrepant subjects, as predicted.

This predicted pattern of results was found only in the mismatching priming condition. It was not found in either the nonmatching priming condition or the yoked (mismatching) condition. (There were significant differences between the mismatching priming condition and the other priming conditions for each of the dependent measures.) These results indicate that in order to activate people's self-discrepancies and induce the emotional–motivational states associated with them, it is necessary to activate actual/own:self-guide *mismatches*. It is not sufficient simply to activate any attribute in the self-guide.

The major purpose of Study 3 in this series was to determine whether the hypothesized processes and effects found in nonclinical samples would also be found in clinical samples. As discussed earlier, this study involved depressed and social-phobic clinical samples as well as a normal undergraduate sample. As in Study 2, on the basis of random assignment, some subjects in each sample were primed with mismatching attributes, whereas the remaining subjects were primed with nonmatching or yoked (mismatching) attributes. As in Study 1, each subject was primed with both ideal mismatching attributes and ought mismatching attributes.

The results replicated those of Study 1 and Study 2. The depressed subjects, who had the highest level of actual:ideal discrepancy, generally experienced an increase in the dejection-related syndrome, whereas the social phobic subjects, who had the highest level of actual:ought discrepancy, generally experienced an increase in the agitation-related syndrome. Moreover, as in Study 1, ideal mismatching priming produced a dejection-related syndrome in all subjects and ought

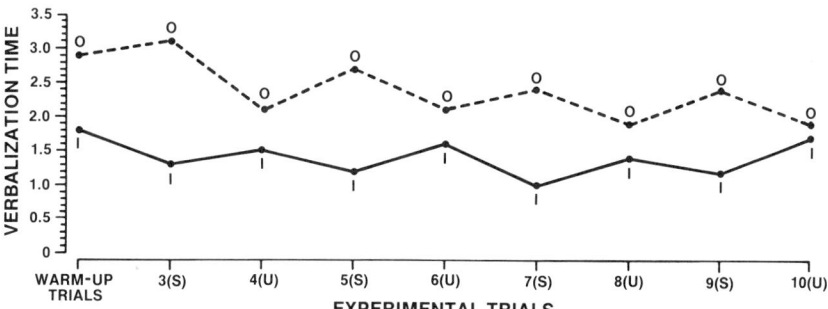

Fig. 3. Total verbalization time (in sec) during warm-up and experimental trials for subjects in the mismatch priming condition. (I = actual/own:ideal/own-discrepant subjects' central tendency; O = actual/own:ought/other-discrepant subjects' central tendency; S = subject-related trial; U = subject-unrelated trial.)

mismatching priming produced an agitation-related syndrome in all subjects, regardless of a subject's predominant discrepancy. Again, this finding provides strong support for the proposal that the causal mediator is the automatic activation of types of discrepant attributes that reflect types of negative psychological situations associated with particular kinds of emotional–motivational states. The results also suggest that individuals who possess more of a particular type of discrepancy are more likely to suffer from the problem associated with that type of discrepancy, perhaps because activation of a mismatch spreads to other mismatches.

V. Summary and Concluding Remarks

People's self-concepts are a major source of their emotional–motivational predispositions. Self-discrepancy theory suggests, however, that it is often not the *content* of self-concepts, per se, that is critical for emotional–motivational predispositions. Rather, the *relations* between self-concept attributes and the attributes contained in other self-beliefs, such as self-guides. The theory proposes, moreover, that these relations between self-beliefs are critical because they embody or represent specific types of psychological situations that are associated with particular kinds of emotional–motivational states.

What matters, then, is not so much what self-concept an individual possesses, but what *patterns of self-beliefs* she or he possesses and the psychological situations represented by these patterns. Indeed, evidence was presented demonstrating that patterns of self-beliefs independent of the self-concept are predictive of emotional predispositions. It was found in the Van Hook and Higgins (1988) studies that people who had discrepancies between two self-guides (e.g., ideal/own vs. ought/other) were vulnerable to experiencing a particular type of negative psychological situation: a double approach–avoidance conflict. And it was also found that particular symptoms are associated with this type of psychological situation—confusion and uncertainty about goals and self-identity, distractibility, rebelliousness, and so on. Other studies found that the combination high actual:ideal discrepancy and strong beliefs about the negative consequences of possessing such a discrepancy was highly related to depressive symptomatology. In addition, the combination of *low* can:ideal/own and high actual:can discrepancy was found to be predictive of especially high levels of disappointment, dissatisfaction, and anger at self. This latter combination, which represents the psychological situation of failing to live up to one's positive potential, exemplifies that patterns among more than two self-state representations can be psychologically meaningful and predictive of particular problems. It also demonstrates that sometimes it is lower, rather than higher, discrepancies between self-state representations that are associated with greater suffering (e.g., low vs. high can:ideal/

own discrepancy). What is critical is the psychological situation that is represented by a particular pattern of self-beliefs rather than the self-concept or even the magnitude of self-discrepancies per se.

There are other reasons as well to go beyond the self-concept in trying to understand the psychological underpinnings of emotional predispositions in general and emotional vulnerabilities in particular. Perhaps most important, a consideration of people's self-concepts alone does not provide a model for predicting distinct vulnerabilities from the same level of negative actual self-attributes. In order to make discriminant predictions, it is necessary to consider how the self-concept attributes are related to other types of self-beliefs and the psychological situations represented by these relations.

Considerable correlational and experimental evidence with undergraduates and clinical samples was presented that strongly supports the following conclusions: (1) the greater the magnitude and accessibility of people's actual:ideal discrepancies, both momentarily and chronically, the greater their experience of dejection-related symptoms (e.g., sadness, dissatisfaction, and lowered behavioral and physiological responses); and (2) the greater the magnitude and accessibility of people's actual:ought discrepancies, both momentarily and chronically, the greater their experience of agitation-related symptoms (e.g., fear, threat, and heightened behavioral and physiological responses). These distinct associations were found even for individuals who possessed both types of self-discrepancies. Thus, distinct patterns of relations between the same self-concept but different self-guides will produce different emotional–motivational states when activated.

Self-discrepancy theory, in its present form, is a general theory relating different patterns of self-beliefs to different kinds of emotional–motivational predispositions. Most of the research testing the theory has examined the relation of dyadic belief patterns, such as actual/own:self-guide discrepancies, to emotional problems. Future research needs to expand the boundaries of our theory-testing in a number of directions. First, the types of psychological situations reflected in triadic (or even more complex) belief patterns need to be considered. The studies described earlier that tested the combination of actual:ideal discrepancy and beliefs about the consequences of possessing such a discrepancy and that tested the combination of can:ideal/own discrepancy and actual:can discrepancy represent an initial step in this direction.

Second, positive psychological situations need to receive more attention. For example, we have found that actual:ideal/own matches are especially predictive of high self-esteem (Moretti & Higgins, 1987). We have also found that low actual:ideal/own discrepancy is associated with feeling satisfied, and low actual:ought/other discrepancy is associated with feeling secure.

Third, the implications of the motivational predispositions associated with particular self-belief patterns for behavior and action need to be considered more fully. Our previous research (Higgins *et al.*, 1986a; Strauman & Higgins, 1987) has found that the dejection produced by actual:ideal discrepancies is associated with slower responding (decreased writing speed; decreased rate of verbal output) and that the agitation produced by actual:ought discrepancies is associated with quicker responding (increased writing speed; increased rate of verbal output). But the implications of the distinct motivational states associated with different self-belief patterns for more significant behaviors have only begun to be considered (e.g., Higgins, Simon, & Wells, 1988).

When considering the motivational implications of self-discrepancy theory, and especially the motivational implications of the positive psychological situations represented by actual:self-guide matches, it is important to recognize that people are not only motivated to reduce discrepancies or avoid experiencing negative psychological situations. They are also motivated to experience positive psychological situations. There is a common misconception that discrepancies are necessary to motivate people, that people with low or no self-discrepancies would have no driving force. With rare exception, people with low or no self-discrepancies typically possess a high level of matching attributes that represent a positive psychological situation, such as actual/own:ideal/own matches, representing the presence of positive outcomes. Although these matches are chronically available to the individual, they will only produce the experience of the positive psychological situation if they are activated. Thus, in order to experience the positive emotions associated with their self-congruencies, people are motivated to instantiate, and thereby activate, their self-congruencies.

People with self-congruencies, then, are motivated to enact or display their congruent self-attributes in order to activate the positive psychological situation represented by the congruency. A fuller understanding of the motivational implications of people's self-belief patterns, therefore, must include consideration of the motivational nature of congruencies as well as discrepancies. As mentioned earlier, it must also recognize that unpleasant emotions can be associated with either increased motivation or decreased motivation (e.g., dissatisfaction vs. hopelessness), and increased motivation can produce action or inaction (e.g., extreme fear leading to flight or fight vs. freeze or faint).

To address these issues from the perspective of self-discrepancy theory, one needs to (1) distinguish among different types of self-belief patterns, (2) identify the psychological situation represented in each pattern, and then (3) demonstrate that activation of a particular pattern (e.g., by priming one of its constituents) produces the emotional–motivational symptoms associated with the psychological situation embodied in the pattern. At least with adults, the mental representations of chronic self-belief patterns can be very complex (see Higgins, 1989). And given that self-evaluative processes can themselves involve multiple stages with multiple affects (see Higgins *et al.*, 1986b), the momentary psychological situations that people experience can also be very complex. Given the observed complexity of people's emotional–motivational states, a model that can capture this complexity is needed.

Acknowledgments

Support for writing this chapter, and for conducting the research it describes, was provided by National Institute of Mental Health Grant MH39429.

References

Abelson, R. P. (1983). Whatever became of consistency theory? *Personality and Social Psychology Bulletin,* **9,** 37–54.
Abramson, L. Y., Seligman, M. E. P., & Teasdale, J. D. (1978). Learned helplessness in humans: Critique and reformation. *Journal of Abnormal Psychology,* **87,** 49–74.
Adler, A. (1964). *Problems of neurosis.* New York: Harper & Row.
Allport, G. W. (1955). *Becoming.* New Haven, CT: Yale University Press.
Anderson, N. H. (1968). Likableness ratings of 555 personality-trait words. *Journal of Personality and Social Psychology,* **9,** 272–279.
Aronson, E. (1969). The theory of cognitive dissonance: A current perspective. In L. Berkowitz (Ed.), *Advances in experimental social psychology* (Vol. 4). New York: Academic Press.
Asch, S. E. (1952). *Social psychology.* Englewood Cliffs, NJ: Prentice-Hall.
Bandura, A. (1977). Self-efficacy: Toward a unifying theory of behavioral change. *Psychological Review,* **84,** 191–215.
Bandura, A. (1982). The self and mechanisms of agency. In J. Suls (Ed.), *Psychological perspectives on the self* (Vol. 1). Hillsdale, NJ: Erlbaum.
Bandura, A., & Schunk, D. H. (1981). Cultivating competence, self-efficacy and intrinsic interest through proximal self-motivation. *Journal of Personality and Social Psychology,* **41,** 586–598.
Bargh, J. A. (1984). Automatic and conscious processing of social information. In R. S. Wyer, Jr. & T. K. Srull (Eds.), *Handbook of social cognition* (Vol. 3, pp. 1–43). Hillsdale, NJ: Erlbaum.
Bargh, J. A., Bond, R. N., Lombardi, W. J., & Tota, M. E. (1986). The additive nature of chronic and temporary sources of construct accessibility. *Journal of Personality and Social Psychology,* **50,** 869–878.
Bargh, J. A., Lombardi, W. J., & Higgins, E. T. (1988). Automaticity of chronically accessible constructs in person × situation effects on person perception: It's just a matter of time. *Journal of Personality and Social Psychology,* **55,** 599–605.
Bargh, J. A., & Pietromonaco, P. (1982). Automatic information processing and social perception: The influence of trait information presented outside of conscious awareness on impression formation. *Journal of Personality and Social Psychology,* **43,** 437–449.
Bargh, J. A., & Pratto, F. (1986). Individual construct accessibility and perceptual selection. *Journal of Experimental Social Psychology,* **22,** 293–311.
Beck, A. T., Rush, A. J., Shaw, B. F., & Emery, G. (1979). *Cognitive therapy of depression.* New York: Guilford Press.
Beck, A. T., Ward, C. H., Mendelson, M., Mock, J., & Erbaugh, J. (1961). An inventory for measuring depression. *Archives of General Psychiatry,* **4,** 561–571.
Bentler, P. M. (1980). Multivariate analysis with latent variables: Causal modeling. *Annual Review of Psychology,* **31,** 419–456.
Bertenthal, B. I., & Fischer, K. W. (1978). Development of self-recognition in the infant. *Developmental Psychology,* **14,** 44–50.

Blatt, S. J., D'Afflitti, J. P., & Quinlan, D. M. (1976). Experiences of depression in normal young adults. *Journal of Abnormal Psychology*, **86,** 203–223.

Bramel, D. (1968). Dissonance, expectation, and the self. In R. P. Abelson, E. Aronson, W. J. McGuire, T. M. Newcomb, M. J. Rosenberg, and P. H. Tannenbaum (Eds.), *Theories of cognitive consistency: A sourcebook* (pp. 355–365). Chicago: Rand McNally.

Brim, O. G. (1976). Theories of the male-life crisis. *Counseling Psychologist: Counseling Adults*. Special Issue.

Bruner, J. S. (1964). The course of cognitive growth. *American Psychologist*, **19,** 1–15.

Carver, C. S., & Scheier, M. F. (1981). *Attention and self-regulation: A control-theory approach to human behavior*. New York: Springer-Verlag.

Case, R. (1985). *Intellectual development: Birth to adulthood*. New York: Academic Press.

Cohen, J., & Cohen, P. (1975). *Applied multiple regression/correlation analysis for the behavioral sciences*. Hillsdale, NJ: Erlbaum.

Collins, A. M., & Loftus, E. F. (1975). A spreading-activation theory of semantic processing. *Psychological Review*, **82,** 407–428.

Coopersmith, S. (1967). *The antecedents of self-esteem*. San Francisco: Freeman.

Derogatis, L. R., Lipman, R. S., Rickels, K., Uhlenhuth, E. H., & Covi, L. (1974). The Hopkins Symptom Checklist (HSCL): A self-report symptom inventory. *Behavioral Science*, **19,** 1–15.

Duval, S., & Wicklund, R. A. (1972). *A theory of objective self-awareness*. New York: Academic Press.

Dweck, C. S., & Elliot, E. S. (1983). Achievement motivation. In P. H. Mussen (Ed.), *Handbook of child psychology: Vol. 4. Socialization, personality, and social development* (pp. 643–691). New York: Wiley.

Ellis, A. (1962). *Reason and emotion in psychotherapy*. New York: Lyle Stuart.

Epstein, S. (1973). The self-concept revisited: Or a theory of a theory. *American Psychologist*, **28,** 404–416.

Epstein, S. (1978). Avoidance–approach: The fifth basic conflict. *Journal of Consulting and Clinical Psychology*, **46,** 1016–1022.

Erikson, E. H. (1963). *Childhood and society* (2nd ed.). New York: W. W. Norton & Co. (Original publication, 1950)

Feffer, M. (1970). Developmental analysis of interpersonal behavior. *Psychological Review*, **77,** 197–214.

Festinger, L. (1942). A theoretical interpretation of shifts in level of aspiration. *Psychological Review*, **49,** 235–250.

Festinger, L. (1957). *A theory of cognitive dissonance*. Evanston, IL: Row, Peterson.

Fischer, K. W. (1980). A theory of cognitive development: The control and construction of hierarchies of skills. *Psychological Review*, **87,** 477–531.

Fiske, S. T., & Dyer, L. M. (1985). Structure and development of social schemata: Evidence from positive and negative transfer effects. *Journal of Personality and Social Psychology*, **48,** 839–852.

Flavell, J. H., Botkin, P. T., Fry, C. L., Wright, J. W., & Jarvis, P. E. (1968). *The development of role-taking and communication skills in children*. New York: Wiley.

Freud, S. (1961). The ego and the id. In J. Strachey (Ed. and Trans.), *Standard edition of the complete psychological works of Sigmund Freud* (Vol. 19, pp. 3–66). London: Hogarth Press. (Original work published 1923)

Greenwald, A. G., & Pratkanis, A. R. (1984). The self. In R. S. Wyer & T. K. Srull (Eds.), *Handbook of social cognition* (Vol. 3, pp. 129–178). Hillsdale, NJ: Erlbaum.

Hamilton, A. M. (1960). A rating scale for depression. *Journal of Neurology and Neurosurgery in Pscyhiatry*, **23,** 56–62.

Harter, S. (1983). Developmental perspectives on the self-system. In P. H. Mussen (Ed.), *Handbook of child psychology, Volume IV: Socialization, personality and social development* (pp. 275–385). New York: John Wiley & Sons.

Harter, S. (1986). Cognitive-developmental processes in the integration of concepts about emotions and the self. *Social Cognition,* **4,** 119–151.

Hayes-Roth, B. (1977). Evolution of cognitive structures and processes. *Psychological Review,* **84,** 260–278.

Heider, F. (1958). *The psychology of interpersonal relations.* New York: Wiley.

Heilizer, F. (1977). A review of theory and research on Miller's response competition (conflict) models. *The Journal of General Psychology,* **97,** 227–280.

Higgins, E. T. (1981). Role-taking and social judgment: Alternative developmental perspectives and processes. In J. H. Flavell & L. Ross (Eds.), *Social cognitive development: Frontiers and possible futures.* Cambridge: Cambridge University Press.

Higgins, E. T. (1987). Self-discrepancy: A theory relating self and affect. *Psychological Review,* **94,** 319–340.

Higgins, E. T. (1989). Continuities and discontinuities in self-regulatory and self-evaluative processes: A developmental theory relating self and affect. *Journal of Personality,* in press.

Higgins, E. T., & Bargh, J. A. (1987). Social cognition and social perception. *Annual Review of Psychology,* **38,** 369–425.

Higgins, E. T., Bargh, J. A., & Lombardi, W. (1985a). The nature of priming effects on categorization. *Journal of Experimental Psychology: Learning, Memory and Cognition,* **11,** 59–69.

Higgins, E. T., Bond, R. N., Klein, R., & Strauman, T. (1986a). Self-discrepancies and emotional vulnerability: How magnitude, accessibility, and type of discrepancy influence affect. *Journal of Personality and Social Psychology,* **51,** 5–15.

Higgins, E. T., & King, G. (1981). Accessibility of social constructs: Information processing consequences of individual and contextual variability. In N. Cantor & J. Kihlstrom (Eds.), *Personality, cognition, and social interaction.* Hillsdale, NJ: Erlbaum.

Higgins, E. T., King, G. A., & Mavin, G. H. (1982). Individual construct accessibility and subjective impressions and recall. *Journal of Personality and Social Psychology,* **43,** 35–47.

Higgins, E. T., Klein, R., & Strauman, T. (1985b). Self-concept discrepancy theory: A psychological model for distinguishing among different aspects of depression and anxiety. *Social Cognition,* **3,** 51–76.

Higgins, E. T., Klein, R., & Strauman, T. (1987). Self- discrepancies: Distinguishing among self-states, self-state conflicts, and emotional vulnerabilities. In K. M. Yardley & T. M. Honess (Eds.), *Self and identity: Psychosocial perspectives* (pp. 173–186). New York: Wiley.

Higgins, E. T., Rholes, W. S. & Jones, C. R. (1977). Category accessibility and impression formation. *Journal of Experimental Social Psychology,* **13,** 141–154.

Higgins, E. T., Simon, M., & Wells, R. S. (1988). A model of evaluative processes and "job satisfaction": When differences in standards make a difference. In R. Cardy, J. Newman, & S. M. Puffer (Eds), *Advances in information processing in organizations* (Vol. 3). Greenwich, CT: JAI Press, in press.

Higgins, E. T., Strauman, T., & Klein, R. (1986b). Standards and the process of self-evaluation: Multiple affects from multiple stages. In R. M. Sorrentino & E. T. Higgins (Eds.), *Handbook of motivation and cognition: Foundations of social behavior* (pp. 23–63). New York: Guilford Press.

Higgins, E. T., & Tykocinsky, O. (1987). *Vulnerabilities from self-beliefs about the past, present, and future.* Unpublished manuscript, New York University.

Higgins, E. T., Van Hook, E., & Dorfman, D. (1988). Do self attributes form a cognitive structure? *Social Cognition,* **6,** 177–207.

Hoge, D. R., & McCarthy, J. D. (1983). Issues of validity and reliability in the use of real–ideal discrepancy scores to measure self-regard. *Journal of Personality and Social Psychology,* **44,** 1048–1055.

Holt, R. R. (1976). Drive or wish? A reconsideration of the psychoanalytic theory of motivation. In M. M. Gill & P. S. Holzman (Eds.), Psychology versus metapsychology: Psychoanalytic essays in memory of George S. Klein. *Psychological Issues,* **9**(4), 158–197.

Horney, K. (1946). *Our inner conflicts: A constructive theory of neurosis.* London: Routledge & Kegan Paul.
Horowitz, M. (1976), *Stress response syndromes.* New York: Jason-Aronson.
Huttenlocher, J., & Higgins, E. T. (1978). Issues in the study of symbolic development. In W. A. Collins (Ed.), *Minnesota symposia on child psychology* (Vol. 2, pp. 98–140). Hillsdale, NJ: Erlbaum.
Jacobs, D. (1971). Moods–emotion–affect: The nature of and manipulation of affective states with particular reference to positive affective states and emotional illness. In A. Jacobs & L. B. Sachs (Eds.), *The psychology of private events.* New York: Academic Press.
James, W. (1948). *Psychology.* New York: The World Publishing Company. (Original publication, 1890)
Kelly, G. A. (1955). *The psychology of personal constructs.* New York: W. W. Morton.
Kemper, T. D. (1978). *A social interactional theory of emotions.* New York: Wiley.
Klein, G. S. (1970). *Perception, motives and personality.* New York: Knopf.
Kuiper, N. A., Derry, P. A., & MacDonald, M. R. (1982). Self-reference and person perception in depression: A social cognition perspective. In G. Weary & H. Mirels (Eds.), *Integrations of clinical and social psychology.* New York: Oxford University Press.
Lazarus, A. A. (1968). Learning theory and the treatment of depression. *Behavior Research and Therapy,* **6,** 83–89.
Lecky, P. (1961). *Self-consistency: A theory of personality.* New York: The Shoe String Press.
Levinson, D. J. (1978). *The seasons of a man's life.* New York: Ballantine Books.
Lewin, K. (1935). *A dynamic theory of personality.* New York: McGraw-Hill.
Lewin, K. (1951). *Field theory in social science.* New York: Harper.
Lewis, M., & Brooks-Gunn, J. (1979). *Social cognition and the acquisition of self.* New York: Plenum.
Liebowitz, M. R., Gorman, J. M., Fyer, A., & Klein, D. F. (1985). Social phobia: Review of a neglected disorder. *Archives of General Psychiatry,* **42,** 729–736.
Maccoby, E. E., & Martin, J. A. (1983). Socialization in the context of the family: Parent-child interaction. In P. H. Mussen (Ed.), *Handbook of child psychology: Vol 4. Socialization, personality, and social development* (pp. 643–691). New York: Wiley.
Magaro, P., & Smith, P. (1981). The personality of clinical types: An empirically derived taxonomy. *Journal of Clinical Psychology,* **37,** 796–809.
Mahler, M. S., Pine, F., & Bergman, A. (1975). *The psychological birth of the human infant.* New York: Basic Books.
Markus, H., & Nurius, P. (1986). Possible selves. *American Psychologist,* **41,** 954–969.
Markus, H., & Wurf, E. (1987). The dynamic self-concept: A social psychological perspective. *Annual Review of Psychology,* **38,** 299–337.
Merton, R. K. (1957). *Social theory and social structure.* Glencoe, IL: The Free Press.
Miller, G. A., Galanter, E., & Pribram, K. H. (1960). *Plans and the structure of behavior.* New York: Holt, Rinehart & Winston.
Miller, N. E. (1944). Experimental studies of conflict. In J. McV. Hunt (Ed.), *Personality and the behavior disorders* (Vol. 1). New York: Ronald Press.
Miller, N. E. (1959). Liberalization of basic S-R concepts: Extensions to conflict behavior, motivation, and social learning. In S. Koch (Ed.), *Psychology: A study of a science: Vol. 2. General systematic formulations, learning, and special processes* (pp. 196–292). New York: McGraw-Hill.
Moretti, M., & Higgins, E. T. (1987, June). *Attribute valence vs. guide discrepancy as predictors of depression and self-esteem.* Paper presented at the annual meeting of the Canadian Psychological Association, Vancouver, British Columbia, Canada.
Morse, S. J. & Gergen, K. J. (1970). Social comparison, self-consistency, and the concept of self. *Journal of Personality and Social Psychology,* **16,** 148–156.
Mowrer, O. H. (1960). *Learning theory and behavior.* New York: Wiley.
Murray, H. A. (1938). *Exploration in personality.* New York: Oxford University Press.

Piaget, J. (1951). *Play, dreams and imitation in childhood.* New York: Norton.
Piaget, J. (1965). *The moral judgment of the child.* New York: Free Press. (Original trans, published 1932)
Piers, G., & Singer, M. B. (1971). *Shame and guilt.* New York: W. W. Norton.
Plutchik, R. (1962). *The emotions: Facts, theories, and a new model.* New York: Random House.
Radke-Yarrow, M., Zahn-Waxler, C., & Chapman, M. (1983). Children's prosocial dispositions and behavior. In P. H. Mussen (Ed.), *Handbook of child psychology: Vol. 4. Socialization, personality, and social development* (pp. 643–691). New York: Wiley.
Rogers, C. R. (1959). A theory of therapy, personality, and interpersonal relationships, as developed in the client-centered framework. In S. Koch (Ed.), *Psychology: A study of a science: Vol. 3. Formulations of the person and the social context* (pp. 184–256). New York: McGraw-Hill.
Rogers, C. R. (1961). *On becoming a person.* Boston: Houghton Mifflin Company.
Rosenberg, M. (1965). *Society and the adolescent self-image.* Princeton, NJ: Princeton University Press.
Roseman, I. J. (1984). Cognitive determinants of emotion: A structural theory. *Review of Personality and Social Psychology,* **5,** 11–36.
Rotter, J. B. (1942). Level of aspiration as a method of studying personality. 1: A critical review of methodology. *Psychological Review,* **49,** 463–474.
Ruble, D. N., & Rholes, W. S. (1981). The development of children's perceptions and attributions about their social world. In J. D. Harvey, W. Ickes, & R. F. Kidd (Eds.), *New directions in attribution research* (Vol. 3). Hillsdale, NJ: Erlbaum.
Schafer, R. (1967). Ideals, the ego ideal, and the ideal self. In R. R. Holt (Ed.), Motives and thought: Psychoanalytic essays in honor of David Rapaport. *Psychological Issues,* 5(2–3), 131–174.
Schlenker, B. R. (1985). Identity and self-identification. In B. R. Schlenker (Ed.), *The self and social life* (pp. 65–100). New York: McGraw-Hill.
Selman, R. L., & Byrne, D. F. (1974). A structural-developmental analysis of levels of role-taking in middle childhood. *Child Development,* **45,** 803–806.
Shantz, C. U. (1983). Social cognition. In P. H. Mussen (Ed.), J. H. Flavell & E. M. Markman (Vol. Eds.), *Carmichael's manual of child psychology. Vol. 3: Cognitive Development* (4th ed., pp. 495–555.). New York: Wiley.
Shapiro, D. (1965). *Neurotic styles.* New York: Basic Books.
Snygg, D., & Combs, A. W. (1949). *Individual behavior.* New York: Harper & Row.
Sorrentino, R. M., & Higgins, E. T. (1986). Motivation and cognition: Warming up to synergism. In R. M. Sorrentino & E. T. Higgins (Eds.), *Handbook of motivation and cognition: Foundations of social behavior* (pp. 3–19). Hillsdale, NJ: Erlbaum.
Srull, T. K., & Wyer, R. S. (1979). The role of category accessibility in the interpretation of information about persons: Some determinants and implications. *Journal of Personality and Social Psychology,* **37,** 1660–1672.
Srull, T. K., & Wyer, R. S., Jr. (1980). Category accessibility and social perception: Some implications for the study of person memory and interpersonal judgments. *Journal of Personality and Social Psychology,* **38,** 841–856.
Stein, N. L., & Jewett, J. L. (1982). A conceptual analysis of the meaning of negative emotions: Implications for a theory of development. In C. E. Izard (Ed.), *Measuring emotions in infants and children* (pp. 401–443). New York: Cambridge University Press.
Strauman, T. J. (1989). Self-discrepancies in clinical depression and social phobia: Cognitive structures that underlie affective disorders? *Journal of Abnormal Psychology,* in press.
Strauman, T. J., & Higgins, E. T. (1987). Automatic activation of self-discrepancies and emotional syndromes: When cognitive structures influence affect. *Journal of Personality and Social Psychology,* **53,** 1004–1014.
Strauman, T. J., & Higgins, E. T. (1989). Self-discrepancies as predictors of vulnerability to distinct syndromes of chronic emotional disease. *Journal of Personality,* in press.

Sullivan, H. S., (1953). *The collected works of Harvey Stack Sullivan (Vol. 1)*. Edited by H. S. Perry and M. L. Gawel. New York: W. W. Norton & Co.

Swann, W. B., Jr. (1983). Self-verification: Bringing social reality into harmony with the self. In J. Suls & A. G. Greenwald (Eds.), *Social psychological perspectives on the self* (Vol. 2, pp. 33–66). Hillsdale, NJ: Erlbaum.

Van Hook, E., & Higgins, E. T. (1988). Self-related problems beyond the self-concept: Motivational consequences of discrepant self-guides. *Journal of Personality and Social Psychology, 55,* 625–633.

Warren, R. E. (1972). Stimulus encoding and memory. *Journal of Experimental Psychology, 94,* 90–100.

Watson, D., & Friend, R. (1969). Measurement of social-evaluative anxiety. *Journal of Consulting and Clinical Psychology, 33,* 448–457.

Weiner, B. (1986). Cognition, emotion, and action. In R. M. Sorrentino & E. T. Higgins (Eds.), *Handbook of motivation and cognition: Foundations of social behavior*. New York: Guilford Press.

Wells, L. E., & Marwell, G. (1976). *Self-esteem: Its conceptualization and measurement*. Beverly Hills, CA: Sage.

Werner, H. (1957). *Comparative psychology of mental development*. New York: International Universities Press.

Werner, H., & Kaplan, B. (1963). *Symbol formation*. New York: Wiley.

Wicklund, R. A., & Gollwitzer, P. M. (1982). *Symbolic self-completion*. Hillsdale, NJ: Erlbaum.

Wiener, N. (1948). *Cybernetics: Control and communication in the animal and the machine*. Cambridge, MA: M.I.T. Press.

Wyer, R. S. & Srull, T. K. (1981). Category accessibility: Some theoretical and empirical issues concerning the processing of social stimulus information. In E. T. Higgins, C. P. Herman, & M. P. Zanna (Eds.), *Social cognition: The Ontario Symposium*. Hillsdale, NJ: Erlbaum.

Wyer R. S. Jr., & Srull, T. K. (1986). Human cognition in its social context. *Psychological Review, 93,* 322–359.

Wylie, R. C. (1961). *The self-concept*. Lincoln: University of Nebraska Press.

Wylie, R. C. (1979). *The self-concept* (rev. ed.). Lincoln: University of Nebraska Press.

MINDING MATTERS: THE CONSEQUENCES OF MINDLESSNESS–MINDFULNESS

Ellen J. Langer

DEPARTMENT OF PSYCHOLOGY
HARVARD UNIVERSITY
CAMBRIDGE, MASSACHUSETTS 02138

I. Overview

How much ostensibly thoughtful action is best described as mindless? Enough time has elapsed since we raised the issue in 1978 (Langer, Blank, & Chanowitz, 1978) to warrant our asking the question again. The increased experience and additional reflection coming with this passage of time suggests that it is worthwhile to reconsider the concepts of mindlessness and mindfulness and refine (and even revise to some extent) our understanding of these basic modes of human life.

Social psychology is now replete with examples of minimal information processing. The discipline has joined cognitive psychology in the realization that individuals can perform seemingly complex tasks with little if any active mental involvement. In the 1960s, social psychologists used the lay scientist metaphor to describe ordinary behavior, but it is now clear that this description was incomplete. Although people are certainly capable of acting mindfully, they frequently respond in a routinized, mindless way. In much of everyday life, people rely on distinctions drawn in the past; they overly depend on structures of situations representative of the underlying meaning without making new distinctions. This mindlessness holds the world still and prevents an awareness that things could be otherwise.

Now that we have a better understanding of the different forms information processing may take, it becomes important to consider the consequences of whether information is processed mindfully or mindlessly. This is the concern of the present article. Data are reported herein indicating that mindlessness may be severely limiting. Research points to how mindlessly held categories limit human performance and even have a negative impact on physical health. Findings are also described that suggest new ways to use mindlessness to one's advantage. Finally, research is discussed that suggests how mindlessness can be prevented.

This article also seeks to develop a clearer theoretical understanding of the mindful and mindless modes. In doing so, some of their general attributes are more fully elaborated, while some previously proposed features are significantly modified.

The implicit position of this article is that in spite of our increased awareness of limited information processing, people in general still are far more mindless than psychologists have assumed. The explicit position is that through mindful social psychological means such as changing expectations and other cognitive restructuring, human potential may be extended far beyond currently accepted limits.

II. Mindlessness and Mindfulness

Most researchers deal with the way information is processed, and so they might wish to label what I call "mindlessness" as *minimal information processing*. I believe that this is too narrow a conception, however, because the evidence suggests that the actor's general state of mind is relevant, and it, too, must be taken into account. It is my proposal that mindlessness and mindfulness are not merely ways of responding but are basic states of mind. In this view, particular patterns of response do not, in themselves, fully constitute mindlessness or mindfulness; rather, these response patterns are symptomatic of them. Mindlessness and mindfulness are proposed to be basic underlying states of the organism as a whole (states of being) and, as such, involve affective as well as cognitive factors. Accordingly, while mindlessness–mindfulness entail all that is implied by cognitive inflexibility–flexibility, they also include *more*.

Moreover, we speak of mindlessness instead of minimal information processing because the distinction between mindfulness and mindlessness is not just quantitative but also qualitative. It is not just that less information is attended to. The information that has been mindlessly processed is not readily available for conscious consideration. As we show in this article, this distinction may be of great consequence when issues of self-esteem are relevant.

I view mindfulness as a state of alertness and lively awareness, which is specifically manifested in typical ways. Generally, mindfulness is expressed in active information processing, characterized by cognitive differentiation: the creation of categories and distinctions. The act of creating distinctions tacitly creates new categories and vice versa. The distinctions drawn may be judged to be major or minor, but they are mindfully drawn just the same. Mindfulness may be seen as creating (noticing) multiple perspectives, or being aware of context. When in this state, the person is becoming more and more differentiated while differentiating the external world. The entire individual is involved in creating. In contrast, in a mindless mode, the individual relies on categories that have already been formed and distinctions that have already been drawn.

Mindlessness is a state of reduced attention. It is expressed in behavior that is rigid and rule-governed rather than rule-guided. The individual becomes mindlessly trapped by categories that were previously created when in a mindful mode. This entrapment limits people both physiologically and behaviorally. Physiological consequences are poor health; behavioral consequences impose unnecessary restrictions on performance. It is important to reemphasize that mindlessness involves rigidity on both cognitive and emotional levels. Moreover, it must be noted that this rigidity is unintentional—it is inflexibility by default rather than by design.

In terms of information theory, mindfulness may be seen as entropy-reducing and mindlessness as entropy-constant. Further, mindfulness is proposed to be capacity-increasing and mindlessness to be capacity-fixing. Thus, this theory differs from automatic–controlled processing theory in assuming (at least for heuristic purposes) that capacity is blind rather than fixed. As is discussed later in some detail, this difference in the assumptions made by these two approaches, as well as their difference in molar as opposed to molecular focus, partly explain how the concepts of mindlessness and mindfulness differ from the concepts of automatic and controlled processing in the work of Schneider and Shiffrin (1977, Shiffrin & Schneider, 1977).

An initial response to the foregoing theory is likely to be that mindlessness is often necessary because there seems to be a forced choice between being mindful of everything, which for most people is impossible, or being mindless of some things to assist mindfulness in regard to others. The baseball player cannot simultaneously think about how to hold the bat, where to hit the ball, and why she or he is playing the game in the first place all at once. Having overlearned how to hold the bat, the player now may proceed to notice which fielders are off-guard to make possible a wise decision as to where to hit the ball. The player, no longer mindful of rudimentary skills, is able to be mindful of something else. Thus, it seems that mindlessness is essential to advanced learning.

A proper consideration of mindfulness, however, reveals that it is not necessary to reach such a conclusion. Mindfulness is a state of being. The person whose mind–body organism is in a mindful mode, in a global sense, is said to be in a mindful environmental interaction in specific channels as the situation demands. For instance, if changed circumstances (e.g., drizzle) cause other ways of gripping the bat to be more adaptive, a player in an overall mindful mode will become aware of this and actively direct attention toward the desirable modification. To be mindful in regard to a specific area (X) does not require that attention be consciously and creatively deployed there continuously; rather, it means that one will be adaptively responsive concerning X and can quickly respond through the deliberate, discriminative mode as appropriate. (As an aside, experts typically do *not* take the basics for granted; they remain alert to potential changes in the situation.)

Thus, we can speak of two values of mindfulness in relationship to specific areas: expressed and latent (or potential). The former occurs when conscious, discriminative attention is deployed in dealing with that area. The latter type of mindfulness, the latent type, is present anytime the relationship of the organism to the area is such that with a change in circumstance, the expressed mode will appropriately activate. In a mindful state of being, an individual would relate to most areas in either the expressed or potential type of mindfulness. However, a person could be in a mindful state in regard to some areas and yet be mindlessly related to other areas. This could occur for information that was initially processed in a mindless way because, according to past research, mindlessly processed information does not always come up for reconsideration, even when it is advantageous to reconsider it (Chanowitz & Langer, 1981; Langer & Imber, 1979).

Research (described herein) suggests that there may be a way to learn about the world that enables us to hold it constant sufficiently to take action (e.g., to proceed beyond the basics) but that does not render the information unavailable when reconsideration would be advantageous. That is, we may be able to form categories and continue to use those that we feel are adaptive in a way that does not lead us to be mindless. This alternative way of learning about the world, which may prevent mindlessness without necessitating expressed mindful consideration of everything, is discussed after examination of the negative consequences of mindlessness and placement of the mindlessness–mindfulness concept in its social-psychological context.

The contention that mindlessness is necessary at times also seems to be implied by my earlier work, suggesting that mindfulness is effortful (cf. Langer, 1978). However, I have gradually revised my views on this point and now believe that mindfulness is *not* more effortful than mindlessness, and may even be essentially effortless. Consequently, whereas I at one time believed it was beneficial to be mindless some of the time (in order to take rest), I no longer believe in the necessity for such supposedly restful mindless interludes. (Perhaps of relevance is a study of arthritis patients in which increased mindfulness resulted in greater happiness [Langer, Field, Pachas, & Abrams, 1988c]). What I do propose is that effort is involved in switching from a mindless to a mindful mode, analogous to the force required to change the direction of a moving object, even when in a frictionless medium. Hence, mindfulness may often appear effortful only because of the effort required to break out of a mindless mode; however, the mindful mode itself may be effortless and not capacity-consuming but capacity-increasing.

Several areas in social psychology make use of research on minimal information processing indicating that people often try to reduce their cognitive activity. These include findings suggesting that (1) people search for stable dispositional attributions rather than cognitively more complex situational or interactional attributions (Jones & Davis, 1965; Jones & Nisbett, 1972; Smith & Miller, 1983); (2) people seek a sufficient explanation for an event rather than seek or infer multiple sufficient causes (Carlston, 1980; Kanouse, 1972); (3) even when given the opportunity to consider more information, people often do not take it (Bargh, 1982; Kiesler, 1966; Newtson, 1976); (4) people tend to show a proclivity both to form illusory correlations (Chapman & Chapman, 1967; Crocker, 1981; Chapman, 1967; Hamilton, 1981; Ward & Jenkins, 1965); and to use judgmental heuristics (Nisbett & Ross, 1980; Tversky & Kahneman, 1974). These diverse research results all speak to the general tendency of people to use minimal cues to guide their behavior. It is not that people never seek out information; we know from the daily sale of newspapers, the popularity of travel to foreign lands, the widespread desire to hear gossip, and even the popularity of games like chess and bridge that they do. This research is only interesting in the face of common observations of people actively engaged in thoughtful action.

Newer work is now appropriately examining *when* people behave mindlessly and when they use more complex strategies. For example, Langer, Blank, and Chanowitz (1978), and Harkness, DeBono, and Borgida (1985) have shown that personal involvement results in the use of more complex reasoning strategies. Moreover, these studies indicate that this choice in processing strategies occurs when the information is first encoded.

McAllister, Mitchell, and Beach (1979) also found that when an outcome is personally relevant, people are more likely to use complex decision strategies. Researchers have identified this trend in a variety of settings. For example, Cvetkovitch (1978) observed it in a gambling situation and Chaiken (1980) noted the same trend in persuasive messages. In a similar vein, Janis and Mann (1977) found that people who expect to justify their decisions are more mindful decision makers.

In Tetlock's (1983) study of the effects of accountability on thought, he found that subjects became more mindful when they expected to have to justify their opinions to an unknown audience. Under these circumstances, their thoughts became more differentiated or complex. Apparently, it is potentially too costly under these conditions not to prepare oneself for a wide variety of possible criticisms. Under friendlier circumstances, however, our single-minded views of the world typically suffice. At the least, in these situations people can unthinkingly offer the socially accepted justifications if any are requested.

While the importance of the decision and accountability for it may increase the likelihood that it will be mindfully considered, it does not ensure that it will be. Indeed, as Janis (1972) has shown us, decisions that affect international security may be made mindlessly by our country's highest leaders, engaged in groupthink. Decisions that led to some of the worst fiascos in American history were made mindlessly.

Along similar lines, Charlan Nemeth (1986) has reported that persistent exposure to the majority opinion leads many people to accept that opinion mindlessly. However, persistent exposure to the minority view may result in greater mindfulness, presumably because they attend to more aspects of the situation, so that majority opinions are then reappraised. Without minority views expressed, mindlessness is often the rule.

On the other hand, the work reviewed by Taylor and Fiske (1978) on the "top of the head" phenomenon and the work by Abelson and his colleagues on scripts (e.g., Abelson, 1981; Schank & Abelson, 1977) has shown us that successful social behavior may be accomplished by minimal information processing. Whether the consequences are positive or negative, the fact of minimal information processing seems clear.

Indeed, in 1978, I proposed that *mindfulness* may occur only under one or more of the following conditions: (1) when significantly more effort is demanded by the situation than was required on previous occasions, (2) when the external factors in the situation disrupt initiation of the mindless sequence, (3) when external factors prevent the completion of the behavior, or (4) when negative or positive consequences are experienced that are sufficiently discrepant with the consequences of prior enactments of the same behavior (Langer, 1978).

Research now bears out these hypotheses (cf. Abele, 1985; Berscheid, Graziano, Monson, & Derner, 1976; Dweck & Diener, 1978; Enzle & Shopflocher, 1978; Hastie, 1984; Lalljee, Watson, & White, 1982; Mikula & Schlamberger, 1984; Pyszczynski & Greenberg, 1981; Wong & Weiner, 1981). More specifically, this research suggests that unless people are explicitly questioned, unless they experience an unexpected failure or a novel consequence, or unless they expect future interaction for which information may be relevant, people do not process as much information as many cognition researchers once thought.

III. Mindlessness–Mindfulness and Health

Concern regarding the pervasiveness of mindlessness becomes important when we look at the relationship between mindfulness–mindlessness and health. There are essentially two ways in which the mindfulness–mindlessness variable is hypothesized to affect health, one direct and one indirect. The indirect influence involves mindful use of one's mindlessness, and we return to this when we discuss performance deficits. For the moment, let us consider the direct effect of mindlessness on the body.

It is useful, I think, to make the strong claim that the body begins to die as the mind ceases to deal with novelty. Longitudinal studies typically find that scores on IQ tests fall prior to death (Abrahms, 1976; Birren, 1968; Hall, Savage, Bolten, Pidwell, & Blessed, 1972; Jarvik & Blum, 1971; Jarvik & Falek, 1963; Riegel, Riegel, & Meyer, 1967). Although mindfulness and intelligence as measured by IQ tests are quite distinct (thoughts considered unintelligent may be creatively produced), they are obviously related (so-called intelligent thoughts probably yield more novel associations). This "terminal drop," as it is called, may indicate a causal relationship from mindlessness to illness, and not, as usually supposed, the other way around.

We tested this relationship in a recent prospective experimental investigation. We were interested in seeing whether a mindfullness treatment would promote longevity in a group of elderly residents of a nursing home (Alexander, Langer, Newman, Chandler, & Davies, 1988).

With colleagues especially interested in the effects of transcendental meditation (TM) on health for the elderly, we conducted an experiment (Alexander *et al.*, 1988) in which we adapted our mindfulness idea to meet the more established program used for the practice of TM. In examining this experiment, it is important to distinguish between active and inactive states of mind. In the active state, the mind is either interacting with the environment or with itself (as in operational thought). As was discussed earlier, there are two basic modes of such activity: (1) mindfulness, an alert, flexible mode, and (2) mindlessness, which, relative to the former, is dull and inflexible. There also appear to be two basic modes in which the mind can be inactive (restful). The more familiar is sleep, characterized by dullness. The other is a state of restful alertness (Alexander *et al.*, 1988), which appears to arise through meditative procedures.

Three groups were designed to be as similar as possible in structure. There was a TM group, a high-mindfulness group, and a low-mindfulness (or relaxation) control group. All subjects sat with their eyes closed twice a day for 20 minutes for 12 weeks and practiced following their instructions. Of course, while this is not likely to be the optimal setting for mindfulness, it permitted a comparison of both of the hypothesized alert groups with the low alertness–relaxation control group. In essence, the mindful group was asked to construct novel thoughts.

Because the mind and body are mutually interrelated, it has been hypothesized that the restfully alert and orderly mental state achieved through TM would be accompanied by integrated physiological states conducive for increased health, and there is considerable research supportive of this hypotheses (Orme-Johnson & Farrow, 1977). We therefore expected both the TM group and the actively mindful group to live longer than comparison subjects. The results were striking. Three years later, no one had died in the TM group and 87.5% of the mindful group was still alive, compared with 62.5% of the baseline group. When we assessed longevity as a function of rated alertness, we found the expected relationship between the alertness of one's mind and health. The mindfulness treatment also resulted in an increase in perceived control.

Reviewing our earlier study on the effects of decision making for elderly adults (Langer & Rodin, 1976; Rodin & Langer, 1977), we find hints of a relationship between mindfulness and health. We originally looked at that nursing home study in terms of perceived control. Thus, it is in order briefly to explicate the relationship between control and mindfulness (see Chanowitz & Langer, 1980; Langer, 1983; and Piper & Langer, 1984 for a fuller discussion of this point).

The mindfulness concept is not meant to replace the concept of control. One could be mindful and yet not experience control. Yet, to the extent one experiences control, one is mindful. The only control that makes sense is mindful. A sense of control can be achieved through successfully meeting novel challenges. Everyday, routine, and expected successes do not strengthen one's sense of control. Perceiving control is not just feeling comfortable. It is *mastering*—going from the unknown to the known. The person must be mindful to develop the experience of control. And mindfulness typically, but not necessarily, gives rise to feelings of control. Mindfully considering all the ways one is helpless obviously would not lead to feelings of control. Yet mindlessly taking any one of these ways of being helpless as necessarily true may be worse still. In any case, because it is painful, people are likely to be mindful of as little negative content as they can.

Control and mindfulness exist in an interactive and reciprocal relationship to each other. Perceiving control results in greater risk taking (for example, Langer, 1975). Risk taking is necessarily mindful. When mindful, the individual is in a position to notice more in the environment. And this openness may enable the individual to see opportunities for control that the mindless person would overlook (see the aforementioned Alexander *et al.*, 1988, study).

In the Langer and Rodin (1976) experiment we encouraged decision making, provided decisions to make, and gave subjects a plant to take care of. Comparison subjects were treated the same way except that they were given a staff-supported rather than a self-supporting communication. The results revealed that the decision-making group was happier, more alert, and more active than the comparison group. In an 18-month follow-up to that study (Rodin & Langer, 1977), we found that the experimental group also lived longer; 15% of this group had died, compared to 30% of the comparison group.

The fact of psychological death is not new (see Seligman, 1975, for example). What is new here is that we are suggesting a cognitive mechanism that might have led to these deaths. Those psychological factors that reciprocally and interactively lead to mindlessness (e.g., depression, perceived lack of control, acute low self-esteem) may promote ill health or premature death. For example, although mindful depression is possible, when one is feeling depressed, one often retreats into familiar and away from risk-taking situations. The familiar is safe. However, if unpredictable events are avoided, there is little opportunity for mindfulness. And it is mindfulness that we believe to be essential for survival.

Consider recent work by Pennebaker and his colleagues. Pennebaker and Hoover (1985) found that people who had traumatic sexual experiences tended to keep those experiences to themselves. The consequences of this inhibition were health problems. Pennebaker and O'Heeron (1984) found that death of a spouse was more likely to cause illness in those who did not confide in others about the experience. Confiding helps people to organize their thoughts about the event (Meichenbaum, 1977) or can give meaning to the trauma (Silver & Wortman, 1980). Both of these processes are clearly mindful. New thought about any content, if it is self-sustaining, should result in physiological benefits if it continues.

Another experiment we conducted with the elderly may help us assess this hypothesis. In this study we found that progressively increasing the cognitive demands made on subjects over 3 weeks resulted in improvements in long- and short-term memory (Langer, Rodin, Beck, Spitzer, & Weinman, 1979). Once again the follow-up investigation suggested that this mindfulness treatment may be good for one's health. When we returned 2 years later, we found that only 7% of the mindfulness group had died versus approximately 30% of each of two comparison groups. If we consider that several of the people who left the nursing home to go to the hospital had died, the numbers are even more striking. Of the mindfulness group, 14% had died or had been discharged to the hospital, compared to 53% of each of two comparison groups. Additional measures on those still living revealed that the group purported to be more mindful was indeed more mindful. For example, they spontaneously mentioned more traits when questioned about their roommates and more details when describing their rooms (Langer, Beck, Janoff-Bulman, & Timko, 1984).

In that same investigation, we also looked at the relationship between mindfulness and labeled senility. At this time, the medical community did not have a clear sense of this disorder, its parameters, or its subcategories. Because we were not taking computerized axial tomography (C A T) scans to make possible confident physical diagnoses, we chose to consider people whose behavior alone had led the nursing home staff (i.e., community doctors) to affix the label "senile." We felt that at the least, the *label* "senile" had psychological significance. We began by looking at mindlessness–mindfulness as discrete categories and considered that people who enter nursing homes are either mindless or mindful. If they face excessive routine, they may suffer excessive mindlessness. Based on our previous investigations, we believed that such mindlessness apparently results in premature death. Therefore, we were inclined to believe that, Alzheimer's disease aside, labeled senility may indicate *mindfulness,* and thus an adaptive response to an overly routinized environment.

It certainly appears less than ideally adaptive for tiresome old people to keep discussing what seems to be the same things over and over again, and to notice aspects of the environment the rest of us think of as trivial. These elderly adults may be breaking down familiar categories that their nonsenile counterparts continue to take for granted and ignore. The *content* of this senility is clearly socially maladaptive, but the *process* still may be biologically adaptive. It is the bizarre content that leads us to a diagnosis of senility for elderly adults. And it is the label *senility* that leads us to overlook anything that may be positive about this disorder. Nevertheless, the processes employed by the elderly adult that result in the label *senile* may be characterized as mindful.

Measures that were taken support this mindfulness interpretation. For example, senile labeled subjects found more novel uses for familiar objects than the comparison group did. Moreover, the uses were judged to be more creative by raters who were unaware of the group from which the responses came.

Data in other areas lend support for this hypothesized relationship between senility and mindfulness. For example, Jonsson, Malhammer, and Waldton (1976) found that senile subjects did not show the habituation response shown by most of the nonsenile control group. *Habituation* entails seeing the stimulus as constant (familiar). If a stimulus is (mindfully) seen anew on each presentation, habituation may not occur.

Given that senile subjects appear to have more potential for mindfulness than expected, it might be predicted that those labeled senile would live longer than their nonsenile counterparts. This is what we found. Holding disease constant, those elderly labeled senile lived an average of 2 to 6 years longer, depending on the study, than their nonsenile counterparts. (Langer *et al.*, 1984). These results nicely support our prospective study on the relationship between mindlessness and longevity.

Brain physiology, chemistry, and anatomy have been found to be far more plastic than previously assumed. Such plasticity has already been shown for animals. The brains of rats have been shown to vary as a function of the complexity of the environment in which they were reared. Rats reared either in social or in nonsocial but complex environments have wider dendritic fields than rats reared in isolation (Fiala, Joyce, & Greenough, 1978; Krech, Rosenzweig, & Bennett, 1962). Volkman and Greenough (1972; Greenough & Volkman, 1973) have shown that animals reared in complex environments develop about 15% more dendritic material than control animals. Cummins and Walsh (1976) have shown that there is a higher frequency–volume of synapses in the visual cortex of rats reared in complex environments. Rosenzweig, Bennet, and Diamond (1972) have shown that environmental complexity introduced in *adulthood* can alter the thickness of the cortex.

Nottebohm also found startling results in a 1984 study of the singing of canaries. Knowing that only male canaries sing, he and his colleagues injected females with testosterone. They too started to sing. Similarly, when males were castrated before they ever started to sing, they never learned. He and Steven Goldberg injected females with either testosterone or a neutral control treatment, cholesterol. They then injected them with a radioactive material for labeling the cells that are incorporated into the DNA of dividing cells. They repeated the process for 30 days. In addition to what they were looking for, they found a massive increase in the number of neurons in *both* conditions. Nottebohm believes that females might need new neurons to learn new songs. Be that as it may, they found this rebirth of neurons occurs in adult birds annually with the learning of each *new* song.

Our data dealing with elderly populations (Alexander *et al.*, 1988; Langer &

Rodin, 1976; Langer *et al.*, 1978; Langer *et al.*, 1984; Rodin & Langer, 1977) suggest that the plasticity demonstrated in animals may be true for humans. Although animals certainly form categories, it may be wiser at this stage in our understanding not to depend too heavily on this metaphor. It is presented here simply to suggest that the advantages of complexity and novelty (i.e., of maximizing differentiation) may be rather far-reaching.

In a recent study, Jasnowski and Langer (1988) looked at the relationship between mindfulness and the immune system. We administered a new mindlessness–mindfulness scale that we are developing along with a test of differential T cells. Apparently, T cells regulate B cell (humoral) mediated immune function. T4 helpers enhance immune function, whereas T8 suppressors subdue it. Levels of T4s have been related to combatting infections (McClelland, Patel, Brown, & Kelner, 1985). We found a significant relationship between T4 helpers and mindfulness.

Whether mindfulness relies on the immune system or not for its expression, it is clear from a number of our own studies that mindfulness is beneficial for physical health. Although there is not enough evidence to be confident about what the precise physiological correlates of mindfulness are, the fact of a relationship between states of mind and states of the body for humans seems clear. Mindfulness–mindlessness is a predictable dimension of state of mind that differentiates states of the body.

Physiological explanations, while important, do not represent deeper truths but simply other truths. (This may be worth remembering for psychologists as the study of neuroscience grows.) With this in mind, we considered another set of experiments examining the relationship between mindlessness–mindfulness and health. In this work, we examine a mindful use of one's mindlessness. Essentially, we considered the effects of healthy premature cognitive commitments on physical health. This will become more meaningful to the reader after a review of the more basic work in the area.

IV. Mindlessness–Mindfulness and Performance

A. MINDLESSNESS THAT RESULTS FROM PRACTICE

Early research on mindlessness–mindfulness is reviewed elsewhere (Langer, 1978, 1983, 1989). Therefore, discussion here is brief, to help make the point that mindlessness limits human performance. Initially, we used a compliance paradigm, to see if people were processing more than a minimum of the information they were given. Results suggested that they were not unless the favor they were asked for was large. (See Folkes, 1984; Langer *et al.*, 1978, Study 1; Langer, Chanowitz, & Blank, 1985b). That first set of studies did not assess any debilitating consequences of mindlessness. However, this has been the major consideration of all subsequent experiments on the topic.

In an early investigation, we examined the experimental situation itself. It was hypothesized that in at least some experiments, subjects who confirm the social psychologists' hypotheses pick up strong cues intentionally provided by the experimenter. These cues suggest action, thus enabling them to proceed mindlessly. The study we conducted to test this hypothesis used the popular Asch–Kelley warm–cold paradigm. Here subjects listen to a speaker who they were led to expect to be personally warm or cold. The original hypothesis was that subjects would be influenced by the label. We found that those who were influenced by the label and saw the speaker as warm or cold, respectively, did not process much of what the speaker actually said (Langer & Newman, 1979). Instead, they appear to have responded mindlessly.

When we find subjects in our laboratories behaving mindlessly, we suspect that the populations they represent also respond mindlessly, for there is no reason for subjects to be mindless when the population is mindful. The problem Helen Newman and I raised, however, was that the novelty of the experimental situation may provoke mindfulness. In this case, we would not know whether mindful subjects were representative of the population or not. The point is that by not knowing the correspondence between sample and population, we may be misled into thinking that mindlessness is less pervasive than it may be.

If mindlessness is pervasive and most people are mindless much of the time, then they are likely to be responding to an abstracted notion of "person" built up over the course of their frequent interactions with people. Lois Imber and I reasoned that if people were mindless in this way, then in interaction with a "deviant," two things should happen. First, the novel deviant should provoke mindfulness, so subjects in this case would be expected to be accurate in their perceptions of common characteristics of the "deviant" individual. Second, if people are typically mindless, these accurate perceptions should be inaccurately judged as atypical—because typically in normal individuals they go unnoticed, This is precisely what we found (Langer & Imber, 1980). When mindless, people did not notice characteristics that were there to be seen, and when it was called to their attention, their prior mindlessness led them to misjudge what they now first encountered.

Not only do people cease to have part of the world available when it has been mindlessly processed, but renewed consideration of it may be debilitating. One can test this simply enough for oneself by thinking about walking while trying to walk (cf. Baumeister, 1984). Cynthia Weinman and I found that this is even true for intellectual behavior. In an experiment, we asked people to tell us about either a novel or a familiar issue when they either did or did not have time to first think about their answer. Time to think, not surprisingly, resulted in a better performance when discussing the novel issue. However, time to think about the familiar issue resulted in worsened performance (Langer & Weinman, 1981).

In another investigation, Lois Imber and I examined the process involved here (Langer & Imber, 1979). We found that with repeated practice, the individual components of a task become relatively unavailable for conscious cognitive work. The result of this mindless task performance is a heightened vulnerability to aspects of the environment that lead one to question one's competence.

When interpersonal factors subtly led subjects to question their ability, those who had no experience at the task and those who had overlearned it now performed poorly. They did not have the components of the task available for evidence of task competence. Over time, with repeated practice, a rigid structure was formed. But the group for whom the parts of the task were still available—a moderately practiced group—was not vulnerable. When the components of the tasks were made available, in a second study, the debilitations experienced by the overlearned subjects were eliminated (Langer & Imber, 1979).

Perhaps more unusual, however, was the finding that this rigid relationship one forms with information may happen on initial exposure to the information and not just with repeated experience.

B. MINDLESSNESS THAT RESULTS AFTER A SINGLE EXPOSURE

We have called the product of this single-exposure mindlessness a "premature cognitive commitment" (Chanowitz & Langer, 1981). Because they occur on a single exposure to information, premature cognitive commitments help distinguish mindlessness from similar concepts, such as habit, functional fixedness, and overlearning. When an individual is presented with information without motivation to question it, she or he may form a premature cognitive commitment. Here, the individual accepts the information unquestioningly. Later, if creative (or simply other) use of that information is required, it will not occur to the individual to reconsider it. The information, in essence, only exists in the single, rigid form in which it was initially encoded. Alternative understandings of the information are not available. This lack of creative use of the information, just as in the preceding study, occurs even when such reconsideration could prevent decrements in performance.

Chanowitz and Langer (1981) compared (1) subjects who were given no reason to mindfully consider information they were presented about a perceptual disorder to (2) other subjects given reason to consider it. All subjects then "discovered" that they had the disorder. Tests revealed that all subjects took in the same information about the disorder. Nevertheless, those who uncritically accepted the information performed less well on follow-up tasks that required the abilities that were supposed to be limited by the disorder.

A second study revealed that performance also may be enhanced by providing individuals with positive premature cognitive commitments. In either case, though, once people form a premature cognitive commitment to information, it will not occur to them to reconsider other meanings for that information or other ways it could be used. The rigid relationship between information and the experience it represents is the same whether it is built up over time or occurs because the individual has made a premature cognitive commitment to the information on a single exposure.

In a more recent study, Strube, Berry, and Moergen (1985) studied premature cognitive commitments and the Type A behavior pattern. They hypothesized that Type A's have made premature cognitive commitments to the idea that they should take control in situations. If consciously asked to consider the decision mindfully, Type A's, under most circumstances, would decide to take control. However, if the other person was believed to be better, the Type A's would give up control. On the other hand, if this decision is mindlessly enacted, there will be times when Type A's are taking control in the presence of someone more able. This would clearly be to their disadvantage. Strube *et al.* found that when explicitly asked to consider who should be in control, Type A's behaved like Type B's and relinquished control to someone more able. However, when not explicitly provoked, Type A's performed mindlessly at a cost.

People's beliefs about their efficacy guide their behavior. Bandura (1981) believes that it is probably good that people suspend further efficacy appraisals if successful performances can be enacted mindlessly. Mindless performance here decreases the likelihood that people will engage in excessive redundant self-referent thought. It is bad when mindless self-judged inefficacy leads to avoidance of situations that in fact could prove enriching. There may be costs, however, for mindless successful performance as well, if even more successful performance could be achieved if only it occurred to the individual to consider it.

In fact, a mindful response is probably the most efficacious response unless two unlikely conditions are both met: (1) if the individual has discerned the very best response, and (2) if the circumstances do not change. A negative side of success, ironically, then, may be that it limits greater success in changing situations because it often occasions mindlessness.

One can easily point to instances that seem to contradict the assumption that mindfulness may be superior to mindlessness in particular cases and not just in general. For example, take the case of placebos. It is clear that mindless belief in a pill is likely to be more effective than mindful consideration of the possibility that the pill is *only* a placebo. However, if one mindfully considered placebos, one might realize that if the pill is inert, the individual her- or himself must be responsible for effecting the physiological improvement (cf. Davison & Valins, 1969). This realization could reasonably instigate a search for a direct way to bring about physiological improvement without appealing to a magical pill procedure that relies on other people for its success.

When people look for something, they are surely more likely to find it than if they do not even think to question whether or not it is possible. If circumstances are always changing, and there may be an even better response possible than the one mindlessly relied on, then in almost every case it may be advantageous to be mindful.

V. Mindlessness–Mindfulness versus Related Concepts

It should be clear by now that when we speak of mindlessness, we are not just speaking of minimal information processing of specific content. Mindlessness may also characterize the state of being of the organism. That is, to return to our baseball example, we could be mindless with respect to the content of how to hold the bat while we are still in the state of being mindful of something else. Regardless of this difference between minimal information processing work and mindlessness–mindfulness work, the heterogeneity of the situations used in all of the work mentioned earlier on minimal information processing has been important in suggesting the pervasiveness of mindlessness.

To avoid confusion, it is probably important to explicitly distinguish mindlessness from other phenomena that rely on minimal information processing. For example, we should briefly examine long-studied notions of set, expectation, labels, and roles. Similarly, work on habit, functional fixedness, and automaticity should be addressed.

According to the present understanding, mindless behavior is enacted with conscious attention to only a few cues that come to represent a scenario. Sets, labels, expectations, roles, and the like work to direct attention to certain information and consequently away from other information. The result of the operation of these factors (sets, labels, etc.) may be considered minimal information processing, in that the individual is directed by these factors to specific information and away from a vast amount of potential information. However, roles, sets, labels, and the like may be enacted mindlessly or mindfully. The state of reduced conscious cognitive activity is not postulated by researchers working on the effects of these other information–determining variables.

Consider *set,* for example. One can have a set and process new information in its light, or one can rely on past information consistent with the set and be closed to new information. For example, the same behavior may be interpreted as shy or snobbish, depending on whether one has a set to see a snob or a shy person. If one is set to see a snob, for example, behavior of the target person will be interpreted in that light. If one has repeatedly interacted with this person, the interaction may proceed mindlessly. If so, the new snobbish behavior may not be noticed. If one is mindful, on the other hand, new evidence of snobbishness will be processed. Thus, to this extent, mindlessness and mindfulness are independent of sets: one can have a set and process new information in keeping within set or one can rely on a set and not take in any information.

Sets, roles, expectations may be in the service of mindlessness. They permit attention to part of the total picture. Repeated experience may further reduce attention as the behavior becomes mindlessly enacted. Needs, values, and other motivational factors have been shown to affect or determine sets and expectations (cf. Bruner, 1951; Bruner, Goodnow, & Austin, 1956). They should not affect mindlessness, except in so far as they determine the original material to be encoded. Thus, mindlessness is a mode of information processing, whereas sets, roles, expectations, and labels are structures that may be mindfully or mindlessly employed.

Like automaticity, habit, and functional fixedness, mindlessness concerns rigid invariant behavior that appears to be relatively effortless. However, unlike these, repetition is not a necessary part of the etiology of mindlessness. (Some researchers [e.g., Nisbett & Wilson, 1977] do speak of automaticity that does not rely on repetition, but when they do, automaticity is instead taken to be involuntary.) Moreover, these other concepts refer solely to a way of responding. In addition to this focus, the study of mindlessness has as a major concern the state of mind of the responder. As such, a different set of research questions comes to mind than that addressed by this earlier work. Our different perspective, for example, led us to questions of the relationship between mindfulness and health.

Now with a better understanding of mindlessness–mindfulness, it may be worthwhile to give special attention to a comparison between Schneider and Shiffrin's work (1977; Shiffrin & Schneider, 1977) on automatic and controlled processing and mindlessness and mindfulness theory. This comparison would be instructive to social psychologists who are tempted single-mindedly to apply cognitive constructs to social behavior.

The most striking similarity between mindlessness–mindfulness and automatic–controlled processing is that both sets of concepts, like those mentioned earlier, distinguish between an active information processing mode and a less active mode. It is this similarity that gives rise to the possibility of overassimilating one view into the other. A clear understanding of the difference between the two pairs of constructs will serve as a caution against reductionism in general. One result of overassimilating one view into the other is misreading mindfulness as a capacity-consuming mental process. As this article makes clear, mindfulness–mindlessness theory, at least for heuristic purposes, does not assume the existence of limited capacity. In contrast, the notion of limited capacity is central to automatic–controlled processing theory.

The concept of limited capacity so crucial to automatic–controlled processing theory is typically assumed without question. However, this assumption is not without controversy in the cognitive psychology literature. Navon (1984), like me, does not accept the idea of limited capacity. He argues rather convincingly that the concept of capacity is post hoc. Whenever one exceeds a capacity, the earlier capacity is said to have been in error. In a different way, Cheng's work (1985) also is at odds with that of Schneider and Shiffrin. Her position is that *all* processing uses capacity. Because limits are really indeterminate, it may be best at this point in our discipline's inquiry not to unnecessarily limit ourselves with fixed ideas about limits. We may advance human potential more if, for heuristic purposes, we take capacity to be unlimited.

The most obvious way automatic–controlled processing differs from mindlessness and mindfulness is in their respective levels of analysis. The former is much more molecular in its approach than the latter. The different approaches are a result of interest in different dependent measures. The molecular approach used to study automatic versus controlled processing was selected because it enables a molecular study of memory. The original question it addressed concerned serial versus parallel processing, where the task was one of memory scanning. In contrast, the molar approach used in the study of mindlessness–mindfulness addresses molar social and health behavior. This difference, however, is not the only one.

Essentially, automatic–controlled processing goes on within a single context. (While this is true for cognitive research generally, it is less true for social psychological research. See Bargh, 1984.) Thoughtful consideration of the definition of mindfulness suggests that, in contrast to processing within a single context, mindfulness is a choice of contexts. The mindlessness–mindfulness distinction is concerned with how we create information or assign meaning to to-be-processed information, primarily from the outside world. Automatic–controlled processing is concerned with how we deal with information we have already categorized. That is, automatic–controlled processing deals with information already understood and interpreted within a context. As such, it deals with information that is in memory. For example, when a subject performs a letter task automatically, she or he has already determined that the letter is a letter. If it were unclear to the subject whether the target was a letter or a number (e.g., "1"), then the first conscious determination of it as one or the other would be mindful before it was automatically treated in a way consistent with that determination.

Another way of seeing that the concepts are separate is to consider mindful–automatic processing and mindless–controlled processing. For example, when we see an ambiguous figure like one that resembles both a rabbit and a duck (Wittgenstein, 1953), it may be said to be mindful to determine what it is. However, the ambiguous figure is automatically perceived sometimes as a rabbit and sometimes as a duck. The same phenomena happens when we see the ambiguous Necker cube. Even though we try hard to determine its orientation in three-dimensional space, the figure automatically changes its orientation. These examples have important implications because they show the distinct levels of information processing. We can be simultaneously mindful (on a molar level) and automatic (on a molecular level).

The possibility of mindless–controlled processing also exists. Memorizing for an exam may serve as an example of mindless–controlled processing. Such memorizing takes place within a single context, and no new distinctions are being drawn, so it is mindless. Memorizing uses up our "capacity," and it is effortful, so it is controlled processing. This example raises yet one more difference between the mindless–mindful concept and automatic–controlled processing.

Controlled processing is effortful. Neither *mindfulness,* in which one is fully engaged in distinction making, nor *mindlessness,* in which one is fully unengaged, is hypothesized to be effortful. The transition from mindlessness to mindfulness may be effortful, but mindfulness is relatively effortless. On this molar level, what is also hypothesized to be effortful is the in-between state of boredom. Boredom is expected to result at that point in an activity in which the activity could be performed mindlessly, but conditions external to the person discourage it. For example, if one needed simply to move items along on a conveyer belt, one might perform the task mindlessly. However, imagine that as the items move along, a sharp knife falls to cut each item in half. The potential cost of losing a finger may keep the person attentive to the present context. However, paying attention to something without drawing new distinctions is likely to be effortful. If the person mindfully engaged herself in finding new ways to do the task, the time would pass quickly. If she or he did not create any new distinctions *and* did not allow him- or herself to perform the task mindlessly, it is expected that she would experience boredom. Be that as it may, the important point now is that mindfulness is not necessarily difficult.

Mindfulness has been misunderstood to be more effortful than mindlessness. Again, it is hypothesized that neither one is effortful. Mindfulness may seem effortful when the content of that mindfulness is either difficult or negative. When one struggles to solve a problem and gives up out of exhaustion, it may not be the mindfulness of the activity (novel distinction making) that was tiring. It is more likely to be either the individual's inability to let go of prior categories when trying to solve the difficult problem or the emotional strain one endures when the person thinks that he or she *should* be able to solve a problem that is tiresome. Some people leave what they think of as the strain and tension of thinking in their work to engage in recreation. However, recreation is often as mindful as the work left behind.

Another, previously mentioned, difference between the theories is that mindfulness–mindlessness theory does not assume a fixed level of capacity. Automatic processing in cognitive psychology serves a positive function, in that it allows for controlled processing by not consuming limited capacity. Within mindfulness–mindlessness theory, capacity is variable, so that a mindful mode can enlarge the capacity, while a mindless mode fixes the capacity on the present level and therefore may unnecessarily limit capacity. If, as Navon (1984) argues, limits can only be determined in a post hoc way, then the two theories would become more similar. In the meantime, automatic processing may be seen as the construct that maintains the concept of limited capacity in cognitive psychology.

One further difference to note about automatic–controlled processing and mindlessness–mindfulness concerns the way in which automatic processing comes about. Automatic processing results from repetition, whereas the work on premature cognitive commitments shows that mindlessness may also come about during a single exposure to information. In addition to typically being quantitatively different, research has demonstrated that mindfulness and mindlessness are qualitatively different from each other, in that once information has been mindlessly processed, it is no longer available for active conscious use (Chanowitz & Langer, 1981; Langer & Imber, 1979).

The penultimate distinction to be drawn is that once information has gone from controlled to automatic, according to Schneider and Shiffrin, it is expected to stay in that mode. However, one of the major points of mindlessness–mindfulness theory is that information that has been mindlessly accepted could be (should be) reconsidered mindfully if it occurred to the person to do so. But no matter how hard we may try to stop and/or change automatic processing, it is almost impossible to do so (otherwise, it would not be automatic).

Thus far, we have noted that automatic–controlled processing theory and mindlessness–mindfulness theory differ with respect to ideas concerning capacity and effortfulness. They differ in the level of analysis they concern (molecular vs. molar) and in etiology (repetition vs. repetition and single instance). Perhaps most important, automatic processing seems to be an advantage for molecular cognitive processing, while mindlessness appears to be costly for social adaptiveness and health.

VI. Misconceptions about the Advantages of Mindlessness and the Disadvantages of Mindfulness

Certain commonplace views of mindlessness make it seem advantageous and mindfulness disadvantageous. Belief in the advantages of mindlessness and in the disadvantages of mindfulness seems to be due to the confusion between automatic processing and mindlessness, which were differentiated in the preceding section. Automatic processing has the advantage of enabling controlled processing. As stated before, automatic processing and mindlessness are not the same thing. Whereas automatic processing is primarily a good thing, mindlessness is primarily disadvantageous. Mindlessness does not enable mindfulness. In fact, mindlessness inhibits mindfulness. Once information is mindlessly accepted, it does not readily come to mind for mindful reconsideration.

Advantages and disadvantages are relative concepts. They are meaningless until a comparison group and/or a criterion is specified. Mindfulness certainly seems disadvantageous when one is mindfully considering negative content. However, this may be because the wrong comparison is being made. Mindfully considering negative thoughts feels less good than mindfully considering positive thoughts, but it is not clear that having one negative thought from one perspective is less negative than having several negative thoughts. For example, thinking of all the ways the elevator may crash the next time you are in it may not be more negative than simply being sure it will crash. Moreover, if one is mindfully considering the issue, there is at least the possibility that positive content will present itself for consideration.

Obsessions and phobias cannot be equated with mindfulness. In order to be mindful, it is not sufficient to think much. Mindfulness enables seeing the old in a new way or novel distinction-making, and does not involve repetition of old distinctions and/or conceptual structures. To the extent that obsessing yields new thoughts, it would be mindful. However, people with these pathologies are caught within a single context, and at least in that way they are mindless rather than mindful. They may mindlessly engage in controlled processing in their everyday life. Mindfulness has been misunderstood to be difficult and as such made mindlessness seem advantageous by contrast.

Linville (1987) provides some data that speaks to this point. She found that subjects who were more mindless with respect to their self-understanding (i.e., those lower in self-complexity) experienced greater mood swings than those subjects with more differentiated views of themselves. She suggests that differentiation (mindfulness) may serve as a buffer against negative thoughts.

Tesser (1978) has found that mindfulness results in attitude polarization. If an attitude is positive, it becomes more positive after mindful consideration, but if it is negative, it becomes more negative. This would suggest a disadvantage of mindfulness. One must realize that evaluation, however, does not reside in the stimulus. Negative affect that seems to result from mindful consideration of negative content actually is the result of a mindless acceptance of the information as negative. The negative content could be neutrally or positively reframed.

To paraphrase Dewey's remarks about diversity (Dewey, 1957), "Mindfulness does not itself imply conflict, but it implies the possibility of conflict."

There may be a disadvantage to being mindful if the people around you see the world from within a single perspective. There are clear costs to being different (see Goffman, 1963; Jones et al., 1984; Yukor, 1987). It would seem that the answer to these problems should be to increase the mindfulness of the larger group rather than to decrease the mindfulness of the more mindful members.

Mindlessness at first seems comfortable. However, it is a mistake to confuse mindlessness with serenity or mindfulness with competitive behavior. Being calm or driven is orthogonal to the mindless–mindful distinction. In fact, anxiety relies on mindlessness. It may be mindful to notice that a stimulus is potentially threatening. However, the anxiety-provoking stimulus is potentially simultaneously many things, which is why it does not lead everyone to feel anxious. The fear-provoking distinction drawn in the past, where it may have proved helpful, may not occasion discomfort unnecessarily. Mindlessness holds the stimulus constant, even when circumstances change. If mindfulness were reflexive, so that the individual chose about what to be mindful, the presumed problems of mindfulness would be solved.

Not only are the advantages of mindlessness the disadvantages of mindfulness, but also the advantages of mindfulness from one perspective are, no doubt, disadvantages of mindfulness from another. For example, a positive corollary of mindfulness is flexibility, an advantage. Inflexibility then would seem to be a disadvantage of mindlessness. However, cast a different way, consistency would seem to be an advantage of mindlessness and inconsistency a disadvantage of mindfulness. This kind of reframing can be done with any descriptor as soon as one looks at it from more than one perspective.

VII. An Alternative View

A tenth-century Chinese encyclopedia divides animals into the following categories: (1) belonging to the Emperor, (2) embalmed, (3) tame, (4) suckling pigs, (5) sirens, (6) fabulous, (7) stray dogs, (8) included in the present classification, (9) frenzied, (10) innumerable, (11) drawn with a very fine camelhair brush, (12) et cetera, (13) having just broken the water pitcher, (14) that from a long way off look like flies (T'ai P'ing, A.D. 978, as cited in Borges, 1967).

The alternative view described in this section encourages us to look at reality as a social construction in which facts are treated as probability statements rather than as absolute truths that are independent of us and fixed. The construction of reality consists of creating discontinuous categories out of a continuous dimension.

Mindfulness involves the creation of categories. Mindlessness yields entrapment by those categories. A look at some of the broader categories we mindlessly use (e.g., mind–body) may reveal more control available than people have assumed over one's psychological and physical health and well-being. I would like to argue that strong advantages would follow if, for heuristic purposes, if not fact, we consider that reality is a continuity on which we impose our categories, thereby making it discontinuous. Even categories themselves (e.g., male–female, old–young, plant–animal, animate–inanimate—all categories) are essentially so many single undifferentiated dimensions until we mindfully act on them to create smaller discrete categories. Sometimes, we create these categories ourselves, and sometimes they are just mindlessly accepted by us as they are given to us by others.

Categories were considered to be well-defined until Brown (1956), Rosch (1973), and then Smith and Medin (1981) made clear that the boundaries between categories were fuzzy and that more and less prototypical instances of categories exist. According to their view then, categories are really probabilities. For example, a penguin is less likely to be considered a good example of a bird than is a robin. However, while this may be true, it is not what we mean when we speak of the potential importance of treating the world probabilistically or conditionally. Even Rosch's natural categories, which are structured probabilistically, are still categories and should be reconsidered and recategorized.

Arbitrary or nonarbitrary recategorization may prove beneficial. The advantages to recategorizing may be seen when an outsider to a field looks inside. The outsider has different categories and sees what the insider may be blind to. For instance, when Roger Brown, social psychologist and psycholinguist, looked at schizophrenia, he found that these patients were linguistically normal despite popular belief to the contrary by people in the field. It was not their linguistic skills, but rather the content of their speech, that was bizarre. Clinicians, too close to the problem, were trapped by their categories. Brown gave them new categories, and schizophrenia became known as a thought disorder and not a language disorder.

It would seem that the source of evidence determines the understanding of an object or event. This has become quite apparent in the physical sciences, where matter appears as either waves or quanta, depending on the observational parameters. That is, matter may be seen as continuous or discrete. Both serve different useful purposes. It may be time for social psychologists to switch to a conception of reality as continuous. Such as change may reveal new understandings about human potential.

Bridgman (1927), the father of operationism, noted that a "concept is synonymous to the corresponding set of operations." That is, concepts are inseparable from the method used to produce the data on which they are based. As Kagan (1986) writes,

> (A)n observer can describe a fir tree in the forest as an object with an essence or as sets of relations among molecules that are under continuous and dynamic change. . . . When the evidence for the tree originates in vision, it appears unchanging. . . . But if the evidence about the tree comes from a summary of a week's measurements of the amounts of oxygen and carbon dioxide exchanged with air, it will seem more obvious that the tree consists of a set of relationships.

On the one hand is Platonic idealism, which assumes a real essence behind every construct, and on the other is a skeptical materialism, which says all that science has is a cluster of correlated events. Science does not give us the essence of objects. Regardless of the ultimate truth of this statement, it would be efficacious for us now to treat our facts as probability statements of sets of relations. This would lead to a greater freedom to create from these relations.

This view than encourages us to take the world we live in as a social construction. This becomes a more reasonable perspective when one considers that once a distinction is drawn, once a discrete category is formed from a continuous reality, it takes on a reality of its own. When one looks back at the distinction, of course, it seems always to have been there because it always could have been. Thus, the world we experience does indeed appear to be independent of us.

The act of creating categories or forming discontinuities is an adaptive and inevitable process (cf. Brown, 1956; Bruner et al., 1956). As research presented suggests, it also may be prevalent because mindfulness may be necessary for survival. However, we may create the absolutes that then entrap us and limit us. Whether one is responding mindlessly because of reliance on a structure built up over time or during a single exposure, when dealing with the world or any of its parts mindlessly, one is acting within a single context without active awareness of alternative conceptions. *Mindfulness* is essentially sensitivity to or awareness of contexts. Without this awareness, one cannot manipulate the context in which one finds oneself. One cannot improve performance, judgment, self-esteem, or health.

One distinction many have single-mindedly held is that between the mind and the body. Obviously, these categories have helped us learn much throughout history. However, mindlessly using this distinction may be limiting human potential. It would seem to our advantage now to consider a new category in which the mind and body are seen as one. If the mind and the body are taken as one, then wherever the mind is, so to speak, the body will be also (cf. Langer, Chanowitz, Rhodes, Jacobs, Palmerino, & Thayer, 1988a, 1988b). This simple idea may explain many anomalous findings and suggests interesting new experiments.

A. CONTEXTS AS PREMATURE COGNITIVE COMMITMENTS

To best understand the potential importance of this mind–body idea, one should first recognize that contexts may be best understood as premature cognitive commitments. For example, roller coasters are fun; bumpy plane rides are not. The difference in our reaction in these two contexts is likely to be attributable to different premature cognitive commitments regarding perceived control (Miller, 1980). If we view contexts in this light, the ways they may be changed to enhance human performance may become more evident. At the least, they lead one to ask: If behavior is context dependent, who controls the context? The degree of potential control available may be ascertained from experiments that explicitly or implicitly vary context. They more than hint at how performance may be unnecessarily limited.

In an experiment assessing Helson's adaptation-level theory, Donald Brown (1953) considered an interesting variation. Subjects judged a series of weights as very light to very heavy, after lifting an anchor weight. Consistent with Helson's theory, the judged weight varied as a function of the distance of the anchor in weight from the series.

Brown's interesting condition was the following. Some subjects were asked to make matters easier for the experimenter by picking up and moving the tray upon which the weights sat after the first round of weights to be judged had been removed. The question was, if weights were influenced by other weights, would subjects in this condition be influenced by the weight of the tray? The tray was not part of the weight-lifting context, yet it seemingly exists in some absolute way independent of the perceiver's psychology. If context determines our experience of stimuli, then the tray should have no influence. And, in fact, the judgment of weight was not influenced by the weight of the tray.

Karsten (1928) was interested in mental satiation. She put subjects in "semi-free situations" in which they were given tasks to perform, but they were instructed that they could stop working on them whenever they wanted to. For example, subjects were drawing until satiated. They apparently could not go on drawing. Then the context changed. They were asked by the experimenter to turn the page over and draw the last picture they drew on the back so the experimenter could identify it, or a subject was asked to draw it on the back to show the experimenter how fast he could draw it. The subject had no difficulty performing the satiated behavior in the new context. In another instance, Karsten had subjects write ababab . . . until they had had enough writing. When exhausted, the subjects were immediately asked to sign their names and addresses for someone collecting handwriting samples. In this new context, the subjects did so quite easily. Perhaps even more interesting was the study in which Karsten had subjects read poems until they were hoarse. The hoarseness disappeared when subjects complained to her of how they hated the task.

These task thus were of two types: continuous activities (such as drawing) and tasks that came to a quick end but were repeated (such as reading a short poem). Karsten found that satiation only occurred within context for both kinds of tasks. When the identical action took on a different meaning, it was performed as if it were a completely new action. That is, with a change in context, satiation effects disappear. Presenting the premature cognitive commitment explanation for satiation effects is not meant to imply that it is better than the original field theory explanation. Reconsidering Karsten's studies in this light, however, may lead to new and useful experimental hypotheses.

On the anecdotal side, drug counselors observe that heroin addicts are less likely to report withdrawal if they do not consider themselves addicts. By contrast, of course, those who do self-label themselves as addicts suffer tremendous withdrawal problems.

Along similar lines, researchers studied deaths that purportedly resulted from drug overdose. Many drug users die from a dose that should not be fatal to them. Siegel, Hirsan, Krank, and McGully (1982) argue that the failure of tolerance on the day of the overdose is a function of context. If a drug is given in the presence of cues that are associated with sublethal doses, death is less likely than when it is given without cues associated with the drug at an earlier time. In each study they ran, those in the different testing situation were more likely to die than those in the familiar situation. Situations may always be perceived as familiar or as unfamiliar. For humans, then, who controls the perceived familiarity of situations? By choosing to perceive situations as unfamiliar, people give up a good deal of control.

Marlatt and Rohsenow (1980) seem to appreciate the importance of context in their work on substance abuse. They varied whether or not subjects expected to receive alcohol (vodka and tonic) or no alcohol (tonic) and whether they actually did receive alcohol or not. Subjects were placed in a taste testing context and were instructed to sample the liquids ad lib and rate them. Despite the physiological effects of the drug, expectancy was the major influence. It determined how much they drank, how aggressively they behaved, and how intoxicated they seemed. In a similar study, Wilson and Abrams (1977) found that the groups of men who believed they had consumed alcohol, whether or not the belief was veridical, showed a tendency for reduced heart rate.

Another area of research that may be understood within this framework is that of state-specific learning. This literature suggests that if the body is returned to a previous physiological state, the state of mind relevant to that state will also return.

For example, Peterson (1977), administered verbal learning tasks to Army personnel who were either sober or who were in an alcohol state (10/mL/kG). The following day, these subjects were asked to recall the material they had learned the day before while they were in the same or a different drug state. Those who were in the same drug state, either sober or the alcohol state, recalled more of the learned material than those whose state had changed.

B. ONE EXPLANATION FOR MANY ANOMALOUS FINDINGS

These studies bring to mind other literatures that now may be understood within a single perspective. The psychological deaths mentioned earlier, deaths due to loss of control and loss of a spouse, for example, may be reconsidered now, along with previously unexplained findings such as voodoo deaths (Cannon, 1942), placebos, spontaneous remissions, and findings in the hypnosis and faith-healing literatures, to name a few. In each case, the findings may be explained in terms of premature cognitive commitments.

In a typical medical study, one or more drugs in pill form may be pitted against an inert pill, a placebo. The person who takes the pill is kept unaware of whether the pill is "real" or inert. If one takes a placebo, thinking that it is physical medication, and one gets better, the illness is taken to be "only psychological." If, on the other hand, one took physical medication thinking it were only a placebo, many would argue that the drug would still have the same effect as it did without the psychological instructions. A strong statement of mindfulness–mindlessness theory would predict that the drug would not be effective. This is probably a more popular view than one might admit. If people did not at least partially believe it, it would not seem unethical to actually do the study. The perception of the study as unethical depends on the assumption that one may be able through instructions to eradicate the medicinal effects of the drug.

The fact of vast improvement with an inert drug is often overlooked because placebos are used to assess the effects of "real" drugs. Rather than solely use placebos as a baseline to assess the effectiveness of medically active drugs, one should also look at the effectiveness of "inert" substances over disease independently.

Similarly, the abilities of nonhypnotized subjects are not fully exploited because they are used to disprove findings attributed to hypnosis. The same is true with respect to spontaneous remissions. Major and minor symptoms appear and then disappear for seemingly no good reason. Physicians typically do not know why this happens, and they define these spontaneous remissions as part of the disease process. The major way in which the medical community devotes research efforts to spontaneous remissions is through its consideration of them, again, as control groups against which to measure the effectiveness of various medical treatment regimens. Each of these—placebos, hypnosis, and spontaneous remissions—should be regarded as evidence that psychological factors may alter physiology. Moreover, what these different areas may have in common is that their effectiveness may rely on premature cognitive commitments.

Placebos will work if the individual has a premature cognitive commitment regarding the efficacy of medication and single-mindedly believes the particular pill will work. If there is any doubt that the pill will be effective, it probably will not work. With or without a pill, no matter how the mind assumes a healthy position, the body should be healthy as well.

In the *Principles of Psychology,* James (1890) describes Dr. Carpenter, who said of himself that

> He has frequently begun a lecture whilst suffering neuralgic pain so severe as to make him apprehend that he would find it impossible to proceed; yet no sooner has he by a determined effort fairly launched himself into the stream of thought, than he has found himself continuously borne along without the least distraction, until the end had come, and the attention has been released, when the pain has recurred with a force that has overmastered all resistance making him wonder how he could have ever ceased to feel it.

If one can take the mind off of the pain, it apparently goes away (see Kanfer & Goldfoot, 1966). Similarly, if one can reinterpret the stimulus, the pain may go away (e.g., Langer, Janis, & Wolfer, 1975). The context determines the pain. This may be seen in research by Beecher (1956), who reported on the relationship between the severity of wounds and pain in a civilian and soldier population. He compared the frequency of pain severe enough to require medication in soldiers wounded in World War II and a matched group of civilians. Although the soldiers had extensive wounds, 32% required medication compared to 83% of the civilians.

In the case of medical treatments, often the belief consists of full confidence in the medicine. Yet sometimes people improve without the aid of medicine, also because of frame of mind.

Ullrich (1984) reported that those cholecystectomy patients who had been assigned to hospital rooms with windows facing fall-colored trees (data were collected from May to October), had shorter postoperative stays and took fewer pain relievers than those assigned to rooms that faced a brick wall.

The French periodical *Presences* (1955) reported that although there were 30,000 doctors in France, there were 40,000 healers. Faith healing is just one more anomaly to which most of the medical community turns a cold shoulder. But, as psychologists, should we? Faith healing may be a function of expectations, and expectations depend on context. We as psychologists have certainly seen the dramatic effect of expectations.

In addition to all of his experiments on the helplessness that follows from expectations of no control, Seligman (1975) described numerous examples of deaths that apparently result without clear physical justification, due to expectations. Richter (1957) brought the phenomenon into the laboratory. In a well-known study, he placed rats in ice water. These animals swam for approximately 40 hours. In contrast, rats that were first given helplessness training died within 1 or 2 hours. Upon autopsy, it was found that the rats died a parasympathetic death, as though they just gave up.

The key to understanding spontaneous remissions may be in appreciating what is meant by the word *spontaneous*. *Spontaneous* means self-operating. The question becomes, how does the body repair itself? The answer may be that health is restored when there is a healthy change in context. Most explanations that have been advanced to explain how some bodies repair themselves rely on healing mechanisms that take time to work. These cannot explain the anecdotal examples that also abound that suggest a more immediate effect. A context change, of course, would not necessarily take time. It would depend on one's premature cognitive commitment.

With respect to diseases like cancer, it is the rare person who can think of him- or herself as healthy again after the diagnosis has been made. This is alarming even if our hypothesis is incorrect. The reason this is alarming is that medical research may be largely dealing with only half of a chi-square contingency table. There may be healthy undiagnosed people walking around with cancer, for example, whose data could change the meaning of this or, for that matter, any other disease.

To make this more meaningful, consider an extraordinary finding reported by Lorber (1981). He studied people with severe hydrocephalus, which is an excess of cerebrospinal fluid in the skull. These people showed normal and some above-normal development on various intelligence tests and everyday functioning, despite the fact that approximately 95% of the cranial area for them is filled with fluid. This renders the thickness of the cortex to be only a tiny fraction of what it is in most people. The conclusion, of course, is that the brain is far more plastic than traditional research methods led us to assume.

C. EXTENDING HUMAN POTENTIAL

It is not clear yet how one can give oneself different premature cognitive commitments—social placebos. However, these social placebos that are given to us by others may be used in two ways. First, as one would imagine, one may "take" a social placebo to return performance to baseline. This is similar to the way placebos have been used in the medical arena. Second, they can be used to extend performance beyond baseline.

Our recent research efforts have focused on reversing degenerative processes. At present, only one of these investigations has been completed. Thus, I limit my discussion to it. In this experiment, Mark Dillon, Ron Kurtz, Martin Katz, and I (1988b) considered the potential effect of exploiting premature cognitive commitments regarding vision in order to improve vision. Our subjects were men enrolled in officer candidate school. Those in the experimental group got into fatigues and assumed the role of an air force pilot. They then "flew" a very convincing simulated plane. We believed, and later verified, that this population would believe that pilots are persons with exceptional vision. However, we said nothing about vision during the experiment. Subjects took an eye test as part of a general physical examination to give us our baseline measures.

Comparison subjects, also in fatigues, engaged in similar procedures, but for them the simulator was broken, so they had a much less involving part to play. Because they were less likely to feel like pilots, comparison subjects were not expected to change as much as experimental subjects. A test of vision was unobstrusively worked into the scenario for both groups. Interestingly, the results revealed improvement over 20/20 vision for 40% of the experimental group. No one in the comparison group improved.

In replications and extensions of this study, we systematically controlled for motivation and arousal. We again exploited experimental subjects' understanding of "pilot." We also tapped into another rigid, although less widely held belief ("exercise improves"). Here we simply had another group of experimental subjects perform a set of eye exercises that we described as vision improving. Both experimental groups improved; and control groups did not, in spite of the fact that they were explicitly encouraged to improve their vision.

These results are certainly exciting. However, until more of these limit-extending results are found, the data do not warrant fully accepting (or, of course, rejecting) the validity of a broader hypothesis—that for most of us, the mind–

body distinction is a premature cognitive commitment. At any rate, I do feel that the data are sufficient to state that the commonly held conception of the relation between the mind and the body is too narrow and rigid. For example, if one considers the reality of psychological deaths, findings on spontaneous remissions and placebos, there is a good deal of evidence already that speaks to how much control the mind has over the body.

Before we try to extend performance, we should become more aware in yet another way than we currently are of the ways in which our own behavior may reflect our own premature cognitive commitments. That is, many of our views represent single-minded understandings of the world. If we improve behavior based on those understandings, we will simultaneously worsen behavior that was mutually incompatible with it. An example may make this clearer.

Men have been found to be more field independent than women. Thus, if we were interested in extending performance we would, at the start, give women remedial treatments to make them more field independent. Or on the other hand, if we truly accepted that behavior may be multidimensional, we would probably explain those same findings by seeing women as more field sensitive than men. If so, then of what should the remedial help consist? I would argue that this is not a small problem. In fact, I think premature cognitive commitments are at issue virtually any time one individual or group negatively evaluates the behavior of another individual or group. That is, a positive construal of the behaviors may account for all the same data that is mutually exclusive with one's current understanding. The actors are acting on one construal; their negative evaluators on another.

Be that as it may, the research seems clear that premature cognitive commitments prevent us from seeing the world from alternative perspectives. If most of the world we know is learned when we were children, and henceforth remains unchanged, one can only imagine how different these categories would be if they had initially been created through an adult lens.

VIII. Preventing Mindlessness

Clearly, people cannot mindfully consider everything around them (even if it may be to their advantage to almost always mindfully consider something). Yet, if a person makes a premature cognitive commitment to information when it is not important to do otherwise, research tells us that debilitation could result if creative use of that information later became necessary. Research also suggests that there may be a way out of this dilemma.

Alison Piper and I considered how premature cognitive commitments result in single-minded understandings of the world. We reasoned that if one were initially to learn about the world with a view toward its multidimensionality, this could be effective in preventing mindlessness. The facts of this world that most people take as unconditional absolute truths, we, as scientists, know are instead probability statements. If these facts were initially presented conditionally, would they be available for creative use in the future?

To test this, we introduced subjects to certain objects, either unconditionally or conditionally. In the unconditional condition, this simply amounted to naming the object (for example, "this is an X"). The conditional instruction was just as simple ("this could be an X"). One of these objects in one study was (could be) a dog's chew toy. A need for an eraser was then created. The question was who would think to use the dog's chew toy to meet this novel use. It was expected that, if asked, all of the subjects would see that it could serve this function.

We were most interested in discovering to whom it would occur without being asked. The results were straightforward; only those subjects introduced to the object in question conditionally thought to use it creatively. Of course, this result was made possible by the unfamiliarity of the object. It is likely that a familiar object would already have been introduced unconditionally.

In order to make sure that subjects did indeed process this information conditionally, we added a second novel need. If subjects were understanding "could be" as conditional and not just temporarily unknown ("it *is* something, but I just don't know what it is"), then the second need should be responded to creatively. If it were only temporarily unknown, then after the first need was met, it would no longer be unknown (e.g., "Now I know what it is. It is an eraser"). In this case, the conditional group on this measure would look similar to the unconditional group. They did not. The results suggest that people can learn conditionally (Langer & Piper, 1987).

Now that it looked as though mindlessness could be prevented without having to mindfully attend to all that might eventually become relevant, we asked if some people quite naturally learn the world this way. We considered dyslexia in this context. Dyslexia, as most people know, is a reading disorder. We reasoned that if a dyslexic could not be sure if, for example, a "d" were a "d" and not a "b" at any moment, this individual would be unlikely to take the world for granted and treat it mindlessly if that could be helped.

In this next experiment, we compared dyslexics and normals. For half of each group, we introduced objects either conditionally or unconditionally. Once again, we found a mindful response for the normal conditional group that was lacking for the unconditional group. Most interesting is the preliminary finding that dyslexics may be mindful even in the explicitly unconditional condition (Langer, Piper, & Friedus, 1987).

Many of us have already learned most of the ideas we hold about people, places, and things in this unconditional way. Therefore, while it is meaningful to know that it may be possible to prevent mindlessness, one may want to know if one's current mindlessness may be reversed.

In our research concerned with interpersonal mindlessness, we essentially taught subjects to consider multiple explanations for events. In so doing, we attempted to reduce prejudice by increasing discrimination (Langer, Bashner, & Chanowitz, 1985a). In comparison with a control group asked to explain various situations in a single way, the experimental group was asked for alternative or multiple explanations for several single events. The premature cognitive commitment that says people who are deaf, for example, are less competent, would result in not hiring the hearing impaired. In contrast, mindfulness would lead to more differentiated discrimination. Here, by analogy, if loud noise were a problem, it would occur to the individual that it might be most advantageous to hire this deaf person.

We found that groups encouraged to be mindful were indeed less likely to engage in indiscriminate discrimination. Of course, if mindlessness were prevented in the first place, the problem may never have arisen.

In another experiment (Piper & Langer, 1984), we asked people to watch television either from multiple perspectives or as they typically do. More specifically, we gave subjects different perspectives to assume, to contrast with their own for 1 hour each night for a week of televiewing. The perspectives included those of a politician, a director, a psychologist, a lawyer, a doctor, and a child. Intentionally changing contexts or premature cognitive commitments is certainly mindful. This mindful televiewing resulted in characters of a target TV show (a soap opera) being seen as more complex and less stereotypic than the single perspective group (cf. Langer & Piper, 1987). If something so fully scripted, like television soap operas, can be watched mindfully, perhaps anything can. It certainly may be worth finding out.

IX. Conclusions

To recapitulate, the findings from our research thus far suggest that mindlessness–mindfulness may be a central dimension in human functioning, the understanding of which may lead to new understandings of human potential. The mindless–mindful distinction differs from similar conceptualizations in that it (1) relies on a molar unit of analysis—entire ongoing social situations, and not just motor behavior, such as typewriting or similar discrete behavior; and (2) focuses on the state of mind of the actor, in addition to behavior, rather than just on the latter. This approach yields the following observations: (1) Mindfulness involves sensitivity to contexts, whereas mindlessness involves submergence in a context; (2) mindless behavior, typically less variable than mindful behavior, is pervasive—much of the typical day may be passed mindlessly and most of our views represent single-minded conceptions; (3) mindlessness may come about on a single exposure to information as well as with repeated experience; (4) the distinction between mindlessness and mindfulness is *qualitative* rather than just quantitative—mindless thought–behavior is not just typically faster, it is not available for mindful consideration; and (5) most important, the consequences may be far-reaching. Mindlessness has some advantages, but it may be *extremely maladaptive*. These disadvantages appear to be both *psychological* and *physical*. As we have said, this mind–body distinction itself may represent a premature cognitive commitment. If so, then perhaps the most extreme consequence of mindlessness is that it *limits human potential*. Whether the characterization of the mind–body distinction as a premature cognitive commitment turns out to be true or not, mindfully reconsidering the relationship, in any case, should continue to lead to new ways to extend human performance.

In the meantime, one should note that the debilitations that result from ignorance of the distinction between mindlessness and mindfulness appear to be real and may be severe. To name a few that research has documented, mindlessness may result in poor judgment, inarticulate speech, heightened sensitivity to competence-questioning aspects of the environment, unnecessarily low self-esteem, poor vision, and premature death. However, even when we are succeeding, prior mindlessness may have led us to behave within an unnecessarily restricted range. And this appears to be true for both overt and physiological responding.

Now that we know that mindlessness can be so debilitating, it is time to uncover the specific situations that do and do not occasion it. And as we do, we should be looking to find out which individuals in these situations are more or less likely to be influenced by the situation. Attention to the common elements in those situations that encourage or support a mindful state and attention to those individuals able to be mindful even in situations that do not support mindfulness would be helpful in findings ways to restructure other situations to prevent mindlessness. In so doing, it may give us control over the contexts that now control us.

When operating within a single-minded awareness, one cannot manipulate the context in which one finds oneself. However, with adequate awareness of context, it may be possible to extend human performance far beyond currently accepted limits. At the least, research tells us that such a mindful pursuit is likely to prove good for one's health.

References

Abele, A. (1985). Thinking about thinking: Causal, evaluative and finalistic cognitions about social solutions. *European Journal of Social Psychology,* **15,** 315–332.

Abelson, R. (1981). Psychological status of the script concept. *American Psychologist,* **36,** 715–729.

Abrahms, J. (1976). Health status as a variable in aging research. *Experimental Aging Research,* **2,** 63–71.

Alexander, C., Langer, E., Newman, R., Chandler, H., Davies J. (1988). Aging, mindfulness, and transcendental meditation. *Journal of Personality and Social Psychology,* in press.

Bandura, A. (1981). Self-referent thought: The development of self-efficacy. In J. H. Flavell & L. D. Ross (Eds.), *Development of social cognition*. Cambridge, England: Cambridge University Press.
Bargh, J. (1982). Attention and automaticity in the processing of self-relevant information. *Journal of Personality and Social Psychology*, **43**, 428–436.
Bargh, J. (1984). Automatic and conscious processing of social information. In R. Wyer & T. Srull (Eds.), *Handbook of social cognition* (Vol. 3). Hillsdale, NJ: Erlbaum.
Baumeister, R. (1984). Choking under pressure. *Journal of Personality and Social Psychology*, **46**, 610–620.
Beecher, H. K. (1956). Relationship of significance of wound to pain experience. *Journal of the American Medical Association*, **161**, 1609–1613.
Berscheid, E., Graziano, W., Monson, T., & Derner, M. (1976). Outcome dependency: Attention, attribution, and attraction. *Journal of Personality and Social Psychology*, **34**, 978–989.
Birren, J. (1968). Increment and decrement in the intellectual status of the aged. *Psychiatric Research Reports*, **23**, 207–214.
Borges, J. L. (1967). *Libro de los seres imaginarios* [Book of imaginary beings] (p. 88). Buenos Aires: Editorial Kirsa.
Bridgman, P. W. (1927). *The logic of modern physics*. New York: Macmillan.
Brown, D. (1953). Stimulus-similarity and the anchoring of the subjective self. *American Journal of Psychology*, **66**, 199–214.
Brown, R. (1956). *Words and things*. New York: Free Press.
Bruner, J. (1951). Personality dynamics and the process of perceiving. In R. R. Blake & G. V. Ramsey (Eds.), *Perception: An approach to personality* (pp. 121–147). New York: Ronald.
Bruner, J., Goodnow, J., & Austin, G. (1956). *A study of thinking*. New York: Wiley.
Cannon, W. (1942). "Voodoo" death. *American Anthropologist*, **44**, 161–181.
Carlston, D. (1980). Events, references, and impression formation. In R. Hastie, T. M. Ostrom, E. B. Ebbesen, R. S. Wyer, D. L. Hamilton, & D. E. Carlston (Eds.), *Person memory* (pp. 89–120). Hillsdale, NJ: Erlbaum.
Chaiken, S. (1980). Heuristic vs. systematic information processing and the use of source vs. message cues in persuasion. *Journal of Personality and Social Psychology*, **39**, 752–766.
Chanowitz, B., & Langer, E. (1981). Premature cognitive commitment. *Journal of Personality and Social Psychology*, **41**, 1051–1063.
Chanowitz, B., & Langer, E. (1980). Knowing more (or less) than you can show: Understanding control through the mindlessness/mindfulness distinction. In M. E. P. Seligman & J. Garber (Eds.), *Human helplessness*. New York: Academic Press.
Chapman, L., & Chapman, J. (1967). Genesis of popular but erroneous diagnostic observations. *Journal of Abnormal Psychology*, **72**, 193–204.
Cheng, P. W. (1985). Restructuring versus automaticity: An alternative account of skill. *Psychological Review*, **92**, 414–442.
Crocker, J. (1981). Judgment of covariation of social processes. *Psychological Bulletin*, **90**, 272–279.
Cummins, R., & Walsh. R. (1976). Synaptic changes in differentially reared mice. *Australian Psychologist*, **2**, 229.
Cvetkovitch, G. (1978). Cognitive accommodation, language, and social responsibility. *Social Psychology*, **41**, 149–155.
Davison, G. C., & Valins, S. (1969). Maintenance of self-attributed and drug-attributed behavior change. *Journal of Personality and Social Psychology*, **11**, 25–33.
Dewey, J. (1957). *Human nature and conduct*. New York: Modern Library.
Dweck, C., & Diener, C. (1978). An analysis of learned helplessness: Continuous changes in performance, strategy, and achievement cognitions following failure. *Journal of Personality and Social Psychology*, **36**, 451–462.
Enzle, M., & Shopflocher, D. (1978). Instigation of attribution processes by attributional questions. *Journal of Personality and Social Psychology*, **4**, 595–599.

Folkes, V. (1984). Mindlessness or mindfulness: A partial replication and extension of Langer, Blank & Chanowitz. *Journal of Personality and Social Psychology,* **48,** 600–604.

Fiala, B. A., Joyce, J. N., & Greenough, W. T. (1978). Environmental complexity modulates growth of granule cell dendrites in developing but not adult hippocampus of rats. *Experimental Neurology,* **59,** 372–383.

Goffman, E. (1963). *Stigma*. Englewood Cliffs, NJ: Prentice-Hall.

Greenough, W., & Volkman, F. (1973). Patterns of dendritic branching in occipital cortex of rats reared in complex environments. *Experimental Neurology,* **40,** 491–508.

Hall, E., Savage, R., Bolten, N. Pidwell, D., & Blessed, G. (1972). Intellect, mental illness, and survival in the aged: A longitudinal study. *Journal of Gerontology,* **27,** 237–244.

Hamilton, D. (1981). Illusory correlation as a basis for stereotyping. In D. L. Hamilton (Ed.), *Cognitive processes in stereotyping and intergroup behavior*. Hillsdale, NJ: Erlbaum.

Harkness, A., DeBono, K., & Borgida, E. (1985). Personal involvement and strategies for making contingency judgments: A stake in the dating game makes a difference. *Journal of Personality and Social Psychology,* **49,** 22–32.

Hastie, R. (1984). Causes and effects of causal attribution. *Journal of Personality and Social Psychology,* **46,** 44–56.

James, W. (1980). *Principles of psychology* (Vol. 2). London: Macmillan.

Janis, I. (1972). *Victims of groupthink*. Boston: Houghton-Mifflin.

Janis, I., & Mann, L. (1977). *Decision making*. New York: Free Press.

Jarvik, L., & Blum. J. (1971). Cognitive decline as a predictor of mortality in discordant twin pairs: A twenty year longitudinal study of aging. In E. Palmore & F. Jeffers (Eds.), *Prediction and life span*. Lexington, MA: Heath Lexington.

Jarvik, L., & Falek, A. (1963). Intellectual stability and survival in the aged. *Journal of Gerontology,* **18,** 173–176.

Jasnowski, M., & Langer, E. (1988). *Mindfulness/mindlessness and salivary immunoglobin A*. Unpublished manuscript, Harvard University, Cambridge.

Jones, E. L., & Davis, K. E. (1965). From acts to dispositions: The attributional process in person perception. In L. Berkowitz (Ed.), *Advances in experimental social psychology* (Vol. 2). New York: Academic Press.

Jones, E., Farina, A., Hastorf, A., Markus, H., Miller, D., & Scott, R. (1984). *Social stigma*. New York: W. H. Freeman.

Jones, E., & Nisbett, R. (1972). *The actor and the observer: Divergent perceptions of the causes of behavior*. Morristown: General Learning Press.

Jonsson, C., Malhammer, G., & Waldton, S. (1976). Abnormalities in the orienting response in senile dementia. *Actra Psychiatrica Scandinavia,* **54,** 323–332.

Kagan, J. (1986). *Meaning and procedure*. Unpublished manuscript, Harvard University, Cambridge.

Kanfer, E., & Goldfoot, E. (1966). Self-control and tolerance of noxious stimulation. *Psychological Reports,* **18,** 79–85.

Kanouse, D. (1972). Language, labelling, and attribution. In E. E. Jones, D. Kanouse, H. Kelly, R. Nisbett, S. Valons, & B. Deiner (Eds.), *Attribution: Perceiving the causes of behavior*. Morristown, NY: General Learning Press.

Karsten, A. (1928). Mental satiation. In J. de Rivera (Ed.), *Field theory as human science*. New York: Gardner Press.

Kiesler, C. (1966). Conflict and the number of choice alternatives. *Psychology Reports,* **18,** 603–610.

Krech, D., Rosenzweig, M., & Bennet, E. (1962). Relations between brain chemistry and problem solving among rats raised in enriched and impoverished environments. *Journal of Comparative and Physiological Psychology,* **55,** 801–807.

Lalljee, M., Watson, M., & White, P. (1982). Explorations, attributions, and the social context of unexpected behavior. *European Journal of Social Psychology,* **12,** 17–19.

Langer, E. (1975). The illusion of control. *Journal of Personality and Social Psychology*, **32**, 311–328.
Langer, E. (1978). Rethinking the role of thought in social interaction. In J. Harvey, W. Ickes, & Kidd (Eds.), *New directions in attribution research*. New Jersey: Erlbaum.
Langer, E. (1983). Playing the middle against both ends: The usefulness of adult cognitive activity as a model for cognitive activity in childhood and old age. In S. Yussen (Ed.), *The development of reflection*. New York: Academic Press.
Langer, E. (1989). *Mindfulness*. Reading, MA: Addison-Wesley.
Langer, E., Bashner, R., & Chanowitz, B. (1985a). Decreasing prejudice by increasing discrimination. *Journal of Personality and Social Psychology*, **49**, 113–120.
Langer, E., Beck, P., Janoff-Bulman, R., & Timko, C. (1984). The relationship between cognitive deprivation and longevity in senile and nonsenile elderly populations. *Academic Psychology Bulletin*, **6**, 211–226.
Langer, E., Blank, A., & Chanowitz, B. (1978). The mindlessness of ostensibly thoughtful action: The role of placebic information in interpersonal interaction. *Journal of Personality and Social Psychology*, **36**, 886–893.
Langer, E., Chanowitz, B., & Blank, A. (1985b). Mindlessness–mindfulness in perspective: A reply to Valerie Folkes. *Journal of Personality and Social Psychology*, **48**, 605–607.
Langer, E., Chanowitz, B., Rhodes, M., Jacobs, S., Palmerino, M., & Thayer, P. (1988a). Nonsequential development and aging. In C. Alexander & E. Langer (Eds.). *Human growth beyond formal operations*. New York: Oxford University Press, in press.
Langer, E., Dillon, M. & Kurtz, R., & Katz, M. (1988b). *Believing is seeing: Using mindlessness to improve vision*. Unpublished manuscript, Harvard University, Cambridge.
Langer, E., Field, S., Pachas, W., & Abrams, E. (1988c). *A mindful treatment for arthritis*. Unpublished manuscript, Harvard University, Cambridge.
Langer, E., & Imber, L. (1979). When practice makes imperfect: The debilitating effects of overlearning. *Journal of Personality and Social Psychology*, **37**, 2014–2025.
Langer, E., & Imber, L. (1980). The role of mindlessness in the perception of deviance. *Journal of Personality and Social Psychology*, **39**, 360–367.
Langer, E., Janis, I., & Wolfer, J. (1975). Reduction of psychological stress in surgical patients. *Journal of Experimental Social Psychology*, **11**, 155–165.
Langer, E., & Lindsay, P. (1988). *The MMQ: A scale to measure mindlessness/mindfulness*. Unpublished manuscript, Harvard University, Cambridge.
Langer, E., & Newman, E. (1979). The role of mindlessness in a typical social psychology experiment. *Personality and Social Psychology Bulletin*, **5**, 195–299.
Langer, E., & Piper, A. (1987). The prevention of mindlessness. *Journal of Personality and Social Psychology*, **53**, 280–287.
Langer, E., Piper, A., & Friedus, J. (1987). *Preventing mindlessness: A positive side of dyslexia*. Unpublished manuscript, Harvard University, Cambridge.
Langer, E., & Rodin, J. (1976). The effects of enhanced personal responsibility for the aged: A field experiment in an institutional setting. *Journal of Personality and Social Psychology*, **34**, 191–198.
Langer, E., Rodin, J., Beck, P., Spitzer, L., & Weinman, C. (1979). Environmental determinants of memory improvement in late adulthood. *Journal of Personality and Social Psychology*, **37**, 2014–2025.
Langer, E., & Weinman, C. (1981). When thinking disrupts intellectual performance: Mindlessness on an overlearned task. *Personality and Social Psychology Bulletin*, **7**, 240–243.
Linville, P. (1987). Self-complexity as a cognitive buffer against stress-related illness and depression. *Journal of Personality and Social Psychology*, **52**, 663–676.
Lorber, M. (1981, April). The disposable cortex. *Psychology Today*.
Marlatt, G. A., & Rohsenow, D. J. (1980). Cognitive processes in alcohol use: Expectancy and the

balanced placebo design. In Nancy K. Mello (Ed.), *Advances in substance abuse: Behavioral and biological research* (Vol. 1, pp. 159–199). Greenwich, CT: Jai Press.

McAllister, D., Mitchell, T., & Beach, L. (1979). The contingency model for the selection of decision strategies: An empirical test of the effects of significance, accountability, and reversibility. *Organizational Behavior and Human Performance*, **24**, 228–244.

McClelland, D. C., Alexander, C., & Marks, E. (1982). The need for power, stress, immune function, and illness among male prisoners. *Journal of Abnormal Psychology*, **91**, 61–70.

McClelland, D. C., Patel, V. G., Brown, D., & Kelner, S. (1985). *The relationship of blood sugar levels to helper and suppressor T cell percentages in normals and insulin dependent diabetics*. Unpublished manuscript.

Meichenbaum, D. (1977). *Cognitive-behavior modification: An integrative approach*. New York: Plenum.

Mikula, G., & Schlamberger, K. (1984). What people think about an unjust event. *European Journal of Social Psychology*, **15**, 37–49.

Miller, S. (1980). Why having control reduces stress: If I can stop the roller coaster, I don't want to get off. In J. Garber & M. Seligman (Eds.), *Human helplessness: Theory and applications* (pp. 71–96). New York: Academic Press.

Navon, D. (1984). Resources—a theoretical soup stone? *Psychological Review*, **91**, 216–234.

Nemeth, C. (1986). Differential contributions of majority and minority influence. *Psychological Review*, **93**, 23–32.

Newtson, D. (1976). Foundations of attributions: The perception of ongoing behavior. In J. Harvey, W. Ickes, & R. Kidd (Eds.), *New directions in attribution research* (Vol. 1, pp. 223–242). Hillsdale, NJ: Erlbaum.

Nisbett, R., & Ross, L. (1980). *Human inference: Strategies and shortcomings*. Englewood Cliffs, NJ: Prentice-Hall.

Nisbett, R., & Wilson, N. (1977). Knowing more than you can tell. *Psychological Review*, **84**, 231–259.

Nottebohm, F. (1984). New neurons form adulthood. *Science*, **224**, 1325–1326.

Orme-Johnson, D. W., & Farrow, J. T. (Eds.) (1977). *Scientific research on the Transcendental Meditation and TM-Sidhi Program: Collected papers* (Vol. 1). Livingston Manor, NY: MIU Press.

Pennebaker, J., & Hoover, C. (1985). Inhibitions vs. cognitions: Towards an understanding of trauma and disease. In R. J. Davidson, G. E. Schwartz, & G. D. Shapiro (Eds.), *Consciousness and self-regulation*. New York: Plenum.

Pennebaker, J., & O'Heeron, R. (1984). Confiding in others and illness rates among spouses of suicide and accidental death. *Journal of Abnormal Psychology*, **93**, 473–476.

Peterson, R. (1977). Retrieval failures in alcohol state dependent learning. *Psychopharmacology*, **55**, 141–146.

Piper, A., & Langer, E. (1984). Aging and mindful control. In M. Baltes & P. Baltes (Eds.), *Aging and control*. Hillsdale, NJ: Erlbaum.

Presences, no. 1, (1955). Paris.

Pyszczynski, T., & Greenberg, J. (1981). Role of discomfort expectancies in the instigation of attributional process. *Journal of Personality and Social Psychology*, **40**, 31–38.

Richter, C. P. (1957). On the phenomenon of sudden death in animals and man. *Psychosomatic Medicine*, **19**, 191–198.

Riegel, K., Riegel, R., & Meyer, G. (1967). A study of the drop-out rates in longitudinal research on aging: The prediction of death. *Journal of Personality and Social Psychology*, **5**, 342–348.

Rodin, J., & Langer E. (1977). Long-term effects of a control-relevant intervention among the institutionalized aged. *Journal of Personality and Social Psychology*, **35**, 897–902.

Rosch, E. (1973). On the internal structure of perceptual and semantic categories. T. E. Moore (Ed.). *Cognitive development*. New York: Academic Press.

Rosenzweig, M., Bennet, E., & Diamond, M. (1972). Brain changes in response to experience. *Scientific American,* **226**(2), 22–29.

Schank, R., & Abelson, R. (1977). *Scripts, plans, goals, and understanding.* Hillsdale, NJ: Erlbaum.

Schneider, W., & Shiffrin, R. M. (1977). Controlled and automatic human human information processing: I. Detection, search, and attention. *Psychological Review,* **84**, 1–66.

Schwartz, G., & Shapiro, J. D. (Eds.). (1985). *Consciousness of self-regulation,* New York: Plenum.

Seligman, M. E. P. (1975). *Helplessness: On depression, development, and death.* San Francisco: W. H. Freeman and Co.

Shiffrin, R. M., & Schneider, W. (1977). Controlled and automatic human information processing: II. Perceptual learning, automatic attending, and a general theory. *Psychological Review,* **84**, 127–190.

Siegel, S., Hirsan, R., Krank, M., & McGully, Y. (1982). Heroin overdose death: Contribution of drugs as actual environmental cues. *Science,* **216**, 436–437.

Silver, R., & Wortman, C. (1980). Coping with undesirable life events. In J. Garber & M. Seligman (Eds.), *Human helplessness: Theory and application.* New York: Academic Press.

Smith, E., & Medin, D. (1981). *Categories and concepts.* Cambridge: Harvard University Press.

Smith, E., & Miller, F. (1983). Mediation among attributional inferences and comprehension processes: Initial findings of a general method. *Journal of Personality and Social Psychology,* **44**, 492–505.

Strube, M., Berry, J., & Moergen, S. (1985). Relinquishment of control and the type A behavior pattern: The role of performance evaluation. *Journal of Personality and Social Psychology,* **49**, 831–842.

Taylor, S. E., & Fiske, S. (1978). Salience, attention, and attribution: Top of the head phenomenon. In L. Berkowitz (Ed.), *Advances in experimental social psychology* (Vol. 11). New York: Academic Press.

Tesser, A. (1978). Self-generated attitude change. In L. Berkowitz (Ed.), *Advances in experimental social psychology* (Vol. 11, pp. 289–338). New York: Academic Press.

Tetlock, P. (1983). Accountability and complexity of thought. *Journal of Personality and Social Psychology,* **45**, 74–83.

Tversky, A., & Kahneman, D. (1974). Judgement under uncertainty: Heuristics and biases. *Science,* **185**, 1124–1131.

Ullrich, R. S. (1984). View through a window may influence recovery from surgery. *Science,* **224**, 420–421.

Volkman, F., & Greenough, W. (1972). Rearing complexity affects branching of dendrites in the visual cortex of the rat. *Science,* **176**, 1445–1447.

Ward, W., & Jenkins, H. (1965). The display of information and the judgement of contingency. *Canadian Journal of Psychology,* **19**(3), 231–241.

Wilson, G., & Abrams, D. (1977). Effects of alcohol on social anxiety and physiological arousal: Cognitive versus pharmacological procedures. *Cognitive Therapy and Research,* **1**, 195–210.

Wittgenstein, L. (1953). *Philosophical investigations* (G. E. M. Anscomge, Trans.) New York: Macmillan.

Wong, P., & Wiener, B. (1981). When people ask "why" questions and the heuristics of attributional search. *Journal of Personality and Social Psychology,* **40**, 650–663.

Yukor, H. (Ed.). (1987). *Attitudes towards persons with disabilities.* New York: Springer.

THE TRADEOFFS OF SOCIAL CONTROL AND INNOVATION IN GROUPS AND ORGANIZATIONS

Charlan Jeanne Nemeth

DEPARTMENT OF PSYCHOLOGY
UNIVERSITY OF CALIFORNIA
BERKELEY, CALIFORNIA 94720

Barry M. Staw

SCHOOL OF BUSINESS ADMINISTRATION
UNIVERSITY OF CALIFORNIA
BERKELEY, CALIFORNIA 94720

I. Introduction

In both small groups and larger organizations, one of the most significant psychological tendencies is a strain toward uniformity, a tendency for people to agree on some issue or to conform to some behavioral pattern. Such uniformity, we argue, has both necessary and desirable elements, particularly with regard to attainment of goals and harmony. It also has detrimental elements. Uniformity may result in decreases in innovation, in the detection of error, or in the willingness or ability to adapt to changing circumstances. We first explore forces for uniformity and attempt to understand why they occur and what personal and situational elements foster them. We then explore the realm of dissent and investigate ways in which it can contribute to the functioning of small groups and larger organizations.

In this article, the description of research on social influence moves rather freely between laboratory settings and organizational contexts. The laboratory studies follow several well-developed research paradigms, with variations in conditions and resultant findings occurring in a cumulative fashion. In contrast, organizational studies of social influence have tended to draw on a wide variety of psychological and sociological theories, resulting in a more disparate set of findings, which have rarely been drawn together. Whereas the social psychological work has typically been experimental, the organizational research ranges from quantitative experiments and surveys to more qualitative case studies. Thus, our integration of work on social control and innovation will necessitate mixing results with varying levels of internal and external validity.

In our discussion of social control and innovation, we also move freely between the microscopic and the macroscopic. Our goal has not been to show how basic principles of social influence can be simply generalized from laboratory groups to functioning organizations, because this would no doubt be misleading. Instead, we have attempted to show (1) how studies of organizational behavior can profit from knowledge of more basic social influence processes, and (2) how experimental group research can be enriched by an understanding of more complex organizational processes. We therefore will alternate between social psychological research and organizational work in illustrating concepts in social control and innovation. We avoid specifying how the microscopic processes aggregate to explain more global behavior because so little is known about such composition rules. In contrast, we draw analogies between group and organizational phenomena and speak to the differences, where they are relevant. Thus, this essay is pretheoretic in nature—an effort to weave together disparate literatures so as to further the work in each subarea, creating a bridge on which future integrative research and theory can be built.

II. Some Theoretical Considerations of the Strain toward Uniformity

In 1950, Festinger noted the importance of pressures for uniformity in his now-classic paper on informal social communication. After studying spontaneous patterns of communication in small groups, Festinger observed the power of pressures toward agreement or conformity and argued that such pressures arise out of two major considerations. The first he termed "social reality," referring to our dependence on the opinions of others for maintaining confidence in the positions that we hold. As noted by Festinger, there are beliefs that can be validated by physical reality (e.g., one can determine if a surface is fragile versus unbreakable by hitting it with a hammer) and beliefs that depend on others for social validation (e.g., knowing who "should" win a Presidential election). For social beliefs, subjective validity depends on whether others share one's views; they provide the anchor or comparison point by which one can validate his or her own opinion. Of course, as Festinger pointed out, it is not necessary to have complete unanimity before one's opinion is considered valid, nor are all people equally important in providing social validation. Some people serve as more important reference groups, their opinions and agreement being especially important in determining subjective confidence in a position.

A second pressure toward uniformity, termed "group locomotion" by Festinger, arises from the desire or need for the group to move toward some goal. It should be clear that groups can be immobilized by dissent and disagreement. When there is consensus on both the goal and the ways to achieve that goal, there is an impetus to move, to locomote, toward that goal.

From the foregoing considerations, it is evident that the strain toward uniformity can be a very persuasive and powerful process in small groups and organizations. Because almost all attitudes, beliefs, and opinions rely on subjective rather than objective realities, and because most groups and organizations do have goals toward which they attempt to locomote, members of collectivities find themselves subject to pressures toward agreement, toward behaving in accordance with existing norms and patterns of behavior. The questions, of course, are, "How is such uniformity achieved? Whose position does each member adopt? And what are the consequences of the pressures for uniformity for both small groups and organizations?"

As we explore the ways in which people come to share the same or similar viewpoints, we note that the agreement can be a result of compromise, or mutual movement toward a central point; it can be the result of movement to, or adoption of, a viewpoint that has already been established by others. It can occur around the position held by those in power or those who constitute a numerical majority. These are the statistically "usual" ways in which uniformity of viewpoints and actions can be achieved. However, agreement could be on the position originally held by a newcomer, by a statistical minority, or by someone (or someones) low in power. While these forms of influence are less usual, they can be important mechanisms for groups and organizations to adapt to changing circumstances, to detect new solutions to old problems, and to evidence creativity.

In this article, we explore the various ways in which influence processes achieve uniformity. We then look to the broader issues regarding the quality of decision making and performance as a function of social influence processes.

III. Ways of Achieving Uniformity

A. DEVELOPMENT OF NORMS AND AGREEMENT BY "COMPROMISE"

Agreement can be achieved via compromise, and the early work by Sherif (1935) on the formation of norms manifests such a process. In attempting to understand how people come to share viewpoints, Sherif studied ad hoc groups (people with no past or established way of viewing a particular issue) with regard to their developing judgments on an ambiguous perceptual issue. The *autokinetic effect* was chosen, which is simply the phenomenon that when an individual is shown a stationary pinpoint of light in an otherwise dark room, the light appears to move, and it may appear to move in any direction. This is an illusion of movement and one on which people initially disagree. Sherif's questions were simply, "What would happen if an individual were placed in such a highly ambiguous situation, one that lacked any external frames of reference? Would the person's judgments be highly variable or would they reflect a subjective frame of reference? When a group of individuals was placed in a similar situation, would it be erratic or would it, too, show a subjectively determined frame of reference, a shared way of viewing things?

Sherif simply asked individuals to indicate the direction of the movement of light. Alone, each person judged the movement of light to be quite erratic; over time, they established their own anchoring points and ranges around which most observations were made. Thus they created their own "norm." When placed with other individuals, Sherif found that the judgments of others affected the perceptual judgments made. This was studied in two ways. In one situation, individuals first made their judgments alone and then were placed with others in a group. In a second situation, the individuals first made judgments of the light movement in a group and then made further judgments by themselves.

Sherif found that when individuals first made judgments in the group setting, they then adhered to the group norm, even when making judgments alone. However, if they first made judgments alone, there still was some tendency for convergence when placed in groups, but the tendency was less marked than when they faced the situation in the group first. Thus, group influence on the autokinetic task was particularly powerful when it was part of the origination of the norm.

In summary, Sherif found that individuals, when faced with an ambiguous situation in group setting, tended to converge in their judgments until a shared frame of reference was achieved. That frame of reference then continued to operate even when individuals were no longer subject to social influence. It is important to note that the agreement reached in such settings occurred as a result of mutual compromise. The norm was somewhere "in between" original individual judgments. As we look at some of the elements present in such a setting that may have fostered such a process of compromise, it is important to note that the situation was highly ambiguous; there was not even a prior history for such judgments. No one could claim expertise or superior ability, nor was there any prior commitment to a particular point of view. It is of interest to note that when the individual norms were developed after the group experience, there was the greatest degree of convergence. This is consistent with the notion that a relative lack of prior history or commitment fosters maximum compromise and agreement in a social context.

B. PERPETUATION OF NORMS: THE SOCIAL-PSYCHOLOGICAL AND ORGANIZATIONAL PERSPECTIVES

In a good deal of subsequent research, both by Sherif and others, there is evidence that once a norm is established, newcomers come to share that norm. Thus, such norms continue even as new members are added and old members leave. In studies by Jacobs and Campbell (1961), for example, an arbitrary norm was created by several confederates influencing the judgment of naive subjects. As the confederates exited the study, however, their influence on group norms continued to be felt. As generations of fresh subjects judged the movement of light, their judgments continued to be influenced by the judgments of the confederates who had originated the group norm, albeit with decreasing strength. That is, as newcomers entered the study, they *slowly* brought the group norm originally created by confederates down to a baseline level. In reflecting on the Jacobs and Campbell study, there are two contrasting phenomena being demonstrated. On the one hand, their data showed how arbitrary norms can be created and persist well beyond the point at which they are directly supported by their originators. On the other hand, their research demonstrated how new entrants to a group bring with them a source of reality, a way of influencing social norms so that they are more in line with external phenomena.

As we move to the organizational context, we find that cultures arise in organizations in quite similar ways to those in which norms develop in groups. An organizational culture (1) provides meaning to behavior and events surrounding individual members, (2) supplies a way to distinguish one firm or collectivity from another, (3) is a vehicle for solidarity and support, and (4) offers continuity over time. And, just as the originators of norms may exert strong influence on subsequent group judgments, an organization's founder is thought to be crucial for development of its culture (Schein, 1985). The founder's management style sets the tone for interpersonal relationships and his or her priorities set the ordering of values for the collectivity. As a firm grows, the founder's personal style and preferences are likely to be modeled and emulated by a management team (people probably hired by the founder) and diffused throughout the organization. Thus, even after the founder passes from the scene, as in the normative transmission studies, the organization is likely to carry his or her imprint (see, e.g., Martin, 1982, for a discussion of Thomas Watson's long-standing influence on IBM; and Schein, 1985, for other detailed case examples of the role of the founder on organizational culture).

Directly extrapolating the normative transmission studies to field settings requires some caution, however. As Weick and Gilfillan (1971) have noted, one reason that beliefs may persist in actual situations is that they have a logical underpinning. They may be warranted, given their ease of use and availability, constituting one of many possible solutions to an environmental problem. Therefore, norms that are totally arbitrary are less likely to persist than those with some environmental justification, even if the latter, over time, are not optimal solutions to external problems.

Zucker (1977) directly addressed the issue of normative transmission in an organization-like setting. She showed that simply running the Jacobs and Campbell experiment with some changes in social labelling produced greater persistence of the norm. Subjects were run in conditions in which they were subjected to simple social influence (i.e., the judgments of other peers, as in the Jacobs and Campbell study) or to judgments in the context of an organization. For the latter, two forms of organizational context were used. Individuals either joined what was described as an ongoing organization or joined an organization with some minimal hierarchy (e.g., the person with the longest tenure in the group was given the title of "light operator"). Zucker found that individuals maintained their beliefs longest, and that these beliefs were most resistant to change, when they operated in an organization with hierarchy followed by the nonhierarchical organization and the nonorganizational context. Thus, the transmission of norms may be strengthened by the institutional character of formal organizations.

A factor that may additionally promote the transmission of norms in organizations is the selection of members. Unlike the normative transmission studies, the perpetuation of beliefs in organizations is not simply a matter of observation and imitation of behavior. Ongoing organizations have norms even before new individuals ever become members, and the selection process favors those who share such norms. First, individuals have been found to self-select themselves into organizations on the basis of the organizations' presumed values and characteristics (Holland, 1976). Second, the organization usually makes a concerted effort to find those who fit in, in terms of values and skills, with the current organizational membership (Schneider, 1987). Thus, a substantial amount of cultural transmission generally occurs before individuals ever enter the confines of the organization.

C. UNIFORMITY VIA POWER AND STATUS

While originators of group norms and organizational selection affect the transmission of beliefs over time, it is clear that there are other immediate sources of influence that can either maintain or modify the original norms. Persons who hold positions of power or who are viewed as higher in status are powerful sources of influence, and agreement is often achieved by adopting the positions they propose. To illustrate the power of such processes, consider the classic studies by Milgram (1963, 1965, 1974) on obedience to an authority figure. In these studies, the authority was a scientist presumably studying the relationship between punishment and learning. The individual (who assumed he was participating in such an experiment) was in fact being tested for his obedience to this scientist. The "scientist" instructed him to shock the "learner" each time that the learner erred and, further, to increase the intensity of the shock with each error. Given that the subject believed that the shocks were painful, Milgram investigated when the people would resist the authority who instructed them to continue the shocks. Would they stop after 150 volts, when the learner first asked to be freed? Would they increase the intensity until the learner no longer responded (at 300 volts)? Would they continue to the end (i.e., 450 volts)? In fact, 63% of the actual subjects continued to the end and delivered 450 volts. These individuals were businessmen, professional men, white-collar workers and blue-collar workers.

Such obedience to an authority, particularly one who had no real power to reward or punish the individuals themselves, was unexpected. Most people predicted that individuals would defy the experimenter at some point. Psychiatrists, for example, predicted that most would defy the authority at 150 volts. They were wrong. Further, this willingness to obey authority was found even with changes in the subject population or the setting. When women served as subjects, the results were similar. Even when the authority figure was of less high status (i.e., in which the experimenter was in a run-down building in downtown Bridgeport, Connecticut, rather than at Yale), 40% of the individuals still obeyed the authority fully (Milgram, 1974).

The results of such studies are even more compelling when one considers the relative lack of power held by Milgram's authority figure. There was no past or future with this individual; he had no real reward or coercive power over the subjects. In ongoing formal organizations, there is very real reward and coercive power. Raises, promotions, reprimands and firings are obvious examples. There is a past and, so the employee hopes, a future with those individuals whose power is embedded in the hierarchy. In a typical bureaucracy, roles are specified by those in command, and exceptions to standard procedures or role specifications are referred up the hierarchy for resolution. General policies are formulated at the highest levels, given specification by middle management, and finally implemented by those lower in the hierarchy. In fact, influence can be so evident and orderly in such a system that it is commonly labeled a "machine model" or mechanistic approach to organization.

Although a large number of organizations emphasize hierarchical power and orderly decision making, there do exist other organizations with more organic structures (Burns & Stalker, 1961), with power not so firmly unidirectional, or with its subparts not so neatly supporting a common goal or theme. To illustrate the contrast, one could place, at one extreme, military and religious organizations with undeniable hierarchies and common goals. At the other extreme would be educational organizations (e.g., universities), with a set of very loosely coupled departments, minimally connected by a common budget and location (Weick, 1976). Most organizations no doubt fall between these two end points.

Though most organizations have a formal hierarchy and a communication system that is better designed for downward than for upward flow of influence, even the most bureaucatic organizations display some power complexities. One such complexity (noted by Mechanic, 1962) is that participants lower in an organizational hierarchy sometimes have substantial latitude in the means by which they implement orders. They also vary in their capacity to influence those formally in charge. As an illustration, Crozier (1964) found that maintenance workers in a large factory possessed virtual immunity from supervisory pressures because they were the only ones who could keep the plant running. Another complexity is that power can emanate from many disparate sources in formal organizations. Not only may each department or division have its own agenda in trying to influence organizational priorities, so too will external constituencies such as suppliers, customers, and regulatory agencies exert control (Mintzberg, 1983). Thus, many organizations can best be described as a confluence of shifting coalitions (Cyert & March, 1963) and power centers rather than a simple hierarchical structure.

Research on organizational power has demonstrated that power comes from the ability to provide resources for the system and to help the system cope with major sources of uncertainty (Hickson, Hinings, Lee, Schneck, & Pennings, 1971; Hinings, Hickson, Pennings, & Schneck, 1974; Pfeffer & Salancik, 1974). This implies that shifts in the power structure are a way in which organizations can adapt or align themselves with changes in the environment. Those who possess critical skills and on whom the organization depends most will, according to this view, attain the greatest power, influencing the way the organization is structured and behaves. The problem with this "critical contingencies" approach to power (Hickson et al., 1971), however, is that power can be self-perpetuating. Even though the environment of the organization changes markedly, those in power may still control the organization's decision processes, thus preserving their influence over the formation of goals, policies, and the allocation of resources. The power structure can be shaken by reality (just as a group's arbitrary set of beliefs eventually return to baseline over time), but the adjustment process often substantially lags behind changes in environmental conditions.

D. UNIFORMITY VIA CONFORMITY TO MAJORITY VIEWS

Much as we have seen that original norms and persons in power can ensure uniformity in viewpoint, there is a more tacit form of influence provided by peers. In the sequence of studies that Milgram conducted on the willingness of people to provide painful shocks to a "learner," an important but often neglected study showed the power of peers, even in the absence of an authority figure. In this study (Milgram, 1974), the authority figure (the experimenter) left the decision of shock intensity to a group of three individuals; one of these was a naive subject and the other two were paid accomplices of the experimenter. In this situation, the shock that was to be given to the learner was the *lowest* level suggested by the three individuals, thereby giving the naive subject complete control over the shock allocation. Even here, however, individuals increased their shock level in response to the increasing shock level suggested by the confederates. They did not adopt the exact position proposed by the confederates, but they "lagged" with increasing intensity. Thus, at Trial 5, when the two confederates suggested

Lever 5 (i.e., 75 volts), the mean response of the naive subjects was Lever 4 (i.e., 60 volts). By trial 30, when the confederates were suggesting Lever 30 (450 volts), the mean lever pulled was 14.13 (over 210 volts). Of 40 individuals, 10 went beyond Lever 25, and 7 went to Lever 30, the maximum intensity.

Majority opinion and its power over the viewpoints of individuals, or minorities of individuals, has a long history in social psychology, and it was perhaps most systematically explored in the years following the classic studies by Solomon Asch (1951, 1955). In the original studies, individuals were asked to choose which of 3 comparison lines was equal in length to a standard line. Alone, people had no difficulty. When confronted with an erroneous majority view, however, many individuals ignored the evidence of their own senses and agreed with the erroneous majority view. Approximately one-third of the responses were in such error. These early studies provided the paradigm and impetus for hundreds of studies investigating why conformity occurs and the ways in which such conformity can be increased or decreased (see generally, Allen, 1965).

As research proceeded, the theoretical developments were sparse, but two main reasons for conformity served as guiding forces for the research. One explanation, termed "informational influence" (Deutsch & Gerard, 1955), is that people accept the viewpoints of others as information about reality. The second explanation, termed "normative influence," is that people want to gain approval or avoid disapproval via conformity. Numerous studies have demonstrated the reasonableness of the distinction between informational and normative influence (see, generally, Allen, 1965). Thus, for example, conformity increases in face-to-face groups (Deutsch & Gerard, 1955); it increases with increasing size of the majority—though incrementally less after three or four individuals (Asch, 1955; Gerard, Wilhemy, & Conolley, 1968; Tanford & Penrod, 1984). It increases with increased expertise on the part of the majority (Mausner, 1954), with greater task difficulty (Blake, Helson, & Monton, 1957), and with ambiguity in the stimulus situation (Crutchfield, 1955). While such factors may promote or impede the degree of conformity, the studies underscore a pervasive tendency for individuals to follow a majority position, even an erroneous majority position. They do so with regard to the judgment of factual items, be it visual (Asch, 1956), auditory (Olmstead & Blake, 1955) or from memory (Deutsch & Gerard, 1955); they do so with regard to opinion items, ranging from the relatively unimportant to the highly important (see, generally, Allen, 1965).

The power of this conformity process is also evident in nonexperimental settings. Kalven and Zeisel (1966), for example, studied actual jury deliberations. These researchers collected information on the first ballot of the 12 jurors and also on the final verdict rendered. The majority position on the first ballot was found to be highly predictive of the final verdict. In fact, when a majority of persons (7–11) favored "guilty," the percentage of "guilty" verdicts was 86%, 9% were "hung" (that is, did not render a verdict), and only 5% rendered a "not guilty" verdict. Similarly, when a majority of persons favored "not guilty," 91% of the verdicts were "not guilty," 7% "hung," and only 2% rendered a "guilty" verdict.

Given the power of majority opinion, consider then the situation confronting newcomers in organizations. They are often painfully aware of the forces for conformity when they arrive at their jobs. They must learn not only the skills and the tasks in order to execute their roles, but also the nuances of organizational life—the norms of dress, speech, and behavior that are associated with being accepted and getting ahead in the system. As described by most scholars of organizational socialization (e.g., Schein, 1978; Van Maanen & Schein, 1979), the individual must progress through various stages in his or her organizational life, moving from outsider to trusted insider in the firm. Though subject to controversy and subjected to little empirical validation, many of these stage models do highlight common themes in organizational socialization. As summarized by Wanous (1980), individuals must confront and accept organizational reality, achieve role clarity, locate oneself in the organizational context, and detect signposts of successful socialization. In short, the newcomer must make sense of the organization's demands and develop strategies to cope with them. Observing the behavior of others—particularly the majority of others—is one way of learning these demands and coping strategies.

Social influence is especially strong in terms of what Schein (1968) has termed "pivotal norms." These norms relate most closely to the central concerns of the organization (e.g., belief in nuclear power by a utility company) or reflect upon the identity of the firm (e.g., conservative dress that implies fiduciary responsibility in banking). Similar to Hollander's (1960) contention that one needs to both conform and show competence in order to achieve status, Schein (1968) argues that conformity in terms of pivotal norms is essential to gaining organizational acceptance and subsequent influence. The degree of conformity mandated by the situation differs according to one's role in the organization, however. Those in managerial positions are subject to influence over a wider range of attitudes and behavior. Theirs is a pervasive role, and, as such, any loose comments or demeanor, even off-the-job, can bring reprimand and recrimination. Blue-collar jobs, on the other hand, tend to be more restricted roles, in which behavior is expected to conform to expectations only within the confines of the organization. Thus, one would expect much greater internalization of norms for those in pervasive rather than restricted roles. One would also expect greater selectivity on the basis of nonperformance (e.g., background and personality) criteria for those entering pervasive roles. As Kanter (1977) has noted, managers tend to reproduce themselves, using similarity in attitudes and demographic characteristics as a means of reducing uncertainty in the hiring process.

As recognized in the conformity literature, ambiguity also contributes to uniformity in beliefs. We have previously noted that individuals seek consensus in their opinions of ambiguous stimuli. It is equally apparent that individuals' work attitudes are affected by the judgments of others. In tests of what has been called the social-information-processing (SIP) approach to job attitudes (Salancik & Pfeffer, 1978), it has been demonstrated that job attitudes depend on the social labeling of work (whether it is seen as desirable or not) and the opinions of others (whether one's cow-orkers appear satisfied or not). After several laboratory and field validations of the SIP perspective (Griffin, 1983; O'Reilly & Caldwell, 1979; White & Mitchell, 1979), it is now believed that objective job characteristics are only one (albeit important) determinant of work attitudes. Other, just as important, social influences include the definition of work by management, coworkers, unions, family, and the larger society, including direct and indirect communications from each of these sources.

Ambiguity concerning the definition of performance can also contribute to uniformity in organizations. Generally, as one progresses up the hierarchy of an organization, work tasks become increasingly amorphous, and there are ambiguous criteria for evaluation. Managing a product, long-range planning, and market analysis, for example, are not as easily judged as manual activities involving production or direct sales. And, as criteria for evaluation become more ambiguous, the reliance on personal characteristics, demeanor, and "potential" in performance evaluations increases. Under such conditions, pressures toward conformity may increase for the individual because adherence to the norms of the organization and conforming to the tastes of the supervisor can become surrogates for promotion criteria (Evan, 1961). Those seeking upward advancement in ambiguous settings (e.g., staff vs. line jobs) can therefore be expected to attend closely to any cues related to social approval as well as the more visible norms of organizational behavior (Pfeffer, 1977).

E. UNIFORMITY VIA DISSENTING, MINORITY VIEWS

Up to now, we have concentrated on the influence exerted by norms and by persons holding positions of relative power and influence. To some extent, this is reflective of the bulk of the research endeavors, both in social psychology and in organizational behavior. There has been a tendency in those literatures to assume that influence flows from the stronger to the weaker, from those with more authority to those with less authority, as well as from the numerical majority to the minority. Nonetheless, as we have seen, some organizational researchers have recognized the multidirectionality of social influence. Some social psychologists have also tried to understand ways in which those lower in power or fewer in number exert influence.

In the early 1970s, Moscovici and Faucheux (1972) and Moscovici and Nemeth (1974) argued that social influence, as studied by social psychologists, tended to be equated with conformity. From this perspective, the individual or the minority was seen as a passive agent. They could conform to the wishes and viewpoints of the majority, or they could resist such influence by remaining independent. However, these theorists reasoned that a consideration of social change rather than social control led one to the inescapable conclusion that minorities do influence majorities, that originally deviant views can come to prevail. After 15 years of research on the ways in which minorities come to exercise such influence, one finding that has been consistently replicated is that minorities must be consistent over time in order to exercise influence (see generally Maass & Clark, 1984).

In an early experimental study on minority influence, Moscovici, Lage, and Naffrechoux (1969) asked individuals in groups of 6 to judge the color and the perceived brightness of a series of blue slides. Two of the 6 individuals, unbeknownst to the naive subjects, were confederates who consistently judged the blue slides to be "green." In such a condition, naive subjects reported nearly 9% "green" responses. When those two confederates were inconsistent in their judgment—that is, when they judged two-thirds of the slides to be "green" and one-third to be "blue," no influence was manifest. Less than 1% of the responses were "green," a finding that is insignificantly different from the control group (i.e., individuals who were exposed to no dissenting viewpoints and who consistently judged the slides to be "blue").

Subsequent research has shown that the behavioral style exhibiting consistency is more subtle than simple repetition. For example, Nemeth, Swedlund, and Kanki (1974) had individuals in groups of 6 judge the color and brightness of a series of 20 blue slides. In three of the conditions, the two confederates were not repetitious in their judgments. On half of the trials, they reported the slides to be "green" and on half of the trials they reported them to be "green-blue." However, the pattern of the responses differed by condition, with a resulting differential in subjects' perception of consistency. In one condition, the two confederates judged the 10 "dim" slides to be "green" and the 10 "bright" slides to be "green-blue." In a second condition, the pattern was reversed (that is, the "dim" slides were judged to be "green-blue" and the "bright" slides were judged to be "green"). In a third condition, these 10 "green" and 10 "green-blue" judgments were randomly paired with the slides, that is, without regard to brightness. In the conditions in which the confederates patterned their judgments to a property of the stimulus (in this case, brightness), they exerted considerable influence. Naive subjects judged the slides to contain "green" over 25% of the time. When the judgments were random, influence was negligible. Less than 1% of the responses contained "green," a finding insignificant from the 0% "green" response of the control group.

Subsequent research refined the concept of consistency, with distinctions, for example, between rigidity and consistency (Mugny, 1982; Ricateau, 1971). Inflexible, extreme positions, it was found, could produce resistance instead of influence. Furthermore, there is some evidence that nonrepetitive behavioral styles that still preserve the perception of consistency may be more effective than repetition. Nemeth and Brilmayer (1987), for example, show that compromise "at the last minute" may produce both manifest and latent influence. Levine et al. (Levine, Saxe, & Harris, 1976; Levine, Sroka, & Snyder, 1977) offer evidence that a conformer-turned-deviant is more influential than a consistent deviant. Yet, most researchers find that, on balance, the perception of consistency of position over time is a necessary if not sufficient condition for minorities to exercise influence (Maass & Clark, 1984).

Additional research concentrated on the importance of perceived confidence on the part of the minority. Some work documented that minorities have some advantages and that, in particular, the fewer the number, the more they are presumed to be confident when they maintain a deviant position (Nemeth, Wachtler, & Endicott, 1977). Other work documented the impact of behavioral acts indicating confidence. In one study, for example, Nemeth and Wachtler (1974) investigated influence exerted by a confederate in a simulated jury deliberation, who took a deviant position with regard to compensation on a personal injury case. Prior to the deliberation, that person either chose the head seat at the table, chose a side seat, was assigned to the head seat or was assigned to a side seat. It was found that the act of taking the head seat, an act that translated into perceived confidence, rendered that individual far more effective. Though his arguments were the same, he significantly swayed majority opinion more when he chose the head seat than when he chose a side seat, or when he was assigned to a seat, be it a head or side seat.

In addition to research emphasizing the importance of behavioral style for minority influence, studies have repeatedly documented that the influence exerted by minorities tends to be latent rather than manifest. We use this important work when we discuss performance issues. In most studies of minority influence, latent influence is greater than manifest influence. For example, people may show little movement to the minority position in public, yet they may often show considerably greater adoption of the position when asked later, in a slightly different way or on a related issue. In the early study by Moscovici et al. (1969), less than 9% of the public responses were "green" when individuals were exposed to the minority who consistently judged the slide to be "green." When subjects were asked subsequently to place a series of "blue-green" stimuli into the categories of "blue" or "green," well over half of these individuals showed a pattern consistent with the influence. They called more "blue-green" stimuli "green" than did a control group.

In the Nemeth and Wachtler (1974) study on jury deliberations, individuals did not move publicly to the compensation position advocated by the confederate. They thought his position was ridiculously low and would not agree to that position. However, they privately lowered their judgments of compensation on that case and they gave less compensation to the plaintiff in an entirely new case. Other work corroborates greater private than public changes to minority views

(Maass & Clark, 1984), and there is evidence that individuals show more influence on indirect judgments than on those directly related to the minority position (Mugny, 1982). Thus, there is considerable evidence that minorities exert more influence than is outwardly manifested.

Although the minority can exert influence, they tend not to have that influence acknowledged or recognized. Even when individuals are influenced by the minority's judgments, such as when they come to judge blue stimuli as "green," they still see the minority as being incorrect and has having poor color vision (Nemeth et al., 1974). Further, there is evidence that the minority that maintains its position is actually disliked, ridiculed, and held with disdain. In the early work by Schachter (1951), for example, people increased their communication to a deviant who maintained a differing position; when unsuccessful in getting him to rescind, they cut off communication and rejected him sociometrically. More recently, studies in minority influence show consistent dislike of the minority and there are anecdotal reports of threats toward a minority who maintains a position even on a hypothetical issue (Nemeth & Wachtler, 1974, 1983).

Such dislike appears to be exacerbated when deviance is viewed as impeding group locomotion toward desired goals. Thus, when group performance, as opposed to individual performance, will be rewarded, people are more rejecting of an interfering deviant (Berkowitz & Howard, 1959). When the group's existence appears threatened due to the behavior of a deviant, rejection is greater (Lauderdale, 1976). It also appears that such dislike may bear some relationship to status. As Levine (1988) has pointed out, when the person interfering with the goal attainment is of high status, he or she is less likely to be defined as a deviant and punished (Giordano, 1983; Hollander & Willis, 1967).

The work on minority influence in organizational settings has, to date, been quite sparse. In an excellent review essay, however, Zald and Berger (1978) have argued that research on this topic should borrow liberally from the study of political processes in nations and communities. They describe organizational coups, in which executives manage to oust the president of a corporation; bureaucratic insurgencies, in which middle managers or professionals gain political support for a change in the organization's direction or procedures; and mass movements, in which large numbers of those at the bottom of the hierarchy resist or confront the organization on issues of concern. However, very little research has been completed on these topics, due no doubt to the difficulties of gaining access for such research.

There has been more work done on *whistle- blowing*—in which the person does not simply argue his or her position within the organization, choosing instead to take the case to outside authorities or the press. Both Graham (1986) and Near and Miceli (1987) have outlined a host of determinants of whistle-blowing activity, ranging from personal responsibility and morality, to assessments of the seriousness of the issue and the likely consequences of one's actions. As in the case of deviants in small-group research, whistle-blowers do not fare well in organizations. Both anecdotal and quantitative evidence shows that they are typically demoted, reassigned to isolated and powerless positions, or fired. Graham (1984) did find that the credibility of the whistle-blower, based on education and pay, was inversely related to retaliation, and Near and Miceli (1986) found that retaliation is lessened if there is some support from supervisors or management. However, Near and Miceli (1985) showed that retaliation was more likely if the reported wrongdoing represented a critical and nonsubstitutable resource—something on which the organization was dependent. Thus, even though whistle-blowers are more likely to act when they see an organization's wrongdoing as serious, this is exactly the condition in which retaliation is likely to be greatest against the dissenting individual.

IV. The Costs and Benefits of Achieving Uniformity

Up to this point, we have underscored and reviewed the extensive research literature documenting the strain toward uniformity among individuals. They may achieve such uniformity by compromising and accommodating to a position somewhere in the middle. They often achieve it either by agreement to an already established norm or by agreement with the position held (1) by those in power, (2) by those higher in status, and/or (3) by those enjoying a numerical majority. Less often, they achieve it by agreement with the position initially held by a numerical minority or by a person low in power or status. The questions then arise, "What are the consequences of such uniformity?" and "Are those consequences different, depending on the form that the influence process takes?"

One of the more obvious advantages of the achievement of uniformity is that people are under less strain; there is greater harmony. In addition, there is far greater efficiency when the norm, or the wishes, will and viewpoint of those in power, is accepted and adopted. Everyone is in agreement, and therefore the group can locomote toward its goals, this being a necessary element for the survival of the group or organization.

On the other hand, there are numerous disadvantages of such influence processes. Some disadvantages are due to the common assumption that truth is correlated with consensus, thus consensus views may be maintained even in the face of changing circumstances or new facts.

Other disadvantages derive from the particular influence process that led to the consensus. When consensus is achieved because of power, status or numerical superiority, people appear relatively unreflective in their adoption of the proposed viewpoint. People are more likely to adopt the viewpoints of the majority than of the minority, for example, regardless of whether that majority is correct or incorrect (Nemeth & Wachtler, 1983). When the influence source is a minority, however, there is evidence of greater originality and divergent thought, permitting the detection of more solutions (Nemeth & Kwan, 1985, 1987; Nemeth & Wachtler, 1983). We first explore the issue related to consensus in general and then proceed to the particular forms of influence, primarily concentrating on the potential contributions of dissent.

A. THE DISADVANTAGES OF CONSENSUS: BREEDING RIGIDITY RATHER THAN CHANGE

With uniformity, individuals and organizations often have difficulty adjusting to shifts in the environment. They neither heed negative data as soon as the data are evident nor shift resources from unproductive to more appropriate ventures as quickly as they should. In the small-group literature, one of the best-known examples is Janis's (1971) historical and archival analysis of cabinet-level decision making that led to political "fiascoes" (e.g., the Bay of Pigs). Janis labeled as "groupthink" that mode of thinking in which concurrence seeking becomes so dominant that it tends to override realistic appraisal of alternative courses of action. Janis (1971) offers evidence that groupthink is encouraged by harmonious and cohesive groups that are relatively isolated from contrary views and that have a directive leader who signals a preference for a given course of action. Other symptoms and by-products of groupthink are an illusion of invulnerability, a belief in the group's morality, stereotyped views of others, strong conformity pressure accompanied by self-censorship, direct pressure on dissenters, and even an illusion of unanimity where it does not exist. The net effect of these symptoms is that decision-making groups do not completely survey the alternatives, examine the risks of their preferred courses of action, or search the information well; they exhibit selective bias, and, on balance, they render poor decisions. Thus, pressures for uniformity may cause a rush to judgment and an inability to make careful, deliberate, and divergent decisions.

While Janis's work on groupthink has shown how social influences can interfere with effective group decision making, separate streams of research have examined social influence on organizational decisions. One example is research on behavior in escalation situations (Brockner & Rubin, 1985; Staw & Ross, 1987; Tegar, 1980). These are situations in which negative results have been received, but in which there is a possibility of recouping one's losses by increasing one's commitment of time, effort, or resources. Several studies have shown that individuals responsible for prior losses invest more in a losing course of action than those facing the same economic decisions without the burden of prior losses (e.g., Bazerman, Beckum, & Schoorman, 1982; Staw, 1976). The most well-documented psychological mechanism accounting for this effect is that of individual or self-justification. However, as one moves from isolated individual action to behavior in social situations, such as an organization, the question arises as to whether the tendency for escalation would be nullified by countervailing forces or whether it would be amplified by social pressures.

In organizations, decision makers may persist in a losing course of action just because they do not want to admit an error *to themselves*. They may invest further because they do not want their mistakes exposed *to others*. Usually, organizations put a premium on success and tend to devalue the careers of those who have failed. Therefore, important moderators of justification in organizations are job security and public identification with a project. Fox and Staw (1979) found in a role-playing exercise that those most worried about keeping their administrative positions tended to commit more resources to a losing course of action. Though not yet researched, it would also be expected that those whose organizational identities are staked to a project (via its origination or advocacy) would remain most committed during its decline. Through explicit and public identification (e.g., "that's Jim's baby"), organizations may thus lock managers into support for a course of action, even if private beliefs are not so unwavering (cf., Kiesler, 1971; Salancik, 1977).

Behavioral norms of the organization may also govern the degree of commitment in escalation situations. Staw and Ross (1980) found that observers of behavior in an escalation situation judged continuing commitment rather than withdrawal to be the behavior most befitting of managerial leadership. Thus, one organizational reason that managers may fall so readily into escalation traps is because consistency in behavior fits existing norms of positive leadership, as exemplified in the phrases "sticking to your guns," "holding the course" or "weathering the storm."

Staw and Ross (1987) have argued that organizational commitment to a course of action often follows a temporal pattern. It begins at the individual level, due to psychological motivations and biases. However, as negative data start to pile up, individual forces for commitment may be superseded by social and structural forces binding the person to the course of action.

Such a pattern was evidenced by British Columbia's decision to hold the World's Fair, Expo 86. As originally advocated by the Premier of British Columbia, Expo was supposed to operate close to the financial break-even point. But as plans for the fair started to become realized, the magnitude of expected losses grew dramatically. At first, efforts were made to minimize the financial hazards by providing more positive estimates of revenues and minimization of costs. Yet, as more dire financial projections were finally accepted (and even the fair's director recommended cancellation), plans for Expo did not change. Politically, it was too late. The fortunes of too many businesses in the province were tied to Expo; it was popular with the voters; and the future of the Premier and his political party were aligned with it. Finally, the question of whether to hold or to cancel the fair also became tied to the very identity of the city of Vancouver—was it reliable in its commitments? Was it "world class" and equal to Toronto and Montreal? Eventually, plans were made to cope with the expected deficit of $300 million (by installing a provincial lottery), and the fair was constructed and held as scheduled (Ross & Staw, 1986).

Escalation situations such as those in the Expo case graphically show how organizational action is more than a simple summation of individual behavior. Errors were no doubt made by key individuals in pursuing the fair, but organizational action in persisting in the course of action was probably due in large part to social influence. The inability of organizations to make proper decisions and to react to changes in their environment is not just collective stupidity or a lack of leadership. It is a more complex consequence of social influence, expressed both in overt pressure on office holders and in political maneuvering, as well as the more tacit effects of shared identity.

B. DISADVANTAGES OF PARTICULAR WAYS OF ACHIEVING CONSENSUS

One of the difficulties in discussing the advantages or disadvantages of influence processes is that, to a large extent, the evaluative judgments depend on whether the source of influence is correct or incorrect, wise or foolish. Thus, if the numerical majority was correct, we would, by and large, welcome the conformity process. If it were the dissenter who had the best ideas or who was most correct, one would then value the role of minority influence.

One of the concerns repeatedly raised in the literature on conformity is the extent to which individuals abdicate the information even from their own senses and adopt an erroneous majority viewpoint. In the Asch (1956) studies on length of lines, for example, some individuals reported that they "saw" the "equality" of lines as proposed by the majority. However, many reported that they knew the majority judgment was incorrect; yet, they followed that judgment in order to belong and to avoid disapproval. Such reactions tend not to occur when the influence source is a minority. Here, approval is not a primary motivation because movement to the minority position, while perhaps incurring the minority's approval, would also incur the disapproval of the majority, which one is deserting. People follow a minority viewpoint primarily when they believe it to be true or correct. Further, there is a far greater tendency to accept a majority viewpoint, regardless of its correctness, than a minority viewpoint (Nemeth & Wachtler, 1983).

1. Promoting Independence

Given the power of majority influence and the tendency for people to adopt majority views even when they are wrong, there has been a concern and emphasis on how to promote independence, particularly when it comes to holding a correct viewpoint rather than succumbing to majority error. One antidote to such conformity and an aid to independence appears to be exposure to a dissenting minority, even when the minority is incorrect.

In some of Asch's (1956) early studies, instead of having the individual face a unanimous disagreeing majority, he placed the individual in a group with a dissenter, one who gave the correct answer and agreed with the naive subject. With a dissenter, the amount of conformity was drastically reduced from 32% to 5%. Perhaps the most interesting finding comes from the condition in which the dissenter was not an ally, but was even more extreme than the majority, disagreeing with both the majority and the naive subject. Even here, conformity was greatly reduced, at least for visual items. For opinion items, Asch (1956) found little effect from exposure to the extreme dissenter. Allen and Levine (1969) have confirmed these results in a study manipulating veridical dissent (supporting the views of the subject) as well as extreme erroneous dissent. Again, both kinds of dissent from the majority reduced conformity on visual and information items, with only veridical dissent reducing conformity on opinion items. Thus, it appears that the presence of a dissenter, even an erroneous one and one who does not agree with you, can reduce the likelihood of conformity. Any break in the unanimity of the majority, even by error, may signal the appropriateness of independent judgment.

More recent evidence by Nemeth and Chiles (1988) suggests that dissent may promote independence more broadly and even in subsequent settings. In that study, three naive individuals were exposed to a confederate who (consistently or inconsistently) called blue stimuli "green." Others were exposed to no dissent. In a subsequent setting, these individuals found themselves in a minority position, faced with a majority judgment that was in error. Three others consistently judged red slides to be orange. If the individuals were not previously exposed to dissent, conformity was very high. On over 70% of the trials, they agreed with the majority's erroneous judgment of orange. When they had been exposed to dissent, whether it was consistent or inconsistent, conformity was drastically reduced; there was less than 25% conformity. In fact, those exposed to consistent dissent showed almost complete independence. They did not differ significantly from control subjects who made their judgments alone.

Still other research points to the possibility that dissent may not only aid independence by reducing the tendency for conformity, but also actually stimulate originality. In a study by Nemeth and Kwan (1985), subjects were exposed to an erroneous majority or minority view that blue slides were "green". Subsequent to this setting, they gave associations to the words "green" and "blue." Using normative data for such word associations, Nemeth and Kwan (1985) found that those exposed to the minority judgment gave not only more associations to each of the words but also significantly more original associations. Their associations were statistically less frequent. Thus, for example, associations to the word "blue" might include "sky" for those exposed to the majority, whereas it might include "jeans" for those exposed to the minority view.

2. Independence and Spontaneity in the Work Setting

Independence is also important in organizations because these goal-directed entities often make a conscious effort to control and channel individual behavior at work. Sets of rules, regulations, and penalties are usually in place to assure attendance and at least minimal performance. To gain a higher level of productivity, many organizations have also instituted some form of incentive system or goal-setting techniques. Although these social control efforts contribute to physical presence and dependable work performance (e.g., Locke, Shaw, Saari, & Latham, 1981), they have not been shown to contribute to more spontaneous and innovative behavior. This is important because, as Katz and Kahn (1966) noted,

> No organizational planning can foresee all contingencies within its own operations, can anticipate with perfect accuracy all environmental changes, or can control perfectly all human variability. The resources of people for innovation, for spontaneous cooperation, for protective and creative behavior are thus vital to organizational survival and effectiveness. An organization which depends solely upon its blueprint of prescribed behavior is a very fragile system.

So far, a small literature has developed on extra-role behavior—actions that are not required by the organization, but nonetheless are seen by managers as beneficial. Participation in social events, making suggestions, volunteering for extra work, and helping coworkers are all positive activities that are neither written into the job description nor extrinsically rewarded. Smith, Organ, and Near (1983) showed that several of these behaviors can be integrated on an organizational altruism scale and distinguished empirically from organizational compliance. O'Reilly and Chatman (1986) similarly separated intra-role and extra-role behaviors, demonstrating that the conduct of prescribed duties have different predictors than that of more prosocial behaviors. Compliance motives were shown to relate to intra-role behavior, whereas both identification and internalization were the strongest correlates of extra-role activities.

Indirectly related to the study of extra-role behavior is the literature on intrinsic motivation. In numerous task experiments, it has been shown that efforts at social control can reduce the individual's intrinsic motivation to perform an activity (see, e.g., Deci, 1975 or Staw, 1976). The application of contingent monetary rewards may increase the role behavior that is directly reinforced, but after the reinforcers are eliminated and surveillance reduced, time voluntarily spent on the task is often diminished. Extrinsic rewards have also been found to reduce performance on creativity tasks—situations in which the best behavior is not inherently obvious or the result of simple increases in effort (Amabile, 1983).

In many organizations, spontaneous and innovative behavior may also fall victim to social control attempts. Whereas extrarole behavior includes a set of actions that managers want from employees but are unwilling to pay for, innovative and spontaneous behavior includes actions that are not planned by nor necessarily approved by supervisors. It is thus quite likely not only that dependable role behavior and innovative activity are driven by different determinants, but also that they may be inimical to each other. For example, symbols of authority, rules, and penalties may induce compliance but drive out various (often functional) forms of deviance. Although monetary rewards and goal-setting are currently thought to be reliable techniques for increasing performance, they may likewise inhibit more spontaneous and innovative behaviors that are not prescribed by management.

Very little research has so far addressed the relation between social control and spontaneous, innovative work behavior. One lead is however provided by Hornstein (1986), who interviewed middle managers about their experiences with courageous acts—instances in which individuals spoke out against supervisors or championed unpopular positions. He found that courageous acts seemed to be less determined by independence or self-reliance than by a sense of identification with the immediate task. Hornstein argued that when self-identity is bound strongly to organizational welfare and job confidence is high, individuals are more likely to speak out when they realize that current practices are not in the best interest of the organization.

In a university setting, Staw and Bell (1988) found that students who were most committed to the school were more likely to make suggestions for its improvement. However, they also found that the number of suggestions varied inversely with satisfaction toward the school. Thus, those who were involved or somehow attached to the organization, but who had grievances or criticisms about it, were most valuable as a source of ideas. This points to the danger of many organizational development activities designed simply to reduce dissatisfaction, because they may quiet the very foes of the system that the organization needs. These results also remind us that most organizations contain many sources of innovation not associated with new technology or product development—sources that are probably suppressed by traditional modes of structure and control.

V. Dissent, Performance, and the Quality of Decision Making

Up to now, we have concentrated on the forces for uniformity and the potentially deleterious consequences of particular ways of achieving that consensus—in particular, conformity to erroneous views and a relative lack of spontaneity and innovation. We have noted the importance of exposure to dissent in overcoming some of these deleterious consequences. However, we also find that dissent makes indirect positive contributions as well. In particular, there is evidence that dissent, even when erroneous, contributes to the detection of truth and to the improvement of both performance and decision making.

A. PERMITTING TRUTH FROM A DISSENTER

Consider the scenario in which the dissenter's position is itself correct, and the majority, the authority, or the norm is incorrect or at least less appropriate to the situation at hand. In such cases, one would want to foster recognition and acceptance of the truth held by this minority. This is not easy to achieve, however. Sometimes, the dissenter is unwilling to voice his or her position. Other times, the majority is reluctant to accept the dissenter's position even though it is correct.

A study by Staw and Boettger (1988) illustrates the former. These authors used the term "initiative" to describe cases in which the individual, in a sense, knows more than the organization. These are cases in which the prevailing knowledge about how to do a job is wrong, and the person defies accepted practice or higher authority to correct the error. Initiative may therefore constitute extraordinarily high performance, the kind that Katz and Kahn saw as essential to organizational functioning. Yet, unlike extra-role behaviors that are unpaid but generally desired by supervisors, acts of initiative are often viewed as subversive activities—behaviors that undercut the established order and prescriptions of the organization.

Staw and Boettger designed an experiment in which business students were asked to play the role of a communications officer in the school. In this staff role, subjects were charged with writing a promotional brochure used to attract incoming students. They were given a first draft of a paragraph describing the features of the school and asked to rewrite the description for the brochure. Unfortunately, the draft they were given was not only poorly written but also included content that was both inappropriate and erroneous. Included as selling points for the school were several features known from a previous student survey to be important drawbacks of attending the school. Thus, subjects were asked to work on a task in which the basic assumptions were flawed and would be detrimental to the program.

One independent variable in the Staw and Boettger study was the salience of alternatives to the prescribed task. Half of the subjects were primed before the experiment by having them rate numerous selling points of the business school, while half received no priming. A second independent variable was the authority level of the person who wrote the school descriptions—whether it was a secretary or the associate dean. The third manipulated variable was goal setting—whether subjects were told to make sure grammatical errors were corrected or simply instructed to "do your best."

The results of the initiative experiment showed very strong effects for priming and goal setting. When an erroneous goal for improving the grammar of the brochure was given, few content changes were offered by subjects. Likewise, when subjects were not primed with alternative content for the brochure, they used the majority of the ideas from the previous draft of the school description, including those rated at the bottom in appropriateness. These results are disconcerting because most natural settings do not include any specific encouragement for alternative approaches; instead, such settings actively focus attention on established, though perhaps erroneous, goals. Moreover, natural settings do not usually include task models that are as blatantly false or undesirable as the ideas included in the school descriptions used in this study. Tasks and procedures are typically buttressed by precedent, rationale, and the specific goals of the organization. Thus, it is likely that initiative is held at a very low level by social influences present in most work settings.

Even where the dissenter does show initiative, in the sense that he or she proposes an answer that is correct, available studies suggest that the recognition of that correctness is not easy if the individual has lower status or is a member of a numerical minority. In studies by Torrance (1959), for example, the issue of correctness versus status was directly studied with Navy bomber crews that consisted of a pilot, a navigator, and a gunner. Pilots had high status and gunners relatively low status. In those studies, individuals attempted to solve a horse-trading problem: an individual buys a horse for $60, sells it for $70, buys it back for $80 and sells it again for $90. The question was how much profit did he make? (It turns out that the correct answer ($20) is not obvious even to college-educated students). In the Navy crews, the navigator was most likely to judge it correctly. However, Torrance was interested in how groups of 3 would decide on the correct answer, given that at least one member knew it. The group solution depended on who knew the correct answer. When the pilot had the correct judgment, 94% of the 3 member groups accepted it; when it was the navigator who held the correct judgment, 80% accepted it; however, when the gunner held the correct answer, only 63% of the groups accepted it. Acceptance of the correct answer was directly related to the status of the person holding the correct answer.

B. PERMITTING UNTRUTH FROM A DISSENTER: THE IMPORTANCE OF PROCESS

While a good deal of research, both in small groups and in organizations, recognizes that majorities or authorities can be in error and that dissent can be a corrective, some recent work suggests that dissent, regardless of its accuracy, contributes to group performance. Rather than concentrating on the truth or error of the minority position, several researchers have documented the importance of dissent as it aids the decision-making process. Janis (1972) for example, has concentrated on the usefulness of dissent in preventing the negative consequences of conformity and unreflective information processing. In his model of groupthink, he outlined several techniques to prevent excess concurrence-seeking, including the assignment of a critical-evaluator role to each member, assigning a member to the role of devil's advocate, examining more carefully dissenting views, and reconsidering decisions even after consensus has been reached. Most of these suggestions involve the usefulness of dissent in processing more divergent information and considering a wider range of alternatives.

More recently, Nemeth (1986) proposed that dissenting minority views do more than retard the negative consequences of conformity and concurrence-seeking. She argued that minority views, even when they are wrong, foster the kinds of attention and thought processes that lead to the detection of new truths and raise the quality of decision making. One element of this is that minorities, if they persist over time, stimulate the majority to exert more cognitive effort and to think in more divergent ways about an issue. Thus, regardless of the specific decisions or judgments that are reached, the decision-making process will, on balance, be improved by the presence of a minority.

Nemeth does not consider all forms of disagreement to lead to decision-making improvements, however. She specifically contrasts minority influence with the influence rendered by majorities. The latter tend to stimulate *convergent* thought processes. People exposed to majority judgments focus on the position from the viewpoint proposed by the majority, and as such, they are often blind to alternative perspectives. To the extent that the majority is correct, convergence of thought and quick adoption of their views can be useful, but to the extent that it is incorrect or only partially correct, such convergence can be deleterious to effective decision-making.

Several studies corroborate these hypotheses. In early research by Nemeth and Wachtler (Nemeth, 1976; Nemeth & Wachtler, 1983) the detection of truths was investigated as a result of majority versus minority influence in an embedded-figures task. Individuals in groups of six were shown a series of slides in which there was a standard figure and six comparison figures. Subjects alone were able to detect the standard in the one "easy" comparison figure; the others were more difficult. Depending on the condition, either two members (a minority) or four members (a majority) repeatedly judged the figure to be embedded in one of the difficult figures as well as in the easy figure. Again depending on the condition, this judgment was either correct (i.e., the comparison figure did indeed contain the standard) or incorrect (i.e., the comparison figure did not contain the standard). It turns out that the correctness of the judgments was found to have little impact on subjects' behavior. Whether the source constituted a numerical majority or minority, however, made a great deal of difference. People simply adopted the majority judgment. Of particular interest, however, was the kind of influence that was exerted by the minority. While individuals did not follow the minority judgment, they did detect the standard in novel comparison figures—that is, those that were not suggested by the minority. And they were correct. They detected embedded figures that were correct, that they would not have detected when alone, and that were not suggested by any confederate. Thus, there is evidence for the notion that people follow the majority more than the minority and they do so even when the majority is incorrect. However, in response to a minority judgment, the individuals appear to search the stimulus array more carefully and, in the process, detect correct solutions that otherwise would have gone undetected.

A second study by Nemeth and Kwan (1987) investigated both the strategies used in problem solving and the detection of correct solutions. Groups of four individuals were shown a series of six-letter strings (e.g., "tNOWap") and asked to name the first three-letter word that they noticed. Because all letter strings contained three capital letters that formed a word from left to right, brief exposures elicited this word as the first one noticed. In the example, this would be "NOW." After five such slides, feedback was given to the individuals. In the "majority" condition, the experimenter then pointed out that *three* of the individuals first noticed the word formed in capital letters from right to left (e.g., "won" in the present example) and that *one* person first noticed the word formed in capital letters from left to right (e.g., "now"). In the minority condition, individuals were told that one person first saw the word formed by the backward sequencing ("won") and that three persons first noticed the word formed by forward sequencing ("now").

Subsequent to these minority and majority treatments, individuals were given a series of 10 slides and were asked to write down all the words they could discern from the given string of letters. They were given 15 seconds for each slide. In confronting this task, there are three primary strategies. Using the example, "tNOWa," it is clear that some words can be formed by the rather usual "forward" sequence (e.g., "no," "tow"). Words can also be formed by the strategy suggested by the influence source (i.e., the "backward" strategy, exemplified by "ant," "on"). Finally, words can be formed by a mixed strategy, which is a combination of forward and backward (e.g., "not," "want").

The results of the Nemeth and Kwan experiment showed that the individuals exposed to the majority view excelled in the usage of the backward sequencing. The majority strategy for problem solving was followed exactly. However, this was at the expense of using the more usual forward sequencing. Thus, their overall performance was equivalent to the control individuals (those not exposed to any information on others' solutions). By contrast, those exposed to the minority view used all three strategies. They used forward, backward, and mixed strategies in the service of a significantly better performance than either those in the majority condition or the control condition.

In subsequent studies (e.g., Nemeth *et al.*, 1989), there is evidence for superior recall of information as a consequence of exposure to minority views. Further, this superior recall is not only on information relevant to the disagreement but even on subsequent information. Thus, the studies by Nemeth and her associates show that it is not opposition, per se, that provides a creative contribution to individual thought and performance. Rather, it is opposition by a minority rather than a majority. It is the minority who is usually ridiculed and derided, who is presumed to be incorrect, and who rarely prevails even when correct. But unlike the majority opposition, which constrains and focuses attention, minority influence can stimulate reappraisal of the situation, help to increase consideration of facts from multiple perspectives, and improve the detection of correct solutions.

C. UTILIZING DISSENT FOR OPTIMAL PERFORMANCE

From both a theoretical and a practical point of view, it is important to know how one can use varying viewpoints and, in particular, dissenting minority views to aid the decision-making process. One relatively obvious way of obtaining multiple perspectives is to utilize Janis's (1972) advice and assign a devil's advocate. Another is simply to form groups based on heterogeneity of viewpoints, as suggested by the work of Hoffman and Maier (1961a,b). In their work investigating homogeneity versus heterogeneity on the basis of personality, demographics, and attitudes, they have found that not all forms of heterogeneity are related to improvements in decision making. On balance, however, the evidence is that heterogeneity, particularly when it involves differing perspectives or viewpoints, improves decision making. Heterogeneity, they argue, provides benefits in terms of increasing the necessary resources for group problem solving; it brings a broader range of skills and abilities to bear on decision-making tasks. The issue, of course, is whether or not these skills, abilities, and perspectives are used.

In contrast to work on heterogeneity, which emphasizes the presence of differing views or abilities within the group, the Nemeth (1986) formulation (previously described) emphasizes the stimulation of individual members to consider multiple perspectives. Such stimulation appears to arise as a result of exposure to a minority view and, in particular, a minority view that persists over time. From this theoretical vantage point, the existence of a single contrasting view argued consistently by a minority of individuals might result in better information processing and decision making than the presence of multiple views in a group. Such a hypothesis remains speculative, but there is indirect support from a study by Nemeth and Nolan (1987), in which recall was improved by exposure to a consistent minority view rather than exposure to a plurality of viewpoints.

In the organizational literature, there is little empirical research on the role of minority influence. We do not know whether the presence of minority opinion serves as a stimulant to the decision making of those in power or those in the majority, or whether the simple existence of multiple perspectives has an additive effect on capabilities of the organization. Theoretically, a case can be made for either position.

The "stimulant" position is taken by Hirschman (1970), who argued that participant dissent or voice is a major means by which organizations come to improve themselves. Freeman and Medoff (1984) have also posited that unions often act as a constructive voice in industrial firms, prompting them to become more systematic and efficient. Finally, while much of the research on the effects of work participation has tried (often futilely) to demonstrate benefits in terms of individual work performance (e.g., Locke & Schweiger, 1979), it can be argued that participation schemes have a more system-wide impact. The scope and form of organizational participation (e.g., through worker ownership, board membership, works councils, unionization) may affect the goals the organization seeks, the actions it takes, and its structural design, in lieu of simple main effects on productivity (Strauss, 1982).

Many scholars of organizational behavior have argued that formal mechanisms should be instituted to protect dissent. For example, Waters (1980) has advocated the creation of an ombudsman office so that individuals would have a place to go for support, especially in trying to change an organization's illegal or unethical practices. Aram and Salipante (1987) have argued for a more active board of directors for considering ethical, social, and legal conflicts. Finally, several schemes have been suggested to formalize the role of dissent in decision making, ranging from use of recognized "corporate devil's advocate" (Herbert & Estes, 1977) to a structured debate in the Hegelian tradition (Mason, 1969), to a strategic assumption analysis (Mitroff & Emshoff, 1979) by which the unstated assumptions of an organization are challenged and substantiated (Graham, 1986). All of these suggestions are essentially efforts to use minority influence as a stimulant to those currently in power or as a way to challenge the unstated assumptions (Argyris, 1982) governing the organization.

It is conceivable that minority views in an organization might also increase, additively, the capacity of the organization to make good decisions. However, this statement would be true only to the extent that firms listened to or somehow used minority input in the decision-making process. More likely, dominant parties exclude minority input until a time of crisis develops—periods in which it is apparent that the prevailing wisdom and assumptions are no longer accurate or have not kept pace with environmental changes. Tushman and Romanelli (1985) have argued that organizations go through long periods of convergence (or normalcy), punctuated by brief times of discontinuity or metamorphosis. It is quite likely that the role of minorities is especially important during these upheavals in which the power structure and set of assumptions guiding the organization are subject to change. Thus, the existence of minorities may be more closely related to the capacity of organizations to survive occasional crises than to their steady-state productivity.

The long-run adaptiveness of having multiple points of view and diverse skills is based on a social-evolutionary model of organizations (Campbell, 1969). When an organization's environment radically shifts over time (e.g., via changes in consumer tastes and preferences, the regulatory environment, or the world competitive structure), there is the need for some mechanism to bring forth alternative perspectives that best fit the new setting. The existence of minority viewpoints provides the organization with alternative procedures and strategies. As the environment shifts, minorities may either come to power themselves or provide the new set of assumptions needed to effect radical changes. Organizations with sources of diversity and the ability to attend to them are thus more likely to survive or prosper following unsettling events (such as dramatic changes in world oil prices) than organizations possessing a more uniform view of its world. Some indirect evidence for this adaptive function of heterogeneity comes from research on the survival rates of various forms of organizations. Population ecologists have found a greater survival rate for generalists (multifunction or diversified firms) as opposed to specialists (single-purpose and more centralized organizations) when environments shift abruptly over time (Aldrich, 1979; Hannan & Freeman, 1977). Although firms possessing fewer attributes (specialists) are likely to be most efficient during stable times, they are least likely to be able to adapt to radically new conditions facing the organization over time.

Obviously, the stimulant and adaptive contributions of minorities do not come without costs. Just as psychological research has shown the efficiency value of homogeneity and the interpersonal difficulties associated with heterogeneity (Byrne, 1971), organizational studies have shown that the demography of managers (e.g., in terms of age and tenure) can adversely affect attitudes and behavior in the firm. Demographic heterogeneity has been shown to be associated with lower cohesion in superior–subordinate relations (Tsui & O'Reilly, 1987), higher managerial turnover (Wagner, Pfeffer, & O'Reilly, 1984), and even with lower ratings of innovation by external analysts (O'Reilly & Flatt, 1987). The latter finding poses the greatest challenge to the assumed benefits of minority influence. It is possible that O'Reilly and Flatt's (1986) innovation ratings are simply a product of positive halo, since they are highly correlated with measures of ongoing performance. It is also possible that the costs of heterogeneity exceed the benefits, except during times of crisis. Thus, the net advantage of heterogeneity would not be evident with cross-sectional analyses or longitudinal studies of short duration, unless measures were gathered before and after a major market or industry change. Finally, it is conceivable that few organizations have the capability to manage or weather the costs of heterogeneity while waiting for its benefits. For each of these reasons there may not be a simple relationship between organizational heterogeneity and innovation.

D. INTEGRATING THE DIFFERENTIATION

Though heterogeneity provides a greater number of inputs and ideas, they are of little use if lack of cohesion and common direction prevent their implementation. A well-known study by Lawrence and Lorsch (1967) illustrates this fact. In their study, Lawrence and Lorsch demonstrated that it was not enough to have a differentiated (or heterogeneous) organization in order to cope with a changing environment. There also need to be mechanisms by which the firm could become integrated. Thus, as differentiation increases (e.g., by having more diverse members and points of view), it is necessary to build in mechanisms to provide integration (e.g., communication aids, conflict-resolution techniques, norms for openness), or there will not be gains in effectiveness. Supporting this argument, Lawrence and Lorsch found that high differentiation *and* high integration were associated with organizational performance in rapidly changing environments.

Although maintaining differentiation and integration is no doubt very useful for organizational adaptiveness, the process is probably much more complex than that originally outlined by Lawrence and Lorsch. Kanter's (1988) discussion of the characteristics of innovative, high-technology companies illustrates this point. She notes that innovative companies often design specific structures that are meant to stimulate diversity—for example, by having a decentralized structure with numerous competing pockets of influence, by keeping roles ambiguous and procedures unformalized so that individuals can work according to their own priorities and interpretations of goals, by separating subunits doing innovative work from sources of central control, by providing some measure of job security so as to minimize fearful adherence to procedures, and by rewarding successful risk taking with both monetary and social rewards. However, in addition to these mechanisms for stimulating diversity, Kanter notes several procedures that high-technology companies often use for channeling organizational efforts in a unified direction. People with innovative ideas are often forced to mobilize other people and resources toward their own particular projects. They must "tin-cup" around the organization, pleading for slack resources that can be hidden in others' budgets, sometimes maintaining secrecy of the nature or scope of the project until success is more assured (e.g., via the famous "skunk-works" at Data General). Innovators may also need to seek aid or sponsorship from those with formal power. As their projects become increasingly promising, more and more people will want to "sign-on" or be associated with the venture, and it will eventually gain top management endorsement. Of course, very few projects actually evolve in this way, from the idea to the implementation stage. Most perish early for lack of support and the resources to carry them forward.

From a social-evolutionary perspective (Campbell, 1969), variety-generating mechanisms, such as those that foster greater diversity in ideas and minority opinions, can potentially aid the adaptiveness of an organization. Yet, there also need to be mechanisms for selection/retention—ways in which the organization can cull the good ideas from the impractical, as well as mechanisms to channel resources to the best of the available alternatives. Thus, organizational innovation may be characterized as a "funneling" process (Staw, 1988). The more diversity and heterogeneity the organization tolerates, the broader the mouth of the funnel for capturing new ideas. The more fine-grained or the stronger the selection mechanisms, the fewer the number of ideas reaching the stage of implementation. The trick of adaptiveness, of course, is to maximize the number of good ideas reaching fruition. Unfortunately, too few organizations know how to maintain both substantial diversity *and* strong selection processes. This may be one reason why a simple association of heterogeneity with innovativeness has not always been found. Diversity, by itself and without a way of culling and carrying forward those projects that are most promising, is thus as likely to lead to misdirection and inefficiency as innovation and adaptiveness.

VI. Social Control and Social Changes: Some Final Thoughts

John Stuart Mill (*On Liberty*, 1859/1979) long ago recognized the importance of open confrontation of viewpoints, of the allowance of diversity, variety, and choice. For him, the adversarial system of competing ideas served democratic principles, but it also was a vehicle for the finding of truths, as well as for the vitality of the positions reached. Like Lord Macauley (1830), he believed that "Men are never so likely to settle a question rightly as when they discuss it freely."

This article provides some empirical underpinnings for Mill's approach. Minority influence can both add to the problem-solving capacity of groups and serve as an intellectual stimulant to the parties involved. By contrast, majority influence can narrow the alternatives and quality of decisions made and stifle innovation when it is expressed via various means of social control. As we have seen, social control in organizational contexts may also lead individuals to defend established courses of action beyond their useful lives, reduce individual initiative to correct organizational errors, and eliminate the diversity that is a prerequisite for organizational adaptiveness.

No doubt, some degree of social control is essential for both groups and organizations. Hence, it is typical to think of cohesion and diversity as opposing processes that need to be traded off in any particular situation. A contingency model is often thereby formulated, in which the composition and processes of the social unit are selected to fit best the problem being solved or the units' demands for efficiency versus adaptiveness (e.g., Maier, 1967; Weick, 1983). While such contingency models are useful, a more productive approach might be to think of the forces for cohesion and diversity as allies rather than tradeoffs. We follow Hackman (1976) in noting that what currently exists for a social unit does not necessarily represent its potential. Groups and organizations can be made more effective by finding new mechanisms, not current or standard practices, that can increase both cohesion *and* diversity. Influence as a stimulus to thought is but one concept, and the funnel model of innovation is but one metaphor that can aid in this reformulation.

Acknowledgments

This manuscript was written jointly and equally by both authors. It was supported in part by National Science Foundation Grant No. BNS 851200 to Charlan Nemeth and in part by research funding provided to Barry Staw by the Institute of Industrial Relations, University of California. These sources of support are gratefully acknowledged.

References

Aldrich, H. E. (1979). *Organizations and environments*. Englewood Cliffs, NJ: Prentice-Hall.
Allen, V. L. (1965). Situational factors in conformity. In L. Berkowitz (Ed.), *Advances in experimental social psychology* (Vol. 2, pp. 133–175). New York: Academic Press.
Allen, V. L., & Levine, J. M. (1969). Consensus and conformity. *Journal of Experimental Social Psychology*, **5**, 389–399.
Amabile, J. M. (1983). *The social psychology of creativity*. New York: Springer-Verlag.
Aram, J. D., & Salipante, P. F. (1987). An evaluation of organizational due process in the resolution of employee/employer conflict. *Academy of Management Review*, **6**, 197–204.
Argyris, C. (1982). *Reasoning, learning, and action: Individual and organization*. San Francisco: Jossey-Bass.
Asch, S. E. (1951). Effects of group pressures upon the modification and distortion of judgments. In H. Guetzkow (Ed.), *Groups, leadership, and men*. Pittsburgh, PA: Carnegie Press.
Asch, S. E. (1955). Opinions and social pressure. *Scientific American*, **193**, 31–35.
Asch, S. E. (1956). Studies of independence and conformity: A minority of one against a unanimous majority. *Psychological Monographs*, **70**(9, Whole No. 416).
Bazerman, M. H., Beckum, R. I., & Schoorman, F. D. (1982). Performance evaluation in a dynamic context: A laboratory study of the impact of a prior commitment to the ratee. *Journal of Applied Psychology*, **67**, 873–876.
Berkowitz, L., & Howard, R. C. (1959). Reactions to opinion deviates as affected by affiliation need (n) and group member interdependence. *Sociometry*, **22**, 81–91.
Blake, R. R., Helson, H., & Mouton, J. S. (1957). The generality of conformity of behavior as a function of factual anchorage difficulty of task and amount of social pressure. *Journal of Personality*, **25**, 294–305.
Brockner, J., & Rubin, J. Z. (1985). *Entrapment in escalating conflicts*. New York: Springer-Verlag.
Burns, T., & Stalker, G. (1961). *The management of innovation*. London: Tavistock Publications.
Byrne, D. (1971). *The attraction paradigm*. New York: Free Press.
Campbell, D. T. (1969). Variation and selective retention in sociocultural evolution. *General Systems: Yearbook of the Society for General System Research*, **16**, 69–85.
Crozier, M. (1964). *The bureaucratic phenomenon*. Chicago: University of Chicago Press.
Crutchfield, R. S. (1955). Conformity and character. *American Psychologist*, **10**, 191–198.
Cyert, R. M., & March, J. G. (1963). *A behavioral theory of the firm*. Englewood Cliffs, NJ: Prentice-Hall.
Deci, E. L. (1975). *Intrinsic motivation*. New York: Plenum.
Deutsch, M., & Gerard, H. (1955). A study of normative and informational social influences on individual judgment. *Journal of Abnormal and Social Psychology*, **51**, 629–636.
Evan, W. M. (1961). Organizational man and due process of law. *American Sociological Review*, **26**, 540–547.
Festinger, L. (1950). Informal social communication. *Psychological Review*, **57**, 271–282.

Fox, F. V., & Staw, B. M. (1979). The trapped administrator: Effects of job insecurity and policy resistance upon commitment to a course of action. *Administrative Science Quarterly, 24,* 449–471.
Freeman, R. B., & Medoff, J. L. (1984). *What do unions do?* New York: Basic Books.
Gerard, H. B., Wilhelmy, R. A., & Conolley, E. S. (1968). Conformity and group size. *Journal of Personality and Social Psychology,* **8,** 79–82.
Giordano, P. C. (1983). Sanctioning the high-status deviant: An attributional analysis. *Social Psychology Quarterly,* **46,** 329–342.
Graham, J. W. (1984, August). *Organizational response to principled organizational dissent.* Paper presented at the annual meeting of the Academy of Management, Boston.
Graham, J. W. (1986). Principled organizational dissent: A theoretical essay. In B. M. Staw & L. L. Cummings (Eds.), *Research in organizational behavior* (Vol. 8, pp. 1–52). Greenwich, CT: JAI Press.
Griffin, R. A. (1983). Objective and social sources of information in task redesign: A field experiment. *Administrative Science Quarterly,* **28,** 184–200.
Hackman, J. R. (1976). Group influences on individuals. In M. D. Dunnette (Ed.), *Handbook of industrial and organizational psychology* (pp. 1455–1525). Chicago: Rand-McNally College Publishing Company.
Hannan, M. T., & Freeman, J. (1984). The population ecology of organizations. *American Journal of Sociology,* **82,** 929–964.
Herbert, T. T., & Estes, R. W. (1977). Improving executive decisions by formalizing dissent: The corporate devil's advocate. *Academy of Management Review,* **2,** 662–667.
Hickson, D. J., Hinings, C. R., Lee, C. A., Schneck, R. E., & Pennings, J. M. (1971). A strategic contingencies theory of intraorganizational behavior. *Administrative Science Quarterly,* **16,** 216–229.
Hills, F. S., & Mahoney, T. A. (1978). University budgets and organizational decision making. *Administrative Science Quarterly,* **23,** 454–465.
Hinings, C. R., Hickson, D. J., Pennings, J. M., & Schneck, R. E. (1974). Structural conditions of intraorganizational power. *Administrative Science Quarterly,* **19,** 22–44.
Hirschman, A. O. (1970). *Exit, voice, and loyalty: Responses to decline in firms, organizations, and states.* Cambridge, MA: Harvard University Press.
Hoffman, L. R., & Maier, N. R. F. (1961a). Quality and acceptance of problem solutions by members of homogeneous and heterogeneous groups. *Journal of Abnormal and Social Psychology,* **62,** 401–407.
Hoffman, L. R., & Maier, N. R. F. (1961b). Sex differences, sex composition and group problem solving. *Journal of Abnormal and Social Psychology,* **63,** 453–456.
Holland, J. L. (1976). Vocational preferences. In M. D. Dunnette (Ed.), *Handbook of organizational and industrial psychology* (pp. 521–570). Chicago: Rand-McNally.
Hollander, E. P. (1960). Competence and conformity in the acceptance of influence. *Journal of Abnormal and Social Psychology,* **61,** 365–369.
Hollander, E. P., & Willis, R. H. (1967). Some current issues in the psychology of conformity and nonconformity. *Psychological Bulletin,* **68,** 62–76.
Hornstein, H. A. (1961). *Managerial courage.* New York: Wiley.
Jacobs, R. C., & Campbell, D. T. (1961). The perpetuation of an arbitrary tradition through several generations of a laboratory microculture. *Journal of Abnormal and Social Psychology,* **62,** 649–658.
Janis, I. L. (1971). Groupthink. *Psychology Today,* 5(6), 43–46ff.
Janis, I. L. (1972). *Groupthink: Psychological studies of policy decisions and fiascoes* (2nd ed). Boston: Houghton- Mifflin.
Kalven, H., Jr., & Zeisel, H. (1966). *The American jury.* Boston: Little Brown.
Kanter, R. M. (1977). *Men and women of the corporation.* New York: Basic Books.

Kanter, R. M. (1988). When a thousand flowers bloom: Structural, collective, and social conditions for innovation in organization. In B. Staw & L. L. Cummings (Eds.), *Research in organizational behavior* (Vol. 10, pp. 169–211). Greenwich, CT: JAI Press.
Katz, D., & Kahn, R. L. (1966). *The social psychology of organizations.* New York: Wiley.
Katz, D., & Kahn, R. L. (1978). *The social psychology of organizations* (2nd ed.). New York: Wiley.
Kiesler, C. A. (1971). *The psychology of commitment.* New York: Academic Press.
Lauderdale, P. (1976). Deviance and moral boundaries. *American Sociological Review,* **41,** 660–676.
Lawrence, P. R., & Lorsch, J. W. (1967). *Organization and environment: Managing differentiation and integration.* Boston: Graduate School of Business Administration, Harvard University.
Levine, J. M. (1988). Reaction to opinion deviance in small groups. In P. Pauls (Ed.), *Psychology of group influence: New perspectives.* Hillsdale, NJ: Erlbaum, in press.
Levine, J. M., Saxe, L., & Harris, H. J. (1976). Reaction to attitudinal deviance: Impact of deviate's direction and distance of movement. *Sociometry,* **39,** 97–107.
Levine, J. M., Sroka, K. R., & Snyder, H. N. (1977). Group support and reaction to stable and shifting agreement/disagreement. *Sociometry,* **40,** 214–224.
Locke, E. A., & Schweiger, D. M. (1979). Participation in decision making: One more look. In B. M. Staw (Ed.), *Research in organizational behavior* (Vol. 1, pp. 265–339). Greenwich, CT: JAI Press.
Locke, E. A., Shaw, K. N., Saari, L. M., & Latham, G. P. (1981). Goal setting and task performance. *Psychological Bulletin,* **90,** 125–152.
Maass, A., & Clark, R. D. (1984). Hidden impact of minorities: Fifteen years of minority influence research. *Psychological Bulletin,* **95,** 428–450.
Macauley, T. B. (1830). In R. Southey (Ed.), *Colloquies on the progress and prospects of society.* London: J. Murray Publishing Company.
Maier, N. R. F. (1967). Assets and liabilities in group problem solving: The need for an integrative function. *Psychological Review,* **74,** 239–249.
Martin, J. (1982). Stories and scripts in organizational settings. In A. Hastorf & A. Isen (Eds.), *Cognitive social psychology.* New York: Elsevier.
Mason, R. O. (1969). A dialectical approach to strategic planning. *Management Science,* **15,** 403–414.
Mausner, B. (1954). The effect of prior reinforcement on the interaction of observer pairs. *Journal of Abnormal and Social Psychology,* **49,** 65–68.
Mechanic, D. (1962). Sources of power of lower participants in complex organizations. *Administrative Science Quarterly,* **7,** 349–362.
Milgram, S. (1963). Behavioral study of obedience. *Journal of Abnormal and Social Psychology,* **67,** 371–378.
Milgram, S. (1965). Some conditions of obedience and disobedience to authority. *Human Relations,* **18,** 57–76.
Milgram, S. (1974). *Obedience to authority,* New York: Harper and Row.
Mill, J. S. (1979). *On liberty.* New York: Penguin Press. (Original work published 1859)
Mintzberg, A. (1983). *Power in and around organizations.* Englewood Cliffs, NJ: Prentice-Hall.
Mitroff, I. I., & Emshoff, J. R. (1979). On strategic assumption making: A dialectical approach to policy and planning. *Academy of Management Review,* **4,** 1–12.
Moscovici, S., & Faucheux, C. (1972). Social influence, conformity bias and the study of active minorities. In L. Berkowitz (Ed.), *Advances in experimental social psychology* (Vol. 6, pp. 149–202). New York: Academic Press.
Moscovici, S., Lage, E., & Naffrechoux, M. (1969). Influence of a consistent minority on the responses of a majority in a color perception task. *Sociometry,* **32,** 365–380.

Moscovici, S., & Nemeth, C. (1974). Social influence II: Minority influence. In C. Nemeth (Ed.), *Social psychology: Classic and contemporary integrations* (pp. 217–249). Chicago: Rand-McNally.

Moscovici, S., & Neve, P. (1971). Studies in social influence: I. Those absent are in the right: Convergence and polarization of answers in the course of a social interaction. *European Journal of Social Psychology*, **1**, 201–214.

Mugny, G. (1982). *The power of minorities*. London: Academic Press.

Near, J. P., & Miceli, M. P. (1985). Organizational dissidence: The case of whistle-blowing. *Journal of Business Ethics*, **4**, 1–16.

Near, J. P., & Miceli, M. P. (1986). Retaliation against whistle-blowers: Predictors and effects. *Journal of Applied Psychology*, **71**, 137–145.

Near, J. P., & Miceli, M. P. (1987). Whistle-blowers in organizations: Dissidents or reformers? In L. L. Cummings & B. M. Staw (Ed.), *Research in organizational behavior* (Vol. 9, pp. 321–368). Greenwich, CT: JAI Press.

Nemeth, C. (1976, July). *A comparison between conformity and minority influence*. Paper presented to the International Congress on Psychology, Paris, France.

Nemeth, C. (1986). Differential contributions of majority vs. minority influence. *Psychological Review*, **93**(1), 23–32.

Nemeth, C., & Brilmayer, A. G. (1987). Negotiation vs. influence. *European Journal of Social Psychology*, **17**, 45–56.

Nemeth, C., & Chiles, C. (1988). Modelling courage: The role of dissent in fostering independence. *European Journal of Social Psychology*, **18**, 275–280.

Nemeth, C., & Kwan, J. (1985). Originality of word associations as a function of majority vs. minority influence processes. *Social Psychology Quarterly*, **48**, 277–282.

Nemeth, C., & Kwan, J. (1987). Minority influence, divergent thinking and the detection of correct solutions. *Journal of Applied Social Psychology*, **9**, 788–799.

Nemeth, C., Mayseless, O., Sherman, J., & Brown, Y. (1989). *Improving recall by exposure to consistent dissent*. Unpublished manuscript, University of California, Berkeley.

Nemeth, C., & Nolan, M. (1987). *Consistency, dissent and recall*. Unpublished manuscript. University of California, Berkeley.

Nemeth, C., & Nolan, M. (1987) *Minority consistency and enhancement of recall*. Unpublished manuscript, Department of Psychology, University of California, Berkeley.

Nemeth, C., Swedlund, M., & Kanki, B. (1974). Patterning of the minority's responses and their influence on the majority. *European Journal of Social Psychology*, **4**, 53–64.

Nemeth, C., & Wachtler, J. (1974). Creating perceptions of consistency and confidence: A necessary condition for minority influence. *Sociometry*, **37**, 529–540.

Nemeth, C., & Wachtler, J. (1983). Creative problem solving as a result of majority vs. minority influence. *European Journal of Social Psychology*, **13**, 45–55.

Nemeth, C., Wachtler, J., & Endicott, J. (1977). Increasing the size of the minority: Some gains and some losses. *European Journal of Social Psychology*, **1**, 11–23.

Olmstead, J. A., & Blake, R. R. (1955). The rise of simulated groups to produce modifications in judgment. *Journal of Personality*, **23**, 335–345.

O'Reilly, C. A., & Caldwell, D. (1979). Informational influence as a determinant of perceived task characteristics and job satisfaction. *Journal of Applied Psychology*, **64**, 157–165.

O'Reilly, C. A., & Chatman, J. (1986). Organizational commitment and psychological attachment: The effects of compliance, identification and internalization on personal behavior. *Journal of Applied Psychology*, **71**, 492–499.

O'Reilly, C. A., & Flatt, S. (1987). *Executive team demography, organizational innovation, and firm performance*. Unpublished manuscript, School of Business Administration, University of California, Berkeley.

Pfeffer, J., & Salancik, G. R. (1974). Organizational decision making as a political process: The case of a university budget. *Administrative Science Quarterly*, **19**, 135–151.

Pfeffer, J. (1977). Toward an examination of stratification in organizations. *Administrative Science Quarterly*, **22**, 553–567.
Ricateau, P. (1971). Processus de categorisation d'autrui et les mechanismes d'influence. *Bulletin de Psychologie*, **24**, 909–919.
Ross, J., & Staw, B. (1986). Expo 86: An escalation prototype. *Administrative Science Quarterly*, **31**, 274–297.
Salancik, G. R. (1977). Commitment and the control of organizational behavior and belief. In B. M. Staw & G. R. Salancik (Eds.), *New directions in organizational behavior* (pp. 1–54). Malabar, FL: Krieger Publishing.
Salancik, G., & Pfeffer, J. (1978). A social information processing approach to job attitudes and task design. *Administrative Science Quarterly*, **23**, 224–253.
Schacter, S. (1951). Deviation, rejection, and communication. *Journal of Abnormal and Social Psychology*, **46**, 190–207.
Schein, E. H. (1968). Organizational socialization and the profession of management. *Industrial Management Review*, **9**, 1–15.
Schein, E. H. (1978). *Career dynamics: Matching individual and organizational needs*. Reading, MA: Addison Wesley.
Schein, E. H. (1985). *Organizational culture and leadership*. San Francisco: Jossey-Bass.
Schneider, B. (1987). The people make the place. *Personal Psychology*, **40**, 437–453.
Sherif, M. (1935). A study of some factors in social perception. *Archives of Psychology*, **27**(187), 1–60.
Smith, C. A., Organ, D. W., & Near, J. P. (1983). Organizational citizenship behavior: Its nature and antecedents. *Journal of Applied Psychology*, **69**, 653–663.
Staw, B. M. (1976). Knee-deep in the big muddy: A study of escalating commitment to a chosen course of action. *Organizational Behavior and Human Performance*, **16**, 27–44.
Staw, B. M. (1988). A funnel model of innovation. In M. West & J. Fair (Eds.), *Integrating individual and organizational approaches to innovation*. Chichester, England: Wiley.
Staw, B. M., & Bell, N. (1988). *Functions of dissatisfaction*. Unpublished manuscript, School of Business Administration, University of California, Berkeley.
Staw, B. M., & Boettger, R. (1988). *Doing what you're told . . . but little else: The role of initiative in work performance*. Unpublished manuscript, School of Business Administration, University of California, Berkeley.
Staw, B. M., & Ross, J. (1980). Commitment of an experimenting society: An experiment on the attribution of leadership from administrative scenarios. *Journal of Applied Psychology*, **65**, 249–260.
Staw, B. M., & Ross, J. (1987). Behavior in escalation situations: Antecedents, prototypes, and solutions. In L. L. Cummings & B. M. Staw (Eds.), *Research in organizational behavior* (Vol. 7, pp. 39–78). Greenwich, CT: JAI Press.
Strauss, G. (1982). Workers participation in management: An international perspective. In B. M. Staw & L. L. Cummings (Eds.), *Research in organizational behavior* (Vol. 4, pp. 173–265). Greenwich, Connecticut: JAI Press.
Tanford, S., & Penrod, S. (1984). Social influence model: A formal integration of research on majority and minority influence. *Psychological Bulletin*, **95**, 189–225.
Tegar, A. (1980). *Too much invested to quit*. New York: Pergamon.
Tom, V. R. (1971). The role of personality and organizational images in the recruiting process. *Organizational Behavior and Human Performance*, **16**, 573–592.
Torrance, E. P. (1959). The influence of the experienced members of small groups on the behavior of the inexperienced. *Journal of Social Psychology*, **49**, 249–257.
Tsui, A. S., & O'Reilly, C. A. (1987). *Beyond simple demographic effects: The importance of relational demography in superior–subordinate dyads*. Unpublished manuscript, School of Business Administration, University of California, Berkeley.

Tushman, M. L., & Romanelli, E. (1985). Organizational evolution: A metamorphosis model of convergence and reorientation. In L. L. Cummings & B. M. Staw (Eds.), *Research in organizational behavior* (Vol. 7). Greenwich, CT: JAI Press.

Van Maanen, J., & Schein, E. H. (1979). Toward a theory of organizational socialization. In B. M. Staw (Ed.), *Research in organizational behavior* (Vol. 1). Greenwich, CT: JAI Press.

Wagner, W. G., Pfeffer, J., & O'Reilly, C. A. (1984). Organizational demography and turnover in top management groups. *Administrative Science Quarterly, 29,* 74–92.

Wanous, J. P. (1980). *Organizational entry.* Reading, MA: Addison-Wesley.

Waters, J. A. (1980). Catch 20.5: Corporate morality as an organizational phenomenon. In W. C. Hamner (Ed.), *Organizational shock* (pp. 372–386). New York: Wiley.

Weick, K. E. (1976). Educational organizations as loosely coupled system. *Administrative Science Quarterly, 21,* 1–19.

Weick, K. E. (1983). Contradictions in a community of scholars: The cohesion–accuracy tradeoff. *The Review of Higher Education, 6,* 253–267.

Weick, K. E., & Gilfillan, D. P. (1971). Fate of arbitrary traditions in a laboratory microculture. *Journal of Personality and Social Psychology, 17,* 179–191.

White, S. E., & Mitchell, T. R. (1979). Job enrichment versus social cues: A comparison and competitive test. *Journal of Applied Psychology, 64,* 1–9.

Zald, M. N., & Berger, M. A. (1978). Social movements in organizations: Coup d'etat, insurgency and mass movements. *American Journal of Sociology, 83,* 823–861.

Zucker, L. G. (1977). The role of institutionalization in cultural persistence. *American Sociological Review, 42,* 726–743.

CONFESSION, INHIBITION, AND DISEASE

James W. Pennebaker

DEPARTMENT OF PSYCHOLOGY
SOUTHERN METHODIST
   UNIVERSITY
DALLAS, TEXAS 75275

I. Introduction

The pain I was feeling was something I have never felt before in my life. I never actually thought that *my* Julie would be leaving me. It was like someone taking my heart and squeezing out all of the feelings I have for her. Why is this happening to me? Everything was so perfect for us. We had everything in the world together. Our love was unbreakable. (18-year-old freshman on the break-up of a relationship.)

I love my parents. We have a perfect family life. My parents always support me in whatever I do. . . . My father has been such a bastard, I know that he has something going with his secretary. My mother takes it out on me. I have to wear the clothes she wants, date the boys she wants. I'm even at SMU because she went here, even though I wanted to go to UT. (20-year-old college junior.)

There was a burst of gunfire and my buddy fell to the ground, half of his head blown off. I looked up and a Gook was running into a shed carrying a machine gun. I ran to the shed, jumped through the door and fired, hitting them in both legs. It was a woman who had shot my buddy and who was bleeding on the ground. We stared into each other's eyes. I ripped off her clothes and made love to her. Before I knew it, I could hear choppers overhead—ours. I pulled out my knife and slit her throat. I loved her. I killed her. (33-year-old Vietnam veteran.)

Today, my mother sent me a care package and I was very excited until I opened it. It was all old things that I had left in my room, bills, old letters, etc. I began to realize that my past could follow me anywhere. My mother sent me an old book I used to have on commonly mispelled words. It allmost ofended me. That was such a reminder of all the old habits and imature actions I felt like a child again [sic]. (18-year-old college freshman.)

> They were throwing babies from the second floor window of the orphanage. I can still see the pools of blood, the screams, and the thuds of their bodies. I just stood there afraid to move. The Nazi soldiers faced us, with their grins. (68-year-old concentration camp survivor, recounting the last days of the Lodz Ghetto, 1942.)

These excerpted transcripts come from individuals who have participated in our studies dealing with traumatic experiences. When given the opportunity, people readily divulge their deepest and darkest secrets. Even though people report that they have lived with these thoughts and feelings virtually every day, most note that they have actively held back from telling others about these fundamental parts of themselves. Indeed, these people report that they have never before discussed these feelings and events with anyone.

This article explores the nature of confession and inhibition. Over the past several years, my colleagues and I have learned that confronting traumatic experiences can have meaningful physiological and psychological benefits. Conversely, not confiding significant experiences is associated with increased disease rates, ruminations, and other difficulties. This pattern of findings has helped us in developing a useful theory of active inhibition that shares many of the assumptions of learning theory, psychodynamic models, and more recent cognitive perspectives.

The article is divided into four general sections. The first section examines the nature of confession per se. When given the opportunity, what secrets do people divulge? Why and how do they do it? The second section focuses on the physiological and psychological effects of confronting (or actively avoiding) past traumatic experiences. Based on a number of laboratory and field studies, it is clear that requiring people to write or talk about traumas is associated with both immediate and long-term health benefits. Using the first two sections as a base, the third section presents a formal theory of active inhibition. The links between the theory and Freud, animal learning, and cognitive perspectives are discussed. The final section of the article is devoted to a reexamination of catharsis, the development and breakdown of the self, and the role of psychosomatics in social psychology.

II. The Parameters of Trauma and Confession

A. BACKGROUND

There is little doubt that traumatic experiences are physically and psychologically unhealthy. The early work of Selye (1976) pointed to the biological effects of psychological traumas on rats and humans. Numerous studies that have examined major life events in general (e.g., Holmes & Rahe, 1967), or specific life events such as rape, war, or natural disaster, repeatedly demonstrate their negative effects on physical and psychological health (for reviews, see Figley & McCubbin, 1984; Sowder, 1985; VandenBos & Bryant, 1987).

In recent years, a number of researchers have suggested that social, cognitive, and individual difference factors can buffer the deleterious effects of life events. For example, friends and acquaintances (e.g., Cobb, 1976), intimate relationships (e.g., Hatfield, 1982), and other forms of social support have been shown to reduce stress in a number of ways (Cohen & McKay, 1984). The stability of individuals' views of themselves (Brown, 1988; Swann, 1987), their ability to find meaning in the events (Janoff-Bulman, 1985; Silver, Boon, & Stones, 1983), and other techniques influencing cognitive appraisal can blunt or exaggerate the stress response (Lazarus & Folkman, 1984). Finally, certain individual differences, such as hardiness (Kobasa, 1982), self-complexity (Linville, 1987), low levels of psychic conflict (Emmons & King, 1988), and optimism (Scheier & Carver, 1985) have been found to reduce the physiological effects of massive life stressors.

An important dimension to coping with stressors that may underlie many of these approaches concerns the degree to which people discuss or psychologically confront traumas after their occurrence. Jourard (1971), for example, argued that self-disclosure of upsetting experiences serves as a basic human motive (see also Derlega, 1984). As such, most people naturally discuss daily and significant experiences with others. Even major traumas such as the death of a friend, a shared natural disaster, or a house fire are usually discussed in detail with close friends. Less socially acceptable traumas, however, can be far more difficult to confide: marital infidelity, embezzlement, being the perpetrator or victim of rape. Whereas talking about a trauma with others can strengthen social bonds, provide coping information and emotional support, and hasten an understanding of the event, the inability to talk with others can be unhealthy for a number of reasons that are discussed herein later.

Across several correlational studies, we have consistently found that not confiding any type of traumatic event is associated with illness episodes and measures of subjective distress. For example, among individuals whose spouses have died unexpectedly by suicide or automobile accident, the more the survivors have talked with others about their spouse's death, the healthier they report being and the less they ruminate about their spouse a year after the death (Pennebaker & O'Heeron, 1984). Among a sample of 200 white-collar workers in a large corporation, we found that experiencing any type of trauma in childhood that was not discussed with others was correlated with current diagnosed health problems, ranging from hypertension and cancer to bouts of influenza and diarrhea (Pennebaker & Susman, 1988). As can be seen in Fig. 1, comparable findings have emerged among college student samples (Pennebaker, Colder, & Sharp, 1988a; Pennebaker & Hoover, 1985). In all of these studies, the magnitude of the confiding–illness relationship was either unaffected or became stronger when measures of social support (e.g., number of close friends) were statistically controlled.

These preliminary findings, then, strongly implicate the beneficial role of

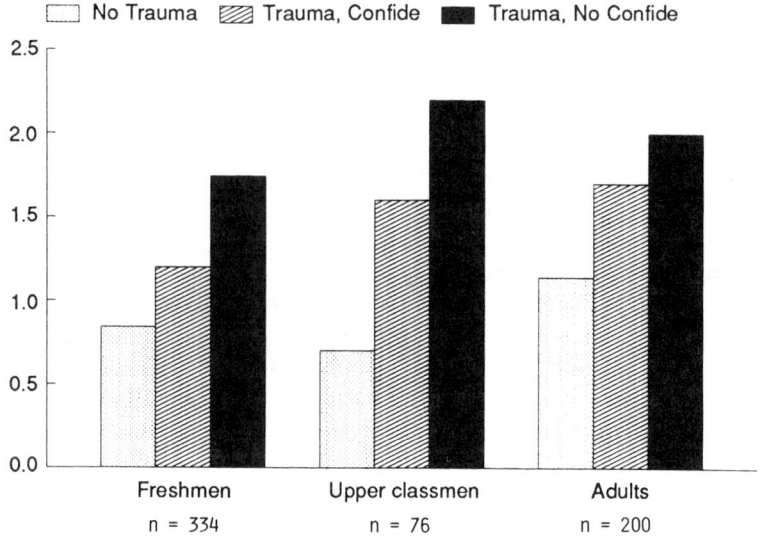

Fig. 1. Illness measures among subjects who reported experiencing no traumatic experiences, traumatic experiences that were all confided, or traumas that were not confided. In the freshman sample, the y-axis refers to actual number of health center visits in the 4 months following completion of the trauma questionnaire. For the upperclass student sample, the y-axis refers to number of self-reported visits to a physician in the 6 months preceding the completion of the trauma questionnaire. The y-axis for the adult sample reflects number of self-reported major and minor illnesses in the previous year.

talking about traumatic experiences and, conversely, the danger of not confiding. An obvious difficulty in evaluating correlational studies such as these is that they are necessarily confounded with social support, cognitive style, or individual differences. In order to remedy this, we have conducted a number of laboratory experiments wherein disclosing traumatic or upsetting experiences is manipulated.

B. INDUCED CONFESSION IN THE LABORATORY: THE GENERAL PARADIGM

Since 1984, we have run several types of studies that require individuals either to write or to talk about their most upsetting personal experiences and, when possible, topics that they have not discussed with others. Some of the studies require students to disclose traumatic experiences on a single occasion while various autonomic nervous system or brain wave activities are monitored. Other experiments, which examine long-term health or immune system function, require individuals to write about traumatic experiences for 15 to 20 minutes each day for 3 or 4 consecutive days. This section first outlines our subject selection procedures and general disclosure instructions. It concludes with a discussion of the ethics and safeguards of conducting studies such as these.

1. Subject Recruitment

Most of the studies that are discussed in this section have used psychology students who receive extra credit for their participation. Typically, the senior investigator addresses the eligible classes and notes that participants may be required to write or talk about the most traumatic experiences of their entire lives. Prospective subjects are assured that their disclosures will be anonymous and confidential. To participate in the experiment, subjects later sign up for the experiment on a form that includes a warning: "NOTE—In this study, you may be expected to write (or talk) about deeply personal experiences."

The night before the actual study, subjects are telephoned and again told that the study may involve their writing (or talking) about extremely upsetting experiences. Further, they are warned that the study may make them cry or feel depressed. They are strongly encouraged not to participate in the study if they have any qualms. Despite these repeated warnings and the availability of other, less-threatening studies, over 90% of the subjects appear for the experiment on the following day. It should be noted that the phone call also forces subjects to think about the topics that they will disclose on the following day.

Based on several questionnaires completed by all introductory psychology students, our subjects do not differ from those who do not sign up for the study in any systematic way. That is, there are no differences in gender or in scores on the Marlowe-Crowne Social Desirability Scale, the Beck Depression Inventory (BDI), symptom or health measures, or scales that tap self-esteem, positive affect, adjustment to college, and so on.

2. General Procedure

At the appointed time, subjects meet individually with an experimenter who again warns them about the study and encourages them to withdraw and receive full credit. After assurances of anonymity are made, subjects, who are randomly assigned to write (or talk) about traumas, are told:

> Once you are escorted into the experimental cubicle and the door is closed, I want you to write continuously about the most upsetting or traumatic experience of your entire life. Don't worry about grammar, spelling, or sentence structure. In your writing, I want you to discuss your deepest thoughts and feelings about the experience. You can write about anything you want, but whatever you choose, it should be something that has affected you very deeply. Ideally, it should be about something you have not talked with others about in detail. It is critical, however, that you let yourself go and touch those deepest emotions and thoughts that you have.
>
> I should warn you that many people find this study quite upsetting. Many people cry during the study and feel somewhat sad or depressed during and after it.

There are, of course, variations in these instructions, depending on the study; these are discussed later. If subjects participate in a single-session, within-subject experiment, they write/talk both about traumatic topics and about superficial topics, such as their plans for the remainder of the day, in a counterbalanced order. In the multiple-session, between-subjects studies, subjects assigned to write about traumatic experiences are free to write about the same or different traumas during each of the 3 or 4 sessions.

After receiving their writing assignment, subjects are escorted to one of several small experimental cubicles by an experimenter who is blind to condition. In the cubicles, subjects are alone for the entire writing/talking period. When the writing time is over, the experimenter returns to the room, asks the subjects to place their assigned identification code on the writing sample, and to place their essay and relevant questionnaires into a large box as they leave the writing area.

Three aspects of this procedure should be highlighted. First, great effort is made by the lead experimenter to establish rapport with each subject. In all of our studies, we have tried to convey a sense of grave importance of the research and our abiding concern for the subject. When giving the trauma instructions, we attempt to be as intense and serious as possible. Our goal, then, is to have the subjects walk into the cubicle with the belief that they are about to reveal their deepest secrets in an honest way.

Second, it is critical that the writing or talking sessions occur in a unique and isolated environment. The writing or talking area is quiet and, once subjects begin writing, the door is shut to give them the impression of solitude. As is discussed later in the article, we are convinced that the more distinct the writing situation (i.e., the more removed from the real world), the more likely people will be to express their deepest thoughts and feelings.

Third, we use every technique that we can think of in our aim to give a sense of anonymity. Subjects place their own essays into a large box with a small slit in it; no names are ever used or asked for by the experimenters; each subject is assigned a unique ID number.

3. Debriefing and Ethical Considerations

As is discussed in the following section, many subjects in our experiments are profoundly affected by their participation. Each debriefing session, which lasts between 20 minutes and an hour, is conducted by a clinician, a graduate student with clinical training, or the author. The general format of the session is based on the debriefing approach of Aronson and Carlsmith (1968). Much of the time is spent exploring how the subjects are feeling at the moment, as well as any problems they may be experiencing directly or indirectly from the experiment. In addition, all subjects are told about the various counseling services offered by the university. The ultimate goal of the debriefing at this point is to make them feel good about the study and the critical role that they have played.

In the multiple-session studies, we are particularly interested in following each subject's health center visits. Because visits could be influenced by our debriefing, we do not tell the subjects of the exact aims of the study (i.e., looking at long-term health). Nevertheless, we are honest in telling them that we cannot inform them of the exact nature of the study for fear of biasing our results. In all of these studies, however, subjects are contacted between 6 weeks and 4 months after the writing phase to evaluate how they are doing. At this time, subjects are told the exact nature of the research, what we were looking for, and what we found.

Because of the sensitive nature of this research, only the author reads each of the writing samples each night during the course of the study to be certain that no one is in imminent psychological or physical danger. Of the 300+ people that we have run using this paradigm, 2 have shown sufficient instability to warrant our excusing them from the remainder of the study and referring them to our staff clinical psychologist who serves as a consultant to the project.

C. HOW AND WHAT PEOPLE DISCLOSE

This is an extremely powerful paradigm. This section first discusses the immediate psychological impact on the subjects. It then provides an overview of the topics that subjects typically disclose and how they go about disclosing them. It concludes with a summary of individual differences related to degree of disclosure.

1. Immediate Impact on the Subjects

In the two experiments in which we have asked subjects to talk about traumatic experiences into a tape recorder for no more than 5 minutes during a single session (Pennebaker, Hughes, & O'Heeron, 1987), over 25% have cried. In these same experiments, when subjects were asked to rate how upsetting or stressful their disclosures had been, using a 7-point scale on which 7 is *extremely upsetting*, the mean rating has been 5.3.

Averaging across the three multiple-session, between-subjects experiments in which subjects have been asked to write about their upsetting experiences for 3 or 4 days (Pennebaker & Beall, 1986; Pennebaker et al., 1988a; Pennebaker, Kiecolt-Glaser, & Glaser, 1988b), subjects in the primary trauma conditions have rated their essays as extremely personal (mean = 5.4, where 7 = *personal*) and emotional (mean = 5.3), compared to control subjects, who wrote about superficial topics (control means = 2.4 for personal and 2.3 for emotional).

Self-reports also indicate that repeated writing greatly increases general feelings of sadness and depression. After each day's writing, for example, subjects are asked to report the degree to which they are currently feeling each of several emotions. Not surprisingly, in comparison with controls, trauma subjects report being significantly more sad, depressed, frustrated, and guilty. Taken together, these findings would indicate that disclosing upsetting experiences is not immediately uplifting—as might be predicted from the perspective of a simple venting or emotional catharsis (e.g., Scheff, 1979).

On the last day of writing and again on follow-up questionnaires 4 months later, subjects are asked how valuable and meaningful the study has been for them as well as the likelihood that they would participate in the study again. Overall, trauma subjects rate the studies as quite valuable and meaningful (4.4, where 7 = *valuable* and *meaningful*) relative to controls (2.3). When asked whether they would participate again knowing what they do now, approximately 98% of the trauma subjects and 93% of the controls have answered affirmatively.

2. Topics of Disclosure

The topics that trauma subjects in the various studies have written or talked about have varied considerably. Table I includes a rough breakdown of categories for four of the experiments. Because many of the topics could be classified in multiple ways, the percentages for each of the studies exceed 100%. As can be seen, the majority of subjects disclose issues surrounding interpersonal conflict and intimacy and loss through death or divorce. Note also that a slightly different pattern emerges for topic of disclosure when individuals talk into a tape recorder on one occasion than when subjects write for 4 consecutive days.

The data in Table I fail to convey the uniqueness and power of the stories that our subjects have disclosed. The following sketches provide a flavor of the essays and transcripts from our studies:

> A female who has lived in fear for several weeks because of the physical and psychological harassment of a jealous woman who has apparently hired two thugs.

> A male who, in his high school years, was repeatedly beaten by his stepfather. After attempting suicide with his stepfather's gun, the stepfather further humiliated the subject by laughing at his failed attempt.

> A female who, in a fit of rage at her father, accused him of marital infidelity in front of her mother. The accusation, which apparently was true and unknown to the mother, led to the separation and divorce of the parents and overwhelming guilt on the part of the daughter.

> A female who, at the age of 10, was asked to clean up her room because of her grandmother, who was to visit the home later that evening. The girl did not do so. That night, the grandmother slipped on one of the girl's toys and broke her hip. The grandmother died a week later during a hip operation.

> A male who, at age 9, was calmly told by his father that he was divorcing the boy's mother because their home life had been disrupted ever since the boy had been born.

Story after story reveals deceit, tragedy, and misery. The feelings of horror, fear, and rage associated with rape, incest, and family violence are featured in every study. The despair and loneliness of the death of a family member, of moving to a new town in childhood, or in coming to college are commonplace. Problems surrounding alcohol and other drug abuse by students and their parents, eating disorders, and suicidal thoughts regularly surface in each experiment.

A grim irony is that these studies have been conducted at Southern Methodist University—a school with a disproportionate number of upper-middle-class students with above-average entering Scholastic Aptitude Test (SAT) scores. That

TABLE I
PERCENTAGE OF TOPICS DISCLOSED IN THE TRAUMA CONDITIONS ACROSS FOUR STUDIES[a]

Topic	Pennebaker & Beall (1986)	Pennebaker, Kiecolt-Glaser, & Glaser (1988b)	Pennebaker, Hughes, & O'Heeron (1987) Study 1	Pennebaker, Hughes, & O'Heeron (1987) Study 2
Death				
Family member	6	6	10	13
Friend	18	4	15	10
Pet	4	3	0	0
Family				
Divorce–separation	3	6	15	10
Conflict–fights	13	8	8	9
Interpersonal conflicts				
Opposite sex	19	15	23	13
Same sex	4	2	4	2
Illness–accident				
Relative–friend	3	0	15	13
Self	7	16	0	8
Failure–humiliation	6	5	0	5
Academic				
Coming to college	4	19	3	8
Grades–teachers	5	3	13	13
Sexual traumas	3	9	5	7
Psychological–behavioral				
Eating disorders	0	4	4	0
Alcohol–drugs	5	2	0	2
Suicidal thoughts	3	6	0	0
Existential	1	7	0	0
Total codable essays or tapes	119	100	20	39

[a] The Pennebaker & Beall and the Pennebaker, Kiecolt-Glaser, & Glaser studies required trauma subjects to write four essays. The two experiments of the Pennebaker, Hughes, & O'Heeron study involved subjects' talking into a tape recorder for 3 to 5 minutes during a single session. Percentages for each study exceed 100% due to multiple coding of some topics.

so many of these students are currently living with significant traumas hints at an even higher rate of problems among individuals in the population at large.

3. The Ways People Disclose Traumas

When we began this research, one of the more startling discoveries was *how* individuals disclosed traumas. Whether writing or talking, when subjects begin addressing the most intimate aspects of their lives their mode of presentation changes. Across the various studies, individuals in the trauma conditions talk faster, write more words per essay, and use more first-person pronouns than those in the control conditions.

Subjectively, most people who talk or write about traumas appear to enter a different level of consciousness during the study. In the studies in which subjects talked into a tape recorder about both traumas and their plans for the day (Pennebaker *et al.*, 1987), we were struck by how subjects' voice qualities changed as a function of topic. Often, as subjects began to disclose the most intimate aspects of their traumas, they began to whisper and to accelerate their speech dramatically. In many cases, their voice characteristics were so different (e.g., tone, volume, even accent) from their normal ways of speaking that they sounded as though they were different people.

In our writing studies, we frequently find that people change their handwriting style when writing about different topics even within the same essay. It is not uncommon for subjects to switch from cursive writing to block lettering for a given topic and then return to the original writing style after completing a particularly significant topic. Some examples of changes in lettering, which are included in Fig. 2, include differences in the slanting of letters, pen pressure, and markouts.

We believe that these changes in presentation style reflect the psychological state that accompanies a "letting-go" or disinhibition. When the normal social or cognitive constraints of disclosing personal experiences are lifted, a different aspect of the self emerges. This change may be similar to the trance states discussed by Erickson, Rossi, and Rossi (1976), or Csikszentmihalyi's (1975) flow experience. We should emphasize that not all of our subjects demonstrate these pronounced presentational changes during the studies. They are, however, far more likely to occur among subjects who rate themselves (or are rated by judges) as disclosing deeply personal topics that they have not discussed with others before the study.

4. Individual Differences

As just suggested, there are large individual differences in the ways and the degree to which that people disclose traumatic experiences. As with any long-term research project, our approach to an individual difference measure of disclosure has gradually changed. In the first of several studies that have examined correlates of degree of disclosure, three independent judges rated each tape recording of 39 subjects who disclosed traumatic experiences, as to the degree to which the recording was personal and emotional (Pennebaker *et al.*, 1987, Study 2). These ratings were summed, yielding a degree-of-disclosure score. The disclosure score was then correlated with a number of individual difference measures that had been completed prior to the study.

Overall, degree of disclosure was positively (and significantly) correlated with the Cognitive and Somatic Anxiety Questionnaire (CSAQ from Schwartz, Davidson, & Goleman, 1978), the Maudsley measure of obsession and compulsion (Rachman & Hodgson, 1980), and the MMPI Psychasthenia scale. Disclosure was unrelated to the Marlowe–Crowne Social Desirability Scale (Crowne & Marlowe, 1964) and to gender. This pattern of results indicates that individuals characterized as high in negative affectivity, or NA (Watson & Clark, 1984), are more likely to disclose deeply personal aspects of themselves within a brief 5-minute disclosure period.

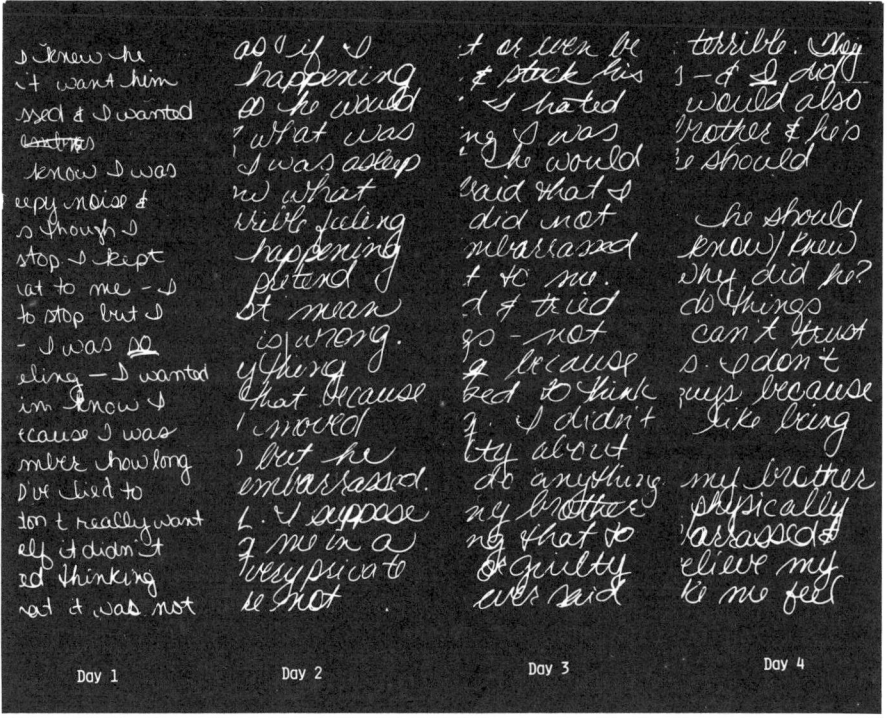

Fig. 2. Change in handwriting of a female describing the same episode over the 4 days of writing (from Pennebaker *et al.*, 1988b).

More recently, we have changed our focus to consider the degree to which individuals disclose issues that they have previously held back in telling others. In other words, we are more interested in the subjective state of disinhibition than in disclosure per se. In one study (e.g., Pennebaker et al., 1988b), we required 25 subjects to write about their deepest traumas for 4 consecutive days. After each writing session, subjects rated the degree to which they wrote about things that they had previously held back from telling others. Unlike judges' ratings of degree of disclosure, writing about previously inhibited topics was inconsistently related to the CSAQ, and negatively correlated with the Marlowe-Crowne.

Finally, as is discussed in greater detail below, we have recently moved to a physiologically based measure of disinhibition or degree of disclosure. Based on earlier studies, we have consistently found that individuals who are objectively rated as high disclosers also have low skin conductance levels (SCLs) during the time they confront traumas relative to times that they talk or write about superficial topics. Degree of disinhibition–disclosure, then, can also be defined by the difference in SCL between confronting traumatic versus trivial topics. In a recent study of 24 subjects (Pennebaker & Sharp, 1988), this difference score was uncorrelated with the Taylor Manifest Anxiety Scale, the Marlowe-Crowne, and gender.

III. Confession: Its Effects on Mind and Body

The general laboratory paradigm that we have used is clearly powerful in eliciting stories of previously undisclosed experiences. Indeed, a brief reading of the technique might suggest that forcing people to dredge up unpleasant experiences could have negative physical and psychological effects. Our studies provide overwhelming evidence to the contrary. In this section, we examine three classes of experiments that deal with the effects and correlates of confronting traumatic experience on long-term health and immune function, autonomic activity, and brain wave activity.

A. LONG-TERM HEALTH AND IMMUNE FUNCTION

Our first question concerning the impact of disclosing traumatic experiences on physical health evolved from a series of survey studies. For example, in a survey of 200 employees of a large corporation, we found that individuals who had experienced traumatic experiences in childhood *and* who had not confided these traumas to others were significantly more likely to have contracted cancer, hypertension, ulcers, and even major bouts with influenza than were people either who had not had traumas or who had confided them (Pennebaker & Susman, 1988). These effects held when controlling for social support, age, and recent traumatic experiences. Similarly, in a survey of 19 individuals who had suffered the death of their spouse due to an automobile accident or suicide, a comparable pattern obtained (Pennebaker & O'Heeron, 1984). That is, those individuals who had talked with others about their spouses' death were significantly healthier in the year following the death than those who had not talked with others.

Based on these and other surveys (e.g., Pennebaker & Hoover, 1985), we sought to manipulate experimentally disclosure among a normal college population in order to learn what aspects of disclosing traumatic events could influence long-term health. In the study (Pennebaker & Beall, 1986), 46 healthy undergraduates were asked to write either about the most traumatic and stressful experiences of their lives or about trivial assigned topics for 4 consecutive days. Of those assigned to write about traumatic events, one experimental group wrote about the facts surrounding the traumas but not their feelings about the traumas (trauma-factual condition), another about their feelings concerning the traumas but not the facts (trauma-emotion), and a third about both their feelings and the facts concerning the traumas (trauma-combination group). Across the four experimental sessions, subjects in the trauma-emotion and the trauma-combination conditions reported feeling the most upset after writing and demonstrated increases in systolic blood pressure, compared to the control and trauma-factual subjects.

Most important, however, was that subjects in the trauma-combination cell visited the Student Health Center for illness in the 6 months following the experiment significantly less than those in the other conditions (see Fig. 3). Six-months follow-up questionnaires also showed a consistent pattern indicating that trauma-combination and trauma-emotion subjects felt healthier, reported fewer illnesses, and fewer days of restricted activity due to illness.

Although the study suffered from some weaknesses, it indicated that written—and anonymous—disclosure of traumatic experiences, while initially unpleasant for the individual, could reduce physician visits and improve health perceptions. Further, for long-term benefits to accrue, it appeared to be important for people to disclose not only the event but also the emotions aroused by the event.

In a recent extension of these findings, Janice Kiecolt-Glaser, Ronald Glaser, and I sought to learn if writing about traumatic experiences had a direct impact on immune function (Pennebaker *et al.*, 1988b). Over 4 consecutive days, 50 healthy undergraduates were randomly assigned to write either about the most upsetting events of their lives or about superficial topics. Blood samples were drawn from the participants before the first day of writing, the last day of writing, and a third time 6 weeks later. Using a blastogenic procedure, two related immune assays (relying on the mitogens Con A and PHA) were performed on the blood samples that measured the action of T lymphocytes. In addition to the immune assays, we were also able to collect health center records for physician visits and self-report data from all of the subjects over the course of the study.

Two important results emerged from the immune study. First, compared to controls, individuals who wrote about traumas exhibited improved immune function from before to after the experiment (see Fig. 4). As in the earlier study, trauma subjects also evidenced a significant drop in health center visits for illness after participating in the experiment relative to controls. (This pattern of health-related results has also recently been replicated by Murray, Lamnin, & Carver, 1988). Second, subjects in the trauma group were asked each day, "To what degree did you write about something which you have previously held back telling others?" Those who reported confronting previously inhibited topics were labeled High Disclosers and those below the median in response to the item were called Low Disclosers. As would be predicted, High Disclosers showed significantly greater immune improvements than Low Disclosers from before to after the writing portion of the study.

Taken together, both correlational and experimental findings with both normal

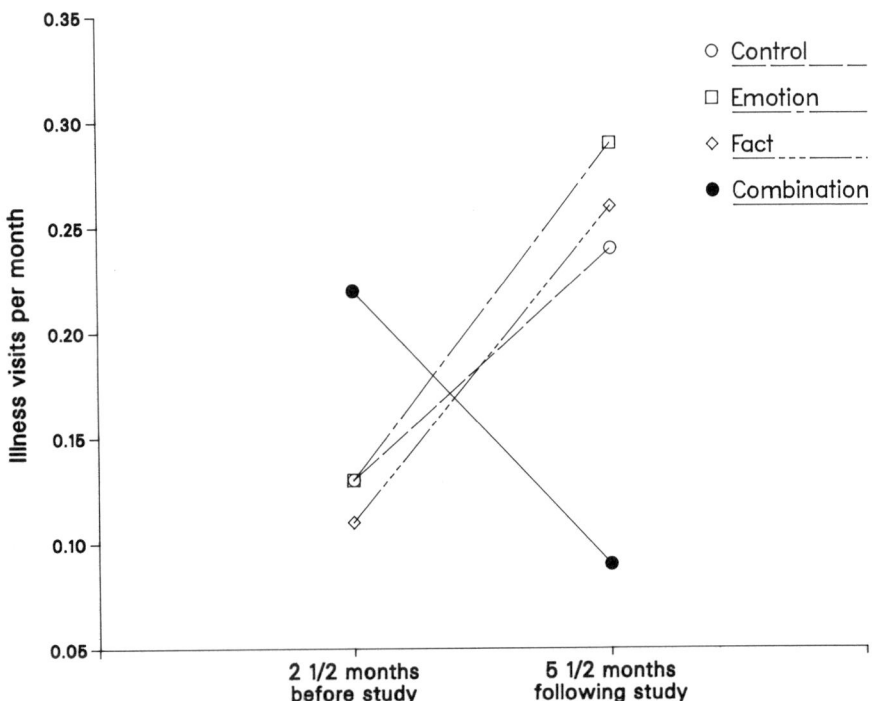

Fig. 3. Number of health center visits for illness per month as a function of writing topic (from Pennebaker & Beall, 1986).

and distressed samples indicate that confronting traumas—by either talking with others or writing—is associated with improved health status. In many respects, the writing studies offer a relatively pure test of the value of confronting traumas because people did not receive social support or other types of social feedback about their writing.

B. AUTONOMIC NERVOUS SYSTEM CORRELATES

In the past several years, a number of investigators have directly and indirectly studied the links between confession, emotional expressiveness, and autonomic activity. For example, polygraph researchers and practitioners have been interested in learning which autonomic indices reliably change when individuals do not "confess." Across a number of studies, measures of electrodermal activity are consistently superior to cardiovascular measures (e.g., heart rate, blood pressure) in discriminating between experimental subjects' telling lies from telling the truth

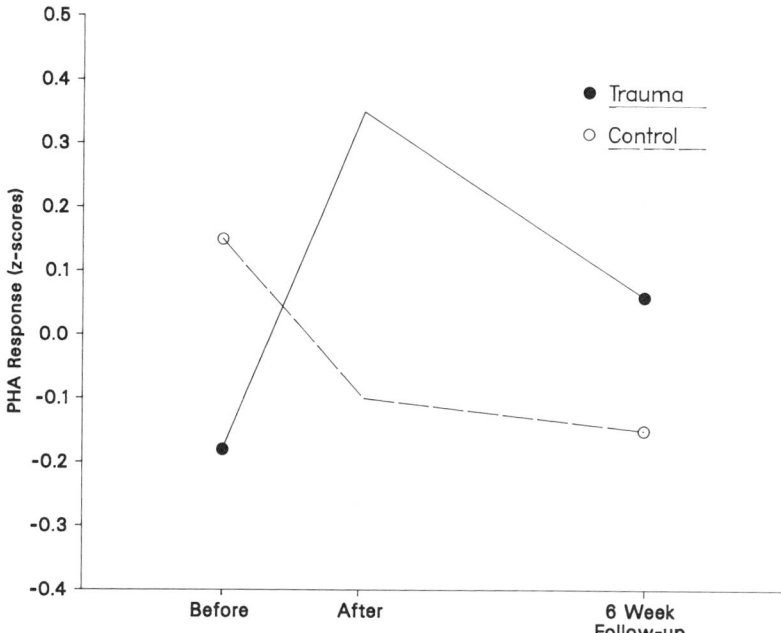

Fig. 4. Mean mitogen response to phytohemagglutinin (PHA) stimulation averaging across three concentration levels (5, 10, and 20 μg/ml of PHA) using blastogenesis. Higher numbers reflect greater immunocompetence (adapted from Pennebaker et al., 1988b).

(see Waid & Orne, 1981 for an excellent review of this literature). Typically, during deception, skin conductance levels increase—which is associated with greater perspiration on the palms of the hand and soles of the feet.

In an important comparison of autonomic measures, Fowles (1980) summarized a large number of studies that indicated that electrodermal activity is associated with behavioral inhibition, whereas cardiovascular measures are linked to behavioral activation. The observations made by Fowles, which are based on the work of Gray (1975), square with work on emotional expression. For example, individuals who are emotionally expressive tend to have lower electrodermal activity than nonexpressive subjects (e.g., Buck, 1984). Using a within-subject design, we have found that SCL is highest when individuals naturally inhibit facial expressions during periods of deception (Pennebaker & Chew, 1985).

In an extension of these ideas, we have examined the links between disclosure of traumatic events and autonomic activity. We predicted that individuals who "let go" and disclosed the most upsetting experiences of their lives would exhibit lower SCLs than when asked to talk about superficial topics. In the first two experiments (Pennebaker, Hughes, & O'Heeron, 1987), subjects talked into a tape recorder about the most traumatic experiences of their lives, as well as their plans for the afternoon, for 3–5 minutes while SCL, heart rate, blood pressure, finger temperature, and corrugator EMG were periodically monitored. Independent judges listened to the recordings and assessed the degree to which each subject discussed events that were objectively personal and emotional. The ratings, then, served as an indicator for degree of disclosure.

Across the two studies, high disclosers evidenced lower SCL levels when talking about traumas than when discussing their plans for the day. Low disclosers evidenced the opposite pattern: higher SCLs during the traumatic topics. In other words, those subjects who "let go" and revealed the most personal and emotional sides of themselves could be discriminated on the basis of SCL drops. Interestingly, none of the other physiological measures differed as a function of degree of disclosure.

Do the autonomic changes in the lab relate to long-term health changes? We have just completed a large-scale study with 33 survivors of the Holocaust (mean age = 65, 17 males, 16 females) to answer this question (Pennebaker & Barger, 1988; Tiebout, 1987). As part of an ongoing archival project sponsored by the Dallas Memorial Center for Holocaust Studies, participants gave a 1–2 hour interview about their experiences during World War II. During the interview, the survivors were videotaped while SCL and heart rate (HR) were continuously monitored.

I cannot begin to express the magnitude of trauma that these individuals endured or the degree to which most currently live with their painful memories. Most of our survivors came from Poland (64%) and were Jewish (97%). Virtually all were displaced from their homes in 1939 and moved to ghettos. Between 1939 and 1942, virtually all witnessed or endured random beatings and saw friends and relatives carried to their deaths. Between 1942 and 1945, most were herded into cattle cars and sent to one of several concentration camps. For 2 to 3 years, they lived with starvation, disease, and constant fear. The majority witnessed the deaths of children, close friends, and family members. No clear picture emerges why our participants survived while the overwhelming majority of their cohort did not. Some were on the brink of death when liberated by the Allies. About 30% escaped the ghettos or work camps and lived in hiding. Another 10–15% secured menial jobs in munition factories or as servants in Nazi officers' homes.

In the weeks following the interview, independent judges rated each videotape on a minute-by-minute basis as to the degree to which the participant was addressing a traumatic topic. Hence, if survivors were talking about the weather or their old neighborhood, their trauma score would be a 1 (on a 5-point scale). The maximum rating (5) was reserved for overwhelming horrors, such as watching their parents carried away to be killed. Across the 33 participants, interrater agreement was acceptable (mean $r = .60$). The mean trauma ratings were then entered, along with mean SCL and HR from the same 1-minute interval. For each subject, then, we were able to compute within-subject correlations reflecting the relationship between objectively coded trauma and both SCL and HR.

The logic of this approach was based on the idea that some people would "let go" while talking about significant traumas (and, thus, evidence negative correlations between trauma rating and SCL), and others would not. Further, based on our previous studies, we predicted that it would be better for one's physical health in the long run to disclose the deepest, most personal aspects of their experiences. In order to assess changes in long-term health, participants were contacted by phone 2 weeks before their interview and again 6–14 months after the interview. During the phone interviews, subjects were asked whether they had any continual health problems that required medical attention (for the preinterview survey) and whether they had been to a physician for illness since the interview (63% had).

Overall, our predictions were borne out. The higher the rated trauma–SCL correlation, the more the participants visited a physician following the interview ($r[31] = .34, p = .05$), after controlling for the preinterview health status and the length of time between the interview and the follow-up interview. Similarly, the higher the participants' overall SCLs during the interview, the more physician visits ($r[31] = .57, p < 0.01$). Interestingly, the average level of rated trauma during the entire interview was unrelated to physician visits and mean SCL. As predicted, the trauma–HR correlations, as well as overall HR levels were unrelated to illness visits.

The results of the Holocaust project tie together much of the previous research that we have conducted on the effects of disclosure. Individuals differ tremendously in how they respond physiologically to disclosing traumatic experience. Drops in skin conductance during disclosure signal that the individuals are letting go and, perhaps, coming to terms with their experiences (cf. Horowitz, 1976). Based on previous studies, this reduced autonomic activity indicates an overall reduction in inhibition or conflict concerning the events. Heightened SCL during disclosure, on the other hand, is indicative of ongoing conflict about the event. These people are not coming to terms with the event and are, perhaps, holding back or suppressing fundamental thoughts or feelings concerning their experiences.

C. CENTRAL NERVOUS SYSTEM ACTIVITY: CORTICAL CONGRUENCE

Although we have demonstrated that confronting traumas is correlated with short-term autonomic and longer-term health changes, we have not yet addressed *why* such relations exist. We believe that the ultimate answer lies in the fundamental cognitive changes that occur during and following our experiments. As is discussed in later sections, there are a number of ways by which to examine changes in cognitive function. A good departure point, however, is to consider how the brain might differentially process individuals' confronting traumas versus superficial topics.

It is beyond the scope of this article to discuss the organization and structure of the cerebral cortex. In recent years, however, a number of researchers have argued that different types of complex information can be processed concurrently and independently in different brain regions (e.g., Davidson, 1984; Gazzaniga, 1986; Luria, 1980). Further, information is differentially processed in the left versus the right hemispheres (Springer & Deutsch, 1986). Gazzaniga (1986), among others, suggests that conscious thought is highly dependent on processing in the language areas of the brain, which are typically located in the left temporal cortex. Emotions, especially negative feelings, are processed in the right frontal areas (Davidson, 1986).

Extrapolating from the work of Davidson, Gazzaniga, and others, it is useful to consider how the brain must process traumatic experiences under different conditions. For example, people who have experienced an upheaval in their lives must process a tremendous amount of sensory, visual, auditory, emotional, linguistic, and other types of information at multiple levels in several brain regions. Based on clinical experience, this process often takes days or weeks, depending on the severity of the trauma.

Imagine what must occur, however, if individuals actively try *not* to process certain parts of the trauma. The suppression of a complex thought is bound to be only partially successful (Wegner, 1988). Some components of an aversive thought will be processed in other regions of the cortex. For example, negative emotions will be processed in the right frontal lobe, which may or may not be available to consciousness. That is, if the language centers are overburdened with other types of information (often obsessive low-level thoughts or compulsive behaviors such as paying bills, or cleaning out the refrigerator), parts of the trauma will be processed but not linguistically organized (cf. Kihlstrom, 1987).

If these ideas are true, we would predict that one effect of confronting traumatic events would be to bring about more coherent and efficient processing of information (i.e., *cortical congruence*). Our metaphorical model of cortical congruence would predict that brain wave activity on the two sides of the head would be more highly correlated when individuals write about traumas than about superficial events. Further, we would predict this relationship to be stronger for high disclosers.

In order to test the cortical congruence idea, 24 undergraduates wrote about the most traumatic experiences of their lives and about their plans for the day for 8 minutes each (Pennebaker & Sharp, 1988). Four times during each essay, subjects were asked to continue thinking about their writing topics while shutting—and not moving—their eyes. During each silent period, SCL, HR, and brain wave activity were monitored. Brain wave activity (EEG) was collected from four sites: the left and right frontal cortex and the left and right parietal cortex (F3, F4, P3, P4 international electrode placements). The EEG data were later period-analyzed on a second-by-second basis, thus yielding 20 1-second alpha and beta frequency periods for each task and for each electrode site. By simply correlating the frontal (left with right) and parietal (left with right) period analysis data across the 20 time-units for each subject and each task, we could assess the cortical congruence. That is, the more highly correlated the two corresponding lobes, the greater the cortical congruence.

As predicted, we found that writing about traumatic experiences was associated with higher interhemispheric correlations than writing about superficial topics for both frontal and parietal lobes ($F[1, 22] = 10.5, p < .01$). More intriguing, however, was the comparison between high and low disclosers. Based on the findings of the Pennebaker *et al.* (1987) project, we split subjects at the median into high and low disclosers, based on their mean SCLs during the trauma and the trivial tasks. Those whose SCLs were lower on the trauma than the trivial tasks were deemed high disclosers, the remainder low disclosers. As can be seen in Fig. 5, the overall interaction ($p < .01$) indicates that high disclosers evidence relatively greater cortical congruence when confronting traumas than lower disclosers.

D. SUMMARY

When individuals are required to confront traumatic experiences, significant changes occur within the body. While talking or writing about traumas, compared with superficial topics, individuals evidence greater congruity in brain wave activity across the cerebral hemisphere, lower SCL, and improved immune function. These effects are most pronounced for high disclosers—that is, individuals who disclose extremely personal topics that they previously have actively held back from telling others.

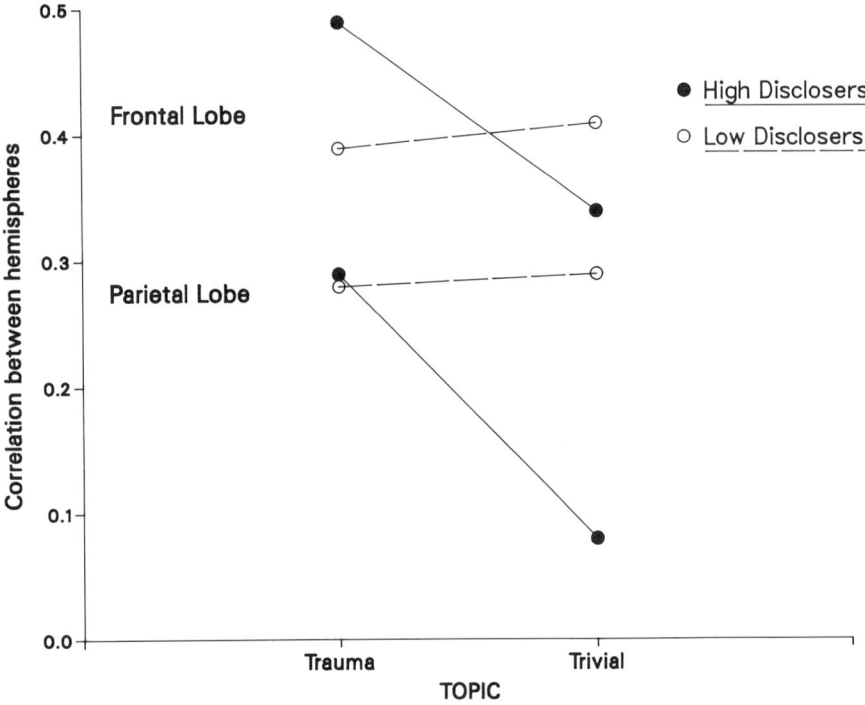

Fig. 5. Mean within-subject correlations between left and right hemispheric EEG during writing about traumas versus superficial topics for high versus low disclosers. Correlations are averaged over alpha and beta frequencies (from Pennebaker & Sharp, 1988).

IV. A Theory of Inhibition and Confrontation

The various findings that we have presented indicate that failing to confront traumas can be physically harmful, whereas talking or writing about them can be helpful. As we have conducted the various studies, we have gradually developed a general theory of inhibition and confrontation. After presenting the basic tenets of the theory, we consider how it is related to other models and perspectives.

A. THE THEORY

The basic ideas of our theory deal with two overlapping issues often seen when individuals face traumatic experiences. The first general process deals with inhibition; the second with confrontation.

1. Active Inhibitory Processes

These processes have the following characteristics:

1. To actively inhibit one's thoughts, feelings, or behaviors requires physiological work. By active inhibition, we mean that individuals must consciously restrain, hold back, or in some way exert effort to *not* think, feel, or behave. Note that this definition of inhibition deviates from that used by many animal learning psychologists, who often consider inhibition as an automatic, noneffortful response.

2. In the short run, inhibition is reflected by increases in SCL. Over time, the work of inhibition serves as a cumulative stressor on the body, which increases the probability of illness and other stress-related physical and psychological problems. Active inhibition can be viewed as one of many general stressors that affect the mind and body. Obviously, the harder one must work at inhibiting, the greater the stress on the body.

3. Active inhibition is also associated with potentially deleterious changes in information processing. In holding back significant thoughts and feelings associated with an event, individuals typically do not process the event fully. By not talking about an inhibited event, for example, individuals usually do not translate the event into language which, as is discussed in the next section, aids in the understanding and assimilation of the event. Consequently, significant experiences that are inhibited are likely to surface in the forms of ruminations, dreams, and associated cognitive symptoms.

2. Cognitive Consequences of Confrontation

In considering traumatic experiences, the opposite pole of active inhibition is confrontation. For lack of a better term, *confrontation* refers to individuals' actively thinking and/or talking about significant experiences, as well as acknowledging relevant emotions. Psychologically confronting traumas negates the effects of inhibition, both physiologically and cognitively.

1. The act of confronting a trauma immediately reduces the physiological work of inhibition. During confrontation, reduction in autonomic activity such as SCL is evident. Over time, if individuals continue to confront and thereby resolve the trauma, the overall physiological work is reduced, thereby lowering the overall stress level on the body.

2. More significant, however, is that confronting a trauma helps individuals to understand and ultimately assimilate the event. By talking or writing about previously inhibited experiences, individuals translate the event into language. Once encoded linguistically, individuals can more readily understand, find meaning in, or attain closure of the experience.

B. LINKS TO OTHER PERSPECTIVES

As should be clear, our work has been heavily influenced by investigators in psychoanalysis, social cognition, psychophysiology, and animal research. This section briefly outlines the similarities and differences of our theory with those in other areas.

1. The Psychoanalytic Tradition

Much of Freud's work was based on studying individuals who had experienced traumatic events in childhood. His early work with Breuer (Breuer & Freud, 1895/1966), for example, focused on the *cathartic method,* whereby patients were encouraged to talk in a stream-of-consciousness manner about their deepest thoughts and feelings surrounding the probable causes of their symptoms. The success of the cathartic method was attributed to the discharge of repressed emotions surrounding the event. Despite the apparent early successes of the cathartic method, Freud later came to believe that the mere expression of repressed emotions did not bring about a permanent cure (Freud, 1920/1966). Although our approach is similar to the cathartic method in several ways, it differs in emphasizing the value of conscious thoughts and feelings rather than the sole expression of pent-up emotions.

A particularly promising evolution in the psychoanalytic approach has been put forward by Mardi Horowitz (1976, 1987). Using a variety of clinical and experimental techniques, Horowitz has developed an elaborate model that incorporates a number of features from cognitive psychology. According to Horowitz, stressful events are processed along three interdependent systems roughly corresponding to perception–cognition, emotion, and cognitive-behavioral control. Although repressed thoughts and feelings can influence the symptoms of traumatic experience, Horowitz is most concerned with the cognitive problems surrounding stress responses.

Drawing heavily on a completion tendency akin to the Ziegarnik effect, Horowitz posits that individuals suffer from ruminations and negative emotions if they are unable to psychologically finish a trauma. By working through an upsetting event—either naturally or in therapy—the individuals ultimately complete the trauma and assimilate it into their self-concepts or schemata. Indeed, this process naturally occurs in a series of stages following a trauma: denial, working through, and assimilation. Although Horowitz has focused heavily on certain types of psychological symptoms often associated with posttraumatic stress disorder (PTSD), he has not considered the underlying physiological causes and effects of inhibition per se.

2. Cognitive Approaches

As the work of Horowitz suggests, a number of perspectives associated with our understanding responses to traumas have been heavily influenced by cognitive models. Features of three overlapping models are particularly relevant to our theory of inhibition and confrontation. These include general information-processing approaches from social psychology, clinically based cognitive models, and work on the suppression of thoughts.

a. Information-Processing Approaches. Many social psychologists have found strict information-processing approaches particularly appealing because of their abilities to link perception, thought, and memory to a variety of phenomena. Recently, for example, Wyer and Srull (1986) have argued that thought can be likened to an elaborate computer program. Central to their argument is the idea that most thoughts are guided by immediate as well as long-term goals. Consequently, most thoughts are focused on completing either externally imposed or intrinsically generated plans and goals. When people do not have any salient goals at a particular time, thoughts are generated in a semirandom manner. Like other similar approaches (e.g., Martin & Tesser, 1988), the Wyer and Srull model is useful in considering how traumas can both disrupt goals and bring about a reordering of new goal information. Indeed, if we assume that understanding an important event is a basic human goal (which is consistent with a variety of theories—Horowitz, 1976; Janoff-Bulman, 1985; Silver & Wortman, 1980), we can better appreciate why so many of our thoughts deal with a trauma after it has occurred. Despite the general appeal of most information-processing approaches, they do not deal with the problem of how or why people actively avoid thinking about specific events.

b. The Suppression and Repression of Thoughts. An interesting approach to remedy this problem has been suggested by Dan Wegner and his colleagues (Wegner, 1988; Wegner, Schneider, Carter, & White, 1987). In this work, Wegner considers the problem of how and why people try to suppress thoughts. Across a number of studies, Wegner finds that people are remarkably bad at not thinking about topics. For example, when told not to think of white bears, people think about them almost as much as if they were told to think of the bears. According to Wegner, the failure of thought suppression lies in the fact that a person must, at some level, be aware of a thought in order to suppress it. Further, the most common thought-suppression strategy is distraction. The problem with distraction is that whatever a person uses to avoid the suppressed thought becomes inexorably tied to the suppressed thought. Over time, then, virtually everything soon reminds the person of the suppressed thought.

Following from Wegner's work, one value of writing or talking about traumatic experiences is that it stops the work of suppression. Indeed, as we found with individuals whose spouses had died unexpectedly, the more they talked about the death, the less they reported ruminating about it (Pennebaker & O'Heeron, 1984).

A parallel approach to understanding thought suppression has been to examine nonconscious mental processes. Unlike suppression, which refers to the conscious avoidance of thoughts, unconscious mental processes include those thoughts, memories, or schemas that are beyond awareness. In an impressive survey of the literature, Kihlstrom (1987) argues that certain perceptual-cognitive and motoric skills can be automatized through experience, thus rendering them nonconscious. Experienced typists, for example, have great difficulty in writing out the correct key sequence of their typewriters because the automatic act of typing has caused their implicit knowledge of the keyboard to become unconsciously coded (cf. Bargh, 1984). Interestingly, the only way that experienced typists are able to reproduce which letters go with which keys is to consciously reconstruct the letters by imagining typing words or letters in their minds.

One can readily appreciate how significant traumas in childhood and beyond may become so rehearsed through ruminative thinking or repeated experience that they evolve into nonconscious mental structures that affect how individuals perceive and think about their worlds on a daily basis. One benefit of writing or talking about traumatic experiences, then, may be to reconstruct and/or make concrete some of the preconscious or nonconscious mental processes that guide the person's conscious thoughts.

c. Cognitively Oriented Clinical Perspectives. Over the past three decades, a number of clinical and personality psychologists have pointed to the importance of considering cognitive processes in the evaluation and treatment of mental disorders. Beck (1976), Ellis (1962), Meichenbaum (1977), and others have argued that individuals often develop maladaptive ways of perceiving and thinking about themselves and their worlds. Through early experience or other means, for example, individuals may unconsciously assume that they are bad people. Although not necessarily aware of this assumption, these people will experience tremendous conflict when they succeed or are held in high esteem by others. The purpose of therapy, then, is to make these fundamental assumptions about the world explicit and ultimately to change them.

An interesting application of this perspective to PTSD can be seen in Epstein's (1980, 1988) cognitive-experiential self-theory. Epstein emphasizes preconscious cognitions that determine the automatic assessment of daily events. Three fundamental motives affect the structure of preconscious cognitions: (1) need for pleasure and avoidance of pain, (2) need for a sense of coherence to assimilate reality, and (3) need for a favorable level of self-esteem. Suffering a traumatic experience, according to Epstein, serves as a "personality smasher" in that it destabilizes or invalidates one or more of the basic preconscious cognitive structures. In order to cope with the trauma, PTSD sufferers may reorganize their self-system using fear, anger, withdrawal, or dissociation as organizing schema. Following a war-related trauma, for example, a person may assimilate the experience around the belief that the world is threatening. Although memories and thoughts about the war experiences may become understandable, the individual now interprets all stimuli as potentially dangerous, thus resulting in states of chronic hyperalertness and anxiety.

As with other cognitive therapists, Epstein believes that an important solution to PTSD is to train people to recognize their preconscious interpretations of events. He also suggests that PTSD victims should be encouraged to confront their fears, in an effort to extinguish them. Finally, they must be exposed to experiences that counteract their views that the world is malevolent, using a varicty of counterlearning techniques. Interestingly, although our writing and talking techniques have not found direct evidence of counterlearning, it appears that confronting traumatic experience in the laboratory influences preconscious interpretations of events and, indirectly, promotes the extinction of the powerful emotions associated with them.

3. Animal Learning and Psychophysiology

The concept of inhibition has featured prominently in the history of animal learning. Pavlov (1927), Spence (1936), and Hull (1950) considered inhibitory processes as the major factor in the weakening of conditioned responses normally seen in extinction. Whereas early learning theorists viewed inhibition as an automatic or nonvoluntary process, more recent thinkers have considered inhibition to be a powerful voluntary and controllable phenomenon (cf. Terrace, 1972).

For several years, Jeffrey Gray (1975) has been investigating the physiological substrates of inhibition and activation. Using paradigms that involve passive avoidance (wherein the animal must not perform a learned behavior in order to avoid punishment), he reports that there is an increase in activity in the behavioral inhibition system (BIS), which is located in the septum and hippocampus. Further, when the activity of the BIS is blocked by drugs or destroyed, rats exhibit a marked decline in the ability to inhibit behaviors. Other studies suggest that the frontal cortex is also directly related to inhibition (e.g., Luria, 1980). As in the famous case of Phineas Gage, when the human frontal lobe is destroyed, individuals become more impulsive and less inhibited, without appreciable loss of cognitive functioning.

More recently, Fowles (1980) has argued that autonomic measures selectively tap psychological processes associated with inhibition and activation. Inhibition, according to Fowles, is reflected in heightened electrodermal activity such as SCL. Variations in activation, on the other hand, can be seen in cardiovascular activity. In the studies in our own laboratory, we have consistently found that when individuals disclose traumatic experiences, SCLs drop, whereas cardiovascular measures (e.g., HR, blood pressure) are either unaffected or increase.

A particularly exciting development has been research linking individual difference measures of inhibition with physiological activity. For example, measures of repressive coping style are associated with overall increased autonomic activity (Weinberger, Schwartz, & Davidson, 1979), major heart problems (Lane & Schwartz, 1987), and disruptions in immune function (Jamner, Schwartz, & Leigh, 1988). Other measures of inhibition, such as level of socialization (Waid & Orne, 1982), lack of emotional expressiveness (Buck, 1984; Notarius & Levenson, 1979), and suppressed hostility (Dimsdale, et al., 1986) have also been found to predict increased autonomic activity and/or long-term health problems.

V. Implications and Future Directions

Our findings surrounding inhibition and confrontation raise a number of questions about emotion, cognition, and psychosomatic processes. This section examines some classical theoretical problems relevant to social psychology. It begins by reconsidering the classic debate about the nature of catharsis. It then focuses on some central issues surrounding the development and reconstruction of the self. Finally, I argue for a more physiologically based approach to social psychology.

A. CATHARSIS VERSUS INSIGHT

Do our collective studies support the value of catharsis or of insight in the reduction of stress? Ironically, our technique of writing or talking about traumatic experience is remarkably similar to Breuer and Freud's cathartic method. Unfortunately, the definition of catharsis has evolved to mean the mere venting of negative emotions (e.g., Scheff, 1979) rather than the expression of both emotions and thoughts. Using the venting definition of catharsis, most well-controlled studies indicate that negative emotional expression is either harmful or has no effect (e.g., Berkowitz, 1982).

Close examination of our studies points to the fact that the mere expression of negative feelings exacerbate those feelings immediately after each study. In other words, venting quickly increases reports of depression, sadness, anger, and guilt. Although negative feelings are temporarily increased, the adverse side effects of venting do not persist over time. By the same token, we have not found that venting has appreciably improved physical health.

Taken together, we think that the value of our cathartic method lies in the insight people get from expressing and becoming aware of both their deepest emotions and their related thoughts. In short, the health effects apparently reflect insight rather than venting. Recall from the Pennebaker and Beall (1986) experiment, only those subjects who wrote about their thoughts and emotions evidenced improved health relative to subjects who wrote only about their emotions or about facts surrounding their traumatic experiences.

More persuasive are the open-ended responses that subjects give on follow-up questionnaires about the long-term effects of participating in our studies. In our most recent study (Pennebaker et al., 1988a), 71 of the 80 experimental subjects responded to an open-ended question on the follow-up questionnaire, "Now that the experiment is completed, could you tell us how it may have influenced you in the long run?" Only 7 (10%) discussed the value of venting by reporting such things as, "I purged some of my feelings," or, "I had a chance to get my feelings out in the open." The vast majority (76%) described the long-term effects by referring to their achieving insight. Examples include,

"It made me think things out and really realize what my problem is," "It helped me look at myself from the outside," and "It was a chance to sort out my thoughts." The remaining 14% used both venting and insight terms or used terminology unrelated to either approach.

An illustrative case distinguishing between venting and insight concerns a 33-year-old male's insomnia caused by intense feelings of anger. Unable to sleep, the subject got up and, at my instruction, wrote about his deepest feelings concerning the cause of his anger. In his writing, he discussed his plans for revenge on the person who had offended him. His venting was indeed graphic with allusions to torture, mutilation, and artistic humiliation. Although the subject returned to bed, he found that he was even more obsessed with feelings of rage. He then returned to his writing pad and wrote about his anger from a self-reflective perspective. That is, he explored why he was so upset, why the offending person touched such a raw nerve, and so on. On completing the second essay, he returned to bed and fell immediately to sleep. As this case study illustrates, the awareness and understanding of the emotion decreased its intensity. The mere expression, however, intensified it (see Berkowitz, Green, & Macaulay, 1962 for a similar distinction between self-reflective versus expressed hostility).

B. RECONSTRUCTING THE SELF

Writing about traumatic and other significant feelings clearly can bring about long-term changes in psychological and physiological health. Why is this remarkably simple technique so powerful? As discussed previously, a critical dimension to confronting personal experiences is that it forces the assimilation of a variety of types of information. Suppressed thoughts and emotions, conflicting beliefs and self-perceptions, and unflattering self-views face the writer. When confronted with an array of important information, the person struggles, and usually succeeds to some degree, to reorder it. The assimilation of information within the writing paradigm raises a number of intriguing issues about how fundamental aspects of the self can be broken down and reconstructed. Indeed, processes akin to our writing technique are apparent in psychotherapy, thought reform, and education.

1. Psychotherapy

According to both cognitive and psychodynamic clinical psychologists, one of the goals of psychotherapy is to understand the underlying causes of current symptoms and, depending on the theorist, to force a realignment of basic belief and perceptual structures (cf. Epstein, 1988; Meichenbaum, 1977). A common technique used to achieve this goal is to get the client to talk about, analyze, and interpret significant early experiences—especially if they are directly relevant to the presenting symptoms. As most clinicians note, this process is far easier to accomplish if the client's defenses are lowered and the client displays a high degree of trust in the therapist (or transference).

Interestingly, the writing technique appears to accomplish some of these same goals without the traditional client–therapist relationship. When individuals write about traumas, their defenses are almost automatically lowered—because it is difficult to accomplish the task otherwise. Writing about traumas also forces individuals to dredge up psychological conflicts and intimate emotions that few other topics arouse. Once the defenses are lowered and conflicting aspects of the self are salient, the individual actively seeks to resolve the conflicts.

Obviously, the writing approach should not be construed as an alternative to psychotherapy. Psychotherapy may accelerate the assimilation process, in that a clinician can point to conflicts that the client cannot (or will not) see. An interesting study by Murray, Lamnin, and Carver (1988) points to another benefit. In their study, healthy college students either wrote about traumatic experience, about superficial topics, or were seen in a therapy session on two occasions, a week apart. The nondirective therapy was superior to trauma writing in bringing about positive moods immediately after each of the sessions. In other words, the therapists were able to bring about a comparable degree of disclosure compared with the trauma writing, but their contact with the subjects forestalled feelings of sadness or depression. Unfortunately, the authors were able to collect follow-up measures on only about half of their sample. With their reduced sample, however, both writing about traumas and brief psychotherapy reduced subsequent health problems relative to control subjects.

Although not a substitute for therapy, we think that writing about traumatic and/or significant experiences can be considered a form of psychic preventive maintenance. Given our findings, it may be puzzling why more people do not use it spontaneously. In our surveys, we find that about 8–20% of college students keep a diary or journal—at least occasionally. However, even among journal-keepers, many do not record many of their deepest thoughts and feelings. In interviewing several, most report that they often forget to keep their diaries during stressful periods because it is too painful. Indeed, like the subjects in our experiments, journal writers know that writing about traumatic and upsetting experiences often results in sadness, depression, and a period of serious introspection.

2. Thought Reform and Brainwashing

Consider briefly those religious, political, and self-help institutions that have produced impressively dedicated followers by bringing about fundamental value and belief changes. A common feature of many "born-again" movements, political thought reform groups, and self-help groups, such Alcoholics Anonymous or the more commercial ventures such as "est" (now called The Forum) is the public confession of personal traumas and shortcomings. Even in many of the more traditional religions, the confession of sins is strongly encouraged—either in the form of talking to a priest or directly to one's god in the form of prayer.

Based on our findings, one can readily appreciate why public confession is so effective. When individuals publicly confront their most intimate experiences, they are in the position of having to assimilate them within the context of the values of the group. The goals and the values of the group, then, become part of the information that the member must incorporate into his or her new self-concept.

An interesting implication of this idea is that attitude change should be most enduring when persuasive messages are used in conjunction with the evocation and generation of significant personal experiences. Note that this approach is fundamentally different from most attribution or dissonance-reduction models. That is, attitudes can be assimilated into one's basic value system through the fundamental reconstruction of the self (cf. Spence, 1987 for a discussion of similar processes seen in psychotherapy).

3. Education

The primary goal of undergraduate education is to get our students to incorporate the theories and facts that we teach them into their understanding of the world. We all secretly hope that each of our eager students will assimilate our views and, when we meet them in 20 years, they will profusely thank us for changing their world views. Why does this so rarely happen? The secret may lie, in part, on the way we teach. Our lectures and movies force the students to be passive recipients of information. Our multiple choice exams actively discourage the integration of information. Even many of our most passionate lectures fail to get our students to incorporate our ideas into their basic value systems.

The work we have done on traumatic experience suggests a relatively simple alternative form of education. Specifically, students should be actively encouraged to write or talk about our facts and theories within the context of their most personal experiences. Indeed, we have developed a class with multiple course sections, where, in one of the sections, students are required to write about their deepest thoughts and feelings associated with the topic of the lecture and reading on that particular day during the first 15 minutes of class. Preliminary findings indicate that absentee rates are lower, test grades are higher, and class discussions are significantly livelier in the experimental section (see also Graves & Stuart, 1985, and Elbow, 1981, using a similar application in English courses for grade school and college, respectively).

C. SOCIAL PSYCHOLOGY AND PSYCHOSOMATICS

Fortunately, the social cognition revolution in social psychology is running low on ammunition. Perhaps its major failure has been to overlook the fundamental role of conflict, inhibition, and stress. We often forget that information processing takes place in the brain, which is an exquisite biochemical organ intimately linked with the rest of the body. During periods of conflict or, perhaps, information overload, the brain uses more energy, which, in turn, affects all other parts of the body. Emotion, stress, and disease are the direct results—and sometimes the causes—of cognitive activity.

Changes in health and psychophysiological activity provide a fascinating glimpse at the ways people think and respond to daily events. As psychosomatic researchers have long known, illness is not a random occurrence. Indeed, most illnesses covary with significant changes in people's social lives, such as divorce, loss, rejection, and social conflict—that is, the very stuff of social psychology. One reason we have not adopted a more psychosomatic approach is that we are used to thinking in cause–effect terms that span only seconds or minutes. If we are under massive stress today and then get sick a week later, we often scan our environment for a more proximal cause, such as what we ate or who we saw a few hours before our illness.

In considering the health effects of stress, social psychologists must move away from relying solely on self-reports of symptoms, distress, or general health complaints and focus more on objective physiological measures. As we and others have found, self-reports are notoriously colored by mood states and neuroticism (e.g., Costa & McCrae, 1985; Pennebaker, 1982; Watson & Pennebaker, 1988). Indeed, many of our presumed independent variables such as perceived stress are conceptually identical to our dependent measures, such as complaints about health.

Within the past few years, technology has changed significantly, which will allow social psychologists to consider biological markers as viable measures. Whereas the measurement of simple autonomic activity used to cost tens of thousands of dollars, it can now be achieved for less than a thousand and involves minimal training. Similarly, rapid advances in psychoimmunology is providing both short-term and long-term markers of immune function at rapidly lowering costs (e.g., Kiecolt-Glaser & Glaser, 1988). In short, we can now expand the domain of social cognition, group, and personality research by considering the body.

Acknowledgments

I am indebted to Dan Wegner for his comments on the manuscript. Preparation of this manuscript was made possible by National Science Foundation grant BNS 8606764.

References

Aronson, E., & Carlsmith, M. J. (1968). Experimentation in social psychology. In. G. Lindzey & E. Aronson (Eds.), *Handbook of social psychology* (Vol. 2). Reading, MA: Addison-Wesley.

Bargh, J. A. (1984). Automatic and conscious processing of social information. In R. S. Wyer & T. K. Srull (Eds.), *Handbook of social cognition* (Vol. 3, pp. 1–43). Hillsdale, NJ: Erlbaum.

Beck, A. T. (1976). *Cognitive therapy and the emotional disorders.* New York: International Universities Press.

Berkowitz, L. (1982). Aversive conditions as stimuli to aggression. In L. Berkowitz (Ed.), *Advances in experimental social psychology* (Vol. 15, pp. 249–288). New York: Academic Press.

Berkowitz, L., Green, J. A., & Macaulay, J. R. (1962). Hostility catharsis as the reduction of emotional tension. *Psychiatry: Journal for the Study of Interpersonal Processes, 25,* 23–31.

Breuer, J., & Freud, S. (1966). *Studies on hysteria.* New York: Avon. (Original work published 1895)

Brown, J. D. (1988). *Self-concept certainty as a buffer against stressful life events.* Unpublished manuscript, Southern Methodist University, Dallas.

Buck, R. (1984). *Communication of emotion.* New York: Guilford.

Cobb, S. (1976). Social support as a moderator of life stress. *Psychosomatic Medicine, 38,* 300–314.

Cohen, S., & McKay, G. (1984). Social support, stress and the buffering hypothesis: A theoretical analysis. In A. Baum, S. E. Taylor, & J. E. Singer (Eds.), *Handbook of psychology and health* (pp. 253–267). Hillsdale, NJ: Erlbaum.

Costa, P. T., Jr., & McCrae, R. R. (1985). Hypochondriasis, neuroticism, and aging: When are somatic complaints unfounded? *American Psychologist, 40,* 19–28.

Crowne, D. P., & Marlowe, D. (1964). *The approval motive: Studies in evaluative dependence.* New York: Wiley.

Csikszentmihalyi, M. (1975). *Beyond boredom and anxiety.* San Francisco: Jossey-Bass.

Davidson, R. J. (1984). Affect, cognition, and hemispheric specialization. In C. E. Izard, J. Kagan, & R. Zajonc (Eds.), *Emotion, cognition, and behavior.* New York: Cambridge University Press.

Davidson, R. J. (1986, October). *EEG measures of cerebral asymmetry: Conceptual and methodological issues.* Paper delivered at the annual meeting of the Society for Psychophysiological Research, Montreal.

Derlega, V. (1984). Self-disclosure and intimate relationships. In V. Derlega (Ed.), *Communication, intimacy, and close relationships* (pp. 1–9). Orlando: Academic Press.

Dimsdale, J. E., Pierce, C., Schoenfeld, D., Browne, A., Zusman, R., & Graham, R. (1986). Suppressed anger and blood pressure: The effects of race, sex, social class, obesity, and age. *Psychosomatic Medicine, 48,* 430–436.

Elbow, P. (1981). *Writing with power.* New York: Oxford University Press.

Ellis, A. (1962). *Reason and emotion in psychotherapy.* New York: Lyle Stuart.

Emmons, R. A., & King, L. A. (1988). Conflict among personal strivings: Implications for psychological and physical well-being. *Journal of Personality and Social Psychology, 54,* 1040–1048.

Epstein, S. (1980). The self-concept: A review and the proposal of an integrated theory of personality. In E. Staub (Ed.), *Personality: Basic issues and current research.* Englewood Cliffs, NJ: Prentice-Hall.

Epstein, S. (1987). *The self-concept, the traumatic neuroses, and the structure of personality.* Unpublished manuscript, University of Massachusetts, Amherst.

Erickson, M. H., Rossi, E. L., & Rossi, S. I. (1976). *Hypnotic realities: Induction of clinical hypnosis and forms of indirect suggestion.* New York: Irvington.

Figley, C. R., & McCubbin, H. I. (Eds.). (1984). *Stress and the family: Coping with catastrophe.* New York: Bruner/Mazel.

Fowles, D. C. (1980). The three arousal model: Implications of Gray's two-factor theory for heart rate, electrodermal activity, and psychopathy. *Psychophysiology, 17,* 87–104.

Freud, S. (1966). *Introductory lectures on psychoanalysis.* New York: Norton. (Originally published 1920)

Gazzaniga, M. (1986). *The social brain.* New York: Plenum.

Graves, D., & Stuart, V. (1985). *Write from the start: Tapping your child's natural writing ability.* New York: New American Library.

Gray, J. (1975). *Elements of a two-factor theory of learning.* New York: Academic Press.

Hatfield, E. (1982). Passionate love, compassionate love, and intimacy. In M. Fisher & G. Stricker (Eds.), *Intimacy.* New York: Plenum.

Holmes, T. H., & Rahe, R. H. (1967). The social readjustment scale. *Journal of Psychosomatic Research,* **11,** 213–218.

Horowitz, M. J. (1976). *Stress response syndromes.* New York: Jacob Aronson.

Horowitz, M. J. (1987). *States of mind.* New York: Plenum.

Hull, C. L. (1950). Simple qualitative discrimination learning. *Psychological Review,* **57,** 303–313.

Jamner, L. D., Schwartz, G. E., & Leigh, H. (1988). Repressive coping predicts monocyte, eosinophile and serum glucose levels: Support for the opioid-peptide hypothesis. *Psychosomatic Medicine,* in press.

Janoff-Bulman, R. (1985). The aftermath of victimization: Rebuilding shattered assumptions. In C. R. Figley (Ed.), *Trauma and its wake.* New York: Brunner/Mazel.

Jourard, S. M. (1971). *The transparent self.* New York: Van Nostrand-Reinhold.

Kiecolt-Glaser, J. K., & Glaser, R. (1988). Behavioral influences on immune function: Evidence for the interplay between stress and health. In T. Field, P. McCabe, & N. Schneiderman (Eds.), *Stress and coping* (Vol. 2). Hillsdale, NJ: Erlbaum, in press.

Kihlstrom, J. F. (1987). The cognitive unconscious. *Science,* **237,** 1445–1452.

Kobasa, S. (1982). The hardy personality: Toward a social psychology of stress and health. In G. S. Sanders & J. Suls (Eds.), *Social psychology of health and illness,* (pp. 3–32). Hillsdale, NJ: Erlbaum.

Lane, R. D., & Schwartz, G. E. (1987). Induction of lateralized sympathetic input to the heart by the CNS during emotional arousal: A possible neurophysiologic trigger of sudden cardiac death. *Psychosomatic Medicine,* **49,** 274–284.

Lazarus, R. S., & Folkman, S. (1984). *Stress, appraisal, and coping.* New York: Springer.

Linville, P. W. (1987). Self-complexity as a cognitive buffer against stress-related illness and depression. *Journal of Personality and Social Psychology,* **52,** 663–676.

Luria, A. R. (1980). *Higher cortical functions in man* (2nd ed.). New York: Basic Books.

Martin, L. L., & Tesser, A. (1988). Toward a motivational and structural theory of ruminative thought. In J. S. Uleman & J. A. Bargh (Eds.), *The direction of thought: The limits of awareness, intention, and control.* New York: Guilford, in press.

Meichenbaum, D. (1977). *Cognitive behavior modification.* New York: Plenum.

Murray, E. J., Lamnin, A., & Carver, C. S. (1988). *Psychotherapy versus written confession: A study of cathartic phenomena.* Unpublished manuscript, University of Miami, Coral Gables, FL.

Notarius, C. I., & Levenson, R. W. (1979). Expressive tendencies and physiological response to stress. *Journal of Personality and Social Psychology,* **37,** 1204–1210.

Pavlov, I. (1927). *Conditioned reflexes.* New York: Oxford.

Pennebaker, J. W. (1982). *The psychology of physical symptoms.* New York: Springer-Verlag.

Pennebaker, J. W., & Barger, S. D. (1988). *Autonomic and health effects of traumatic disclosure among survivors of the Holocaust.* Unpublished manuscript, Southern Methodist University, Dallas.

Pennebaker, J. W., & Beall, S. K. (1986). Confronting a traumatic event: Toward an understanding of inhibition and disease. *Journal of Abnormal Psychology,* **95,** 274–281.

Pennebaker, J. W., & Chew, C. H. (1985). Deception, electrodermal activity, and inhibition of behavior. *Journal of Personality and Social Psychology,* **49,** 1427–1433.

Pennebaker, J. W., Colder, M. L., & Sharp, L. K. (1988a). *Accelerating the coping process.* Unpublished manuscript, Southern Methodist University, Dallas.

Pennebaker, J. W., & Hoover, C. W. (1985). Inhibition and cognition: Toward an understanding of trauma and disease. In R. J. Davidson, G. E. Schwartz, & D. Shapiro (Eds.), *Consciousness and self-regulation* (Vol. 4, pp. 107–136). New York: Plenum.

Pennebaker, J. W., Hughes, C., & O'Heeron, R. C. (1987). The psychophysiology of confession: Linking inhibitory and psychosomatic processes. *Journal of Personality and Social Psychology,* **52,** 781–793.

Pennebaker, J. W., Kiecolt-Glaser, J. K., & Glaser, R. (1988b). Disclosure of traumas and immune function: Health implications for psychotherapy. *Journal of Consulting and Clinical Psychology,* **56,** 239–245.

Pennebaker, J. W., & O'Heeron, R. C. (1984). Confiding in others and illness rate among spouses of suicide and accidental death victims. *Journal of Abnormal Psychology,* **93,** 473–476.

Pennebaker, J. W., & Sharp, L. K. (1988). *EEG activity during the disclosure of traumatic and superficial topics.* Unpublished manuscript, Southern Methodist University, Dallas.

Pennebaker, J. W., & Susman, J. R. (1988). Disclosure of traumas and psychosomatic processes. *Social Science and Medicine,* **26,** 327–332.

Rachman, S. J., & Hodgson, R. J. (1980). *Obsessions and compulsions.* Englewood Cliffs, NJ: Prentice-Hall.

Scheff, T. J. (1979). *Catharsis in healing, ritual, and drama.* Berkeley: University of California Press.

Scheier, M. F., & Carver, C. S. (1985). Optimism, coping, and health: Assessment and implications of generalized outcome expectancies. *Health Psychology,* **4,** 219–247.

Schwartz, G. E., Davidson, R. J., & Goleman, D. (1978). Patterning of cognitive and somatic processes in the self generation of anxiety: Effects of meditation versus exercise. *Psychosomatic Medicine,* **40,** 321–328.

Selye, H. (1976). *The stress of life.* New York: McGraw-Hill.

Silver, R. L., Boon, C., & Stones, M. H. (1983). Searching for meaning in misfortune: Making sense of incest. *Journal of Social Issues,* **39,** 81–102.

Silver, R. L., & Wortman, C. B. (1980). Coping with undesirable life events. In J. Garber & M. E. P. Seligman (Eds.), *Human helplessness: Theory and applications* (pp. 279–375). New York: Academic Press.

Sowder, B. J. (Ed.) (1985). *Disasters and mental health: Selected contemporary perspectives.* Rockville, MD: National Institutes of Mental Health.

Spence, D. P. (1987). *The Freudian metaphor: Toward paradigm change in psychoanalytic theory.* New York: Norton.

Spence, K. W. (1936). The nature of discrimination learning in animals. *Psychological Review,* **43,** 427–449.

Springer, S. P., & Deutsch, G. (1986). *Left brain, right brain.* New York: Freeman.

Swann, W. B. (1987). Identity negotiation: Where two roads meet. *Journal of Personality and Social Psychology,* **53,** 1038–1051.

Terrace, H. S. (1972). Conditioned inhibition. In R. A. Boakes & M. S. Holliday (Eds.), *Inhibition and learning* (pp. 99–119). London: Academic Press.

Tiebout, J. (1987). *Effects of publicly testifying about traumatic events of physical and psychological health.* Unpublished master's thesis, Southern Methodist University, Dallas.

VandenBos, G. R., & Bryant, B. K. (Eds.) (1987). *Cataclysms, crises, and catastrophes: Psychology in action.* Washington, DC: American Psychological Association.

Waid, W. M., & Orne, M. T. (1981). Cognitive, social, and personality processes in the physiological detection of deception. In L. Berkowitz (Ed.), *Advances in experimental social psychology* (Vol. 14). New York: Academic Press, 61–106.

Waid, W. M., & Orne, M. T. (1982). Reduced electrodermal response to conflict, failure to inhibit dominant behaviors, and delinquent proneness. *Journal of Personality and Social Psychology,* **43,** 769–774.

Watson, D., & Clark, L. A. (1984). Negative affectivity: The disposition to experience aversive emotional states. *Psychological Bulletin,* **96,** 465–490.

Watson, D., & Pennebaker, J. W. (1988). Health complaints, stress, and distress: Exploring the central role of negative affectivity. *Psychological Review,* in press.

Wegner, D. M. (1988). Stress and mental control. In S. Fisher & J. Reason (Eds.), *Handbook of life stress, cognition, and health*. Chichester, England: Wiley.

Wegner, D. M., Schneider, D. J., Carter, S. R., & White, T. L. (1987). Paradoxical effects of thought suppression. *Journal of Personality and Social Psychology,* **53,** 5–13.

Weinberger, D. A., Schwartz, G. E., & Davidson, R. J. (1979). Low-anxious, high-anxious, and repressive coping styles: Psychometric patterns and behavioral and physiological responses to stress. *Journal of Abnormal Psychology,* **88,** 369–380.

Wyer, R. S., & Srull, T. K. (1986). Human cognition in its social context. *Psychological Review,* **93,** 322–359.

A SOCIOCOGNITIVE MODEL OF ATTITUDE STRUCTURE AND FUNCTION

Anthony R. Pratkanis

BOARD OF PSYCHOLOGY
UNIVERSITY OF CALIFORNIA
SANTA CRUZ, CALIFORNIA 95064

Anthony G. Greenwald

DEPARTMENT OF PSYCHOLOGY
UNIVERSITY OF WASHINGTON
SEATTLE, WASHINGTON 98195

I. Introduction

In 1935, Gordon Allport declared that attitude is "social psychology's most indispensable concept." That observation remains true today, as evidenced by common practices within the discipline of social psychology. Attitudes receive prominent treatment by social psychology textbook authors. They are often used to explain such diverse phenomena as prejudice, interpersonal attraction, consumer behavior, organizational behavior, human sexuality, mass communications, social influence, and the self-concept. As McGuire (1969) points out, attitudes are often a high-volume research area for psychology, accounting for large amounts of psychological research at given times. And as Katz and Stotland (1959) noted, the attitude concept finds employment in all the major theoretical schools of social psychology including field, behavioral, cognitive, mathematical, and expectancy-value approaches.

A. BUT IS THE ATTITUDE CONCEPT REALLY NEEDED?

The history of attitude research presents a paradox (see Katz & Stotland, 1959). Despite the perceived importance and the popularity of the attitude construct, it has been severely criticized, with some calling for it to be abandoned. Disillusionment with the attitude concept stems from three basic concerns.

1. Attitudes appear to be poor predictors of behavior toward their objects. In his definition of attitudes, Allport (1935) explicitly specified that attitudes direct behavior. Not surprisingly, it is generally assumed that attitudes should predict behavior. Weakness of empirical support for this behavior-prediction assumption has been the basis for several prominent critiques, including those of LaPiere (1934), Festinger (1964), Wicker (1969), and Abelson (1972).

   2. *Attitudes appear not to be a selective force in information processing.* In their 1948 textbook, Krech and Crutchfield advanced the proposition that attitudes guide perceptual and cognitive processes. The two most often stated principles regarding attitude-guided information processing are that persons selectively (1) seek information that agrees with their attitudes while avoiding disagreeing information (e.g., Festinger, 1957) and (2) remember attitude-agreeable (as opposed to disagreeable) information (e.g., Levine & Murphy, 1943). However, the empirical evidence for these two principles has been consistently weak (see Freedman & Sears, 1965; Frey, 1986; Pratkanis, 1984; Waly & Cook, 1966).

   3. *Attitudes may be epiphenomenal.* Few would disagree with the observation that attitudes are pervasive, as evidenced by (1) the ease with which people report evaluative reactions to a wide range of objects, (2) the difficulty of identifying categories of objects within which evaluative judgments are not made, and (3) the prominence of the evaluative dimension in judgments of meaning (Osgood, Suci, & Tannenbaum, 1957). This pervasiveness of attitudes, however, does not guarantee that attitudes are important in explaining social behavior. As Bem (1967) suggested, attitudes might be epiphenomenal, cognitive illusions that are constructed after the fact of behavior.

B. WHY THE PARADOX OF ATTITUDE IMPORTANCE?

   It is our position that social psychology's fondness for the attitude construct and the tenuous empirical status of that construct are related. The popularity of attitudes has promoted an indiscriminate use of the term. As Greenwald (1989) argues, almost any conceivable entity, from sensory qualities (such as odors and tastes) through concrete objects (such as persons and things) and abstract thoughts (such as social roles and political ideologies) to behavior (intentions to act), and even attitudes (e.g. attitudes towards prejudice), can serve as an attitude object. Furthermore, in survey contexts, researchers have used the term *attitude* even more broadly to refer to almost any social or motivational disposition, including personality constructs (such as self-efficacy, time orientation, and authoritarianism) and motives (such as need for power, affiliation, and achievement; see Robinson & Shaver's, 1973, collection of attitude scales).

   As Blumer (1955; see also Bain, 1928; Symonds, 1927) argued, the attitude concept fails to meet the criteria of a scientific concept. Its popularity has produced a watered-down concept incapable of effective prediction. The root of this problem began with early efforts at defining "attitude," and it culminates today in the two most popular ways of conceptualizing attitude structure and function—the tripartite model and the principle of cognitive consistency.

1. Early History of the Definition of Attitude

The 1930s saw two prominent proposals for the definition of attitude: (1) the oft-cited definition by Allport (1935) guided conceptual development of the attitude construct; (2) the other, by Thurstone (1931) guided the development of attitude measures (cf., Edwards, 1957; see Ostrom, 1989, for a review of this history).

For the 1935 *Handbook of Social Psychology,* Allport undertook to survey the (then relatively brief) history of attitude research. He found, much as have more recent reviewers (e.g., Fleming, 1967), that the early usage of the term *attitude* was extensive and diverse, extending to such conceptions as adaptedness (by evolutionary biologists such as Spencer), muscular preparedness (by Lange and Baldwin), cognitive set (by the Wurzburg school), dynamic motivation (by Freudians), and mental processes that determine response (by sociologists such as Thomas and Znaniecki). Allport offered an integrative definition of attitude as "a mental and neural state of readiness, organized through experience, exerting a directive or dynamic influence upon the individual's response to all objects and situations with which it is related" (p. 810). Allport's characterization of attitude was more than a definition; it was an implicit theory of attitude structure and function; it assumed that attitudes guide behavior by orienting and energizing the organism to act.

In contrast, Thurstone (1931) defined attitude as "the affect for or against a psychological object" (p. 261). This definition was minimally theoretical, and left the conceptual formulation of attitude (i.e., attitude structure and function) as a task for subsequent investigation. For similar reasons, we start from a position that is much like Thurstone's, defining attitude as a *person's evaluation of an object of thought.*

2. The Tripartite Model of Attitude Structure

For the most part, attitude researchers have been reluctant to suggest that one model of attitude is superior to others. Accordingly, many researchers have supported definitions that (1) permit a broad array of research operations for attitude measurement and (2) put no apparent boundaries on the sort of entity that can be regarded as an attitude (e.g., Allport, 1935; DeFleur & Westie, 1963; Greenwald, 1968b). The model of attitude structure that has been most often advanced by social psychologists (perhaps due to its breadth) is in terms of a tripartite entity; in it, an attitude is conceived as having three components—affective, cognitive, and conative (or behavioral). As Rosenberg and Hovland (1960) describe, "We here indicate that attitudes are predispositions to respond to some class of stimuli with certain classes of responses and designate the three major types of responses as cognitive, affective, and behavioral'' (p. 3).

Although such a broad model of attitude may be of value in the early stages of a concept's development (see Smith, Bruner, & White, 1956, p. 34), the tripartite now deters research progress for at least two reasons. First, operations and measures have not been linked with theoretical constructs, resulting in little consensus concerning the meaning of the terms of the tripartite model. For example, *affect* has been variously described as an evaluation, subjective feelings, and physiological correlates. The conative component has been variously assessed using observed action, verbal self-report of past action, and self-report of intentions. Any given research investigating the conative component can purportedly be investigating the attitude–behavior relationship, the relationship of the conative to other attitude components, or the relationship between behavior and the conative component of attitude.

A second concern with the tripartite model is that its breadth severely limits the model's predictive and explanatory power. The triparite model is not strong enough to specify the conditions under which expected attitude effects are most likely to occur. As a consequence, most of the research on the tripartite model has addressed the question of validation (cf. Breckler, 1984; Kothandapani, 1971; Ostrom, 1969) as opposed to investigating the implications of the model for predicting attitude effects (see the line of research beginning with Norman, 1975, for an exception). (For further critical discussion of the tripartite model, see Ajzen, 1989; Breckler & Wiggins, 1989; Cacioppo, Petty, & Geen, 1989; and Zanna & Rempel, 1988).

3. Consistency Theories of Attitude Functions

During the era of consistency theories in the 1950s and 1960s (culminating in Abelson *et al.*, 1968), social psychologists believed that an attitude should induce a *correspondence* of response. *Positive* attitudes result in *positive* feelings, thoughts, and behaviors toward an object, whereas *negative* attitudes engender the opposite, *negative* response. Of course, the expectation that all attitude effects are consistency effects may cause one to overlook other (possibly important) attitudinal effects and processes.

Consistency theories also posit that individuals are motivated to maintain balance and consistency among cognitive elements and interpersonal relationships. This "drive for consistency" postulate finds a parallel in Allport's definition of attitude—when an attitude is invoked, an individual is driven to act consistently with the implications of the attitude. As research on consistency processes progressed, the original "motive for cognitive consistency" was gradually replaced by one implicating the role of self-esteem maintainence and self-justification as a guide for cognitive processes (see Aronson, 1969, 1984; Greenwald & Ronis, 1978). However, the attitude construct has yet to be updated to reflect these developments.

C. OVERVIEW OF THE SOCIOCOGNITIVE MODEL OF ATTITUDE

This chapter seeks to resolve the paradox of attitude importance (1) by reviewing research to determine whether or when the pessimism concerning the predictive power of attitudes is warranted and (2) by using the results of this review to develop and support a sociocognitive model of attitudes. This model proposes (1) that attitudes have a *cognitive* representation (as opposed to a tripartite structure) and (2) that attitudes serve to relate a person to the *social* world (i.e., serve a social function [Cooley, 1912; Katz, 1960; Smith, Bruner, & White, 1956; Tetlock, 1988] rather than a cognitive consistency function).

1. The Cognitive Representation of Attitude Structure

According to the sociocognitive model of attitude, an attitude is represented in memory by (1) an object label and rules for applying that label, (2) an evaluative summary of that object, and (3) a knowledge structure supporting that evaluation. This representation operates in accordance with principles of social cognition (cf. Wyer & Srull, 1984). The sociocognitive model of attitude is similar in form to those proposed to account for findings obtained in the impression formation literature (see in particular, Fiske & Pavelchak, 1986, and also Anderson & Hubert, 1963; Carlston, 1980; Dreben, Fiske, & Hastie, 1979).

2. The Functions of an Attitude

The sociocognitive model offers a two-part answer (see Herek, 1986 for a similar proposal) to the functionalist's (Smith, Bruner, & White, 1956) question, "Of what value is an attitude to a person?" First, an attitude is used to make sense of the world and to help the organism operate on its environment. In terms of structure, the evaluative summary serves a *heuristic* function (a simple strategy for appraising an object) and the knowledge structure supporting an evaluation serves a *schematic* function (organizes and guides memory for events and complex action toward an object). Second, an attitude is held in service of perhaps the most important attitude object—the self. An attitude is used to define and maintain self-worth. We attach different labels to this self-related function of attitude, depending on the audience (public, private, or collective) that is observing the attitude and its expression.

3. Chapter Overview

Sections II, III, and IV describe the cognitive components of the sociocognitive model and discuss its role in the prediction of attitude effects. Section V describes various research findings indicating that attitudes serve self-related functions. In anticipation of our conclusion, we find that the cause for concern about the attitude concept (described previously) is not warranted. Attitudes are successful predictors of a wide range of cognitive processes; they influence processing of episodic information in a predictable fashion; and they are related to important social behaviors under specifiable conditions.

II. Identification of the Attitude Object: Engaging Attitude Functions

Attitude researchers and theorists implicitly assume that an attitude object is represented in semantic memory. Earlier theorists (see Cantril, 1932; Newcomb, Turner, & Converse, 1965; Scott, 1969; Scott, Osgood, & Peterson, 1979) attempted to describe the properties of an attitude object by using such terms as abstractness and inclusiveness. More recently, Greenwald (1989) has used his levels-of-representation framework (see Greenwald, 1988) to describe the representation of attitude objects at one of four cognitive levels: (1) physical objects, (2) categories, (3) propositions, and (4) schemata. Few research endeavors, however, have investigated these distinctions.

According to the sociocognitive model, an attitude object is represented in memory by a label (e.g., "militant feminist," "Ariel the dog," "the pesticide controversy") and a set of rules and operations for applying that label (such as categorization processes described by Smith & Medin, 1981). Object identification is the first step to accessing the evaluative and knowledge components of an attitude and thereby engaging the heuristic and schematic attitude functions.

A. THE DIFFICULTY OF (CORRECTLY) IDENTIFYING ATTITUDE OBJECTS

An implicit assumption of much previous work on attitudes is that persons consistently and consensually apply the same rules and operations for labeling an attitude object. On the contrary, the labeling of an attitude object can be highly variable across persons, places, and times. For any given situation, (1) objects may be difficult to identify in compact verbal labels, (2) multiple attitude objects can be potentially salient, and (3) different object labels can be applied simultaneously by the researcher and by the research subject. When these problems occur in a research situation, the attitude measured by the researcher cannot be expected to be more than weakly predictive of social behavior (see also, Kelman, 1974; Salancik, 1982).

For example, consider the classic attitude–behavior study published in 1934 by LaPiere (see also Dillehay's 1973 critique). In this study, a young Chinese couple travelled with LaPiere, seeking accommodation at many hotels and restaurants. LaPiere sought to relate the hotel and restaurant proprietors' attitudes toward Chinese (assessed with a mailed questionnaire) to their behavior of providing accommodations or service to the Chinese couple. LaPiere found little relationship between his measure of attitude and the proprietors' behavior toward the Chinese couple.

LaPiere assumed that the salient attitude object was "members of the Chinese race." However, the couple (who were described as personable and charming) could have been identified as customers, as middle-class people, as friendly examples of the Chinese race, as a young married couple, etc. LaPiere further assumed that the proprietor's behavior was dependent primarily on attitudes toward Chinese. The proprietor's behavior may have been influenced as much (or more) by attitudes toward other objects, such as the woman's perfume, income generated from the business, the reputation of the restaurant, or other patrons. It is also possible that proprietors did not possess a representation of an object corresponding to the label, "Chinese people."

LaPiere's research is not an isolated example of the observation that object labels are labile. Object labels can be changed and modified as a function of disconfirming evidence (Weber & Crocker, 1983), dissonance reduction (Abelson, 1959), decision structuring (Farquhar & Pratkanis, 1987; Plott & Levine, 1978; Schattschneider, 1960), and social influence (Billig, 1987; Ries & Trout, 1981). Different object labels can be applied to the same stimulus as a result of simple priming manipulations (Berkowitz & Rogers, 1986; Higgins & King, 1981; Iyengar & Kinder, 1987).

Although variability in object identification hinders behavior prediction, it may have functional value for the person. Greenwald (1980), in his description of the *totalitarian ego*, notes that rewriting history (of which modifying an object label is one example) can serve to maintain an organization of knowledge by eliminating the need for drastic restructuring in the face of disconfirming information. The maintenance of an organization of knowledge is useful for preserving access to stored information and for achieving a sense of coherence of perception. The ease with which object labels are changed may also serve to protect and maintain positive self-regard. Objects can be redefined for the self's benefit. For example, an attack on a cherished opinion can be dodged by changing the topic (e.g., "It's not that I hate all Lithuanians, just the pushy ones.") and a desired reference group can be embraced by adopting their conceptual system.

B. OBJECT IDENTIFICATION: IMPROVING THE PREDICTIVE UTILITY OF ATTITUDES

Much recent research on attitudes has been an attempt to specify the conditions under which attitudes predict behavior. The success of these programs has been achieved, in part, by proposing techniques for reducing the multiple and variable meanings that can be associated with an attitude object in a given setting. Four general classes of techniques for increasing the likelihood of engaging one particular object label (over other potentially competing labels) can be identified, all of which improve predictive power.

1. Increasing the Level of Object Specificity

Early attitude measurement theorists such as Thurstone and Likert stressed the importance of precisely delimiting the attitude object for successful scale construction (see Mueller, 1986). To assist in implementing this admonition, Payne (1951) proposed a number of suggestions (such as avoiding double-barrelled questions and eliminating items with hidden meaning) for increasing the clarity of an attitude object for survey respondents. Similarly, Ajzen and Fishbein (1977) report evidence that attitude–behavior correlations are stronger when there is correspondence in the level of specificity between attitude and behavior in terms of the *action* to be performed, the *target* at which the action is directed, the *context* in which it is to be performed, and the *time* at which it is to be performed.

2. Increasing the Salience of an Attitude Object

Numerous research programs have developed manipulations for increasing the salience and relevance of a given attitude object (in contrast to the salience of competing objects). For example, Borgida and Campbell (1982) found higher attitude–behavior consistency for a global attitude object (the environment) when it was explicitly linked to a behavior (increasing the amount of campus parking). Snyder (1982) reviews evidence showing that there is a stronger attitude–behavior relationship (1) with low self-monitors than with high self-monitors who may be influenced by competing concerns such as impression management, (2) when the situation demands that the subject think about the attitude object, thus increasing the salience of a given object, and (3) when the representation of the attitude object is explicitly made relevant for the behavior. Granberg (1985) has demonstrated the role of object salience for predicting social judgment. In his study, subjects' identification of Ted Kennedy's position on abortion varied as a function of their own attitude toward abortion and toward Kennedy, plus their perception of the Democratic position on abortion, and their perception of Kennedy as a liberal and as a member of the Catholic Church. Granberg found that he could manipulate the strength of any of these factors by increasing their salience prior to the judgment task.

3. Specifying the Nature of the Object Representation

Two studies by Lord, Lepper, and Mackie (1984) demonstrate the value of specifying the object representation for increasing attitude–behavior correlations. In their two studies, subjects first provided their attitudes toward specific University social clubs and toward homosexuals. In a later session, subjects were given an opportunity to interact with prototypical (i.e., the best examplar of the category) and nonprototypical members of these two social groups. The results showed that attitudes were more predictive of behavior toward prototypical members.

4. Controlling for the Effects of Competing Objects

Davidson and Morrison (1983) have developed a within-subjects procedure for attitude assessment, which takes into consideration some of the more salient attitude objects that may be in competition with the object of investigative interest. In a study demonstrating the technique, married couples completed an attitude survey concerned with four contraceptive methods. One year later, subjects reported which birth control methods they had used during the year. Davidson and Morrison found that attitudes were moderately related to behavior (explaining 55.5% of the variance) when analyzed in the traditional manner of relating attitudes to behavior across subjects. However, considerably more variance in behavior (77.5%) was explained when the analysis compared a single person's attitude toward all objects and used the most positive attitude as a predictor of behavior.

C. ATTITUDES AS PREDICTORS

The preceding four sets of research findings have identified a condition that improves the predictive power of an attitude. An attitude is a better predictor when an object label is held consistently across time and situations and when that label is shared by both the researcher and the subject. Consistent object identification allows consistent access to the evaluative and knowledge components of an attitude.

Nevertheless, the difficulties in producing strong attitude–behavior correlations, and the necessity for clearly specifying an attitude object, may prompt some to believe that attitudes are only weakly connected to behavior and other dependent variables. To the contrary, however, the need for well-controlled research settings to demonstrate strong attitude–behavior relations may mean only that the influence of attitudes on behavior is so pervasive that it is difficult to isolate the effects of a single attitude. To paraphrase Shakespeare, perhaps attitude should be considered a construct that predicted "not wisely, but too well."

III. Attitude as Heuristic

Historically, as Mueller (1986) notes, there has been substantial agreement that evaluation (i.e., affect for or against) is the most essential component of the attitude concept, distinguishing it from other mental constructs (see McGuire, 1989 as an exception). In the sociocognitive model of attitude, the evaluative component is represented in memory by a simple evaluative summary of an object. This summary, typically expressed by words such as "like/dislike," "agree/disagree," and "good/bad," plays an important role in the appraisal of social objects.

A. ATTITUDE HEURISTIC DEFINED

Attitude theorists have long noted that attitudes serve a cognitive or knowledge function. For example, Lippmann (1922) viewed public opinion as an economical simplifier of a complex world. Smith, Bruner, and White (1957) posited that opinions serve an object appraisal function: "An attitude provides a ready aid in 'sizing up' objects and events in the environment" (p. 41). Katz (1960) has suggested that attitudes satisfy a knowledge function, providing adequate structure to the social world. McGuire (1969) noted that attitudes serve as "a simplified and practical manual of appropriate behavior toward specific objects" (p. 158). Katona (1975) has specified a principle of affect generalization—good things produce good consequences and bad things produce bad consequences. Pettigrew (1979) concluded that past research on prejudice indicates that people often commit an ultimate attribution error—that is, the attribution of good and bad qualities to liked and disliked groups of people (respectively).

Pratkanis (1989) used the term *attitude heuristic* to refer to the use of an attitude in knowing. A heuristic is a simple, but often only approximate, strategy for solving a problem. Some examples include, "If the experimental results are null, then the design is inadequate." and "If the person is from the South, he or she must be intellectually backward." Heuristics differ from detailed sets of procedures or algorithms, which invoke complex sets of rules for problem-solving (see Sherman & Corty, 1984; Tversky & Kahneman, 1974).

An attitudinal heuristic uses the stored evaluation of an object as a cue to solving the problem of how to act in relation to the object. Attitudes are used to assign objects to a favorable class (for which strategies such as favoring, approaching, praising, cherishing, and protecting are appropriate) or to an unfavorable class (for which strategies such as disfavoring, avoiding, blaming, neglecting, and harming are used). An example is: "I dislike Reagan, therefore the federal deficit is the result of his 'charge card' economic policies." Such attitude heuristics operate according to the principles of balance theory (Heider, 1958; Zajonc & Burnstein, 1965), although it is not necessary to assume a motivation to maintain consistency (see Wyer, 1974).[1]

---

[1]Wyer (1974) notes that balance principles describe social inference processes when they summarize a subject's prior experience with the type of objects about which inferences are made. Thus, an attitude heuristic should be viewed as a summary of past experience as opposed to a motivation to maintain balance among cognitive elements (as traditionally assumed by balance theory).

B. CONCEPTUAL MEMORY PROCESSES

According to Pratkanis (1989), conceptual processes are often affected by the use of an attitude as a heuristic. Conceptual or semantic memory is knowledge of the world, consisting of facts, ideas, and concepts. According to Tulving (1983),

> [Semantic memory] is a mental thesaurus, organized knowledge a person possesses about words and other verbal symbols, their meaning and referents, about relationships among them, and about rules, formulas, and algorithms for the manipulation of symbols, concepts, and relations. (p. 21)

The contents of conceptual memory are relatively permanent, are accessed automatically, and are context free (i.e., not linked to a temporal event). Conceptual memory tasks include the processes of comprehension, categorization, inference, judgment, and reasoning. It can be contrasted with episodic memory which is "a system that receives and stores information about temporally dated episodes or events, and temporal–spatial relations among them." (Tulving, 1983, p. 21). Episodic memory is involved when an individual attempts to recall yesterday's happenings, a list of experimental nonsense syllables, or a persuasive message presented in a laboratory setting.

C. ELEVEN USES OF ATTITUDE AS A HEURISTIC IN CONCEPTUAL PROCESSING

Pratkanis (1989) classified 11 reliable effects of attitudes on conceptual processes. This list is reproduced here.

1. Interpretation and Explanation

Attitudes are used to interpret and explain social events. For example, Smith (1947) found that pro- and anti-Soviet individuals rated the credibility of Soviet news items in accord with their attitudes. Cooper and Jahoda (1947) and Kendall and Wolf (1949) demonstrated that prejudiced individuals misunderstood cartoons presenting a bigoted person in an unfavorable manner. Hastorf and Cantril (1954) found that interpretations of a Princeton–Dartmouth football game varied as a function of support for the two opponents. Manis (1961) showed that attitudes affected the interpretation of a message such that subjects mistakenly attributed an own-attitude-consistent position to an admired person on the issue of college fraternities. Regan, Straus, and Fazio (1974) found that subjects made internal attributions when an actor behaves consistently with attitudinal expectations (i.e., liked actors perform positive behaviors and disliked actors perform negative behaviors), but the subjects made external attributions when an actor behaved inconsistently with attitude-based expectations.

2. Halo Effects: Expectations and Inferences

A favorable or unfavorable person impression biases expectations and inferences about that person. For example, much research shows that people who are evaluated as attractive are expected to be "better" than those not so evaluated (Hatfield & Sprecher, 1986) and that liked individuals are expected to possess positive traits, whereas disliked individuals are assumed to possess negative ones (see Lott & Lott, 1972; Lott, Lott, Reed, & Crow 1970). Similarly, in surveys of economic expectations, Katona (1975) finds that good events such as the end of World War II and the end of the Cuban missile crisis are typically associated with optimistic expectations concerning the economy, whereas negative events such as the U-2 incident and the Berlin crisis induce economic pessimism.

3. Syllogistic Reasoning

Attitudes toward the conclusion of a syllogism can influence the ability to determine whether the syllogism is logically valid (cf. Evans, Barston, & Pollard, 1983; Feather, 1964; Gordon, 1953; Janis & Frick, 1943; Lefford, 1946; Morgan, 1945; Morgan & Morton, 1943, 1944). For example, Thistlewaite (1950) asked respondents to state whether syllogisms such as the following were valid:

> *Given:* If production is important, then peaceful industrial relations are desirable. If production is important, then it is a mistake to have Negroes for foreman and leaders over Whites.
> *Therefore:* If peaceful industrial relations are desirable, then it is a mistake to have Negroes for foreman and leaders over Whites.

For this syllogism, prejudiced individuals (who agree with the conclusion) are more likely to indicate (incorrectly) that the logic is valid compared to less prejudiced individuals.

4. Responses to Persuasive Communications

Greenwald (1968a) has found that individuals with an unfavorable attitude toward the topic of persuasive communication are more likely to counterargue a message, whereas those with a favorable attitude are more likely to provide consonant cognitive responses. This pattern of results has been frequently obtained in studies of persuasion (see Petty, Ostrom, & Brock, 1981). Similarly, Waly and Cook (1965) found that an argument was considered more effective and plausible by those who agreed (as opposed to disagreed) with the position expressed in the argument (see Lord, Lepper, & Ross, 1979, for a more recent example).

5. Interpersonal Attraction

Byrne (1971) repeatedly finds that individuals with attitudes similiar to one's own are viewed as attractive. In a typical experiment, subjects receive information about others' attitudes. Attitude similarity is manipulated by varying the proportion of shared attitudes between the subject and a stimulus person. The more shared attitudes, the more attractive the subject rates the stimulus person. (See Rosenbaum, 1986, for an alternative repulsion interpretation of these findings).

6. Judgment of Social Stimuli

One's own attitude provides a reference point for the judgment of social stimuli. For example, Vroom (1960) found that individuals with a positive attitude toward an organization viewed that organization's goals as similar to their own. Granberg and Jenks (1977) found that survey respondents perceived the position of their preferred candidate in the 1972 Presidential election (McGovern or Nixon) on nine sociopolitical issues to be highly similar to their own position on these issues. Edwards (1941) and Vallone, Ross, Lepper (1985) obtained results indicating that attitudes influence the judgment of bias in the source of a message. Sherif and Hovland (1961) present additional evidence that attitudes bias social judgments.

7. False Consensus of Opinion

Wallen (1943) found that subjects believe their attitude position to be more popular than it actually is. In this first "false-consensus" study, students were asked to give both their opinions on, and their estimate of, the percentage of students who supported the Selective Service, the St. Lawrence Seaway Project, and war with Germany. The results showed that the respondents estimated the attitudes of others so that their own opinion coincided with that of the estimated majority. The false-consensus effect has been replicated often (cf. Fields & Schuman, 1976; Granberg, Jefferson, Brent, & King, 1981; Ross, Greene, & House, 1977; Sherman, Chassin, Presson, & Agostinelli, 1984). Goethals (1986) presents evidence indicating that the false-consensus effect, like some of the other effects listed in this section, may also serve the self-functions of attitude described in Section V.

8. Fact Identification

The use of an attitude can lead to the selective reconstruction of past events. For example, 2½ years after the event, Eberhart and Bauer (1941) assessed memory for a riot involving the Chicago police and a crowd of striking employees of the Republic Steel Company. Eberhart and Bauer found that subjects with a prolabor attitude were more likely to remember that the crowd was unarmed and that the police brutally shot peaceful citizens, whereas antilabor subjects recalled the opposite. Similarly, Pratkanis (1988a) found that subjects misidentified facts consistent with their attitudes. Given pairs of statements such as (1) Ronald Reagan maintained an "A" average at Eureka college and (2) Ronald Reagan never achieved above a "C" average at Eureka college (a fact), subjects were most likely to identify as true those statements that agreed with their attitudes (see also Smith, 1968).

9. Estimates of Personal Behavior

Past personal behavior is often revised to be consistent with current attitudes. For example, Bem and McConnell (1970) changed attitudes on the student control of their university, using a counterattitudinal essay procedure. The results showed that subjects erred by overestimating the extent to which their premanipulation attitudes (as assessed earlier by Bem and McConnell) were similar to their current attitudes. Although there is disagreement over the psychological mechanisms involved, this finding has been often replicated (cf. Aderman & Brehm, 1976; Goethals & Reckman, 1973; Ross & Shulman, 1973; and Shaffer, 1975a,b). Markus (1985) has found a similar effect in a national survey of teenagers and parents, conducted in 1965, with follow-up collections in 1973 and 1982. He found that current attitudes on policy issues, such as legalization of marijuana, women's roles, and rights of the accused biased the recall of past attitudes on these issues.

Ross, McFarland, and Fletcher (1981) provide another example of the use of attitudes in the selective estimation of the frequency of past personal behavior. In their studies, subjects received persuasive messages that either derogated or promoted daily toothbrushing and frequent bathing. Those who heard the antitoothbrushing and antibathing messages estimated that they toothbrushed and bathed less often than those who heard the promessages. Ross, McFarland, Conway, and Zanna (1983) have replicated this effect, but they find that it is less likely to occur when the domain of recall is objective, as opposed to ambiguous (i.e., recall of the frequency of exercise versus how vigorous exercise was perceived to be).

10. Information Error Technique

The fact that attitudes produce errors in judgments led Hammond (1948) to suggest an *information error technique* as an indirect measure of attitudes (see Kreman, 1949; Kubany, 1953; Parrish, 1948; Weschler 1950a,b). In this technique, respondents are asked, under the guise of an information survey, to select which of two statements is true. In reality, both responses are incorrect—for example (taken from Weschler, 1950a): "During the strike wave of April 1948, the percentage of estimated working time lost was (1) 1.1% or (2) 2.2%?" (The correct answer is 1.6%). Respondents frequently chose the error most consistent with their attitudes. Given that lost working time is viewed as negative, individuals with a probusiness attitude indicate that the strike produced considerable downtime, whereas the prolabor supporter attributes less lost time to the strike.

11. Prediction of Future Events

Hadley Cantril (1940) once observed, "What people want to happen, they tend to think will happen" (p. 406). The Gallup (1972) poll has asked the following question of nationally representative samples before the Presidential elections of 1944, 1948, 1952, 1960, and 1968: "If you were to guess at this time, who do you think will win the next presidency, a Republican or Democrat?" The results, averaged across the years, indicate that 63.3% of the Democrats believe that a Democrat will win the next election (versus 19.5% predicting a Republican victory, with the rest undecided), whereas 57.0% of the Republicans believe a Republican will win (versus 26.3% predicting a Democratic win, with the rest undecided). This partisan attitude effect held for all elections except the Truman–Dewey Presidential election of 1948 (see also Granberg & Brent, 1983).

D. IMPLICATIONS OF THE ATTITUDE HEURISTIC FOR BEHAVIOR

Fazio (1986) has proposed a model of the attitude–behavior relationship that implicates the heuristic function of attitude. According to Fazio, attitudes are used to selectively perceive and interpret an object. This selective perception of the object then comprises part of the individual's definition of the situation (in conjunction with norms and other perceptions). This definition of the situation subsequently determines the direction and nature of behavior toward the attitude object. Fazio's (1986) model suggests three factors that influence the magnitude of the attitude–behavior relationship: (1) probability of retrieving the attitude object from memory (see previous section on engaging attitude functions), (2) strength of the attitude-object–evaluation relationship, and (3) opportunity and ability to execute the attitudinal strategy (i.e., act in accordance with one's attitude-based perceptions).

1. Attitude Strength Increases Attitude–Behavior Consistency

Attitude researchers have suggested many terms for the strength of an attitude, including certainty, confidence, conviction, crystallization, extremity, intensity, magnitude, salience, and stability (see Abelson, 1988; Raden, 1985). There is a growing literature indicating that the stronger an attitude (as measured in a variety of ways), the more predictive it is of behavior (Fazio & Zanna, 1978a,b; Petersen & Dutton, 1975; Sample & Warland, 1973) and of conceptual cognitive processes (Fazio, 1989; Pratkanis, 1988). Fazio (1989) has conceptualized attitude strength as a continuum ranging from nonattitudes to highly accessible attitudes. A nonattitude (Converse, 1970) is an attitude (evaluation) that is not stored in memory, but is created (computed) when a person is asked to evaluate an object. Highly accessible attitudes are those for which the evaluation is activated automatically and quickly (as evidenced by short evaluative judgment latencies) by an encounter with the attitude object. Fazio (1986; 1989) has identified situational manipulations that increase the accessibility of weakly held attitudes and reports that highly accessible attitudes are more predictive of behavior.

2. Situational and Personal Constraints Decrease Attitude–Behavior Consistency

Situational influences may overpower even the most highly accessible attitude (see Schuman & Johnson, 1976). For example, organizational researchers have found that job satisfaction is only mildly related to job performance and moderately related to absenteeism and turnover (cf. Iaffaldano & Muchinsky, 1985), although it is reasonable to assume that job attitudes should be highly accessible. In explaining these low correlations, researchers have identified numerous situational factors, such as family responsibilities, other employment opportunities, personal health, technological constraints, the task structure, and so on that restrict an employee's opportunity for action consistent with an attitude (see Baron, 1986; Cotton & Tuttle, 1986; Schminke, 1986).

Similarly, an individual may not possess (or believe he or she possesses) the abilities and skills for acting consistently with an attitude (see Abelson's 1982 discussion of attitudes, scripts, and behavior). For example, complex knowledge structures are needed in order to interact with some attitude objects (e.g., the oenophile's knowledge of Napa Valley and Santa Cruz Mountains microclimates or the gambler's understanding of casino games; see next section). In some cases, knowledge needed to act on an attitude may not just be missing, but may actually contradict the attitude. Devine (1988; see also Goldberg, Gottesdiener, & Abramson, 1975 for a similar example) has identified the interesting case of the white liberal for whom an attitude (e.g., support for racial equality) conflicts with knowledge (i.e., derogatory racial stereotypes taught by society), resulting in a complex relationship between attitudes, knowledge, and social perceptions. Recently, Ajzen (1988; see also Rogers, 1983) has pointed out that it may not be enough to know how to act toward an attitude object; one must also believe that one can perform the behavior (i.e., self-efficacy), if given the opportunity to act on an attitude.

IV. The Schematic Function of Attitudes

Attitude theorists have suggested a number of formats for describing knowledge structures supporting an attitude. For example, expectancy-value theorists (Fishbein & Ajzen, 1975; Rosenberg, 1956) describe attitudinal knowledge in terms of a multiattribute belief structure typically expressed by the linear-additive equation $A_O = \sum_{i=1}^{n} b_i e_i$, where A_O is the attitude toward some object, O; b_i is the subjective probability that O is related to attribute i; e_i is the evaluation of attribute i; and n is the number of beliefs. Cognitive-oriented theorists (e.g., Katz & Stotland, 1959; Newcomb, Turner, & Converse, 1965; Scott, 1969; Scott, Osgood, & Peterson, 1979) have prepared lists of cognitive dimensions and properties (e.g., differentiation, integration, coherence, ambivalence) on which attitudinal knowledge structures are assumed to differ. Although such specifications are a logical first step for distinguishing attitudes, there has been far too little successful empirical and theoretical work to distinguish the meaning of one property from another and to indicate which properties are useful for predicting attitude effects. For example, in a review of studies investigating differentiated and integrated attitudinal knowledge, Ajzen (1989) finds that including such properties does little to improve behavior prediction.

According to the sociocognitive model of attitude, attitudinal knowledge can be quite varied, consisting of any (or all) of the following information: arguments for and against a given proposition, esoteric and technical knowledge about the domain, subjective beliefs, information on how to behave toward the object, goals and wishes about the object, the social meaning of adopting a certain attitude position, and personal episodes. The specific contents and organization of this knowledge is an important determinant of attitude and memory effects.

A. THE SCHEMATIC FUNCTION DEFINED

One early proposition for relating attitudinal knowledge to attitude effects, suggested both by Watson and Hartmann (1939) and by Levine and Murphy (1943), was that attitudes serve as a frame of knowledge for encoding and reconstructing a persuasive message. In support of this proposition, early studies obtained what can be termed an "attitude and selective learning effect"—superior recall for information that agrees with one's attitude. For example, Levine and Murphy (1943) found that a procommunist message was learned better by communists, whereas an anticommunist message was learned better by capitalists (see Watson & Hartmann, 1939, for a similar finding using religious attitudes).

Pratkanis (1989) referred to the use of an attitude to organize and guide memory for events as the attitude's *schematic function*. A schema is an organization of a subset of knowledge relevant to a limited domain. It consists of both *content* (an organization of information) and *procedure* (the use of this information in knowing). In contrast to a heuristic, which is one simple rule, a schema is an organization of a set of procedures and data within a domain.

A frequent finding in learning and memory research is that persons with well-developed schemas demonstrate superior episodic memory for terms and information related to the schematized domain. (As just one example, see the research of Voss and his colleagues on expertise and memory [Chiesi, Spilich, & Voss, 1979; Spilich, Vesonder, Chiesi, & Voss, 1979; Voss, Vesonder, & Spilich, 1980]). The schema is presumably used both during encoding (to aid in comprehension, interpretation, and elaboration of to-be-learned materials) and during retrieval (to provide internal cues that serve as covert mnemonics for recall and reconstruction of an event [Hastie, 1981; Taylor & Crocker, 1981]).

B. ATTITUDES AND EPISODIC MEMORY

Over four dozen studies spread over nearly 50 years of research have yielded little reliable support for the attitude and selective learning effect obtained by Watson and Hartmann (1939) and by Levine and Murphy (1943). In contrast to the effects of attitudes on conceptual processes, the influence of attitudes on episodic memory (the recall of temporally located and dated materials) has been inconsistent (see Pratkanis, 1984; Roberts, 1985 for reviews). Some studies have replicated the Watson-and-Hartmann–Levine-and-Murphy finding that agreeable information is learned best (cf. Edwards, 1941; Jones & Kohler, 1958; Weldon & Malpass, 1981); others have demonstrated no attitude and learning relationship (cf. Brigham & Cook, 1969; Greenwald & Sakumara, 1967; Smith & Jamieson, 1972; Waly & Cook, 1966); still others have found better recall of attitudinally extreme compared to moderate information (cf. Doob, 1953; Judd & Kulik, 1980; Postman & Murphy, 1943); and at least one study has yielded a negative attitude and learning correlation (Cacioppo & Petty, 1979). Similarly, Greenwald (1968a) reported that persuasion researchers also typically fail to find consistent correlations between message agreeableness and recall of message content. Although the pattern of attitude and episodic learning results is complex, there is growing evidence that the knowledge structures supporting an attitude plays an important role in attitudinal learning (see Pratkanis, 1989).[2]

---

[2]Attitudes can also influence learning via mechanisms other than the knowledge structure supporting an evaluation. For example, Pratkanis (1988) discusses how the use of an attitude as a heuristic can influence memory when recall is primarily an inference or guess about the past (see as examples, Edwards, 1941; Lydon, Zanna, & Ross, 1988; Read & Rosson, 1982). Attitudes can also motivate the biased processing of a persuasive communication, resulting in a selective recall of the communication (see Cacioppo & Petty, 1979).

C. BIPOLAR ATTITUDE STRUCTURE

Around 2500 years ago, the Sophist Protagoras observed, "There are two sides to every question." Any opinion or argument can be opposed by a counterargument (see Billig, 1987, for an exposition of the Protagoras maxim). Much more recently, Judd and Kulik (1980; see also Doob, 1953; Postman & Murphy, 1943) found that people, despite their own personal beliefs, can learn and recall information on both sides of an issue, thereby providing empirical evidence for Protagoras's bipolar model of attitude.

In Judd and Kulik's (1980) study, college students saw 54 Thurstone-scaled attitude statements on the topics of women's rights, capital punishment, and majority rule in South Africa. Subjects stated their agreement with each statement and then rated each one for the degree it reflected an extremely pro or extremely anti position. A day later, subjects attempted to recall the statements. Items rated at the extremes of either the agree–disagree or the pro–anti continuum were (1) most rapidly rated and (2) most easily recalled. These results suggested that

> Attitudes thus may act as bipolar schemas that contain representations or expectations of very agreeable and disagreeable points of view. Information that closely matches these expectations is more easily judged and recalled than is information that, although relevant, does not match as well. (Judd & Kulik, 1980, p. 570)

In other words, a knowledge structure supporting an attitude (evaluation) contains not only arguments, beliefs, and expectations supporting one's own position, but may also contain opposing information (and perhaps counterarguments refuting this opposing material).[3] Persons with such a bipolar structure should demonstrate superior learning and faster encoding for information that fits the knowledge frame—that is, information that is consistent with either a pro or an anti position, rather than just agreeable information.

Further support for bipolar attitude schemas comes from a variety of sources. Hymes (1986) reasoned that subjects who are neutral on abortion should be aschematic (i.e., lacking well-defined knowledge on this issue) whereas pro- and anti-abortion advocates should possess a bipolar schema for the issue. Consistent with this supposition, Hymes found that pro- and anti-abortion advocates were better in categorizing information as either pro- or anti-abortion than were neutral subjects.

Pratkanis (1984) also provided data in support of the bipolar hypothesis for some attitude domains. In one study, college students were asked to list arguments for and against 1 of 10 controversial social issues (e.g., nuclear power, gun

---

[3]A bipolar knowledge structure should not be confused with ambivalence of belief. *Ambivalence* refers to the endorsement of conflicting (opposing) beliefs about an issue, whereas the term *bipolar* refers to knowledge of supporting and opposing arguments (regardless of personal endorsement).

control, abortion, draft registration, death penalty). Although subjects' opinions on these issues tended to be distributed across the attitude continuum, the results revealed that 82.7% of the subjects could generate at least one argument on both sides of an issue. (However, subjects typically listed more arguments agreeing with their own position, consistent with the findings of Feather, 1969.)

In two additional experiments, Pratkanis (1984) obtained recall, recognition, and reaction-time data consistent with an assumed bipolar schematic structure. In those studies, subjects first stated their agreement with pro, neutral, and anti statements on the issues of nuclear power, defense spending, and welfare. Results for free recall and recognition of the statements revealed no attitude-selective learning effect—the correlation between recall and statement agreement was −.04 in Experiment 1 and .02 in Experiment 2. However, subjects tended to recall better, evaluate faster, and recognize more quickly those items rated at either extreme of the agreement scale.

McGuire's (1964) work on resistance to persuasion can be viewed as showing that bipolar attitude structures are better "inoculated" against attitude change than unipolar ones. McGuire found that attitudes toward *cultural truisms* (issues such as toothbrushing and X-ray exams) could be easily changed, presumably because subjects had little in the way of an organized structure containing either attitude-supporting or (especially) attitude-opposing knowledge. By providing exposure to opposing arguments, McGuire created bipolar knowledge structures. These inoculated (bipolar) structures effectively resisted the effects of otherwise highly persuasive attacking messages (see also Wood, 1982).

D. UNIPOLAR ATTITUDE STRUCTURE

Pratkanis (1984) reasoned that some attitudes may be supported by unipolar knowledge structures. A positive unipolar structure consists exclusively of knowledge favorable to (supporting) its object.[4] For example, a sports fan typically possesses an elaborate knowledge structure containing technical and esoteric information. With unipolar attitudes, persons with positive attitudes have much more knowledge than those with less favorable (or neutral) attitudes. Consequently, with unipolar attitudes, an attitude and selective learning effect should be expected. A person with a positive attitude possesses knowledge structures that are useful for encoding and recalling domain-related information, whereas those persons with a neutral attitude lack such structures and should process domain-related information poorly.

[4]Unipolar structures may also be associated with negative attitudes (although such structures have not yet been the focus of research). In such cases, knowledge associated with the attitude is unfavorable toward and derogatory of the object. Negative unipolar structures may arise under conditions of strong societal censorship (such as attitudes toward birth control during the Middle Ages: see Ranum & Ranum, 1972).

Three criteria distinguish unipolar (versus bipolar) attitude structures: (1) lack of controversy (versus controversy); (2) population distribution of attitude ranging from neutral to just one extreme (versus extreme-to-extreme distribution); and (3) linear relationship between attitude and amount of attitude-relevant knowledge (versus a tendency to find curvilinear relationships).

Three studies have compared the roles of unipolar versus bipolar knowledge structures in the learning of attitude-related materials. Pratkanis (1984) asked subjects to complete a relationship judgment task similar to the one used in self-reference research (see Rogers, Kuiper, & Kirker, 1977). In this task, subjects answered questions with the stem, "Is this word or phrase related to _____ ?" Subjects answered such questions for 72 words, 12 of which were related to each of six topics (welfare, defense spending, nuclear power, sports, music, and religion). For example, words related to defense spending included pentagon, freeze, and domino; words related to sports included screen, touchdown, and forward. After a filler task, subjects attempted free recall of the words and completed a survey to assess their attitudes and knowledge concerning the six domains.

The results revealed that the topics of sports and music were unipolar in nature. Few subjects endorsed negative statements concerning these activities, and the correlation between attitude and knowledge measures was linear and positive. In contrast, the topics of welfare, nuclear power, and defense spending showed the bipolar pattern. Attitudes were distributed across the full range of the scale and subjects with extreme attitudes professed to know more about the issue. Knowledge structures supporting religion were complex, not clearly fitting either the unipolar or bipolar pattern.[5] The recall results showed that subjects with more knowledge of bipolar and unipolar topics demonstrated superior free recall of topic-related terms (an "attitude-reference" effect). This effect took the form of an attitude-selective learning effect for unipolar topics—that is, a positive attitude–recall correlation. However, for bipolar topics, subjects tended to recall better information at both extremes of the attitude scale, thus yielding no linear attitude–learning relationship.

Pratkanis (1987) replicated these unipolar–bipolar results using persuasive communications, rather than word-and-phrase stimuli. In this study, subjects completed an attitude–knowledge survey and then attempted to learn and recall messages that were anti-nuclear-power, pro-defense-spending, promusic, and prosports. Each message consisted of a series of arguments in support of the message conclusion (e.g. "nuclear power plants have a high risk of accidental

---

[5]Religion may be a superordinate category spanning multiple categories corresponding to denominations and sects (e.g., Catholic, Mennonite, Zen Buddhist). Unipolar attitudes may exist at the denominational level. Similarly, sports and music can be viewed as superordinate categories. Unlike religion, however, attitudes toward various types of sports and music are typically positively correlated (e.g., the sports fan enjoys baseball, football, and basketball, whereas the religious person rarely identifies with more than one denomination).

meltdown;" "the simple Bach chorale moves the soul"). For sports and music, few subjects endorsed the negative end of the attitude continuum and there were positive correlations between attitudes and knowledge. For the issues of defense spending and nuclear power, subjects were distributed along the attitude continuum, and subjects with attitudes at the extremes of the continuum professed the most knowledge about the domain. For the two unipolar messages (sports and music), there was an attitude-selective learning effect—subjects who held positive attitudes toward sports and music showed superior learning of the message. For the bipolar messages (defense spending and nuclear power), subjects with extreme attitudes on the topic demonstrated a tendency to recall the information best.

Pratkanis, Syak, and Gamble (1987) investigated the relationship between attitude toward social drinking and recall of persuasive communications concerning drinking. The domain of social drinking is interesting because, in regards to social policy, it is bipolar (i.e., most people can provide arguments for and against drinking). However, knowledge concerning drinking activities is distributed in a unipolar pattern. Persons who have prodrinking attitudes are more likely to know technical details such as how to fix exotic drinks, the number of gallons in a keg of beer, and the names of various liquors. Pratkanis, Syak, and Gamble asked subjects to learn three communications: one favoring social drinking, one opposing social drinking, and one of a technical nature on how to make an exotic drink called a Pousse-cafe. The results showed that attitudes were not related to the learning of the pro- or anti-social-drinking message. However, subjects with prodrinking attitudes demonstrated superior learning of the technical Pousse-cafe message. Subjects with prodrinking attitudes also possessed greater technical knowledge concerning drinking (as assessed by an objective test), and this greater knowledge moderated the attitude–learning results.

Previous research has identified other unipolar attitude objects. For example, Greenwald and Pratkanis (1984) reviewed evidence that a subject's judgments about self tend to be overly positive and are made rapidly when they set the subject apart from others in a favorable direction and that self-relevant information (which is usually positive) is recalled efficiently. Gustafson (1957) found that members of various ethnic groups were better at learning the accomplishments of in-group members in American history. Liben and Signorella (1980) and others found that children with traditional gender-role attitudes (compared to those who have not as yet developed these attitudes) demonstrate superior memory for materials that protray traditional sex roles. Becker and Byrne (1985) reviewed research on sexual attitudes, and they presented a pattern of memory results that are similar to those obtained with attitudes toward social drinking—erotophiles obtained higher test scores in a college sexuality course, retained more information from a birth-control lecture, and were better at recalling erotica than erotophobes. Saegert and Young (1983) find that health food enthusiasts score well on general nutrition tests.

E. ADDITIONAL USES OF ATTITUDINAL KNOWLEDGE

The foregoing research indicates that attitudes can be used to guide and organize memory for events. However, attitude knowledge structures may serve other purposes. As discussed in Section III,D, attitudinal knowledge can guide usage of (or complex behavior toward) an object. Such knowledge structures should contain technical and action-oriented information, possibly organized in a script-format (Abelson, 1976, 1982). As illustrated by McGuire's (1964) inoculation research, attitudinal knowledge, especially that of a bipolar nature, can be of use in arguing the merits of a proposal. Attitudinal knowledge can also by used to describe the utility of an object, resulting in a structure listing the benefits and drawbacks of an object similar to that proposed by expectancy-value theorists (e.g., Fishbein & Ajzen, 1975). The varied usage of attitudinal knowledge suggests that the type of knowledge structure supporting an attitude may be not just a function of the topic domain (as demonstrated by Pratkanis), but also a function of personality variables (see, for example, Olson & Zanna's, 1979 research on repressor's and selective exposure), an understanding of intent to persuade (see Adler *et al.,* 1980), and the roles and tasks a person must perform in a given situation (see, for example, Tetlock's 1988 research on accountability and cognitive structure, Sidanius's, 1988 discussion of attitude function and political sophistication, and Bosso's, 1987, account of the life cycle of the pesticide issue).

V. The Self-Functions of Attitudes

The functional theories of Smith, Bruner, and White (1956) and of Katz (1960) explicitly linked the possession of an attitude to the definition and appraisal of the self-concept. Smith *et al.* (1956) suggested that attitudes serve to defend the self through two functions: *externalization* (holding an attitude in order to protect the self) and *social adjustment* (holding an attitude in order to maintain relationships with others). Katz suggested the self-related functions of *ego-defensive* (similar to Smith *et al.*'s externalization) and *value-expressive* (holding an attitude as an act of self-expression).

The functional approach to attitudes has not yet generated an impressive volume of research. After a brief flurry of research, mostly addressing the ego-defensive functions (e.g., Katz, McClintock, & Sarnoff, 1957; Stotland, Katz, & Patchen, 1959), the functional approach has been relegated to a position as a passing remark in the attitude chapters of many social psychological texts. One reason for this empirical neglect is that attitude functions were never explicitly linked with empirical operations (Shavitt, 1989, and Snyder & DeBono, 1989), perhaps as a general reflection of the weakness of the self metaphors of the 1950s and 1960s at linking conceptual definitions to research procedures (Pratkanis & Greenwald, 1985).

The sociocognitive perspective agrees with early functional models on the importance of the self in determining attitude structure and functioning. In this section, we use the Greenwald and Pratkanis (1984) view of the self to specify the self-functions of an attitude. Unlike some critics of functional theories, we believe that considerable evidence has accumulated in support of the proposition that attitudes are held in service to the self, although much of this evidence is linked to other theoretical perspectives and is typically not recognized as functional research.

A. THE THREE FACETS OF THE SELF AND THEIR ATTITUDE FUNCTIONS

The self has come to be viewed as a major factor in motivation as persons seek to establish and maintain positive self-identities. In a recent analysis, Greenwald and Breckler (1985; see also Breckler & Greenwald, 1986; Greenwald, 1982; Greenwald & Pratkanis, 1984) identified three classes of strategies for establishing and maintaining self-esteem, termed the *ego tasks,* of the public, private, and collective facets of the self. The public self's strategy is to maintain and establish self-worth by earning favorable evaluations from others (a public audience); the private self achieves self-worth by meeting or exceeding internalized evaluative standards (the approval of a private audience); and the collective self establishes self-worth by seeking to attain the goals of reference groups (a collective audience). Greenwald (1989) has suggested that a wide variety of attitudes readily participate in these strategies for establishing and maintaining self-regard.

When the *public* facet of the self is emphasized, the person should display attitudes that are agreeable to others. Such attitudes can be used to earn the approval of others and, via this public-self strategy, self-regard. The public self's strategy corresponds to Smith *et al.*'s *social adjustment* function ("[O]ne will more readily and forthrightly express acceptable attitudes while inhibiting or modulating the expression of less approved ones" [pp. 41–42]).

The *private* facet of the self earns self-regard by meeting or exceeding internalized criteria of success. One strategy for achieving this goal is to maintain attitudes that are consistent with other attitudes and with one's self-concept. Katz's (1960) *value-expressive* function ("the individual derives satisfactions from expressing attitudes appropriate to his personal values" [p. 170]) can thus be interpreted as a manifestation of the private facet of the self.

The *collective* facet of the self establishes self-worth by helping to achieve the goals of important reference groups (family, church, profession, work group, etc.) An obvious strategy toward that end is to value objects that are identified with those groups. Attitudes that are shaped by this strategy may be said to serve a group solidarity or *social identification* function. This last function is not one that appears in either the Smith *et al.* or the Katz original list. Smith (1980) later extended the meaning of social adjustment to include mediation of self–other relationships and social identification. However, the present list of self-functions was anticipated by Kelman's (1961) three influence processes of compliance (public), internalization (private), and identification (collective).

B. EVIDENCE FOR THE SELF-RELATED FUNCTIONS OF ATTITUDES

Much evidence exists in social psychology to demonstrate that attitudes are used to define, appraise, and maintain the self-concept. We review eight domains of empirical inquiry. (See also Herek, 1987; Shavitt, 1989; Snyder & DeBono, 1989, for recent discussions on operationalizing attitude functions).

1. Self-Definition and Verification

Research from a number of theoretical perspectives indicates that attitudes are used to define one's self. Cialdini *et al.* (1976) find that people tend to BIRG (bask in reflected glory) by expressing positive attitudes toward winning football teams (e.g., donning team insignia). Conversely, Tesser and Campbell (1983) report that subjects express negative attitudes toward persons whose performance is threatening to their own self-esteem. Swann's self-verification (1983) and Wicklund and Gollwitzer's (1982) symbolic self-completion theories both suggest that attitudes toward physical objects and people can be used to maintain one's self-concept. C. Snyder and Fromkin (1980) review studies indicating that attitudes can be adopted as a strategy for establishing uniqueness (see also Abelson & Prentice, 1989). Goethals (1986) finds that strategies for maintaining a positive self-image can result in both a false-consensus and a false-uniqueness effect.

2. The Self-Justification of Dissonant Acts

In a reformulation of dissonance theory, Aronson (1969, 1984; see also Greenwald & Ronis, 1978) stated that dissonance is most powerful as a motivator of human behavior when the self-concept is threatened. In such cases, attitudes can be adopted and expressed as one possible means of reconciling undesirable acts to a positive self-concept. Aronson (1984) interprets the literature on dissonance as indicating that attitudes are adopted as a means of justifying the self's involvement in (1) escalating commitment to a failing course of action (Brockner

& Rubin, 1985); (2) the performance of a self-discrepant act for insufficient justification (Festinger & Carlsmith, 1959); (3) the overexpenditure of effort (Aronson & Mills, 1959); and (4) cruelty (Lerner, 1980).

3. Selective Exposure

As noted previously, early research, based on cognitive dissonance theory, has revealed that the selective-exposure effect is not particularly easy to obtain. Recently, Frey (1986) has reviewed evidence showing that selective exposure is more likely to occur under conditions of (1) perceived free choice and (2) commitment. For example, Sweeney and Gruber (1984) found that committed Nixon supporters (who supposedly chose their attitudes freely) reportedly paid less attention and knew less information about the Watergate proceedings. In the terminology of a revised dissonance theory (Aronson, 1969; Greenwald & Ronis, 1978), selective exposure occurs when the possession of an attitude has implications for self-evaluation.

4. Impression Management

According to Schlenker (1980), attitudes are used for impression management purposes; people express attitudes in order to claim desirable self-images and to reject undesirable ones. As evidence for this proposition, Schlenker points to research indicating that subjects (1) are differentially persuaded by a communication as a function of the nature of an audience observing the attitude expression (Braver, Linder, Corwin, & Cialdini, 1977); (2) express attitude similarity and liking for others as an ingratiation tactic (Jones, 1964); and (3) modify their opinions in anticipation of a persuasive communication, to gain strategic self-presentational advantage (Cialdini & Petty, 1981).

5. Self-Monitoring

Snyder and DeBono (1989) use the Self-Monitoring scale (Snyder, 1974; Snyder, 1987) to operationalize attitude functions. They reasoned that for high self-monitors (who strive to be the person called for by the situation), attitudes will serve primarily a social adjustment function, whereas for low self-monitors (who attempt to use an internal standard as a guide for behavior), attitudes will serve a value-expressive purpose. In a program of research, Snyder and DeBono (1989) found that high self-monitors are most persuaded by appeals targeted to the social adjustment function (e.g., image advertising and messages describing widespread social agreement for a position) and that low self-monitors are most persuaded by appeals targeted to the value-expressive function (e.g., reason-why advertising and messages relating an issue to underlying values). In a similar vein, Scheier and Carver (1983) review evidence showing that when public self-consciousness is high, people modify the expression of their attitudes to fit the situation, whereas when private self-consciousness is high, people act in accordance with their attitudes.

6. Symbolic Attitudes

Recent research in the area of AIDS and racial integration have found that attitudes are often held for symbolic reasons (i.e., related to values that are important for self-definition), in contrast to instrumental concerns (i.e., direct and immediate consequences of interacting with an object). Pryor, Reeder, Vinacco, and Russo (1987) found that attitudes toward a heterosexual AIDS victim were a function of both the instrumental value of interacting with the victim (as measured by procedures developed by Fishbein & Ajzen, 1975) and symbolic reasons (e.g., the belief in AIDS as a homosexual affliction and one's own level of homophobia). Similarly, Kinder and Sears (1981) found that whites' support for a black mayoral candidate was largely determined by symbolic factors (e.g., traditional white Protestantism morality), as opposed to direct racial threats (e.g., loss of job or property-value). Although racial attitudes may serve symbolic (value-expressive) purposes, they can also result, as Pettigrew (1958, 1959) found, from conformity to group norms, thus serving social adjustment and identification functions. (For a further discussion of symbolic attitude research, see Bobo, 1983; Herek, 1986; Sears & Kinder, 1985; Sniderman & Tetlock, 1986).

7. Social Status, Social Role, and Attitudes

Attitudes often serve to maintain the social status and role occupancy of the self. For example, Lieberman (1956) found that workers who became company foremen developed promanagement attitudes (i.e., positive attitudes toward the company as a place to work, toward top management, and toward the company's incentive system), whereas workers who became union stewards developed pro-union attitudes (i.e., positive attitudes toward the labor union, toward top union officers, and toward seniority, as opposed to ability, as a criterion for advancement). When the foremen and stewards returned to their original rank-and-file worker roles, their attitudes tended to revert back to their previous positions. Similarly, Frederickson (1969) found that the role occupancy of local government officials (in particular, legislators, elected executives, appointed executives, labor representatives, and arbitrators) was an important factor in determining attitudes toward various labor relations issues. Herman and Hulin (1972) found that various job-related attitudes were a function of status and departmental membership within an organization.

8. The Maintenance of In-Groups and Out-Groups

Attitudes can serve as a means of maintaining boundaries between groups and of defining one's self within the collective (see Tajfel, 1981, and Turner, 1987 for a theory of self-categorization into a social group). Abelson and Prentice (1989) refer to this as the "badge value of attitudes"—the adoption of highly visible attitudes, important for maintaining social identification with the group. Social groups often expect members to adopt certain attitudes (e.g., acceptance of distinctive religious garb, ethnic food preferences, shared beliefs about outgroups) as a means of defining the group's distinctiveness and for identifying the individual with the group. For example, Hurtado and Gurin (1987) found that support for bilingualism (i.e., using Spanish and English as means of communication) among individuals of Mexican descent living in the United States served to promote ethnic identity. Approval of bilingualism was more strongly associated with a Chicano (i.e., mestizo–mestiza, *la raza*) as opposed to an "upwardly mobile" identity.

C. THE IMPORTANCE OF THE SELF FOR UNDERSTANDING ATTITUDES

The self plays an important role in establishing the contents and organization of attitude structure and in specifying the conditions under which certain attitude effects will occur.

1. The Self and Attitude Structure

The pursuit of positive self-regard can affect the label, evaluation, and knowledge associated with an attitude object. As noted in Section II,A, objects can be labelled and identified to the self's advantage. Functional theories of attitude change (see Insko, 1967; Kiesler, Collins, & Miller, 1969, for reviews) have suggested, and much of the foregoing research has demonstrated, that object evaluations are created and maintained in service to the self. Attitudinal knowledge structures may develop as a result of the persistence of an ego task. For example, social-adjustive attitudes should contain information about how other people value the object; value-expressive attitudes should be associated with knowledge of the relationship between an attitude and other attitudes and the self; and social-identification attitudes should be associated with knowledge about how reference-group members value the attitude object.

2. The Self and Attitude Prediction

The research on self-functions has identified another condition that improves the predictive power of an attitude. People are more likely to act in accord with their attitudes when those attitudes are important (either situationally or chronically) for their self-concepts. Furthermore, people are likely to act on these attitudes, not solely in an evaluatively consistent manner, as suggested by cognitive consistency theories, but in a fashion that increases self-worth (which in some cases may give the appearance of inconsistency).

VI. Concluding Remarks

A. WHAT IS AN ATTITUDE?

According to a sociocognitive model, an attitude is represented in memory by (1) an object label and procedures for applying that label, (2) a summary evaluation of that object, and (3) a knowledge structure supporting that evaluation. This cognitive representation relates a person to the social world by serving to make sense of the environment (heuristic and schematic functions) and to establish, maintain, and enhance positive self-regard (social adjustment, value-expressive, and social identification functions).

B. HOW WARRANTED IS THE PESSIMISM CONCERNING ATTITUDES?

Contrary to popular belief in social psychology, attitudes are *not* epiphenomenal but *are* predictive of large classes of social behavior. Attitudes are found to predict: (1) conceptual cognitive processes such as inference, judgment, and reasoning in a wide variety of circumstances; (2) behavior when the evaluation of an object is readily used to interpret the situation and the person has the ability (knowledge) and opportunity to act in accord with these perceptions; (3) memory for a persuasive communication via the knowledge structure supporting an evaluation; and (4) selective exposure to information when the self is implicated in the further processing of that information. In general, attitudes are better predictors when there is consistent and consensual identification of the attitude object.

C. WHY THEN ALL THE CONCERN ABOUT ATTITUDES?

Approximately 20 years ago, there was a flourishing of books and articles on attitudes (Abelson *et al.*, 1968; Fishbein, 1967; Greenwald, Brock, & Ostrom, 1968; McGuire, 1969, to list a few). At this time, there was broad acceptance of a definition of attitude that was stated in terms of the venerable tripartite of affect, behavior, and cognition. Attitude theory was strongly dominated by cognitive-consistency principles that were associated with the concepts of balance, congruity, and dissonance.

As we have seen in this article, attitudes are complexly related to behavior, to selective exposure for information, and to memory for a persuasive communication. The major theories of attitudes, popular 20 years ago, are unable adequately to describe and summarize the conditions under which attitudes produce such effects. It is a mistake to assume that attitudes are poor predictors of social processes merely because our theories of attitude have not succeeded in describing those relationships.

D. WHITHER THE COURSE OF ATTITUDE RESEARCH?

Greenwald, Pratkanis, Leippe, and Baumgardner (1986) view scientific progress as both the search for qualifying conditions on existing effects and the development of increasingly powerful theories to describe those conditions. In this sense, the course of attitude research can certainly be viewed as scientific progress. In 1935, Allport proclaimed the importance of the attitude concept for social psychology. After approximately three decades of attitude research, multiple commentaries were published announcing that attitudes were apparently not as predictive of social behavior as originally assumed and that it was time to consider abandoning the attitude concept. Research in the 1970s responded to these critiques by addressing the question, "Under what condition does an attitude predict a given effect?" (see Zanna & Fazio, 1982). This later research has achieved rather promising results, as previously unruly attitude effects are increasingly brought under experimental control.

The sociocognitive model of attitude represents our attempt to resolve the paradox of attitude importance and to integrate research findings by specifying the conditions under which significant attitude effects occur. As a summary of attitude effects, it is hoped that the sociocognitive model of attitude will generate further formulations about the relationship of attitudes to social behavior and will serve to maintain the conception that attitudes function powerfully to guide interaction in a complex social world.

VII. Summary

The history of attitude research presents a paradox. As early as 1935, attitude was proclaimed as social psychology's most indispensable construct. That faith in the attitude construct remains strong today. At the same time, the predictive utility of attitudes has been widely questioned, as researchers have had difficulty demonstrating strong positive relationships of attitudes (1) to behavior, (2) to memory for persuasive messages, and (3) to selection among items of controversial information.

The present thesis is that pessimism concerning the predictive utility of the attitude construct is unwarranted. We review evidence from diverse areas of social psychology to demonstrate that attitudes frequently serve three functions: *heuristic* (attitudes provide a simple strategy for appraising an object), *schematic* (attitudes organize and guide complex behavior towards an object and memory for events), and *self-related* (attitudes are used to define and maintain self-worth). These functions are used to construct a sociocognitive model of attitude (as a replacement of previous approaches). According to this model, an attitude is represented in memory by (1) an object label and procedures for applying that label (which needs to be engaged for attitude effects to occur), (2) an evaluation associated with that structure (which guides the heuristic function), and (3) a knowledge structure supporting that evaluation (which serves the schematic function). As a cognitive representation, attitudes are used to relate an individual to the social world.

Acknowledgments

This article is an elaboration of two previous chapters appearing as Greenwald (1989) and Pratkanis (1989). The authors thank Cheryl Boglarsky, David Douglass, Rebecca Slaton, M. Brewster Smith, and Marlene E. Turner for comments on an earlier draft.

References

Abelson, R. P. (1959). Modes of resolution of belief dilemmas. *Journal of Conflict Resolution,* **3,** 343–352.
Abelson, R. P. (1972). Are attitudes necessary? In B. T. King & E. McGinnies (Eds.), *Attitudes, conflict, and social change* (pp. 19–32). New York: Academic Press.
Abelson, R. P. (1976). Script processing in attitude formation and decision-making. In J. S. Carroll & J. W. Payne (Eds.), *Cognition and social behavior* (pp. 33–45). Hillsdale, NJ: Erlbaum.
Abelson, R. P. (1982). Three modes of attitude–behavior consistency. In M. P. Zanna, E. T. Higgins, & C. P. Herman (Eds.), *Consistency in social behavior* (pp. 131–146). Hillsdale, NJ: Erlbaum.
Abelson, R. P. (1988). Conviction. *American Psychologist,* **43,** 267–275.
Abelson, R. P., Aronson, E., McGuire, W. J., Newcomb, T. M., Rosenberg, M. J., & Tannenbaum, P. H. (Eds.) (1968). *Theories of cognitive consistency: A sourcebook.* Chicago: Rand-McNally.
Abelson, R. P., & Prentice, D. A. (1989). Beliefs as possessions: A functional perspective. In A. R. Pratkanis, S. J. Breckler, & A. G. Greenwald (Eds.), *Attitudes structure and function* (pp. 361–381). Hillsdale, NJ: Erlbaum.
Aderman, D., & Brehm, S. S. (1976). On the recall of initial attitudes following counterattitudinal advocacy: An experimental reexamination. *Personality and Social Psychology Bulletin.* **2,** 59–62.
Adler, R. P., Friedlander, B. Z., Lesser, G. S., McRingoff, L., Robertson, T. S., Rossiter, J. R., & Ward, S. (1980). *Research on the effects of television advertising on children.* Lexington, MA: Lexington Books.
Ajzen, I. (1989). Attitude structure and behavior. In A. R. Pratkanis, S. J. Breckler, & A. G. Greenwald (Eds.), *Attitudes structure and function* (pp. 241–274). Hillsdale, NJ: Erlbaum.

Ajzen, I., & Fishbein, M. (1977). Attitude–behavior relations: A theoretical analysis and review of empirical research. *Psychological Review*, **84**, 888–918.

Allport, G. W. (1935). Attitudes. In C. Murchison (Ed.), *The handbook of social psychology* (pp. 798–844). Worcester, MA: Clark University Press.

Anderson, N. H., & Hubert, S. (1963). Effects of concomitant verbal recall on order effects in personality impression formation. *Journal of Verbal Learning and Verbal Behavior*, **2**, 379–391.

Aronson, E. (1969). The theory of cognitive dissonance: A current perspective. In L. Berkowitz (Ed.), *Advances in experimental social psychology* (Vol. 4, pp. 1–34). New York: Academic Press.

Aronson, E. (1984). *The social animal*. New York: W. H. Freeman and Co.

Aronson, E., & Mills, J. (1959). The effect of severity of initiation on liking for a group. *Journal of Abnormal and Social Psychology*, **59**, 177–181.

Bain, R. (1928). An attitude on attitude research. *American Journal of Sociology*, **33**, 940–957.

Baron, R. A. (1986). *Behavior in organizations*. Boston: MA: Allyn & Bacon.

Becker, M. A., & Bryne, D. (1985). Self-regulated exposure to erotica, recall errors, and subjective reactions as a function of erotophobia and Type A coronary-prone behavior. *Journal of Personality and Social Psychology*, **48**, 760–767.

Bem, D. J. (1967). Self-perception: An alternative interpretation of cognitive dissonance phenomena. *Psychological Review*, **74**, 183–200.

Bem, D. J., & McConnell, H. K. (1970). Testing the self-perception of dissonance phenomena: On the salience of premanipulation attitudes. *Journal of Personality and Social Psychology*, **14**, 23–31.

Berkowitz, L., & Rogers, K. H. (1986). A priming effect analysis of media influences. In J. Bryant & D. Zillman (Eds), *Perspectives on mass media* (pp. 57–81). Hillsdale, NJ: Erlbaum.

Billig, M. (1987). *Arguing and thinking: A rhetorical approach to social psychology*. Cambridge: Cambridge University Press.

Blumer, H. (1955). Attitudes and the social act. *Social Problems*, **3**, 59–65.

Bobo, L. (1983). Whites' opposition to busing: Symbolic racism or realistic group conflict? *Journal of Personality and Social Psychology*, **45**, 1196–1210.

Borgida, E., & Campbell, B. (1982). Belief relevance and attitude–behavior consistency: The moderating role of personal experience. *Journal of Personality and Social Psychology*, **42**, 239–247.

Bosso, C. J. (1987). *Pesticides and politics: The life cycle of a public issue*. Pittsburgh, PA: University of Pittsburgh Press.

Braver, S. L., Linder, D. E., Corwin, T. T., & Cialdini, R. B. (1977). Some conditions that affect admissions of attitude change. *Journal of Experimental Social Psychology*, **13**, 565–576.

Breckler, S. J. (1984). Empirical validation of affect, behavior, and cognition as distinct components of attitude. *Journal of Personality and Social Psychology*, 47, 1191–1205.

Breckler, S. J., & Greenwald, A. G. (1986). Motivational facets of the self. In R. M. Sorrentino & E. T. Higgins (Eds.), *Handbook of motivation and cognition* (pp. 145–164). New York: Guilford Press.

Breckler, S. J., & Wiggins, E. C. (1989). On defining attitude and attitude theory: Once more with feeling. In A. R. Pratkanis, S. J. Breckler, & A. G. Greenwald (Eds.), *Attitude structure and function* (pp. 407–427). Hillsdale, NJ: Erlbaum.

Brigham, J. C., & Cook, S. W. (1969). The influence of attitude on the recall of controversial materials: A failure to confirm. *Journal of Experimental Social Psychology*, **5**, 24–243.

Brockner, J., & Rubin, J. Z. (1985). *Entrapments in escalating conflicts: A social psychological analysis*. New York: Springer-Verlag.

Byrne, D. (1971). *The attraction paradigm*. New York: Academic Press.

Cacioppo, J. T., & Petty, R. E. (1979). Effects of message repetition and position on cognitive response, recall, and persuasion. *Journal of Personality and Social Psychology*, **37**, 97–109.

Cacioppo, J. T., Petty, R. E., & Geen, T. R. (1989). Attitude structure and function: From the tripartite to the homeostasis model of attitudes. In A. R. Pratkanis, S. J. Breckler, & A. G. Greenwald (Eds.), *Attitude structure and function* (pp. 275–309). Hillsdale, NJ: Erlbaum.

Cantril, H. (1932). General and specific attitudes. *Psychological Monographs*, **42**, (5, Whole No. 192).

Cantril, H. (1940). America faces the war: A study in public opinion. *Public Opinion Quarterly*, **4**, 387–407.

Carlston, D. E. (1980). Events, inferences, and impression formation. In R. Hastie, T. M. Ostrom, E. B. Ebbesen, R. S. Wyer, D. L. Hamilton, & D. E. Carlston (Eds.), *Person memory: The cognitive basis of social perception* (pp. 89–119). Hillsdale, NJ: Erlbaum.

Chiesi, H. L., Spilich, G. J., & Voss, J. F. (1979). Acquisition of domain-related information in relation to high and low domain knowledge. *Journal of Verbal Learning and Verbal Behavior*, **18**, 257–273.

Cialdini, R. B., Borden, R. J., Thorne, A., Walker, M. R., Freeman, S., & Sloan, L. R. (1976). Basking in reflected glory: Three (football) field studies. *Journal of Personality and Social Psychology*, **34**, 366–375.

Cialdini, R. B., & Petty, R. E. (1981). Anticipatory opinion effects. In R. E. Petty, T. M. Ostrom, & T. C. Brock (Eds.), *Cognitive responses in persuasion* (pp. 217–235). Hillsdale, NJ: Erlbaum.

Converse, P. E. (1970). Attitudes and non-attitudes: Continuation of a dialogue. In E. R. Tufte (Ed.), *The quantitative analysis of social problems* (pp. 168–189). Reading, MA: Addison-Wesley.

Cooley, C. H. (1912). Valuation as a social process. *Psychological Bulletin*, **9**, 441–450.

Cooper, E., & Jahoda, M. (1947). The evasion of propaganda: How prejudiced people respond to anti-prejudice propaganda. *Journal of Social Psychology*, **23**, 15–25.

Cotton, J. L., & Tuttle, J. M. (1986). Employee turnover: A meta-analysis and review with implications for research. *Academy of Management Review*, **11**, 55–70.

Davidson, A. R., & Morrison, D. M. (1983). Predicting contraceptive behavior from attitudes: A comparison of within- versus across-subjects procedures. *Journal of Personality and Social Psychology*, **45**, 997–1009.

DeFleur, M. L., & Westie, F. R. (1963). Attitude as a scientific concept. *Social Forces*, **42**, 17–31.

Devine, P. G. (1989). Automatic and controlled processes in prejudice: The role of stereotypes and personal beliefs. In A. R. Pratkanis, S. J. Breckler, & A. G. Greenwald (Eds.), *Attitude structure and function* (pp. 181–212). Hillsdale, NJ: Erlbaum.

Dillehay, R. C. (1973). On the irrelevance of the classical negative evidence concerning the effect of attitudes on behavior. *American Psychologist*, **28**, 887–891.

Doob, L. W. (1953). Effects of initial serial position and attitude upon recall under conditions of low motivation. *Journal of Abnormal and Social Psychology*, **48**, 199–205.

Dreben, E. K., Fiske, S. T., & Hastie, R. (1979). The independence of evaluative and item information: Impression and recall order effects in behavior-based impression formation. *Journal of Personality and Social Psychology*, **37**, 1758–1768.

Eberhart, J. C., & Bauer, R. A. (1941). An analysis of the influences on recall of a controversial event: The Chicago Tribune and the Republic Steel strike. *Journal of Social Psychology, S.P.S.S.I. Bulletin*, **14**, 211–228.

Edwards, A. L. (1941). Political frames of reference as a factor influencing recognition. *Journal of Abnormal and Social Psychology*, **36**, 34–50.

Edwards, A. L. (1957). *Techniques of attitude scale construction*. New York: Appleton-Century-Croft.

Evans, J. St. B. T., Barston, J. L., & Pollard, P. (1983). On the conflict between logic and belief in syllogistic reasoning. *Memory and Cognition*, **11**, 295–306.

Farquhar, P. H., & Pratkanis, A. R. (1987). *Decision structuring with unavailable options*. Unpublished manuscript. Carnegie-Mellon University, Pittsburgh, PA.

Fazio, R. H. (1986). How do attitudes guide behavior? In R. M. Sorrentino & E. T. Higgins (Eds.), *Handbook of motivation and cognition* (pp. 204–242). New York: Guilford Press.
Fazio, R. H. (1989). On the power and functionality of attitudes: The role of attitude accessibility. In A. R. Pratkanis, S. J. Breckler, & A. G. Greenwald (Eds.), *Attitude structure and function* (pp. 153–179). Hillsdale, NJ: Erlbaum.
Fazio, R. H., & Zanna, M. P. (1978a). On the predictive validity of attitudes: The roles of direct experience and confidence. *Journal of Personality, 46,* 228–243.
Fazio, R. H., & Zanna, M. P. (1978b). Attitudinal qualities relating to the strength of the attitude–behavior relationship. *Journal of Experimental Social Psychology, 14,* 398–408.
Feather, N. T. (1964). Acceptance and rejection of arguments in relation to attitude strength, critical ability, and intolerance of inconsistency. *Journal of Abnormal and Social Psychology, 69,* 127–136.
Feather, N. T. (1969). Attitude and selective recall. *Journal of Personality and Social Psychology, 12,* 310–319.
Festinger, L. (1957). *Theory of cognitive dissonance.* Stanford, CA: Stanford University Press.
Festinger, L. (1964). Behavioral support for opinion change. *Public Opinion Quarterly, 28,* 404–417.
Festinger, L., & Carlsmith, J. M. (1959). Cognitive consequences of forced compliance. *Journal of Abnormal and Social Psychology, 58,* 203–210.
Fields, J. M., & Schuman, H. (1976). Public beliefs about the beliefs of the public. *Public Opinion Quarterly, 40,* 427–448.
Fishbein, M. (Ed.) (1967). *Readings in attitude theory and measurement.* New York: Wiley.
Fishbein, M., & Ajzen, I. (1975). *Belief, attitude, intention and behavior: An introduction to theory and research.* Reading, MA: Addison-Wesley.
Fiske, S. T., & Pavelchak, M. A. (1986). Category-based versus piecemeal-based affective responses: Developments in schema-triggered affect. In R. M. Sorrentino & E. T. Higgins (Eds.), *Handbook of motivation and cognition.* New York: Guilford.
Fleming, D. (1967). Attitude: The history of a concept. *Perspectives in American history, 1,* 287–365.
Frederickson, H. G. (1969). Role occupancy and attitudes toward labor relations in government. *Administrative Science Quarterly, 14,* 595–606.
Freedman, J. L., & Sears, D. O. (1965). Selective exposure. In L. Berkowitz (Ed.), *Advances in experimental social psychology* (Vol. 1, pp 57–97). New York: Academic Press.
Frey, D. (1986). Recent research on selective exposure to information. In L. Berkowitz (Ed.), *Advances in experimental social psychology* (Vol. 19, pp. 41–80). New York: Academic Press.
Gallup, G. H. (1972). *The Gallup Poll: Public opinion 1935–1971.* New York: Random House.
Goethals, G. R. (1986). Fabricating and ignoring social reality: Self-serving estimates of consensus. In J. M. Olson, C. P. Herman, & M. P. Zanna (Eds.), *Relative deprivation and social comparison* (pp. 135–157). Hillsdale, NJ: Erlbaum.
Goethals, G. R., & Reckman, R. F. (1973). The perception of consistency in attitudes. *Journal of Experimental Social Psychology, 9,* 491–501.
Goldberg, P. A., Gottesdiener, M., & Abramson, P. R. (1975). Another put-down of women? Perceived attractiveness as a function of support for the feminist movement. *Journal of Personality and Social Psychology, 32,* 113–115.
Gordon, R. L. (1953). The effect of attitude toward Russia on logical reasoning. *Journal of Social Psychology, 37,* 103–111.
Granberg, D. (1985). An anomaly in political perception. *Public Opinion Quarterly, 49,* 504–516.
Granberg, D., & Brent, E. (1983). When prophecy bends: The preference–expectation link in U.S. Presidential elections, 1952–1980. *Journal of Personality and Social Psychology, 45,* 477–491.

Granberg, D., Jefferson, N. L. Brent, E. E., & King, M. (1981). Membership group, reference group, and the attribution of attitudes to groups. *Journal of Personality and Social Psychology,* **40,** 833—842.

Granberg, D., & Jenks, R. (1977). Assimilation and contrast effects in the 1972 election. *Human Relations,* **30,** 623–640.

Greenwald, A. G. (1968a). Cognitive learning, cognitive response to persuasion, and attitude change. In A. G. Greenwald, T. C. Brock, & T. M. Ostrom (Eds.), *Psychological foundations of attitudes* (pp. 147–170). New York: Academic Press.

Greenwald, A. G. (1968b). On defining attitude and attitude theory. In A. G. Greenwald, T. C. Brock, & T. M. Ostrom (Eds.), *Psychological foundations of attitudes* (pp. 361–388). New York: Academic Press.

Greenwald, A. G. (1980). The totalitarian ego. *American Psychologist,* **35,** 603–618.

Greenwald, A. G. (1982). Ego task analysis: An integration of research on ego-involvement and self-awareness. In A. Hastorf & A. M. Isen (Eds.), *Cognitive social psychology* (pp. 109–147). New York: Elsevier North-Holland.

Greenwald, A. G. (1988). *Levels of representation.* Unpublished manuscript. University of Washington, Seattle, WA.

Greenwald, A. G. (1989). Why attitudes are important: Defining attitude and attitude theory 20 years later. In A. R. Pratkanis, S. J. Breckler, & A. G. Greenwald (Eds.), *Attitude structure and function* (pp. 429–440). Hillsdale, NJ: Erlbaum.

Greenwald, A. G., & Breckler, S. J. (1985). To whom is the self presented? In B. R. Schlenker (Ed.), *The self and social life* (pp. 126–145). New York: McGraw-Hill.

Greenwald, A. G., Brock, T. C., & Ostrom, T. M. (Eds.). (1968). *Psychological foundations of attitudes.* New York: Academic Press.

Greenwald, A. G., & Pratkanis, A. R. (1984). The self. In R. S. Wyer & T. K. Srull (Eds.), *The handbook of social cognition* (pp. 129–178). Hillsdale, NJ: Erlbaum.

Greenwald, A. G., Pratkanis, A. R., Leippe, M. R., & Baumgardner, M. H. (1986). Under what conditions does theory obstruct research progress? *Psychological Review,* **93,** 216–229.

Greenwald, A. G., & Ronis, D. L. (1978). Twenty years of cognitive dissonance: Case study of the evolution of a theory. *Psychological Review,* **85,** 53–57.

Greenwald, A. G., & Sakumara, J. S. (1967). Attitude and selective learning: Where are the phenomena of yesteryear? *Journal of Personality and Social Psychology,* **7,** 387–397.

Gustafson, L. (1957). Relationship between ethnic group membership and the retention of selected facts pertaining to American history and culture. *Journal of Educational Sociology,* **31,** 49–56.

Hammond, K. B. (1948). Measuring attitudes by error-choice: An indirect method. *Journal of Abnormal and Social Psychology,* **43,** 38–48.

Hastie, R. (1981). Schematic principles in human memory. In E. T. Higgins, C. P. Herman, & M. P. Zanna (Eds.), *Social cognition* (pp. 39–88). Hillsdale, NJ: Erlbaum.

Hastorf, A. H., & Cantril, H. (1954). They saw a game. *Journal of Abnormal and Social Psychology,* **49,** 129–134.

Hatfield, E., & Sprecher, S. (1986). *Mirror, mirror: The importance of looks in everyday life.* Albany, NY: State University of New York Press.

Heider, F. (1958). *The psychology of interpersonal relations.* New York: Wiley.

Herek, G. M. (1986). The instrumentality of ideologies: Toward a neofunctional theory of attitudes. *Journal of Social Issues,* **42,** 99–114.

Herek, G. M. (1987). Can functions be measured? A new perspective on the functional approach to attitudes. *Social Psychology Quarterly,* **50,** 285–303.

Herman, J. B., & Hulin, C. L. (1972). Studying organizational attitudes from individual and organizational frames of reference. *Organizational Behavior and Human Performance,* **8,** 84–108.

Higgins, E. T., & King, G. (1981). Accessibility of social constructs: Information-processing consequences of individual and contextual variability. In N. Cantor & J. F. Kihlstrom (Eds.), *Personality, cognition, and social interaction* (pp. 69–121). Hillsdale, NJ: Erlbaum.

Hurtado, A., & Gurin, P. (1987). Ethnic identity and bilingualism attitudes. *Hispanic Journal of Behavioral Sciences,* **9,** 1–18.

Hymes, R. W. (1986). Political attitudes as social categories: A new look at selective memory. *Journal of Personality and Social Psychology,* **51,** 233–241.

Iaffaldano, M. T., & Muchinsky, P. M. (1985). Job satisfaction and job performance: A meta-analysis. *Psychological Bulletin,* **97,** 251–273.

Insko, C. A. (1967). *Theories of attitude change.* New York: Appleton-Century-Crofts.

Iyengar, S., & Kinder, D. R. (1987). *News that matters.* Chicago: University of Chicago Press.

Janis, I. L., & Frick, F. (1943). The relationship between attitudes toward conclusions and errors in judging the logical validity of syllogisms. *Journal of Experimental Psychology,* **33,** 73–77.

Jones, E. E. (1964). *Ingratiation.* New York: Appleton-Century-Crofts.

Jones, E. E., & Kohler, R. (1958). The effects of plausibility on the learning of controversial statements. *Journal of Abnormal and Social Psychology,* **53,** 27–33.

Judd, C. M., & Kulik, J. A. (1980). Schematic effects of social attitudes on information processing and recall. *Journal of Personality and Social Psychology,* **38,** 569–578.

Katona, G. (1975). *Psychological economics.* New York: Elsevier.

Katz, D. (1960). The functional approach to the study of attitudes. *Public Opinion Quarterly,* **24,** 163–204.

Katz, D., McClintock, C., & Sarnoff, I. (1957). The measurement of ego defense as related to attitude change. *Journal of Personality,* **25,** 465–474.

Katz, D., & Stotland, E. (1959). A preliminary statement to a theory of attitude structure and change. In S. Kock (Ed.), *Psychology: A study of a science* (Vol. 3, pp. 423–475). New York: McGraw-Hill.

Kelman, H. C. (1961). Processes of opinion change. *Public Opinion Quarterly,* **25,** 57–78.

Kelman, H. C. (1974). Attitudes are alive and well and gainfully employed in the sphere of action. *American Psychologist,* **29,** 310–324.

Kendall, P. L., & Wolf, F. M. (1949). The analysis of deviant cases in communications research. In P. F. Lazarsfeld & F. N. Stanton (Eds.), *Communications research 1948–49* (pp. 152–179). New York: Harper & Brothers.

Kiesler, C. A., Collins, B. E., & Miller, N. (1969). *Attitude change: A critical analysis of theoretical approaches.* New York: Wiley.

Kinder, D. R., & Sears, D. O. (1981). Prejudice and politics: Symbolic racism versus racial threats to the good life. *Journal of Personality and Social Psychology,* **40,** 414–431.

Kothandapani, V. (1971). Validation of feeling, belief, and intention to act as three components of attitude and their contribution to prediction of contraceptive behavior. *Journal of Personality and Social Psychology,* **19,** 321–333.

Krech, D., & Crutchfield, R. S. (1948). *Theories and problems of social psychology.* New York: McGraw-Hill.

Kreman, E. O. (1949). *An attempt to ameliorate hostility towards the Negro through role playing.* Unpublished master's thesis, The Ohio State University, Columbus, OH.

Kubany, A. J. (1953). A validation study of the error-choice technique using attitudes on national health insurance. *Educational and Psychological Measurement,* **13,** 157–163.

LaPiere, R. T. (1934). Attitudes versus action. *Social Forces,* **13,** 230–237.

Lerner, M. J. (1980). *The belief in a just world.* New York: Plenum.

Lefford, A. (1946). The influence of emotional subject matter on logical reasoning. *Journal of General Psychology,* **34,** 127–151.

Levine, J. M., & Murphy, G. (1943). The learning and retention of controversial statements. *Journal of Abnormal and Social Psychology,* **38,** 507–517.

Liben, L. S., & Signorella, M. L. (1980). Gender-related schemata and constructive memory in children. *Child Development*, **51**, 11–18.
Lieberman, S. (1956). The effects of changes in roles on the attitudes of role occupants. *Human Relations*, **9**, 385–402.
Lippmann, W. (1922). *Public Opinion*. New York: Harcourt, Brace & Co.
Lord, C. G., Lepper, M. R., & Mackie, D. (1984). Attitude prototypes as determinants of attitude–behavior consistency. *Journal of Personality and Social Psychology*, **46**, 1254–1266.
Lord, C. G., Lepper, M. R., & Ross, L. (1979). Biased assimilation and attitude polarization: The effects of prior theories on subsequently considered evidence. *Journal of Personality and Social Psychology*, **37**, 2098–2109.
Lott, A. J., & Lott, B. E. (1972). The power of liking: Consequences of interpersonal attitudes derived from a liberalized view of secondary reinforcement. In L. Berkowitz (Ed.), *Advances in experimental social psychology* (Vol. 6, pp. 109–148). New York: Academic Press.
Lott, A. J., Lott, B. E., Reed, T., & Crow, T. (1970). Personality-trait descriptions of differentially liked persons. *Journal of Personality and Social Psychology*, **16**, 284–290.
Lydon, J., Zanna, M. P., & Ross, M. (1988). Bolstering attitudes by autobiographical recall: Attitude persistence and selective memory. *Personality and Social Psychology Bulletin*, **14**, 78–86.
Manis, M. (1961). The interpretation of opinion statements as a function of message ambiguity and recipient attitudes. *Journal of Abnormal and Social Psychology*, **63**, 76–81.
Markus, G. B. (1985). *Stability and change in political attitudes: Observed, recalled, and explained.* Unpublished manuscript. University of Michigan.
McGuire, W. J. (1964). Inducing resistance to persuasion. In L. Berkowitz (Ed.), *Advances in experimental social psychology* (Vol. 1, pp. 191–229). New York: Academic Press.
McGuire, W. J. (1969). The nature of attitudes and attitude change. In G. Lindzey & E. Aronson (Eds.), *The handbook of social psychology* (Vol. 3, pp. 136–314). Reading, MA: Addison-Wesley.
McGuire, W. J. (1989). The structure of individual attitudes and of attitude systems. In A. R. Pratkanis, S. J. Breckler, & A. G. Greenwald (Eds.), *Attitude structure and function* (pp. 37–69). Hillsdale, NJ: Erlbaum.
Morgan, J. J. B. (1945). Attitudes of students toward the Japanese. *Journal of Social Psychology*, **21**, 219–227.
Morgan, J. J. B., & Morton, J. T. (1943). Distorted reasoning as an index of public opinion. *School and Society*, **57**, 333–335.
Morgan, J. J. B., & Morton, J. T. (1944). The distortion of syllogistic reasoning produced by personal convictions. *Journal of Social Psychology*, **20**, 39–59.
Mueller, D. J. (1986). *Measuring social attitudes: A handbook for researchers and practitioners.* New York: Teachers College Press.
Newcomb, T. M., Turner, R. H., & Converse, P. E. (1965). *Social psychology: A study of human interaction*. London: Routledge & Kegan.
Norman, R. (1975). Affective–cognitive consistency, attitudes, conformity, and behavior. *Journal of Personality and Social Psychology*, **32**, 83–91.
Olson, J. M., & Zanna, M. P. (1979). A new look at selective exposure. *Journal of Experimental Social Psychology*, **15**, 1–15.
Osgood, C. E., Suci, G. J., & Tannenbaum, P. H. (1957). *The measurement of meaning*. Urbana, IL: University of Illinois Press.
Ostrom, T. M. (1969). The relationship between the affective, behavioral, and cognitive components of attitude. *Journal of Experimental Social Psychology*, **5**, 12–30.
Ostrom, T. M. (1989). Interdependence of attitude theory and measurement. In A. R. Pratkanis, S. J. Breckler, & A. G. Greenwald (Eds.), *Attitude structure and function* (pp. 11–36). Hillsdale, NJ: Erlbaum.
Parrish, J. A. (1948). *The direct and indirect assessment of attitudes as influenced by propagandized radio transcripts*. Unpublished master's thesis, The Ohio State University, Columbus, OH.

Payne, S. L. (1951). *The art of asking questions.* Princeton, NJ: Princeton University Press.
Petersen, K. K., & Dutton, J. E. (1975). Centrality, extremity, intensity: Neglected variables in research on attitude–behavior consistency. *Social Forces,* **54,** 393–414.
Pettigrew, T. F. (1958). Personality and sociocultural factors and intergroup attitudes: A cross-national comparison. *Journal of Conflict Resolution,* **2,** 29–42.
Pettigrew, T. F. (1959). Regional differences in anti-Negro prejudice. *Journal of Abnormal and Social Psychology,* **59,** 28–36.
Pettigrew, T. F. (1979). The ultimate attribution error: Extending Allport's cognitive analysis of prejudice. *Personality and Social Psychology Bulletin,* **5,** 461–476.
Petty, R. E., Ostrom, T. M., & Brock, T. C. (1981). *Cognitive responses in persuasion.* Hillsdale, NJ: Erlbaum.
Plott, C. R., & Levine, M. E. (1978). A model of agenda influence on committee decisions. *American Economic Review,* **68,** 146–160.
Postman, L., & Murphy, G. (1943). The factor of attitude in associative memory. *Journal of Experimental Psychology,* **33,** 228–238.
Pratkanis, A. R. (1984). *Attitudes and memory: The heuristic and schematic functions of attitudes.* Unpublished dissertation, Ohio State University.
Pratkanis, A. R. (1987). [Unipolar and bipolar attitudes in learning persuasive communications]. Unpublished raw data. Carnegie-Mellon University, Pittsburgh, PA.
Pratkanis, A. R. (1988). The attitude heuristic and selective fact identification. *British Journal of Social Psychology* **27,** 257–263.
Pratkanis, A. R. (1989). The cognitive representation of attitudes. In A. R. Pratkanis, S. J. Breckler, & A. G. Greenwald (Eds.), *Attitude structure and function* (pp. 71–98). Hillsdale, NJ: Erlbaum.
Pratkanis, A. R., & Greenwald, A. G. (1985). What is the self? *Journal for the Theory of Social Behavior,* **15,** 311–329.
Pratkanis, A. R., Syak, P., & Gamble, E. (1987). *The role of technical knowledge in attitudinal learning.* Paper presented at the annual meeting in May of the Midwestern Psychological Association, Chicago, IL.
Pryor, J. B., Reeder, G. D., Vinacco, R., & Russo, T. K. (1987). *The instrumental and symbolic functions of attitudes towards AIDS victims.* Unpublished manuscript, Illinois State University.
Raden, D. (1985). Strength-related attitude dimensions. *Social Psychology Quarterly,* **48,** 312–330.
Ranum, O., & Ranum, P. (Eds.). 1972. *Popular attitudes toward birth control in pre-industrial France and England.* New York: Harper and Row.
Read, S. J., & Rosson, M. B. (1982). Rewriting history: The biasing effects of attitudes on memory. *Social Cognition,* **1,** 385–397.
Regan, D. T., Straus, E., & Fazio, R. (1974). Liking and the attribution process. *Journal of Experimental Social Psychology,* **10,** 385–397.
Ries, A., & Trout, J. (1981). *Positioning: The battle for your mind.* New York: Warner.
Roberts, J. V. (1985). The attitude–memory relationship after 40 years: A meta-analysis of the literature. *Basic and Applied Social Psychology,* **6,** 221–241.
Robinson, J. R., & Shaver, P. R. (1973). *Measures of social psychological attitudes.* Ann Arbor, MI: Institute for Social Research, University of Michigan.
Rogers, R. W. (1983). Cognitive and physiological processes in fear appeals and attitude change: A revised theory of protection motivation. In J. T. Cacioppo & R. E. Petty (Eds.), *Social psychophysiology: A sourcebook* (pp. 153–176). New York: Guilford Press.
Rogers, T. B., Kuiper, N. A., & Kirker, W. S. (1977). Self-reference and the encoding of personal information. *Journal of Personality and Social Psychology,* **35,** 677–688.
Rosenbaum, M. E. (1986). The repulsion hypothesis: On the nondevelopment of relationships. *Journal of Personality and Social Psychology,* **51,** 1156–1166.
Rosenberg, M. J. (1956). Cognitive structure and attitudinal affect. *Journal of Abnormal and Social Psychology,* **53,** 367–372.

Rosenberg, M. J., & Hovland, C. I. (1960). Cognitive, affective, and behavioral components of attitudes. In C. I. Hovland & M. J. Rosenberg (Eds.), *Attitude organization and change* (pp. 1–14). New Haven, CT: Yale University Press.

Ross, L., Greene, D., & House, P. (1977). The "false-consensus effect": An egocentric bias in social perception and attribution process. *Journal of Experimental Social Psychology*, **13**, 279–301.

Ross, M., McFarland, C., Conway, M., & Zanna, M. P. (1983). Reciprocal relation between attitudes and behavior recall: Committing people to newly formed attitudes. *Journal of Personality and Social Psychology*, **45**, 257–267.

Ross, M., McFarland, C., & Fletcher, G. J. O. (1981). The effect of attitude on the recall of personal history. *Journal of Personality and Social Psychology*, **40**, 627–634.

Ross, M., & Shulman, R. F. (1973). Increasing the salience of initial attitudes: Dissonance versus self-perception theory. *Journal of Personality and Social Psychology*, **28**, 138–144.

Saegert, J., & Young, E. A. (1983). Nutrition knowledge and health food consumption. *Nutrition and Behavior*, **1**, 103–113.

Salancik, G. R. (1982). Attitude–behavior consistencies as social logics. In M. P. Zanna, E. T. Higgins, & C. P. Herman (Eds.), *Consistency in social behavior* (pp. 51–73). Hillsdale, NJ: Erlbaum.

Sample, J., & Warland, R. (1973). Attitude and prediction of behavior. *Social Forces*, **51**, 292–304.

Schattschneider, E. E. (1960). *The semi-sovereign people*. New York: Holt, Rinehart & Winston.

Scheier, M. F., & Carver, C. S. (1983). Two sides of the self: One for you and one for me. In J. Suls & A. G. Greenwald (Eds), *Psychological perspectives on the self* (Vol. 2, pp. 123–157). Hillsdale, NJ: Erlbaum.

Schlenker, B. R. (1980). *Impression management*. Monterey, CA: Brooks/Cole.

Schminke, M. (1986). *Power and opportunity in the turnover decision*. Unpublished doctoral dissertation. Carnegie-Mellon University, Pittsburgh, PA.

Schuman, H., & Johnson, M. P. (1976). Attitudes and behavior. In A. Inkeles, J. Coleman, & N. Smelser (Eds.), *Annual review of sociology* (Vol. 2, pp. 161–207). Palo Alto, CA: Annual Reviews.

Scott, W. A. (1969). Attitude measurement. In G. Lindzey & E. Aronson (Eds.), *The handbook of social psychology* (Vol. 2, pp 204–273). Reading, MA: Addison-Wesley.

Scott, W. A., Osgood, D. W., & Peterson, C. (1979). *Cognitive structure: Theory and measurement of individual differences*. Washington, DC: V. H. Winston & Sons.

Sears, D. O., & Kinder, D. R. (1985). Whites' opposition to busing: On conceptualizing and operationalizing group conflict. *Journal of Personality and Social Psychology*, **48**, 1141–1147.

Shaffer, D. R. (1975a). Some effects of consonant and dissonant attitudinal advocacy on initial attitude saliency and attitude change. *Journal of Personality and Social Psychology*, **32**, 160–168.

Shaffer, D. R. (1975b). Another look at the phenomenological equivalence on pre- and post-manipulation attitudes in the forced compliance experiment. *Personality and Social Psychology Bulletin*, **1**, 497–500.

Shavitt, S. (1989). Operationalizing functional theories. In A. R. Pratkanis, S. J. Breckler, & A. G. Greenwald (Eds.), *Attitude structure and function* (pp. 311–337). Hillsdale, NJ: Erlbaum.

Sherif, M., & Hovland, C. I. (1961). *Social judgment*. New Haven, CN: Yale University Press.

Sherman, S. J., Chassin, L., Presson, C. C., & Agostinelli, G. (1984). The role of evaluation and similarity principles in the false consensus effect. *Journal of Personality and Social Psychology*, **47**, 1244–1262.

Sherman, S. J., & Corty, E. (1984). Cognitive heuristics. In R. S. Wyer & T. K. Srull (Eds.), *The handbook of social cognition* (Vol. 1, pp. 189–286). Hillsdale, NJ: Erlbaum.

Sidanius, J. (1988). Political sophistication and political deviance: A structural equation examination of context theory. *Journal of Personality and Social Psychology*, **55**, 37–51.

Smith, D. D. (1968). Cognitive consistency and the perception of others' opinions. *Public Opinion Quarterly,* **32,** 1–15.

Smith, E. E., & Medin, D. L. (1981). *Categories and concepts.* Cambridge, MA: Harvard University Press.

Smith, G. H. (1947). Beliefs in statement labelled fact and rumor. *Journal of Abnormal and Social Psychology,* **42,** 80–90.

Smith, M. B. (1980). Attitudes, values, and selfhood. In M. M. Page (Ed.), *Nebraska symposium on motivation 1979* (pp. 305–350). Lincoln, NB: University of Nebraska Press.

Smith, M. B., Bruner, J. S., & White, R. W. (1956). *Opinions and personality.* New York: Wiley.

Smith, S. S., & Jamieson, B. D. (1972). Effects of attitude and ego-involvement on the learning and retention of controversial material. *Journal of Personality and Social Psychology,* **22,** 303–310.

Sniderman, P. M., & Tetlock, P. E. (1986). Symbolic racism: Problems of motive attribution in political analysis. *Journal of Social Issues,* **42,** 129–150.

Snyder, C. R., & Fromkin, H. L. (1980). *Uniqueness: The human pursuit of difference.* New York: Plenum.

Snyder, M. (1974). The self-monitoring of expressive behavior. *Journal of Personality and Social Psychology,* **30,** 526–537.

Snyder, M. (1982). When believing means doing: Creating links between attitudes and behavior. In M. P. Zanna, E. T. Higgins, & C. P. Herman (Eds.), *Consistency in social behavior* (pp. 105–130). Hillsdale, NJ: Erlbaum.

Snyder, M. (1987). *Public appearances/Private realities: The psychology of self-monitoring.* New York: W. H. Freeman and Co.

Snyder, M., & DeBono, K. G. (1989). Understanding the functions of attitudes: Lessons from personality and social behavior. In A. R. Pratkanis, S. J. Breckler, & A. G. Greenwald (Eds.), *Attitude structure and function* (pp. 339–359). Hillsdale, NJ: Erlbaum.

Spilich, G. J., Vesonder, G. T., Chiesi, H. L., & Voss, J. F. (1979). Text processing of domain-related information for individuals with high and low domain knowledge. *Journal of Verbal Learning and Verbal Behavior,* **18,** 275–290.

Stotland, E., Katz, D., & Patchen, M. (1959). The reduction of prejudice through the arousal of insight. *Journal of Personality,* **27,** 507–531.

Swann, W. B. (1983). Self-verification: Bringing social reality into harmony with the self. In J. Suls & A. G. Greenwald (Eds), *Psychological perspectives on the self* (Vol. 2, pp. 33–66). Hillsdale, NJ: Erlbaum.

Sweeney, P. D., & Gruber, K. L. (1984). Selective exposure: Voter information preferences and the Watergate affair. *Journal of Personality and Social Psychology,* **46,** 1208–1221.

Symonds, P. M. (1927). What is an attitude? *Psychological Bulletin,* **24,** 200–201.

Tajfel, H. (1981). *Human groups and social categories.* Cambridge: Cambridge University Press.

Taylor, S. E., & Crocker, J. (1981). Schematic bases of social information processing. In E. T. Higgins, C. P. Herman, & M. P. Zanna (Eds), *Social cognition* (pp. 89–134). Hillsdale, NJ: Erlbaum.

Tesser, A., & Campbell, J. (1983). Self-definition and self-evaluation maintenance. In J. Suls & A. G. Greenwald (Eds), *Psychological perspectives on the self* (Vol. 2, pp. 1–31). Hillsdale, NJ: Erlbaum.

Tetlock, P. E. (1989). Structure and function in political belief systems. In A. R. Pratkanis, S. J. Breckler, & A. G. Greenwald (Eds.), *Attitude structure and function* (pp. 129–151). Hillsdale, NJ: Erlbaum.

Thistlethwaite, D. (1950). Attitude and structure as factors in the distortion of reasoning. *Journal of Abnormal and Social Psychology,* **45,** 442–458.

Thurstone, L. L. (1931). The measurement of social attitudes. *Journal of Abnormal and Social Psychology,* **26,** 249–269.

Tulving, E. (1983). *Elements of episodic memory*. New York: Oxford Press.
Turner, J. C. (1987). *Rediscovering the social group: A self-categorization theory*. Oxford: Basil Blackwell Ltd.
Tversky, A., & Kahneman, D. (1974). Judgments under uncertainty: Heuristics and biases. *Science*, **185**, 1124–1131.
Vallone, R. P., Ross, L., & Lepper, M. R. (1985). The hostile media phenomenon: Biased perception and perceptions of media bias in coverage of the Beirut massacre. *Journal of Personality and Social Psychology*, **49**, 577–585.
Voss, J. F., Vesonder, G. T., & Spilich, G. J. (980). Text generation and recall by high-knowledge and low-knowledge individuals. *Journal of Verbal Learning and Verbal Behavior*, **19**, 651–667.
Vroom, V. H. (1960). The effects of attitudes on perception of organizational goals, *Human Relations*, **13**, 229–240.
Wallen, R. (1943). Individuals' estimates of group opinion. *Journal of Social Psychology*, **17**, 269–274.
Waly, P., & Cook, S. W. (1965). Effects of attitude on judgment of plausibility. *Journal of Personality and Social Psychology*, **2**, 745–749.
Waly, P., & Cook, S. W. (1966). Attitude as a determinant of learning and memory: A failure to confirm. *Journal of Personality and Social Psychology*, **4**, 280–288.
Watson, W. S., & Hartmann, G. W. (1939). The rigidity of a basic attitudinal frame. *Journal of Abnormal and Social Psychology*, **34**, 314–335.
Weber, R., & Crocker, J. (1983). Cognitive processes in the revision of stereotypic beliefs. *Journal of Personality and Social Psychology*, **45**, 961–977.
Weldon, D. E., & Malpass, R. S. (1981). Effects of attitudinal, cognitive and situational variables on recall of biased communications. *Journal of Personality and Social Psychology*, **40**, 39–52.
Weschler, I. R. (1950a). An investigation of attitudes toward labor and management by means of the error-choice method: I. *Journal of Social Psychology*, **32**, 51–62.
Weschler, I. R. (1950b). A follow-up on the measurement of attitudes toward labor and management by means of the error-choice method: II. *Journal of Social Psychology*, **32**, 63–69.
Wicker, A. W. (1969). Attitudes versus actions: The relationship of verbal and overt behavioral responses to attitude objects. *Journal of Social Issues*, **25**, 41–78.
Wicklund, R. A., & Gollwitzer, P. M. (1982). *Symbolic self-completion*. Hillsdale, NJ: Erlbaum.
Wood, W. (1982). Retrieval of attitude-relevant information from memory: Effects on susceptibility to persuasion and on intrinsic motivation. *Journal of Personality and Social Psychology*, **42**, 798–810.
Wyer, R. S. (1974). *Cognitive organization and change: An information processing approach*. Hillsdale, NJ: Erlbaum.
Wyer, R. S., & Srull, T. K. (1984). *Handbook of social cognition*. Hillsdale, NJ: Erlbaum.
Zajonc, R. B., & Burnstein, E. (1965). The learning of balanced and unbalanced social structures. *Journal of Personality*, **33**, 153–163.
Zanna, M. P., & Fazio, R. H. (1982). The attitude–behavior relation: Moving toward a third generation of research. In M. P. Zanna, E. T. Higgins, & C. P. Herman (Eds.), *Consistency in social behavior* (pp. 283–301). Hillsdale, NJ: Erlbaum.
Zanna, M. P., & Rempel, J. K. (1988). Attitudes: A new look at an old concept. In D. Bar-tal & A. W. Kruglanski (Eds.), *The social psychology of knowledge* (pp. 315–334). New York: Cambridge University Press.

INTROSPECTION, ATTITUDE CHANGE, AND ATTITUDE-BEHAVIOR CONSISTENCY: THE DISRUPTIVE EFFECTS OF EXPLAINING WHY WE FEEL THE WAY WE DO

Timothy D. Wilson
DEPARTMENT OF PSYCHOLOGY
UNIVERSITY OF VIRGINIA
CHARLOTTESVILLE, VIRGINIA 22903

Dana S. Dunn
DEPARTMENT OF PSYCHOLOGY
MORAVIAN COLLEGE
BETHLEHEM, PENNSYLVANIA 18018

Dolores Kraft
Douglas J. Lisle
DEPARTMENT OF PSYCHOLOGY
UNIVERSITY OF VIRGINIA
CHARLOTTESVILLE, VIRGINIA 22903

I. Introduction

The ability to introspect is uniquely human. Other species may have thoughts, feelings, and motives, but as far as we know, they do not occupy their time by reflecting on the nature of these states. Because introspection is a mark of what it is to be human, and one of the highest achievements of evolution, it is tempting to view it as a generally accurate and error-free enterprise. The first experimental psychologists made this assumption by using introspective reports to study thought and perception (e.g., Titchener, 1912). Only the introspections of respondents who had undergone a good deal of training were trusted, but reports from these self-observers were the sole source of data for theories of the mind.

The use of introspective reports by the structuralists failed, due largely to the unreliability of the reports. This failure was widely criticized, and was partly responsible for the rise of behaviorism (e.g., Watson, 1913). With the waning of behaviorism and the rise of cognitive science, the use of verbal reports on attitudes, thoughts, and feelings have again become commonplace, as has a renewed debate over the validity of these reports (Ericsson & Simon, 1980, 1984; Lieberman, 1979; Nisbett & Ross, 1980; Nisbett & Wilson, 1977b; Smith & Miller, 1978; Wilson, 1985b; Wilson & Stone, 1985).

As well as being viewed as error-free, introspection has traditionally been considered to be a beneficial activity. Self-reflection is an integral part of most forms of psychotherapy, and some decision theorists have advocated increased reflection as an aid to better decision making (e.g. Janis & Mann, 1977). Many people deliberately become more reflective when faced with important decisions, and they may even make long lists outlining their thoughts and feelings about each alternative. Indeed, in this harried, hectic world of ours, it seems that we could prevent much mindless behavior by taking the time to be more contemplative about our actions (Langer, 1978).

Recent research in social psychology has corroborated the usefulness of certain kinds of self-reflection, particularly focusing on one's attitudes and beliefs. Snyder and his colleagues, for example, have found that instructing people to think about their attitudes increased the consistency between attitudes and behavior, presumably by increasing the salience of the attitude and its implications for behavior (Snyder & Kendzierski, 1982; Snyder & Swann, 1976; see also Fazio, Chen, McDonel, & Sherman, 1982). Research generated by self-awareness theory (Duval & Wicklund, 1972; Wicklund, 1975) has also demonstrated that self-focused attention increases attitude–behavior correlations (e.g. Pryor, Gibbons, Wicklund, Fazio, & Hood, 1977; Scheier, Buss, & Buss, 1978). Finally, Tesser (1978) has shown that thinking about one's attitudes increases their strength.

Just as assumptions about the accuracy of introspection have been challenged, however, so have claims about its beneficial effects. Theodore Roethke observed that "Self-contemplation is a curse/That makes an old confusion worse" (1975, p. 249). Mario Vargas Llosa, a judge at the Berlin Film Festival, found it less than useful to introspect about why he liked or disliked films in the competition:

> I went to every screening with a fresh pack of notecards that I would dutifully cover with my impressions of each and every film. The result, of course, was that the movies ceased to be fun and turned into problems, a struggle against time, darkness and my own esthetic emotions, which these autopsies confused. I was so worried about evaluating every aspect of every film that my entire system of values went into shock, and I quickly realized that I could no longer easily tell what I liked or didn't or why. (Vargas Llosa, 1986, p. 23)

In this article, we present evidence consistent with the observations of Roethke and Vargas Llosa that introspection can be disruptive. Our focus is on one type of introspection—thinking about the reasons for one's feelings. We attempt to demonstrate that this type of thought can cause people to change their minds about how they feel and lead to a disconnection between their attitudes and their behavior.

When people think about why they feel the way they do, we suggest that they feel compelled to give a "good story" to explain their feelings. The reasons they come up with emphasize cognitions about the attitude object, and the reasons are often incomplete or incorrect. Further, these cognitions often consist of a biased sample of reasons that imply a different attitude than the one subjects previously held. Unaware that their reasons are a biased sample, subjects change their attitude in the direction implied by their reasons. Because the reasons consist of beliefs about the attributes of the attitude object, this new attitude has a heavy cognitive flavor. Behavior often remains affectively driven, however, resulting in reduced attitude–behavior consistency.

We have chosen with care the word "disruptive" to describe the effects of thinking about reasons because this term has fewer pejorative connotations than adjectives like "harmful" or "detrimental." We present evidence suggesting that under some circumstances, people are better off not thinking about why they feel the way they do. Our argument should not be viewed, however, as a general condemnation of introspection. We do not recommend that people studiously avoid introspecting about the reasons behind their feelings. Indeed, a strength of our model is that it specifies when it is best to introspect in this manner and when it is not. Thus, we question the universal applicability of Socrates's oft-quoted statement that "the unexamined life is not worth living" (Loomis, 1942, p. 56) but we stop far short of suggesting that the examined attitude is not worth having.

II. Thinking about Reasons Reduces Attitude–Behavior Consistency

Asking people to think about reasons was initially used as a means of changing inferences about people's internal states in self-attribution experiments (Wilson, Hull, & Johnson, 1981; Wilson & Linville, 1982). Thinking about reasons was found to change people's reported attitudes, traits, and moods. In Wilson *et al.*'s (1981) Study 2, for example, some subjects were rewarded for playing with an interesting puzzle, while others were not. Differences in reported liking for the puzzle were found only among subjects who were asked to think about why they were motivated to play with the puzzle. Among subjects who did think about reasons, an overjustification effect (Lepper & Greene, 1978) occurred: Those who were rewarded reported less interest in the puzzles than did those who were not rewarded. Among subjects who did not think about reasons, no differences in reported liking were found in the reward versus no-reward conditions.

In these early studies, thinking about reasons typically had no effect on behavioral measures of people's attitudes, such as the amount of time Wilson *et al.*'s (1981) subjects played with the puzzles in a free-time period. This led us to believe that thinking about reasons might adversely affect attitude–behavior consistency (the consistency question was equivocal in the early studies because the n's were too small to allow meaningful tests of differences in attitude–behavior correlations). Several subsequent studies were thus performed to test the hypothesis that thinking about reasons reduces attitude–behavior consistency.

In each experiment, subjects either had or were given direct experience with an attitude object, then their verbally reported attitudes and behaviors toward the attitude object were assessed. The attitude reports were always private and anonymous, whereas the behaviors, as far as subjects knew, were not monitored

TABLE I

SUMMARY OF STUDIES EXAMINING THE EFFECTS OF THINKING ABOUT REASONS ON ATTITUDE–BEHAVIOR CONSISTENCY[a]

Study	Attitude object	Setting
1. Wilson et al. (1984), Study 1	Puzzles	Laboratory
2. Wilson et al. (1984), Study 2a	Vacation pictures	Laboratory
3. Wilson et al. (1984), Study 2b	Vacation pictures	Laboratory
4. Wilson et al. (1984), Study 3	Dating partner	Laboratory/field
5. Wilson (1985a)	Vacation pictures	Laboratory
6. Wilson & Dunn (1986b), Study 1	Beverages	Field
7. Wilson & Dunn (1986b), Study 2	Puzzles	Laboratory
8. Wilson, Kraft, & Dunn (1988a), Study 2	Walter Mondale	Laboratory
9. Wilson, Kraft, & Lisle (1988b)	Beverage	Laboratory
10. Millar & Tesser, 1986	Puzzles	Laboratory

[a]Some of the correlations were computed on a within-subjects basis, while others were computed between-subjects. The significance tests have all been converted to z's for ease of comparison.

or observed by the experimenter. Each study included a reasons condition in which subjects were instructed to introspect, before their attitudes were assessed, about why they felt the way they did about the attitude object. In the control conditions, subjects were not given any instructions about how to think about the attitude object. Control subjects typically spent an equivalent amount of time on a filler task, often a questionnaire with which they thought about their reasons for something unrelated to the attitude object, such as their decision about which college to attend.

In Study 1 by Wilson, Dunn, Bybee, Hyman, and Rotondo (1984), for example, subjects familiarized themselves with five different types of paper-and-pencil puzzles, rated how interesting each type of puzzle was, and then were given the opportunity to play with whichever puzzles they chose in a free-time period. Subjects who were randomly assigned to the reasons condition were instructed at the outset to think about *why* they liked or disliked each type of puzzle. After familiarizing themselves with the puzzles, but before rating them, these subjects wrote down the reasons for their preferences, ostensibly to organize their thoughts. Instead of thinking about reasons, subjects in the control condition completed a filler questionnaire unrelated to the puzzles. The main dependent measure was the within-subject correlation between each person's ratings of the five puzzles and the amount of time he or she spent playing with each puzzle type in the free-time period. As predicted, the instructions to think about reasons significantly reduced the average correlation between attitudes and behavior (mean r's = .54 and .17 in the control and the reasons conditions, respectively).

TABLE I (continued)

	Attitude–behavior correlation		Significance of difference	
Behavioral measure	Control condition	Reasons condition	z	p
Playtime with puzzles	.54	.17	2.10	.04
Facial expressions	.57	−.05	1.77	.08
Facial expressions	.53	−.03	2.06	.04
Persistence of relationship	.62	.10	2.32	.02
Facial expressions	.22	−.09	1.56	.12
Beverages purchased	.59	.41	1.61	.11
Playtime with puzzles	.53	.25	2.48	.01
No. of fliers taken	.46	−.43	2.52	.01
Am. of beverage consumed	.76	.22	2.86	.004
Playtime with puzzles	.43	−.02	2.54	.01

Wilson et al.'s (1984) Studies 2 and 3 established the generalizability of the disruptive effects of thinking about reasons. In Study 2 (actually two studies—one plus a replication), subjects viewed a series of color slides of vacation scenes. Subjects in the reasons condition were instructed to think about why they liked or disliked the pictures, while subjects in the control condition were simply told to watch the slides as if they were seeing a movie in a theater. The latter subjects exhibited a fair degree of consistency between their attitudes (reports of how much they enjoyed the slide show) and behavior (ratings made by hidden observers of the pleasantness of subjects' facial expressions during the slide show), $r = .55$. As predicted, subjects who thought about reasons showed no consistency, $r = -.01$ (these correlations are averaged across the two slide show studies).

Wilson et al.'s (1984) third study demonstrated that the effect of thinking about reasons is not limited to mundane attitudes such as those about puzzles or vacation pictures, nor is it limited to behaviors assessed in the laboratory. Students involved in steady dating relationships were either asked to list all the reasons they could think of as to why they felt the way they did about their dating partners, or were not given any instructions to introspect. Once again, thinking about reasons significantly undermined attitude–behavior consistency; in this case, the correlation was between how well-adjusted subjects said their relationship was and whether they were still going out with their dating partner several months later. This correlation was .62 in the control condition, but only .10 among those who thought about reasons.

The effects of thinking about reasons on attitude–behavior consistency has proven to be a very robust phenomenon. Table I lists 10 studies that have found a reduction in consistency due to a reasons analysis. Consistency has been undermined with highly self-relevant attitudes (feelings about one's dating partner) and more mundane attitudes (interest in puzzles), with a variety of behavioral measures, and in both laboratory and field situations. In addition, the effect has been replicated by other researchers (Millar & Tesser, 1986).

We should acknowledge that the list of experiments in Table I is selective. It does not include our initial studies that were not designed to examine differences in correlations (two studies by Wilson et al., 1981, and one by Wilson & Linville, 1982), nor does it include our failures—a few studies that found no differences between reasons and control conditions. The purpose of Table I is to illustrate the range of settings, attitude objects, and measures with which the phenomenon has been demonstrated. To illustrate better the robustness of the effect of thinking about reasons, we averaged across all the known studies in this area, including our initial and all subsequent studies, and our successes as well as our failures. Using the method of adding z's (Mosteller & Bush, 1954; Rosenthal, 1978), it is apparent that thinking about reasons does reduce attitude–behavior consistency, $z = 4.45, p < .00002$.

III. Why Does Thinking about Reasons Reduce Attitude–Behavior Consistency?

A. THINKING ABOUT REASONS IS DISRUPTIVE; FOCUSING ON FEELINGS IS NOT

In attempting to explain why thinking about reasons reduces attitude–behavior consistency, our first step was to compare the effects of thinking about reasons with another type of introspection, to see if the disruptive effects we found were specific to thinking about reasons. As previously mentioned, there is some evidence that it is, in that several researchers have found that another form of introspection—inducing people to focus on their feelings—*increases* attitude–behavior consistency (Carver & Scheier, 1981; Fazio et al., 1982; Snyder, 1982; Wicklund, 1982).

There are several differences between our research and self-focus research, making it unclear whether the different effects that were found were due to the different forms of introspection used or to some other factor. For example, the different types of studies began with different levels of attitude–behavior consistency in the control conditions, in which people did not introspect about their beliefs and feelings. We began with attitudes about which there was high attitude–behavior consistency, and we found that thinking about reasons reduced it. The self-focus studies typically began with low consistency, and they found that focusing on one's feelings increased it. One possibility, then, is that if an attitude is weak or nonsalient (and thus does not predict behavior), then any form of introspection—be it focusing or thinking about reasons—might increase its accessibility, and improve attitude–behavior consistency. If the attitude is already accessible and predictive of behavior, then either type of introspection might call to mind competing thoughts and feelings, reducing the accessibility of the initial attitude and lowering attitude–behavior consistency.

Alternatively, the initial accessibility of the attitude may be less important than the type of introspection that is performed. Though there are surface similarities between focusing on an attitude and thinking about reasons, there are important differences between these types of introspection. The former involves a retrieval of affect, while the latter involves a retrieval not only of how one feels but also of thoughts and beliefs about those attributes of the attitude object that might explain the affective reaction. The question of why these different types of introspection can have different effects is discussed shortly. It is first necessary to establish that the discrepancy between the findings of our studies and self-focus studies is due to differences in the types of introspection people perform and not due to other differences between the studies, such as the initial accessibility of attitudes.

Wilson and Dunn (1986a) performed two studies in which focusing instructions were pitted against instructions to think about reasons, holding constant the initial accessibility of people's attitudes. There were three conditions in each study: One in which people were asked to think about *why* they felt the way they did about the attitude object, one in which they were asked to focus on *how* they felt about the attitude object (using instructions very similar to those used by Snyder & Swann, 1976), and a control condition in which subjects did not receive any introspection instructions. Study 1 was a field experiment, in which the subjects were students waiting in line for dinner at a college cafeteria, and the attitude objects were beverages served at the cafeteria. Study 2 was a replication of Wilson *et al.*'s (1984) puzzle experiment.

The results of the two studies are summarized in Table II. In both studies, thinking about reasons reduced attitude–behavior correlations relative to control

TABLE II
EFFECTS OF ANALYZING REASONS VERSUS FOCUSING ON FEELINGS ON ATTITUDE–BEHAVIOR CONSISTENCY[a]

Study	Condition		
	Focus	Control	Reasons
Wilson & Dunn (1986a), Study 1	.63	.59	.41
Wilson & Dunn (1986a), Study 2	.54	.53	.25

[a]The correlations were computed on a within-subject basis and then averaged after converting them to z-scores. The entries in the table have been converted back to correlation coefficients.

subjects, while focusing led to slight increases in correlations. Averaging across studies, the correlations in the reasons condition were significantly lower than the correlations in both the control and the focus conditions. The correlations in the focusing conditions were not significantly higher than the control correlations, possibly due to the fact that our control subjects had direct experience with the attitude objects (unlike most prior studies that used focusing manipulations), which might have caused people to focus naturally on their attitudes (Fazio & Zanna, 1981).

The important finding for our purposes was that thinking about reasons had a significantly different effect than focusing on feelings, at least when attitude–behavior correlations began at a high level. (It is possible that both thinking about reasons and focusing on feelings would increase correlations that began at a low level.) This finding has also been obtained in an experiment by Millar and Tesser (1986), which is discussed in detail later. Because the initial salience of people's attitude was held constant in the Wilson and Dunn (1986a) and Millar and Tesser (1986) studies, it cannot be argued that either type of introspection (e.g., focusing or analyzing) reduces the accessibility of salient attitudes.

B. THINKING ABOUT REASONS CAN CAUSE ATTITUDE CHANGE

Thus, our first clue is that there is something about thinking about reasons—as opposed to focusing on feelings—that reduces attitude–behavior consistency. Our second clue is that thinking about reasons causes a change in people's reported attitudes.

The lowering of a correlation between attitudes and behavior can occur for at least three reasons: (1) People could change their attitudes but not their behavior, (2) people could change their behavior but not their attitudes, or (3) people could change both their attitudes and their behavior, but in different directions. The available evidence suggests that thinking about reasons reduces attitude–behavior consistency for the first of these reasons: People change their minds about how they feel, but do not change their behavior. The effects of thinking about reasons on attitudes and behavior were examined in 20 studies that have used reasons analysis manipulations: the 10 summarized in Table I; 2 by Wilson et al., 1981; 1 by Wilson and Linville, 1982; 1 plus a replication by Tesser, Leone, and Clary, 1978; and 5 unpublished studies. Analyzing reasons changed self-reported attitudes in 11 of the 20 studies, whereas behavior changed in only 3 of the 20. (By "change," we mean that the average reported attitude in the reasons analysis condition was significantly different than the average reported attitude in the control condition.) This summary is somewhat misleading, because it includes three studies in which the reasons-analysis manipulation failed to affect any dependent variable, including attitude–behavior consistency. When these studies are eliminated from the summary, thinking about reasons changed reported attitudes in 11 of 17, whereas behavior changed in only 3 of 17.

In addition, in four of the studies (Wilson et al.'s [1984] Studies 1 and 3, Wilson & Dunn's [1986a] Studies 1 and 2), we coded the reasons people gave in the reasons conditions according to how positive an attitude toward the stimulus they conveyed. The positivity of subjects' reasons correlated significantly more with their subsequent attitudes than with their behavior. That is, people's reasons were more apt to predict the attitudes they reported than how they behaved.

Oddly, however, in some studies thinking about reasons caused a reduction in attitude–behavior correlation, in the absence of significant differences between reported attitudes or behavior in the reasons versus the control conditions. In the Wilson et al. (1984) couples study, for example, the predicted drop in correlation was found, but there were no differences in the mean reported level of adjustment of the relationship between the reasons analysis and control subjects; nor was there a difference (thankfully!) in the percentage of couples who had broken up several months later. One explanation for this pattern of results is that thinking about reasons caused people to change their minds about how they felt, but that the *direction* of this change differed from subject to subject. In the couples study, for example, thinking about reasons might have caused some subjects to report a more positive attitude toward their relationship and others to report a more negative attitude. Assuming that their behavior was unaffected by the reasons manipulation, this change in attitude would explain the drop in attitude–behavior consistency. The mean level of reported adjustment, however, averaged across subjects, would be indistinguishable from the mean level of reported adjustment in the control condition.

The only way to detect such a pattern of change would be to measure attitudes twice; once before a reasons analysis manipulation and once after. We did this in two recent studies, to test the possibility that thinking about reasons can cause change in a positive direction for some subjects but a negative direction for others. In the first study (Wilson, Kraft, & Dunn, 1988a), during a mass testing session, subjects rated their attitudes toward several possible candidates for President in 1988. Several weeks later, they were seen individually in the laboratory, where they rated their attitudes again toward six of these candidates. Before rating their attitudes in the lab, half of the subjects wrote down their reasons for preferring or not preferring each candidate, while the other half completed a filler questionnaire.

As in Wilson et al.'s (1984) couples study, people did not become uniformly more positive or negative toward the attitude object as a result of thinking about reasons. The average amount of change in a positive or negative direction was minimal, and it was no greater in the reasons than in the control condition. To test the possibility that the reasons manipulation caused change in a positive direction for some subjects but a negative direction for others, we computed the absolute value of the difference between each subject's attitude at Time 1 and

Time 2. As predicted, subjects in the reasons condition showed a greater amount of absolute change than did control subjects (M's = .76 and .56, respectively, $p < .05$).[1]

This finding was replicated in a second study (Wilson & Kraft, 1988) in the context of a phone survey. Subjects were telephoned and asked to give their attitudes toward some social issues. Two sets of issues were used. Some subjects were asked for their attitudes toward the death penalty, a national health insurance, and busing to achieve school integration, while others were asked for their attitudes toward abortion and President Reagan.[2] Half of the subjects were first asked to give reasons for why they felt the way they did about each issue; the other half were not. All subjects had rated their attitudes toward the same six issues several weeks earlier during a mass testing session, allowing us to test the amount of attitude change that occurred in each condition. Once again, people in the reasons-analysis condition did not become uniformly more positive or negative on any of the issues, but they did exhibit significantly more change when the direction of this change is ignored.

IV. Self-Persuasion via Self-Reflection

Thinking about reasons thus appears to reduce attitude–behavior consistency by changing attitudes, while behavior remains unchanged. What remains to be explained is *why* thinking about reasons changes attitudes, particularly why it can cause change in a positive direction for some people and a negative direction for others. In this section, we discuss in detail the mediating factors that we propose as responsible for the disruptive effects of thinking about reasons. Though empirical support has been found for several of our proposed mechanisms, some are speculative. The processes we propose do implicate some important boundary conditions on the effects of thinking about reasons, however, and we have accumulated a good deal of evidence for one of these boundary conditions.

Our argument is as follows: First, when asked to explain their feelings, people feel compelled to come up with a reasonable-sounding answer (reasonable to themselves and to others). Second, when people attempt to explain an attitude, they do not always know exactly why they feel the way they do. Therefore, the

---

[1] These results are only for those subjects who were relatively unknowledgeable about the candidates. As is discussed later, no differences were predicted for subjects who were knowledgeable, and none were found.

[2] These subjects were also asked their attitudes toward U.S. support for the Contras in Nicaragua. As it happened, we did our survey during the Spring of 1987, when there was an increasing amount of media attention to the diversion of funds to the Contras from arms sales to the Iranians. As a result, this was the one issue of the six we used in which control subjects showed a change in attitude between Time 1 and 2. In order to test our hypothesis that thinking about reasons causes attitude change, it is necessary that control subjects not change their attitudes. Therefore, this issue was eliminated from the final analyses.

reasons they come up with sound plausible, but they might not correctly explain their feelings, or they might only be a subset of the actual reasons underlying their attitude. If the reasons people generate are only a subsample of the correct reasons, they may be a *biased* sample, because what is easiest to verbalize or what is available in memory at any given time may well not be representative of the entire set of reasons. Unaware that their reasons are incomplete or incorrect, people view them as representative of their feelings and adopt the attitude they imply. In the following section, we explain this set of hypotheses in greater detail, and we suggest the way in which it accounts for attitude change in both positive and negative directions and for a reduction in attitude–behavior consistency.

A. PEOPLE ARE RARELY AT A LOSS FOR REASONS

When we ask people in our studies to explain the reasons for their attitudes, almost never do people respond by saying, "I don't know." This may, of course, be a function of the experimental context in which subjects find themselves. Subjects may not know why they feel the way they do, but they construct an explanation to avoid looking foolish or inarticulate. It is difficult to assess the extent to which people's readiness to give reasons is driven by social desirability concerns, because the best way to know if they have reasons is to ask them. We believe that there is more to this readiness than social desirability, however. First, to minimize social desirability concerns, we tell subjects in our studies that we want them to think about their reasons in order to organize their thoughts, and we explain that no one will ever read what they write. Second, as is discussed later, we have replicated the effects of thinking about reasons on attitude–behavior consistency in studies in which subjects are never directly asked to introspect, but in which they are placed in conditions that should trigger a reasons analysis.

Even if people's readiness to give reasons in our studies is due to a desire to avoid looking foolish, it is important to note that this desire should be present in many situations other than psychology experiments. It is common in everyday life to be asked to explain one's feelings ("Why did you like the movie?"). Such questions are as likely to raise social desirability concerns in these contexts as they are in psychology experiments.

B. THE REASONS PEOPLE GIVE ARE OFTEN INCOMPLETE OR INCORRECT

People's explanations of their own feelings, judgments, and behaviors are often incorrect (Nisbett & Wilson, 1977b; Wilson & Stone, 1985). While there is some controversy over the extent of this inaccuracy (e.g., Ericsson & Simon,

1980; Smith & Miller, 1978), few authors would dispute the claim that people often have difficulty knowing the exact causes of their affective states. For example, imagine asking people to explain exactly why they love their spouses. It is unlikely that most people could accurately state that Trait A contributes precisely X% to their feelings, while Trait B contributes precisely Y%.

In an upcoming section on boundary conditions, we argue that some types of attitudes are easier to explain than others, and are thus more susceptible to the disruptive effects of thinking about reasons. For the moment, however, we simply suggest that there is a (sometimes substantial) margin of error in people's explanations of their attitudes.

C. EXPLAINING ATTITUDES BRINGS TO MIND A BIASED SAMPLE OF REASONS

We suggest that thinking about reasons often focuses people's attention on a biased sample of attributes of the attitude object that are not representative of a person's prior attitude. When thinking about reasons, people's main goal seems to be to construct a plausible-sounding "good story" to explain their attitudes. In our culture, such good stories use beliefs about the attributes of the attitude object to justify an attitude; for example, "I liked the movie because of the skilled acting and the involving plot," "I dislike this candidate because of his proposed economic programs" (Nisbett & Wilson, 1977b). These are precisely the types of reasons people give in our studies (e.g., Wilson et al., 1984). In terms of the traditional definition of attitudes as consisting of both an affective and a cognitive component, people give explanations that emphasize the cognitive component.

What is interesting about this is that there is ample evidence that attitudes are often caused by factors other than rational cognitions about the attributes of the attitude object. These other influences on attitudes include mere exposure (Zajonc, 1968), classical conditioning (Staats & Staats, 1958; Zanna, Kiesler, & Pilkonis, 1970), operant conditioning (Insko & Cialdini, 1971), halo effects (Nisbett & Wilson, 1977a), and attitudes stemming from people's core values, such as their religious beliefs or the beliefs of their parents (Ellsworth & Ross, 1983; Herek, 1986; Rokeach, 1973; Sears, 1983). When people in our studies are asked to think about reasons, rarely if ever do they mention such factors.

Thus, beliefs are given as explanations of affect rather than affect as explanations of beliefs, even when the latter causal sequence is correct. For example, Nisbett and Wilson (1977a) manipulated how likeable a college instructor was, and they found that how much subjects liked him influenced their ratings of specific characteristics, such as his physical appearance and mannerisms. When people were asked to explain their attitudes, however, they were much more likely to say that they liked him because he was physically attractive than they were to give the correct causal account, which was that they thought he was physically attractive in part because they liked him. There appears to be a strong cultural norm in our society to explain attitudes in terms of cognitions about the attributes of the attitude object. It is much more common to hear people say, "I like the candidate because of his liberal views" than, "I like the candidate because my parents were Democrats."

Other factors may be overrepresented in people's accounts of their reasons because they are easy to verbalize, more available in memory, or flattering. Some factors are more difficult to verbalize or even recognize than others. A subject in Wilson *et al.*'s (1984) couples study, for example, might find the fact that her partner is physically attractive easier to verbalize than the fact that when she is depressed, he fails to be supportive. In addition, when asked to think of reasons, people may focus too much on stimulus characteristics that are available in memory. For example, a couple who had just had a fight might focus on the negative aspects of their relationship when asked to analyze it, when as a whole their relationship is going well.

D. PEOPLE ADOPT THE ATTITUDE IMPLIED BY THEIR BIASED SET OF REASONS

Attitude change appears to occur through a process of self-persuasion, in which people convince themselves that the biased sample of reasons they just generated is representative of their attitude, possibly due to a general insensitivity to sample bias (Hamill, Wilson, & Nisbett, 1980). Thus, the woman who finds it easier to verbalize her dating partner's attractiveness than his lack of responsiveness may convince herself that she likes him more than she thought she did, because all of the reasons that she thinks of are positive. Similarly, the couple who just had a fight might convince themselves that their relationship is on the rocks, since all the attributes that come to their minds are negative.

Perhaps the most controversial part of our self-persuasion hypothesis is the idea that people come up with reasons that do not match their initial affect toward the attitude object. Consistency theories, as well as common sense, suggest that when asked to explain their feelings, people will search for reasons that are consistent with their affect, not inconsistent. We agree that such consistency drives can be operative; it is unlikely that a person who has extremely positive feelings toward his dating partner will come up with all negative reasons when asked to explain his feelings. Indeed, we make no claims that asking people to think about reasons will change love to hate or Democrats to Republicans. We do argue that people often equivocate about their attitudes, and that on many issues, they have a range of positions that are acceptable (C. Sherif, M. Sherif, & Nebergall, 1965; M. Sherif & Hovland, 1961). Our argument is that the attitude people have at any given moment is influenced by the reasons they bring to mind when trying to explain it. Cognitions that were not previously a central part of the attitude may be overemphasized, leading to some attitude change. Thus, while we do not claim to be able to turn love into hate, we do claim that people's attitudes can become somewhat more positive or negative as a result of having to explain their feelings.

We will return to this point when we discuss the boundary conditions on the effects of thinking about reasons, suggesting that people are most apt to bring to mind cognitions that conflict with their initial affect for certain kinds of attitudes. At present, it is important to note that there is evidence for the fact that attitude change can result from having a biased sample of reasons in memory (Salancik, 1974; Seligman, Fazio, & Zanna, 1980). Seligman *et al.*, for example, asked subjects to think of reasons why they liked their dating partner. Unlike in our studies, these researchers attempted to bias the types of reasons subjects considered by the way the question was asked: Subjects answered either the question, "I go out with this person *because I* . . . " or, "I go out with this person *in order to* . . . " The former question elicited reasons that were primarily internal (i.e., having to do with one's own feelings and commitment), while the latter question elicited reasons that were primarily external (i.e., having to do with factors other than love and commitment, such as the desire to impress one's friends).

As predicted, subjects seem not to have realized that they had generated a biased set of reasons, and as a result, they adopted the attitude these reasons implied. That is, subjects who answered the "because I" question reported significantly more love and expressed more of an intention to marry their partners than did subjects who answered the "in order to" question. Salancik (1974) found similar results when the attitude object was a college course that subjects were taking.

Thus, our reasons analysis studies can be considered replications of the Salancik (1974) and Seligman *et al.* (1980) studies, with two major differences. First, we did not direct subjects' reasons in any particular direction. Interestingly, subjects seem to come up with biased samples on their own, resulting in attitude change. Second, we included behavioral measures in our studies, and we found that the new attitudes subjects reported typically did not predict their behavior.

Finally, our argument about self-persuasion via self-reflection may help explain why attitude change is not in a common direction in some of our studies. What is easiest to verbalize or most available in memory might be positive for one person but negative for another. For example, in the Wilson, Kraft, and Dunn (1988a) study on political attitudes, what was easiest to verbalize or most available in memory about a particular political candidate may have been positive for some people ("He came across well on TV last week") but negative for others ("He sleeps around"). Even if the same event is available in memory for all subjects, different subjects might interpret it quite differently, leading to attitude change in opposite directions (e.g., "He showed courage and leadership in his decision to sell arms to the Iranians," vs. "He sure bungled that one").

V. How and When Does Thinking about Reasons Influence Behavior?

To recap our argument to this point, we suggest that thinking about reasons brings to mind a biased sample of cognitions about the attitude object, producing attitude change in the direction of this biased sample. As reviewed earlier, this change seems to be expressed on self-report measures of attitudes but not on behavioral measures, resulting in reduced attitude–behavior consistency. In this section, we explain why thinking about reasons often does not influence behavior, and we outline the conditions under which it will.

One possibility invokes Campbell's (1963) differential threshold argument. Campbell argued that different types of attitudinal responses have different thresholds; that is, some require more effort or motivation to perform. From lowest to highest threshold, he argued, are (1) autonomic–muscular reactions (e.g., galvanic skin response—GSR), (2) verbal reports about feelings toward the stimulus, (3) verbal reports about one's behavioral intentions, and (4) overt, locomotor behavior. Some attitudes may be sufficiently strong to influence verbal reports, but not strong enough to be expressed behaviorally. Campbell (1963) reinterpreted some classic demonstrations of attitude–behavior inconsistency, such as LaPiere's (1934), in terms of his differential threshold argument. Rather than being signs of logical inconsistency, he argued, some studies simply show that an attitude is weak, and thus it exceeds the threshold for verbal reports but not for behavior.

It is possible that the attitude change in our studies is another example of this phenomenon. Thinking about reasons may only cause weak, momentary attitude change, which is sufficient to change people's attitude reports but is insufficient to budge them behaviorally. Such a view would be relatively trivial, demonstrating that we succeeded only in moving people a bit on 7-point attitude scales, but not on more consequential, behavioral dependent measures. There is reason to believe, however, that the differential threshold view cannot account fully for the effects of thinking about reasons on attitude–behavior consistency. When people have thought about reasons, the cognitive component of the attitude is at the forefront of their minds. If they then have the opportunity to behave toward the attitude object, we argue that this cognitive component *will* drive their behavior, at least initially. Why, then, have we found so much attitude–behavior inconsistency among people who have thought about reasons?

Our argument rests on our earlier suggestion that thinking about reasons turns attitudes into responses that are based primarily on cognitions about the attitude object. As argued by Millar and Tesser (1986), behavior as well as attitudes can be the result of either the affective or the cognitive component of an attitude. As seen shortly, Millar and Tesser (1986) found that thinking about reasons influenced behavior as well as attitudes, as long as the behavior was a function of the cognitions made salient by the reasons analysis manipulation. We agree that cognitively based behaviors can be influenced by thinking about reasons.

We suggest, however, that behavior that immediately follows a reasons analysis is apt to be cognitively driven, but that this behavior becomes more affectively driven over time. When people think about reasons, the cognitions that become salient may determine people's attitude reports and their *initial* behavior. As they continue to interact with the attitude object, however, their basic affective reaction to it is more likely to reassert itself, thereby driving their behavior in a way that is likely to be inconsistent with their previously stated, cognitively based attitude.

An example of this process can be found in our studies that used Fazio's puzzle paradigm. In these studies, subjects think about why they feel the way they do about five different types of puzzles. As a result of this reasons analysis, they use different criteria to evaluate the puzzles, and indeed end up evaluating them differently than do people in control conditions who do not think about reasons (Wilson & Dunn, 1986a; Wilson et al., 1984). After evaluating the puzzles subjects are left alone during a free-time period, where they can play with any of the puzzles they choose.

We originally reported that subjects in the reasons-analysis conditions choose to play with the same puzzles as subjects in the control conditions, and as a result, they exhibited less consistency between their evaluations and their behavior (Wilson & Dunn, 1986a; Wilson et al., 1984; see also Millar & Tesser, 1986). This is true if one averages subjects' behavior toward the puzzles during the entire 15-minute free-time period. According to our new hypothesis about the sequence of behavior, however, we might expect that something like the following occurred: Subjects who thought about reasons brought to mind thoughts about the objective attributes of the puzzles, and they used these thoughts to evaluate them. When faced with the choice of which puzzles to play with in the free-time period, their *initial choice* was likely to be determined by these salient cognitions about the puzzles, and thus be consistent with their evaluations. As they played with these puzzles, however, their affect had a chance to reassert itself, and they discovered that they did not like these puzzles all that much after all (e.g., "This puzzle is challenging and is cleverly constructed, but you know, I think I really prefer some of the other ones"). Thus, their later choices of puzzles were more affectively driven, and thus inconsistent with their previous evaluations.

To test this possibility, we reanalyzed the data from the Wilson et al. (1984) and Wilson and Dunn (1986a) puzzle studies. First, we looked at subjects' first choice of which puzzle to work on in the free-time period. As seen in Table III, subjects in the reasons conditions did tend to make different choices as to which puzzle to play with first than did subjects in their corresponding control conditions. This different pattern of first choices was not significant in the Wilson et al. (1984) study, which had a relatively small sample size, but it was significant in the Wilson and Dunn (1986a) study, which had a larger sample size. Combining across studies, using the method of adding z's (Rosenthal, 1978), the difference was significant ($z = 2.25$, $p = .02$).

The differences reported in Table III do not indicate whether subjects' first choices of puzzles corresponded to their liking ratings, as we have predicted. To test this hypothesis, we examined subjects' reported liking for the first puzzle they chose to play with in the free-time period. If we are right—that subjects initially played with the puzzles they thought were the most interesting in both the control and the reasons conditions—there should be no difference in reported liking for the first puzzle they played with. This hypothesis was confirmed. The mean liking ratings of the first puzzles subjects played with, in the reasons versus the control conditions, was 5.46 versus 4.69 in the Wilson *et. al* (1984) study and 5.67 versus 5.72 in the Wilson and Dunn (1986a) study (t's < 1.17).

We also expect that as subjects in the reasons condition played with the puzzles, their affective reactions reasserted themselves, causing them to end up playing with ones they had not rated very highly to begin with (accounting for the low attitude–behavior correlations we found in this condition). To test this possibility, we examined the ratings subjects gave to the puzzles they played with after their first choice, with the prediction that these ratings would be lower in the reasons than in the control conditions. This prediction was confirmed. The mean liking for the puzzles that subjects played with after their first choice, in the reasons versus the control conditions, were 3.28 versus 4.99 in the Wilson *et al.* (1984) study and 4.28 versus 4.50 in the Wilson & Dunn (1986a) study. Though the difference between conditions was significant only in the Wilson *et al.* (1984) study ($t(21) = 2.65$, $p < .02$), the overall difference combined across studies is significant ($z = 2.48$, $p < .02$).

Thus, we have found evidence for behavioral change as a result of thinking about reasons, suggesting that Campbell's (1963) differential threshold view is not a satisfactory account of our results. An advantage of our hypothesis concerning initial versus later behavior change is that it specifies when behavior change should result from thinking about reasons and when it should not. If subjects have a relatively long period of time in which to interact with the attitude

TABLE III
PERCENTAGE OF PUZZLES PLAYED WITH FIRST, BY CONDITION

Puzzle	Wilson *et al.* (1984)		Wilson & Dunn (1986a)	
	Control ($n = 13$)	Reasons ($n = 13$)	Control ($n = 47$)	Reasons ($n = 49$)
A	54	54	30	35
B	0	15	4	22
C	31	8	49	31
D	15	15	15	6
E	0	8	2	6

object, as in the puzzle studies and the Wilson et al. (1984) couples study (in which the behavioral measure was whether subjects had broken up several months later), then people's affective response toward the stimulus has a chance to reassert itself, resulting in attitude–behavior inconsistency. If the behavioral measure is a short-term one, such as subjects' initial choice between different attitude objects, this choice might well be driven by the new, cognitively based attitude, resulting in attitude–behavior consistency.

Such a result was found in a recent study by Wilson, Lisle, and Schooler (1988c). Subjects in this study evaluated a set of five posters of the sort commonly found in college students' rooms (the attitude measure), and they were allowed to choose one to take home (the behavioral measure). Because the behavioral measure was not a long-term one, in which affect had a chance to reassert itself, we predicted that thinking about reasons would influence both subjects' liking ratings and their choice of which poster to keep. This prediction was confirmed. Interestingly, as is discussed in detail in a later section, subjects in the reasons condition came to regret their choice of poster more after taking it home. As our time-course hypothesis suggests, subjects' affect toward the posters had more of a chance to reassert itself once they got the poster home, thus they were more apt to regret a choice that had been cognitively determined.

This hypothesis can be used to reinterpret some of the results of our earlier studies summarized in Table I. As already seen, one reason the Fazio puzzle paradigm has been so successful in demonstrating that thinking about reasons reduces attitude–behavior consistency is that the behavioral measure was a long-term one. Further, it may explain why the results of Study 1 by Wilson and Dunn (1986a) were weak. In this study, subjects waiting in line at a college dining hall were asked to think about why they liked or disliked several beverages, and the behavioral measure was which beverages they purchased with their dinners. Because the behavioral measure was a short-term one, we might expect that it would be influenced by any attitude change that occurred as a result of thinking about reasons. As predicted, attitude–behavior consistency was relatively high in the reasons conditions of this study.[3]

---

[3]Some of the other studies in Table I are difficult to classify in terms of our hypothesis about the time frame of the behavior. Three studies used facial expressions while watching a slide show as the behavioral measure, which seem not to have changed as a result of thinking about reasons. Unlike the other studies, however, the behavior measure was assessed before the self-report measure, preventing a test of the hypothesis that behavior was initially consistent with self-reports but became less so as time passed. Another study reported in Table I seems inconsistent with the time-frame hypothesis: Study 2 by Wilson, Kraft, and Dunn (1988a). Here, the behavioral measure was the number of fliers subjects took for the 1984 Presidential candidates. This appears to be a short-term behavioral measure, yet the number of fliers subjects took in the reasons condition was not consistent with their reported attitude. The reason for this may be due to Millar and Tesser's (1986) distinction between behaviors that are affectively versus cognitively driven. Some behaviors, such as seeing a picture of Mondale and Ferraro and having to commit oneself to posting these pictures around the campus, may elicit an immediate affective response that is inconsistent with one's cognitions about the attitude object.

To summarize, we suggest that when people are asked to think about reasons, they feel compelled to give a good story as an explanation of their feelings. These reasons are often a biased sample of cognitions about the attitude object, which imply a different attitude than subjects held previously. Unaware that their reasons are a biased sample, subjects change their attitude in the direction implied by their reasons. The attitude change that occurs is not necessarily in a uniformly positive or negative direction. Wilson, Kraft, and Dunn (1988) and Wilson and Kraft (1988) found that some subjects changed in a positive direction, others in a negative direction as a result of thinking about reasons. The change that occurs seems to direct subjects' initial behavior, as indicated by our reanalysis of the Wilson et al. (1984) and Wilson and Dunn (1986a) puzzle studies. Over time, however, behavior seems to snap back, possibly because subjects' affective response toward the stimulus has a chance to reassert itself.

One advantage of this account is that it implies several boundary conditions on the disruptive effects of thinking about reasons. Before discussing these, however, it is important to discuss an alternative explanation of the effects of thinking about reasons, which Millar and Tesser (1986) have offered.

MILLAR AND TESSER'S (1986) MISMATCH HYPOTHESIS

Millar and Tesser (1986) have recently advanced a somewhat different account of why thinking about reasons reduces attitude–behavior consistency. Consistent with our arguments, they suggest that analyzing reasons causes people to think about attributes of the attitude object, which increases the salience of the cognitive component of the attitude. Also similar to our position, they argue that people's attitude is a function of those thoughts or feelings about the attitude object that are salient in memory at any given time. Their focus, however, is on the traditional breakdown of attitudes into affective and cognitive components. Rather than saying that attitude change results from bringing to mind a biased sample of cognitions, they suggest that thinking about reasons increases the salience of the cognitive component of an attitude at the expense of the affective component.

More specifically, Millar and Tesser (1986) suggest that (1) the attitudes people report depend on which attitude component is salient in memory, because the affective and cognitive components of attitudes often conflict; (2) thinking about reasons increases the salience of the cognitive component, such that attitude reports become cognitively driven; (3) behavior is often affectively driven (as was the case, they argue, in previous reasons analysis studies); (4) when people think about reasons, attitude–behavior consistency will thus suffer, because attitude reports become a function of the cognitive component of attitudes, whereas behavior is a function of the affective component. This reasoning explains why

Wilson and Dunn (1986a) found different effects of analyzing reasons versus focusing on affect. The attitude reports of people who thought about reasons became cognitively driven, whereas their behavior remained affectively driven, resulting in low attitude–behavior correlations. When people focused on their affect, the affective component of their attitude determined their attitude reports, which thus matched their affectively driven behavior.

The mismatch hypothesis received additional support in an experiment by Millar and Tesser (1986). As in the Wilson and Dunn (1986a) study, some subjects thought about why they liked or disliked a set of puzzles, while others focused on how they felt about the puzzles, without justifying their feelings. The reasons-analysis manipulation increased the salience of the cognitive component of subjects' attitudes, reasoned Millar and Tesser (1986), while the affective-focus manipulation increased the salience of the affective component. In addition, Millar and Tesser manipulated whether subjects' behavior toward the puzzles was cognitively or affectively driven. In the affective-behavior condition, subjects were allowed to work on any of the puzzles they chose during a free-play period (as in Wilson and Dunn's study), with the assumption that their choice of puzzles was motivated chiefly by a desire to play with the ones they found most pleasing. In the cognitive-behavior condition, subjects were told that the puzzles were designed to increase their analytic ability, and that they would receive a test of analytic ability immediately after the free-time period. The assumption here was that the subjects' choice of puzzles would be a function of their beliefs about which puzzles would best prepare them for the analytic abilities test, and thus would be more cognitively driven.

Millar and Tesser's (1986) 2×2 design created two cells in which the components driving attitudes and behavior matched (one in which both attitudes and behavior were cognitively driven, and one in which both attitudes and behavior were affectively driven), and two mismatch cells, in which attitudes and behavior were each driven by different components. The main dependent measure was the mean within-subject correlation between each subject's ratings of the puzzles and the amount of time he or she spent playing with each one in the free-time period. As predicted, and as seen in Fig. 1, attitude–behavior consistency was high in the matching cells and low in the mismatch cells. It thus appears that another way in which thinking about reasons lowers attitude–behavior consistency is that people phrase their attitude reports in cognitive terms, while (often, at least) their behavior is a function of their affect.

We view the Millar and Tesser position and ours as complementary, with empirical evidence supporting both. The chief difference is as follows: While both positions argue that attitudes become more cognitively based as a result of thinking about reasons, we suggest that this is because people bring to mind a biased sample of cognitions, while Millar and Tesser (1986) argue that a preexisting cognitive component is emphasized at the expense of a conflicting affective component. This is potentially an important distinction, because it implies different boundary conditions on the effects of thinking about reasons. According to our position, thinking about reasons will be particularly disruptive when an attitude is primarily affective in nature, with few supporting cognitions. Under these conditions, we suggest, people are not used to phrasing their attitude in cognitive terms, and forcing them to do so is most likely to be disruptive—that is, they are most likely to generate a set of cognitions that is a biased sample of the factors underlying their attitudes. Evidence for this hypothesis is presented shortly. According to the Millar and Tesser position, thinking about reasons should be most disruptive when people initially have conflicting affective and cognitive components to their attitudes. A subsequent set of studies by Millar and Tesser (1988) found support for this hypothesis. Thus, our position and Millar and Tesser's appear to be nonoverlapping and noncontradictory, with empirical support for both.

A second difference between our position and Millar and Tesser's (1986) concerns the conditions under which the cognitively based attitude that results from thinking about reasons will conflict with behavior. Millar and Tesser (1986) suggest that behaviors that are affectively determined will conflict with this new attitude, whereas behaviors that are cognitively driven will not. We argue that, in addition to the nature of the behavior (whether it is affectively or cognitively determined), one must consider its time course. People's initial behavioral response, we suggest, will often follow from their new, cognitively based attitude, whereas over time, behavior becomes more affectively driven.

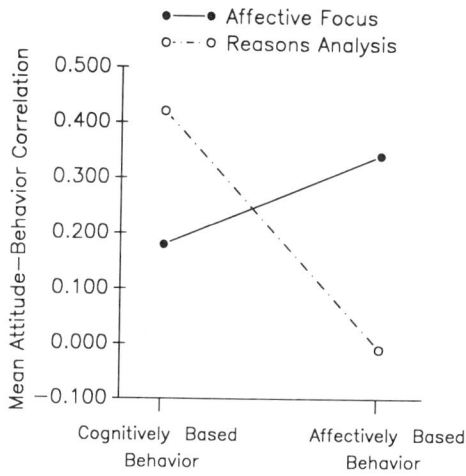

Fig. 1. Effects on attitude–behavior consistency of (1) analyzing reasons versus focusing on affect and (2) cognitively versus affectively mediated behavior. Adapted from Millar and Tesser with permission. Copyright 1986 by American Psychological Association.

VI. Boundary Conditions on the Effects of Thinking about Reasons

Any good explanation of an effect specifies the boundary conditions that limit it. Several such boundary conditions are implied by our explanation of why thinking about reasons can change attitudes and lower attitude–behavior consistency, and there is empirical evidence for some of these delimiting conditions.

A. AFFECTIVELY VERSUS COGNITIVELY BASED ATTITUDES

We suggested earlier that some types of attitudes may be more susceptible to the effects of thinking about reasons than others. Any attitude that people find easy to explain, so that they do not come up with a biased set of cognitions, should be relatively unaffected by thinking about reasons. An example of such an attitude, we suggest, is one that is based on a relatively small number of well-thought-out cognitions about the attitude object, such that people can easily call upon these cognitions when asked to explain the attitude. Other kinds of attitudes are more difficult to explain. For example, some attitudes have a strong, amorphous affective component with few supporting cognitions, and it is difficult to know where this affect came from. Attempts to explain this type of attitude may be particularly apt to lead to a biased set of reasons. Most of the attitudes examined in our studies seem to be of this latter type, such as people's feelings about their dating partner or their liking for a set of vacation pictures.

This distinction is similar to one made by Zajonc (1980), Zajonc and Markus (1982), and Zanna and Rempel (in press) concerning the affective and cognitive underpinnings of attitudes. These authors argue, in contrast to the traditional attitude theory, that some attitudes are primarily affectively based, in that they have strong affective components without a large number of beliefs supporting the attitude. As discussed earlier, attitudes can be affective because they are the result of minimal cognitive processing, such as mere exposure, classical conditioning, or operant conditioning, or because they stem from people's core values such as their moral or religious beliefs. We refer to any attitude that is grounded by strong emotions rather than a logical analysis of the evidence as "affectively based."

Other attitudes conform more to the traditional definition, in that they have strong affective and cognitive components. (Whether an attitude can consist of only a cognitive component—with little or no accompanying affect—is an interesting question that is not considered here.) Many of these, which we refer to as "cognitively based attitudes," result from a careful analysis of the relevant facts. For example, people might evaluate a political candidate by compiling and evaluating information about the candidate's stance on the issues. Such attitudes are typically accompanied by affect, but the affect follows from a careful analysis of the attributes of the attitude object, and it is likely to be subordinate to the cognitive component of the attitude.

Earlier, we argued that thinking about reasons is disruptive because people construct an explanation of their feelings, and this explanation often implies a somewhat different evaluation of the attitude object than they previously held. This process would only be expected to occur, however, if people were not fully aware of what had caused their affect, forcing them to construct the most plausible explanation. If people knew why they felt the way they did, then the reasons they brought to mind would be the correct ones, and the reasons would be consistent with their affect. We suggest that people with cognitively based attitudes can more easily recall the correct reasons for their attitudes because they are more likely to have worked out carefully how they feel by deliberating about the attributes of the attitude object. Thus, they should be less susceptible to the disruptive effects of analyzing reasons.

People are less likely to know the determinants of their affective attitudes. Important determinants such as mere exposure are apt to be overlooked because they are implausible; that is, they are not part of their implicit theories about what causes people to feel the way they do (Nisbett & Wilson, 1977b). For example, few people recognize the extent to which their political preferences result from the party identification of their parents (Campbell, Converse, Miller, & Stokes, 1960; Hyman, 1959). Even if people originally knew the determinants of their feelings, as time passes, it is often the affect that remains in memory while its causes are forgotten (Lingle & Ostrom, 1981; Zajonc, 1980). Further, if the processes underlying an affective reaction are minimal or inaccessible (as in the mere exposure effect), it is unlikely that people could easily verbalize the nature of these processes. Finally, attitude objects are often complex and multidimensional, and it is simply too difficult to sort out from among the many possibilities the extent to which different attributes influence our feelings, as in our earlier example of people's inability to know exactly why they feel the way they do about their spouses.

Thus, people are more apt to be misled when trying to explain affectively based attitudes, increasing the likelihood that they will come up with a biased set of reasons. Further, because affective attitudes are dominated by a strong, amorphous affective component, the very act of trying to translate this affect into a logical-sounding verbal code may be disruptive. Attempting to recast such attitudes in cognitive terms probably contributes to the distortions and disruptions that occur. In short, we argue that thinking about reasons can turn a gut reaction into an opinion based on a biased sample of cognitions about the attitude object. When people already have an informed opinion (i.e., a cognitively based attitude that is already phrased in a logical, verbal code), having to verbalize reasons should be easier and less disruptive.

We do not mean to argue that people are unaware of the causes of all of their affectively based attitudes and fully aware of the causes of all of their cognitively based attitudes. Sometimes people have an affective reaction resulting from a single, powerful source, and this source is easy to identify. Zanna and Rempel (in press), for example, present the case of the attitude toward drunk driving of a parent whose child was killed by an intoxicated driver. The parent's attitude is likely to be based on an intense emotional reaction, not on an appraisal of facts and statistics about accident rates of intoxicated drivers; nonetheless, the parent will know full well the reason for the attitude. Conversely, there are undoubtedly cognitively based attitudes that people have difficulty explaining, because they consist of so many complex beliefs that it is difficult to know how much each one contributes to the attitude. Our claim is that people are more likely to know why they feel the way they do if their attitude is based on a careful appraisal of the attributes of the attitude object than if it is not; that is, the dimension of affectively versus cognitively based attitudes is correlated with people's ability to explain them accurately, though not perfectly so.

A thorny issue with regard to the distinction between affectively and cognitively based attitudes is whether they differ only in terms of the nature of their underpinnings, or whether they also differ in terms of their strength. Are affectively based attitudes typically weaker or stronger than cognitively based ones? Are they more or less accessible or available in memory? These are important questions, because how strong or accessible an attitude is may also determine its susceptibility to disruption by thinking about reasons.

B. WEAK VERSUS STRONG ATTITUDES?

Just because an attitude is not based on a set of well-thought-out cognitions does not mean that it is affectively based. There are many issues about which people care little and do not have well-articulated attitudes. This type of response is unlikely to have strong cognitions or strong affect, and it is best characterized as a nonattitude (Converse, 1970; Hovland, 1959) or a weak attitude with low accessibility (Fazio, 1986; Fazio & Zanna, 1981). Thus, there are at least three types of attitudes: (1) those that are strongly held and based on a set of well-thought-out cognitions about the attitude object (cognitively based attitudes), (2) those that are strong but grounded primarily on an affective reaction to the stimulus (affectively based attitudes), and (3) those that are weak and inaccessible, with few supporting cognitions or affective bonds (nonattitudes).

It is possible that attitudes that are weakly held are also highly susceptible to a reasons-analysis manipulation. This argument is based on Fazio's model of attitude accessibility (Fazio, 1986). Fazio distinguishes between attitudes that are based on direct experience with the attitude object (and thus are strong and accessible) versus attitudes that are not based on direct experience (and thus are weak and inaccessible). The latter type of attitude has been demonstrated (1) to be less likely to predict behavior, (2) to be held with less confidence, and (3) to take longer to be expressed than strong attitudes (Fazio, 1986; Fazio & Zanna, 1981). Generalizing from Fazio's work, weak attitudes may also be more susceptible to alteration by attitude-change techniques, including our reasons-analysis manipulation.

It may well be the case that weak attitudes are more susceptible to change. Our studies suggest, however, that our effects are not *limited* to weak attitudes; the effects can occur with relatively strong attitudes. In virtually all of our studies, we began with attitudes that predicted behavior well (and thus were strong, according to the Fazio model), and we found that thinking about reasons undermined attitude–behavior consistency. Indeed, many of these studies used a paradigm developed by Fazio to create strong attitudes, in which subjects were given direct experience with a set of puzzles. Thinking about reasons has been found to change people's attitudes toward these puzzles and to reduce the consistency between these new attitudes and their subsequent behavior, even though the attitudes were strong at the outset.

Instead of weak attitudes being those that are most susceptible to the disruptive effects of thinking about reasons, we suggest that it is those that are affectively based. It is not a simple matter, however, to operationalize the difference between an attitude that is weak versus one that is strong but affectively based. Measures have been developed to assess separately the affective and cognitive components of attitudes (e.g., Rosenberg, 1956, 1960), but responses on these measures might not reflect the extent to which an attitude is *based* on one or the other component. In principle, people could know a good deal about the issues in a political campaign, for example, but their attitudes could still be based on intense emotional reactions to the candidates rather than on their beliefs about the issues.

Indirect evidence for the existence of such attitudes does exist, chiefly from studies that have shown that it is the affective component of an attitude that correlates the best with people's behavior and preferences (Abelson, Kinder, Peters, & Fiske, 1982; Seligman *et al.*, 1979). It is not an easy matter to demonstrate, however, that a particular attitude is affectively based, and it is particularly difficult to demonstrate that two attitudes are equal in strength but differ in the extent to which their underpinnings are affective.

We return to a discussion of this difficulty after describing several tests of the hypothesis that thinking about reasons will only influence attitudes that are affectively based. Our first four tests divided subjects on the basis of their knowledge about or experience with the attitude object. We assumed that people who were unknowledgeable or inexperienced would be more likely to have affectively based attitudes. There is an obvious danger to operationalizing affectively versus cognitively based attitudes by dividing people on the basis of their experience with the attitude object, because people's attitudes may differ in many respects other than their affective basis, such as their strength or accessibility. Most of the attitude objects we chose, however, were of sufficient importance and salience to people that it seemed unlikely that people would have weak attitudes. Some evidence for this assumption is presented, as is a fifth study that manipulated whether attitudes were affectively or cognitively based.

C. EMPIRICAL TESTS

1. The Couples Study Revisited

People who have a lot of experience with an attitude object are more likely to have opinions that are based on a careful appraisal of the attributes of the attitude object, thus any introspection that brings these attributes to mind should have little impact. People who are inexperienced should be more likely to have affectively based attitudes that are the result of quick appraisals or such factors as classical conditioning or mere exposure. These people probably are less knowledgeable about why they feel the way they do, and they are more apt to be misled by being asked to give reasons.

For example, the participants in the Wilson et al. (1984) couples study differed in the amount of time they had been dating. In a reanalysis of this study, we performed a median split on the length of the couple's relationship (median = 5.1 months), with the assumption that those who had been dating for a relatively short time would be more likely to have affectively based attitudes. It is possible that instead they had weak attitudes. Anyone who has observed an 18-year-old in love would probably agree, however, that these attitudes can be very strong, but they may consist of relatively few cognitions. The couples who had been dating for a relatively long time were assumed to have attitudes that were more cognitively based, in the sense that they had had more opportunity to develop a set of cognitions about their partners, and they could more easily verbalize these thoughts.

We predicted that our reanalysis of the Wilson et al. (1984) study would show that thinking about reasons reduced attitude–behavior consistency only for those couples who had been dating for a relatively short period of time. As seen in Table IV, this prediction was confirmed. An a priori contrast was performed on

TABLE IV
Effects of Analyzing Reasons and Length of Dating Relationship on Attitude–Behavior Consistency[a]

	Newer relationships		Longer relationships	
	Control	Reasons	Control	Reasons
Individuals as the unit of analysis	.57	−.19	.57	.56
Couples as the unit of analysis	.62	−.21	.64	.63

[a] Data from Wilson et al. (1984, Study 3). Couples were classified as having "newer" or "longer" relationships on the basis of a median split on the length of time they had been dating (median = 5.1 months).

the correlations in Table IV that assigned a weight of -3 to the reasons–new relationship group and a weight of 1 to the other three groups. This contrast was significant when individuals were the unit of analysis and marginally significant when couples were the unit of analysis (z's = 2.55 and 1.74, p's = .01 and .08, respectively).

2. Attitudes toward Walter Mondale

Wilson, Kraft, and Dunn (1988a) conducted a series of additional tests of our hypothesis that thinking about reasons is most apt to influence affectively based attitudes. In one study, subjects were divided on the basis of their knowledge about the candidates in the 1984 Presidential election. Half of the subjects in each group were asked to think about why they felt the way they did about Walter Mondale, while the others completed a filler questionnaire. The chief dependent measure was attitude–behavior consistency (the behavioral measure of subjects' attitude was the number of Mondale–Ferraro fliers they were willing to take to post around the campus). Thinking about reasons again decreased consistency for unknowledgeable subjects but not for knowledgeable ones (see the first row of Table V). A planned comparison that assigned a weight of -3 to the reasons–unknowledgeable cell and weights of 1 to the other three cells was significant ($z = 3.41, p = .001$).

3. Attitudes toward the 1988 Presidential Candidates

The two studies just reviewed showed that knowledge moderates the effects of thinking about reasons on attitude–behavior consistency. The next two studies tested the hypothesis that knowledge also moderates the effects of thinking about reasons on attitude change. As reviewed earlier, Wilson, Kraft, and Dunn (1988a) performed a study in which attitudes toward six of the candidates for President

TABLE V
EFFECTS OF ANALYZING REASONS AND KNOWLEDGE ON ATTITUDE–BEHAVIOR CONSISTENCY AND ATTITUDE CHANGE[a]

	Condition			
	Unknowledgeable		Knowledgeable	
Correlation between:	Control	Reasons	Control	Reasons
Attitude–behavior consistency	.46	$-.43$	.66	.53
Absolute value of change in attitude	.55	.76	.72	.60

[a]Entries in the first row are from Wilson, Kraft, and Dunn (1988a, Study 1); entries in the second row are from Wilson, Kraft, and Dunn (1988a, Study 2).

in 1988 were measured twice, once in a mass testing session and once in the laboratory. In our earlier discussion of this study, we reported that subjects who thought about reasons were significantly more apt to change their minds about the candidates than subjects in the control condition. These results, however, were reported only for subjects who were relatively unknowledgeable about the candidates. As predicted, there was not a significant difference between the absolute value of change among those subjects who were knowledgeable about the candidates, as seen in the second row of Table V. An analysis of variance on these change scores yielded a significant Reasons Condition × Knowledge interaction ($p < .05$), though our standard planned comparison, as described previously, was significant only at the .12 level.

4. Attitudes toward Posters

The Wilson, Lisle, and Schooler (1988c) study allows a further test of the hypothesis that knowledge about the attitude object moderates the effects of thinking about reasons on attitude change. In brief, subjects were asked to examine and rate their liking for five posters that were of two different types: Two were reproductions of Impressionist art, whereas three were of a more "pop" style, such as a photograph of a cat with the caption, "Gimme a Break." We predicted that under normal conditions, the art posters would be the most affectively pleasing, and thus most preferred by subjects. When subjects thought about why they liked or disliked the posters, however, we predicted that they would focus on their cognitions about the posters, which would be easier to verbalize about the popular ones. Thus, we expected that subjects in the reasons condition would change their attitudes toward the posters, becoming more positive toward the popular ones and less positive toward the art posters.

This prediction was made, however, only for people who were relatively unknowledgeable about art, and thus should find it most difficult to verbalize their cognitions. People who are knowledgeable about art should find it easier to verbalize why they feel the way they do, and thus they should be less apt to bring to mind a biased set of reasons. This prediction was confirmed. For unknowledgeable subjects, thinking about reasons caused an increase in liking for the popular posters and a decrease in liking for the art posters. Thinking about reasons had relatively little impact on knowledgeable subjects. A contrast that tested the overall predicted pattern of results was highly significant ($F[1,31] = 12.96$, $p = .001$).

Thus, four studies have found that knowledge about the attitude object moderates the effects of thinking about reasons. The explanation for these findings, we suggest, is that unknowledgeable people had attitudes that were more affective in nature, and thus more apt to be disrupted by an attempt to explain them. Clearly, however, people who are unknowledgeable might differ in other ways from people who are knowledgeable. It would thus be desirable to manipulate the basis of an attitude, rather than relying on an individual difference variable. This strategy was used in the next study reviewed here.

5. Manipulating the Basis of an Attitude

A study by Wilson and Kraft (1988) attempted to create attitudes toward the same stimuli that were affectively based for some people and more cognitively based for others. Subjects were told that the purpose of the study was to look at the kinds of impressions people form of clinical psychology graduate students, to see if these impressions were related to the students' therapeutic skills. As a means of creating affectively based attitudes toward the students, some subjects were exposed to a mere exposure manipulation, in which they were given no information about the students other than their photographs. The frequency with which subjects saw these photographs was manipulated, so that subjects saw the photographs of some students only once, others 25 times. Subjects in the cognitive-information group received brief profiles about each student that described her career goals, research interests, and leisure-time activities, in the absence of any photographs. These profiles were pretested such that they caused a range in liking for the students equal to the range in the mere exposure condition.

Half of the subjects in each condition received our standard reasons manipulation, in which they wrote down why they liked or disliked each of the clinical psychology graduate students. Subjects in the control condition completed a filler questionnaire. All subjects then rated their liking for the students on 7-point scales. We predicted that the reasons manipulation would have relatively little impact on the subjects in the cognitive-information condition, because they would have formed their attitudes by integrating a relatively small number of pieces of information about the students (e.g., "She likes to bowl and read science fiction books"). When asked to give reasons, it should have been relatively easy for these people to verbalize why they felt the way they did.

It should have been more difficult for subjects in the mere exposure condition to verbalize why they felt the way they did, for at least two reasons: (1) It is unlikely that subjects knew that their attitudes were influenced by the frequency with which they saw the photographs, thus they were unaware of the major determinant of their attitudes; (2) the nonverbal information they received (i.e., the photographs) was more difficult to verbalize than were the profiles. Therefore, subjects in the mere exposure condition were hypothesized to be more apt to be misled by thinking about reasons, and thus more apt to change their minds about how they felt.

This prediction was confirmed, as seen in Table VI. For subjects who saw the profiles, thinking about reasons had little effect on their attitudes ($p = .37$). For subjects in the mere exposure condition, however, thinking about reasons changed their attitudes in a negative direction ($p < .001$). A contrast testing the overall prediction that thinking about reasons would not affect attitudes in the

TABLE VI
EFFECTS OF THINKING ABOUT REASONS
ON AFFECTIVELY AND COGNITIVELY BASED
ATTITUDES[a]

	Control	Reasons
Profiles	4.84	4.72
Mere exposure	5.23	4.78

[a]Adapted from Wilson & Kraft (1988). Liking ratings were made on 7-point scales. The higher the number, the greater the liking.

profile condition but would in the mere exposure condition was highly significant ($p < .001$). Interestingly, what seems to have happened in the mere exposure condition is that the affective advantage of repeated exposure to a stimulus was lost when people thought about why they felt the way they did. When subjects did not think about reasons, they liked the person they saw 25 times about 1 standard deviation more than the person they saw only once. When subjects thought about their reasons for liking or disliking the target people, they liked the person they saw 25 times only slightly more than the person they saw once.

6. Summary and Implications

The first four studies reviewed in this section indicated that thinking about reasons is most apt to change attitudes and lower attitude–behavior consistency when people are relatively unknowledgeable about the attitude object. We argued that the unknowledgeable people were less likely to know why they felt the way they did than knowledgeable people, and thus they were more likely to be misled when asked to think about reasons. The reason unknowledgeable people were less apt to know why they felt the way they did, we suggested, was because their attitudes were more affectively based. Wilson and Kraft's (1988) study created attitudes that were either affectively based (i.e., the result of a mere exposure manipulation) or cognitively based (i.e., based on profiles of the clinical psychology students). As in the other studies, thinking about reasons influenced only the former type of attitudes.

We have discussed at length the possibility that it is not affectively based attitudes that are most susceptible to disruption, but those that are weak or inaccessible. There are several sources of evidence against this possibility. In several of the studies we have just presented, there is evidence that people who were unknowledgeable had relatively strong attitudes, in that these attitudes predicted their behavior well. Further, Wilson and Kraft's (1988) study manipulated the basis of attitudes, and we found that those resulting from mere exposure were changed by thinking about reasons, whereas those resulting from reading the profiles were not. Finally, in some of our earlier studies, we had created strong attitudes by giving subjects direct experience with the attitude object, using Fazio's procedure for doing so (e.g., Regan & Fazio, 1977). Thinking about reasons was found to change attitudes in these studies and to undermine attitude–behavior consistency, suggesting that it is not just weak attitudes that are susceptible to these effects. On balance, then, the evidence points to our distinction between affectively and cognitively based attitudes as a moderator of the effects of thinking about reasons. This issue is far from settled, however. It is not a simple matter just to assess the affective and cognitive bases of attitudes, and to distinguish these characteristics from attitudinal strength. A fertile area for future research would be to develop such assessment techniques.

Our research indicating that some types of attitudes are more likely to be changed by thinking about reasons, it should be noted, helps explain the inconsistency we referred to earlier between our self-persuasion hypothesis and consistency theories. We have argued that when people are asked to explain an attitude, they often come up with a biased set of cognitions about the attitude object, which causes them to change their minds about how they feel. As noted earlier, consistency theories suggest that when people are asked to explain an attitude, they would think of reasons that are consistent with the phenomenon they are attempting to explain.

People will generate a consistent set of beliefs, we argue, for some types of attitudes—namely those that are cognitively based—and thus are already grounded on a set of well-thought-out, integrated beliefs. When people are asked to explain an affectively based attitude, however, they do not have a ready-made set of consistent beliefs to call upon. In fact, there is evidence that when people are relatively unknowledgeable about an attitude object—and thus are likely to have affectively based attitudes—their beliefs about the attitude object are relatively inconsistent (Lusk & Judd, 1988). As we have seen, the reasons people do come up with are also likely to be biased in a number of respects. Previous studies have shown that if people are duped, through linguistic devices, into generating a set of biased reasons, they adopt the attitude implied by these reasons (Salancik, 1974; Seligman *et al.*, 1980). It is thus not surprising that if people come up with a biased sample of reasons on their own, a similar type of attitude change occurs.

D. PREDICTING BEHAVIOR THAT IS AFFECTIVELY VERSUS COGNITIVELY DRIVEN

An additional boundary condition was suggested by Millar and Tesser (1986). They demonstrated that thinking about reasons reduces the ability of attitudes to predict affectively based behavior but not cognitively based behavior. Because analyzing reasons heightens the salience of the cognitive component of the attitude, behavior that is motivated chiefly by these cognitions will follow from attitude reports. Millar and Tesser (1986) did not have a no-introspection control group, thus it is unclear whether thinking about reasons actually increased correlations with cognitively based behaviors or simply did not lower them. In either case, an important boundary condition has been established.

It will take further research to delineate better which types of behavior are motivated primarily by affect and which by the cognitive component of attitudes. Millar and Tesser (1986) describe affectively based behaviors as "consummatory" (i.e., those performed to obtain pleasure or avoid pain) and cognitively based behaviors as "instrumental" (i.e., those performed to achieve some goal associated with the attributes of the attitude object, such as working on puzzles to develop one's analytic ability). As with the basis of attitudes, it would be extremely difficult to estimate what percentage of people's behavior is motivated chiefly by affect versus cognition. Enough behavior seems to emanate from the heart rather than the head, however, that this boundary condition does not trivialize the effects of thinking about reasons.

E. OTHER BOUNDARY CONDITIONS

There are several other potential boundary conditions of thinking about reasons that have yet to be tested empirically. For example, the reasons analyses performed by subjects in our studies were relatively brief. Perhaps if people were to spend more time analyzing their motives, and if they were more motivated to do so (e.g., if they were facing an important decision), they could more successfully integrate with their affect the cognitions that result from thinking about reasons. Similarly, the analysis of reasons in our studies has been carried out solitarily. It may be that if we discuss our motives with another—such as a friend, spouse, or psychotherapist—the other person can be more objective, seeing inconsistencies and distortions that are not obvious to us. Finally, it may be that some people are better at introspection than others. Just as there are individual differences in the extent to which people focus on themselves (Fenigstein, Scheier, & Buss, 1975), there might be differences in skill at analyzing reasons. We included Fenigstein et al.'s (1975) private self-consciousness scale in one of our reasons-analysis studies (Wilson et al., 1984, Study 1), and we found that thinking about reasons lowered attitude–behavior correlations both for people high and for people low in private self-consciousness. A more direct measure of skill at introspection (rather than a measure of the frequency of self-focus), however, might predict which individuals are most susceptible to the disruptive effects of thinking about reasons.

VII. Alternative Explanations for the Disruptive Effects of Thinking about Reasons

There are other possible explanations for the disruptive effects of thinking about reasons. Four such possibilities are considered here, along with evidence for and against each one.

A. DOES THINKING ABOUT REASONS INCREASE DISCREPANCIES BETWEEN THE AFFECTIVE AND THE COGNITIVE COMPONENTS OF ATTITUDES?

We argued earlier that thinking about reasons causes people to recast their attitudes in cognitive terms, and that these attitudes then conflict with behavior that is affectively based (particularly when enough time has elapsed for people's affective reaction to reassert itself). We have also tested an additional hypothesis about why thinking about reasons can lower attitude–behavior consistency. When people have a cognitively based attitude, we suggest, they are more apt to have a set of cognitions about the attitude object that are well integrated with their affect. For example, people whose attitudes toward a political candidate are based on a careful appraisal of the candidate's stance on the issues are likely to have cognitions that are consistent with their affective reaction, because their affect stems from these cognitions.

When people have affectively based attitudes, they are less likely to have spent time integrating their thoughts with their feelings, and they are thus more likely to have beliefs that conflict with their affect (e.g., "He may have voted the wrong way on a few bills in Congress, but I really like him"). Under normal conditions, people with affectively based attitudes probably focus on those beliefs that are consistent with their affect; that is, the affect swamps the cognitions. When asked to explain their attitudes, however, they may focus on their beliefs, highlighting their inconsistency with their affect ("Why do I feel the way I do? Well, now that I think about it, his position on some key issues is different from mine"). If so, thinking about reasons may not only change people's minds about how they feel, it may also create an attitude with discrepant affective and cognitive components. This would help explain why thinking about reasons reduces attitude–behavior consistency, because there is ample evidence that attitudes with discrepant components are unstable and poor predictors of behavior (Norman, 1975; Rosenberg, 1968).

Evidence for part of this proposed sequence of events was recently obtained by Lusk and Judd (1988). In two studies, they found that subjects who were relatively knowledgeable about politics had beliefs about political candidates that were intercorrelated; that is, their knowledge about the candidates was integrated into a schema that was evaluatively consistent. Subjects who were unknowledgeable had beliefs that were more apt to be inconsistent. To the extent that the unknowledgeable people had attitudes that were more affectively based, this supports our contention that affectively based attitudes are less apt to be supported by a set of consistent beliefs.

To see if thinking about reasons highlights discrepancies between the affective and cognitive components of affectively based attitudes, we measured the affective and cognitive components of attitudes separately in four of our studies: a survey of attitudes toward marijuana by Wilson and Dunn (1986b); Wilson, Kraft, and Dunn's (1988a) studies of attitudes toward the 1984 and 1988 Presidential candidates; and Wilson Kraft's (1988) study that manipulated the affective versus cognitive basis of attitudes. In the first three of these studies, subjects were divided on the basis of their knowledge about or experience with the attitude object, as a means of operationalizing the affective versus cognitive basis of their attitudes. In the fourth study, we manipulated the basis of their attitudes, as discussed previously.

In the last three studies, the affective and cognitive components of attitudes were assessed using techniques described by Rosenberg (1960). In the first, the affective component was assessed with semantic differential scales, and the cognitive component was assessed with a previously developed measure of beliefs about marijuana (Schlegel, 1975). The consistency between subjects' affective and cognitive responses was assessed by standardizing their responses on each measure, and then computing the absolute value of the difference between them.

Thinking about reasons increased the discrepancy between the affective and cognitive components of attitudes in three of the four studies when attitudes were affectively based (see Table VII). Averaging across studies, this difference was significant ($z = 2.02$, $p = .04$). Thinking about reasons had relatively little impact on attitudes that were cognitively based. A contrast testing the overall predicted pattern of results (with a contrast weight of 3 in the reasons–affective attitude cell and -1 in each of the remaining cells) was also significant across studies ($z = 2.93$, $p = .003$). These differences, however, were not very large. Even though the difference between the affective–reasons and affective–control conditions was significant across studies, it failed to reach significance in any of the individual studies. Further, as seen at the bottom of Table VII, the difference in discrepancy scores between these conditions averaged only .10 standard deviation units.

Thus, some weak support for our hypothesis concerning the consistency between the affective and cognitive components has been obtained. Clearly this effect is not very strong, however, and it is unlikely that it fully accounts for the reductions in attitude–behavior consistency we have found. As discussed earlier, these reductions appear to be due in large part to the fact that when people think about reasons they recast their attitudes in cognitive terms, though their behavior is often affectively driven.

B. DOES THINKING ABOUT REASONS LOWER CONFIDENCE IN ATTITUDES?

Analyzing the reasons for one's feelings might cause people to consider alternative points of view, shaking their confidence in their attitudes. Unable to explain fully why she is attracted to her dating partner, for example, a person might begin to question the strength or nature of her feelings. Fazio and Zanna (1981) demonstrated that attitudes held with low confidence are poor predictors of behavior, thus a loss of confidence precipitated by thinking about reasons would explain the reductions in attitude–behavior consistency found in our studies.

This hypothesis is implied in the earlier quote from Mario Vargas Llosa, who "could no longer easily tell what I liked or didn't" after analyzing the films at the Berlin Film Festival. It is echoed by a character in a novel by Iris Murdoch, who observed that "not everything is improved and clarified by being dug up" (Murdoch, 1986, p. 422). Finally, in the first study (of which we are aware) that used a reasons-analysis manipulation, some evidence was found for this hypothesis. Carper and Doob (1953) asked subjects for their level of agreement with six attitude statements having to do with the equal access to governmental services by American citizens. Half of the subjects were first asked to explain why they felt the way they did, whereas the others were not. Interestingly, those who thought about reasons were more apt to erase their subsequent attitude

TABLE VII
EFFECTS OF THINKING ABOUT REASONS AND KNOWLEDGE ON THE CONSISTENCY BETWEEN THE AFFECTIVE AND COGNITIVE COMPONENTS OF ATTITUDES[a]

	Affectively based		Cognitively based	
	Control	Reasons	Control	Reasons
Wilson & Dunn (1986b)	.48	.56	.46	.45
Wilson, Kraft, & Dunn (1988a), Study 1	.63	.85	.85	.67
Wilson, Kraft, & Dunn (1988a), Study 2	.70	.65	.54	.75
Wilson & Kraft (1988)	.62	.79	.58	.50
Mean	.61	.71	.61	.59

[a] Cell entries are the absolute value of the difference between subjects' standardized affective response and standardized cognitive response.

responses than those who did not, suggesting that they became less certain about how they felt.[4]

We have tested the reduced-confidence hypothesis in several of our studies, however, and have not found any support for it. Several different measures of confidence and clarity of attitudes have been used. In five studies, subjects were simply asked how confident they were in their attitudes. In three, we included measures of the latitude of acceptance and latitude of rejection of people's attitudes, where they endorsed from a list of attitude statements all that they found acceptable and all they found objectionable as descriptions of their position (Sherif & Hovland, 1961). Finally, we measured how long it took subjects to answer the questions about their attitudes in two studies, with the assumption that low confidence would be reflected by longer response times.

As seen in Table VIII, no evidence has been found that thinking about reasons reduces confidence in attitudes. The only significant difference on any of the confidence measures was such that subjects who thought about reasons expressed *more* confidence in their attitudes than did subjects in the control condition (Wilson, 1985a; $p = .01$). It seems, then, that introspecting about reasons does not reduce attitude–behavior consistency by lowering confidence in one's attitudes.

C. DOES THINKING ABOUT REASONS INCREASE THE COGNITIVE DIFFERENTIATION OF ATTITUDES?

Schlegel and DiTecco (1982) have recently distinguished between attitudes that have a differentiated versus an undifferentiated cognitive component. People who are knowledgeable about or experienced with an attitude object, they argued, are likely to have complex, multidimensional beliefs that are not easily represented on unidimensional, affective scales. That is, experienced people are apt to view the attitude object as consisting of many different dimensions, some good and some bad, making it difficult to express their attitudes on a single affective scale. Their responses on such scales, Schlegel and DiTecco reasoned, will thus be poor predictors of their behavior. People with little knowledge about or experience

---

[4]Carper and Doob (1953) did not find any difference in the mean level of agreement with the attitude statements between those who thought about reasons and those who did not, and as a result they concluded that the use of reasons questions in attitude surveys "can be heartily recommended" (p. 517). Our studies suggest that attitude change may in fact have occurred, but it was in a positive direction for some subjects and a negative direction for others. In fact, one of the issues used by Carper and Doob—whether there should be a national health insurance—was also used in the survey conducted by Wilson and Kraft (1988). We, too, found no differences in the mean level of agreement between reasons and control subjects. We had assessed subjects' attitudes several weeks before the manipulation, however, and thus could assess the absolute value of change in attitudes. As predicted, subjects who thought about reasons did show more such absolute change than control subjects.

with an attitude object will have undifferentiated, unidimensional cognitive structures that are consistent with their affect. Responses on affective scales by inexperienced people will thus capture their attitudes more accurately and be better predictors of their behavior.

Schlegel and DiTecco (1982) conducted a survey on attitudes toward marijuana that supported their hypotheses. People inexperienced with marijuana tended to have undifferentiated attitudes (as assessed by a hierarchical factor analysis on ratings of their beliefs), and affective measures of their attitudes were good predictors of their reported use of marijuana 1 year later. People experienced with marijuana had more differentiated beliefs, and affective measures did not predict their behavior very well. Behavior by experienced people could be predicted if multidimensional attitude scales were used.

Schlegel and DiTecco's (1982) work provides a possible explanation of the disruptive effects of thinking about reasons. Thinking about reasons may make cognitions about the attitude object more differentiated, by forcing people to consider different aspects of the stimulus. Thus, people in the reasons-analysis conditions may end up with more differentiated attitudes than control subjects, making their responses on single-evaluative-attitude measures less predictive of

TABLE VIII
THE EFFECT OF THINKING ABOUT REASONS ON CONFIDENCE IN ONE'S ATTITUDES

Study	Control condition	Reasons condition	Significance of difference
Confidence questions[a]			
Wilson et al. (1984)	5.38	5.48	$t(24) = -.46$
Wilson (1985a)	7.73	8.20	$t(102) = -2.60*$
Wilson et al. (1988b)	7.60	7.32	$t(37) = .57$
Wilson et al. (1988b)	7.56	7.00	$t(34) = 1.21$
Wilson & Dunn (1986b)	7.00	7.61	$t(30) = -1.32$
Latitude of acceptance[b]			
Wilson (1985a)	2.08	2.21	$t(103) = .50$
Wilson et al. (1988b)	2.05	2.63	$t(37) = 1.51$
Wilson et al. (1988b)	2.61	2.83	$t(34) = .47$
Latitude of rejection[c]			
Wilson (1985a)	5.87	6.00	$t(103) = -.28$
Wilson et al. (1988b)	6.15	6.05	$t(37) = .14$
Wilson et al. (1988b)	5.11	5.50	$t(34) = -.57$
Response time to attitude questions(s)[b]			
Wilson et al. (1984)	4.61	4.78	$t(24) = .25$
Wilson & Dunn (1986b)	8.67	7.92	$t(141) = -1.23$

[a]Higher numbers reflect confidence. All ratings were made on 9-point scales except for those in the Wilson et al. (1984) study, which were made on 7-point scales.
[b]Smaller numbers reflect greater confidence.
[c]Larger numbers reflect greater confidence.
*$p < .05$.

their behavior. If so, the low attitude–behavior correlations we have found would essentially be a measurement problem, correctable if multidimensional attitude measures rather than single affective scales were used.

We suggest, however, that the type of short-term reasons analyses that people perform in our studies do not produce multidimensional attitudes. Thinking about reasons for 10 minutes is not sufficient to turn an unknowledgeable person into a knowledgeable person who has a well-integrated, differentiated belief structure. To see if thinking about reasons increases attitude differentiation, we replicated Schlegel and DiTecco's (1982) survey, with the addition of a reasons-analysis manipulation (Wilson & Dunn, 1986b). Over 300 students were given the same survey about attitudes toward marijuana, and they were divided into knowledgeable and unknowledgeable groups, based on their reported use of marijuana. Before filling out the survey, half of the respondents were asked to describe why they liked or did not like to smoke marijuana (reasons-analysis condition), while the other half described why they chose the college they did (control condition).

Following Schlegel and DiTecco (1982) a hierarchical factor analysis was performed on subjects' beliefs about marijuana in each of the four Knowledge × Reasons-Analysis cells. (A principal axes factor solution with oblique rotation was used to derive first-order factors. Higher-order factors were then derived by factor analyzing in the same way the correlations among the rotated first-order factors.) This analysis yielded four measures of attitude structure in each cell: (1) attitude differentiation (the number of lower-order factors resulting from the hierarchical factor analysis), (2) attitude organization (the total communality of the factor solution divided by the total normalized variance), (3) attitude centrality (the variance explained by the most general factor divided by the total commonality of the solution), and (4) attitude complexity (the number of factors at each level of the solution weighted by the variance at each level, multiplied by the number of levels, divided by the degree of organization). These indices of cognitive structure are virtually identical to Zajonc's (1960), except that Schlegel and DiTecco (1982) prefer the label ''organization'' to Zajonc's label of ''unity.''

As seen in Table IX, Schlegel and DiTecco's (1982) results were replicated: People experienced with marijuana had attitudes that were more differentiated

TABLE IX
MEASURES OF ATTITUDE INTEGRATION

Condition	Differentiation	Organization	Centrality	Complexity
Unknowledgeable				
Control	3	.624	.333	7.598
Reasons analysis	3	.621	.333	7.329
Knowledgeable				
Control	4	.581	.250	8.957
Reasons analysis	4	.579	.250	9.176

and complex and less central than people inexperienced with marijuana. (The organization index revealed few differences between knowledgeable and unknowledgeable subjects in either our study or Schlegel and DiTecco's.) The results show no evidence, however, that thinking about reasons increases the dimensionality of attitudes: The measures of differentiation, organization, centrality, and complexity were virtually identical in the control and the reasons-analysis conditions. Further, there was no evidence in this study or in two others (Wilson, Kraft, & Dunn, 1988a, Study 2; Wilson et al., 1984, Study 3) that the behavior of people who think about reasons can be predicted from multidimensional measures of attitudes. These results suggest that the disruptive effect of thinking about reasons on attitude–behavior consistency is not a measurement problem that can be corrected with the inclusion of multidimensional attitude scales.

D. DEMAND CHARACTERISTICS AND SELF-PRESENTATIONAL CONCERNS

Perhaps asking people to think about reasons heightens self-presentational concerns, compelling people to report an attitude they thought was socially acceptable, but which they knew was not their true attitude. Alternatively, people may have felt an implicit demand to report a new attitude after thinking about reasons. In either case, attitude–behavior correlations would suffer, because behavior (which subjects did not know was being assessed) would reflect people's true attitudes, whereas their reports would reflect attitudes that they wanted or thought they were expected to hold.

Tetlock and Manstead (1985) have cogently pointed to the difficulties of distinguishing between impression management versus intrapsychic explanations. It is relatively clear, however, that neither concerns about one's public image nor demand characteristics were responsible for the changes in reported attitudes in people who thought about reasons. In all of our studies (with the exception of Wilson and Kraft's [1988] phone survey) subjects' attitude reports were made privately and anonymously. In one study, subjects never marked their responses on paper; they pressed buttons that supposedly sent their responses directly to a computer that immediately aggregated all subjects' responses (Wilson et al., 1984, Study 1). Thus, there is every reason to believe that subjects were candid in their responses.

Nor is it likely that demand characteristics can account for our results. In one study, subjects thought their reasons-analysis, attitude, and behavioral responses were part of three separate studies (Wilson & Dunn, 1986a, Study 1), thus it is unlikely that they viewed the reasons-analysis manipulation as an attempt to change their attitudes. In addition, subjects were told in most of our studies that they would not hand in the paper on which they wrote down their reasons, as its only purpose was to organize their thoughts. Typically, when the experimenter enters the room after subjects have completed the reasons questionnaire, he or she casually deposits the questionnaire in a trash can, saying that it will not be needed anymore. Further, in one study, the subjects never wrote down what their reasons were (Wilson et al., 1984, Study 2).

Perhaps the best evidence against a demand characteristic or self-presentational interpretation comes from a measure used in the Wilson, Lisle, and Schooler (1988c) study. In this study, the attitude object was a set of five posters commonly purchased by college students. At the end of the study, subjects were allowed to choose one of the posters to take home, and they thought the experimenter would not know which one they took. If subjects who thought about reasons reported new attitudes purely for self-presentational reasons or due to demand characteristics, one would not expect this change to show up on the measure of which poster they chose to take home. (Because they thought we would not know which poster they chose, they presumably chose the one they genuinely liked the best.) Not only did subjects in the reasons condition change their minds about which posters they liked the most, however; they also tended to choose different posters to take home. Thus, demand characteristics or self-presentational concerns appear not to have played a major role in the attitude change that occurred in this study.

VIII. Conditions under Which People Think about Reasons

An important issue in research on analyzing reasons concerns the conditions under which a reasons analysis is performed. In our studies, people were instructed to think about reasons, and the effects of this reasons analysis were then examined. This manipulation has ecological validity, in that it is fairly common in everyday life to be asked to explain one's feelings ("Why do you like her? Why didn't you like the movie?"). Nonetheless it is important to examine other conditions triggering a reasons analysis. We do not go through our daily lives constantly examining our motives and reasons; indeed, Langer (1978) argued that much of the time, we follow well-learned scripts in a relatively mindless fashion. When are people likely to think about the reasons for their feelings?

Though there has been little research on this specific question, the issue of when people attempt to explain other people's behavior has received a considerable amount of attention. Causal attributions about other people are apt to be made when (1) people are explicitly asked to make attributions, as in our reasons-analysis studies; (2) an unexpected event occurs, such as when a friend behaves in an uncharacteristic manner (Clary & Tesser, 1983; Hastie, 1984; Lau & Russell, 1980; Pyszczynski & Greenberg, 1981; Wong & Weiner, 1981); (3) a stimulus person has hedonic relevance to the observer (Berscheid, Graziano, Monson, &

Dermer, 1976; Harvey, Yarkin, Lightner, & Town, 1980; Monson, Keel, Stephens, & Genung, 1982), and (4) people experience a lack of control (Pittman & Pittman, 1980).

The factor that has received the most attention, and seems to be most predictive of whether causal attributions about other people are made, is the unexpectedness of someone else's behavior. This same factor might also determine when an analysis of reasons for our own behavior and feelings occurs. People have many expectations about how they will feel toward an attitude object; for example, most people fully expect to enjoy the next chocolate bar they eat, and they expect their next trip to the dentist to be unpleasant. If their reactions to future chocolate bars and trips to the dentist were consistent with their expectations, there is little reason to think about why. If, however, their reactions violated their expectations (a scintillating dentist appointment!), they are likely to try to explain these reactions.

If having unexpected feelings triggers a reasons analysis, and the other conditions for the disruptive effects of thinking about reasons are met (such as the attitude being affective), then the following sequence of events should occur: (1) People notice that their reaction to a stimulus is not what they expected it to be, (2) they attempt to explain their unexpected reaction, (3) they recast their attitude in cognitive terms, resulting in low attitude–behavior correlations.

We have conducted three experiments to test this hypothesized sequence of events, as part of a research program on the effects of expectations about one's own affective reactions (Wilson, Lisle, Kraft, & Wetzel, in press). We describe portions of this research that bear directly on the hypothesis that having unexpected affective reactions triggers a reasons analysis. Rather than instructing people to think about reasons in these studies, we manipulated people's expectations about how they would feel toward an attitude object, then we violated these expectations in some conditions, with the assumption that a reasons-analysis would be triggered. Two control conditions were included in each study: (1) One group was given expectations about how they would feel, just as in the unexpected reaction condition, but these expectations were confirmed rather than disconfirmed; (2) another control group was given no expectations about how they would feel. The main dependent measure was, as in most of our previous studies, the correlation between subsequent attitudes and behavior. To check our assumption that having unexpected feelings triggers a reasons analysis, subjects in all conditions completed a thought-listing questionnaire at the end of the experiment (Brock, 1967; Cacioppo & Petty, 1981; Greenwald, 1968), on which they listed all the thoughts they could recall having when they were first exposed to the attitude object.

In Study 1, for example, subjects were asked to taste a beverage, and they were told that a very high percentage of people had liked the beverage. Some subjects received a pleasant-tasting lemonade—thus there was no discrepancy between their affective reaction and their expected reaction. Other subjects received a fairly unpleasant concoction of lemonade, water, and salt—thus there was a discrepancy between their affective reaction and their expected reaction. Finally, a no-expectation control condition was included in which subjects were not told about other subjects' reactions, with half of the control subjects receiving the pleasant drink and half the unpleasant drink. The attitude measure in this study was subjects' rating of how much they enjoyed the beverage, whereas the behavioral measure was the amount of the beverage subjects drank during a free-time period when they thought the study was over.

Two other studies have also been conducted to assess the effects of violating affective expectations, using (1) different attitude objects (single-panel cartoons and reproductions of modern art) and (2) a different way of manipulating people's expectations. In Study 2, subjects viewed and rated 20 cartoons, and they received feedback indicating that the ones they disliked were all from the same magazine. They then saw four new cartoons that were supposedly from this same magazine, but were (according to pretest subjects) fairly funny. Thus, they expected to dislike the new cartoons, but these expectations were disconfirmed. Subjects in the expected-reaction condition received feedback indicating that the ones they had liked from the first set were from the target magazine—thus they expected to like the four new cartoons. Subjects in the no-expectation condition did not see any cartoons from the target magazine before viewing the four new ones. The attitude measure was subjects' ratings of how funny the new cartoons were, while the behavioral measure was the mirth they expressed on their faces while viewing the new cartoons.

Study 3 had the same design as Study 2, except that subjects viewed reproductions of paintings rather than cartoons. They saw new paintings at the end of the study that were ostensibly all of the same (fictitious) style, labeled the Schematic Style. As in Study 2, subjects initially rated 20 paintings, and some subjects received feedback indicating that the ones they liked were all of the Schematic Style. Others received feedback that the ones they disliked were of the Schematic Style, while the remainder were not told that any of the first 20 were Schematic paintings. The new Schematic paintings all subjects subsequently saw had been given low ratings by pretest subjects, thus some subjects had unexpected reactions to them, others had expected reactions, and some had no expectations about how they would react. There was no behavioral measure in this study, thus attitude–behavior correlations could not be assessed. The thought-listing task was included, to see if having unexpected reactions triggered a reasons analysis.

Our main hypothesis was that subjects in the unexpected-reaction conditions would think about why their reactions were not what they expected them to be, and that this reasons analysis would result in low correlations between their attitudes and behavior. Subjects in the expected-reaction conditions should respond similarly to those with no expectations. Since their feelings toward the attitude objects were consistent with their expectations, there was no reason to think about why—thus, no reasons analysis was expected to occur, and attitude–behavior correlations were expected to be high.

As seen in Table X the predicted pattern of attitude–behavior correlations occurred: They were high in the no-expectation and expected-reaction conditions, and low in the unexpected-reaction conditions. Averaging across studies, the correlation in the unexpected reaction condition was significantly lower than both the correlation in the no-expectation condition and the correlation in the expected-reaction condition (p's < .05).

Subjects' responses on the thought-listing task were coded in each study to test the hypothesis that the lowered correlations in the unexpected-reaction conditions were caused by a reasons analysis. As it happened, the coders achieved acceptable reliability only on a rather broad categorization of the reported thoughts, namely a division of the thoughts into those that concerned the attitude object (e.g., the beverage in Study 1) and those that did not. The number of thoughts in each category, as well as the total number of thoughts reported, are displayed in Table X. As predicted, subjects in the unexpected-reaction conditions reported the most thoughts, while subjects in the no-expectation and expected-reaction conditions reported very similar numbers of thoughts. The total number of thoughts reported by subjects in the unexpected-reaction condition was significantly higher than the total number of thoughts reported in each of the other two conditions (p's < .05).

To summarize the results of these studies, the last part of our prediction—that having unexpected reactions triggers a reasons analysis, which leads to low attitude–behavior consistency—has been supported. We also obtained evidence that having unexpected reactions triggers more thoughts than having expected

TABLE X
EFFECTS OF EXPECTED AND UNEXPECTED AFFECTIVE REACTIONS ON
ATTITUDE–BEHAVIOR CORRELATIONS AND REPORTED THOUGHTS[a]

	Condition		
	No expectation	Expected reaction	Unexpected reaction
Attitude–behavior correlations	.69†	.70†	.11‡
Thoughts about the attitude object (.86)	3.22†	3.24†	4.05†
Thoughts not about the attitude object (.72)	1.57†	1.55†	2.08†
Total thoughts (.89)	4.79†	4.78†	6.12‡

[a]The correlations were averaged over two studies, the reported thoughts over three studies. Correlations or means in the same row that have different superscripts, † and ‡, differ from each other at the .05 level of significance. The numbers in parentheses after each category are the reliabilities of the coders' ratings, averaged across studies.

reactions or having no expectations. The evidence for the hypothesis that this increase in thinking involves more of a reasons analysis, however, could not be tested because our coders were unable to achieve sufficient reliability when attempting to categorize the thoughts as reasons. The results of our initial work in this area are promising, however, and suggest that further tests of the hypothesis be performed, with more reliable measures of people's tendency to think about reasons.[5]

It is important to reiterate that these studies are also useful in ruling out a demand characteristic or self-presentational interpretation of our earlier experiments, in which subjects were asked to think about their reasons for liking or disliking an attitude object. Despite our efforts to convince subjects that their reasons analyses were private and that no one would ever see their reasons, it is possible that they were still concerned with putting their best reasons forward. Further, simply asking subjects to think about reasons might imply to them that they should rethink their position and possibly change their minds. In the set of studies just reviewed, however, subjects were never asked to think about reasons. Instead, the situation was set up so that a reasons analysis should be triggered naturally (i.e., by manipulating the unexpectedness of subjects' affective reactions). As predicted, this both increased the number of thoughts subjects had and lowered their attitude–behavior consistency.

IX. How and When Will Thinking about Reasons Get Us into Trouble?

We began this article with a discussion of introspection as a uniquely human trait. In the course of our review, we have seen that one type of introspection—thinking about the reasons for one's feelings—can change people's minds about how they feel and lower the consistency between their attitudes and subsequent behavior. We have used the word "disruptive" to describe these effects, in part because we wish to avoid a general condemnation of introspection. We do believe, however, that it is not always to people's advantage to turn an affective response into a cognitive one, as seems to occur as a result of thinking about reasons. In our next, concluding, section, we discuss further when it is advantageous and

---

[5]An interesting issue in this area of research is whether people *notice* that their reactions to an attitude object differ from their expected reactions. If an expectation is very strong, and the valence of the attitude object is ambiguous, people assimilate the valence of the attitude object to their expectation, without ever realizing that a discrepancy existed (Wilson et al., in press). For example, the expectation that a movie will be excellent might cause people to rate a mediocre movie very highly, without realizing that it was not as good as they expected it to be. We would not expect a reasons analysis to occur in cases in which people do not realize that their expectations have been violated. The unexpected-reaction conditions reported here were ones in which people were predicted to notice the discrepancy between their expectations and their actual reactions.

when it is not to think about the reasons for one's feelings. In this section, we describe two empirical demonstrations that the attitude change that results from thinking about reasons can be disadvantageous to the person doing the introspecting.

A. THE FUNCTION OF ATTITUDE OBJECTS

The primary function of many attitude objects is to give pleasure. When deciding what flavor of ice cream to buy, whether to paint the living room yellow or blue, or whom to date on Saturday night, the overriding goal is to make the choice that is most affectively pleasing. It is precisely these types of attitude objects, we suggest, about which one should avoid thinking about reasons. If we spend too much time thinking about *why* we prefer vanilla to rocky road, *why* yellow seems preferable to the blue, or *why* we like Bob more than Joe, we may recast our feelings in cognitive terms, and thereby lose sight of what our preferences are.

Wilson, Lisle, and Schooler (1988c) performed two experiments to test this hypothesis. Two conditions needed to be satisfied in these studies: (1) Stimuli needed to be used whose function was primarily affective—that is, people's main criterion for choosing among them is the extent to which they are affectively pleasing; (2) a criterion needed to be found for assessing the validity of people's preferences or choices. To demonstrate that thinking about reasons can be undesirable, a standard of judgment needs to be found by which people's preferences can be evaluated.

In Wilson, Lisle, and Schooler's (1988c) first study, the attitude object was a food item—various kinds of strawberry jams. This seems to satisfy the criterion that it be a stimulus whose function is largely affective. The standard of judgment we used was evaluations of the jams made by taste experts at *Consumer Reports* magazine. These taste experts rated 44 jams according to 16 sensory attributes (e.g., aroma, sweetness, bitterness), and the jams were rank ordered by *Consumer Reports* on the basis of these ratings.

For our study, we chose five of the jams that were wide apart in their rankings by the *Consumer Reports* experts (ranging from the first to the last). Subjects tasted a sample of each of the jams and rated how much they liked it, ostensibly as part of a consumer psychology experiment. We assumed that in the absence of a reasons analysis, subjects would rate the jams according to their affective reaction toward each one, and that these affective reactions would correspond well to the ratings of the *Consumer Reports* taste experts. This is what happened; the average within-subject rank-order correlation between control subjects' liking ratings and the ranking of the taste experts was .55, which was significantly greater than zero.

Half of the subjects received our standard reasons-analysis manipulation, in which they were asked to think about why they liked or disliked each jam. We predicted that thinking about reasons would (1) turn what was an affective response into a more cognitive one, and (2) change subjects' minds about how they felt. This prediction was confirmed, in that subjects in the reasons condition gave three of the jams lower ratings and two higher ratings than did control subjects. More importantly, the change that occurred was in a direction *away* from the rankings made by the *Consumer Reports* experts: The average rank order correlation between liking ratings and the rankings of the experts was only .11 in the reasons condition, which was significantly lower than the corresponding mean correlation in the control condition.

Wilson, Lisle, and Schooler's (1988c) Study 1 thus provides initial evidence that thinking about reasons can be disadvantageous. To the extent that the ratings made by the *Consumer Reports* experts can be considered an objective standard of quality, thinking about reasons caused subjects to make evaluations that corresponded less to this objective standard. That is, compared to control subjects, they were more apt to rate "good" jams as poor and "poor" jams as good. This study is only a first step, however, in demonstrating that it can be disadvantageous to think about reasons. It is true that analyzing reasons moved attitude judgments away from an objective standard of quality, but it is not clear that is very consequential or even undesirable to subjects. As long as they think they like a particular jam, what difference does it make that it was ranked low by a panel of experts?

The cost might be that if subjects in the reasons condition went to the store and purchased the jam they rated the highest, they might later regret this choice. That is, after prolonged exposure to the jam, their affective reaction to it might reassert itself, and they might end up displeased with their choice. Though they initially persuaded themselves that the jam was good as a function of thinking about reasons, over time they may realize that the jam really was not that good after all.

Wilson, Lisle, and Schooler (1988c) tested this possible sequence of events in a second study. The stimuli used in Study 2 were posters of the sort commonly found in the rooms of college students. As discussed earlier, these posters were of two general types. Two were reproductions of Impressionist art, and three of a more "pop" style (e.g., photographs of cats with cute quotations). Subjects were shown the five posters, completing either a reasons or a filler questionnaire, and then they rated their liking for each one. Finally, we told subjects that they could choose one poster to take home as a reward for being in the study. Additional copies of the posters were rolled up and placed in the corner of the room, and subjects made their choice unobserved by the experimenter.

The two art posters were most affectively pleasing to subjects, as reflected by the fact that subjects in the control condition rated these higher than the popular posters, and the fact that 95% of them chose one of the art posters to take home. We hypothesized again that thinking about reasons for liking the posters would change people's minds about how they felt, presumably by turning an affective response into a more cognitive one. This prediction was confirmed: Subjects in the reasons condition rated the art posters lower and the popular posters higher than did control subjects, and they were significantly more likely to choose one of the popular posters to take home.

These results still do not demonstrate that the change in attitudes that occurred were in any way disadvantageous for subjects in the reasons condition. As in the jam study, there may not be any undesirable consequences of changing one's mind about which attitude object is the best. A follow-up measure, however, suggested that there are such negative consequences to thinking about reasons. Subjects were telephoned approximately 3 weeks after they were in the study and asked a series of questions about their satisfaction with their choice of poster (e.g., whether they still had the poster and whether they had hung it up). Subjects in the reasons condition indicated that they were significantly less pleased with their choice than did subjects in the control condition, suggesting that an initial affective reaction to the poster (which, as indicated by control subjects, was most positive toward the art posters) had had a chance to reassert itself. As discussed earlier, the results of the poster study were moderated by people's knowledge about art. As predicted, they were stronger for subjects who were unknowledgeable.

This result is important, because it suggests that people ought not to be too introspective about many personal and consumer decisions, particularly if they are not very knowledgeable in that domain. Trying to think about the reasons for one's preferences can change people's minds about how they feel, leading to a choice that they later regret. In other words, some things are best left unanalyzed. This view was well-stated in an article by Anna Quindlen, in which she discusses her attitude toward rock and roll:

> Some people overanalyze rock-and-roll, just as they overanalyze everything else. They say things like "Bruce Springsteen is the poet laureate of the American dream gone sour," when all I need to know about Bruce Springsteen is that the saxophone bridge on "Jungleland" makes the back of my neck feel exactly the same way I felt the first time a boy kissed me. . . . Rock-and-roll is a lot like sex: If you talk seriously about it, it takes a lot of the feeling away—and feeling is the point. (Quindlen, 1987, p. C12)

B. STIMULI WITH AFFECTIVE AND PRACTICAL FUNCTIONS

It is important to note that the two Wilson, Lisle, and Schooler (1988c) studies used stimuli with a primarily affective function. With stimuli such as jams and posters, there is little else to consider other than the extent to which they give pleasure. That is, people need only heed the affective component of their attitudes, and they probably should avoid forms of introspection that emphasize cognitions about the attitude object. For many other kinds of stimuli, however, both affective and practical considerations are important, and we may be better advised to heed both the affective and cognitive components of our attitudes.

For example, consider the decision of which car to buy. Clearly, there is an affective component to this choice. People's attachment to their automobile has been described as "truly passionate," stemming from "a deep-seated desire to include the car in the family and to emphasize our strong, symbolic attachment with these objects of affection" (Marsh & Collett, 1987, p. 18). Unlike jams or posters, however, there are many attributes of cars other than their affective appeal that probably ought to be considered, such as their price, safety, frequency of repair, and fuel consumption. In fact, many of the major decisions we make in life—whom to marry, what job to accept, what house to buy—involve a weighting of both the affective and cognitive components of our attitudes toward the alternatives.

An interesting area of future research would be to examine the effects of thinking about reasons on decisions involving stimuli such as these. Because the cognitive component of attitudes is important in these decisions, introspection (such as analyzing reasons) that emphasizes this component may be useful. If thinking about reasons obscures people's affect too much, however, they may well end up making a decision they later regret. It appears that a balance between thinking about reasons and "listening to one's heart" is the best strategy for these types of decisions.

X. Summary and Conclusions

A. UNANSWERED QUESTIONS

Throughout this article, we have pointed out areas in which further evidence is needed to nail down a particular hypothesis or conclusion, and there is no need to repeat these comments here. One important unanswered question, however, bears mentioning. It is clear that asking people to think about reasons will often produce attitude change, particularly for affectively based attitudes. The direction of this change, however, has been difficult to predict. In some of our studies, people who think about reasons end up with an attitude that is significantly more negative or positive, on the average, than the attitudes of control subjects. In the Wilson, Lisle, and Schooler (1988c) poster study, for example, subjects who thought about reasons reported greater liking for the popular posters and less liking for the art posters than did control subjects. In the Wilson and Kraft (1988) study that manipulated the basis of attitudes, subjects who were in the mere-exposure condition became more negative toward the clinical psychology students than control subjects. In other studies, thinking about reasons causes changes in both a positive and a negative direction, averaging out to no difference when compared to control subjects. This result was found in Wilson, Kraft, and Dunn's (1988a) study on attitudes toward the 1988 Presidential candidates, and in Wilson and Kraft's (1988) survey of attitudes toward social issues. (Presumably, this bidirectional change also occurred in Wilson et al.'s [1984] couples study).

We suggest that the reason the direction of attitude change is difficult to predict is closely related to our hypothesis about the generation of a biased sample of reasons. We have argued that people's reasons are often biased in the direction of such factors as what seems most plausible as a cause, what is easiest to verbalize, and what is most available in memory. Because it is difficult to know what is available in memory for any given subject at any given time, it is not surprising that the direction of the resulting attitude change has been difficult to predict. In the Wilson et al. (1984) couples study, for example, we had no way of knowing whether positive or negative reasons were most available to any given couple.

It would be possible, of course, to predict the direction of attitude change by manipulating the types of reasons that are available to subjects. This is precisely what was done by Salancik (1974) and by Seligman et al. (1980), by means of the wording of the questions subjects were asked about their reasons. As predicted, subjects became more positive toward the attitude object when intrinsic reasons were elicited and more negative when extrinsic reasons were elicited. Thus, if thinking about reasons is ever to be used as an attitude-change technique, those who use it should attempt to manipulate (or at least predict) the types of reasons subjects bring to mind, in order to know the direction of any attitude change that occurs.

B. RECOMMENDATIONS

We are now in a better position to recommend when people should introspect about the reasons for their feelings and when they should not (qualified, of course, by the proverbial call for further research). First, our data imply that it might not be good to think about reasons to the extent that we value consistency between attitudes and behavior. This is a complicated notion, however, for several reasons. First, it is clear that thinking about reasons will not always reduce attitude–behavior consistency. Some of the boundary conditions that have been established empirically are that analyzing reasons has little effect on people knowledgeable about the attitude object (presumably because they have better access to the actual causes of their attitudes), and analyzing reasons does not lessen the ability of attitudes to predict cognitively based behavior (Millar & Tesser, 1986). Second, we presented evidence that people do respond consistently with their new attitudes immediately after thinking about reasons, before their affective reaction to the stimulus has a chance to reassert itself.

Even when thinking about reasons does reduce attitude–behavior consistency, this outcome is not always to be avoided. To assess the desirability of analyzing reasons, we must consider for whom it is desirable or undesirable—the person doing the introspection or the social scientist attempting to predict behavior—as well as the nature of the attitude that is being analyzed.

1. Desirability to the Social Scientist of Asking People to Think about Reasons

There is little doubt that it can be undesirable for social scientists to ask their respondents to think about reasons. The goal of a good deal of research in the social sciences—including psychology, sociology, economics, political science, and consumer research—is to predict people's behavior from their verbally reported attitudes. Occasionally, in these areas of research, people are asked to explain why they feel the way they do. If "why" questions are asked before people report their attitudes, attitude–behavior consistency will often suffer. For example, if people are asked to think about why they prefer a particular consumer good before reporting their preferences, their preferences may not predict their future purchasing behavior. Unless consumers have a well-developed cognitive structure about the product (which is unlikely when a new product is being test marketed), asking them to justify their preferences in cognitive terms will hinder the goal of marketing researchers—the prediction of consumer behavior.

Similarly, if members of the electorate have attitudes toward a candidate that are primarily affectively based, asking them to think about the reasons for their feelings could lower the correlation between their attitudes and their voting behavior. The use of "why" questions may be justified more easily when researchers are certain that the attitudes they are assessing are the result of a conscious scrutiny of the issues, so that people can accurately report why they feel the way they do.

2. Desirability to the Individual Who Thinks about Reasons

As we have seen, whether or not a reasons analysis is desirable to the person doing the analyzing depends on the nature of the attitude under examination. Several of our studies have shown that if the attitude is based on a good deal of knowledge about the attitude object, then thinking about reasons will not change people's attitudes or lower attitude–behavior consistency. Wilson and Kraft's (1988) mere-exposure study suggested that this is because knowledgeable people are more apt to have attitudes that are based on cognitive information that is easy to verbalize, whereas people who are unknowledgeable are more apt to have affectively based attitudes.

When an attitude is affectively based, and when the function of the attitude object is primarily affective, the Wilson, Lisle, and Schooler (1988c) studies demonstrated that it is best to avoid a reasons analysis. The preferences of subjects who thought about why they liked certain strawberry jams changed in a direction away from an objective standard of quality, and subjects who thought about why they liked or disliked a set of posters were more apt to regret their decision as to which poster to take home. Even when an attitude is affectively based, however, we must qualify our conclusion that it best not to try to explain it. First, we noted that for many important decisions, such as what car to buy or whom to marry, it is probably best to weigh both one's affect toward the alternatives and one's beliefs about their attributes. Here, people probably ought to strike a balance between listening to one's heart and being very deliberative and introspective. Exactly how to accomplish this—or even whether such a balancing is desirable for these types of decisions—is an important avenue of future research.

Further, some affectively based attitudes are themselves undesirable (either to the people who hold them or to the people around them); thus it may be good to disrupt them by thinking about reasons. Our argument here is that analyzing reasons is an attitude-change technique that may be useful in changing undesirable attitudes. It is difficult, as discussed by Zajonc and Markus (1982), to change an affectively based attitude by presenting people with logical, persuasive arguments. If people with such attitudes were asked to explain why they feel the way they do, however, the act of constructing an explanation might produce some attitude change. It is unlikely that thinking about reasons is a powerful way to change attitudes; in some of our studies, the amount of change was small, and the extent to which this change persists over time is not clear. Nonetheless, it may be a useful way of unfreezing an affectively based attitude by making people reconsider it in cognitive terms.

There are at least two sorts of harmful attitudes that might be changed by thinking about reasons—those that are undesirable from the individual's perspective, and those that are undesirable from a societal perspective. Either type of attitude might change in a desirable direction if people attempt to justify it. For example, Tesser, Leone, and Clary (1978) asked people who were anxious about speaking in public to think about why they felt the way they did when giving a speech, and then they asked subjects to give a brief speech. Subjects who thought about reasons reported feeling significantly less anxious during their speech than did subjects in a control, no-introspection condition. Thus, a feeling that was undesirable from the subjects' perspective—speech anxiety—was changed by asking people to justify it (see also Leone & Baldwin, 1983; Leone, Minor, & Baltimore, 1983). When people think about their reasons for their anxieties, they presumably find it difficult to think of logical, rational reasons, and this inability to justify their negative affect succeeds in changing it. It is not clear how long-lasting such change is, thus we are not suggesting that thinking about reasons be adopted as a powerful therapeutic technique. Nonetheless, the Tesser *et al.* (1978) study is a good example of a case in which analyzing reasons can have beneficial rather than undesirable consequences.

Analyzing reasons may also be useful as a way of challenging attitudes that are harmful from a societal perspective. Generalizing from the Tesser *et al.* (1978) study, people asked to justify their racist attitudes might find it difficult to do so, and thus they might moderate their beliefs. Again, we are not suggesting that this will necessarily produce long-lasting reductions in prejudicial attitudes; indeed, the available evidence suggests that changes in attitudes will be more likely to occur than changes in behavior. With undesirable feelings such as racial prejudice, however, it is desirable to unfreeze the attitude, even if behavioral change does not immediately follow.

It is best not to think about reasons when the function of the attitude object is to give us pleasure, when our attitude is affectively based, and when we have no desire to change our feelings. If a couple is quite happy with their feelings toward each other, attempts to justify these feelings may not be productive. Many affectively based attitudes cause no discomfort (unlike speech anxiety) and cause no harm to others (unlike racial prejudice), including feelings about our spouses, friends, and hobbies—not to mention strawberry jams and art posters. When asked to report these types of feelings, people would do well to follow the advice one of us recently received in a fortune cookie: "Answer just what your heart prompts you."

Acknowledgments

The writing of this chapter and the research it reports were supported by grants from the National Science Foundation (BNS-8316189) and the National Institute of Mental Health (MH41841). We would like to thank several people who read a previous draft of this chapter and who provided extremely valuable feedback, including Robert Abelson, Gene Borgida, Bella DePaulo, Arie Kruglanski, Richard Petty, Jonathan Schooler, Jeanne Smith, Mark Snyder, Claude Steele, Abe Tesser, and Chris Wetzel.

References

Abelson, R. P., Kinder, D. R., Peters, M. D., & Fiske, S. T. (1982). Affective and semantic components in political person perception. *Journal of Personality and Social Psychology*, **42**, 619–630.
Berscheid, E., Graziano, W., Monson, T., & Dermer, M. (1976). Outcome dependency: Attention, attribution, and attraction. *Journal of Personality and Social Psychology*, **34**, 978–989.

Brock, T. C. (1967). Communication discrepancy and intent to persuade as determinants of counterargument production. *Journal of Experimental Social Psychology, 3,* 269–309.

Cacioppo, J. T., & Petty, R. E. (1981). Social psychological procedures for cognitive response assessment: The thought listing technique. In T. Merluzzi, C. Glass, & M. Genest (Eds.), *Cognitive assessment.* New York: Guilford.

Campbell, A., Converse, P. E., Miller, W. E., & Stokes, D. E. (1960). *The American voter.* New York: Wiley.

Campbell, D. T. (1963). Social attitudes and other acquired behavioral dispositions. In S. Koch (Ed.), *Psychology: A study of science* (Vol. 6, pp. 94–172). New York: McGraw-Hill.

Carper, J., & Doob, L. W. (1953). Intervening responses between questions and answers in attitude surveys. *Public Opinion Quarterly, 17,* 511–519.

Carver, C. S., & Scheier, M. F. (1981). *Attention and self-regulation: A control-theory approach to human behavior.* New York: Springer-Verlag.

Clary, E. G., & Tesser, A. (1983). Reactions to unexpected events: The naive scientist and interpretive activity. *Personality and Social Psychology Bulletin, 9,* 609–620.

Converse, P. E. (1970). Attitudes and non-attitudes: Continuation of a dialogue. In E. R. Tufte (Ed.), *The quantitative analysis of social problems* (pp. 168–189). Reading, MA: Addison-Wesley.

Duval, S., & Wicklund, R. A. (1972). *A theory of objective self-awareness.* New York: Academic Press.

Ellsworth, P. C., & Ross, L. (1983). Public opinion and capital punishment: A close examination of the views of abolitionists and retentionists. *Crime and Delinquency, 29,* 116–169.

Ericsson, K. A., & Simon, H. A. (1980). Verbal reports as data. *Psychological Review, 87,* 215–251.

Ericsson, K. A., & Simon, H. A. (1984). *Protocol analysis: Verbal reports as data.* Cambridge, MA: MIT Press.

Fazio, R. H. (1986). How do attitudes guide behavior? In R. M. Sorrentino & E. T. Higgins (Eds.), *The handbook of motivation and cognition: Foundations of social behavior* (pp. 204–243). New York: Guilford Press.

Fazio, R. H., Chen, J., McDonel, E., & Sherman, S. J. (1982). Attitude accessibility, attitude–behavior consistency, and the strength of the object–evaluation association. *Journal of Experimental Social Psychology, 18,* 339–357.

Fazio, R. H., & Zanna, M. P. (1981). Direct experience and attitude–behavior consistency. In L. Berkowitz (Ed.), *Advances in experimental social psychology* (Vol. 14, pp. 161–202). New York: Academic Press.

Fenigstein, A., Scheier, M. F., & Buss, A. H. (1975). Public and private self-consciousness: Assessment and theory. *Journal of Consulting and Clinical Psychology, 43,* 522–527.

Greenwald, A. G. (1968). Cognitive learning, cognitive response to persuasion, and attitude change. In A. Greenwald, T. Brock, & T. Ostrom (Eds.), *Psychological foundations of attitudes* (pp. 148–170). New York: Academic Press.

Hamill, R., Wilson, T. D., & Nisbett, R. E. (1980). Insensitivity to sample bias: Generalizing from atypical cases. *Journal of Personality and Social Psychology, 39,* 578–589.

Harvey, J. H., Yarkin, K. L., Lightner, J. M., & Town, J. P. (1980). Unsolicited interpretation and recall of interpersonal events. *Journal of Personality and Social Psychology, 38,* 551–568.

Hastie, R. (1984). Causes and effects of causal attribution. *Journal of Personality and Social Psychology, 46,* 44–56.

Herek, G. (1986). The instrumentality of attitudes: Toward a neofunctional theory. *Journal of Social Issues, 42,* 99–114.

Hovland, C. I. (1959). Reconciling conflicting results derived from experimental and survey studies of attitude change. *American Psychologist, 14,* 8–17.

Hyman, H. H. (1959). *Political socialization.* Glencoe, IL: Free Press.

Insko, C. A., & Cialdini, C. A. (1971). *Interpersonal influence in a controlled setting: The verbal reinforcement of attitude.* New York: General Learning Press.

Janis, I. L., & Mann, L. (1977). *Decision making: A psychological analysis of conflict, choice, and commitment.* New York: Free Press.

Langer, E. (1978). Rethinking the role of thought in social interaction. In J. H. Harvey, W. Ickes, & R. F. Kidd (Eds.), *New directions in attribution research* (Vol. 2, pp. 35–58). Hillsdale, NJ: Erlbaum.

LaPiere, R. T. (1934). Attitudes vs. actions. *Social Forces*, **13**, 230–237.

Lau, R. R., & Russell, D. (1980). Attributions in the sports pages: A field test of some current hypotheses in attribution research. *Journal of Personality and Social Psychology*, **39**, 29–38.

Leone, C., & Baldwin, R. T. (1983). Thought-induced changes in fear: Thinking sometimes makes it so. *Journal of Social and Clinical Psychology*, **1**, 72–83.

Leone, C., Minor, S. W., & Baltimore, M. L. (1983). A comparison of cognitive and performance-based treatment analogues: Constrained thought versus performance accomplishments. *Cognitive Therapy and Research*, **7**, 445–454.

Lepper, M. R., & Greene, M. (1978). *The hidden costs of reward: New perspectives on the psychology of human motivation.* Hillsdale, NJ: Erlbaum.

Lieberman, D. A. (1979). Behaviorism and the mind: A (limited) call for a return to introspection. *American Psychologist*, **34**, 319–333.

Lingle, J. H., & Ostrom, T. M. (1981). Principles of memory and cognition in attitude formation. In R. E. Petty, T. M. Ostrom, & T. C. Brock (Eds.), *Cognitive responses in persuasion* (pp. 399–420). Hillsdale, NJ: Erlbaum.

Loomis, L. R. (Ed.). (1942). *Plato: Apology, Crito, Phaedo, Symposium, Republic* (B. Jowett, Trans.). New York: Walter J. Black.

Lusk, C. M., & Judd, C. M. (1988). Political expertise and the structural mediators of candidate evaluations. *Journal of Experimental Social Psychology*, **24**, 105–126.

Marsh, P., & Collett, P. (1987, June). Driving passion. *Psychology Today*, 16–24.

Millar, M. G., & Tesser, A. (1986). Effects of affective and cognitive focus on the attitude–behavior relationship. *Journal of Personality and Social Psychology*, **51**, 270–276.

Millar, M. G., & Tesser, A. (1988). The effects of affective-cognitive consistency and thought on the attitude-behavior relation. *Journal of Experimental Social Psychology*, in press.

Monson, T. C., Keel, R., Stephens, D., & Genung, V. (1982). Trait attributions: Relative validity, covariation with behavior, and prospect of future interaction. *Journal of Personality and Social Psychology*, **42**, 1014–1024.

Mosteller, F. M., & Bush, R. R. (1954). Selected quantitative techniques. In G. Lindzey & E. Aronson (Eds.), *Handbook of social psychology: Vol. 1. Theory and method* (pp. 289–334). Cambridge, MA: Addison-Wesley.

Murdoch, I. (1986). *The good apprentice.* New York: Viking Press.

Nisbett, R. E., & Ross, L. D. (1980). *Human inference: Strategies and shortcomings of social judgment.* Englewood Cliffs, NJ: Prentice-Hall.

Nisbett, R. E., & Wilson, T. D. (1977a). The halo effect: Evidence for unconscious alteration of judgments. *Journal of Personality and Social Psychology*, **35**, 250–256.

Nisbett, R. E., & Wilson, T. D. (1977b). Telling more than we can know: Verbal reports on mental processes. *Psychological Review*, **84**, 231–259.

Norman, R. (1975). Affective–cognitive consistency, attitudes, conformity, and behavior. *Journal of Personality and Social Psychology*, **32**, 83–91.

Pittman, T. S., & Pittman, N. L. (1980). Deprivation of control and the attribution process. *Journal of Personality and Social Psychology*, **39**, 377–389.

Pryor, J. B., Gibbons, F. X., Wicklund, R. A., Fazio, R. H., & Hood, R. (1977). Self-focused attention and self-report validity. *Journal of Personality*, **45**, 514–527.

Pyszczynski, T. A., & Greenberg, J. (1981). Role of disconfirmed expectancies in the instigation of attributional processing. *Journal of Personality and Social Psychology, 40,* 31–38.

Quindlen, A. (1987, February 25). Life in the 80s. *The New York Times,* p. C12.

Regan, D. T., & Fazio, R. H. (1977). On the consistency between attitudes and behavior: Look to the method of attitude formation. *Journal of Experimental Social Psychology, 13,* 38–45.

Roethke, T. (1975). *The collected poems of Theodore Roethke.* Garden City, NY: Anchor Books.

Rokeach, M. (1973). *The nature of human values.* New York: The Free Press.

Rosenberg, M. J. (1956). Cognitive structure and attitudinal affect. *Journal of Abnormal and Social Psychology, 53,* 367–372.

Rosenberg, M. J. (1960). A structural theory of attitude dynamics. *Public Opinion Quarterly, 24,* 319–341.

Rosenberg, M. J. (1968). Hedonism, inauthenticity, and other goals toward expansion of a consistency theory. In R. P. Abelson, E. Aronson, W. J. McGuire, T. M. Newcomb, M. J. Rosenberg, & P. H. Tannenbaum (Eds.), *Theories of consistency: A sourcebook* (pp. 73–111). Chicago: Rand McNally.

Rosenthal, R. (1978). Combining results of independent studies. *Psychological Bulletin, 85,* 185–193.

Salancik, G. R. (1974). Inference of one's attitude from behavior recalled under linguistically manipulated cognitive sets. *Journal of Experimental Social Psychology, 10,* 415–427.

Scheier, M. F., Buss, A. H., & Buss, D. M. (1978). Self-consciousness, self-report of aggressiveness, and aggression. *Journal of Research in Personality, 12,* 133–140.

Schlegel, R. P. (1975). Multidimensional measurement of attitudes toward smoking marijuana. *Canadian Journal of Behavioral Science, 8,* 387–396.

Schlegel, R. P., & DiTecco, D. (1982). Attitudinal structures and the attitude–behavior relation. In M. P. Zanna, E. T. Higgins, & C. P. Herman (Eds.), *Consistency in social behavior: The Ontario Symposium* (Vol. 2, pp. 17–49). Hillsdale, NJ: Erlbaum.

Sears, D. O. (1983). The persistence of early political predispositions: The roles of attitude object and life stage. In L. Wheeler & P. Shaver (Eds.), *Review of personality and social psychology* (Vol. 4, pp. 79–116). Beverly Hills, CA: Sage.

Seligman, C., Fazio, R. H., & Zanna, M. P. (1980). Effects of salience of extrinsic rewards on liking and loving. *Journal of Personality and Social Psychology, 38,* 453–460.

Seligman, C., Kriss, M., Darley, J. M., Fazio, R. H., Becker, L. J., & Pryor, J. B. (1979). Predicting summer energy consumption from homeowners' attitudes. *Journal of Applied Social Psychology, 9,* 70–90.

Sherif, C. W., Sherif, M., & Nebergall, R. E. (1965). *Attitude and attitude change.* Philadelphia: W. B. Saunders.

Sherif, M., & Hovland, C. I. (1961). *Social judgment: Assimilation and contrast effects in communication and attitude change.* New Haven: Yale University Press.

Smith, E. R., & Miller, F. D. (1978). Limits on perception of cognitive processes: A reply to Nisbett and Wilson. *Psychological Review, 85,* 355–362.

Snyder, M. (1982). When believing means doing: Creating links between attitudes and behavior. In M. P. Zanna, E. T. Higgins, & C. P. Herman (Eds.), *Consistency in social behavior: The Ontario Symposium* (Vol. 2, pp. 105–130). Hillsdale, NJ: Erlbaum.

Snyder, M., & Kendzierski, D. (1982). Acting on one's attitudes: Procedures for linking attitude and behavior. *Journal of Experimental Social Psychology, 18,* 165–183.

Snyder, M., & Swann, W. B. (1976). When actions reflect attitudes: The politics of impression management. *Journal of Personality and Social Psychology, 34,* 1034–1042.

Staats, A. W., & Staats, C. K. (1958). Attitudes established by classical conditioning. *Journal of Abnormal and Social Psychology, 57,* 37–40.

Tesser, A. (1978). Self-generated attitude change. In L. Berkowitz (Ed.), *Advances in experimental social psychology* (Vol. 11, pp. 289–338). New York: Academic Press.

Tesser, A., Leone, C., & Clary, G. (1978). Affect control: Process constraints versus catharsis. *Cognitive Therapy and Research*, **2**, 265–274.

Tetlock, P. E., & Manstead, A. S. R. (1985). Impression management versus intrapsychic explanations in social psychology: A useful dichotomy? *Psychological Review*, **92**, 59–77.

Titchener, E. B. (1912). The schema of introspection. *American Journal of Psychology*, **23**, 485–508.

Vargas Llosa, M. (1986, February 16). My son the Rastafarian. *The New York Times Magazine*, pp. 20–28, 30, 41–43, 67.

Watson, J. B. (1913). Psychology as the behaviorist views it. *Psychological Review*, **20**, 158–177.

Wicklund, R. A. (1975). Objective self-awareness. In L. Berkowitz (Ed.), *Advances in experimental social psychology* (Vol. 8, pp. 233–275). New York: Academic Press.

Wicklund, R. A. (1982). Self-focused attention and the validity of self-reports. In M. P. Zanna, E. T. Higgins, & C. P. Herman (Eds.), *Consistency in social behavior: The Ontario Symposium* (Vol. 2, pp. 149–172). Hillsdale, NJ: Erlbaum.

Wilson, T. D. (1985a). [Role of confidence in moderating the effects of analyzing reasons on attitude–behavior consistency.] Unpublished raw data.

Wilson, T. D. (1985b). Strangers to ourselves: The origins and accuracy of beliefs about one's own mental states. In J. H. Harvey & G. Weary (Eds.), *Attribution in contemporary psychology* (pp. 9–36). New York: Academic Press.

Wilson, T. D., & Dunn, D. S. (1986a). Effects of introspection on attitude–behavior consistency: Analyzing reasons versus focusing on feelings. *Journal of Experimental Social Psychology*, **22**, 249–263.

Wilson, T. D., & Dunn, D. S. (1986b). [Thinking about reasons does not increase the complexity of people's attitudes.] Unpublished raw data.

Wilson, T. D., Dunn, D. S., Bybee, J. A., Hyman, D. B., & Rotondo, J. A. (1984). Effects of analyzing reasons on attitude–behavior consistency. *Journal of Personality and Social Psychology*, **47**, 5–16.

Wilson, T. D., Hull, J. G., & Johnson, J. (1981). Awareness and self-perception: Verbal reports on internal states. *Journal of Personality and Social Psychology*, **40**, 53–71.

Wilson, T. D., & Kraft, D. (1988). [The effects of analyzing reasons on affectively- versus cognitively-based attitudes.] Unpublished raw data.

Wilson, T. D., Kraft, D., & Dunn, D. S. (1988a). *The disruptive effects of explaining attitudes: Boundary conditions and mediating processes.* Unpublished manuscript, University of Virginia, Charlottesville.

Wilson, T. D., Kraft, D., & Lisle, D. J. (1988b). *Effects of unexpected affective reactions on amount of thought and attitude–behavior consistency.* Unpublished manuscript, University of Virginia, Charlottesville.

Wilson, T. D., & Linville, P. W. (1982). Improving the academic performance of college freshmen: Attribution therapy revisited. *Journal of Personality and Social Psychology*, **42**, 367–376.

Wilson, T. D., Lisle, D. J., Kraft, D., & Wetzel, C. G. (in press). Preferences as expectation-driven inferences: Effects of affective expectations on affective experience. *Journal of Personality and Psychology*.

Wilson, T. D., Lisle, D. J., & Schooler, J. (1988c). *Some undesirable effects of self-reflection.* Unpublished manuscript, University of Virginia, Charlottesville.

Wilson, T. D., & Stone, J. I. (1985). More on telling more than we can know. In P. Shaver (Ed.), *Review of personality and social psychology* (Vol. 6, pp. 167–183). Beverly Hills, CA: Sage.

Wong, P. T. P., & Weiner, B. (1981). When people ask "why" questions, and the heuristics of attributional search. *Journal of Personality and Social Psychology*, **40**, 650–663.

Zajonc, R. B. (1960). The process of cognitive tuning in communication. *Journal of Abnormal and Social Psychology*, **61**, 159–167.

Zajonc, R. B. (1968). Attitudinal effects of mere exposure. *Journal of Personality and Social Psychology Monograph*, **9**, 1–28.

Zajonc, R. B. (1980). Feeling and thinking: Preferences need no inferences. *American Psychologist,* **35,** 151–175.

Zajonc, R. B., & Markus, H. (1982). Affective and cognitive factors in preferences. *Journal of Consumer Research,* **9,** 123–131.

Zanna, M. P., Kiesler, C. A., & Pilkonis, P. A. (1970). Positive and negative attitudinal affect established by classical conditioning. *Journal of Personality and Social Psychology,* **14,** 321–328.

Zanna, M. P., & Rempel, J. K. (1988). Attitudes: A new look at an old concept. In D. Bar-Tal & A. Kruglanksi (Eds.), *The social psychology of knowledge.* New York: Cambridge University Press, in press.

INDEX

A

Acetylcholine, social psychophysiology and, 50
Action, social psychophysiology and, 50–54
Affect
  anger and, 31, 32
    approaches, 6, 7
    cognitive-neoassociationistic analysis, 7, 9–12
    present research, 16, 28, 31
  confession and, 215
  disruptive effects of explaining why and, 334–336
    alternative explanations, 319–324
    boundary conditions, 308–318
    conditions, 327–329
    hypotheses, 301–307
    self-persuasion, 298, 299
    trouble, 330–334
  self-discrepancy theory and, 94, 117
  social psychophysiology and
    facial EMG, 68–71
    facial response system, 50, 65
    obstacles, 73, 76
    response patterning, 44
  sociocognitive model of attitudes and, 254
Aggression
  anger and, 1, 2, 31, 34
    approaches, 3
    cognitive-neoassociationistic analysis, 7, 8, 10–13
    present research, 13, 14, 18, 21, 28
  mindlessness-mindfulness and, 161
Agitation, self-discrepancy theory and, 94, 123, 125–130
  emotional-motivational problems, 102
  motivation, 97
  negative consequences, 111
  socialization of self-beliefs, 107
Alertness, mindlessness-mindfulness and, 143
Alzheimer's disease, mindlessness-mindfulness and, 145
Anger, 1, 2, 31–34
  approaches, 2, 3, 6, 7
    cognitive processes, 3–6
  cognitive-neoassociationistic analysis, 7
    conceptual distinctions, 7, 8
    evidence, 8, 9
    memory, 11–13
    subsequent cognitive processing, 9–11
  inhibition and, 234, 236, 237
  present research, 13, 14
    experiments, 14–31
  self-discrepancy theory and, 128
  social psychophysiology and, 48
Animal learning, inhibition and, 235
Annoyance, anger and, 2, 31–34
  cognitive-neoassociationistic analysis, 10, 11, 13
  present research, 13, 14, 16, 19, 23–30
Anxiety
  disruptive effects of explaining why and, 337
  inhibition and, 234
  mindlessness-mindfulness and, 156
  self-discrepancy theory and, 101–103, 109, 111
Appraisal, anger and
  approaches, 4–6
  cognitive-neoassociationistic analysis, 7, 9
  present research, 14
Apprehension, social psychophysiology and, 54

345

INDEX

Approach-approach conflict, self-discrepancy theory and, 114
Approach-avoidance conflict, self-discrepancy theory and, 114, 115, 128
Arousal
  anger and, 31
    approaches, 3, 4
    cognitive-neoassociationistic analysis, 9, 10, 12
    present research, 13, 14, 28-30
  self-discrepancy theory and, 95
  social psychophysiology and, 77, 78
    errors of inference, 67
    facial response system, 60, 64, 65
    obstacles, 74-76
Association, social psychophysiology and, 82
  facial EMG, 71
  facial response system, 56-59
Attention
  anger and, 9, 10, 15
  mindlessness-mindfulness and, 139, 140, 142
    related concepts, 151, 152, 154
  social psychophysiology and, 44, 54, 61, 68, 76
Attitudes
  anger and, 10, 26-28
  disruptive effects of explaining why and, 287-289, 334-338
    alternative explanations, 319-326
    boundary conditions, 308-318
    conditions, 327-330
    consistency reduction, 289-296
    hypotheses, 301-307
    self-persuasion, 296-300
    trouble, 330-334
  social control and
    dissent, 200, 202
    uniformity, 177, 184, 185
  social psychophysiology and, 42
    empirical anomalies, 78
    facial response system, 50-53, 58, 59
    obstacles, 76
Attitudes, sociocognitive model of, 245, 273-275
  concept, 245, 246
  heuristic, 253, 254
    conceptual memory, 255
    conceptual processing, 255-259
    implications for behavior, 259, 260
  importance, 246
  object identification, 250
    difficulty, 250, 251
    predictive utility, 251-253
  schematic function, 261, 267
    bipolar attitude structure, 263, 264
    definition, 261, 262
    episodic memory, 262
    unipolar attitude structure, 264-266
  self-functions, 267, 268
    evidence, 269-272
    facets of self, 268, 269
    importance, 272, 273
Attributes
  anger and
    approaches, 3-5
    cognitive-neoassociationistic analysis, 9
    present research, 13, 14
  disruptive effects of explaining why and, 289
    conditions, 326, 327
    self-persuasion, 298, 299
  inhibition and, 239
  mindlessness-mindfulness and, 138, 141
  self-discrepancy theory and, 93, 94, 120, 123-130
    emotional-motivational problems, 100, 101
    motivation, 95-97
    negative consequences, 108, 111
    self-guide, 115
    socialization of self-beliefs, 107
    vulnerability, 112-114, 116, 119
  social psychophysiology and, 78
  sociocognitive model of attitudes and, 254, 261
Authority, social control and, 182, 196
Automaticity
  inhibition and, 234, 235
  mindlessness-mindfulness and, 151-155
Autonomic nervous system
  confession and, 214, 225-228
  inhibition and, 231, 235
Autonomic reactions, disruptive effects of explaining why and, 301
Aversive stimuli, anger and, 1, 2, 31-34
  approaches, 2-7
  cognitive-neoassociationistic analysis, 7, 9, 10, 13

present research, 14, 16, 18–20, 23–28
Avoidance, *see also* Approach-avoidance conflict
 anger and, 7
 inhibition and, 235
Awakening, social psychophysiology and, 71

B

Basking in reflected glory, sociocognitive model of attitudes and, 269
Beck Depression Inventory
 confession and, 215
 self-discrepancy theory and
  emotional-motivational problems, 101, 102
  negative consequences, 108–111
  vulnerability, 119
Behavioral inhibition system, 235
Bias
 disruptive effects of explaining why and, 288, 335
  boundary conditions, 308, 309, 317
  hypotheses, 301, 305–307
  self-persuasion, 297–300
 self-discrepancy theory and, 111
 social control and, 190, 191
 social psychophysiology and, 42
 sociocognitive model of attitudes and, 257, 258
Biosensory processes, social psychophysiology and, 58
Blatt Depressive Experience Questionnaire, self-discrepancy theory and, 101
Blocking, social psychophysiology and, 69
Boredom, mindlessness-mindfulness and, 154
Brain
 confession and, 214, 228, 229
 inhibition and, 240
 mindlessness-mindfulness and, 146
 social psychophysiology and, 61
Brainwashing, inhibition and, 238, 239

C

Capacity, mindlessness-mindfulness and, 140, 152–154

Cardiovascular measures
 confession and, 225, 226
 inhibition and, 235
Categories
 disruptive effects of explaining why and, 329, 330
 mindlessness-mindfulness and, 138, 139
  health, 145, 147
  misconceptions, 157, 158
  related concepts, 153, 154
 self-discrepancy theory and, 124
 social psychophysiology and, 56
 sociocognitive model of attitudes and, 250, 255, 263, 272
Catharsis
 confession and, 218
 inhibition and, 232, 236, 237
Central nervous system, confession and, 228–230
Centrality, disruptive effects of explaining why and, 324
Cerebral cortex, confession and, 228
Cholinesterase, social psychophysiology and, 50
Coalition model of emotion, social psychophysiology and, 60–65
Cognition
 anger and, 2
 confession and, 212–214, 220
 disruptive effects of explaining why and, 287–289, 335–337
  alternative explanations, 319–325
  boundary conditions, 308–312, 314–318
  conditions, 327
  hypotheses, 301, 302, 304–307
  self-persuasion, 298–300
  trouble, 330–334
 inhibition and, 231–234, 236, 237, 240
 mindlessness-mindfulness and, 137–142, 168
  alternate view, 159–165
  health, 144, 145, 147
  performance, 149, 150
  preventing mindlessness, 165, 167
  related concepts, 151, 152, 154, 155
 self-discrepancy theory and, 95, 97, 98, 122–124
 social control and, 198
 social psychophysiology and, 41, 43
  changing zeitgeist, 80

Cognition, social psychophysiology (*cont.*)
  facial EMG, 71
  facial response system, 50, 54, 58, 59, 61
  obstacles, 73-75
  perioral EMG, 73
  response patterning, 44
  sociocognitive model of attitudes and, 245-250, 273
    heuristic, 254, 260
    object identification, 250
    schematic function, 261
    self-functions, 267, 268, 272, 273, 279
Cognitive and Somatic Anxiety Questionnaire, confession and, 221, 222
Cognitive dissonance, social psychophysiology and, 75, 77
Cognitive-neoassociationistic analysis, anger and, 7-13, 31
Cohesion, social control and, 204
Collective self, sociocognitive model of attitudes and, 268
Complexity, disruptive effects of explaining why and, 324
Compliance
  mindlessness-mindfulness and, 147
  social control and, 194, 195
  sociocognitive model of attitudes and, 269
Compromise, social control and, 177, 178, 187, 189
Computerized axial tomography scans, mindlessness-mindfulness and, 145
Conditioning
  disruptive effects of explaining why and, 298, 308, 312
  inhibition and, 235
Confession, 211, 212, 238, 239
  effects, 222, 229
    autonomic nervous system, 225-228
    central nervous system, 228-230
    health, 222-225
  trauma and
    background, 212-214
    disclosure, 217-222
Conformity
  social control and
    dissent, 195, 197, 198
    uniformity, 176, 182-185, 192, 193
  sociocognitive model of attitudes and, 271

Confrontation, inhibition and, 230, 231, 233, 235-237
Confusion, self-discrepancy theory and, 114-116, 128
Consensus
  social control and
    dissent, 197, 198
    uniformity, 189-195
  sociocognitive model of attitudes and, 257, 269, 273
Consistency
  disruptive effects of explaining why and, 288, 289, 336
    alternative explanations, 319, 320, 322
    boundary conditions, 308, 309, 311, 313, 316, 317
    conditions, 327-330
    hypotheses, 301, 302, 304-307
    reduction, 289-296
    self-persuasion, 296, 297, 299
  mindlessness-mindfulness and, 151, 157
  self-discrepancy theory and, 93, 96
  social control and, 186, 187
  social psychophysiology and, 44
  sociocognitive model of attitudes and, 247, 248, 273
    heuristic, 258-260
    object identification, 252-254
    self-functions, 272, 273
Constraints
  confession and, 220
  sociocognitive model of attitudes and, 260
Context
  inhibition and, 239
  mindlessness-mindfulness and, 167, 168
    alternate view, 159-161, 163
    health, 144
    misconceptions, 156
    related concepts, 153, 154
  self-discrepancy theory and, 105
  social control and, 180, 184
Contingency
  mindlessness-mindfulness and, 163
  self-discrepancy theory and
    negative consequences, 109, 110
    socialization of self-beliefs, 105, 106, 108
  social control and, 182, 194, 204
Convergence, social control and, 178, 198, 201

INDEX

Coping
   confession and, 213
   inhibition and, 235
   social control and, 184
Corrugator supercilii, social
    psychophysiology and, 68, 69
Cortical congruence, confession and, 228, 229
Counterlearning, inhibition and, 235
Cues
   anger and, 3, 12
   mindlessness-mindfulness and, 141, 148, 157
   social control and, 185
   social psychophysiology and, 77
    facial EMG, 54–56, 58
    obstacles, 74

D

Debriefing, confession and, 216, 217
Decision making
   disruptive effects of explaining why and, 288
   social control and, 196–198, 200, 201
Dejection, self-discrepancy theory and, 94, 121, 123, 125–127, 129
   emotional-motivational problems, 101
   motivation, 97
   vulnerability, 113, 119
Demographics, social control and, 202
Dendrites, mindlessness-mindfulness and, 146
Depression
   anger and, 8, 9
   confession and, 215, 217, 218
   disruptive effects of explaining why and, 299
   inhibition and, 236, 238
   mindlessness-mindfulness and, 144
   self-discrepancy theory and, 127, 128
    emotional-motivational problems, 101–103
    negative consequences, 109–111
    vulnerability, 118, 119
Deviance
   mindlessness-mindfulness and, 148
   social control and, 186–188, 195
Devil's advocate, social control and, 201
Differentiation
   disruptive effects of explaining why and, 324
   social psychophysiology and, 56

Disclosure
   confession and
    effects, 223, 224, 226, 227, 229
    trauma, 217–222
   inhibition and, 235, 238
Discomfort, self-discrepancy theory and, 99, 107
Disconfirmation, social psychophysiology and, 76, 77
Discrepancies, disruptive effects of explaining why and, 319–321
Discrimination
   mindlessness-mindfulness and, 140, 167
   social psychophysiology and, 56, 57, 82
Disease
   confession and, *see* Confession
   inhibition and, *see* Inhibition
Disinhibition, confession and, 220, 222
Disruptive effects of explaining why, 287–289
   alternative explanations, 319
    cognitive diffentiation, 322–325
    confidence in attitudes, 321, 322
    demand characteristics, 325, 326
    discrepancies, 319–321
   attitude-behavior consistency, reduction of, 289–296
    boundary conditions, 308–312, 318
    empirical tests, 312–317
    predicting behavior, 317, 318
   conditions, 326–330
   hypotheses, 301–307
   recommendations, 335–338
   self-persuasion, 296–300
   trouble, 330, 331
    attitude objects, 331–333
    stimulus function, 333, 334
    unanswered questions, 334, 335
Dissent, social control and, 175, 195, 196
   integrating differentiation, 202–204
   performance, 200–202
   permitting truth, 196, 197
   permitting untruth, 197–200
   uniformity, 176, 185–190, 193
Dissociation, inhibition and, 234
Dissonance
   inhibition and, 239
   sociocognitive model of attitudes and, 251, 269, 270, 273
Distortion, social psychophysiology and, 66
Distractibility, self-discrepancy theory and, 115, 128

INDEX

Distraction
  anger and, 29
  inhibition and, 233
Distress
  anger and, 21, 24, 26-28, 30, 33
  self-discrepancy theory and, 93, 97, 106
Dreams, social psychophysiology and, 71
Drive, social psychophysiology and, 74, 75
Duncan Multiple Range test, anger and, 26
Dyslexia, mindlessness-mindfulness and, 166

E

Education, inhibition and, 239
Effectors, social psychophysiology and, 47
Efference, social psychophysiology and
  empirical anomalies, 78
  facial response system, 48-50, 52, 60, 61, 63
Ego-defensive functions, sociocognitive model of attitudes and, 267
Ego tasks, sociocognitive model of attitudes and, 268, 272
Elaboration, social psychophysiology and, 56
Electrodermal activity, social psychophysiology and, 67
Electroencephalographic activity
  confession and, 229
  social psychophysiology and, 71
Electromyographic activity
  confession and, 226
  social psychophysiology and, 82
    affect, 68-71
    facial response system, 50-60
    perioral EMG, 71-73
    response patterning, 45, 47
Electrooculargraphic activity, social psychophysiology and, 71
Emblems, social psychophysiology and, 48
Emotion
  anger and, 2
    approaches, 3-6
    cognitive-neoassociationistic analysis, 8-11
    present research, 13, 14
  confession and
    effects, 223, 225, 226, 228
    trauma, 218, 221
  disruptive effects of explaining why and, 310
  inhibition and, 232, 235-238, 240
  mindlessness-mindfulness and, 139
  self-discrepancy theory and, 93-95, 120, 122-130
    emotional-motivational problems, 99-104
    motivation, 95-98
    negative consequences, 109, 111
    self-guide, 115
    socialization of self-beliefs, 104, 108
    vulnerability, 112, 113, 116-120
  social psychophysiology and, 41-43, 82
    changing zeitgeist, 80
    empirical anomalies, 78, 79
    errors of inference, 65
    facial EMG, 68, 69, 71
    facial response system, 48, 50, 54, 58-65
    obstacles, 74
    perioral EMG, 73
    response patterning, 44
Encoding
  mindlessness-mindfulness and, 149, 152
  social psychophysiology and, 44, 54
  sociocognitive model of attitudes and, 261-264
Enzymes, social psychophysiology and, 50
Episodic memory, sociocognitive model of attitudes and, 255, 262
Escalation, social control and, 190-192
Escape, anger and, 7
Evaluation, social psychophysiology and, 56, 57
Excitation
  anger and, 3
  social psychophysiology and, 45, 62
Externalization
  social psychophysiology and, 63, 64
  sociocognitive model of attitudes and, 267
Extinction, inhibition and, 235

F

Facial electromyographic activity, social psychophysiology and, 68-71, 82
Facial response system, social psychophysiology and, 46-48
  coalition model of emotion, 60-65
  efference, 48-50

perioral EMG, 54–57
persuasive appeals, 58–60
skeletomuscular patterning, 50–54
Fatigue, anger and, 8
Fear
  anger and
    approaches, 3
    cognitive-neoassociationistic analysis, 7–9, 11, 12
  confession and, 227
  inhibition and, 234
  self-discrepancy theory and, 97, 109
  social psychophysiology and, 48
Fear of Negative Evaluation Scale, self-discrepancy theory and, 102
Feedback
  anger and, 5, 6, 15
  confession and, 225
  disruptive effects of explaining why and, 328
  self-discrepancy theory and, 93, 95
  social control and, 199
  social psychophysiology and, 50, 54, 61
Feelings
  anger and, 19–21, 23, 29, 31–33
  disruptive effects of explaining why and, 335, 337, 338
    alternative explanations, 319, 321
    consistency reduction, 292, 294
    self-persuasion, 297, 299
    trouble, 331
  self-discrepancy theory and, 93
  social psychophysiology and, 64, 78
Flexibility, mindlessness-mindfulness and, 138, 157
Frame of reference, social control and, 177, 178
Frustration, confession and, 218

G

Gain mechanisms, social psychophysiology and, 64
Gating, social psychophysiology and, 64
Goals
  inhibition and, 233, 238, 239
  social control and, 175
    dissent, 196, 197
    uniformity, 176, 177, 182, 188, 194, 195
  sociocognitive model of attitudes and, 261, 268

Groups
  social control and, 175, 176
  uniformity, 176–179, 188
  sociocognitive model of attitudes and, 271, 272
Guilt
  confession and, 218
  inhibition and, 236

H

Habituation, mindlessness-mindfulness and, 146
Handwriting, confession and, 220, 221
Heart rate, confession and, 226, 227, 229
Heterogeneity, social control and, 200, 202–204
Heuristics, sociocognitive model of attitudes and, 249, 253, 254, 275
  conceptual memory, 255
  conceptual processing, 255–259
  implications for behavior, 259, 260
Hierarchy, social control and, 181, 182
Hippocampus, inhibition and, 235
History and Background Questionnaire, self-discrepancy theory and, 110, 111
Homogeneity, social control and, 200
Hopkins Symptom Checklist, self-discrepancy theory and, 101, 102, 108–110
Hostility
  anger and, 1, 2
  cognitive-neoassociationistic analysis, 7, 8, 10, 12
  present research, 14, 24, 27, 28
  inhibition and, 235
Hysterical personality, self-discrepancy theory and, 115

I

Ideals, self-discrepancy theory and, 120, 121, 125–127, 129
  negative consequences, 108–111
  socialization of self-beliefs, 114
  vulnerability, 118, 120
Identity
  social control and, 192, 195
  sociocognitive model of attitudes and, 268, 269, 272

INDEX

Illustrators, social psychophysiology and, 48
Imagery, social psychophysiology and
  facial EMG, 68
  facial response system, 50–54, 59, 60
  response patterning, 44
Immune function
  confession and, 222–225, 229
  inhibition and, 235, 240
Immune system
  confession and, 214
  mindlessness-mindfulness and, 147
Impression management, sociocognitive model of attitudes and, 270
Impulse, anger and, 9
Inconsistency, self-discrepancy theory and, 94
  motivation, 95, 96
  self-guide, 115
  vulnerability, 118
Independence, social control and, 192–195
Inference
  social psychophysiology and, 65–67
  sociocognitive model of attitudes and, 255, 256, 273
Inhibition, 212, 226, 230
  catharsis, 236, 237
  mindlessness-mindfulness and, 144
  perspectives, 232–235
  psychosomatics, 239, 240
  reconstructing self, 237–239
  social psychophysiology and, 45, 62
  theory, 230, 231
Initiative, social control and, 196, 197
Innovation, social control and, 175, 176, 204
  dissent, 195, 202–204
  uniformity, 194, 195
Insight, inhibition and, 236, 237
Instigation, anger and, 7, 8, 13
Intensity
  inhibition and, 237
  social psychophysiology and, 50
Internalization
  social control and, 184, 194
  sociocognitive model of attitudes and, 268, 269
Introspection, disruptive effects of explaining why and, 287, 289, 335–337
  alternative explanations, 322
  boundary conditions, 312, 318
  consistency reduction, 290, 292–294
  self-persuasion, 297
  trouble, 330, 331, 333, 334
IQ, mindlessness-mindfulness and, 142, 143
Irritability, anger and, 2, 31–34
  cognitive-neoassociationistic analysis, 10, 11, 13
  present research, 13, 14, 16, 19, 22, 24, 26–28, 30, 31

L

Labeling
  anger and, 3, 4
  social control and, 179, 185
  sociocognitive model of attitudes and, 249, 273, 275
    object identification, 250, 253
    self-functions, 272
Learned helplessness, anger and, 8
Locomotion, social control and, 176, 177

M

Manipulation
  anger and, 22–24
  confession and, 214, 223
  disruptive effects of explaining why and, 334, 335
    alternative explanations, 320, 321, 324, 325
    boundary conditions, 310–312, 314–316
    conditions, 326, 327
    consistency reduction, 294, 295
    hypotheses, 306
    self-persuasion, 298
    trouble, 331
  social control and, 193, 196
  social psychophysiology and, 48
  sociocognitive model of attitudes and, 251, 252, 257, 260
Marlowe-Crowne Social Desirability Scale, confession and, 215, 222
Memory
  anger and, 10–13, 31
  disruptive effects of explaining why and, 335
    boundary conditions, 309, 310
    self-persuasion, 297, 299, 300
  inhibition and, 233

mindlessness-mindfulness and, 145, 153
self-discrepancy theory and, 123, 124
social psychophysiology and
  facial response system, 50, 54-57
  perioral EMG, 73
sociocognitive model of attitudes and, 249, 274-275
  heuristic, 255, 257, 259
  object identification, 250
  schematic function, 261, 262, 266, 267
Mimicry, social psychophysiology and, 48, 50, 73
Mindfulness, *see* Mindlessness-mindfulness
Mindlessness-mindfulness, 137-142, 167, 168
  alternate view, 157-159
    anomalous findings, 161-164
    context, 159-161
    extending human potential, 164, 165
  health, 142-147
  misconceptions, 155-157
  performance
    practice, 147-149
    single exposure, 149-151
  preventing mindlessness, 165-167
  related concepts, 151-155
Minority views, social control and, 177
  dissent, 196-202
  uniformity, 183, 185-189, 192, 193
Mismatch hypothesis, disruptive effects of explaining why and, 305-307
Motivation
  anger and, 9
  disruptive effects of explaining why and, 301, 318
  mindlessness-mindfulness and, 152
  self-discrepancy theory and, 94-97, 120, 122, 124, 127-130
    emotional-motivational problems, 99-104
    information processing, 98
    negative consequences, 109
    self-guide, 115
    socialization of self-beliefs, 104-108
    vulnerability, 112, 113, 116-118, 120
  social control and, 192, 194
  sociocognitive model of attitudes and, 246-248
    heuristic, 254
    self-functions, 268
Motoneuron, social psychophysiology and, 49, 50

Muscle action potential, social psychophysiology and
  facial EMG, 69
  facial response system, 49-51, 61
Muscles, social psychophysiology and
  facial EMG, 47-51, 55, 57, 58, 61, 65, 68, 69
  perioral EMG, 71, 73
Muscular reactions, disruptive effects of explaining why and, 301

N

Neuromuscular reactions, anger and, 5
Norms
  disruptive effects of explaining why and, 299
  self-discrepancy theory and, 116
  social control and
    dissent, 196
    uniformity, 177-180, 189
  sociocognitive model of attitudes and, 271

O

Obsession, mindlessness-mindfulness and, 156
Optimism, confession and, 213
Orbicularis oculi, social psychophysiology and
  facial EMG, 48, 54, 57, 64
  response patterning, 45
Organization, disruptive effects of explaining why and, 324, 325
Organizations
  social control and, 175, 176
    dissent, 196, 200, 201, 203
    uniformity, 179-182, 184, 185, 188-192, 194, 195
  sociocognitive model of attitudes and, 257, 260
Overlearning, mindlessness-mindfulness and, 149

P

Perceived control, mindlessness-mindfulness and, 143, 144, 159
Performance, social control and, 194-196, 199

Periocular activity, social psychophysiology and, 45, 47, 64, 65
Perioral activity, social psychophysiology and EMG, 71-73
  facial response system, 48, 50, 54-59
Persuasion
  disruptive effects of explaining why and, 296-300, 337
  sociocognitive model of attitudes and, 275
    heuristic, 256
    schematic function, 261, 264, 266, 267
Persuasive appeals, social psychophysiology and, 58-60
Pessimism, sociocognitive model of attitudes and, 249
Phobia
  mindlessness-mindfulness and, 156
  self-discrepancy theory and, 103, 127
Placebo, mindlessness-mindfulness and
  alternate view, 161, 162, 164, 165
  performance, 150
Planned comparison
  anger and, 24, 33
  disruptive effects of explaining why and, 313, 314
Pleasantness index, anger and, 25, 26
Posttraumatic stress disorder, inhibition and, 232, 234
Power, social control and, 180-182
Prediction
  disruptive effects of explaining why and, 334, 335
    alternative explanations, 323
    boundary conditions, 314, 316-318
    conditions, 329
    consistency reduction, 293, 296
    trouble, 333
  sociocognitive model of attitudes and, 246, 250, 275
    heuristic, 259, 260
    object identification, 250-253
    schematic function, 261
Prejudice
  disruptive effects of explaining why and, 339
  sociocognitive model of attitudes and, 254, 255
Priming
  anger and, 33, 34
    cognitive-neoassociationistic analysis, 8, 12
    present research, 14, 16, 18-20, 22, 24, 26, 28, 29
  self-discrepancy theory and, 98, 123-128
  social control and, 196, 197
  sociocognitive model of attitudes and, 251
Private self, sociocognitive model of attitudes and, 268
Psychophysiology, inhibition and, 240
Psychosomatics, inhibition and, 236, 239, 240
Psychotherapy
  disruptive effects of explaining why and, 288, 318
  inhibition and, 237, 238
Public self, sociocognitive model of attitudes and, 268
Punishment
  anger and, 31, 32, 34
    present research, 14-27, 29, 30
  self-discrepancy theory and, 107, 110
  social control and, 180, 188

R

Race, social psychophysiology and, 42
Rapid eye movement, social psychophysiology and, 71
Rationalization, social psychophysiology and, 58
Recall
  disruptive effects of explaining why and, 327
  social psychophysiology and, 56
  sociocognitive model of attitudes and
    heuristic, 258
    schematic function, 262-264, 266
Recognition, sociocognitive model of attitudes and, 264
Reference groups, sociocognitive model of attitudes and, 268, 272
Reflection, disruptive effects of explaining why and, 287, 288
Regulators, social psychophysiology and, 48
Rehearsal, inhibition and, 234
Reinforcement, social control and, 194
Respiratory rhythms, social psychophysiology and, 42
Response patterning, social psychophysiology and, 44-47
Restlessness, self-discrepancy theory and, 94, 102

Retrieval
    social psychophysiology and, 54
    sociocognitive model of attitudes and, 259, 265
Reward
    anger and, 32, 34
    present research, 15, 17, 19–21, 24–27, 29, 30
    disruptive effects of explaining why and, 289, 332
Rigidity, social control and, 186, 190
Risk taking, mindlessness-mindfulness and, 144
Role
    social control and, 184, 194
    sociocognitive model of attitudes and, 271
Role playing, social control and, 191
Routine, mindlessness-mindfulness and, 137, 145

S

Satiation, mindlessness-mindfulness and, 160
Schachter-Singer two-factor theory of emotion, anger and, 14
Schematic function, sociocognitive model of attitudes and, 261–267, 275
Schizophrenia, mindlessness-mindfulness and, 158
Selective exposure, sociocognitive model of attitudes and, 270, 274
Self-awareness, self-discrepancy theory and, 95
Self-beliefs, self-discrepancy theory and, 125, 128–130
    negative consequences, 111
    self-guide, 116
    socialization, 104–108
    vulnerability, 111, 112, 116–120
Self-concept, self-discrepancy theory and, 93–96, 100
Self-discrepancy theory, 93–95, 128–130
    hypothesis 1, 99
        emotional-motivational problems, 99–104
        negative consequences, 108–111
        self-guide, 114–116
        socialization of self-beliefs, 104–108
        vulnerability, 111–114, 116–120
    hypothesis 2, 120–128
        information processing, 97–99
        motivation, 95–97
Self-esteem
    confession and, 215
    mindlessness-mindfulness and, 138, 159, 168
    self-discrepancy theory and, 129
        emotional-motivational problems, 100
        vulnerability, 112–114, 117
    sociocognitive model of attitudes and, 248, 268, 269
Self-guide, self-discrepancy theory and, 121, 122, 125, 126, 128–130
    emotional-motivational problems, 101
    motivation, 95, 96
    socialization of self-beliefs, 105–108
    vulnerability, 112–17
Self-monitors, sociocognitive model of attitudes and, 252, 270, 271
Selves Questionnaire, self-discrepancy theory and, 121, 122, 125
    emotional-motivational problems, 99, 103
    negative consequences, 108, 109
    vulnerability, 112, 118
Semantic memory, sociocognitive model of attitudes and, 250, 255
Semantic processing
    self-discrepancy theory and, 123, 124
    social psychophysiology and, 54–58
Semantic scale, disruptive effects of explaining why and, 320
Senility, mindlessness-mindfulness and, 145, 146
Silent language processing, social psychophysiology and, 71–73
Skeletomuscular patterning, social psychophysiology and, 50
Skin conductance levels
    confession and, 222, 226, 227, 229
    inhibition and, 231
Skin conductance responses, social psychophysiology and, 78, 82
Skin resistance responses, social psychophysiology and, 42
Sleep, social psychophysiology and, 71, 78
Social adjustment, sociocognitive model of attitudes and, 267–272
Social Avoidance and Distress Scale, self-discrepancy theory and, 102
Social change, social control and, 186

Social comparison theory, social psychophysiology and, 79, 80
Social control, 175, 176
　dissent, 195, 196
　　integrating differentiation, 202-204
　　performance, 200-202
　　permitting truth, 196, 197
　　permitting untruth, 197-200
　social changes, 204
　uniformity
　　conformity, 182-185
　　consensus, 190-195
　　costs and benefits, 189, 190
　　minority views, 185-189
　　norms, 177-180
　　power, 180-182
　　theoretical considerations, 176, 177
Social-information processing, social control and, 185
Social psychophysiology, 39, 40, 43, 77, 78, 81-83
　alternative conceptualization, 43
　background, 40-42
　changing zeitgeist, 79-81
　empirical anomalies, 78, 79
　errors of inference, 65-67
　facial EMG, 68-71
　facial response system, 46-48
　　coalition model of emotion, 60-65
　　efference, 48-50
　　perioral EMG, 54-57
　　persuasive appeals, 58-60
　　skeletomuscular patterning, 50-54
　obstacles, 73-77
　perioral EMG, 71-73
　response patterning, 44, 45, 47
Socialization, self-discrepancy theory and, 104-108
Socialization Questionnaire, self-discrepancy theory and, 108, 109
Somatic activity, social psychophysiology and
　empirical anomalies, 79
　facial EMG, 68
　facial response system, 47, 50, 51, 58, 61-65
　perioral EMG, 73
　response patterning, 45
Spatial specificity, social psychophysiology and, 45

Spontaneous remission, mindlessness-mindfulness and, 161-163, 165
Status
　social control and, 180-182, 197
　sociocognitive model of attitudes and, 271
Stimulus
　disruptive effects of explaining why and, 295, 336
　　alternative explanations, 323
　　boundary conditions, 315, 316
　　conditions, 326, 327
　　hypotheses, 305
　　trouble, 331, 333, 334
　mindlessness-mindfulness and, 156, 157, 162
　self-discrepancy theory and, 98, 120
　social psychophysiology and
　　changing zeitgeist, 79, 80
　　facial response system, 48, 54, 56, 61, 64, 65
　　response patterning, 44
　sociocognitive model of attitudes and, 257
Stress
　anger and, 8, 22
　confession and, 213, 217, 223
　inhibition and, 231, 232, 238-240
　social psychophysiology and, 67
Stroop interference effect, self-discrepancy theory and, 123
Syllogisms, sociocognitive model of attitudes and, 256
Symbolic attitudes, sociocognitive model of attitudes and, 271
Symbolic representation, self-discrepancy theory and, 104
Synapses, mindlessness-mindfulness and, 146

T

T cells, mindlessness-mindfulness and, 147
Task performance, social psychophysiology and
　facial response system, 51, 53-55
　response patterning, 44
Taylor Manifest Anxiety Scale, confession and, 222

Temporal specificity, social psychophysiology and, 57
Testosterone, mindlessness-mindfulness and, 146
Thought reform, inhibition and, 238, 239
Traits, social psychophysiology and, 55-57
Transcendental meditation, mindlessness-mindfulness and, 143
Trauma
  confession and
    background, 212-214
    disclosure, 217-222
    effects, 222-229
    laboratory, 214-217
  inhibition and, 230-239
Type A behavior, mindlessness-mindfulness and, 150

U

Uniformity, social control and, 175
  conformity, 182-185
  consensus, 190-195
  costs and benefits, 189, 190
  minority views, 185-189
  norms, 177-180
  power, 180-182
  theoretical considerations, 176, 177
Uniqueness, social psychophysiology and, 44

V

Value expressive functions, sociocognitive model of attitudes and, 267, 268, 272
Verification, sociocognitive model of attitudes and, 269
Violence, anger and, 1
Vulnerability
  mindlessness-mindfulness and, 149
  self-discrepancy theory and, 111-114, 116-120, 129
    emotional-motivational problems, 103
    negative consequences, 110, 111
    self-guide, 114-116
    socialization of self-beliefs, 107, 108

W

Whistle blowing, social control and, 188, 189

Z

Zeitgeist, social psychophysiology and, 79-81, 83

CONTENTS OF OTHER VOLUMES

Volume 1

Cultural Influences upon Cognitive Processes
  Harry C. Triandis
The Interaction of Cognitive and Physiological Determinants of Emotional State
  Stanley Schachter
Experimental Studies of Coalition Formation
  William A. Gamson
Communication Networks
  Marvin E. Shaw
A Contingency Model of Leadership Effectiveness
  Fred E. Fiedler
Inducing Resistance to Persuasion: Some Contemporary Approaches
  William J. McGuire
Social Motivation, Dependency, and Susceptibility to Social Influence
  Richard H. Walters and Ross D. Parke
Sociability and Social Organization in Monkeys and Apes
  William A. Mason
Author Index—Subject Index

Volume 2

Vicarious Processes: A Case of No-Trial Learning
  Albert Bandura
Selective Exposure
  Jonathan L. Freedman and David O. Sears
Group Problem Solving
  L. Richard Hoffman
Situational Factors in Conformity
  Vernon L. Allen
Social Power
  John Schopler
From Acts to Dispositions: The Attribution Process in Person Perception
  Edward E. Jones and Keith E. Davis
Inequity in Social Exchange
  J. Stacy Adams
The Concept of Aggressive Drive: Some Additional Considerations
  Leonard Berkowitz
Author Index—Subject Index

Volume 3

Mathematical Models in Social Psychology
  Robert P. Abelson
The Experimental Analysis of Social Performance
  Michael Argyle and Adam Kendon
A Structural Balance Approach to the Analysis of Communication Effects
  N. T. Feather
Effects of Fear Arousal on Attitude Change: Recent Developments in Theory and Experimental Research
  Irving L. Janis
Communication Processes and the Properties of Language
  Serge Moscovici
The Congruity Principle Revisited: Studies in the Reduction, Induction, and Generalization of Persuasion
  Percy H. Tannenbaum
Author Index—Subject Index

Volume 4

The Theory of Cognitive Dissonance: A Current Perspective
Elliot Aronson
Attitudes and Attraction
Donn Byrne
Sociolinguistics
Susan M. Ervin-Tripp
Recognition of Emotion
Nico H. Frijda
Studies of Status Congruence
Edward E. Sampson
Exploratory Investigations of Empathy
Ezra Stotland
The Personal Reference Scale: An Approach to Social Judgment
Harry S. Upshaw
Author Index—Subject Index

Volume 5

Media Violence and Aggressive Behavior: A Review of Experimental Research
Richard E. Goranson
Studies in Leader Legitimacy, Influence, and Innovation
Edwin P. Hollander and James W. Julian
Experimental Studies of Negro-White Relationships
Irwin Katz
Findings and Theory in the Study of Fear Communications
Howard Leventhal
Perceived Freedom
Ivan D. Steiner
Experimental Studies of Families
Nancy E. Waxler and Elliot G. Mishler
Why Do Groups Make Riskier Decisions than Individuals?
Kenneth L. Dion, Robert S. Baron, and Norman Miller
Author Index—Subject Index

Volume 6

Self-Perception Theory
Daryl J. Bem
Social Norms, Feelings, and Other Factors Affecting Helping and Altruism
Leonard Berkowitz
The Power of Liking: Consequences of Interpersonal Attitudes Derived from a Liberalized View of Secondary Reinforcement
Albert J. Lott and Bernice E. Lott
Social Influence, Conformity Bias, and the Study of Active Minorities
Serge Moscovici and Claude Faucheux
A Critical Analysis of Research Utilizing the Prisoner's Dilemma Paradigm for the Study of Bargaining
Charlan Nemeth
Structural Representations of Implicit Personality Theory
Seymour Rosenberg and Andrea Sedlak
Author Index—Subject Index

Volume 7

Cognitive Algebra: Integration Theory Applied to Social Attribution
Norman H. Anderson
On Conflicts and Bargaining
Erika Apfelbaum
Physical Attractiveness
Ellen Berscheid and Elaine Walster
Compliance, Justification, and Cognitive Change
Harold B. Gerard, Edward S. Connolley, and Roland A. Wilhelmy
Processes in Delay of Gratification
Walter Mischel
Helping a Distressed Person: Social, Personality, and Stimulus Determinants
Ervin Staub
Author Index—Subject Index

Volume 8

Social Support for Nonconformity
Vernon L. Allen
Group Tasks, Group Interaction Process, and Group Performance Effectiveness: A Review and Proposed Integration
J. Richard Hackman and Charles G. Morris
The Human Subject in the Psychology Experiment: Fact and Artifact
Arie W. Kruglanski
Emotional Arousal in the Facilitation of Aggression through Communication
Percy H. Tannenbaum and Dolf Zillmann

The Reluctance to Transmit Bad News
Abraham Tesser and Sidney Rosen
Objective Self-Awareness
Robert A. Wicklund
Responses to Uncontrollable Outcomes:
An Integration of Reactance Theory
and the Learned Helplessness Model
Camille B. Wortman and Jack W. Brehm
Subject Index

Volume 9

New Directions in Equity Research
*Elaine Walster, Ellen Berscheid,
and G. William Walster*
Equity Theory Revisited: Comments
and Annotated Bibliography
J. Stacy Adams and Sara Freedman
The Distribution of Rewards and Resources
in Groups and Organizations
Gerald S. Leventhal
Deserving and the Emergence of Forms
of Justice
*Melvin J. Lerner, Dale T. Miller,
and John G. Holmes*
Equity and the Law: The Effect of a
Harmdoer's "Suffering in the Act"
on Liking and Assigned Punishment
*William Austin, Elaine Walster,
and Mary Kristine Utne*
Incremental Exchange Theory: A Formal
Model for Progression in Dyadic Social
Interaction
L. Lowell Huesmann and George Levinger
Commentary
George C. Homans
Subject Index

Volume 10

The Catharsis of Aggression: An Evaluation
of a Hypothesis
Russell G. Geen and Michael B. Quanty
Mere Exposure
Albert A. Harrison
Moral Internalization: Current Theory
and Research
Martin L. Hoffman

Some Effects of Violent and Nonviolent
Movies on the Behavior of Juvenile
Delinquents
*Ross D. Parke, Leonard Berkowitz,
Jacques P. Leyens, Stephen G. West,
and Richard J. Sebastian*
The Intuitive Psychologist and His
Shortcomings: Distortions in the Attribution
Process
Lee Ross
Normative Influences on Altruism
Shalom H. Schwartz
A Discussion of the Domain and Methods
of Social Psychology: Two Papers by Ron
Harre and Barry R. Schlenker
Leonard Berkowitz
The Ethogenic Approach: Theory
and Practice
R. Harre
On the Ethogenic Approach: Etiquette
and Revolution
Barry R. Schlenker
Automatisms and Autonomies: In Reply
to Professor Schlenker
R. Harre
Subject Index

Volume 11

The Persistence of Experimentally Induced
Attitude Change
Thomas D. Cook and Brian F. Flay
The Contingency Model and the Dynamics
of the Leadership Process
Fred E. Fiedler
An Attributional Theory of Choice
Andy Kukla
Group-Induced Polarization of Attitudes
and Behavior
Helmut Lamm and David G. Myers
Crowding: Determinants and Effects
Janet E. Stockdale
Salience: Attention, and Attribution:
Top of the Head Phenomena
Shelley E. Taylor and Susan T. Fiske
Self-Generated Attitude Change
Abraham Tesser
Subject Index

Volume 12

Part I. Studies in Social Cognition

Prototypes in Person Perception
  Nancy Cantor and Walter Mischel
A Cognitive-Attributional Analysis of Stereotyping
  David L. Hamilton
Self-Monitoring Processes
  Mark Snyder

Part II. Social Influences and Social Interaction

Architectural Mediation of Residential Density and Control: Crowding and the Regulation of Social Contact
  Andrew Baum and Stuart Valins
A Cultural Ecology of Social Behavior
  J. W. Berry
Experiments on Deviance with Special Reference to Dishonesty
  David P. Farrington
From the Early Window to the Late Night Show: International Trends in the Study of Television's Impact on Children and Adults
  John P. Murray and Susan Kippax
Effects of Prosocial Television and Film Material on the Behavior of Viewers
  J. Philippe Rushton
Subject Index

Volume 13

People's Analyses of the Causes of Ability-Linked Performances
  John M. Darley and George R. Goethals
The Empirical Exploration of Intrinsic Motivational Processes
  Edward I. Deci and Richard M. Ryan
Attribution of Responsibility: From Man the Scientist to Man as Lawyer
  Frank D. Fincham and Joseph M. Jaspars
Toward a Comprehensive Theory of Emotion
  Howard Leventhal
Toward a Theory of Conversion Behavior
  Serge Moscovici
The Role of Information Retrieval and Conditional Inference Processes in Belief Formation and Change
  Robert S. Wyer, Jr. and Jon Hartwick
Index

Volume 14

Verbal and Nonverbal Communication of Deception
  Miron Zuckerman, Bella M. DePaulo, and Robert Rosenthal
Cognitive, Social, and Personality Processes in the Physiological Detection of Deception
  William M. Waid and Martin T. Orne
Dialectic Conceptions in Social Psychology: An Application to Social Penetration and Privacy Regulation
  Irwin Altman, Anne Vinsel, and Barbara B. Brown
Direct Experience and Attitude—Behavior Consistency
  Russell H. Fazio and Mark P. Zanna
Predictability and Human Stress: Toward a Clarification of Evidence and Theory
  Suzanne M. Miller
Perceptual and Judgmental Processes in Social Contexts
  Arnold Upmeyer
Jury Trials: Psychology and Law
  Charlan Jeanne Nemeth
Index

Volume 15

Balance, Agreement, and Positivity in the Cognition of Small Social Structures
  Walter H. Crockett
Episode Cognition: Internal Representations of Interaction Routines
  Joseph P. Forgas
The Effects of Aggressive-Pornographic Mass Media Stimuli
  Neil M. Malamuth and Ed Donnerstein
Socialization in Small Groups: Temporal Changes in Individual–Group Relations
  Richard L. Moreland and John M. Levine
Translating Actions into Attitudes: An Identity-Analytic Approach to the Explanation of Social Conduct
  Barry R. Schlenker
Aversive Conditions as Stimuli to Aggression
  Leonard Berkowitz
Index

Volume 16

A Contextualist Theory of Knowledge:
Its Implications for Innovation and Reform
in Psychological Research
  William J. McGuire
Social Cognition: Some Historical
and Theoretical Perspectives
  Janet Landman and Melvin Manis
Paradigmatic Behaviorism: Unified Theory
for Social-Personality Psychology
  Arthur W. Staats
Social Psychology from the Standpoint
of a Structural Symbolic Interactionism:
Toward an Interdisciplinary Social Psychology
  Sheldon Stryker
Toward an Interdisciplinary Social
Psychology
  Carl W. Backman
Index

Volume 17

Mental Representations of the Self
  John F. Kihlstrom and Nancy Cantor
Theory of the Self: Impasse and Evolution
  Kenneth J. Gergen
A Perceptual-Motor Theory of Emotion
  Howard Leventhal
Equity and Social Change in Human
Relationships
  *Charles G. McClintock, Roderick M.
  Kramer, and Linda J. Keil*
A New Look at Dissonance Theory
  Joel Cooper and Russell H. Fazio
Cognitive Theories of Personality
  Alice H. Eagly and Shelly Chaiken
Helping Behavior and Altruism: An
Empirical and Conceptual Overview
  John F. Dovidio
Index

Volume 18

A Typological Approach to Marital
Interaction: Recent Theory and Research
  Mary Anne Fitzpatrick
Groups in Exotic Environments
  Albert A. Harrison and Mary M. Connors
Balance Theory, the Jordan Paradigm,
and the Wiest Tetrahedron
  Chester A. Insko
The Social Relations Model
  David A. Kenny and Lawrence La Voie
Coalition Bargaining
  S. S. Komorita
When Belief Creates Reality
  Mark Snyder
Index

Volume 19

Distraction–Conflict Theory: Progress
and Problems
  Robert S. Baron
Recent Research on Selective Exposure
to Information
  Dieter Frey
The Role of Threat to Self-Esteem
and Perceived Control in Recipient Reaction
to Help: Theory Development and Empirical
Validation
  Arie Nadler and Jeffrey D. Fisher
The Elaboration Likelihood Model
of Persuasion
  Richard E. Petty and John T. Cacioppo
Natural Experiments on the Effects
of Mass Media Violence on Fatal Aggression:
Strengths and Weaknesses of a New
Approach
  David P. Phillips
Paradigms and Groups
  Ivan D. Steiner
Social Categorization: Implications for
Creation and Reduction of Intergroup Bias
  David A. Wilder
Index

Volume 20

Attitudes, Traits, and Actions: Dispositional
Prediction of Behavior in Personality
and Social Psychology
  Icek Ajzen
Prosocial Motivation: Is it Ever Truly
Altruistic?
  C. Daniel Batson
Dimensions of Group Process: Amount
and Structure of Vocal Interaction
  James M. Dabbs, Jr. and R. Barry Ruback

The Dynamics of Opinion Formation
Harold B. Gerard and Ruben Orive

Positive Affect, Cognitive Processes, and Social Behavior
Alice M. Isen

Between Hope and Fear: The Psychology of Risk
Lola L. Lopes

Toward an Integration of Cognitive and Motivational Perspectives on Social Inference: A Biased Hypothesis-Testing Model
Tom Pyszczynski and Jeff Greenberg

Index

Volume 21

Introduction
Leonard Berkowitz

Part I. The Self as Known

Narrative and the Self as Relationship
Kenneth J. Gergen and Mary M. Gergen

Self and Others: Studies in Social Personality and Autobiography
Seymour Rosenberg

Content and Process in the Experience of Self
William J. McGuire and Claire V. McGuire

Information Processing and the Study of the Self
John F. Kihlstrom, Nancy Cantor, Jeanne Sumi Albright, Beverly R. Chew, Stanley B. Klein, and Paula M. Niedenthal

Part II. Self-Motives

Toward a Self-Evaluation Maintenance Model of Social Behavior
Abraham Tesser

The Self: A Dialectical Approach
Carl W. Backman

The Psychology of Self-Affirmation: Sustaining the Integrity of the Self
Claude M. Steele

A Model of Behavioral Self-Regulation: Translating Intention into Action
Michael F. Scheier and Charles S. Carver

Index